Money
Financial Markets
and
Economic Activity

Norman E. Cameron

University of Manitoba

SECOND EDITION

Addison-Wesley Publishers

Don Mills, Ontario • Reading, Massachusetts
Menlo Park, California • New York • Wokingham,
England • Amsterdam • Bonn • Sydney
Singapore • Tokyo • Madrid • San Juan

PROJECT EDITOR: Shirley Tessier
PRODUCTION EDITOR: Valerie Jones
COPYEDITORS: Dennis Bockus/Valerie Jones
PERMISSIONS/PROOFREADING: Gail Copeland
DESIGN AND TYPESET: Pronk&Associates

Canadian Cataloguing in Publication Data

Cameron, Norman E.
   Money, financial markets and economic activity

2nd ed.
Includes bibliographical references and index.
ISBN 0–201–52997–1

1. Finance — Canada.   2. Financial institutions —
Canada.   3. Finance.   4. Financial institutions.
I. Title

HG173.C35 1991   332'.0971   C91-094218-8

A B C D E F – DON – 96   95   94   93   92   91

CONTENTS

PART TWO Lending and Borrowing Behaviour

PART THREE Financial Intermediation

PREFACE TO THE SECOND EDITION

The second edition is much more than an updated reprinting of the first edition. Most ideas have been rewritten in clearer prose, some new ideas have been added, and some old ideas have been dropped as no longer useful.

Nevertheless, the major features of the first edition remain the major features of this edition. This book is still aimed at readers who want to know both the how and the why of the entire financial system — not just of the market for money. This book still emphasizes the importance of risk, and still devotes more space than most texts to analysis of financial market responses to risk. The last third of the book still addresses sophisticated issues of stabilization policymaking under uncertainty.

The book continues to be divided up into a first two-thirds that is mainly microeconomic, and a last third that is macroeconomic. In both parts the openness of our financial system to that of the rest of the world is treated as a key feature. A final chapter is needed on the international financial system only to deal with special international institutions, not to acknowledge for the first time that there is a world outside Canada.

One result of integrating the world financial system into the book throughout is a greater stress than before on the importance and results of arbitrage between different segments of the financial system. The message many readers will get even before Chapter 14 is that there are powerful forces of substitution at work in financial markets that tend to keep relative yields together on similar assets, even as they cause volatile flows of funds between similar markets.

There is one significant deletion in this second edition. In discussing risk, I have replaced the full Tobin–Markowitz analysis (that uses covariances of asset yields) with the somewhat simpler capital asset pricing model approach. The ideas of systematic and unsystematic risk are much easier to explain and apply in practice than is the idea of covariances between asset yields.

There are several additions besides the capital asset pricing model. One is an adapted supply and demand diagram that is used to bring out connections between financial markets. It is particularly useful to bring out the special assumptions that underlie all the arbitrage propositions that are so common and so exotic in financial market analysis.

A second addition is discussion of the option theory approach to understanding financial assets. This discussion includes a non-mathematical explanation of the pricing of options and swaps, and discussion of the Modigliani–Miller proposition as a special example of the put–call parity condition.

A third addition is more analytical treatment of the government's role in the financial system, using more than just the standard notion that governments try to maximize social welfare. The role of political considerations is given much more weight in explaining the structure of regulation that we have — especially the most recent reforms. The incentive effects of such government innovations as flat-rate deposit insurance come under analytical scrutiny as well.

The macroeconomic discussion has become more focused now that macroeconomics itself has settled down (temporarily) into fairly stable new Keynesian and new classical camps. Both views are presented in the review of macroeconomic theory, but the new Keynesian view dominates when discussion turns to what stabilization policy rules should be. The impact of the rational expectations revolution appears in the policy discussion, as distinct from the review of macroeconomics, in two ways: first, in the emphasis on policy rules for future policy rather than on the size of a policy dose in a particular situation; and second, in the game theory approach to policy that was pioneered by Finn Kydland and Edward Prescott in 1977.

Revising this book has taken more time than my most generous estimate, but almost all of it worthwhile. I am grateful to the University of Manitoba for the sabbatical leave which provided time free of other responsibilities, and to the University of Michigan which generously made its excellent facilities available to me during that sabbatical year. Useful comments and criticisms on both style and substance have been provided by Stephen Watson of the Government of Manitoba, by Andrew Alleyne of Great West Life, by colleagues Derek Hum, George Churchman, and John MacCallum of the University of Manitoba, by several former students in my money and banking course (but especially Robert Myskiw and Robert Amano), and by reviewers Paul Boothe, University of Alberta; James Ahiakpor, St. Mary's University; Russell Boyer, University of Western Ontario; Ralph Kolinski, University of Windsor; Pierre L. Siklos, Wilfrid Laurier University; and Peter Sephton, University of New Brunswick, Fredericton. These criticisms have caused me a little extra work, and saved the readers a lot.

Robert Klaise and Ron Doleman of Addison-Wesley have been constructive and supportive throughout, a pleasure to work with. Dennis Bockus and Valerie Jones provided thorough copy-editing to keep the prose consistent and to bring out meaning where it was obscured. I thank you all for your contributions even though I remain responsible for what this book contains.

N.E.C.
Winnipeg, June 1991

PART ONE

Money and Financial Markets

Chapter one

Introduction and Overview

Authors often spend part of their introductory chapters explaining why the subject of their book is worth all the reading to follow. In the 1960s, money and banking texts needed such passages urgently: the monetary mechanism is a somewhat dry subject, banking was downright dull, and the rest of the financial system was very conservative.

Now, the financial system is much livelier. The Economic Council describes the change: "...as Canada entered the 1980s, hardly a week passed without a new financial service being offered, one institution acquiring another, or an institution entering a new field—quite a change from the tranquil days of the 1960s!"[1] The financial sector became a glamour sector of the economy. Wall Street was on everyone's lips in the 1980s even before the October 1987 stock market crash. The best and the brightest from universities headed to financial firms for interesting careers. Hollywood made a blockbuster movie (*Wall Street*) about power and corruption in stockmarket dealing. Deregulation in country after country stirred up competition in places that had not seen much of it for decades. Linkages between financial institutions and markets in different countries created a single, worldwide financial network out of the separate financial systems of each nation.

That was the good news, for as long as it lasted. The bad news has been a sorry record of bankruptcy on a scale not seen since the Great Depression. Over two dozen Canadian financial institutions have failed since 1980 due to fraud, greed, and management folly. Many others have been forced to merge. Provincial governments even took some of the blame. Large banks in Canada and abroad spent the whole decade of the 1980s recovering from the massive bad loans they made to Third World governments in the international lending binge of the

---

[1] *A Framework for Regulation* (Ottawa: Supply and Services, 1987).

Source: Gary Brookins, *Richmond Times Dispatch*, 1990.

late 1970s. As bad as Canadian experience has been, the American experience, captured by the accompanying cartoon, has been far worse: U.S. taxpayers will end up paying over half as much as Canada's entire national debt to bail out government-insured depositors in over a thousand savings and loan firms (S&Ls) that have failed.

No, the financial sector has been anything but dull over the last decade. Authors of money and banking texts can approach their subject without having to whip up readers' interest first.

SECTION 1

Approach of the book

This book looks at the financial sector first and foremost as a system of markets for separate financial assets — for instance, markets for term deposits, for bonds, and for futures contracts. This is to be contrasted with seeing the financial system as just a group of financial institutions, for instance, or as just a set of branch offices, automated teller machines, and electronic telephone networks. In the same way economists see Canada's transportation system as a set of markets for separate transportation services — air, land, water — between Toronto and Winnipeg, between Montreal and Halifax, and so on, rather than as just a set of roads, rails, and airports.

The book explains the behaviour of the financial system in four major stages. The first stage describes the range of financial markets available. This involves much description of institutional facts about individual markets, since few readers will be familiar with many of Canada's financial markets. Because the most fundamental and in some ways the most difficult of financial assets is money itself, money gets special treatment.

The second stage explains the forces behind demand and supply in markets for financial assets. Some of these forces work on households as lenders and borrowers. Some of them work on business firms. Some work on financial institutions serving as intermediaries between other lenders and borrowers. Risk is a major factor influencing lending and borrowing decisions. Considerable time is spent explaining what risk is and how it does and does not matter to lender and borrower decisions.

The third stage explains connections between different markets in the financial system. The financial system has more close substitutes than is usual in other sectors of the economy, which gives rise to unusually fixed structures of relative prices and yields on financial assets.

The fourth and last stage explains the connections between financial markets and non-financial or real markets. This is macroeconomic theory. It leads to discussion of how monetary policy can and should be used.

The approach of focusing on financial markets as the key units of analysis is reflected in frequent use of the basic tool that economists have always used in analyzing markets: the partial equilibrium, supply–demand diagram. Many issues in the book are related back to this simple diagram.

Individual financial markets can have all the attributes we notice in goods markets, such as monopoly power, rivalry, barriers to entry, product differentiation, and the like. A commonly used measure of monopoly power is the combined market share of the four largest participants in the market. Professor Edwin Neave of Queen's University has calculated the four-firm concentration ratios shown in Table 1–1 for some of Canada's more concentrated financial markets. The four largest firms are on the borrowers' side in some markets (for deposits and insurance) and on the lenders' side in others (for loans and mortgages). In general, financial markets have less monopoly power than most markets for goods and non-financial services, because entry is relatively easy, so we will generally treat financial markets as though they were approximately competitive.

SECTION 2

Overview of the book

The following outline is both a prospectus and a summary of the book. It can be usefully read at any point where an overview of the forest is useful, to supplement the inspection of individual trees. The following paragraphs introduce the central ideas as well as the specific types of information that are to be found in this book.

TABLE 1–1: Financial market concentration in Canada

Financial market	Market shares of the largest four participants
Personal savings deposits	37
Domestic personal and commercial loans	63
Consumer credit market (personal loans)	52
Residential mortgage loans	33
Group life insurance	35
Individual life insurance	35
Automobile insurance	21
Property, casualty and direct insurance	17

Source: E.H. Neave, "Canada's Approach to Financial Regulation," *Canadian Public Policy,* March 1989, 2.

Part One: Money and Financial Markets

The fundamental role of even the most primitive financial system is to provide a form of money for the rest of the economy. Money lubricates all transactions in all sectors of the economy. Economies without money must rely on barter transactions, which are possible but inefficient and time-consuming. Chapters 2 and 3 discuss this most basic role of the Canadian financial system. Chapter 2 describes in some detail the current money and payments mechanism in Canada. Chapter 3 presents some history of moneys in Canada, focusing on two innovative payments mechanisms used in our distant past.

Modern financial systems do far more than provide an asset that can serve as money. The Canadian financial system also serves, for instance, to channel funds from savers to borrowers. In so doing, the financial system creates stocks of financial assets and debts, which form a large part of the wealth accumulation of households and firms and even governments. Each form of financial asset has given rise to its own financial market with lenders, borrowers, and equilibrium. Especially over the 1980s, our financial system has become more open to the world outside North America: it channels funds between foreign savers and domestic borrowers and between domestic savers and foreign borrowers. For most of our large-scale financial transactions, it makes sense to think of Canadian financial markets as just one set of booths in a permanent, electronically linked international trade fair of dozens of such booths.

Chapter 4 discusses how a financial system contributes to an economy and identifies the channels through which funds flow from savers to borrowers. Chapters 5 and 6 describe the Canadian financial system — first by looking at the national balance sheet accounts to see who owes what to whom and in what form, and then by a tour of the main groups of financial institutions and financial markets. Chapter 6 also explains the newer financial instruments used in hedging markets to protect against market risks (options, futures contracts, and swaps).

Part Two: Lending and Borrowing Behaviour

Lending and borrowing behaviour mainly reflects choices about spending income now rather than later (*intertemporal* choices). For households, the logic of intertemporal choices is captured in life cycle or permanent income theories of saving and consumption. Such theories explain much of the observed total demand and supply of assets, though they explain little of the mix of lending or borrowing by type of financial asset. Chapter 7 explains the life cycle and permanent income theory of saving, lending and borrowing and briefly reviews the actual pattern of household wealth and debt to see how well the theory is supported.

Much borrowing is done by firms, financial institutions, and governments, to which the life cycle and permanent income theories do not apply. The logic of firms' and financial institutions' borrowing is explained by a version of profit-maximization theory from introductory economics: they borrow when there is a profit to be made between the yield on their assets and the interest cost of their borrowing. Chapter 8 presents two models used to analyze firms and financial institutions. The special situation of governments is also discussed.

The pattern of lending and borrowing by type of financial market is explained in large part by considerations of risk. Both lenders and borrowers would like to avoid risk exposure, if they do not have to give up too much in doing so. A simple way of analyzing the response of lenders and borrowers to uncertainty of yields is to divide that uncertainty into just two parts: systematic risk and unsystematic risk. Unsystematic risk can be removed from an asset portfolio by the appropriate combination of different assets, while systematic risk cannot be removed. Systematic risk is therefore much less desirable in an asset than unsystematic risk.

Chapter 9 presents the mainstream theory of borrower and lender reaction to risk, a theory that leads to the capital asset pricing model.

Part Three: Financial Intermediation

Financial institutions that borrow in their own name and then relend the same funds to other borrowers have become more and more important in the Canadian financial system. Their existence is explained by economies of scale in handling information costs and by some asymmetries of information (that is, borrowers knowing more than lenders do about borrowers' repayment abilities). Chapter 10 outlines some models of financial intermediation and explains the sources of positive spreads between lending and borrowing rates. Banks remain the core financial institutions because of their role in creating most of the money supply, so special attention is paid to the process of deposit expansion when banks acquire extra cash reserves.

Chapters 11–13 describe the major groups of financial institutions, point out the differences in balance sheets, and explain each group's sources of profit and problems of risk management. Actual Canadian financial intermediaries differ substantially on the surface, with different names and regulations and organizational structures. However, they have become much more similar over the last decade as each group has moved farther into other groups' markets.

Part Four: Financial Market Equilibrium

The behaviour of financial institutions and other investors has the effect of tying together yields in many different financial markets, just as prices are tied together for close substitute consumer goods. This behaviour is called **arbitrage**: the willingness of many lenders and borrowers to shift large amounts of wealth between close substitute assets in response to small yield differentials. Arbitrage keeps large yield differentials from arising between markets for close substitute assets. Some sets of yields therefore move together in almost fixed structures. Chapter 14 looks at several yield structures that have been identified by economists.

Flows of funds in the Canadian financial system are influenced by various forms of government intervention. Whether one predicts that government influence is likely to improve or worsen performance of the financial system depends on the approach one chooses to explain a government's use of its influence. Two such approaches are explained and applied in Chapter 15, the social welfare approach and the rational politics approach. One conclusion that emerges is that the current phase of deregulation of the financial system will leave creditors of financial intermediaries with substantially less protection from shareholders' exploitation than was the case in the 1960s.

Part Five: Macroeconomics and Financial Markets

The financial system both makes monetary policy possible and also makes it necessary. The quantity of money created by our financial system influences the rest of the economy in powerful ways: in the longer run it is money that determines prices, while in the shorter run money influences output and employment as well. Left to itself, a modern financial system creating paper money such as ours is likely to worsen business cycle fluctuations. Central banking has arisen in this century to control the process of money creation and mitigate the business cycle. Chapters 16 to 18 provide a quick review of modern business cycle theories. Chapters 19 and 20 explain more specialized monetary topics in greater detail, such as money demand, wealth effects, and interest parity conditions. The effect of adding more financial sophistication to the mainstream aggregate demand model is not large. Between them, chapters 16 to 20 provide the background for discussions of what governments and central banks can and should do to mitigate business cycles.

Part Six: Stabilization Policy in Canada

Experts disagree on what causes business cycle fluctuations, so it is understandable that there is no agreement on what can be done to reduce them. Even economists who agree on causes can disagree on the nature and timing of the impacts of the policies that are used as cures. To a certain extent, the outcome is determined by public expectations about policy. That leaves policymakers in a difficult position as they try to design good monetary policy rules for a small open economy.

Chapter 21 explains in some detail the objectives and procedures of central banking both in Canada and internationally. Chapter 22 explains the policymakers' situation in some detail and considers several alternative policy rules that have been suggested. Chapter 23 reviews what the Bank of Canada has actually done since 1971 in light of the monetary rules available.

Part Seven: The International Financial System

Foreign institutions, foreign borrowers, and foreign financial markets play some role in almost all issues discussed earlier in the book. The "rest-of-the-world" sector is therefore introduced in Chapter 5 and included in discussion in many chapters thereafter. However, it is now useful to think of a single world financial system. Such a financial system has problems similar to those of a national financial system; however, unlike a national financial system, there is no central government that can set up whatever central institutions are needed. Chapter 24 briefly describes the world financial system and discusses its major problem: the creation of an adequate but not excessive world money supply.

SECTION 3

Summary

This book analyzes the financial system as an interlocking network of financial markets, one market for each financial asset. The book first describes the roles and institutional structures of financial markets in Canada, with emphasis on the assets used as money. It then analyzes the behaviour of lenders and borrowers in individual markets, first under certainty and then taking account of risk. Next the book considers how tight interconnections between financial markets affect the structure of the general equilibrium of all financial markets. The last third of the book is monetary macroeconomics; it reviews macroeconomic theory and analyzes the interconnection between financial markets and the real sector of the economy.

Questions and Problems

1. What defines a financial market? How would you tell whether some person or firm or transaction was part of a particular financial market?

2. Identify as many as you can of the types of lenders and borrowers in the financial markets listed in Table 1–1.

3. Which of the financial markets in Table 1–1 have you made use of in the last three years? For each case, were you a borrower or a lender?

4. Both the financial system and the transportation system are described in this chapter as sets of interconnected markets. What other system of the Canadian economy can you describe that way? Go ahead and do so.

Suggestions for Further Reading

Economic Council of Canada. *A Framework for Regulation*. Ottawa: Supply and Services, 1987.

——. *A New Frontier: Globalization and Canada's Financial Markets*. Ottawa: Supply and Services, 1990.

Chapter two

Money and the Payments Mechanism

$\mathbf{M}$oney is the most fundamental part of any financial system, because almost all payments are made with money. This chapter describes the monetary system we now have in Canada; the next chapter provides some historical background on how that system developed.

You should learn in this chapter:

1. the role and costs of barter arrangements;
2. the roles that money plays besides making payments;
3. what particular assets we now consider to be money;
4. how the Canadian payments mechanism works.

SECTION 1

◻ Barter

All parts of the financial system make their contributions to society, but some contributions are larger than others. Without money and a payments mechanism of some sort, we would be reduced to barter, or to not trading at all.

Barter transactions still occur in modern economies, but they are insignificant in total trade. Pure **barter** would be defined as a mutual exchange of goods or services between two parties without any intermediary. Each party takes away from the barter exchange whatever good or service the other party brought to it. The dentist fixes the plumber's tooth in return for the plumber fixing the dentist's water pump, both at (more or less) the same time. This particular transaction requires that the dentist wants his pump fixed at the same time that the plumber wants his tooth fixed. The probability of such a **double coincidence of wants**

11

Trade with Russia could bring new cultural influences. Rank Xerox has been offered racing camels, falcons and goat horns as part of a barter deal for electronic goods. Admitting that there might be a Middle Eastern market for the first two items, the company refused the deal.

Source: Illustration © 1990, Chris Riddell

The Economist, February 24, 1990, p. 57. © 1990, The Economist Newspaper Ltd. Reprinted with permission.

Double coincidence of wants is not always easy to find

is much lower than the probability of the dentist wanting his pump fixed and the plumber wanting money in exchange. *All* plumbers accept money in exchange for fixing pumps, but very few want their teeth worked on instead. Barter transactions are normally more difficult to arrange than monetary transactions because double coincidences of wants are hard to recognize in advance. The dentist with the non-working pump already knows he needs his pump fixed, and he will know one or more plumbers, but it will take him some time even on the telephone to find a plumber who needs dental work of about the same value. People whose time is valuable therefore seldom engage in barter.

Barter is easier to arrange and therefore more frequent if all potential swappers are brought together. One of the few times this happens in Canada is during school lunchtime, when students swap various parts of the lunches they brought: a peanut butter and jam sandwich for a butter tart, an apple for two cookies. The student whose parent regularly packs zucchini sandwiches finds out the hard way that the need for a double coincidence of wants can be a stiff barrier to trade.

Exporting firms and large financial institutions now encounter barter frequently. In international trade, barter crops up under the name *countertrade*. Many developing countries have not been able either to earn or to borrow enough abroad to pay for desired imports with money, so they have turned to barter as an alternative. The deal offered to Rank Xerox (see box) is an example of attempted countertrade. To try to increase the number of barterers and to increase the probability of a double coincidence of wants, many importers and exporters have developed networks of contacts to permit multilateral rather than just bilateral transactions.

In international finance, there is now a large and flourishing barter market in interest rate and currency swaps. This barter market is an exception to the usual situation in that the swaps add to, rather than replace, regular market transactions. A swapper might, for instance, issue a fixed-rate loan in U.S. dollars and then swap that interest obligation for another at floating rates in Swiss francs. Chapter 6 provides more details about these sophisticated arrangements.

SECTION 2

The roles of money

Money fills three distinct roles in a modern economy:

1. a unit of account and standard of deferred payment,
2. a medium of exchange, and
3. a store of value.

Each role will be discussed in turn.

Unit of account

In all economies people must choose at the margin between different pairs of goods or different pairs of inputs. The choices depend in one way or another on the relative values and costs of each pair of alternatives, such as shoes and clothing, or machinists' time and use of drilling equipment. Some way must be found to express relative costs. One way is to use the **exchange rate** (that is, the number of units of item A you should expect to trade for one unit of item B) for each pair of alternatives. The difficulty is that there are so many different pairs of alternatives. How many loaves of bread for one tooth repair? How many chickens for a cow? How many chickens for a textbook? The list of exchange rates required is much too long to be workable in any but a very primitive society.[1]

The number of exchange rates to be remembered can be dramatically reduced if every item has a relative value expressed in terms of one common good called a **unit of account**, or **numeraire**. The unit of account could be anything: dollar bills, wildcat skins, peanuts, or cowrie shells. In modern economies, each nation's basic currency unit serves as its unit of account. In international currency markets and in international trade, the common unit of account is usually the U.S. dollar. With a unit of account, the exchange rate of any two goods is found simply from the ratio of their prices. If an hour of machinist's time has a price of 15 dollar bills and an hour's use of drilling equipment has a value of 30 dollar bills, then their exchange rate is 30:15, or 2:1.

The major benefit of having a unit of account accrues only if everyone uses the same unit. Then only one set of prices is needed. It is to secure this benefit to Canadians that the Currency and Exchange Act, after defining the currency of Canada to be dollars, cents, and mills, goes on in finest legalese:

> Every contract, sale, payment, bill, note, instrument and security for money and every transaction, dealing, matter and thing whatever relating to

---

[1] The general formula for combinations of pairs is that where there are n different goods that can be exchanged, there are $n(n-1)/2$ possible trades of pairs and therefore $n(n-1)/2$ exchange rates. For a simple economy dealing with 1000 items, that means almost half a million exchange rates.

money or involving the payment or the liability to pay any money, that is made, executed or entered into, done or had, shall be made, executed, entered into, done or had according to the currency of Canada, unless it is made, executed, entered into, done or had according to (a) the currency of a country other than Canada; or (b) a unit of account that is defined in terms of the currencies of two or more countries.

Which item serves as unit of account does not make much difference. Usually, the local currency unit is used, but not always. The British government used pounds, shillings, and pence as its unit of account for keeping financial records in the colonies but made most of its payments to troops in Canada with Spanish silver dollars. In Upper Canada, much of the accounting of merchants in outlying areas was done in wildcat skins, or "cats."[2] Some of the merchants' trade was paid for with wildcat skins, but most was paid for with a hodgepodge of foreign coins from other countries. Not until 1858 was Canada's currency unit also used as its unit of account.

In modern economies, many recorded values refer to transactions in some future period, such as interest and principal payments at the maturity date of a loan. There must be some unit of account for such deferred payments. The unit, or **standard of deferred payment**, is normally the domestic currency unit, but that rule can change if rapid inflation is expected. By the third quarter of 1988, for instance, the IMF Survey reported that price inflation in developing countries as a group had accelerated to 63 percent per year, from 28 percent in the first quarter of 1987. That meant that the buying power of those countries' domestic currency units (pesos, australs, cruzados, shekels, etc.) was falling at an average rate of 63 percent per year. Lenders do not like to be paid back in devalued currency units, so they do not want to have deferred payments expressed in domestic currency units when those units are likely to become devalued. Often borrowers and lenders will agree instead on a different standard of deferred payment; usually the different standard is the currency unit of some other, less inflation-prone nation (for example, Swiss francs or U.S. dollars).

The item that serves as unit of account or standard of deferred payment need not have any physical existence. It is used to express value measurements in the same way that the concept of a light-year is used to express distance measurements in astronomy. One does not need to travel a light-year to find the light-year useful as a unit. Similarly, one does not need to hold a dollar coin to find the dollar useful as a unit. We do hold dollar coins and other assets called money, but we do so because of the other two functions money serves: the functions of medium of exchange and store of value.

---

[2] Sources for historical material in this and later sections are E.P. Neufeld, *The Financial System of Canada* (Toronto: Macmillan of Canada, 1972), chapter 1, and E.P. Neufeld, ed., *Money and Banking in Canada* (Toronto: McClelland and Stewart, 1964: Carleton Library Series 17), part 1, especially chapters 1–5 and 14.

Medium of exchange

An asset serves as a **medium of exchange** if it is regularly and generally accepted in exchange for other commodities. A Bank of Canada note, such as the twenty-dollar bill, is a common example. Coins and deposit account balances transferred by cheque are currently the other two main media of exchange in Canada.

The essential property of a medium of exchange is that it be accepted in exchange not principally because of its own intrinsic value (if it has any at all) but because it can be exchanged for other items elsewhere. Assets with this property are said to possess **liquidity**. The wider the range of commodities for which an asset can be exchanged, the more liquid it is. For example, a piggy bank full of pennies is less liquid than the same value in five-dollar bills, because not many sellers want to be paid in thousands of pennies.

Many items can serve as media of exchange at the same time. One of Canada's recurring problems used to be that we had too many kinds of media of exchange. Several colonial acts were passed in attempts to clear up what the exchange rates were between the various currencies in use.[3] Through most of the period up to the 1850s, our forebears had to make do with a hodgepodge of foreign coinage too worn or defaced to use in foreign trade, together with private notes and tokens issued by various merchants and others.

When there are several different media of exchange available, a monetary version of Murphy's law comes into effect. **Gresham's law** says that the worst forms of money will come to be the ones most frequently used. In its short form, Gresham's law says that "bad money drives out good." The good money is that most likely to keep its value, or else that most desirable for some other intrinsic reason (beauty, perhaps, or durability). The bad money cannot disappear from circulation into other uses, particularly as a store of value, so it keeps on being passed from hand to hand. The bad money is therefore what we see being used in trade. The effect can be seen in the list of change received by one shopper in a transaction of 1820, described in the box on page 16.

Another example of Gresham's law, in this case an example of a money being too *good* and therefore disappearing too fast, comes from Nova Scotia. After 1713, the British government paid its garrisons at Annapolis Royal and at Louisbourg in liquor, which was brought up in trade from the Caribbean. Liquor served as a medium of exchange, but obviously it had other uses. Finally, the garrison petitioned the Crown:

> That they be payd in money, or Bills, & not in Rum or Other Liquors, that cause them to be Drunk every day, and Blaspheme the name of God.[4]

---

[3] However, the different colonial legislatures did not manage to agree on the same set of exchange rates; co-ordination of financial legislation across provinces was worse then than it is now.

[4] R.A. Lester, "The Playing Card Currency of French Canada," in E.P. Neufeld, *Money and Banking in Canada*, p. 9.

Back in 1820, an exasperated man complained to his local paper about the change he got after buying sixpence of squash with a twenty-shilling note. He lost threepence in discount on the note itself, and received the following "moneys" in change (at face value):

5 shillings in the note of George Leggett
5 shillings in the note of Wm. Lawson
1 shilling in the team boat note of H.H. Cogswell
1 shilling 3 pence in the note of Adam Esson
1 shilling 3 pence in the note of John A. Barry
three 7 1/2 pence notes of Wm. Smith
7 1/2 pence in silver
3 shillings 6 pence in copper

Source: E.P. Neufeld, *The Financial System of Canada* (Toronto: Macmillan of Canada, 1972), p. 37.

The importance of confidence

The preceding examples show that many items can be used as a medium of exchange. The only necessary requirement is that holders believe the item will be accepted later when they want to spend it — in short, confidence. Confidence in a medium of exchange has all the properties of a self-fulfilling prophecy. If enough people believe a medium of exchange will be accepted, then it will be accepted, precisely because enough people believe it will be accepted. On the other hand, once confidence in a currency starts to slip, it is likely to slip ever more quickly. As holders become more eager to get rid of a kind of money, they agree to higher and higher money prices for other items in exchange. Faster inflation of these money prices undermines confidence in the money even further. Holders become even more eager to spend it at whatever price, and so on. Hyperinflation is often the end result. As we will see in the next chapter on monetary standards, the evolution of different moneys is largely a story of developing less and less expensive ways of generating the confidence necessary to a medium of exchange.

Store of value

The third role of money is as a store of value. A **store of value** is anything that can be bought now and converted into something of value in the future. A car or a house or a share of common stock in a corporation will all have some resale value next year. A bond will be redeemed by its issuer in the future at full face value (unless it is a "junk" bond on which the issuer defaults). Most bank deposits can be redeemed at any time at their face value. All of these items are stores of value. The class of all items that can serve as stores of value are referred to as "assets." Accountants sometimes refer to the class of assets as "capital" items, as opposed to "current" items, such as haircuts, which do not retain any value beyond the current period. The definition of a store of value is very general, and the class of assets is therefore very broad.

Assets that serve as a medium of exchange are always stores of value. In Africa, the cowrie shells used to trade in local markets were stored as wealth in the form of necklaces. Gold coins used for trade in Medieval Europe were also kept in treasuries and strongboxes as stores of value between trades. We Canadians regularly keep part of our accumulated savings in the form of currency and chequing deposits.

In modern economies, assets that serve as a medium of exchange are generally the safest assets, and by definition they are always the most liquid assets, but they are far from the only assets. In fact, the total value of all medium of exchange assets in Canada is only two-thirds of 1 percent of the total value of all assets ($40 billion out of total assets of about $6 000 billion).

SECTION 3

Definitions and measures of money

In general, money is defined to include whatever items serve money's roles. In practice, the role that counts is that of medium of exchange. Each definition of the money supply tries to include in the class of assets called *money* all the assets that fulfill money's role as a medium of exchange. Unfortunately for students of monetary economics, the principle is often interpreted to include assets that are not themselves used in exchange, but are only easily converted into assets that are. In either case, it is the medium of exchange role that is central.

Narrow definitions of **money** exclude all assets not directly used in exchange. M1 is the official measure of narrow money. **Broad** definitions of **money** include also some assets not themselves used as media of exchange, but easily exchangeable (without risk of loss) into assets that are. Broadness is a matter of degree, so there are three official measures of broad money: M2, M3, and M2+. The Bank of Canada reports Canada's official measures of the money supply each week, and Figure 2–1 shows the makeup of each one.

The striking features of Figure 2–1 are that M1 is very much smaller than the broad money measures and that deposits at near banks are now a large share of broad money (in M2+). **Near banks** include trust and mortgage loan companies, credit unions and caisses populaires, and two provincial deposit-taking firms. Near-bank deposits are no longer just a small fringe around bank deposits, a fringe that can be ignored in measuring the money supply. Near-bank chequable deposits are still a much smaller share of total chequable deposits (about one-fifth), so near banks still account for only a small part of narrow money. We will find in chapters 22 and 23 that broad money is the most useful money measure for purposes of monetary policy.

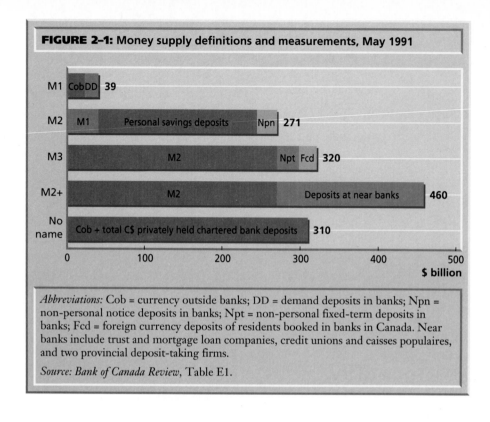

FIGURE 2–1: Money supply definitions and measurements, May 1991

Abbreviations: Cob = currency outside banks; DD = demand deposits in banks; Npn = non-personal notice deposits in banks; Npt = non-personal fixed-term deposits in banks; Fcd = foreign currency deposits of residents booked in banks in Canada. Near banks include trust and mortgage loan companies, credit unions and caisses populaires, and two provincial deposit-taking firms.

Source: Bank of Canada Review, Table E1.

Notes on measuring the money supply

There are many details about money supply measures that Figure 2–1 does not specify. The most important are listed below.

1. All deposit measures exclude deposits held by the federal government, and also deposits held in other financial institutions. Both are excluded so that money supply measures will reflect holdings of the non-bank public.

2. The big chartered banks in Canada each have their own wholly owned mortgage loan company subsidiary, which also issues deposits to finance lending activities. Deposits of such wholly owned near-bank subsidiaries are included in total deposits of the parent bank. As banks come to own other near-bank subsidiaries, still more near-bank deposits will come inside the money supply measures.

3. **Demand deposits** are ordinary chequing accounts that are legally repayable in full on demand. **Notice deposits** are deposits for which the issuing chartered bank has the right to require notice before withdrawal or transfer. Chequable savings accounts are classed as notice deposits because they are legally payable after notice rather than on demand. In practice, chequable savings accounts are treated by many households as an asset very similar to

a personal chequing account, which is a demand deposit. It is difficult in practice to draw a line between deposits that are and deposits that are not media of exchange.

4. Demand deposits are overstated at any point of time by the amount of cheques in process that have been added to the recipient's account but not yet deducted from the payer's account. The overstatement is called the "private sector float." An estimate of the float is subtracted from total recorded demand deposits in arriving at money supply measures. The float is gradually shrinking as electronic arrangements make the cheque-clearing process quicker.

5. In principle, deposits held in non-bank financial institutions should be included along with bank deposits in all the money supply measures. Generally they are not. The reason is that deposit totals in non-bank institutions are not measured as frequently and accurately and quickly (particularly by the thousands of local credit unions and caisses populaires) as by chartered banks. Only a broad-money measure M2+ is reported with all near-bank deposits included, and even that has to rely on estimates of deposits in credit unions for the most recent three or four months.

Growth rates of each money supply measure are tracked over time by economists, who see them as significant causes and indicators of growth of price levels and real incomes.[5] Figure 2–2 shows the growth of monetary aggregates over the 1970s and 1980s. As might be expected from their definitions, the broad-money aggregates move together much of the time. M1 growth deviates for two reasons: M1 growth is much more strongly affected by changes in interest rates than is growth of broad money; and several innovations in types of deposit in the 1970s and 1980s had much more impact on chequing deposits than on the time deposits that make up the bulk of broad money measures.

Money-supply definitions will continue to change as payment habits change, as new types of deposit come into being, as existing types of deposit come to be used in new ways, and as new reporting arrangements allow the Bank of Canada to get accurate measures of non-bank deposits more quickly. The principle underlying all of the future changes in definition is unlikely to change; it will still be to get a definition approximating more closely the elusive concept of the values of all assets serving as (or easily convertible into) media of exchange.

---

[5] Parts Five and Six (especially chapters 22 and 23) explain the role of monetary aggregates in the macroeconomy.

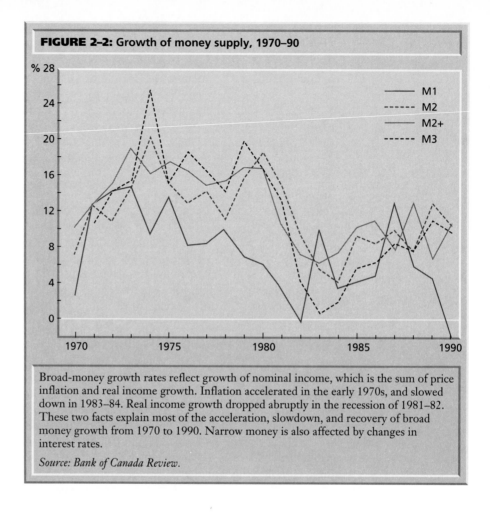

FIGURE 2–2: Growth of money supply, 1970–90

Broad-money growth rates reflect growth of nominal income, which is the sum of price inflation and real income growth. Inflation accelerated in the early 1970s, and slowed down in 1983–84. Real income growth dropped abruptly in the recession of 1981–82. These two facts explain most of the acceleration, slowdown, and recovery of broad money growth from 1970 to 1990. Narrow money is also affected by changes in interest rates.

Source: Bank of Canada Review.

SECTION 4

Money and the payments mechanism in the 1990s

You have learned so far in this chapter that the medium-of-exchange function of money is an important one. This section will describe in some detail the Canadian **payments mechanism** — how money is transferred to make payments, how long the process takes, and what resources are used up in the process.

Cash

We all know how cash is used to make payments. We just hand it over in exchange for the goods we buy. That's all there is to it. It can be that simple because currency and coin are **bearer instruments**. The person who bears them, owns them. Transfer of ownership involves nothing more than transfer of physical possession. When we give a ten-dollar bill to a friend, the friend's ownership of the ten-dollar bill begins the moment he holds the bill in his hand. Almost all assets other than cash are registered somehow, on paper or electronically, as the property of a particular individual. Transfer of ownership of registered assets involves changing the ownership registration. There is a pro and a con to holding bearer instruments rather than registered instruments as assets. The advantage is that making payments with a bearer instrument is easy and, therefore, fast. The buyer of a cup of coffee accepts the cup, hands over payment of 60 cents, and that's it; the transaction is completed. No further checking is required to be sure the 60 cents was not stolen. No further work is needed at the end of the day to transfer legal ownership of the 60 cents from buyer to seller.

The disadvantage of a bearer instrument is its insecurity. Registered chequing accounts are much easier to protect from theft than hundred-dollar bills. To transfer ownership of funds in a chequing account, someone must use special number codes, special signatures, and/or magnetically encoded plastic cards. Transferring ownership of chequing accounts also leaves a trail of records that can be used to trace thefts and mistakes well after the transfer has taken place. Having records available is more important for larger transactions. For smaller amounts, the insecurity of bearer instruments is not so important that we want the extra fuss of a registered asset; however, few of us keep large amounts in bearer form.

The disadvantage of bearer instruments is an advantage for those whose transactions are illegal in some way. Such people do not want any paper trail of documentation left behind them. Illegal transactions are therefore handled almost exclusively with currency, usually in small denominations, since some records are kept of large-denomination bills.

Cash is therefore used in transactions that are either small or illegal. Chequing deposits and credit cards are used for virtually all other payments. We will see below that payments by credit card amount to a form of slightly delayed payment by chequing deposit, so essentially all payments not made in cash are made by transfer of chequing deposit.

Cash has become steadily less important in making payments over the last century, as the use of chequing deposits has spread. Figure 2–3 shows that currency is not declining as a share of the narrow money supply, M1, but the graph is misleading. Over the past 25 years a series of innovations have speeded up the cheque-clearing process, which has allowed each chequing account dollar to handle more and more payments per year. There have been few such innovations for cash. If and when innovations stop increasing the efficiency of chequing accounts, the percentage of M1 that is cash will probably turn downward again.

Chequable deposits

Chequable deposits are issued by banks, by most near banks (trust companies, mortgage loan companies, credit unions and caisses populaires, and two

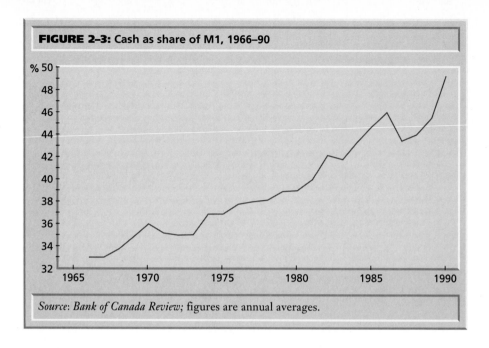

FIGURE 2–3: Cash as share of M1, 1966–90

Source: Bank of Canada Review; figures are annual averages.

provincial bank-type agencies), and even by some brokerage firms. Figure 2–4 shows the relative shares of each class of issuer of chequable deposits in Canada. Banks still dominate, with four-fifths of all chequable deposits.

Some of the deposits listed in Figure 2–4 are demand deposits; some are notice deposits. All are used in the same ways to make payments. Deposits are *registered instruments*, so any transfer of deposits requires a process of reregistering new ownership. New methods of deposit transfer are being developed, but the vast majority of transfers of deposits between people are still initiated by a paper cheque. Canadians write five to ten million cheques every business day, worth between $10 billion and $25 billion.

Cheque transfers

Transfers of deposits are simple to handle when both the payer and the receiver of the cheque have their deposit accounts in the same bank. When I write a cheque on my account that says "Please pay you the sum of $25," and you deposit the cheque in your account in the same bank, the bank interprets the instruction "Please pay $25" as meaning: transfer $25 from my account to yours. The bank makes that adjustment on its books, cancels the cheque by stamping it, and later returns the cheque to me as evidence that my instructions were followed. The same sort of process occurs when telephone and other utility bills are paid through automated teller machines without a cheque, except that the instruction "Please pay" is given electronically rather than on a paper cheque. The process has one extra step when payer and receiver have accounts in different Canadian

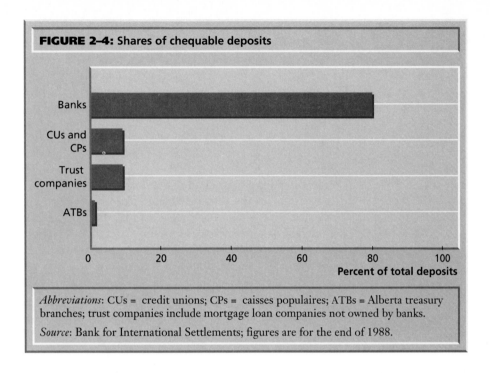

FIGURE 2–4: Shares of chequable deposits

Abbreviations: CUs = credit unions; CPs = caisses populaires; ATBs = Alberta treasury branches; trust companies include mortgage loan companies not owned by banks.

Source: Bank for International Settlements; figures are for the end of 1988.

banking institutions. I can still write a cheque instructing my bank to pay you $25, but the process of getting $25 added to your account in your bank involves (1) my bank deducting $25 from my account, (2) my bank making payment of $25 to your bank, and (3) your bank adding $25 to your account. The interbank payment in step 2 is handled by transfers between banks' deposits rather than between my and your deposits. My bank and your bank both hold deposits in the same institution, the Bank of Canada. My bank pays your bank $25 just by instructing the Bank of Canada to transfer $25 from my bank's account in the Bank of Canada to your bank's account in the Bank of Canada. The process takes milliseconds on the computer that handles such transfers.

Eventually, almost all deposit transfers will be done electronically on a single national payments system connecting all banks' computers. I will pay you $25 by entering the instruction to my bank either on my home computer, on a point-of-sale terminal in your store, or on an automated teller machine, using both my own account identification and yours. After checking that all identification codes are correct, the computer network will do the rest on its own. My account will drop; yours will rise. My bank's account in the Bank of Canada will drop; your bank's account in the Bank of Canada will rise. In this fully automated system, each transaction will be cleared individually and immediately.

Until the arrival of a single national payments mechanism, we will have to live with an avalanche of paper cheques each day. The Canadian Payments Association (CPA) operates a sophisticated **automated clearing and settlement**

system to handle the domestic part of this avalanche.[6] To illustrate the cheque-clearing and settlement process, let us trace two cheques. Both are received by Mr O'Malley and deposited in his Toronto branch of the Royal Bank. The first cheque is written by Acme Chemical, O'Malley's employer, on Acme's account in the Royal Bank. The second cheque is a dividend cheque written by NOVA Corporation on its account in the Toronto Dominion Bank.

1. O'Malley signs his name on the back of both cheques and deposits them in his account at the Royal, using an automated teller machine on his way to work. O'Malley's account is increased by the amount of both cheques.

2. The Royal Bank's courier picks up the cheques received at each Toronto branch and takes them to the Royal's Toronto-area data centre. The dollar amount of each cheque is encoded onto the cheque in machine-readable characters. For each cheque the amount, the payer's account number, and the transit number of the payer's bank are then read into the Royal's computer system to be sorted and tabulated.

3. During the sorting process the cheque from Acme is recognized as being drawn on a Royal Bank account (it has the Royal's transit number on it). The amount is deducted immediately from Acme's account. That cheque has been cleared, and all that remains is to get the cheque back to Acme's accountants.

4. The cheque from NOVA is recognized by its transit number as being drawn on a TD Bank account. It is added to the Royal's pile of other cheques drawn on accounts in the TD Bank. By midnight local time, the Royal has physically exchanged its pile of TD Bank cheques for a similar pile from the TD Bank's Toronto-area data centre drawn on Royal Bank accounts. The difference in value between the two piles is the *net clearing gain* or *loss*; it is recorded with the Canadian Payments Association's central computer and immediately transferred between the Royal's and the TD Bank's accounts with the Bank of Canada.[7]

5. The TD Bank reads into its computer the bundle of cheques received from the Royal. The TD computer deducts the amount of NOVA's cheque to O'Malley from NOVA's account. That cheque is now cleared. All that remains is to send the cheque back to NOVA's accountants.

All stages of the NOVA cheque transfer can be illustrated on a simple and useful balance sheet diagram called a T-account. Figure 2–5 shows the balance sheet changes for the Royal Bank, the TD Bank, and the Bank of Canada that are caused

---

[6] The CPA is an association of 134 deposit-taking institutions as of August 1990. The CPA was set up after the 1980 Bank Act revision to take over operation of the cheque-clearing system from the Canadian Bankers' Association.

[7] Smaller institutions generally do not settle their net clearing gains and losses this directly. Instead they arrange to have their net clearing gains with other CPA members settled by transfer into and out of the Bank of Canada deposit of some larger institution. The institutions that have their own settlement balances at the Bank of Canada are called the "direct clearing members" of the CPA.

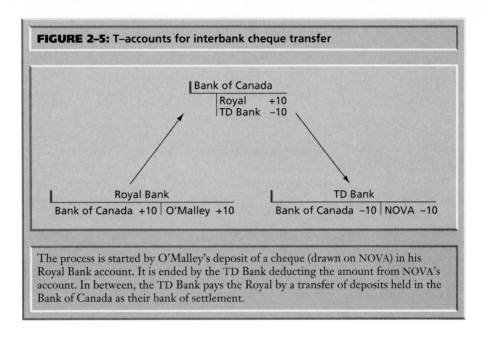

FIGURE 2–5: T–accounts for interbank cheque transfer

The process is started by O'Malley's deposit of a cheque (drawn on NOVA) in his Royal Bank account. It is ended by the TD Bank deducting the amount from NOVA's account. In between, the TD Bank pays the Royal by a transfer of deposits held in the Bank of Canada as their bank of settlement.

by O'Malley's deposit of the cheque from NOVA. Changes in assets appear on the left side of each bank's T-account, changes in debts on the right side. All assets and debts in this diagram are deposits. Names inside the T-accounts refer to owners of deposits if on the right, or to issuers of deposits if on the left. Units are in thousands of dollars. The transfers flow from O'Malley to the Royal, then via the Bank of Canada to the TD Bank, and finally to NOVA. The Bank of Canada serves only as a bank of settlement; its size does not change, only the ownership of its deposits. The Royal Bank grows and the TD Bank shrinks.

Same-day settlement and float

A relatively new feature of the clearing system in Canada is retroactive or same-day settlement. In our example above, the Royal immediately increases O'Malley's account by the amount of the two cheques he deposits. However, the Royal cannot count on the TD Bank settling with it for NOVA's cheque by midnight local time, and NOVA's account would certainly not be decreased by the amount of the cheque until the next day. In the past that meant that O'Malley's deposit in the Royal would have gone up a day before NOVA's account in the TD Bank went down. For that day, total deposits of the two banks together would have been overstated; the amount of the overstatement is called the estimated **float**. Since banks pay interest on deposits, bank interest costs are also exaggerated by any float that exists. In order to eliminate this problem, the automated clearing and settlement system allows for next-day (after midnight) settlements to be dated the previous day. **Same-day settlement** eliminates most

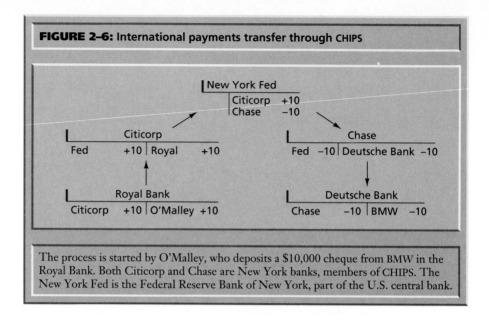

FIGURE 2–6: International payments transfer through CHIPS

The process is started by O'Malley, who deposits a $10,000 cheque from BMW in the Royal Bank. Both Citicorp and Chase are New York banks, members of CHIPS. The New York Fed is the Federal Reserve Bank of New York, part of the U.S. central bank.

of the float and greatly simplifies large-scale banking, where the interest amounts even for a day are no longer trivial.

International payments

Many payments are between firms in different nations. Most such cheques are written in U.S. dollars and are cleared in New York through CHIPS, the Clearing House Interbank Payments System. About $450 billion of payments per *day* are cleared through CHIPS and Fedwire, the other part of the international clearing mechanism. Clearing through CHIPS is similar to clearing through the Canadian system, but with an extra stage. Instead of Canadian and foreign banks holding settlement accounts in the same institution, they both hold correspondent balances in New York banks, which in turn hold settlement balances at the Federal Reserve Bank ("the Fed").

Figure 2–6 shows the path of a cheque received by O'Malley from the automaker BMW. BMW has written the cheque on BMW's account in Deutsche Bank. After O'Malley deposits the cheque, it travels up the diagram through the Royal Bank to the Royal's correspondent bank in New York (Citicorp), across through the New York Fed to the Deutsche Bank's correspondent bank in New York (Chase), and back down through Deutsche Bank to BMW. The two CHIPS banks in New York settle with each other through deposit transfers in their settlement accounts at the New York Fed.

International payments may involve a foreign exchange transaction as well, if the deposits and the cheque are not all in the same currency. If O'Malley's cheque from BMW is in deutschemarks and his deposit is in Canadian dollars, the

Royal will actually sell the deutschemark amount of the cheque in the interbank foreign exchange market before increasing O'Malley's deposit by the amount of Canadian dollars received in exchange.[8]

Credit cards and the payments mechanism

Most wallets and purses that contain currency also contain one or more credit cards. Credit cards are an important part of how we make payments, so some explanation is in order on how credit cards fit in with the payments mechanism described so far.

Imagine a credit-card transaction between Customer and Merchant. Customer uses her VISA card, which is sponsored by the TD Bank. Merchant joined the VISA system through the Royal Bank. To buy a tankful of gas, Customer signs a credit voucher imprinted with her VISA card number and Merchant's VISA number. Merchant treats his copy of the voucher just like a cheque: he deposits it in the Royal Bank. The Royal increases Merchant's chequing account by the voucher amount and sends the voucher, along with the others received that day, to the nearest VISA clearing centre. When the vouchers are processed, the VISA organization first raises the amount owed to VISA by Customer, and then notes the Merchant's bank to which the extra amount is owed. Nothing further happens at this point. The Royal has increased Merchant's deposit and has a future claim on the VISA organization to match it.

At month end, VISA sends to Customer a statement of all her VISA purchases for the month. Some time after that, Customer writes a cheque to the VISA payment centre. VISA decreases the amount owed to VISA by Customer, and allocates the amount of the cheque to the various banks from whose merchants Customer made the purchases. As the cheque is cleared, Customer's deposit in the TD Bank and the TD Bank's settlement deposit in the Bank of Canada are both reduced; the various merchants' banks' settlement deposits are increased and their claims on VISA are reduced.

At the end of the process the net effect is almost the same as if Customer had paid Merchant by cheque. The only remaining difference between payment by cheque and payment with credit cards is that merchants' copies of credit vouchers are not returned to customers even when full payment is made. Only a list of credit vouchers is returned to Customer. That saves a huge amount of paperhandling and courier expense.

Other forms of deposit transfer

Other forms of cheque transfer are available. One is automatic transfer via magnetic tape. This system is used for a wide variety of regular payments from

---

[8] Large (six-figure) amounts are handled as described in the text, individually. Small amounts would not be handled individually, but would be lumped together before being sold by the Royal Bank in the foreign exchange market.

one account into many others. Dividend payments, annuity payments, Canada Savings Bond coupon payments, and the payrolls of millions of Canadians are handled by this method. Also, a range of regular payments from many accounts into one central account are handled this way: prearranged utility-bill payments and house mortgage payments are two examples.[9] For a magnetic tape transfer, either a bank or a computer service company processes the customer's accounts to prepare magnetic tapes of the necessary deposit transfers; a different tape is needed for each institution in which any of the deposits are held. When the time for payment or receipt comes, the tapes are fed into each bank's computer, and the necessary transfers are made electronically. No cheques are issued. Written statements are sent to each participant (for instance, to each employee) just to confirm the transaction. The banks involved experience net clearing gains or losses as a result of tape transfers and handle them just like the net clearing gains and losses from cheque clearing.

A second form of chequeless transfer of deposit is spreading only gradually. The debit card was introduced into Canada by credit unions in 1981–82. A **debit card** is just like a credit card (VISA or Mastercard) except that, in using it to pay merchants' bills, cardholders are authorizing their credit union to deduct (debit) the amount from their chequing account immediately, rather than to add (credit) it to their unpaid credit-card balance for payment at the end of the month. In essence, the debit-card voucher signed by the customer will become just like a cheque written on the customer's account.

What is making the debit card system much different is the new technology of electronic point of sale (POS) terminals in stores. Starting with pilot experiments in various cities in 1989–91, debit cards are replacing cheque payments with electronic transfers for regular retail transactions. In these experiments, retail store clerks use their POS terminals instead of cash registers. The clerks request the customer's bank to transfer the amount of the purchase to the retail store's deposit account. Once the customer has authorized the deposit transfer by entering his or her personal identification number, the deposit transfer takes place instantly. The store's POS terminal prints out one copy of the transaction for the customer and one copy for the store's records. All that remains of the normal cheque-clearing process is that the customer's bank still has to settle with the store's bank by transferring the amount of the purchase between their respective deposits in the Bank of Canada, and that is done electronically, even now, for cheque transfers.

In the system of debit cards plus POS terminals, there are no couriers, no data centres, no shipping of cancelled cheques back to those who wrote them. The pilot experiments are being followed, gradually, by nationwide introduction. Then, for a while, we will have two parallel deposit transfer systems. It remains

---

[9] A retail version of magnetic tape transfers is payment of utility and credit card bills either at automated teller machines or, more recently, via telephone or home computer. In both cases the cheque-clearing process is bypassed.

Source: The Economist, December 16, 1989, p. 79. © The Hulton-Deutsch Collection.

to be seen whether the debit card system will become as popular with the public as the chequing system has been.

The successor to the debit card is likely to be the prepaid **smart card**. Smart cards contain an electronic memory to record the prepaid card balance and deduct from it as the card is used. Such cards are in use for university library copiers in many cities, but the big impact will come from general-usage smart cards issued by VISA and Mastercard and similar companies. These cards will be a plastic and electronic version of travellers' cheques, which are already an equivalent to currency.[10]

There are other forms of deposit transfer that so far are used mainly in international transactions. Money orders, bank drafts, wire transfers, and certified cheques are all alternatives to the ordinary cheque. All are used to make payments that are either large or across national borders. For large interbank transfers, there is an international computer hookup that permits the funds to be relayed to each other instantaneously. This sort of service can be used to get funds between parts of large global firms as well.

[10] For a discussion of these cards and their future, see "A Survey of International Banking," *The Economist* Supplement, April 7, 1990, 33.

▣ Summary

Without money, an economy would have to do all its trading in the form of barter. Pure barter requires a double coincidence of wants, which is quite a restrictive condition. Modern forms of barter do occur occasionally, but usually in barter exchanges where there is some limited form of money involved as well.

Money plays three distinct roles in modern economies: as a unit of account for recording and calculating values, as a medium of exchange for making payments, and as a store of value for postponing spending. The supply of money is defined entirely by money's role as a medium of exchange. The narrow definition (M1) includes only assets used directly to make payments. Broader definitions (M2, M3, and M2+) also include some other assets that are very liquid and close substitutes for narrow money. In Canada, the narrowly defined money supply consists of currency, coin, and chequable demand deposits. Broad moneys include other categories of bank deposits and even, in one case, deposits of non-banks. Broad money measures are very much larger than narrow money and also grow at rates that are often quite different from that of M1.

The current payments mechanism for using our media of exchange consists of two parts. Cash payments, made with currency and coin, are direct physical transfers of bearer instruments between trading parties. Payments by cheque involve transfers of chequing deposits, which are registered assets rather than bearer assets. The bulk of payments in Canada are by cheque. The Canadian Payments Association operates a sophisticated and expensive system of couriers and computers to handle the paperwork of processing millions of cheques each business day.

The paperwork of payments by cheque is greatly reduced by two innovations of the last two decades: credit cards, which replace cheques by non-returnable vouchers; and electronic transfers of funds in any of several forms, which replace cheques with electronic instructions.

Key Terms

barter

double coincidence of wants

money

exchange rate

unit of account (numeraire)

standard of deferred payment

medium of exchange

liquidity

Gresham's law

store of value

narrow money

broad money

near banks

notice deposit

bearer instrument

payments mechanism

float

clearing and settlement
        system

Questions and Problems

1. What swaps or barter transactions have you made during the last month? How inconvenient were they to arrange? Would you rather have received cash instead for what you exchanged?

2. In 1989, just before the loonie was introduced to replace the $1 bill, the Bank of Canada issued uncut sheets of $1 bills, suitable for framing. Were these sheets of bad money or good money, in the sense of Gresham's law?

3. Compare and contrast a change of unit of account with the change from Fahrenheit to Celsius measures of temperature.

4. What is the key requirement for a medium of exchange? Why is it key?

5. List the items you have used or seen used as means of payment. Note the ones that are commonly in circulation. Does Gresham's law predict correctly for the items in your list?

6. How long is it, on average, between the time you add a dollar to your stock of currency (in a purse or wallet) and the time you spend that dollar? How long is the time, on average, between your depositing dollars in your chequing account and then spending them?

7. Trace through the steps you think are required to deal with a cheque that bounces. Some firms charge $5 to $15 for the extra handling such cases involve. Is such a charge justified by extra costs to the firm?

8. Identify the steps in normal cheque clearing that would be eliminated if we all paid by credit card instead.

Suggestions for Further Reading

Bank of Canada. "Recent Developments in Monetary Aggregates," *Bank of Canada Review*; articles with roughly this title appear about once a year.

Neufeld, E.P. *The Financial System of Canada*. Toronto: Macmillan of Canada, 1972.

For an exhaustive treatment of measurements of the money supply, see Peter Martin, *Inside the Bank of Canada's Weekly Financial Statistics: A Technical Guide*, 2nd ed. Vancouver, B.C.: Fraser Institute, 1988, pp. 141ff, or see the *Notes to the Tables* appendix to Table E1 in the *Bank of Canada Review*.

Chapter three

Monetary Standards, Playing Cards, and Army Bills

Chapter 2 has described the roles of money and the particular assets used as money in modern Canada. We have come a long way from the days when all payments were made in heavy coin. The switch to paper money was itself a major innovation with enormous cost savings, and Canada was one of the first countries of the Western world to make the switch. This chapter focuses on Canada's two early experiments with paper money — one in New France after 1685 and one in both Upper and Lower Canada during the War of 1812. The first section of the chapter outlines the various kinds of monetary system that are possible. The final section outlines the main features of Canada's monetary development from 1812 to the present.

You should learn in this chapter:

1. what kinds of money there are;
2. what properties matter if an item is to serve as money;
3. how Canada came to have two of the world's interesting early experiments in the use of paper money;
4. how Canada developed the monetary system that exists today.

SECTION 1

Monetary standards

Money has taken a huge variety of forms because the only fundamental requirement for an asset to serve as money is that enough people have confidence that it will be accepted as payment. There is no limit in principle to the forms of money people might have confidence in. Nevertheless, most forms of money have

33

certain features in common. Money is usually easily portable, transferable, and divisible. These characteristics make the money physically convenient. The other key feature for a form of money to work well is that its supply must be limited and not easily expandable. Usually the moneys that have been convenient have not been limited in supply, and vice-versa. Each economy has had to make its own choice between the two features. The history of the development of money in Western civilization has largely been one of choosing forms that are progressively more convenient but also less naturally limited in supply. The result has been steadily greater efficiency in making payments, but also steadily greater risk of the money supply growing too fast. Argentina in the 1980s has provided the most recent example of a money supply gone berserk, with an annual inflation rate averaging nearly 300 percent from 1980 to 1988, and 3164 percent in 1989.[1] At each stage of monetary reform, government has generally increased its influence over the supply of money. These days, each national economy uses a kind of money for which there is no natural limit on supply, and control over the supply of money is given almost entirely to the government.

Commodity moneys

Early moneys were chosen more for assurance of limited supply than for convenience. **Commodity moneys** were simply some particular commodity such as gold nuggets or cattle or wheat or wildcat skins, that was limited in supply because it was difficult to produce or find. The supply was also limited because some of the commodity was diverted to other uses as decoration, as food, as clothing, or even (in Nova Scotia) as strong drink.

Commodity standards

The next stage in development of money increases the convenience of money, but exposes users to greater risk of oversupply. The commodity becomes standardized, as in the form of minted coins, so that the commodity can be valued by count rather than by weighing or measuring. The extra convenience of minted coins, or **specie**, is obvious. To maintain confidence that each coin contains the standard content of precious metal, minting is certified and each coin stamped by the government (in medieval Europe, usually the king). While the intrinsic value of the coin is the user's guarantee that it will serve as a store of value, coins typically exchanged for even more than their intrinsic value. The business of minting coins was therefore profitable. The profit accrued to the king, and was known as **seigniorage** (from the French *seigneur*). Seigniorage could be increased many times if the king could get away with using less than the standard content of gold or silver (using cheaper base metals instead), so there has always

---

[1] World Bank, *World Development Report, 1990*, and International Monetary Fund, *International Financial Statistics*, May 1991.

been temptation for revenue-hungry kings to "debase" the coinage. The history of money is full of instances of rulers yielding to this temptation.[2]

A monetary system using standardized commodity items such as gold and silver coins is known as a **commodity standard**. The danger in relying on a commodity standard is that users are tempted to cheat. If all silver dollars are treated as equal for exchange purposes, then a silver dollar will still be just as valuable in trade if the user clips a little of the silver off the edges to sell separately. Despite heavy fines and elaborate minting procedures, such as the use of milled edges and fine detail in engraving, the coinage was subject to gradual debasement by less honest users. This problem ended only as commodity standards were replaced by token money.

Token money

The next stage in increasing convenience is **token money**. Token moneys are notes or certificates with little or no intrinsic value, which are guaranteed by the issuer to be convertible into a commodity standard money.

Goldsmiths' receipts were the first form of token money in England, though token moneys had been used much earlier in other countries. A goldsmith's receipt is a token convertible into a specified quantity of gold. The receipt was like any other warehouse receipt but, since gold was used as money, the receipt came to be used as money also. For much of the colonial period up to 1763, the French settlers in Canada used paper tokens in the form of playing cards that were convertible (with a lag) into the silver coin of France. From 1820 to 1914, Canadians used token money in the form of banknotes: paper certificates issued by private banks and convertible into gold coin, or specie.[3]

Token money is more convenient than commodity money both by design and by necessity: the item to serve as a token is chosen precisely for its convenience, and nobody would hold token money in place of the real thing if token money were not more convenient. There is also no incentive to debase token money itself. The token has no intrinsic value; clipping a little off the edge of a banknote only gives the clipper a small strip of worthless paper.

However, limits to oversupply of token money are much weaker than for commodity moneys because the ingredients of token money are so much more readily available. Notes and certificates require only ink and paper. The effective barrier to oversupply of token money lies in the threat of sanctions, should token

---

[2] Seigniorage from our modern money supply is enormous. The annual costs of replacing worn-out banknotes and issuing new ones were $41.5 million in 1990. The annual gain from being the issuer of banknotes is the interest that can be earned from using the banknotes to buy government bonds. That annual interest was $2615 million in 1990. Bank of Canada, *Annual Report 1990* (Ottawa: Bank of Canada), 63ff.

[3] Sources for historical material in this and later sections are E.P. Neufeld, *The Financial System of Canada* (Toronto: Macmillan of Canada, 1972), chapter 1, and E.P. Neufeld, ed., *Money and Banking in Canada* Carleton Library Series 17 (Toronto: McClelland and Stewart, 1964), part 1, especially chapters 1–5 and 14.

Small Change?

The Swedish Bank of Stockholm, founded in 1656, issued the first bank notes in Europe in 1661. These notes became widely used by the public because the copper coinage was very inconvenient to use. The most commonly used coin was worth two dollars and weighed seven pounds. The largest denomination coin, which was worth ten dollars, weighed forty-three pounds. The Swedish bank's notes became very popular soon after they were issued and soon exchanged at a premium above their face value.

Source: T.B. Chudy, *A Study of Free Banking Systems in the Nineteeth Century: Theory and Evidence* (Unpublished Ph.D. dissertation, Simon Fraser University, 1989).

users call for conversion of their tokens into the commodity standard money and should the issuer of the tokens not be able to meet the guarantee. Sanctions against oversupply were weak for many kings and governments. The early history of token moneys was largely one of issuers failing to meet conversion guarantees.

Where token money is convertible into commodity money, the monetary system is described as a form of commodity standard. The most famous of these is the gold standard, the monetary system in use in Britain and many other countries for most of the nineteenth century and up to 1914. Where the token money is convertible into a commodity that is not itself money, the system is known as a **commodity exchange standard**. For example, for the period from 1926 to 1929 in Canada, government-issued Dominion Notes were convertible into 400-ounce gold bars rather than specie. For much of the period from 1945 to 1971, U.S. dollars were convertible into gold bullion rather than specie, and even that only for foreigners.

Fiduciary money

All convertible token money is **fiduciary money** (from the Latin word *fiducia*, meaning trust). The issuer's money is accepted even though it has no intrinsic value, because holders trust the issuer's guarantee that all token money will be convertible into the stated commodity on demand. The weak link is the issuer. Some issuers were not honest. Some honest issuers overestimated the amount of notes they would be able to redeem, just as some borrowers overestimate the amount of loans they will be able to repay. The result was often the bankruptcy of the issuer.

When issuers of token money went into bankruptcy, it was not only the issuers who lost. Holders of the token money got back little or nothing of the "guaranteed" value of their holdings. The whole economy suffered. On several occasions in Canadian history, governments have actually suspended the convertibility of token moneys into commodity money in order to avoid that suffering. The French government twice suspended redemption of its paper money in New France (and, for that matter, in France also). The convertibility of notes issued by private banks was suspended in 1837–38; convertibility of government-issued notes was suspended temporarily in 1914–25, and permanently after 1929. Suspension of convertibility of token moneys removes the only barrier to oversupply. In all periods of suspension except the last, the result was immediate overissue of token money and general price inflation.

Fiat money

The final stage in the progress of moneys from less to more convenient, and from more to less limited in supply, is *fiat money*. A fiat is another word for a law. **Fiat money** is money that is accepted in exchange because a government law is passed to declare it acceptable. Fiat money is not convertible into anything of intrinsic value. Our currency in Canada is a typical example of a fiat money. Bank of Canada notes and coins from the Canadian Mint are money because an Act of Parliament threatens legal penalties for anyone in Canada not accepting them in payment of debts. Bank of Canada notes themselves promise nothing; they merely declare "This note is *legal tender*," and that declaration (with the RCMP and the courts to back it up) makes them acceptable as money. The early paper money of New France was a form of fiat money. It was not convertible into silver coin of France until several months after issue in New France. During that period of several months, the governor threatened to fine anyone not accepting it in payment.

Fiat money can take any form the government wishes, so it is usually made as convenient as technically possible. In Canada, the loonie replaced the one-dollar bill in 1989, for instance, in part because a coin of higher denomination was needed for use in vending machines and parking meters. There is no need to compromise convenience for the sake of ensuring limits to supply, because in the short run the acceptability of fiat money does not rest on assurances of limited supply.

The dark side of fiat moneys is that there is no longer any physical limit on supply. We just have to trust the government not to issue too much. In the light of past history of sovereigns abusing their influence over the supply of money, our modern reliance on fiat moneys is quite a remarkable act of faith. We will discuss in later chapters the arrangements we make in Canada to reduce the chances of excessive monetary growth.

Paper standards

Even fiat moneys are not always the most convenient, so other forms of money have developed alongside fiat money. The other forms are token moneys, convertible into the fiat money. The feature of convertibility makes these token moneys fiduciary, even though the item they are convertible into has no intrinsic value. In Canada, our fiduciary money is bank demand deposits, convertible into currency on demand. The two-level system of fiat and fiduciary money is sometimes known as a **paper standard**. Most modern economies have a paper standard similar to ours in Canada.

Taking a long view of monetary history, we have been very successful in increasing the convenience of money. We have come a long way from the time when a queen's dowry, for example, had to be transported in boxes of coins from one country to another, protected by an armed escort on horseback. Now millions of dollars are transferred instantly between countries by the touch of a computer key. We have also divorced ourselves almost totally from all physical limitations on supply; we have given our governments almost complete control of supply. We now get whatever quantity of money our governments want to issue. The result of both types of progress has been a vigorous, productive financial system and an equally vigorous debate over how governments' monetary powers should be exercised. The next two sections look in more detail at two episodes in our monetary development in Canada that rank among the more successful experiments in world monetary history.

SECTION 2

Playing-card money in Canada, 1685–1763

In the years before 1685, the colony of New France suffered from a chronic currency shortage.[4] The colony received an annual injection of coin from France — the governor's budget allocation — which the governor used to pay the soldiers of the garrison. The soldiers used it to buy goods from local merchants. Local merchants used it to pay their suppliers, who were back in France. Therefore, the colony's coins headed back to France soon after they arrived; many went back on the same ship they came out on. The colony did not have enough currency to handle its normal trade conveniently for the rest of the year. Before 1685, the colonial government had tried several schemes to keep currency in the economy, but none was very successful.

In 1685, it was the governor's turn to feel the pinch. The colonial intendant's (finance minister's) response started a very successful, efficient monetary experiment. For some reason, the French budgetary system changed in 1684, so that the governor and intendant of New France did not receive their funds for 1685 in advance as had been usual in previous years. The funds for 1685 arrived only in early September of 1685.

The intendant had to finance the garrison and meet other expenses for the first eight months. After exhausting his own resources and those of his friends and, as he confided later to a friend, "not knowing to what saint to pay his vows,

---

[4]This section is based on the sources in footnote 1 and the original documents in Adam Shortt, ed., *Documents Relating to Currency, Exchange, and Finance in French Canada* (New York: B. Franklin, 1968).

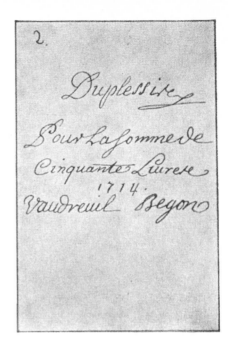

Playing card money, 1714

Source: Courtesy of the Bank of Canada, National Currency Collection. *Photographer:* James Zagon.

money being extremely scarce," he decided to issue paper money, redeemable in French silver coin when the funds arrived.

The paper money consisted of ordinary playing cards cut up into a different shape for each denomination (for the illiterate) and signed by three colonial officials. The intendant did not have the printing facilities or the paper to make more elaborate paper money, and playing cards were both plentiful and durable.

The governor used both carrot and stick to ensure the acceptance of the new money as a medium of exchange. The carrot was his pledge to redeem the cards in September, either in coin or in bills of exchange drawn on the colonial treasury in Paris. The latter arrangement was a very convenient one for merchants with bills to pay in France. The stick was his threat to fine any inhabitant who refused to accept the playing-card money in settlement of debts.

The experiment was popular with everybody except the distant king, who rightly feared loss of control over the expenditures of his colonial officials. When the colony's appropriations finally did come in September, the playing cards were redeemed as promised and then burned. The king forbade repetition of the experiment, but he was far away, and the same problem caused the intendant to issue playing cards again in 1686 and then every year from 1690 to 1719. Because the cards were redeemed as promised, the inhabitants gradually developed enough confidence in them that some cards were hoarded rather than presented for redemption in September. That is, the cards began to be used not only as a medium of exchange, but also as a long-term store of value.

The advantages of card money

Playing-card money was not Canada's first fiduciary money. Private merchants had previously issued their own notes to serve as a circulating means of payment, promising redemption in whatever goods the merchant sold. These notes did circulate but were not accepted by all at par as a medium of exchange. The first money with that status was the card money issued by the state and convertible into currency.

Card money turned out to have some quite unexpected advantages over the silver coinage relied on before. First, it did not leave the colony, since it was worthless elsewhere. Second, it soon eliminated any need to ship coin across the Atlantic Ocean and back again, thereby removing some of the incentive for piracy on the high seas. Within the economy, most of the cards ended up in the hands of the merchants by the fall, since the merchants were the major sellers of goods. The merchants in turn had imported most of the goods from France, and therefore had bills to pay in France. The most convenient method of payment to French suppliers was by endorsing bills of exchange drawn on the colonial treasury in Paris. The merchants therefore redeemed their card money holdings in bills of exchange rather than in coin.

The intendant quickly came to realize that there was little need to send the colony's appropriation out in the form of cash. Mere pieces of paper announcing what total of bills of exchange the intendant could write would be sufficient. When war broke out between France and England, the shipment of coin was forbidden, and all of the cards without exception were redeemed in bills of exchange. The colony had shifted over entirely to a paper-money system, though the paper was still backed by the exchangeability of bills on the treasury in Paris for silver coin. It was a silver exchange standard.

A third advantage of playing-card money to the colony of New France may have been to undermine the morale of the Massachusetts troops sent to capture Quebec in 1690. The Massachusetts troops were promised that they would be paid out of the plunder from Quebec. At some point in their expedition it must have dawned on even the most simple-minded soldier that, in a colony that used playing-card money both as a medium of exchange and as a store of value, much of the plunder would be worthless even if Quebec could be taken. All the paper money in Quebec could not buy a single beer in Massachusetts. The expedition returned home empty-handed. The Massachusetts colony promptly issued its own paper money to pay the troops — the first paper money in the English colonies.

The disadvantages of card money

The system of playing-card money eventually broke down for the reason that most fiduciary-money systems have broken down — overissue. Louis XIV bankrupted the French government with his wars in Europe, so he was forced to suspend conversion of notes of France into silver coin. The card money of New France could be redeemed in paper money of France, but that traded at a substantial discount from its face value in silver coin. Many holders of card money chose not to redeem it at all when that was the alternative. Since new card money had to be issued each year to finance new and large expenditures for the colony's wartime defences, the amount of card money in existence rose steadily, from 4 livres per head in 1702 to 70 livres per head in 1714, an average annual growth rate of 27 percent in the per-capita money supply. Even so, the colonists had more confidence in the card money than they did in the French paper money into which it was convertible. This is a rare case of a fiduciary money being stronger than its backing.

The second card-money episode

The card money was finally redeemed in coin at half face value in 1720, and the first card-money episode was over. The colony immediately returned to the perennial currency shortage that had been typical of the years before 1685, and colonists promptly began to plead for a reissue of card money. Their wish was granted in 1730, and card money was reissued each year thereafter until 1763. Blank cards were used this time. The second card-money experiment worked very well until once again the French government overextended itself and issued paper money to finance large wartime spending. In particular, the army commanders were allowed to issue army orders to pay their bills in the field. These were made legal tender to allow them to circulate as currency, but the amount issued was not controlled by the intendant and was not related to the French government's ability to repay. Since the card money issued by the intendant was subject to a bit more discipline than the army orders, the card money became a superior store of value. Gresham's law came into operation: the superior card money was hoarded, and only the inferior army orders remained in circulation. After New France was ceded to the British in 1763, the card money was eventually redeemed at about one-quarter of face value.

Lessons of the card-money experiment

The lesson drawn from the card-money experiment by the British colonial government was that paper money was dangerous. Not until 1820 was a private bank chartered with the power to issue notes intended for circulation. The notes were to be redeemable on the spot in specie. The card money, by contrast, had been redeemable in the fall, if the ship came in with the colony's appropriations and if the intendant's bills of exchange were honoured in Paris.

In fact, the lesson learned should have been quite different. For most of the 65 years in which the card money was used, the colonists had a stable, safe, and very convenient payment mechanism. In particular, the colony and France saved both lives and resources by not having to ship valuable coin across the sea and back and saved wealth by reducing the number of robberies at sea. The colony's price levels and trading volumes were not subject to unnecessary fluctuations caused by the seasonal flows of currency into and out of the colony.

On the face of it, the success of New France's card-money experiment over so long a period was unlikely. After all, the issuing of new money each year was tied to the government's spending plans, which gave the colonial government control of its own budget constraint. Very often that situation has led to massive overissue and hyperinflation. In New France, fortunately, the colonial government was also subject to an external constraint on its deficits, from the king's treasury in Paris. That outside constraint both limited the issue of card money in New France and gave credibility to the whole experiment. Only when the demands of French wars overrode the constraints of the French treasury (both in Europe and North America) did overissue escalate and credibility shrink. For modern governments of sovereign countries, there is no such outside constraint to rely on to give their currencies credibility.

It is also worth noting that although the card money was convertible directly into silver coin, that feature may not have been necessary after the first few years. As long as local merchants accepted the card money, customers would have confidence in it as a medium of exchange. Merchants in turn needed only to know that they could pay their own bills in France, for which they needed convertibility into bills of exchange on the government in Paris.

SECTION 3

■ Army bills, 1812–14

After the peace of 1763, the British American colonies once again settled into the pattern of chronic currency shortage. "Good" media of exchange, suitable for payments abroad, were shipped to Europe to make those payments. Only "bad" currency stayed behind. The colonists had to make do with worn and defaced coinage of many countries and a variety of merchants' notes, redeemable in merchandise of various sorts and subject to varying discounts from face value. Interest was forming in banks as a source of note issue to replace the merchants' note issue. Three Montreal merchant firms therefore put the following notice in the *Official Gazette* on October 18, 1792:

> The undersigned, having experienced great inconvenience in Canada from the deficiency of specie or some other medium to represent the increasing circulation of the Country, as well as from the variety of money now current, and knowing the frequent loss and general difficulty attending receipts and payments, have formed the resolution of establishing a Bank of Montreal, under the name of the "Canada Banking Company." [5]

---

[5] Quoted in James Stevenson, "The Canadian Banking Company," in E.P. Neufeld, ed., *Money and Banking in Canada*, 28–29.

The scheme fell through for a variety of reasons, and the merchants founded only a bank of deposit rather than a bank of note issue. Twenty years later, however, the British colonial government found itself in the predicament that the French colonial government had been in during its wars. (Incidentally, this was the same predicament that the Canadian government would find itself in during World War I, producing the same response.)

The outbreak of the War of 1812 meant a huge increase in the government's spending for soldiers, munitions, and fortifications. The British imperial government was unlikely to send the necessary funds, as it was still locked in a very expensive struggle with Napoleon. The governor took the advice of his executive council and issued a paper money known as **army bills**. The bills were made available in denominations of 1, 2, 3, 4, 5, 10, 16, 20, 25, 50, 100, and 400 dollars. Interest was paid at 4 percent on bills of $25 and over. Smaller bills were redeemable in coin, larger bills in coin or treasury bills issued in London, at the discretion of the governor. The smaller bills were made out to bearer. The larger bills were made out to individuals but could be transferred by endorsement on the back, like a modern cheque.

The first issue of army bills totalled only 250 000, but as the war progressed the amount outstanding grew to 1 249 000 (a rate of increase of 123 percent per year over the period, much larger than for the French card-money experiment). Fortunately the war was short, so the issue did not have enough time to get out of hand. All the army bills were promptly redeemed at full value (plus interest on the larger bills) at the end of the war.

The army bills proved just as convenient to the colony as had the playing-card money to New France. In both cases, the issue of paper money was successfully used to finance government deficits caused by wars. The difference is only that the War of 1812 was short and the British government was not bankrupted, whereas the French colony's wars were long and the French government was bankrupted on both occasions. The successful ending to the army bills episode served to remove from people's minds the idea that paper moneys inevitably led to overissue and then default. Instead, people remembered the great convenience of a medium of exchange that was easy to use and that would stay in the colony.

SECTION 4

Development of the modern monetary system

Pre-Confederation

After the army bills were paid off and withdrawn from circulation, pressure for introduction of some other convenient money grew quickly. The proposed means was to allow private banks to be set up to issue their own bank notes, redeemable on demand in gold coin. Between 1817 and 1822, five such banks opened their doors, including the Bank of Montreal and the Bank of Nova Scotia. The number of note-issuing banks grew steadily throughout the century. A peak of 60 note-issuing banks was reached in 1900 before a wave of mergers consolidated the Canadian banking system into only eight banks by 1965.

Strangely enough, the army bills episode did not lead quickly to the establishment of a government note issue in the provinces of Upper and Lower Canada. This failure was despite provincial notes having been issued in 1761 in Nova Scotia and in 1790 in Prince Edward Island. Even a domestic Canadian coinage did not appear until 1858. There were several attempts by governors to take over the private banks' note issues, but all these attempts were stoutly opposed by business and banking interests, which favoured both free enterprise and an elastic money supply. The bankers knew a good thing when they saw it; borrowing by issuing bank notes paying zero interest, in order to lend to merchants paying positive interest, was too profitable a business to be shared with government. The government persevered, however, and in 1866 introduced Provincial Notes in the Canadian provinces.

Post-Confederation

After Confederation in 1867, Provincial Notes were replaced by **Dominion Notes**. As these government notes were introduced, banking legislation was changed to allow private banks' notes to be redeemable in either specie or the government notes. Dominion Notes were redeemable only in specie. Canada therefore had a three-tier monetary system: private bank notes convertible into Dominion Notes and Dominion Notes convertible into specie. It was convenient for the banks to have Dominion Notes as an extra form of cash reserves against their note issue, since (like the card money of New France) Dominion Notes did not leave the country to pay for imports.

The three-tier monetary system of chartered bank notes, Dominion Notes, and specie has changed since Confederation to a two-tier system of just Bank of Canada notes (plus a token coinage) and chartered bank chequing deposits. Specie was eliminated by the government suspending convertibility of both Dominion Notes and private bank notes into specie. Convertibility was suspended from 1914 to 1925 because of the urgent needs of war finance during World War I: much of Canada's part in the war was financed by the government printing money, which it could not have done if the money had to stay convertible into specie. Convertibility was suspended permanently after 1929, part of a general breakdown of the international gold standard system in the late 1920s.

Chartered bank chequing deposits were added to our money supply gradually as the public came to use chequing accounts to make payments. Business customers were the first, relying more and more on their chequing deposits (known as *current accounts*) over the period from 1867 to 1935. Household use of cheques was not widespread until after 1958, when personal chequing accounts were introduced.

Bank of Canada notes were added to our monetary system in 1935, when the Bank of Canada was established to take over monetary responsibilities from the Department of Finance. To help it in this function, the Bank of Canada was given a monopoly of note issue. The Bank of Canada therefore took over responsibility for both Dominion Notes and the remaining note issue of the chartered banks and issued its own Bank of Canada notes to replace both as they wore out. By then banks had come to rely more on issue of business chequing deposits to finance their lending activity and less on issue of their own bank notes; private bank notes continued to be issued up to 1935, but they were not important to banks' profits.

The history of any monetary system is mainly a history of currencies and banks. Only in the last 30 years have non-bank financial institutions played any significant role in Canada's monetary system, though non-banks have long been important in other parts of the financial system. Banks still dominate in the market for chequable deposits, but non-bank financial institutions now account for one-fifth of the market. Most of the non-banks have entered the market for short-term deposits only recently, as part of a general movement of all financial institutions to spread themselves over more financial markets. The exceptions are credit unions and caisses populaires; they have always raised their funds by issue of household deposits. Only in 1960 did credit unions and caisses start to issue chequable deposits. However, in the 1980s they seized some initiative from banks by pioneering the issue of debit cards in Canada.

Until 1983, one of the barriers to entry into the market for chequable deposits has been that the cheque-clearing mechanism was operated by the Canadian Bankers' Association. Non-bank institutions wanting to have their cheques cleared for payment had to do so through one of their rival banks. In 1983, responsibility for the cheque-clearing mechanism was transferred to the Canadian Payments Association, a body that includes banks, all credit union centrals, about two dozen trust and mortgage loan companies, and a few other deposit-issuing firms.

The future: a cashless, chequeless society?

Crystal-ball gazing is always dangerous, especially when predicting changes in household habits formed over decades. Still, some parts of the future payments mechanism are already with us in the form of the automated teller machine and the home computer. It seems likely that we will come to make more and more of our future payments the way many of us pay our utility bills today — by punching buttons on a computer. Now the computer we use is the automated teller machine at bank branches and in shopping malls. In the future, we will also use computers in stores and at home. Some people do already. The computers at stores will be point-of-sale (POS) terminals, connected to the banking system computer network. These will replace the modern cash register. By using a telephone hookup, computers at home will be connected to the banking system computer network only when we want them to be. As this trend develops, we can expect to see banks introducing extra charges for handling cheques. That charge will speed up the trend to chequeless transfers considerably. Banks, after all, would like to get out from under the burden of handling all those bits of paper each business day. For institutions that have the necessary computer systems, automated payment of large transactions is already on the way.

It seems unlikely that cash will disappear. Transfer of bearer notes is still a very convenient mechanism of payment, and it is secret. Also, hot dog vendors and ice cream stands will not find it worthwhile to set up POS terminals. Therefore, until we lose our taste for privacy and hot dogs, we will not stop using cash. As electronic payment becomes easier, however, we will find ourselves making fewer and fewer cash payments, and therefore carrying around smaller and smaller amounts of cash.

SECTION 5

◱ Summary

The items that have served as money in the past have generally been easily portable and divisible. The successful items have also been limited in supply. There has been a steady progression in Western civilization from naturally scarce but relatively inconvenient moneys, such as the precious metals, toward lighter and more convenient paper currencies. There has also been a progression toward moneys without any automatic limit on supply other than the good judgment of bankers or governments. Money was initially chosen to be some relatively scarce, low-bulk and high-value commodity. Then the commodity was standardized in the form of coins. Later, token moneys were added by being made convertible into commodity money. In the modern era, token moneys are used by themselves without convertibility into anything else. We supplement our currency issues (a token money) with bank deposits convertible into currency (a token money convertible into a token money). The quantity of token money created now is controlled entirely by the government through its central bank.

The playing-card money of New France was an unplanned but successful early experiment in paper currency. Only the excessive wartime needs of the French government led to the overissue and collapse of the playing-card currency. From 1812 to 1814, the issue and later redemption of army bills to finance wartime spending provided another successful experiment with paper currency. Private note issue by chartered banks followed shortly thereafter.

Canada's monetary system after the army-bills episode consisted initially of coin (specie) and bank notes redeemable in specie. Dominion Notes were added in 1868. Chequable deposits were added to the monetary system gradually through the nineteenth century. In 1935 the Bank of Canada took over the Dominion Notes issue and also the private note issues of chartered banks. Now we have a two-tier token money system consisting of Bank of Canada notes and coin (fiat money) plus bank deposits redeemable in Bank of Canada notes.

Key Terms

commodity money	fiduciary money
specie	fiat money
seigniorage	paper standard
commodity standard	playing-card money
token money	army bills
commodity exchange standard	Dominion Notes

Questions and Problems

1. What sort of societies are likely to use cattle as money, and why?

2. Why is there concern about overissue of token moneys and commodity standard moneys but not about commodity moneys?

3. Does a modern government make more seigniorage from paper money than old-style kings used to make from their coinage?

4. Why did playing cards circulate in French Canada as a medium of exchange? Were they also a store of value?

5. How did Gresham's law make its appearance during the first and second card-money episodes?

6. What limit was there on the issue of private bank notes after 1817? What limit is there on the issue of Bank of Canada notes now?

7. What is the key ingredient necessary for an item to serve as money? Does Monopoly money (from the board game) have that property? Does gold?

Suggestions for Further Reading

McCullough, A.B. *Money and Exchange in Canada to 1900*. Ottawa: Parks Canada and Dundurn Press, 1985.

Neufeld, E.P., ed. *Money and Banking in Canada*. Toronto: McClelland and Stewart, 1964.

———. *The Financial System of Canada*. Toronto: Macmillan of Canada, 1972.

Shortt, Adam, ed. *Documents Relating to Currency, Exchange, and Finance in French Canada*. New York: B. Franklin reprint, 1968.

Chapter four

The Roles of the Financial System

The previous two chapters have described the monetary system. We will now look at the financial system as a whole. The chapter describes each of the several roles that the financial system plays in an economy. Many of the roles of the financial system involve financial flows in the economy, so financial flows are described. Finally, this chapter lays out the features to be looked for in a successfully functioning financial system. In Chapter 15 we look back to see whether Canada's financial system has these features or not. The current chapter is designed to set the financial system into perspective. Chapters 5 and 6 describe the financial system in more detail.

You should learn in this chapter:

1. the various roles a financial system plays in an economy;
2. the basic flows of funds in a financial system;
3. the features to be looked for in a successful financial system.

SECTION 1

◻ The roles of the financial system

Aside from providing useful and interesting employment for those who master the contents of this book, the financial system plays five major roles:

1. it channels saving into real investment;
2. it provides a medium of exchange;
3. it provides a variety of stores of wealth;
4. it provides borrowing facilities;
5. it makes monetary policy possible, and affects its effectiveness.

Channelling saving into real investment

The financial system channels the flow of saving into real investment, a process that is discussed fully in section 2. **Saving** is defined as the flow of income in any year that is not spent on items consumed in that year. **Real investment** is defined as the purchase of durable goods (also called **real assets**), where durable means not consumed in the current year. Real assets include housing, plant and equipment, and inventories.[1] Spending on new financial assets is not real investment; it is referred to as either financial investment or lending.

Some saving requires no channelling at all. Where the saving and real investment spending are both done by the same person or firm, the financial system is not needed. This would be the case if Acme Chemical Ltd. used all its undistributed profit (the part not spent on taxes or dividends) to add to its fleet of trucks, or if the O'Malley family ploughed all the family income it could spare during the year into building a summer home at the lake.

Where the saving is done by someone who does not want to invest in durable goods and where the real investment is planned by someone who cannot finance it all himself or herself, the financial system is needed. It is through lending in the financial system that the saving flow of one group finances the real investment spending of other groups.

The financial system matches up savings not directly reinvested with investments not directly or self-financed. Without it, not much real investment would take place. Without that investment, the economy would have a smaller stock of capital equipment and housing, and therefore lower productivity and a lower standard of living.

Providing a medium of exchange

The financial system creates assets (collectively called "money") that serve as a medium of exchange. Money is an asset used by all sectors of the economy for buying and selling everything else, a specialized device to save the transactions costs of barter (discussed in Chapter 2). As part of its role in providing a medium of exchange, the financial system also operates the payments mechanism by which money is transferred from one holder to another.

Providing a variety of stores of wealth

If we are to postpone spending some of our income until retirement or the next rainy day, we need some store of value into which to put saving. Real assets

---

[1] In introductory macroeconomics, to make models easier to describe, spending on durable consumer goods, such as appliances and cars, is classified as consumption spending rather than real investment even though most appliances and cars are not consumed within the year of purchase. Since saving is defined as income less consumption, spending on durable consumption goods is also deducted from income to arrive at saving measures used in introductory macroeconomics. More sophisticated macroeconomic models do not always use such crude definitions of saving and real investment.

serve as stores of value. Real assets are available in most economies, except where ideology bans private ownership. The financial system also provides a wide variety of **financial assets** that savers can buy instead of real assets. The O'Malley family can buy financial assets (pension annuities) that will generate a level lifetime income stream beginning at retirement. Acme Chemical can buy financial assets (such as treasury bills) that can be easily sold off or cashed in should Acme need to finance losses during recessions. The financial system not only creates a wide variety of assets to suit a wide variety of needs. The financial system also operates many different markets, at considerable expense, to make such assets more easily resaleable, or liquid.

Providing borrowing or credit facilities

The other side of providing savers with a variety of ways to store their wealth is providing borrowers with a range of debts from which to choose. Every financial asset held by a saver is, at the same time, a debt to the person or firm that issued it, so the variety of debts available must be exactly the same as the variety of financial assets. Once people can borrow, they can arrange to buy many durable goods that are too expensive to finance out of current saving. That widens their range of spending choices and increases real investment spending. For instance, the O'Malleys can finance their summer home partly by saving out of current income and partly by taking out a mortgage loan to be repaid from future income. Acme Chemical can draw on its line of credit at the bank to finance a larger fleet of trucks than its current profits alone could finance, repaying the loan from future income.

Stabilizing the economy

In any developed economy, levels of money supply and interest rates have important effects on levels of output, inflation, and unemployment.[2] If the financial system allows the government to exert control over money supply or interest rates or both, the government can affect levels of output, inflation, and unemployment. It is a short but contentious step from there to the idea that the government can use the financial system to *stabilize* output, inflation, and unemployment; that is, to bring about low levels of inflation, more constant unemployment rates, and output levels that stay close to capacity. Stabilization policies are at the core of ongoing macroeconomic debate; we will discuss them at length in Parts Five and Six of this text.

---

[2] Experts disagree on the exact channels by which money supply and interest rates affect the economy, but almost all agree that the effects are important.

SECTION 2

◼ The flow of funds

Flows of funds are the raw material of the financial system. They are explained in introductory and intermediate macroeconomics courses using circular flow diagrams. One of the properties of the circular flow diagram is that each year the economy generates a flow of saving. The flow of saving comes from each of the four major sectors of the economy: households, governments, business firms, and the rest-of-the-world (ROW) sector. Households do not spend all of their disposable income on consumption; what is left is household saving. Governments do not usually spend all of their tax revenues on purchases of *current* goods and services, that is, goods and services consumed this year; what is left is government saving.[3] The business sector pays taxes and dividend payments out of its before-tax profit, but usually has some of its profit left over (undistributed); what is left over is **net business saving**. Business firms also have available all of the revenue set aside as capital consumption allowances; when that is added, the total is *gross* business saving. Finally, the rest-of-the-world (ROW) sector as a whole both adds to and uses up the flow of saving by domestic sectors. Capital inflows add to domestic saving; capital outflows soak up domestic saving. The **net capital inflow** measures the extra contribution of the ROW sector to Canadian saving; this is sometimes called foreign saving.

The sum of foreign saving plus gross domestic saving (household plus government plus gross business saving) gives **gross saving** for the economy, a measure of the total flow of funds into the Canadian financial system each year. Figure 4–1 shows this flow in a modified circular flow diagram. For convenience, the breakdown of income and spending flows between domestic sectors is left out of Figure 4–1; spending is either current spending or real investment spending (by whatever sector), and income is either consumed or saved (by whatever sector). The bottom of Figure 4–1 shows gross saving as the sum of gross domestic saving plus the net capital inflow.

There is only one ultimate destination for gross saving: it must end up somehow financing the flow of real gross investment. In an economy without a financial system, with no lending or borrowing, each individual's saving would be reinvested directly by the same individual. In economies with a financial system, there is another alternative: savers can lend their savings and real investors can borrow from others to finance their real investment. This is **direct lending**. In economies with well-developed financial systems, savers do not need to find real investors to lend to; that is, households do not need to find real estate developers or expanding manufacturing firms. Savers can lend indirectly through

---

[3] In calculating government saving, spending on capital items (roads, airports, etc.) is counted as capital rather than current spending. Both current and capital spending are counted in calculating government surpluses or deficits. The government surplus is therefore government saving less government capital spending. The government deficit is of course just the name we give to a negative surplus.

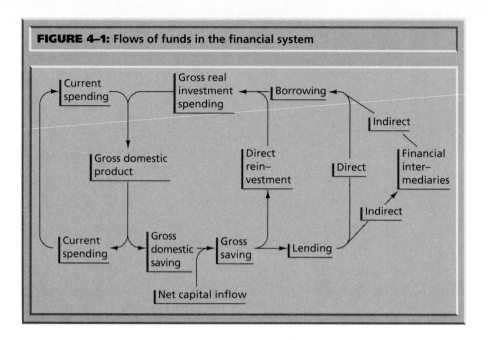

FIGURE 4–1: Flows of funds in the financial system

financial intermediaries such as banks, trust companies, or insurance firms. As a general rule, more developed financial systems have larger shares of gross savings flowing through financial intermediaries to real investors. The benefit of **indirect lending** through financial intermediaries is that savers and real investors need not agree on using the same type of financial asset. Often the kind of financial asset that best suits savers would be too constraining as a debt for real investors. Dealing with financial intermediaries instead of directly with each other, savers and real investors can both have more of the terms and conditions they want.

The three routes that gross saving can take on the way to real gross investment (shown in Figure 4–1) leave quite different paper trails. Direct reinvestment of savers' own funds may leave no paper trail at all: at year end, the saver who is a real investor owns an extra real asset, but may not have some document to prove it. When savers lend directly to real investors, the lender ends up holding a financial claim of some sort (a loan note, a bond, or a share, for instance) issued directly by the real investor. When savers lend indirectly through financial intermediaries, the saver acquires a debt or financial claim issued by a financial institution; the real investor issues its financial claim to the financial institution rather than to the saver. For instance, the O'Malleys might lend their saving to a bank by acquiring a two-year term deposit issued by that bank, and the bank might then lend the funds to Acme Chemical by acquiring a business loan note issued by Acme.

The different routes that gross saving can take on the way to finance gross real investment imply different amounts of asset creation. Direct reinvestment of $100 creates only the real asset worth $100. Direct lending of $100 creates the real asset (worth $100) and also a financial asset worth $100. Indirect lending creates the real asset (worth $100) and also two or more financial assets worth $100 each. Where indirect lending goes through many different institutions, financial assets can be created that are worth in total many times the real investment that is ultimately financed. For instance, in 1988 gross investment of $131 billion was accompanied by a net increase in financial assets of $169 billion. The total recorded stock of real assets of $2218 billion was more than matched by an outstanding stock of financial assets of $3348 billion.[4]

The flow-of-funds constraint

There is a constraint underlying the flow of funds diagram in Figure 4–1 which can be presented in many ways that are useful for the financial analysis of an economy. The constraint, called the **flow-of-funds constraint**, is that gross saving must equal gross real investment.[5] One useful restatement of the constraint is that gross domestic saving less real gross investment must therefore equal foreign saving or the net capital inflow. In everyday language, what we invest that we cannot finance at home, we must finance abroad.

Another restatement of the flow-of-funds constraint has been used widely in the 1980s to analyze the large deficits of that decade.[6] First, break down domestic savings into private saving (S_p) and government saving (S_g). Break down real gross investment spending into private investment (I_p) and government investment (I_g). Let NCI stand for the net capital inflow. The flow-of-funds constraint becomes

$$I_p + I_g = S_p + S_g + NCI.$$

This can be easily rearranged as

$$(I_g - S_g) + (I_p - S_p) = NCI.$$

In order to put this in more familiar form, add government current spending (C_g) to both I_g and S_g. $I_g + C_g$ is total government spending (G). $S_g + C_g$ must equal total government tax revenue (T). Therefore,

$$(I_g + C_g) - (S_g + C_g) = G - T.$$

---

[4] Statistics Canada, *Flow of Funds and National Balance Sheet Accounts, 1988* (Ottawa: Supply and Services, 1990).

[5] Alert readers may have noted that (a) real gross investment refers only to purchase of *new* capital goods, while (b) gross saving can be invested in either new *or already existing* capital goods. Real gross investment can differ from gross saving for individuals and even for whole sectors, but not for the whole economy. For the whole economy total investment in already existing capital goods must be zero: already existing capital goods are fixed in total, so there is no way that all sectors together can either increase or decrease their holdings of existing capital goods.

[6] For instance, the Bank of Canada's *Annual Report* for 1989 contains this passage: "What will essentially determine how the Canadian current account performs across the years will not be the precise stance of monetary policy, but the extent to which Canada can generate its own private and public saving to match its demand for investment." (p. 10).

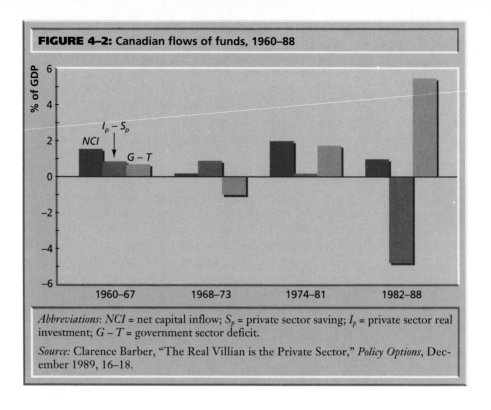

FIGURE 4–2: Canadian flows of funds, 1960–88

Abbreviations: NCI = net capital inflow; S_p = private sector saving; I_p = private sector real investment; $G - T$ = government sector deficit.

Source: Clarence Barber, "The Real Villian is the Private Sector," *Policy Options*, December 1989, 16–18.

The flow-of-funds constraint can then be written as

$$(G - T) + (I_p - S_p) = NCI,$$

or, in English, the government sector deficit plus the private sector deficit must always equal the net capital inflow. When applied to current policy, the flow of funds constraint implies that an economy that has a large net capital inflow (as Canada and especially the U.S. have had over the 1980s) will not be able to reduce it as long as government deficits far exceed private sector surpluses. Even the adjustment of exchange rates, normally considered a powerful adjustment mechanism, will not lower NCI unless somehow either the government or the private sector deficit is reduced.

Figure 4–2 shows the relative sizes of the savings flow ingredients in Canada over the last three decades. The total domestic deficit (private-sector plus government) has been slightly positive through most of Canada's history; we have made up the gap by borrowing abroad. After 1982 the public sector deficit mushroomed, at the same time that the private sector deficit turned into a huge surplus. Net capital inflows into Canada were therefore not much affected. In the United States, by contrast, a similar huge increase in the government deficit in the 1980s was not matched by any extra private sector surplus, so all of the extra government deficit has been financed with enormous net capital inflows.

Over the 1980s foreigners (particularly Japanese and Germans) acquired bonds and shares issued by the U.S. government and by U.S. firms worth hundreds of billions of dollars.

Note before we leave this section that the constraint we have just discussed is not the same thing as an equilibrium condition. The fact that at any point of time the constraint equations described in this section must be true does not mean that the economy is in equilibrium and will have no tendency to change. Far from it. For instance, the flow of funds constraint was satisfied over the period 1974–81 in Figure 4–2, but the recession of 1981–82 followed anyway. The flow of funds constraint was satisfied each year from 1982 to 1988, but 1988 was far different from 1982. The flow of funds constraint does not prevent change in the economy; it only constrains changes to follow certain patterns.

SECTION 3

◻ Evaluation of the financial system

Evaluating our financial system involves comparing the features of our actual financial system with those of an ideal financial system. What features would an ideal financial system have? The answers are generally the same as for any other sector. Differences are only of emphasis. An ideal financial sector would be efficient both in using its inputs and in allocating funds among borrowers. It would be equitable. It would also contribute to economic stability.

Efficiency

An efficient sector gets the maximum output from its inputs and therefore produces its output at the minimum cost. We are familiar with these ideas in the manufacturing sector, from elementary microeconomics. Being efficient and minimizing costs also apply to the financial sector. The output of the financial sector consists of creating and servicing a wide range of financial instruments, and providing a wide range of financial services. Inputs into the financial sector include the thousands of individual Canadians who stream into financial institutions each day to work, the huge array of computing systems that keep track of all the financial system's information, and the buildings that contain them. We do not want the financial system to waste any of those inputs; they could be used to produce more or better financial services, or they could be useful in other sectors of the economy.

The consequences of inefficient use of inputs in the financial sector are high costs to the public and a narrow range of financial assets and services. High costs to the public may be in the form of high service charges or in the form of personal inconvenience such as standing in long lines. A narrow range of financial assets will mean either unnecessary exposure to risk on the part of borrowers and lenders or even transactions foregone (and jobs lost) that would have been

Source: Phil Mallette, *The Financial Post*, September 18, 1989, p. 14.

worthwhile. For instance, imagine the consequences to Canada if our financial system had still not introduced automated teller machines to provide routine deposit and withdrawal facilities, so that all servicing of deposits was still done by individual tellers at bank branch wickets. Imagine the waste and frustration if financial institutions were open only between 10 a.m. and 3 p.m. each day, as used to be the case before extra competition in the 1960s forced banks to keep hours more convenient for customers.

Allocational efficiency

The financial system affects the output level of all other sectors by the way in which it allocates savings among real investment projects. That allocation involves some selection of which investment projects get financed and which do not. If the financial system does not allocate savings to the most productive real investments, output growth in the economy will suffer. Anything that affects an economy's growth rate will be very important in the long run, however small it might appear in the short run, since the effects compound over time. The cartoon above was inspired by some flamboyant dynamic inefficiency from late 1989: the efforts of investment dealers to channel savings into junk bonds, which were used to finance takeover bids and, incidentally, earn very large upfront fees for the dealers. Many of the junk bonds defaulted in late 1989 and 1990, including those issued by Canadian real estate developer Robert Campeau to buy up a huge U.S. chain of retail stores.

As an example of allocational inefficiency, imagine the consequences if financial institutions were barred from lending to small firms with no established earnings record, or firms without real estate to use as collateral. The most productive ventures conceived by such groups would not be financed; the public's saving flow would go instead to finance extra takeover bids and new head offices of large firms. Many of today's large companies (for example, Apple Computers) would never have been started successfully in such a financial system. The economy would be much worse off, like a Third World dictatorship that has used its foreign aid for showy monuments rather than for new roads and schools.

Equity

The third criterion for evaluation is the equity with which the financial system treats savers and borrowers and financial institutions. Democratic societies such as ours believe in equal opportunity for its own sake, quite independent of whether equal opportunity is likely to foster static or dynamic efficiency. That means our financial system should not deny loans or charge more to certain individuals just because of some feature, such as colour or nationality or sex or age, which has nothing to do with the likelihood of repayment or cost of servicing. We call that unfair discrimination. Women, for instance, have successfully protested against the provision of insurance and annuities at different rates for men and women, on the grounds that it is unfair discrimination.

Even countries that carefully try to promote equity in their financial system may not see it as being in their national interest to extend that consideration to outsiders. Foreign-owned financial institutions in all countries frequently protest against unfair discrimination in favour of domestically owned financial institutions. In discussions of the 1980s, both domestic and foreign financial institutions argued for the removal of many discriminatory regulations restricting their range of activity, claiming that the financial system should be a "level playing field." This is an argument based on equity. The detailed legislation that prohibits insider trading (trading by company officials on the basis of special company information not available to the general public) reflects our desire that all traders start on an equal footing. This, too, is a policy based on equity considerations.

Stabilization of the economy

We all have an interest in low inflation and stable output growth at output levels close to capacity. We would like to avoid large fluctuations in both price levels and rates of unemployment. The financial system affects our ability to avoid such fluctuations. The nature of the financial system has an influence on how monetary policy affects the rest of the economy. If there are effective barriers preventing flows of funds between financial markets, for instance, monetary policy will be unable to affect the full range of financial asset yields and will have less impact on aggregate demand and output levels. Also if the financial intermediaries that issue most of our money supply do not hold cash reserves in fixed ratio to their deposits, monetary policy impacts will be more uncertain.

◻ Summary

The financial system serves several roles in any economy. It channels saving flows into real investment. It provides media of exchange and operates the economy's payment mechanism. It provides convenient stores of wealth, and a range of different credit facilities for savers and borrowers. And it may offer the government or central bank an opportunity to influence the economic stability of the economy.

Flows of funds from savers to real investors take different routes. The lending routes, direct or indirect, are made possible by having a financial system. Some lending occurs directly to real investors, but most is made indirectly to real investors through one or more intermediaries. The result of indirect lending can be the creation of many dollars of financial assets and debt for every dollar of real investment financed. The flow of funds in any economy is subject to a flow-of-funds constraint, which has been useful for analyzing recent deficit behaviour in Canada and the United States.

Financial systems can be evaluated just like other sectors. The criteria for any such evaluation are that it should be efficient both in using its inputs and in allocating funds between real investment projects, that it should not discriminate unfairly, and that it should contribute to the stability of output growth and price levels. There is much more agreement on the meaning of the efficiency criteria than on what the other two criteria imply in practice.

Key Terms

saving	net capital inflow
real investment	gross saving
real assets	financial intermediaries
financial assets	direct lending
flow of funds	indirect lending
net business saving	flow-of-funds constraint

Questions and Problems

1. Explain how the financial system performs each of the roles listed in Chapter 4 for you personally.

2. If you treat spending on education as accumulation of human capital (that is, investment in skills), what proportion of your investment is financed by

your own saving and what portion by borrowing? Is the borrowing direct or indirect?

3. Have you been a lender this year? Has your lending been direct or indirect? If the latter, through which intermediary? Do you know where your funds ended up?

4. What do you think the relative sizes of public deficits, private sector deficits, and net capital inflows were in 1940 after the outbreak of World War II but before the United States entered the war?

5. The big banks in Canada and abroad lost large amounts of their wealth on loans to Third World countries in the 1980s as these countries proved unable to repay either interest or principal. Was this an example of allocational inefficiency? Explain your reasoning.

Suggestions for Further Reading

Statistics Canada. *Flow of Funds and National Balance Sheet Accounts*. Ottawa: Supply and Services (annual).

Economic Council of Canada. *A Framework for Financial Regulation*. Ottawa: Supply and Services, 1987.

——. *A New Frontier: Globalization and Canada's Financial Markets*. Ottawa: Supply and Services, 1990.

Chapter five

Financial Markets and Institutions

Any financial system is a complex network of relationships among lenders, borrowers, and firms such as banks and insurance companies (which are both lenders and borrowers). Some organizing idea is required to sort the mass of details into categories before we can describe the financial system. The organizing idea used in this chapter and for most of this book is that the financial system can be usefully seen as a set of markets, one for each type of financial asset. Sections 1 and 2 of this chapter describe the different types of financial markets to be found in Canada. Section 1 also traces some of the connections between Canadian and foreign markets that have made large parts of our financial system truly global rather than national. Section 3 introduces the different types of financial institution currently in place and identifies the main financial markets in which they participate.

You should learn in this chapter:

1. the main distinguishing features of financial markets;
2. the relative sizes of different financial markets and of different participant groups, as revealed in the national balance sheet accounts;
3. the examples of each type of financial market to be found in Canada;
4. the extent of international connections in Canada's financial markets;
5. the kinds of financial institution active in Canada, with their main types of borrowing and lending;
6. how yields are defined and calculated in financial markets.

The national balance sheet view of financial markets

It was pointed out in Chapter 1 that the financial system can be thought of as a set of financial markets, one for each major type of financial asset or debt — one market for term deposits, one for chequable deposits, one for common stocks, and so on. Each financial market has a supply of its asset, a demand for its asset, and an equilibrium yield, which clears the market. Supply and demand both refer to the total outstanding quantities of the asset, rather than to flows of new borrowing or new lending. A summary view of financial markets can therefore be had simply by looking at the total quantities borrowed and loaned in each market. That is what the national balance sheet accounts provide.

The **national balance sheet accounts** are a set of balance sheets for each group in the economy and for the economy as a whole. A **balance sheet** records assets and debts at a point of time such as the year-end and calculates **wealth** (W) as the difference between total assets (A) and total debt (D):

$$W = A - D.$$

Other names sometimes given to wealth are **equity** (for firms) and **net worth** (for households).

Table 5–1 presents an overview of asset markets, drawn from Canada's national balance sheet accounts at the end of 1988. Each column represents a different sector of the economy. Each row represents a different asset or liability. Each cell represents the amount of a particular asset or debt held by or owed by a particular group in the economy. All groups are included, so the table is closed in the sense that each financial asset held by any group is shown somewhere on the table as being owed by another group. For instance, the currency and deposit holdings shown in the seventh row from the top, under financial assets, are also shown in the currency and deposits row under debts as being owed or issued by banks and near banks, by other financial institutions, by governments, and by the rest-of-the-world sectors. Similarly, shares and claims held as assets by people are also shown under debts in the corporate sectors as shares and claims.

The rows of Table 5–1 identify different markets. Each asset row shows the demand for an asset by various sectors; that is, it shows the composition of the lenders for that asset, as of 1988. Each debt row shows the supply of a financial asset by borrowers in various sectors.[1] Take the first financial asset listed, currency and deposits. You see that $540 billion in currency and deposits are

---

[1] It is always true for any financial asset that the total held as an asset must equal the total outstanding as debt; each financial asset is both asset and debt at the same time, just as a coin is both heads and tails. Measured holdings are not always desired holdings, however; if yields are too low, some holders will be trying to unload their asset onto someone else.

TABLE 5–1: An overview of asset markets for 1988 (in billions of dollars)

Sectors	Persons and uninc. business	Non-finan'l corps	Banks and near-banks	Other finan'l institutions	Govern-ments	ROW*	Total
Total assets	1899	1338	580	784	518	447	5566
Real assets	913	956	17	38	294		2218
Housing and consumer durables	643	72		4	1		721
Plant and equipment	79	751	14	26	238		1109
Land	190	133	3	7	55		388
Financial assets	986	382	563	747	224	447	3348
Shorter term:							
Currency and deposits	343	49	51	19	17	62	540
Consumer and trade credit		105	71	17	3	7	201
Loans		9	147	36	18	22	233
Treasury bills and paper	26	22	46	42	16	19	172
Longer term:							
Mortgages	11	6	183	66	4	1	270
Bonds	83	6	28	178	39	150	484
Insurance and pensions	267						267
Shares and claims	209	155	22	348	103	163	1000
Foreign investments			3	19			23
Other assets	47	30	13	20	24	22	156
Total debt	342	990	572	726	499	219	3348
Shorter term:							
Currency and deposits			482	8	2	48	540
Consumer and trade credit	91	89		1	8	12	201
Loans	34	121	4	21	20	32	233
Treasury bills and paper		47		18	108		172
Longer term:							
Mortgages	216	53		1			270
Bonds	1	125	12	28	321		487
Insurance and pensions				266	1		267
Shares and claims		502	50	354	5	90	999
Foreign investments						23	23
Other debts		52	24	29	36	15	156
Wealth or net worth	1557	349	8	58	18	228	2218

Notes
* Rest of the world.

a) Persons and unincorporated businesses includes not only farmers and unincorporated retail store operations and professional practices of doctors and lawyers and the like, but also non-profit institutions such as churches, unions, and universities.

b) Shares includes claims of corporations on affiliated corporations, whether in the form of loans or bonds or shares.

c) Real asset holdings are valued at replacement cost in the national balance sheet. Share values of corporations (shares and claims) are measured as the residual of assets less non-share liabilities, but usually with real assets valued at a "book" value, which is typically less than replacement cost. Shares and claims are therefore undervalued in the national balance sheet. For each sector, the amount of undervaluation is the difference between replacement cost and book value of the sector's real assets. It is this undervaluation that accounts for corporate sectors having any residual wealth after deducting total debts (including shares and claims) from total assets.

d) Assets held in trust by a trustee are treated as being held by the ultimate beneficiary; for example, assets held by trust companies in registered retirement savings plans for individual households are treated as being held directly by households in the first column.

Source: Statistics Canada, *Financial Flow and National Balance Sheet Accounts, 1988* (Ottawa: Supply and Services, 1989). Some totals do not add exactly because of rounding errors in consolidation of this table.

shown in the asset row, assets held by all sectors, though mainly by households. The same $540 billion is also broken down by borrower in the debt row. The debt is mostly issued by domestic banks and near-banks ($482 billion), but also in part by foreign banks in the rest-of-the-world sector ($48 billion), by firms in the other financial institutions sector ($8 billion), and by the federal government ($2 billion of coinage).

Highlights of the national balance sheet table

Table 5–1 shows the relative importance of different financial markets, grouped by type of asset. The main features of financial markets to be noted from Table 5–1 are listed below.

1. Financial markets are big relative to the markets for real assets. Total financial assets exceed total real assets in value ($3348 billion versus $2218 billion); the total of currency and deposits held ($540 billion) exceeds the total value of residential and commercial land ($388 billion).

2. Financial institutions collectively dominate most financial markets either as lenders or as borrowers. Collectively, financial institutions account for over one-third of all financial assets and debts in the table. Table 5–1 shows that total assets of financial institutions ($580 billion + $784 billion) are over half as big as the total recorded value of real assets for the whole economy ($2218 billion). This reflects the extent of development of the Canadian financial system. A wide range of financial assets has been issued by financial institutions, from currency to life insurance policies to term deposits, which suit asset holders' needs better than the alternative of holding only real assets such as land and housing. As the range of financial assets issued has increased, so has the share of financial assets in total assets held by all sectors.

3. Most financial markets have a wide range of types of debtors and lenders, as well as a wide range of participants within each type. Few financial markets are very concentrated or monopolistic, at least when the broad market categories of Table 5–1 are used.

4. Longer-term assets (typically five years or more to maturity) are collectively much bigger in totals outstanding than shorter-term assets (less than five years to maturity). Of the longer-term assets, shares dominate. Of the shorter-term assets, currency and deposits dominate.

5. Households (part of the persons and unincorporated business sector) participate in a fairly narrow range of financial markets. They are important lenders only in the markets for currency and deposits, for life insurance and pensions, and for shares (mainly through mutual fund shares). They are important borrowers only in the markets for consumer credit and mortgage loans.

6. Non-financial corporations and governments do relatively little lending. What lending they do is mainly to affiliated corporations, usually subsidiaries, in the form of shares and other claims.

7. The market for treasury bills and short-term paper is the market in which monetary policy is usually conducted. That fact makes it very important in the financial system, and it is described fully in Chapter 6. However, Table 5–1 shows it to be a small market in total value of assets outstanding.

International connections

There are many international connections reflected in Table 5–1, but some are difficult to see. The ROW column shows that foreign firms and financial institutions are important lenders to Canadian residents by holding shares and claims on associated Canadian firms (mainly, but not entirely, subsidiaries) and on unrelated firms ($163 billion), by holding large quantities of bonds issued (usually abroad) by Canadian provinces and corporations ($150 billion), by holding deposits issued by Canadian banks ($62 billion), by making loans directly to Canadian firms ($22 billion), and by buying Canadian treasury bills and other short-term paper in the wholesale money market ($19 billion).

Foreign lending is very important in the Canadian economy. To see that, we need only look at the volume of funds supplied by the rest of the world to Canadians in international markets, relative to Canada's national output. Per dollar of national output, Canada receives a higher volume of foreign lending than any other member of the G-7 group of nations (United States, Japan, Germany, France, United Kingdom, Italy).[2] Canadians' lending to the rest of the world is shown in the bottom half of the ROW column. Canadians hold a wide range of foreign-issued debts — shares of subsidiaries ($90 billion), loans

---

[2] Economic Council of Canada, *A New Frontier: Globalization and Canada's Financial Markets* (Ottawa: Supply and Services, 1990).

($32 billion), deposits in foreign banks ($48 billion), and a range of other foreign-issued assets such as shares, treasury bills, and bonds. In addition, Canadians lend a lot in the form of foreign currency deposits issued by Canadian banks and near banks: non-financial corporations have $6 billion and households $11 billion of their total currency and deposit holdings denominated in foreign currency.

Canada is even more tightly connected to international financial markets than the above list suggests. Table 5–1 does not reflect at all the large-scale business with foreigners outside Canada undertaken by foreign branches of Canadian banks and insurance companies; nor the constant competition of Canadian with foreign investment dealers and foreign banks to arrange for foreign placement of foreign bond issues; nor the regular use by Canadians of international futures and options markets to hedge against or to speculate on foreign exchange and interest-rate fluctuations; nor the constant flow of information between head offices abroad and the dozens of foreign banks and other financial agencies now working in Canada. Large-scale markets, and even some of the more sophisticated smaller-scale financial markets, became international rather than national over the course of the 1980s. Many Canadian financial markets have long been closely connected to those in the United States; for them, globalization has meant opening up connections outside North America, Europe, and Asia.

SECTION 2

Classification of Canadian financial markets

Each financial market is unique, defined by the kind of financial asset or debt issued in it. Nonetheless, two broad distinctions are useful in discussing financial markets — the distinction between retail and wholesale markets and the distinction between primary and secondary markets. A third grouping of financial markets can be identified using the type of instrument used. Each of the resulting groups is described in this section.

Retail versus wholesale markets

The first distinction is one taken over from the trade sector, between retail and wholesale. Households and smaller firms typically borrow and lend in retail markets. Large firms typically borrow and lend in wholesale markets. Financial institutions often borrow and lend in both.

Retail market transactions are small scale and generally not carried out in any standardized unit larger than the dollar. Retail deposits are as likely to come in amounts such as $1394.52 as in round thousand-dollar amounts. Retail transactions are usually customized to suit the parties to each transaction. For instance, each small business loan has a different size and repayment date. Most retail financial markets have interest rates that are posted for all transactions by financial institutions rather than being negotiated afresh for each new customer. Posted rates are generally set only at discrete quarter-percent levels, such as 11, $11\,^1/_4$, or $11\,^1/_2$ percent, and posted rates are not changed more than weekly.

Wholesale markets are characterized by exactly the opposite features: large-scale, standardized transactions in multiples of some large standard amount. Wholesale markets' interest rates or prices are generally arrived at by impersonal bidding from both sides of the market, and vary continuously over time. Wholesale markets generally operate over the telephone and video screen rather than in person, which means there are fewer barriers to entry. New lenders in the market for corporate bonds need only a set of telephone lines, not a network of branch offices located where the corporations are. Since so many wholesale customers are firms rather than persons, some wholesale markets are referred to more commonly as **institutional markets**.

Retail transactions generally have higher processing costs per dollar lent than wholesale transactions. Another characteristic of many retail financial markets is that they have unequal market power, with many on one side of the market and relatively few on the other. In such markets, households and small businesses will earn less interest on their savings and pay more interest on their debts than if they were in wholesale markets.

Primary versus secondary markets

A second useful division is to distinguish between primary and secondary markets. There is a primary market for each financial instrument that exists. There is a secondary market only for some of them, though the number of secondary markets grows each year. A **primary market** is one in which each transaction involves the buying of a newly created asset or newly issued debt rather than one created or issued at some previous time. For example, buyers of Canada Savings Bonds are buying bonds that the government of Canada issues to them fresh, not bonds that were previously the property of some other bondholder. Similarly, when we buy a pension contract, we buy a new one rather than a secondhand one that was returned by a previous owner. Because new assets and debts are created each time, primary market transactions all imply new borrowing and new lending.

Secondary markets are to primary markets as the used car market is to the new car market. In secondary markets, those transacting are all buying or selling assets already issued some time earlier. For example, in a typical stock market transaction a pension fund may sell its shares in a mining company, and an insurance company may buy them.

Primary markets are obviously important to the economy because they are the markets in which borrowing and lending take place. Without primary markets, funds could not be channelled from saving to real investment. Secondary markets contribute by providing liquidity and by providing current market valuations for all traded assets.

Source: *The Economist*, October 21, 1989, p. 88.
© 1989 Kevin Kallaugher/The Economist Newspaper Ltd.
Reprinted with permission.

Liquidity in an asset refers to how quickly and at what cost it can be converted into money. The existence of a secondary market is a valuable feature for holders of all but the shortest-term assets, since it allows them to sell the assets rather than hold them to the maturity date — that is, it gives the assets greater liquidity.

Records of the sales of assets taking place in secondary markets provide a current market value for such assets. Current market valuation is important both to potential new buyers and sellers, but also to all who need to know today's value of the assets in a trust or pension fund or corporate balance sheet. Looking up a current market valuation in newspaper reports of secondary market trading activity is much cheaper than hiring a professional appraiser to estimate an asset's value.

TABLE 5–2: Classification of financial markets by type

Asset group	Retail markets		Wholesale markets	
	Primary	Secondary	Primary	Secondary
Currency and deposits	Yes	No	Yes	Limited resaleability
Consumer and trade credit (customer credit)	Yes	Not yet	Yes	Limited
Loans	Yes	Not yet	Yes	Yes
Treasury bills and short-term paper	No	Limited, via mutual funds	Yes	Yes
Mortgage loans	Yes	Developing fast	Yes	Yes
Bonds	Mainly Canada Savings Bonds	Yes	Yes	Yes
Life insurance and pensions	Yes	No	No	Yes, for insurance
Shares and claims on associated firms	Yes	Yes	Yes	Yes

Money, capital, and hedging markets

Financial assets that are traded in secondary markets are often grouped by type of financial instrument. The group of markets for short-term liquid assets are known collectively but confusingly as the **money market**. The group of markets for long-term corporate debt and equity and for government debt are known collectively as the **capital market**. The group of markets for insurance, options, and futures contracts are referred to as the **hedging markets**. Other financial markets are not usually grouped together under any collective label. Money, capital, and hedging markets are described in some detail in the next chapter.

Table 5–1 identifies financial markets by the asset traded and shows whether that asset is typically issued for short or long terms. Table 5–2 shows which financial markets are retail or wholesale, primary or secondary. (The main secondary markets are further described in Chapter 6.)

As can be seen from Table 5–2, secondary markets are almost the exception at the retail level, but they are the rule at the wholesale level. Much of the wholesale secondary market activity has developed only in the 1980s. Most of it developed in international markets first and then spread to domestic Canadian markets. It seems likely that secondary markets will soon develop in Canada, even at the retail level, for such assets as loans and consumer credit.

SECTION 3

◻ Financial institutions in Canada

No description of the financial system is complete without a brief tour of the financial institutions that play such an important part in the markets of Table 5–1. Financial institutions are distinguished from non-financial firms by the fact that financial institutions borrow funds mainly in order to lend them again rather than to add to their own productive capacity. Financial institutions issue their own debts and use the funds to buy financial assets rather than real assets such as plant and equipment. The main kinds of debts issued and assets bought by Canada's different types of financial institution are shown in Table 5–3.

Deposit-takers

The first category of firms is singled out by the fact that they raise most of their funds by taking in money in deposits of some sort. The Bank of Canada is apart from the other deposit-takers, because it issues its deposits only to the federal government and to clearing members of the Canadian Payments Association. The other **deposit-takers** issue deposits that are either redeemable on demand and chequable (demand deposits), redeemable with some notice (notice or savings deposits), or else redeemable at a specific future date (term deposits).[3] Even term deposits have relatively short terms, less than five years; this means that each year deposit-taking firms must issue a significant volume of new deposits just to replace old deposits that are maturing.

Within the deposit-taking group are firms of vastly different sizes. The credit unions and caisses populaires are small-scale firms operating only at the retail level and only in Canada. The chartered banks are generally either large domestic banks or smaller subsidiaries of large foreign parent banks. Both groups of banks operate at the wholesale level in Canada and abroad. The domestic banks also have huge retail branch networks. The group of trust and mortgage loan companies contains a few large firms that operate at home and abroad (two of them even maintain their own clearing deposits with the Bank of Canada), but the group also contains many smaller firms closer to credit unions in scale and type of operation.

Contractual savings firms

Contractual savings firms raise funds by taking in regular savings contributions of households under a long-term contract, usually for insurance protection or for a retirement pension. Contractual savings firms provide only statements of

---

[3] The notice requirement for notice deposits is waived in practice in Canada; exercising it would be interpreted as evidence that the bank was poorly managed. On the other hand, term deposits of banks are usually redeemable (at some interest penalty) before maturity.

TABLE 5–3: Main activities of financial institutions

Intermediary	Main debts issued (borrowing)	Main assets bought (re-lending)
Deposit-takers:		
Bank of Canada	Currency and deposits	Gov't of Canada bonds and treasury bills
Chartered banks	Savings and term deposits	Business and consumer loans, mortgages
Credit unions and caisses populaires	Savings and term deposits	Mortgage and consumer loans
Trust and mortgage loan companies	Term deposits	Mortgage loans
Contractual savings institutions:		
Life insurance companies	Life insurance and annuity policies	Mortgage loans, bonds, shares
Trusteed pension plan	Liability to plan contributors	Bonds and shares
Property and casualty insurance companies	General insurance policies	Bonds and shares
Social security funds	Liability to contributors	Provincial bonds, Quebec Crown corporation shares
Miscellaneous:		
Sales finance and consumer loan companies	Short-term paper and bonds	Consumer and business loans
Investment dealers	Loans	Treasury bills and short-term paper
Mutual funds	Shares	Shares and bonds
Venture capital companies	Shares	Shares and bonds of startup companies
Investment companies	Shares	Shares
Public financial institutions	Shares, bonds, and deposits	Mortgages and bonds

liability to policyholders (usually at year-end) rather than anything transferable such as a share or bond certificate. Contractual savings contracts are difficult to cancel, so the flow of funds to contractual savings firms is not nearly as uncertain as it is for deposit-takers. Because their source of funds is so secure, contractual savings firms can afford to invest in longer-term assets than can deposit-takers.

The social security funds (the Canada Pension Plan and the Quebec Pension Plan) are public institutions with the longest-term assets of all.

Other financial institutions

Outside the deposit-takers and the contractual savings firms are a miscellaneous collection of firms. All but the first group of firms in this category tend to buy longer-term assets. The first group of firms, sales finance and consumer loan companies, lend to businesses and consumers to finance retail sales of consumer goods; if they financed their lending by issuing deposits they would look much like banks, but instead they borrow by issuing short-term paper in wholesale money markets.

Investment dealers are the financial equivalent of retailers for the financial system: they make the secondary markets in financial assets work by helping other groups issue and buy and resell (all for fees, of course). Investment dealers must hold some inventory of the assets in which customers trade, for the same reason any retailer must have inventories of the goods to be sold: convenience to the customer.

Mutual funds raise their funds by issuing shares; closed-end funds issue shares only the once, and holders must resell them in the secondary stock market to get their money back; open-end funds issue shares on demand and redeem shares on demand (with a short lag) at a price determined by the current market values of the mutual funds' assets. Venture capital companies, usually owned by a pool of other financial institutions, specialize in lending to starting companies, usually by buying shares and long-term loans. Holding or investment companies invest for long periods by buying shares and making longer-term loans to client companies; holding companies usually exert some managerial influence over management of the companies to whom they lend.

The last group, public financial institutions, also includes a variety of firms. The Alberta treasury branches issue deposits and make loans just like the other deposit-takers. The Canada Deposit Insurance Corporation insures most of the retail deposits issued by the deposit-takers. The Canada Mortgage and Housing Corporation operates like a mortgage lender of last resort, and also insures mortgage loans against default risk on a huge scale. The Farm Credit Corporation, the Export Development Corporation, the Federal Business Development Bank, and a host of provincial financial institutions offer special credit to borrowers in a particular sector or province. Public financial institutions generally raise their funds by issuing bonds, backed by the guarantee of their parent government.

Figure 5–1 shows only the main markets frequented by each different type of financial institution. The larger financial firms in Canada generally take part in many different financial markets, often in several different countries. As a result, different types of deposit-taking firm, for instance, are coming to look much more alike in their financial activity. Differences are coming to be matters of emphasis on particular types of lending or borrowing, which of course can change quickly. There remain some significant legal differences, but even those

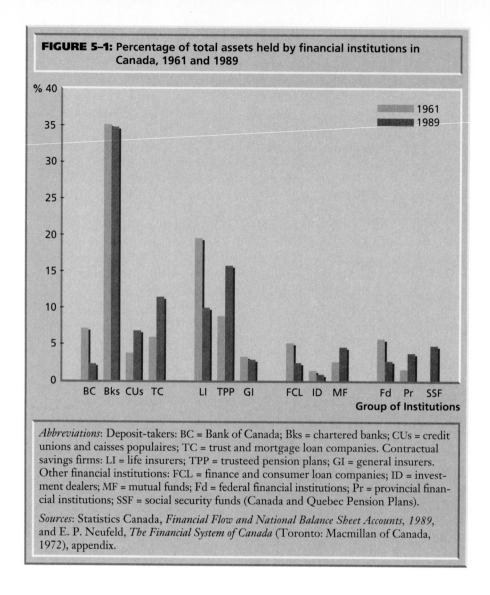

FIGURE 5–1: Percentage of total assets held by financial institutions in Canada, 1961 and 1989

Abbreviations: Deposit-takers: BC = Bank of Canada; Bks = chartered banks; CUs = credit unions and caisses populaires; TC = trust and mortgage loan companies. Contractual savings firms: LI = life insurers; TPP = trusteed pension plans; GI = general insurers. Other financial institutions: FCL = finance and consumer loan companies; ID = investment dealers; MF = mutual funds; Fd = federal financial institutions; Pr = provincial financial institutions; SSF = social security funds (Canada and Quebec Pension Plans).

Sources: Statistics Canada, *Financial Flow and National Balance Sheet Accounts, 1989*, and E. P. Neufeld, *The Financial System of Canada* (Toronto: Macmillan of Canada, 1972), appendix.

have been disappearing fast in the wave of deregulation that swept world financial markets in the 1980s.

Figure 5–1 puts the different types of financial firm into perspective as giants and pygmies by asset size. The contrast between 1961 levels and 1988 levels also shows which have been faster growing and which have been languishing. The chartered banks are the biggest single group, especially now that their large mortgage loan company subsidiaries are consolidated with the parent banks. The banks have not been growing as rapidly as many other groups, however; the banks' main growth has been abroad rather than in Canada. The banks are matched in total assets by the total of all contractual savings firms, which have been growing much faster as a group. Public financial institutions collectively are large enough to matter, but are concentrated in a few special markets. Investment dealers, who play such an important role in the daily functioning of Canada's major secondary markets, look like the pygmies of the financial system in terms of total assets; the importance of their role is out of all proportion to their size.

SECTION 4

▢ Yields

Any further discussion of the financial system will have to be more specific than the broad survey of this chapter. Any specific discussion of financial markets will quickly need to use the concept of yield. The yield of a financial asset is usually its most important attribute. It is therefore time to explain in some detail what a yield is and how it is calculated.

Yield is the return on a financial or real investment, expressed as an average annual fraction or percentage of the invested amount. When yields are used in mathematical formulae, it is almost always the fractional form that is used. Outside formulae, we normally discuss yields in percentage form. Unless otherwise qualified, the yield is calculated for the period an investment is held, rather than for some other period such as the life of the asset. There are alternative yield concepts, which are described later in this chapter, but they are always referred to by a special name (such as coupon yield, dividend yield, yield to maturity, etc.) to distinguish them from the "normal" yield concept defined here.

Financial yield or discount rate

Because there are many different forms in which an investment can provide returns, the formula for calculating yield as an average annual percentage takes many different forms. All the forms are based on the concept of a **present discounted value**. The present discounted value is the current equivalent of some other value that is payable only in the future. To be specific, the present discounted value (PDV) of $100 payable a year from now is the amount in the present that would grow to equal $100 in a year if allowed to grow at $100\,r$ percent per year, where r is the currently available interest rate on assets. This relationship can be expressed in the formula

$$PDV(1 + r) = \$100\,,$$

and therefore the present discounted value itself is $\$100/(1 + r)$. In this expression, the rate r is called the *discount rate*.

The general approach to calculating the yield on an asset is to find the discount rate r that causes the present discounted value of all returns from holding an asset to equal the present discounted value of all costs incurred. If an asset offers returns of $\$R_1$ one year from now, $\$R_2$ two years from now, and $\$R_5$ in five years, and if it costs $\$C$ now, the yield this asset provides is the number r such that

$$\$R_1/(1+r) + \$R_2/(1+r)^2 + \$R_5/(1+r)^5 = \$C.$$

If the asset's cost included also an amount $\$C_1$ payable a year from now, the right-hand side of the equation above would be $\$C_0 + \$C_1/(1+r)$.

The yield r in the preceding equation is in fractional form rather than percentage form; that is, a yield of 10 percent appears as $r = 0.10$ rather than $r = 10$. Calculation of r from such an equation is by process of trial and error, generally. It is messy by hand, but quick by hand calculator or computer. Fortunately, many cases encountered in financial markets are much simpler than the general equation above. The most common examples are given below, all scaled to a standard size of $1000, for convenience:

1. Simple one-year loan:

Assume the loan is for $1000, all to be lent now. That is the cost. Assume the returns come in the form of an interest coupon of $120 payable at year-end, and the principal value of $1000 payable also at year-end. The yield is r such that

$$(\$1000 + \$120)/(1+r) = \$1120/(1+r) = \$1000.$$

In this equation, $1 + r$ must be 1.12, so r must be 0.12, or 12 percent. For this simple one-year case, the yield can be calculated more straightforwardly as just the ratio of one-year gain over current cost, or $r = \$120/\$1000 = 0.12$.

2. Three-month treasury bill or other discount paper:

Any discount paper returns only its principal at maturity; there is no interest coupon. Assume the cost to buy the treasury bill now is $980. Yield is r such that

$$\$1000/(1+r)^{0.25} = \$980.$$

The discount factor $(1+r)$ is raised to the power 0.25 because r is expressed as an annual rate, and the treasury bill matures only 0.25 years in the future. The yield must be 0.0842, or 8.42 percent. As a rough approximation for assets maturing in only part of a year, yield can first be calculated on a part-year basis (for example, a yield per three months) rather than as an annual yield; then the part-year yield must be multiplied by the number of part-year periods in a year (four in the case of a three-month treasury bill). The treasury bill would have a three-month yield of 2.04 percent and an annual yield of 8.16 percent (4×2.04). This rough approximation is usually adequate for yields under 5 percent per year, but not for larger yields.

3. *Two-year bond (held to maturity):*

Assume the bond costs $990 to buy now in the secondary bond market, and the bond provides semi-annual interest coupon payments of $60, plus the repayment of principal of $1000 at the end of two years. The yield r is such that

$$\$60/(1+r)^{0.5} + \$60(1+r)^1 + \$60/(1+r)^{1.5} + \$1060/(1+r)^2 = \$990.$$

Yield can be found by a calculator search or a computer program to be 0.1298, or 12.98 percent.

4. *100 shares of common stock held for six months:*

Let the cost of the shares be $1000 ($10 per share), payable now. Let the expected returns be two quarterly dividend payments of $10, and an expected resale value of $1200 at the end of six months. The yield r is such that

$$\$10/(1+r)^{0.25} + (\$10+\$1200)/(1+r)^{0.5} = \$1000.$$

The yield can be found by trial and error to be 0.491, or 49.1 percent.

5. *Perpetual bond, or a share of stock that is held forever:*

Let the cost be $1000 payable now, and let the return be $90 payable at each year-end forever. The yield r is such that

$$\$90/(1+r) + \$90/(1+r)^2 + \cdots + \$90/(1+r)^n = \$1000,$$

where n approaches infinity. For large values of n (say, 40 or bigger), this equation approximates the much simpler equation $\$90/r = \$1000$, from which it is easy to see that the yield r must be 0.09, or 9 percent.

Alternative concepts of yield

Other yield concepts are sometimes used in financial markets. They are always preceded by some qualifying label to distinguish them from the yield concept explained above. Many of them are useful because they can be calculated with less information than the normal yield concept. Three of them are current yields, yields to maturity, and real yields.

Current or dividend yield: The current yield on a bond or share is calculated by dividing the annual coupon or dividend returns by the bond or share's current market value. Any capital gain or loss is ignored. Current yield is not to be confused with coupon yield on a bond; the coupon yield is found by dividing the annual coupon payments on a bond by the bond's *face value*. Relative to current yields, coupon yields ignore any possible premium or discount of market value from face value.

Yield to maturity (on a bond): These are the yields calculated and reported in the financial press. They differ from normal yields only when the lender has a holding period different from the maturity of the bond. Example 3 on page 75 is an example of a yield to maturity. For assets that have no maturity, such as shares of stock, a yield to maturity does not exist. An investor planning to sell a bond before maturity will, in general, receive a different stream of returns and have a different average annual yield than is calculated for the yield to maturity.

Real and nominal yields: The **real yield** on an asset is the normal financial yield less whatever inflation rate (in fractional form) is expected over the term of investment. The normal financial yield (without subtracting any allowance for inflation) is called a **nominal yield**. Nominal yields treat each dollar of return as having the same purchasing power regardless of when it is received.

SECTION 5

Summary

Two useful ways of classifying financial markets are into retail versus wholesale markets, and into primary versus secondary markets. There are examples of all four combinations in our financial system. Financial markets are also grouped together by type of asset; consequently, we talk about the money market for short-term liquid assets, the capital markets for long-term debts and equity, and the hedging markets for risk-avoidance contracts of various sorts.

The national balance sheet accounts provide a quick summary of total assets and debts outstanding in each financial market. For each asset, the national balance sheet accounts show who the lenders are and who the debtors are. These are the two sides of any financial market. The picture that emerges is of a financial system with many different markets, in most of which there are lenders and debtors from several different sectors. Increasingly these financial markets not only raise funds from primary lenders and lend to primary borrowers, but they also allow trading of previously issued financial assets between holders; more and more financial assets now have secondary as well as primary markets. Households participate in only a few of the markets available. Non-financial corporations also tend to lend in only a few markets, although they borrow in all available forms.

Financial institutions both borrow and lend at the same time; they issue debts to finance financial assets rather than real assets such as housing or plant and equipment. There are a wide range of financial institutions in Canada. Each has a few main types of asset or debt that it buys or issues, though each financial institution typically lends at least small amounts in almost all financial markets. Deposit-taking institutions dominate in short-term lending and borrowing, while contractual savings institutions dominate in long-term lending and borrowing. Public financial institutions generally play very significant roles for narrow parts of the financial system.

Key Terms

national balance sheet accounts
balance sheet
retail markets
wholesale market
institutional market
primary markets
secondary markets
liquidity

money market
capital market
hedging markets
deposit-takers
contractual savings firms
yield
present discounted value
real yield

Questions and Problems

1. What is the equity of Acme Chemical if it has fixed assets that cost $10 million originally, bonds outstanding of $3 million, inventories of $1 million, cash of $0.5 million, and accumulated capital consumption allowances of $4 million?

2. Which Canadian financial markets in Table 5–1 do not have any significant international connections either through lenders or through borrowers?

3. In which financial markets do banks and near banks participate, according to Table 5–1?

4. What are the characteristics of the typical financial market for household financial transactions?

5. What common factors are there among the financial institutions that have increased their share of total assets between 1961 and 1988, according to Figure 5–1?

6. From Tables 5–2 and 5–3, make a table or grid showing which types of financial institution are competing head to head as lenders or borrowers. In which financial markets does this occur?

Suggestions for Further Reading

Neave, G. *Canada's Financial System*. Toronto: Wiley, 1981.

Neufeld, E.P. *The Financial System of Canada*. Toronto: Macmillan, 1972.

McMillan, Alexander. *An Introduction to Canadian Financial Markets: an Analytical Approach*. Scarborough, Ont.: Prentice-Hall Canada, 1989.

Statistics Canada. *Financial Flow and National Balance Sheet Accounts* (annual).

Chapter six

Money Markets, Capital Markets, and Hedging Markets

Charts and tables from the national balance sheet accounts do little to describe the day-to-day workings of financial markets. For the main secondary markets of the financial system (the money market, the capital markets, and the hedging markets), there is a fairly elaborate set of institutions and procedures. Most primary markets are much simpler; for instance, a supplier lends to a customer firm in the 90-day trade credit market simply by letting the firm delay payment of its bill for 90 days.

Money market assets and capital market assets will be generally familiar from the last chapter. Hedging market instruments may be less familiar; many hedging markets are very new, and the instruments traded do not show up much on balance sheets. Financial innovations change each of these markets from one year to the next, but some description of their fundamental characteristics is possible.

You should learn in this chapter:

1. who takes part in the money and capital and hedging markets;
2. what main assets are used in each market;
3. how futures contracts, options, and swaps are used to hedge financial risks;
4. how hedging markets make financial markets more global.

SECTION 1

☐ The money market

The **money market** is relatively small in terms of total assets. It is significant out of all proportion to its size, for two reasons. First, the money market is the market through which monetary policy must start to have its effects on the rest of the economy. Second, changes in money market yields are often used as a signal by rate-setters in other financial markets to adjust their own yields. Changes in retail deposit interest rates follow changes in yields on (wholesale) money market deposits. The money market also influences loan rates. Most bank loans are negotiated with floating rates, which are tied more or less closely to money market yields. International loan rates are usually tied to the **London interbank offer rate** (LIBOR), which is the most influential money market rate of all. Domestic bank loan yields are tied to the banks' prime loan rate, but banks adjust the prime rate to match very closely the changes in short-term money market deposit rates. Money market yield changes serve as signals to these other markets because the money market is a large auction market reflecting demand and supply from many sectors of the economy.

Borrowers and instruments

The money market is a wholesale market for short-term liquid assets. The minimum amount is $100 000; average amounts are in millions. Maturities are short; several assets have been developed just for overnight financing, and the bulk of assets are issued for terms between 30 and 90 days. Money market assets are issued for fixed terms and cannot be redeemed before maturity. Liquidity is provided for the longer-term assets by their being negotiable (easily transferable between holders) in a wide, active secondary market. Money market assets must have very little default risk to be easily resalable and therefore liquid; borrowers must either have an excellent credit rating of their own or else they must have their debts guaranteed by some other firm or large bank that does have an excellent credit rating.[1]

The money market is both primary and secondary. New borrowing is done in the money market by making available new debt either through money market dealers or (for the largest borrowers such as big banks and the federal government) directly. Secondary trading of money market assets is mainly done through money market dealers. As far as lenders are concerned, there is no difference between primary and secondary purchases from a money market dealer. Money market dealers around the world survive by finding the best places for lenders to place short-term funds. If they find that Canadian money market assets offer a better return than U.S., German, or Japanese assets, including the costs of converting in and out of Canadian currency, the world's money market dealers will advise clients to shift funds into the Canadian money market.

The money market has become a global market in the last decade. Listings of money market yields in *The Globe and Mail, The Financial Post,* or the *Financial Times* show yields for assets issued in Canada, the United States, and abroad, denominated in several different currencies (see the accompanying newspaper

---

[1] Assets with significant credit risk cannot be kept liquid because each potential buyer must run through a time-consuming credit check on the issuer before making a decision.

A Guide to Money Market Terms

Bankers' acceptances (BAs)   Paper issued by non-financial firms, without collateral or interest coupon, sold at a discount. Upon acceptance by a large bank, for a fee of about 1/4 percent, repayment of principal at maturity is guaranteed by the bank. BAs are issued by lesser-known firms unable to issue commercial paper on their own or unwilling to incur the large set-up costs of money market borrowing for ocassional trips to the market.

Bearer deposit notes   A form of paper issued by banks that is transferable by mere physical delivery, without re-registration. Bearer deposit notes are issued without interest coupons and are sold at a discount.

Buybacks   A purchase and resale agreement arranged by investment dealers with lenders other than the Bank of Canada. Dealers sell securities to lenders for a few days or more under an agreement to buy them back at a specific price; the price difference provides the yield.

Day-to-day loans   Loans from banks to investment dealers, secured by government bonds as collateral, repayable on at most one day's notice.

Interbank deposits   Very short-term, non-marketable term deposits issued from one bank to another, often sold abroad or in foreign currency.

Note   Unsecured debt with a term usually under five years.

Other call loans   Loans from non-banks to investment dealers, with securities as collateral; repayable on one day's notice but not frequently called.

Paper   Short-term debt without interest coupon, repayable only at maturity, issued in round amounts, sold at a discount; issued by large firms with excellent credit ratings as commercial paper, by sales finance companies (with consumer debts as collateral) as sales finance paper, and by other non-financial firms (with a bank guarantee) as bankers' acceptances.

Purchase and resale agreements (PRAs)   A form of loan from the Bank of Canada to investment dealers who are money market jobbers. Instead of taking government bonds as collateral for a loan, the Bank of Canada actually buys the bonds from money market dealers in need of cash, and sells them back a few days later at an agreed price. The difference between purchase and resale price determines the yield on a PRA. PRAs also appear as special PRAs when the Bank of Canada initiates the loan, and in reverse as sale and repurchase agreements (SRAs).

Special call loans   Loans from banks to investment dealers, with securities as collateral, repayable within 24 hours. These are frequently called by banks as part of daily cash reserve management.

Term   Length of time to final redemption of an asset. Short term is a year or less, long term is over ten years.

Treasury bill (T-bill)   Government debt issued without interest coupon, repayable in round amounts only at maturity, sold at a discount (which provides the yield to buyers); an asset so liquid that financial market professionals often just refer to it as "cash."

Money Markets

Supplied by: Royal Bank of Canada
Indicative wholesale late afternoon rates

Canada

Bank Rate	8.96
Prime Rate	9.75
Call Loan Average	7.00

Bankers Acceptances	Fri	Prev day	Week ago	4 Wks ago
1-month	8.79	8.80	8.94	9.16
3-month	8.78	8.79	8.90	9.09
6-month	8.90	8.98	8.97	9.17
T-Bills				
1-month	8.65	8.67	8.84	9.01
3-month	8.66	8.71	8.82	9.02
6-month	8.82	8.82	8.89	9.05

U.S.

Discount Rate	5.50
Prime Rate	8.50
Fed Funds	5.50

Commercial Paper	Fri	Prev day	Week ago	4 Wks ago
1-month	5.90	5.90	5.80	5.78
3-month	5.95	5.95	5.83	5.80
6-month	6.05	6.05	5.85	5.82
T-Bills				
1-month	5.36	5.39	5.36	5.38
3-month	5.57	5.56	5.53	5.47
6-month	5.74	5.71	5.68	5.61
Commercial CD's				
1-month	6.10	6.08	5.87	5.92
3-month	6.20	6.13	5.95	5.95
6-month	6.30	6.25	6.10	6.05

International

	Fri	Prev day	Week ago	4 Wks ago
Euro deposit rates (Bid)				
US$ - Overnight	5.75	5.75	5.62	5.56
1-month	6.00	5.93	5.81	5.81
3-month	6.12	6.06	5.93	5.93
6-month	6.31	6.25	6.06	6.06
C$ - 3-month	8.50	8.44	8.50	9.06
DM - 3-month	8.93	8.93	5.93	9.00
YEN - 3-month	7.56	7.62	7.62	7.68
£ - 3-month	11.25	11.25	11.25	11.43
London Interbank offer rate				
1-month		6.12	6.06	5.93	5.93
3-month		6.25	6.18	6.06	6.06
6-month		6.43	6.37	6.18	6.18

Canadian & U.S. Govt. Bond Yields

Supplied by: Royal Bank of Canada
Indicative wholesale late afternoon rates

Canadian	Fri	Prev day	Week ago	4 Wks ago
2-YEAR	9.34	9.28	9.17	9.77
5-YEAR	9.62	9.53	9.36	9.37
7-YEAR	9.79	9.74	9.52	9.54
10-YEAR	9.89	9.81	9.61	9.64
25-YEAR	10.16	10.07	9.87	9.95
U.S. treasuries				
2-YEAR	6.97	6.87	6.66	6.84
5-YEAR	7.95	7.88	7.68	7.76
7-YEAR	8.17	8.09	7.90	7.99
10-YEAR	8.27	8.21	8.05	8.13
20-YEAR	8.47	8.42	8.25	8.37
30-YEAR	8.47	8.41	8.26	8.34

Source: The Financial Post, June 10, 1991.

listing as an example). Lenders and borrowers shop around for the best deal inside and outside their own country. Corporate financial officers will not hesitate to lend in U.S. dollars or deutschemarks if the return is better than in Canadian dollars (including the cost of hedging foreign exchange risk, discussed in section 3 below). Banks and large corporations will not hesitate to borrow from foreign banks and in foreign currencies if the rate is better. It is therefore hard to talk of our money market as Canadian any more, and a list of Canadian money market assets shows only part of the picture. Nevertheless, Table 6–1 shows the relative importance of different Canadian money market debts and borrowers.

At the shortest end of the money market, overnight borrowing is done by banks and investment dealers. Banks need to adjust their cash reserve holdings to compensate for the net effects of each day's withdrawals, deposits, and cheque-clearings in order to meet the cash reserve requirement. Investment dealers need to arrange day-to-day financing for their very volatile securities holdings. Banks and other members of the Canadian Payments Association (CPA) borrow overnight through advances from the Bank of Canada and through interbank

TABLE 6–1: Outstanding amounts of money market instruments in Canada, by type of issuer, December 1990 (millions of dollars)

Governments		147 433
Federal treasury bills [a]	133 244	
Provincial and municipal T-bills and paper	14 189	
Banks		44 345
Bank of Canada advances	66	
Bearer deposit notes	8 314	
Certificates of deposit and interbank deposits	35 965	
Investment dealers		3 358
Day-to-day loans	33	
Buybacks	656	
Special and other call loans	2 669	
Sales, finance, and consumer loan companies		
Finance paper		8 265
Other financial firms		
Commercial paper		9 916
Non-financial corporations		54 232
Bankers' acceptances	42 060	
Commercial paper	12 172	
Total		**267 549**

[a] The $5506 million that is held as *required* secondary reserves by the chartered banks is excluded from total federal treasury bills outstanding in order to get a better measure of truly marketable amounts.

Sources: Bank of Canada Review; Statistics Canada, *Financial Institutions,* 1990.

deposits from other banks. Investment dealers borrow overnight to finance their inventories of short-term securities through day loans and "special" call loans from banks or through purchase and resale agreements (PRAs) with the Bank of Canada.

All groups in Table 6–1 use the money market to borrow for terms ranging from several days to a year. The federal government is easily the biggest borrower with its treasury bills (T-bills). Non-financial firms have raised $48 billion with commercial paper and with bankers' acceptances. Banks raise funds by issuing either bearer term deposit notes (BDNs) or certificates of deposit (CDs); the latter are usually non-negotiable and non-redeemable, which makes them the least liquid money market assets. Investment dealers raise funds for longer than overnight by issuing ordinary call loans. Sales finance companies and other non-bank financial firms issue financial paper.

TABLE 6–2: Distribution of money market assets in Canada, January 1991

Sector	Federal treasury bills	Other short-term paper
Households (individuals and unincorporated businesses)	32 657	5 041
Non-financial corporations	9 989	15 425
Financial institutions	56 360	44 259
Bank of Canada	11 124	0
Chartered banks	16 410	8 175
Credit unions and caisses populaires	2 358	3 804
Trust and mortgage loan companies	5 349	5 598
Life insurers	1 051	1 854
Trusteed pension plans	6 860	10 977
Mutual funds	3 909	2 928
Investment dealers	957	574
Other private financial institutions	6 297	8 727
Public financial institutions	2 045	1 602
Governments	8 293	14 491
Rest of the world	14 041	5 982
Total	**121 340**	**85 178**

Sources: Statistics Canada, *Financial Institutions; Bank of Canada Review.*

Lenders in the money market

Table 6–2 shows the relative significance of different lenders as holders of all money market assets other than certificates of deposit; a breakdown of the latter by holder is not available.

Money market assets are to the financial system what currency holdings are to households: a convenient way to store wealth for short periods until it is needed for some other purpose. No financial institution specializes in lending in the money market, just as no household specializes in holding bundles of currency. There is no profit in it. Instead, all financial institutions and large corporations dabble in money market assets with the short-term funds they have on hand at the moment. As a result, holdings of money market assets are widely distributed among many groups.[2] It is precisely the wide distribution of money market assets that makes the Bank of Canada prefer to conduct monetary policy actions in the

---

[2] The large block of treasury bills held by chartered banks is only half voluntary: the rest was required under the 1980 Bank Act to meet secondary reserve requirements.

money market: all groups participate in it, so all groups will notice and, hopefully, respond when money market interest rates change.[3]

Two groups are special in Table 6–2. First, the Bank of Canada pays for its large treasury bill holdings by issuing its own deposits, which end up being held by chartered banks as cash reserve assets against the chartered bank deposits that form part of M1, M2, and M3. It is the Bank of Canada's treasury bill holdings, therefore, that underlie the economy's money supply. Second, holdings of investment dealers make up the inventory of the money market **jobbers** — the investment dealer firms that deal extensively in money market assets and collectively make the money market operate smoothly.[4] It is through the jobbers' traders and telephones that money market deals are made. Money market jobbers hold inventories of money market securities in order to be able to fill customers' orders without delay, which keeps money market assets liquid.

The rest-of-the-world sector's holdings of Canadian money market assets gives only a hint of the close connections between the world's money markets today. Small differences in yield attract large quantities of such investors very quickly. In order to attract foreign lenders, many of the assets listed in Table 6–1 are issued in foreign currencies as well as Canadian dollars. Some of the foreign currency assets are marketed through foreign dealers rather than at home.

Underwriting new issues

Money market dealers operate or "make" the money markets by standing ready to buy and sell the whole range of money market assets out of their own inventory (with a small spread on a large turnover to cover their costs). Most of their trading is secondary, but they handle new issues at the same time. They underwrite new issues of all but the largest borrowers either by agreeing to pay the issuer a set minimum price (this "bought deal" arrangement is a recent innovation) or else without any price commitment, selling the issue on a "best-efforts" basis. Under best-efforts underwriting, the borrower does not find out the actual selling price of the debt (which determines the actual cost of borrowing) until all the issue has been sold. The issuer's uncertainty is higher, and the commissions are smaller.

The largest borrowers operate their own money market desks and are therefore in a position to distribute their new issues directly to money market lenders. For instance, banks issue bearer term deposit notes and certificates of deposit directly to lenders who contact them by telephone and video terminal. The largest Canadian borrower of all, the federal government, even has its own money market dealer: the Bank of Canada auctions off new issues of treasury

---

[3] Money market assets recorded in Table 6–2 as held by households mainly reflect holdings of trust companies on behalf of households, under estate and trust arrangements, rather than direct, discretionary investments of the Joneses and the Smiths. Even this is changing rapidly, however, as personal investment strategies and financial communications systems become more sophisticated.

[4] Holdings of investment dealers are only partly reflected in Table 6–2; many investment dealers' holdings are consolidated with those of their parent banks.

bills for the federal government each Thursday for 90-day, 180-day, and 365-day terms.

Other short-term corporate borrowing

The money market is highly visible, but it does not account for a large proportion of total funds raised. The rest of shorter-term borrowing by firms is done by taking out short-term loans from banks and other lenders and by deferring payment of bills to suppliers (using trade credit). Secondary markets for these assets are still developing. Trade credits are marketable in the money market when guaranteed by a bank, as a bankers' acceptance. Trade credits can also be sold in blocks by creditor companies to factoring or acceptance companies, which exist for that purpose. Bank loans are generally not resaleable, although banks have been selling off parts of big bank loans in recent years, including some Third World loans at hefty discounts.

SECTION 2

 # Capital markets

Borrowers and instruments

Longer-term borrowing of firms, governments, and households is done in capital markets through issuing financial leases, term loans, mortgages, bonds, and shares. Firms can issue all of these assets, governments can issue all but shares, and households are generally limited to issuing mortgages. Figure 6–1 shows the relative sizes of each instrument outstanding as of the end of 1988.

Lenders in capital markets

Table 5–1, the national balance sheet table, has already shown the distribution of shares, bonds, and mortgages among sectors as assets. Holdings of mortgages are dominated by financial institutions, of which trust companies and mortgage loan companies are the most important. Holdings of bonds (other than Canada Savings Bonds, which are relatively short-term assets) are concentrated in pension funds and insurance companies at home and abroad. Most shares are held either by parent firms (that is, for shares of subsidiaries) or by pension and mutual funds. When one asks who owns the parent firms and the pension and mutual funds, the ownership of shares can always be traced back eventually to either a household or a government.

Capital markets differ from each other by more than the parts of the money market. The instruments themselves can be quite different, and market arrangements vary considerably. Each of the five capital market instruments is therefore discussed separately, starting with the least familiar.

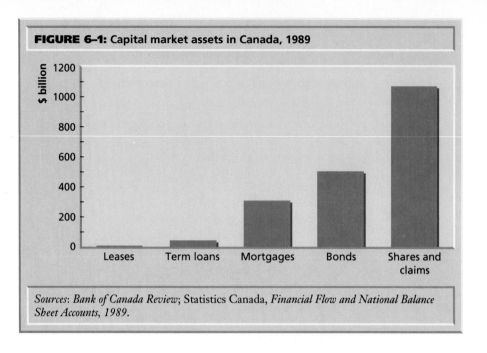

FIGURE 6–1: Capital market assets in Canada, 1989

Sources: Bank of Canada Review; Statistics Canada, *Financial Flow and National Balance Sheet Accounts, 1989.*

Financial leases

Financial leases are the smallest and least straightforward capital market asset and also the one with the least developed secondary market. Financial leases are generally arranged with leasing companies that are themselves subsidiaries of larger financial firms, although trust companies and finance companies also participate directly.

Financial leasing is an arrangement in which the lender buys a large piece of equipment such as an airplane, and at the same time leases it out to a particular user such as Air Canada for its whole expected useful life. Such a financial lease is very similar to lending Air Canada the funds to buy the airplane itself, and charging Air Canada a level annual charge to pay interest and repay the principal. After all, it is Air Canada that looks after all the costs of ownership, such as insurance and maintenance. There are two differences that explain the existence of this market. First, there is no loan to show on Air Canada's balance sheet that might rank ahead of claims of other creditors should Air Canada declare bankruptcy; that may make some of Air Canada's other creditors happier. Second, the lessors of the airplane may have a tax benefit because they nominally own the airplane: they may be able to use tax allowances for depreciating their airplane to reduce their other taxes.

Some larger financial leases are divided up and sold off in parts by originating banks to other holders without the expertise or contacts to generate their own lease contracts; however, there is not yet an active market to resell such subdivided leases.

Term loans

Term loans are loans for periods of one to ten years that do not have the special security of bonds or mortgages. Term loans are a fairly recent innovation themselves in Canada. Only after the Federal Business Development Bank had been extending them for several years did the Canadian chartered banks start any term lending at all. Canadian banks have only recently adopted a widespread U.S. banking practice of reselling parts of a large loan to other lenders. The secondary loan market that banks have thereby created for loans, including term loans, is still very much a wholesale market confined to large lenders and loans of large companies. In international markets there has been a much larger secondary market for term loans of large corporations and banks. There is an active secondary market for floating-rate notes (FRNs), whose interest rates are usually tied to the London interbank deposit offer rate (LIBOR). More recently, a secondary market has developed for term loans with interest rates fixed to maturity.

Mortgages

Mortgages are loans for up to 20 years that have fixed maturity, interest rate either fixed for a few years or floating with market rates, and the security of some piece of real estate that creditors can seize in the event of default by the borrower. A distinctive feature of almost all mortgages is that borrowers are obligated to make level payments that combine interest and repayment of principal, as in a consumer installment loan. Such payments are known as *blended payments*.

The secondary mortgage market is still developing in Canada. Large blocks of residential mortgages have been resold by financial institutions to each other since the 1960s; some trust companies with large branch networks made a business of originating many mortgages and then reselling them to mortgage loan companies to hold to maturity. Then in the 1970s the chartered banks bought up or set up their own mortgage loan subsidiaries and resold bank-originated mortgages to their subsidiaries. Such in-house arrangements greatly slowed down the growth of a secondary mortgage market that would have made all mortgage loans more liquid. However, in 1986 two Canadian banks initiated what is now essentially a retail secondary market for mortgage loans. The two banks pooled together government-guaranteed mortgage loans and sold units in the pool to the general public. Units in a mortgage loan pool are called "mortgage-backed securities." Such securities are growing rapidly.

Mortgage-backed securities are an example of an important class of recent innovations known collectively as **securitization**.[5] When an illiquid asset is

---

[5] Securitization has gone much farther in the United States than in Canada. Mortgage pools started in the U.S. in 1970 and now finance about one-third of all mortgage loans. Small business loans, guaranteed by the Small Business Administration of the U.S. government, have been securitized (pooled and resold) since 1985. Automobile and credit-card loans have also been securitized. All that is absolutely necessary is a guarantee from some creditworthy name to eliminate credit risk for holders.

securitized, first a collection of such assets is pooled together; then a guarantee is arranged for the pool (from government if the assets themselves are government-guaranteed, but otherwise from a large domestic or international bank); finally one or more classes of claims on the pool, known as "asset-backed securities," are created and sold off to finance the pool. Over 15 000 individual and institutional investors had participated in residential mortgage pools by late 1989, raising over $3 billion. The minimum amount of pool units has been around $5000, which puts them within easy reach of retail lenders. In late 1989, the market expanded to finance non-guaranteed mortgages as well.

Since the asset-backed securities are homogeneous and guaranteed against default, it is much easier to keep an active secondary market for them than for the underlying assets, such as the individual mortgage loans. It is interesting that this innovation is one that reduces the share of intermediaries in total assets, even though it involves intermediaries in packaging up and guaranteeing the asset pools underlying asset-backed securities. Securitization has the effect of shifting some flows of funds from indirect lending via financial institutions to direct lending between savers and real investors.

Shares

Shares have no maturity date as a rule, and they promise only contingent payments of dividends — that is, if the company makes a sufficient profit. In return, the least protected or common shareholders get to vote in the election of company directors and, indirectly, for company management and policy.

Shares are basically either common or preferred. *Common shares* share in residual profit without limit, though they receive as cash only the amount declared as dividends.[6] *Preferred shares* usually give up voting rights and also accept a ceiling on the dividend rate in exchange for being paid dividends before the common shareholders. Preferred shares are *callable* or redeemable by the issuer as a rule, so they are not permanent financing.[7] Some are also *retractable* or redeemable at the discretion of the holder, and some are *convertible* into common shares at a fixed price. Convertibility gives the holder the protection of a preferred share and still the right to unlimited capital gains (by converting at the pre-fixed price) if the company is wildly successful. Shares are traded in the stock market through brokers, who generally act as go-betweens rather

---

[6] Dividends provide only a small return on shares: the average is between 3 and 4 percent. Profits not paid out in dividends (retained earnings) go to increase holdings of some asset on the company's balance sheet instead, which will generally increase the market valuation of the company's stock. Shareholders therefore expect to benefit from retained earnings by a capital gain in market price.

[7] Firms must usually agree to some restrictions, such as on the use of assets or issue of new debts, in order to attract purchasers of their preferred shares. Later such restrictions may become onerous, and redeemability provides an acceptable way out for both parties. Term preferred shares did have a specific maturity date set at time of issue; they flourished in the late 1970s because of special tax treatment of dividend income.

than as principals. Shares of larger companies with many shares outstanding are formally "listed" on one or more of Canada's five stock exchanges and often abroad as well; trade in outstanding shares of listed companies is carried out by continuous public auction either on the trading floor of the exchange or on a set of interactive computer terminals in brokers' offices. Other shares trade in the **over-the-counter (OTC) market**, which means over the telephone and video terminal. In the United States, the OTC market is known as the NASDAQ (for National Association of Securities Dealers' Automatic Quotation) system; this computerized system, operating out of dealers' offices, is already close to being a complete video terminal market for some 4500 stocks. Floor traders resist fiercely, but it seems likely that all floor trading will gradually be supplanted by systems such as NASDAQ, even for the biggest and most active stocks; however, the computer system involved will be worldwide and trading will go on 24 hours a day.[8]

New issues of shares are usually bought (*underwritten*) by large groups of brokers acting as principals and then resold at a somewhat higher price to more permanent holders (known as *subscribers* when the issue is new). All new issues even of exchange-listed stocks are marketed over the telephone rather than on the floor of stock exchanges, because they are sold (*subscribed to*) in advance before the shares are physically available to exchange. If and when computerized trading replaces stock exchange trading floors, there will be even less difference between the selling of newly issued and existing shares.

The announcement of the issue of Scudder New Europe Fund shares (shown on p. 90) gives some idea of how global an activity the underwriting of new shares can now be. These mutual fund shares were simultaneously offered in the United States, in Europe, and in Asia, using a different underwriting group in each area.

Bonds

Bonds are generally recognizable by having a fixed redemption payment at maturity (the par value), a stream of semi-annual interest payments (interest coupons), and an elaborate form of promissory note called an *indenture agreement*. The indenture agreement specifies in great detail all the terms and conditions of the loan. In event of default on interest payments, the indenture agreement gives bondholders special rights to take over all or part of the company to secure payment.

Bonds come in two types: *mortgage bonds* and *debentures*. Mortgage bonds have an explicit provision in the indenture agreement allowing bondholders to seize particular real estate assets if the issuer defaults on paying interest or principal, while debentures do not. In recent years many bond issues have had new features added to make them more attractive and to lower the nominal coupon yield required. Some are *convertible* into preferred or even common

---

[8] This was even the view of the chairman of the U.S. Securities and Exchange Commission, in testimony to Congress in mid-1989.

```
All of these securities having been sold, this announcement appears as a matter of record only.
NEW ISSUE                                                    February 22, 1990

                        16,000,000 Shares

              Scudder New Europe Fund, Inc.
                         Common Stock
                          ($.01 par value)

          Scudder, Stevens & Clark, Inc.—Investment Manager
          LB Fonds Beratungsgesellschaft m.b.H.—Economic Adviser for
            Austria and Regional Adviser for Eastern Europe
          (an indirect wholly-owned subsidiary of Österreichische Länderbank Aktiengesellschaft)
          Banco Português de Investimento—Economic Adviser for Portugal

          These securities were offered in the United States, Europe and Asia.
```

United States Offering
8,000,000 Shares

The First Boston Corporation
Prudential-Bache Capital Funding
A.G. Edwards & Sons, Inc.

Bear, Stearns & Co. Inc.   Alex. Brown & Sons Incorporated   Daiwa Securities America Inc.   Dillon, Read & Co. Inc.
Donaldson, Lufkin & Jenrette Securities Corporation   Drexel Burnham Lambert Incorporated   Goldman, Sachs & Co.   Kidder, Peabody & Co.   Lazard Frères & Co.
Merrill Lynch Capital Markets   Montgomery Securities   Morgan Stanley & Co. Incorporated   The Nikko Securities Co. International, Inc.
Nomura Securities International, Inc.   PaineWebber Incorporated   Salomon Brothers Inc   Shearson Lehman Hutton Inc.
Smith Barney, Harris Upham & Co. Incorporated   Wertheim Schroder & Co. Incorporated   Dean Witter Reynolds Inc.
Yamaichi International (America), Inc.   Allen & Company Incorporated   Oppenheimer & Co., Inc.

European Offering
4,000,000 Shares

Credit Suisse First Boston Limited   Prudential-Bache Capital Funding
Banque Indosuez   N M Rothschild & Sons Limited

Asian Offering
4,000,000 Shares

CS First Boston (Hong Kong) Limited   Prudential-Bache Capital Funding

Jardine Fleming International Inc.   ChinTung Limited   Daewoo Securities Co., Ltd.   Daishin Securities Co., Ltd.
Dongsuh Securities Co., Ltd.   G.K. Goh (Stockbrokers) Pte Ltd.   Hanshin Securities Co., Ltd.   Hyundai Securities Co., Ltd.
Kokusai Securities (Hong Kong) Limited   The Lucky Securities Co., Ltd.   New Japan Securities International (H.K.) Ltd.
Okasan International (Asia) Limited   Ssangyong Investment and Securities Co., Ltd.   Tong Yang Securities Co., Ltd.
Wako International (Hong Kong) Limited   Wardley Investment Services (Hong Kong) Limited

Source: The Economist, March 3, 1990, p. 20. © The First Boston Corporation.

shares at a specified price. Like preferred shares, some bonds are *retractable* (at the holder's discretion). Some are *callable* (at the issuer's discretion). Some are *extendible*, the opposite of retractable; it is usually the longer-term issues that are made retractable and the shorter-term issues that are made extendible. Some bonds, called *income debentures*, pay interest only if profits are sufficient, just like preferred shares. Some bonds have been unbundled to sell separately the stream of interest payments and the final repayment of principal; the latter part is referred to as a *stripped bond*, or a deep discount bond (because it sells at a deep discount from the par or redemption value). The set of interest payments (regular, even payments for a specific period of time) is then a standard financial instrument called an *annuity*, an asset normally issued by trust and insurance companies.

The bond market operates like the money market and the OTC stock market. Bond dealers operate as brokers to bring buyers and sellers together over the telephone or computer screen; the bond dealers are generally just the bond division of the same investment dealer firms that operate the money market. In the bond market, dealers sometimes sell out of inventory as in the money market, and sometimes find a seller elsewhere as in the stock market; turnover is less than for money market assets, so dealers do not maintain as large an inventory of assets.

Bond markets are as international as money markets. Bond dealers regularly contact customers at home and abroad. Canadian borrowers and lenders contact both Canadian and foreign dealers in their search for the best terms. Since foreign firms were allowed into the Canadian securities business in 1987, the establishment of subsidiaries of large foreign investment dealers has tied the Canadian bond market even closer to the international bond market. Over the period 1981–87, over one-third of Canadian bonds issued were placed outside Canada and the United States.[9] Between 1984 and 1988, annual trading in Government of Canada bonds by non-residents rose from $9 billion to almost $80 billion.[10]

New issues of bonds are generally underwritten by groups of bond dealers just like new issues of shares. Smaller bond issues may be placed directly with one or two large lenders, in what is called a *private placement*. The Bank of Canada is the underwriter for all federal government bond issues.

SECTION 3

☐ Hedging markets

The most exotic and rapidly growing financial markets have been those that allow users to reduce or *hedge* their risks. The assets traded in hedging markets are often very complex, but for professionals managing millions of dollars of others' money, the set-up cost of learning about them is well worth the extra peace of mind.[11] **Hedging markets** include traditional insurance policies, but much more interesting are the newer markets for forward and futures contracts, for options contracts, and now for currency and interest rate swaps. Insurance markets are discussed briefly to put the other, more exotic markets into some perspective.

---

[9] Economic Council of Canada, *A New Frontier: Globalization and Canada's Financial Markets*, p. 18.

[10] To put this figure into perspective, the total volume of trading in just medium-term Government of Canada bonds (those with terms from three to ten years) is about $550 billion per year. Foreign trading is still relatively small.

[11] For a thorough explanation of the newer hedging instruments, see Bank for International Settlements, *Recent Innovations in International Banking* (Basle: BIS, 1986), available from the Bank of Canada.

Insurance

Insurance contracts are debts whose repayment amount depends on whether or not some real (non-financial) disaster occurs, such as death of a key executive or explosion of a boiler. To the insurer they are contingent debts; to the person or firm insured they are financial assets. By the maturity of the contract the insurer will have paid up in full, either zero if the insured-against disaster did not occur, or the face value of the policy if it did. As financial assets, insurance contracts are generally small scale and unique; for instance, a life insurance policy on the life of a specific executive with a specific past medical history and current health habits. Insurance contracts are not generally transferable or tradable in a secondary market.[12] Transactions costs tend to be high in markets with little standardization and low turnover, and this market is no exception.

Insurance products allow us to eliminate the unfortunate financial consequences of a wide range of uncertain real events. What insurance products cannot protect us against are the financial consequences of changes in future market prices or interest rates. Fluctuations of exchange rates and interest rates became much larger in the 1980s than in previous decades, so investors and borrowers and intermediaries developed a whole new set of hedging instruments to protect themselves against market price risks.

Forward and futures contracts

Futures contracts were developed in the last century to hedge against price risks in farm products, such as corn, wheat, and cotton. *Financial futures* contracts developed mainly in the 1980s in Chicago, London, Philadelphia, Montreal, Tokyo, and other financial centres. A look at the futures market page of any financial newspaper will show the wide range of financial futures currently available.

A **futures contract** is essentially a resaleable version of a forward contract, amended so it can easily be bought and sold in a futures exchange. A **forward contract** is an agreement to complete some financial transaction in the future (for example, buying a currency or borrowing funds), at a price or rate that is set in the forward contract. *Forward exchange contracts* are used to fix in advance the prices of future foreign exchange transactions. For instance, you could arrange now to buy 1 million yen next June, at a price (set now) of 105 yen per Canadian dollar. *Forward rate agreements* are used to fix in advance the rates for future loans or deposits. Forward contracts are arranged between customers and (usually) banks, for terms of a few months to a year or more, and for amounts to suit the customer. Forward contracts are generally unique, cancellable only with agreement of both parties, and not very liquid. They are available in wholesale or retail amounts. In financial jargon, they are issued in an over-the-counter (OTC) market.

---

[12] Insurers can often lay off some of their risks with specialized reinsurance companies. Those insured can assign their policy benefits to other parties in some cases. That is the extent of the secondary insurance market.

Forward Exchange Rates

Supplied by: Royal Bank of Canada
Indicative wholesale late afternoon rates

Friday, March 16, 1990

Per US$	Spot	1-mth	3-mth	6-mth	12-mth
Fri					
Canadian Dollar	1.1820	1.1869	1.1962	1.2086	1.2295
British Pound*	1.6190	1.6100	1.6449	1.6693	1.7098
Deutsche Mark	1.6990	1.6985	1.6983	1.7003	1.7026
Japanese Yen	152.70	152.62	152.40	152.07	151.32
Per C$					
U.S. Dollar	0.8460	0.8425	0.8360	0.8274	0.8133
British Pound*	1.9137	1.9110	1.9675	2.0174	2.1023
Deutsche Mark	1.4374	1.4310	1.4198	1.4068	1.3847
Japanese Yen	129.18	128.59	127.41	125.83	123.08

inverted

Source: The Financial Post, March 19, 1990, p. 31.

Futures contracts are standardized, negotiable versions of forward contracts. Standardization increases the volume of contracts of any given type so that a secondary market can be maintained. A secondary market makes negotiable contracts liquid.[13] Because futures contracts are traded on active secondary markets, it is possible to cancel a futures contract before maturity. In fact, almost all futures contracts are cancelled before maturity. The cancellation of a futures contract is achieved by offsetting it with another contract in the opposite direction. All futures contracts are legally made with the futures market exchange corporation, not with another customer as in stock market trading. Two opposing futures contracts by the same person with the same futures market exchange corporation therefore cancel each other out. An illustration of how cancellation works is given in the box on page 94.

Forward exchange contracts are used as a key component of international money market trading. Dealers attract international lenders by putting together combinations of a particular money market asset and a forward exchange contract; the forward exchange contract serves to convert the proceeds at maturity of the asset back into the lender's home currency. For instance, in order to attract funds from a Japanese bank, a dealer might combine C$1 million in 30-day Canadian commercial paper with a 30-day forward contract to buy C$1 million in yen. The dealer would quote a combined (all-in) yield consisting of the yield on the commercial paper plus the percentage discount or saving of the forward purchase price of the yen below the current (spot) market price of the yen.

---

[13] Standardization has a cost: most hedgers will not be able to find a futures contract for exactly the type and quantity of assets they hold. They will have to settle for the most similar asset available and the nearest $100 000 amount.

How OMERS Buys and Cancels a Futures Contract

Date of trade	Buyer	Futures market corporation	Seller
June 26	OMERS @ $91 ←	International Money Market (IMM) (part of Chicago Mercantile Exchange)	← Canada Trustco @ $91
July 7	G W Life @ $92 →		→ OMERS @ $92

OMERS (the Ontario Municipal Employees' Retirement System, a large pension plan) first buys and later sells the same type of futures contract, at the prices shown per unit of the underlying asset. In this example, assume the underlying asset is a U.S. treasury bill, and that the delivery date is September. Each contract is for $1 million in treasury bills. Both contracts are with the futures market corporation. The opposite parties to the trades (the IMM is not exposing itself to risk) happen to be Canada Trustco in June and Great West Life in July. OMERS' two mutually offsetting contracts are "washed out:" OMERS is no longer held responsible for either buying or delivering the U.S. treasury bill in September. Instead Canada Trustco is held liable to deliver the treasury bill to Great West Life. Canada Trustco receives $91 per $100 of par value in the contract; GW Life pays $92 per $100 of par value. The $1 margin between them per $100 of par value is paid to OMERS as soon as OMERS has completed the second trade. That $1 margin per $100 of par value means $10 000 per contract, since contracts are for $1 million of par value.

Hedging markets are not kept active just by hedgers. Futures contracts attract many speculators as well. If Green is convinced that bond prices will fall and believes that others have not yet realized it, she can profit enormously from her conviction by contracting to sell bonds in the future, using contracts. As others in financial markets come to share Green's conviction, the futures price of bond futures will sag. Green can then buy bond futures at the lower price to cancel her contract, and she pockets the difference. What makes the profit so attractive is that Green need not put up the value of the bonds, but only a *margin*, or "good faith," *deposit* of between 1 and 5 percent of the bonds' value. Her yield will be enormous in percentage terms. Of course, Green could be wrong, in which case her losses could be equally big.

The biggest futures markets are those for Eurodollar deposits (to hedge against changes in short-term interest rates), for U.S. treasury bills (to do the same in a different form), and for the Standard & Poor's 500 composite stock index (to hedge against stock price fluctuations). New futures markets arise each

Pork Bellies, Move Over

The commodities market used to conjure up images of fast-talking Midwesterners trading corn and pork-belly futures. Then it moved upscale, with contracts on everything from Swiss francs to stock indexes being swapped in the "pits." Now the Pacific Stock Exchange wants to add a new item to the list of commodities: Dynamic Random Access Memory microchips.

Yes, the microchip, as in the tiny silicon semiconductors that help run everything from laptop computers to space rockets. The Pacific exchange argues that the chip futures would offer a badly needed hedge against price fluctuations that happen when new computers create excess demand for chips—or overproduction leaves a glut. In mid-1988, a single 256-kilobit chip sold for as much as $17. Today it costs under $2.

Skeptics say that chips shouldn't qualify as commodities, since they're not subject to seasonal fluctuations like crops. But some analysts disagree. Bill Tai of Alex Brown Inc. in San Francisco says computer companies should leap at the chance to cut favorable price and delivery deals ahead of time—and that producers, including the Japanese, will play to protect themselves against unanticipated price drops. If the Commodity Futures Trading Commission approves the request, as expected, the Pacific exchange could start issuing contracts as early as next spring. And California will have put yet another new spin on an old idea.

Source: Newsweek, October 30, 1989, p.70.

year, however. All that is needed to create a new market is to find an item that is both homogeneous and sufficiently important that many regular buyers would like to hedge against movements in its price. The latest such item, the microchip, is discussed in the box above.

Options

Options are contracts that give the holder the right, but not the obligation, to buy or sell a standard quantity of an underlying asset at a specific price, called the *strike price*. **Call options** convey the right to *buy* the underlying asset at the strike price; **put options** convey the right to *sell* the underlying asset at the strike price. Option contracts all have an expiry date, usually no more than a year distant, after which the option is no longer "alive," and the right to buy or sell ceases to exist.[14]

Using the right to buy or sell is known as *exercising* the option. The holder of a

---

[14]The expiry date means different things for American and European options. American options convey rights to buy or sell *on or before* the expiry date; European options convey rights to buy or sell only *on* the expiry date.

call option on shares, for example, exercises the option by buying 100 shares at the strike price from someone who has issued such a call option.

Options are available for stocks, bonds, money market assets, precious metals, currencies, and loans. Some are available on a customized basis from banks, while other, more standardized options are traded in organized options exchanges through investment dealers. Minimum trading quantities are small enough for larger retail customers, but the market is mostly wholesale.

Whereas futures contracts are used to fix future prices or interest rates, options can be used to fix only the minimum or only the maximum future price. Buyers can fix the maximum price by buying a call option on the asset or currency they will need; sellers can fix the minimum price at which they will have to sell by buying a put option.[15] As an example, the insurance company Faithful Life expects a large inflow of funds from its policyholders next month, but fears that the prices of bonds it will want to buy will rise a lot between now and then. Faithful can use a call option to protect itself against that financial risk. Assume, for instance, that Faithful can buy call options on 9.5 percent Canada bonds due in October 2001, with a strike price of $100 per $100 of par value. The cost is $0.90 per $100. With those options in hand, Faithful is guaranteed that the price of the bonds it will need will be no greater than $100.90, the strike price of its options plus the cost of buying the option. If next month the market price of the bonds rises above $100, Faithful will exercise its options and take delivery from the option seller for the strike price of $100. If the market price is still lower than the strike price of the option, then Faithful will be able to buy at the lower market price and will just let the options expire.

Some options contracts are for assets that cannot actually be bought or sold. A stock market index, such as the Standard & Poor's 500 composite index, has regularly reported values but cannot be bought and sold. When call options in such indexes are exercised, the issuer of the option cannot produce a "Standard & Poor's 500 index." Instead, the rules for exercising such options are that the issuer of the option pays the holder whatever profit the holder has made. For example, if the strike price of an index call option is $340 and the market value of the index has risen to $346.31 when the holder wishes to exercise the option, the holder's profit is $6.31 × 500, or $3155.[16] The issuer of the call option must pay $3155 to the holder exercising the option.

The same method of cash payment is used for interest rate options. In order to set a cap or ceiling on possible interest rates for a one-year loan to be taken out in three months, Acme Chemical could buy a call option on interest rates for $100 000 of loan principal with a strike price equal to the desired ceiling rate (for example, 15 percent). If actual loan rates in three months turn out higher than 15 percent, then Acme will exercise its option. The option seller will pay Acme

---

[15] Their maximum or minimum price of course includes the premium paid for the option; the point of the exercise is that the price is no longer uncertain.

[16] The multiple 500 applies to the S&P 500 index option. Other index options use different multiples for calculating profits and losses.

the difference in interest costs for the year on $100 000 of principal at the new, higher interest rates.

Speculators can use options markets as a way to profit from outguessing other market participants, with less downside risk than in futures markets. If the ever-optimistic Green is convinced that the level of the Standard & Poor's 500 stock index will rise by more than others believe, she can buy call options on the S&P 500 index. If Green proves right, the resale value of call options on the S&P 500 index will rise as the others catch up to Green's wisdom. She can then resell her options at a profit. The option costs only a fraction of the level of the index of underlying assets (the stocks making up the S&P 500), yet a one-point rise in the value of the index causes almost a one-point rise in the option value. A ten-point rise in the market value of the S&P 500 from 300 to 310 will raise the value of some call options by eight points, but from a much smaller base such as from 12 to 20. Green's percentage gain from the call option is huge in that case, even with a small change in the index. Yet, if Green turns out to be wrong, she simply lets the option contract expire without exercising it, and she loses no more than her investment in the option contract.[17]

Currently the largest volume of trading in options is for options on Japanese and U.S. stock indexes, on U.S. treasury bonds, and on Eurodollar deposits. The latter two options are actually options on *futures contracts* for treasury bonds and Eurodollar deposits; the logic of futures options is the same as for other options.

Swaps

Swaps started off as a sophisticated form of barter. Through international banks and investment dealers, investors and borrowers found opposite parties willing to exchange one kind of payment stream for another. Nowadays large international banks stand ready to act as principals in swaps rather than just as brokers. In an *interest rate swap*, a borrower committed to some pattern of interest rate payments on a term loan (fixed or floating with LIBOR, or floating with some other benchmark rate) exchanges interest obligations with a bank or another borrower to end up with a different, more desirable pattern of interest payments. The most common interest rate swap is from fixed to floating interest rates. For instance, as of early 1990 the federal government had arranged $3 billion in swaps of its medium-term fixed-interest obligations for floating-rate obligations at the bankers' acceptance rate. The swaps lowered the government's cost of funds to 72 basis points (that is, 0.72 percentage points) below what it would have paid on three-month treasury bills.[18]

---

[17] On the other hand, Green might choose to profit by selling ("writing") a put option on the S&P 500 index. If Green is right, she profits by the original proceeds from selling the put option, since the option will never be exercised. If Green is wrong and the S&P 500 index falls, her option will be exercised. Then she will have to pay the difference between the actual and strike price of the index, however large the difference turns out to be. Her put-option strategy has fixed potential profit with unlimited potential loss.

[18] Reported in Bank of Canada *Annual Report, 1989*, 38.

In a *currency swap*, what is exchanged is the currency in which interest payments are to be made. For instance, a firm that has issued a Swiss franc bond might exchange the Swiss franc interest obligations for a commitment to pay interest in U.S. dollars. Canadian provinces have made extensive use of swaps to reduce their exposure to exchange rate risks on their extensive foreign borrowings. Many firms issued bonds in Australian dollars and swapped the interest payments for U.S. dollars, when the "all-in" cost was lower than for borrowing in U.S. dollars in the first place. *Cross-currency interest rate swaps* involve changing both currency and interest pattern at the same time.

The total number of swaps in force has grown enormously; by the end of 1987, total interest rate swaps were estimated to be above $889 billion, and total foreign currency swaps above $219 billion. Swappers can get out of any one commitment by swapping it for yet another, so swaps have become more liquid as the market has grown.[19]

Hedging markets and globalization

Swaps, forward contracts, and options allow hedging of interest rate and exchange rate risks. Exchange-traded futures contracts and options are not available for terms or expiry dates much beyond a year, but forward contracts and swaps are. Without hedging, longer-term borrowers would feel themselves confined to borrowing at fixed rates in their domestic currency unless foreign rates were very much cheaper and there was some undertaking by the government to keep floating interest rates more stable than they have been over the past decade. With hedging, borrowers can eliminate almost all of the currency and interest rate risks of going abroad or tapping a different market; as a result, borrowers are much more willing than before to switch between financial markets in response to changes in relative yields. A Canadian corporation that can get a good deal on a deutschemark term loan, for instance, no longer has to worry about being committed to deutschemark interest payments for a long period once it knows that they can be swapped immediately for interest payments in Canadian dollars. Similarly, a Japanese lender who finds a good deal on U.K. sterling bonds will not worry about being committed to sterling for the long term when the sterling payments can be swapped for yen payments. The response of borrowers and lenders to changes in any one market's interest rates is therefore more vigorous than it was before the growth of hedging markets. Capital flows between markets are larger. The world's financial markets are tied more closely together into a single global financial system. The implications of such elastic capital flows will be discussed at several points later in this book.

---

[19] Many different permutations of swaps are becoming available. The swaption is an example: a future swap is arranged, which one party to the agreement can exercise or not at will. Almost all of the permutations of swaps involve creative uses of interest rate options together with the basic swap. The basic swaps themselves can be seen as merely combinations of options.

SECTION 4

Summary

The money market and the capital markets are the main secondary markets of the financial system. The money market is relatively small, but it is very active and gives important signals to other financial markets where rates are "posted" and adjust more slowly. Both money and capital markets are "made" by specialized investment dealers who act as principals in the money market, as brokers in the stock market, and as both in the bond market. The sales forces used in the secondary market are also used to distribute new issues of shares, bonds, and money market instruments when groups of dealers agree to underwrite new issues. Federal government treasury bills and bonds are the exception: treasury bills are issued weekly in a special closed-bid auction that is the centrepiece of the money market, while federal bonds are underwritten entirely by the Bank of Canada. The main types of capital market are the bond market, the stock market, and the mortgage market. Markets for term loans and for financial leases are still relatively small.

The last decade has witnessed the very rapid growth of hedging markets for forward and futures contracts, for options, and for swaps — all specifically designed to allow hedging of financial risks, but useful for speculators as well. Hedging markets have been so successful that it is now easy for lenders and borrowers to shift between currencies or between floating-rate and fixed-rate markets in response to changes in relative interest rates, without having to expose themselves to much extra risk. New hedging instruments are being made available each year.

Key Terms

money markets	mortgages
London interbank offer rate (LIBOR)	securitization
	over-the-counter (OTC) markets
purchase and resale agreements (PRAs)	bonds
	hedging markets
treasury bills (T-bills)	futures contracts
jobbers	forward contracts
capital markets	call options
financial leasing	put options
term loans	swaps

Questions and Problems

1. Distinguish between money markets and capital markets.

2. How does the activity or presence of the money market jobbers improve the performance of the money market?

3. What significant difference is there, if any, between a PRA and a collateral loan secured by government bonds?

4. Identify what you consider the two most *different* assets in the money market. Do the same for the capital market. Is the degree of difference roughly comparable in the two markets, or is one market more homogeneous than the other? What do you think follows from your conclusion about the differences in yields that will be observed in each market at any time?

5. Of the two attributes of callability and retractability, which is more attractive to lenders, and why? What will the attribute you have chosen do to the yield that lenders will be willing to accept on assets with that attribute?

6. The "bought deal" took a long time to arrive in Canadian bond markets. Why do you suppose that was?

7. Has the explosive growth of hedging markets in the 1980s increased or decreased the level of risk to which investors are exposed? Explain your conclusion.

8. What item do you expect to become the underlying asset for the next futures market? Why that item?

9. In the Middle Ages, brickyard workers fiercely resisted the introduction of the wheelbarrow. In the 1990s floor traders in stock and other exchanges will fiercely resist the further spread of computerized trading. Explain the parallels and differences between the two situations.

10. What will the spread of computerized trading do to globalization of financial markets? Why, exactly?

Suggestions for Further Reading

Martin, Peter. *Inside the Bank of Canada's Weekly Financial Statistics: A Technical Guide*. Vancouver: Fraser Institute, 1989. Especially useful for a more detailed description of borrowers and instruments than is provided in this chapter.

Bank of International Settlements. *Recent Innovations in International Banking*. Basle: BIS, 1986; available from the Bank of Canada.

Economic Council of Canada. *The New Frontier: Globalization and Canadian Financial Markets*. Ottawa, Supply and Services, 1990.

PART TWO

Lending and Borrowing Behaviour

Chapter seven

Household Wealth, Saving, and Borrowing

Previous chapters have identified Canada's borrowers and lenders and the markets in which they come together. The questions that remain concern *why* households and firms become either borrowers or lenders, for how long, and on what scale. What determines the amount of lending and borrowing that goes on, and hence the amount of wealth and debt outstanding? What will change it? This chapter looks at wealth and at saving and borrowing decisions to answer those questions for households. The next chapter considers the different case of firms and governments.

You should learn in this chapter:

1. the life-cycle permanent-income theory of households' demand for wealth;
2. the basic graphical microeconomic model of intertemporal choice;
3. how actual Canadian saving and wealth patterns both reflect and reject the predictions of life-cycle permanent-income theory.

SECTION 1

▢ Demand for wealth: the life-cycle permanent-income theory

The explanation of household saving and wealth starts by recalling two accounting identities from Chapters 4 and 5. Wealth (W) is defined and measured at any point of time as the total value of assets (A) less total debts (D) outstanding.

$$W = A - D$$

Over time, wealth can grow either because the value of assets grows or because debts are paid off, or both. The flow that increases the stock of wealth between one point of time and another is the flow of net saving. **Net saving** (S) is defined as income (Y) less all consumption (C). Consumption includes both taxes and the current year's consumption or depreciation of capital items such as housing and consumer durables; consequently

$$S = Y - C.$$

When income is measured comprehensively to include not only labour and interest and dividend income, but also all capital gains income from increases in market prices of assets, the relationship between wealth and net saving is simply

$$S = dW,$$

where dW is the change in wealth.[1] The expression dW can be positive or negative.

The definition of net saving brings out a central fact about the process of accumulating wealth: it involves the pain of *not* consuming now, and the pleasure of consuming later instead. The process of dissaving, or reducing wealth, (where Y is less than C, and S is negative) involves the pleasure of consuming more now and the pain of consuming less later. The saving decision is basically a decision about the *timing* of consumption.

A powerful theory of saving behaviour and demand for wealth has been built on this idea. The general form of the theory was first developed by Irving Fisher at Yale University in the early years of this century. A more restricted and more powerful version of the theory was developed in the 1950s by Franco Modigliani as the life-cycle hypothesis and, simultaneously, by Milton Friedman as the permanent-income theory. To see how the theory works, we now look at an imaginary, rational household headed by Sarah Brown.

Choice of lifetime consumption pattern

Sarah Brown is a rational consumer. She is also forward-looking, in that she cares about consumption in the future as well as in the present. Ideally, Brown would like more consumption now *and* more later.

What keeps Brown from choosing an infinite level of consumption in each time period is that she must sooner or later pay for all of her consumption. Of course, she does not have to spend in each future period exactly the income received in that period. She can borrow against future income to raise consumption now, or she can store some current income for a while as extra wealth and defer spending it to later periods. Brown's many options are subject to one overall financing constraint: over her whole lifetime, the total of her consumption spending plus any interest on borrowing must match the total of her income plus any initial wealth plus all interest earned on accumulated wealth. This constraint is expressed formally in economics as

---

[1] Where income measures do not include capital gains, neither do saving flow measures. In that case, dW becomes the sum of measured saving and capital gains.

Total Lifetime Resources: An Algebraic Explanation

Assume for convenience that Brown has initial wealth W_0 and knows for certain that her current and future incomes will be $Y_0, Y_1, \ldots,$ and Y_n. Those are the sources from which she must pay for all of her spending. The total present value of those sources is not just the sum $W_0 + Y_0 + Y_1 + \cdots + Y_n$, because dollars available at different points in time are not of equal value. A dollar of current or present income is better than a dollar of income next year, because current income can earn interest between now and next year. The lower present value of later dollars is captured by *discounting them to the present* for the interest they cannot earn. To discount income that is t years off in the future, multiply the income amount by the discount factor $D = 1/(1 + r)$ once for each of the t years, where r is the fractional form of the annual interest rate that can be earned on wealth. The present discounted value of Brown's initial wealth and of her income stream is her total lifetime resources (TLR). This is shown as

$$TLR = W_0 + Y_0 + Y_1 D + Y_2 D^2 + Y_3 D^3 + \cdots + Y_n D^n.$$

Total lifetime resources is called "total wealth" in Friedman's permanent-income version of this theory. Friedman broke down total wealth into human and non-human wealth. Non-human wealth is what the national balance sheet accounts record — W_0 in the expression above.

The total **present discounted value** of her consumption over all periods must not exceed her total lifetime resources, where **total lifetime resources** is defined as the total present discounted value of her income from all periods plus her initial wealth.

The concept of present discounted value is explained in the box above on total lifetime resources.

Economists have generally assumed for simplicity that income stream and initial wealth are fixed; that is, no decision of Brown's can change them. If so, then Sarah Brown cannot change her total lifetime resources, TLR, and there is a fixed ceiling to the total present discounted value of lifetime consumption that she can arrange. All that Brown can choose is how to spread her consumption total over her remaining lifetime.

Irving Fisher's theory of saving

Fisher derived several useful propositions about saving and consumption behaviour without adding any more assumptions than those above.[2]

The first, obvious proposition is that initial wealth, the lifetime income stream, and the interest or discount rate are the main determinants of a household's average consumption over a lifetime. These three factors determine total lifetime resources.

The second, and much less obvious, proposition is that consumption is *independent* of the time pattern of income for Sarah Brown. She is constrained by her total lifetime resources and not by its composition. If she comes to expect changes in income in any future years that rearrange income between years, but which leave total lifetime resources unchanged, she will not change her lifetime consumption plan at all. Income matters in Sarah Brown's thinking only as it affects her total lifetime resources.

Third, any change in just one year's income can be expected to have a relatively small impact on total lifetime resources, and therefore a small impact on consumption in any one year. It follows that any increase in just one year's income would be mainly saved. Another way of saying that is that the marginal propensity to save out of such a change in income is very large.

Fourth, *future* income will matter to Brown's *current* consumption just as much as current income: both influence total lifetime resources.

Fifth, households such as Sarah Brown's will spread their lifetime income around between years to get the most *total* satisfaction; at the margin in each year, therefore, we can expect to find roughly equal marginal utility per dollar of total lifetime resources. If offered $100 of consumption goods two years from now, or its present discounted value equivalent in consumption goods now, Sarah Brown would be indifferent between the two options.

The accompanying box explains Sarah Brown's choice in algebraic form, for those who would like to see the standard tools of microeconomics at work in the financial system.

Unfortunately, we cannot tell what Irving Fisher's solution implies for the actual amount of saving in any one year without knowing both Sarah's income pattern and her pattern of tastes over time. Does she believe she will enjoy things more when she is young? Does she think life begins at 40? Irving Fisher's theory did not specify. Friedman and Modigliani did specify the nature of tastes and were able to go further.

Friedman's permanent-income theory

Friedman added to Fisher's framework the assumption that households want a steady level of consumption over time, and of course they want as big a steady

---

[2] Irving Fisher, *The Role of Interest* (New York: Macmillan, 1907).

Sarah Brown's Consumption Choice

Sarah Brown makes her household decisions so as to maximize a utility function

$$U = U(C_0, C_1, ..., C_n),$$

where $C_0, C_1, ..., C_n$ are consumption levels in years $0, 1, ..., n$. All consumption levels have positive but declining marginal utility. Brown's financing constraint is that

$$C_0 + C_1 D + C_2 D^2 + \cdots + C_n D^n = TLR,$$

where D stands for the discount factor $1/(1 + r)$ and TLR is total lifetime resources. The optimal conditions for Brown's equilibrium are derived from the first-order conditions for a maximum of $U(C_0, ..., C_n)$ subject to the financing constraint. Solving this problem with calculus yields the following utility-maximizing condition: Sarah Brown will allocate total lifetime resources to consumption in each period such that, at the margin,

$$MU_i/MU_j = [1/(1 + r)]^i /[1/(1 + r)]^j = [1/(1 + r)]^{i-j} = (1 + r)^{j-i},$$

where MU_i/MU_j is the marginal rate of substitution of consumption in periods i and j. If period j is next year and period i is now, for example, $j - i = 1$ and the optimal condition above becomes $MU_0/MU_1 = 1 + r$. The last equation shows that current consumption will have higher marginal utility than next year's consumption by the factor r. If Brown is ever offered a choice on a television game show between extra consumption next year and the same amount of extra consumption now, over and above her previously chosen pattern, she must always prefer the extra consumption now. Brown's condition is usually expressed by economists as one of having positive *marginal rate of time preference* (MRTP).

level as they can afford.[3] The biggest steady level they can afford is the **annuity value** of total lifetime resources (or total wealth, as Friedman called it). An annuity value is the maximum annual amount a lump sum will produce over some specified period (for instance, until death), leaving nothing at the end.[4] Friedman called this annuity amount Brown's **permanent income**, and asserted

---

[3] *A Theory of the Consumption Function* (New York: National Bureau of Economic Research, 1955). Friedman's theory is very well known in economics both in consumption theory and in an extension to the demand for money.

[4] The 30-year annuity value of the lump sum of $1 is $r/[1 - 1/(1 + r)^{31}]$. Where r is 0.05 or 5 percent, the annuity value is about $0.06.

that Brown's consumption each year would equal her permanent income; that is, the marginal propensity to save out of permanent income is zero.

Saving arises in the permanent-income theory as the gap between each year's observed income and its permanent income. Permanent income is constant as long as the figure for total lifetime resources is constant, and so is consumption. Fluctuations in observed income will therefore cause changes not in consumption, but in saving. High-income years, when observed income is above permanent income, will also be high-saving years; low-income years will also be low-saving or dissaving years. Wealth will rise during the high-income years and fall during the lowest-income years. Wealth will be the cumulative result of sequences of high- and low-income years. Wealth will reach a high level once households have experienced most of their (expected) high-income years and before they have run into many low-income years. Wealth will be low for those whose high-income years are still expected in the future. Finally, wealth will end at zero for each rational household as it passes from the scene.

The permanent-income theory suggests that saving will be powerfully affected by any change in income that is not expected to persist. Such changes in income are called *transitory*, as distinct from *permanent*. Transitory income has little or no impact on permanent income and therefore little or no effect on consumption. Almost all of any increase in transitory income is saved. On the other hand, if changes in actual income are expected to persist (that is, to be changes in permanent income), then consumption will rise or fall by the full change in permanent income and saving will not change at all.

Modigliani's life-cycle solution

Franco Modigliani's life-cycle model[5] is more complex but also richer, although it is so similar in approach to the permanent-income theory that they are often lumped together as a single model. Modigliani assumed that households want to spread their consumption out smoothly over their lifetime, but with a rising trend. He also assumed that households have a typical "humped" pattern of labour income over their life cycle, rising until near retirement age and then falling more or less abruptly thereafter. The result is a predicted pattern of negative saving in the early, low-income years of a household's existence, high saving in the middle, high-income years, and negative saving again in low-income retirement years. Wealth initially falls below zero as households borrow against future income, rises to a peak near retirement, and thereafter declines toward zero.

Modigliani's theory has more or less the same implications as Friedman's for the marginal propensity to save out of extra current income: it will be large unless extra income is expected to persist over much of the life cycle. Modigliani's theory

---

[5] The life-cycle approach to saving behaviour was developed by Franco Modigliani and Richard Brumberg, "Utility Analysis and the Consumption Function: An Interpretation of Cross-section Data," in K.K. Kurihara, ed., *Post-Keynesian Economics* (New Brunswick, N.J.: Rutgers University Press, 1954).

also brings out other properties of *aggregate saving*. Aggregate saving is the sum of saving of all households in a given economy. Each household will be saving at the rate appropriate for its point in the life cycle; some will have positive saving, some negative. In a stable economy with no average income growth and no population growth, the sum of saving over all households will be zero. Savers will be exactly offset by dissavers. For aggregate saving to be positive, either income growth or population growth, or both, are necessary; then the high aggregate saving of middle-aged households will be on a relatively larger scale and will more than outweigh the aggregate dissaving of the retired.

One can add many realistic features to the basic story of the humped income pattern in the life-cycle model. The theory can be extended to include many events important to the Brown household: Brown herself marrying, having children, seeing the children off into their own households, and retiring on social security benefits from the Canada Pension Plan and Old Age Security program. These extensions complicate the pattern of desired saving that Sarah Brown will choose, but they do not change the basic conclusions much. Figure 7–1 shows the result of adding such extensions to fit a typical household in Canada. Labour income falls during retirement but not drastically compared with the income level of ten years before retirement. After labour income has flattened out, total income continues to grow due to investment income from accruing wealth. Consumption needs generally rise with time, but fastest in the years with children and more slowly as the children leave home.

The conclusions to be drawn from life-cycle theory are not much changed by the extensions added in Figure 7–1. The basic pattern of hump-saving, and therefore of humped wealth, remains. Saving is not as sharply humped, however: the curve of saving in Figure 7–1 has more of a whale-back shape than a camel-back shape. What changes is mainly the prediction for households' early years: greater realism suggests that household needs, as well as household incomes, are low to start with. Households do not feel much need to run up consumer debts in their early years because there is not much gap between their desired consumption and their income in the early years.

Consumption versus consumption spending

In the permanent-income or life-cycle theory *consumption* is not quite the same as the *consumption spending* we observe and measure. The difference arises in consuming the services of durables such as cars, freezers, or boats. At the point where a household *starts* to use the services of a car, even on a small scale, there will be a large increase in consumer *spending* because cars are lumpy; one cannot easily buy just part of a car. Lumpiness of consumer durables means that young households starting without consumer durables are faced with large increases in consumption spending for quite modest increases in actual consumption. Older households, by contrast, can maintain high levels of consumption with low levels of consumption spending because they already own the necessary consumer durables. Although young households must spend a lot to acquire consumer durables, they will pay for them as far as possible by borrowing against future

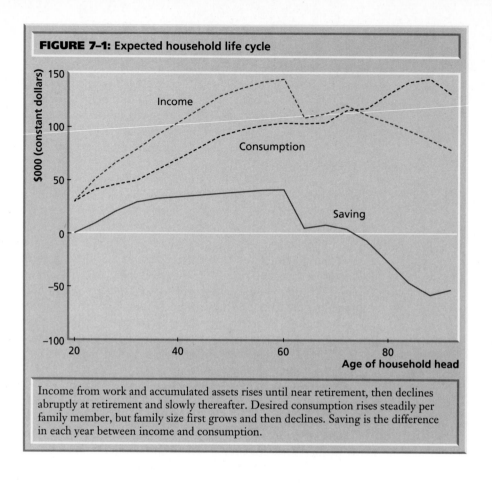

FIGURE 7–1: Expected household life cycle

Income from work and accumulated assets rises until near retirement, then declines abruptly at retirement and slowly thereafter. Desired consumption rises steadily per family member, but family size first grows and then declines. Saving is the difference in each year between income and consumption.

years of higher income. This is most obvious for the largest consumer durable of all, a house: houses are paid for over periods of 20 years and longer.

Implications of the life-cycle permanent-income approach

The three versions of saving theory described above differ in their details, but they have enough in common that economists refer to all three collectively as the **life-cycle permanent-income (LCPI) theory**.

Fisher, Friedman, and Modigliani all assumed that households are forward-looking. By contrast, the simple Keynesian consumption theory of introductory textbooks suggests that households like Sarah Brown's look no further ahead than current income to decide on their saving level. Being forward-looking means acting on *expectations* of the future, since we do not have perfect foresight. Because expectations are psychological variables, they are unobservable and may be quite volatile. Here, however, the expectation is of a whole lifetime income stream; that may be more stable than an expectation of just one year's income.

The LCPI theory suggests that only five variables are important to saving and wealth. The first of these is households' endowment of initial wealth and expected lifetime income.

The second variable is the household's taste for present versus future consumption, which economists measure as the marginal rate of time preference. MRTP is defined as the proportional extra utility of current over future consumption. Fisher left tastes unspecified in his model. Friedman and Modigliani constrained tastes to produce smooth desired consumption paths. It is a plausible assumption that tastes will not change dramatically for the household sector as a whole, though tastes of course vary widely between households. It would take a major social upheaval, like a sweeping new religious movement or the threat of a holocaust to cause much change to our collective taste for present versus future consumption.

The third variable is the interest rate expected by households over their lifetime. Fisher's and Modigliani's theories both imply that the slope of households' desired consumption path depends on the interest rate. Since higher expected interest rates lower the relative cost of later consumption, households tilt their desired consumption paths more steeply, to start with less consumption and end with more. One can see from Figure 7–1 that as the desired consumption path is tilted more steeply around its mid point at about age 50, consumption will be further below income in the early years and further above in the later years. With higher interest rates on wealth, households will save more in the early years and dissave more in retirement. In that case, households accumulate wealth faster up to retirement, and run that wealth down faster after retirement. The impact of even fairly small changes in the expected lifetime interest rate on the time path of accumulated wealth can be dramatic.

The fourth and fifth variables, brought out by Modigliani's version, are the age distribution of the population and the rate of growth of population and per capita income. These affect aggregate saving and therefore aggregate wealth. Neither variable changes rapidly in the short run, but they do differ markedly between nations, and they can cause large changes in the medium run of a decade or two.

SECTION 2

◻ The intertemporal choice diagram

In Sarah Brown's example, her household was faced with an intertemporal choice—the choice between spending income at different points of time. A common way of looking at intertemporal choice problems is to split time up into only two periods so that indifference curve analysis can be brought to bear. Indifference curve analysis brings out the central features of intertemporal choice graphically, in ways familiar to economists. Two period problems can be set up to reflect the same kind of lifetime planning choices as in Brown's multiperiod

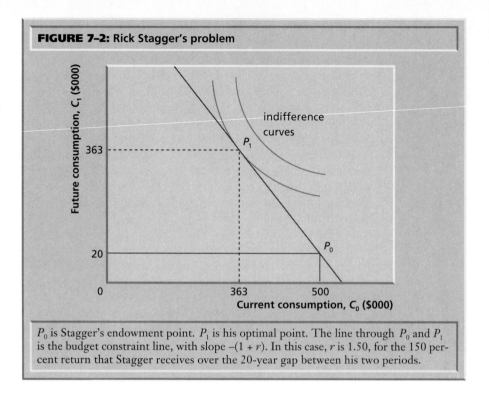

FIGURE 7-2: Rick Stagger's problem

P_0 is Stagger's endowment point. P_1 is his optimal point. The line through P_0 and P_1 is the budget constraint line, with slope $-(1 + r)$. In this case, r is 1.50, for the 150 percent return that Stagger receives over the 20-year gap between his two periods.

model. This section uses indifference curve analysis to treat such a two-period problem: that of Rick Stagger.

Stagger is the 20-year-old lead singer in the latest pop music sensation, Falling Rocks. He thinks of his life as having only two periods: his professional show business career and "afterwards"—his retirement. Each period is 20 years long (Rick does not plan to be around after 60). Stagger has a fantastic income now, thanks to his talents and those of his agent, but after his show business career ends he expects to earn only the average industrial wage plus a modest sum from publishing his memoirs. Let his annual income (Y_0) during his singing career be $500 000, and his annual income afterwards (Y_1) be $20 000. Stagger's utility depends only on current consumption (C_0) and consumption in retirement (C_1). Both amounts of consumption have positive but declining marginal utility. Stagger is well advised by assorted financial representatives and accountants and earns an impressive real after-tax yield on his accumulated saving. A dollar saved at the midpoint of his singing career grows to buy $2.50 of extra consumption at the midpoint of his retirement period ($1.00 of principal plus $1.50 of interest). Note that this is real interest, after allowing for inflation.

Figure 7–2 shows Stagger's situation for the two financial periods on an *intertemporal choice diagram* (sometimes called a Fisher diagram, after Irving Fisher). Current annual consumption, C_0, which is constant over his whole show-business career, is measured along the horizontal axis. Future annual consumption, C_1, over his whole post-show-business existence, is measured along the vertical axis. The point P_0 is the combination of current and future consumption Stagger would have if he spent all his income as it came in, saving nothing. P_0 is called his *endowment point* because it reflects the pattern of income with which he is endowed.

The other possible consumption combinations for Stagger lie in a triangle bounded by the two axes and a financing or *budget constraint* line. The budget constraint line runs through P_0 with a slope of $-(1 + r)$. Since Stagger earns \$1.50 on the dollar or 150 percent per period, r is 1.50 and the slope of Stagger's budget line is -2.50. For every \$1 of current consumption that Stagger gives up (moving to the left of P_0) he will get an extra \$2.50 of future consumption (moving above P_0). Stagger could also borrow against future income, but he would have to give up \$2.50 of future consumption for every \$1 of extra current consumption.

Figure 7–2 also shows a few of Stagger's *indifference curves*, which reflect his tastes for current, relative to future, consumption. Each indifference curve joins together all of the combinations of current and future consumption that Stagger regards as equally desirable (that is, among which he is indifferent). Indifference curves closer to the top right reflect higher levels of satisfaction than those closer to the origin.

The slope of an indifference curve at any point is called the **marginal rate of substitution** (*MRS*). It represents the ratio of change in future consumption to change in current consumption that would leave Stagger's happiness unchanged. For small changes, the *MRS* must equal the negative of the ratio of marginal utility of current consumption (MU_0) to marginal utility of future consumption (MU_1): $MRS = -MU_0/MU_1$. The more attractive current consumption is at the margin (the bigger MU_0), the more extra future consumption will be needed to persuade Stagger to give up \$1 of current consumption, and the steeper will be the indifference curve at that point.

Optimal consumption choice

With the help of his agent, Stagger chooses the point on his budget constraint line with the highest utility. That optimal point, P_1, is the point of tangency of the highest attainable indifference curve and the budget constraint line. The slope of Stagger's indifference curve is the marginal rate of substitution. The slope of the budget line is $-(1 + r)$, whose value in this case is -2.50. At Stagger's optimal point, therefore, $MRS = -MU_0/MU_1 = -2.50$, or $MU_0/MU_1 = 2.50$. For Stagger to want to spend any more of his income now, it must yield at least 2.5 times as much extra satisfaction as the same extra real income would yield in retirement. Otherwise, Stagger would be better off postponing the extra \$1 of current consumption and getting an extra \$2.50 of retirement consumption.

Exactly where the point of tangency P_1 will occur along Stagger's income constraint depends on Stagger's tastes for current and future consumption. If he were a miser, P_1 would involve little current consumption and a lot in the future. If he were a spendthrift, it would involve a lot of current consumption and relatively little in the future. If his tastes were like those of the households assumed by Milton Friedman in the permanent-income hypothesis, who wanted their consumption paths to be flat regardless of the interest rate, Stagger would choose the point shown as P_1 in Figure 7–2: current and future consumption would be equal at $363 000.

With current income of $500 000 and current consumption of only $363 000, Stagger's annual saving during his show business career is the difference of $137 000 per year. By the time he retires, his wealth will have grown to nearly $4.4 million with accumulating interest. During retirement, Stagger will spend all that wealth to supplement his meagre retirement income of $20 000. He will continue to spend $363 000 per year by dissaving $343 000 per year. By age 60, the end of his 20-year retirement period, Stagger will have prudently spent all his wealth and will die with nothing but memories (he does not plan to have a family).

Factors affecting Stagger's saving

Fisher diagrams such as Figure 7–2 can be used to illustrate the effects of changes in current and future income, tastes, and interest rates on saving and the demand for wealth. We will look at two examples: changes in current income and changes in interest rates.

Figure 7–3 shows the effect of higher current but not future income.[6] The endowment point P_0 moves out along the current income axis to P_0'. The new optimal point P_1' has also moved to the right, although not by as much. (Note that it has also moved upward, and lies on a higher indifference curve.) The desired current consumption will increase by only by a fraction of the increase in current income. The marginal propensity to consume out of this current income increase is much less than one, though greater than zero. Current saving increases by the difference between the income increase (dY_0, measured by horizontal movement from P_0 to P_0') and the consumption increase (dC_0, measured by the smaller horizontal movement from P_1 to P_1').

An increase in income that was truly permanent would raise both current and future income. The endowment point would be moved both to the right and upward. Desired current and future consumption would increase in roughly the same proportions as in Figure 7–3, and in roughly the same amount as the rise in income. Saving would not be affected at all.

Change in interest rate

Indifference curve analysis can also be used to illustrate the effect of changes in the expected average interest rate per period. This changes the slope of the

---

[6] This would be an example of a change in transitory income if Stagger's periods did not last so long. It makes little sense, however, to talk of extra income over a whole singing career as "transitory."

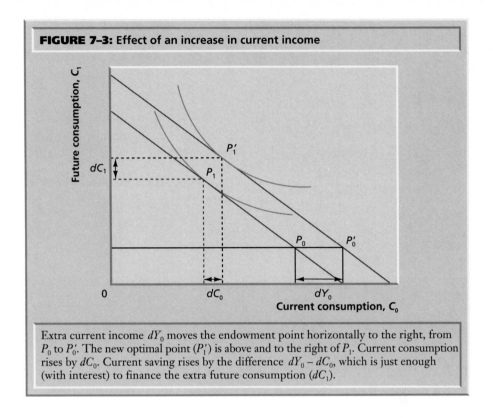

FIGURE 7–3: Effect of an increase in current income

Extra current income dY_0 moves the endowment point horizontally to the right, from P_0 to P_0'. The new optimal point (P_1') is above and to the right of P_1. Current consumption rises by dC_0. Current saving rises by the difference $dY_0 - dC_0$, which is just enough (with interest) to finance the extra future consumption (dC_1).

budget line. Figure 7–4 assumes that Stagger's advisers predict an increase in yield from 150 percent to 200 percent per period. Stagger's budget constraint becomes steeper but his endowment point is not changed. His new constraint line therefore goes through P_0 with a slope of -3.00. Stagger's new optimal point P_1' is higher, so he is better off; savers are always better off from an increase in their yields. In Figure 7–4 we can see that Stagger's current consumption falls. His current saving must therefore rise, since his current income has not changed. He cuts back on current consumption and adds to his planned future consumption until at the margin he enjoys an extra dollar of current consumption just as much as he would enjoy three dollars of extra future consumption. As we noted in discussing the life-cycle theory above, Stagger's lifetime consumption path is made steeper by higher interest rates.

If the indifference curves in Figure 7–4 were more sharply curved, as they would be if Stagger came to regard current and future consumption as less substitutable, the same steepening of the budget line would produce *higher* rather than lower current consumption. The reason is that changes in interest rates have both income and substitution effects on current consumption. The two effects work in opposite directions, and the net effect depends on how sharply curved the indifference curves are. The **substitution effect** is the effect of changing just

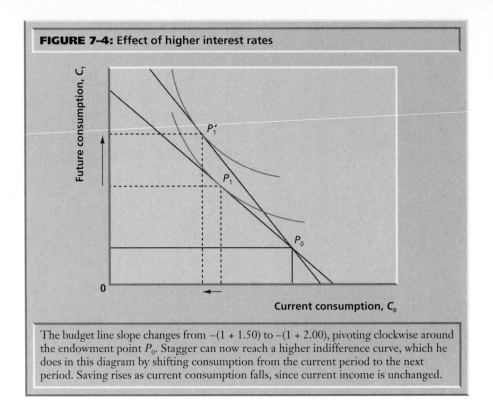

FIGURE 7–4: Effect of higher interest rates

The budget line slope changes from $-(1 + 1.50)$ to $-(1 + 2.00)$, pivoting clockwise around the endowment point P_0. Stagger can now reach a higher indifference curve, which he does in this diagram by shifting consumption from the current period to the next period. Saving rises as current consumption falls, since current income is unchanged.

the relative cost of current versus future consumption: as current consumption is made relatively more expensive, Stagger chooses less of it. Current saving rises. The **income effect** is the effect on Stagger's interest income, ignoring any changes in relative cost. Since Stagger is a saver already, higher interest rates give him greater interest income on his previous saving level. Stagger uses the extra buying power to choose more of both current and future consumption. Higher current consumption with the same current income means that current saving falls.

Which of the income or substitution effects dominates is an empirical matter. Modigliani and Friedman assume that the substitution effect dominates. Empirical research supports them: many econometric models of consumption behaviour show that higher interest rates have significant negative effects on consumption spending.[7] Simulation modelling of life-cycle models shows similar results.

For borrowers (see the example of Casey, below) the income effect of higher interest rates is to lower rather than raise total spending power: borrowers have to

---

[7] See, for instance, Ray C. Fair, *Specification, Estimation, and Analysis of Macroeconomic Models* (Cambridge, Mass.: Harvard University Press, 1984).

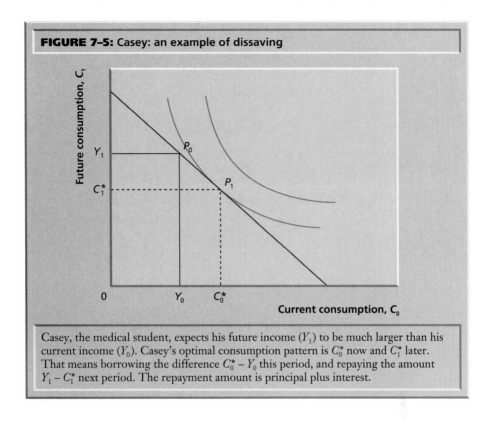

FIGURE 7–5: Casey: an example of dissaving

Casey, the medical student, expects his future income (Y_1) to be much larger than his current income (Y_0). Casey's optimal consumption pattern is C_0^* now and C_1^* later. That means borrowing the difference $C_0^* - Y_0$ this period, and repaying the amount $Y_1 - C_1^*$ next period. The repayment amount is principal plus interest.

pay more in interest to creditors and have less left over for future consumption. They respond by cutting back on both current and future consumption: both their income and their substitution effect is to raise current saving. All borrowers in intertemporal choice diagrams lower their borrowing when interest rates rise, regardless of their tastes; some may even become savers.

An example of dissaving

Some situations give rise to current borrowing rather than current saving. Consider Casey, a medical student with prospects for a large future income (Y_1) and small current income (Y_0). His plight is illustrated in Figure 7–5.

Casey's endowment point is P_0, as given by his expected income stream of Y_0 this period and Y_1 next period. He has no initial wealth. He can borrow against future income at an interest rate of r per period, so his budget constraint runs through P_0 with slope $-(1 + r)$. As with Stagger's, Casey's optimal point P_1 is at the tangency of the budget line with an indifference curve. Unlike Stagger's, Casey's optimum point P_1 has more current consumption (C_0^*) than current income (Y_0), so his current saving is negative: he issues debts to finance what he cannot buy out of his income. His outstanding debt is ($C_0^* - Y_0$) at the end of the current period. Next period, he repays that debt with interest out of Y_1, and spends on future consumption only what is left. Finally, like Stagger, Casey leaves this earth with zero wealth.

You may wish to change Casey's situation, as we changed Stagger's, to show the effect of changes in income, tastes, and interest rates on current saving. These exercises are left to the reader.

Household wealth and saving patterns

The logic of all wealth-holding in the life-cycle permanent-income theory is to save in fat years and dissave in lean years. Knowing the typical pattern of a household's income over its life cycle, we know the distribution of fat years and lean years, so we can use the LCPI theory to predict levels of saving and wealth in each year. From knowing how far apart fat and lean years are, we can also predict how long households will plan to hold their wealth. Length of holding period shows up in the kind of assets in which wealth can be held. This section looks at measures of Canadian household wealth-holding to see how far the implications of LCPI theory hold up in practice.

Patterns of total wealth by age

Figure 7–6 shows the actual income levels and wealth-holdings of a cross section of Canadian households in Statistics Canada's most recent wealth survey. Both conform to the humped life-cycle pattern assumed by Modigliani. However, the pattern of wealth by age in any one year not a good description of how actual Canadian households build up their wealth over a lifetime. The cross-section wealth profile is a much flatter profile than any individual household would expect over its own lifetime. The reason is that cross-section data combine younger households, whose high expected income profiles reflect modern productivity, with older households, whose past income profiles reflect lower past productivity. Even with modest growth in productivity, younger households can be expected to spend, save, and accumulate wealth on a scale about twice that of their parents at the same age. The gap between wealth of current younger groups and current older groups therefore greatly underestimates the extra wealth that today's younger groups expect to accumulate by the time they are 55.

The data in Figure 7–6 confirm the most general prediction of LCPI theory, that households save during their income-earning years and dissave after retirement. Even the under-25 group has positive median wealth, as the simulation result in Figure 7–1 predicted. On the other hand, the over-65 group has an amazingly large median wealth. There is not much sign of their wealth being run down anywhere near zero by time of death. Either households are not saving just for retirement or else they change their minds about consumption once they retire, or perhaps there is some other explanation for this departure from what LCPI theory predicts.

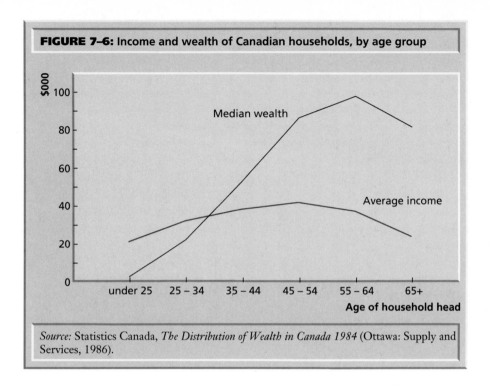

FIGURE 7–6: Income and wealth of Canadian households, by age group

Source: Statistics Canada, *The Distribution of Wealth in Canada 1984* (Ottawa: Supply and Services, 1986).

Some economists have argued that the reason for positive wealth for the under-25 group lies not in their modest needs, but rather in the constraints imposed on them by our financial system. Even if young households wanted to go deep into debt to start with, it is argued, they cannot find lenders to make it possible. Instead they must trim their spending in the early years to fit their low incomes. Figure 7–7 shows that, in fact, over one-fifth of households (families and unattached individuals) have negative wealth. About one-eighth of the next group of households have negative wealth as well. Clearly the constraints on going into debt are not that stringent. However, repayment periods on straight consumer debt are generally no more than three years; it is hard to accumulate a lot of such debts when they are being repaid so quickly.

Wealth composition

LCPI theory implies wealth is stored for use mainly in retirement. For most households, retirement is a long way off, so one would expect them to hold most of their wealth in long-term forms.[8] Older age groups would be expected to hold their wealth in much more short-term forms. Further, LCPI theory suggests that

---

[8] It is possible to hold a long series of short-term assets for long periods, but the transactions costs are large over 20-year periods.

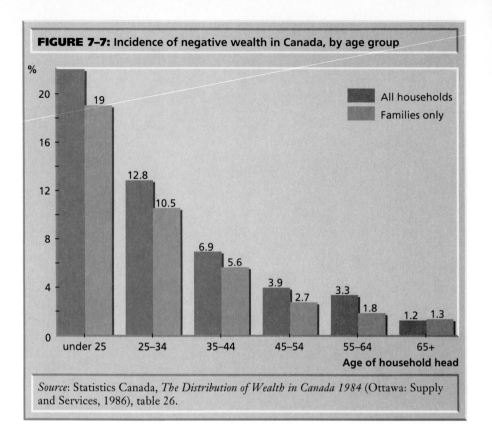

FIGURE 7–7: Incidence of negative wealth in Canada, by age group

Source: Statistics Canada, *The Distribution of Wealth in Canada 1984* (Ottawa: Supply and Services, 1986), table 26.

debts will be incurred for only two reasons: first, to finance pure consumption, as in Casey's example above; second, to spread the payment for long-lived consumer durables and housing over more than just the year of purchase. The cross-section data from Statistics Canada's 1984 wealth survey support all of these predictions.

Table 7–1 shows the proportions of different assets in average total assets, by age of household. The figures are averages rather than medians, so they reflect unduly the asset proportions of the very wealthy in Statistics Canada's sample. The figures for *equity in a business*, for instance, show that while equity in a business is an important share of average total assets, at most one in five households have any such asset at all. Similarly only one in ten households with a head of household under 25 own a house. Table 7–1 also excludes two important classes of asset: consumer durables other than vehicles and the value of insurance policies and pension plan assets.

What is striking about household asset patterns by age is the importance of long-lived assets, particularly housing. The relative importance of vehicles falls steadily as total assets grow tenfold, from $14 500 to the peak of $144 100, but the share of housing and real estate stays high. The next most important asset, though much less common, is equity in a family business, also a very long-

TABLE 7-1: Asset proportions of household portfolios, by age group

Asset type	Under 25	25–34	35–44	45–54	55–64	65+
Physical assets						
Home	40.5	49.7	49.1	41.3	38.2	37.9
Other real estate	4.3	6.2	7.3	9.1	10.5	6.6
Automobiles	18.1	7.6	4.8	4.2	3.6	2.9
Boats, campers, etc.	2.7	1.0	1.1	1.0	0.9	0.5
Equity in a business	17.2	21.1	23.2	24.6	20.2	15.5
(% with any equity)	4.1	13.4	19.3	20.2	16.1	6.6
Financial assets						
Liquid assets	13.7	7.6	7.0	10.8	15.7	26.4
Deposits and cash	11.5	6.2	5.7	8.0	11.7	20.1
Bonds (CSBs, etc.)	2.3	1.4	1.4	2.7	3.9	6.4
Shares	0.6	1.6	1.5	1.8	3.0	3.4
Registered Savings Plans	1.6	2.8	3.4	5.0	5.7	2.7
Other financial assets	1.1	2.5	2.5	2.0	2.4	2.8
Average total assets ($000)	14.5	60.1	107.0	142.2	144.1	94.9

Source: Statistics Canada, *The Distribution of Wealth in Canada 1984* (Ottawa: Supply and Services, 1986), table 26.

term asset. Life insurance and pension assets, excluded from the survey, are also long-term assets. Holdings of short-term assets consist of consumer durables and vehicles, plus holdings of deposits and bonds (almost all Canada Savings Bonds). Holdings of consumer durables and vehicles reflect the pattern of consumption in industrial countries rather than being aspects of lifetime saving plans: we must own these durables to enjoy their services. We keep some on hand because we do not use them all up in the year of purchase. Holdings of deposits and other liquid assets protect us against unexpected dips in income or surges in needs before retirement, but it is remarkable how small liquid assets are in total. With consumer durables and pension plan assets included, liquid assets would look even smaller.

Table 7–1 confirms the LCPI prediction that older households will hold their wealth more in short-term forms. Liquid assets are much more important for the over-65 group. Physical assets are less important. The family business has been sold off and the proceeds put into deposits and Canada Savings Bonds.

Debt levels and composition

The wealth survey data on household debt patterns also support LCPI predictions. Figure 7–7 has already shown that negative wealth occurs frequently only among the younger households. Table 7–2 shows the mixture of debts

TABLE 7–2: Debt patterns of households in Canada, 1984

Debt type	Under 25	25–34	35–44	45–54	55–64	65+
Credit-card debts	$218	$481	$535	$427	$288	$95
Other consumer debts	1 409	3 125	3 850	3 129	1 729	285
Miscellaneous loans	1 046	1 022	1 176	995	1 009	190
Mortgage debts	2 687	12 619	15 615	9 243	4 179	569
Total debts	5 359	17 246	21 176	13 794	7 205	1 423
as % of total assets	36.9	28.7	19.8	9.7	5.0	1.5

Source: Statistics Canada, *The Distribution of Wealth in Canada 1984* (Ottawa: Supply and Services, 1986), table 26.

issued, by age of household. As predicted, the youngest households have the largest debts relative to their total assets. Almost all of the debts in Table 7–2 are incurred to purchase durables of one sort or another. The two exceptions are credit-card debts and miscellaneous loans. Credit-card debts are incurred on about the same scale per capita for all age groups because the convenience of payment by credit card appeals equally to all groups. The miscellaneous loan category means mainly Canada Student Loans for the youngest age group. Canada Student Loans are, of course, the main long-term loan students can use to borrow against future income, unless the student happens to have a block of liquid assets such as bonds to use as collateral. Most of the loans are paid off before households make it into the 25–34 age group. It is probably these loans that account for many of the negative wealth cases among younger households.

The other debts in Table 7–2 reflect the household's financing and consumption of various durable assets, such as housing and cars and recreation vehicles. The kind of debts used to finance different durable assets differ mainly in the length of time allowed for repayment. Almost all are installment debts with level, blended payments. Lenders generally take a claim on the asset being financed as a form of security; most of the items being financed are chattels (a legal word for movable goods), so the loans secured by them are called *chattel mortgages*. Lenders are understandably reluctant to allow their loan values to exceed the value of the security, so lenders insist the loan be repaid at least as fast as the chattel itself depreciates from wear and tear.

In Table 7–2, consumer debts are a much larger fraction of total assets for households under 25 because such households are mainly financing consumer durables. Only one of these households in ten has bought a house. Residential mortgage loans are important for older households because older households much more frequently have houses to be financed. Further, mortgage loans are still a significant proportion of total assets even for the 35–44 age group, because mortgage loans are repaid so much more slowly than other loans: houses depreciate slowly, so mortgage loans can be spread over many more years than can car loans. Even so, mortgage loans are relatively insignificant proportions of total assets for households in the 45–54 age group. By then most of the loan has been repaid.

Inflation, nominal interest rates, and forced saving

Saving done when the saver would really like to be consuming instead is **forced saving**. It may occur when lenders insist on some equity or down payment from consumer borrowers before making loans for consumer durables. Unless the household can borrow the down payment elsewhere, it will have to be saved from current income. There is another, less obvious but more important way in which lending arrangements force higher household saving than households want. It arises because of the way modern financial systems handle inflation.

Inflation distorts many financial arrangements because it distorts our standard of deferred payments, the dollar. Financial assets all involve deferred payments, and for loan contracts the deferred payments are expressed in dollars. When inflation occurs, the dollars in which future payments are made become less valuable; creditors lose and borrowers gain. We could adjust for that in several different ways.[9] In Canada we build a provision for expected inflation into our nominal interest payments. We add an **inflation premium** to our nominal interest rates and leave nominal principal payments untouched.

An inflation premium will be very roughly equal to the rate of inflation expected over the life of the loan; for instance, in late 1990 the inflation premium contained in an 11 percent nominal mortgage interest rate could be around 5 percent; in the late 1970s it was closer to 10 percent. The inflation premium can be thought of as an extra principal payment on a loan, to compensate the lender for the shrinkage of real value the principal will suffer during the year from inflation. But inflation premiums are paid right from the start of the loan rather than at maturity. Borrowers paying regular inflation premiums can therefore be thought of as making regular, extra loan repayments right from the start of the loan. When borrowers make loan repayments from current income, that is a form of saving. When higher inflation premiums raise nominal interest rates, therefore, borrowers can be seen as forced to do more saving. Sometimes the forced saving is more than they can afford, so they decide not to buy a house at all.

Aggregate saving over time

It is a prediction of life-cycle theory that the net total saving rate out of income will rise slowly with the growth rate of either population or real per capita income. The logic is that such growth causes the gross saving of younger, high-saving households to outweigh by a larger degree the gross dissaving of older

---

[9]We could do as the Israelis do for bank deposits and loans payable in shekels: they raise borrowers' payments of both interest and principal at each future date to reflect whatever inflation has occurred by then; this is called indexing for inflation.

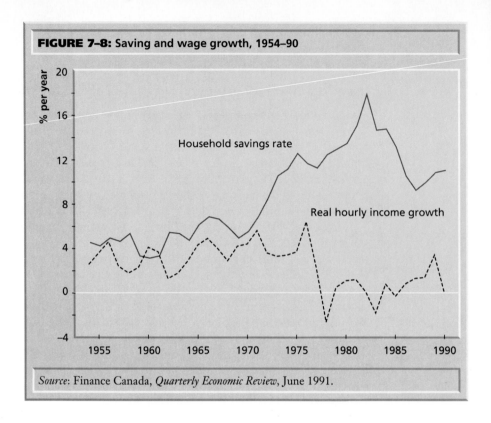

FIGURE 7–8: Saving and wage growth, 1954–90

Household savings rate

Real hourly income growth

% per year

Source: Finance Canada, *Quarterly Economic Review*, June 1991.

households. Faster population growth causes a relatively greater number of younger households, while faster growth of per capita income causes younger households to be operating on a relatively greater scale of lifetime spending and saving than older households.

Effects of growth on saving rates are fairly clear in comparisons across nations. They are also visible over time in Canada. Figure 7–8 shows the time path of the Canadian household saving rate, together with the path of real hourly earnings per person-hour from 1954 on. One interpretation of the data is that the saving rate rose until 1982 largely in response to the rapid income and population growth of the 1950s, 1960s, and early 1970s. When income and population growth stop or slow down, one can expect aggregate saving rates to stop rising and eventually to start falling, though slowly. That is what Figure 7–8 shows happening from 1982 on.

SECTION 4

🔲 Summary

Saving and demand for wealth are means of storing income in order to spend it in later periods. The life-cycle permanent-income theory is based on the idea that households realize this and, in fact, plan their consumption well ahead in order to allocate their lifetime income the most satisfactorily. The rational household of Sarah Brown illustrates the process. Consumption and saving in any year reflect Sarah's tastes for consumption over time and her total lifetime income stream. Income in any one year by itself does not make much difference to consumption in that year, so transitory changes in income cause mainly changes in saving.

Modigliani and Friedman assumed households want to smooth consumption over their lifetimes, rather than have it humped in the middle-aged years the way income is humped. The early and late years of a household's existence are therefore lean years, and the middle-aged years are fat years. Saving is done in the fat years to finance consumption above income levels (dissaving) in the lean years. At the end of a lifetime, they assume that wealth would be zero if households were certain about their time of death.

The interest rate is an important influence on saving and wealth, because it determines how much households will want their consumption path to tilt over their lifetimes. Steeper consumption paths involve more saving in the income-earning years and more dissaving in retirement, so wealth builds up more quickly and then runs down more quickly on either side of retirement. The age distribution and income growth rate are also important to aggregate saving and wealth for a whole society; these variables determine the extent to which saving by younger and middle-aged groups is offset by dissaving of the retired.

When the financial planning problem can be set into just two periods, saving decisions can be illustrated and analyzed on an intertemporal choice diagram. The same conclusions emerge as when many periods are considered.

The actual wealth of Canadian households conforms fairly well to predictions of the LCPI theory both in distribution across age groups and in composition. In particular, the bulk of household assets are long-term assets, many designed to provide for consumption during retirement. There is also a stock of liquid assets to protect against emergencies — unexpected periods of low income or high need. Short-term, liquid assets are a much larger share of total assets for those retired, who are no longer looking as far ahead as the rest. Incidence of negative wealth is fairly high among the youngest group (over one in five), though the median wealth is positive.

Household debts likewise support the LCPI theory's predictions. Only for the youngest group of households is negative wealth at all frequent, so only for them do debts often exceed assets. The kind of debt involved in these cases seems to be Canada Student Loans. The debts reflect mainly the different kinds of durable assets households buy in order to consume (gradually, over several years). Younger households therefore have important consumer and, later, mortgage debts. Older households have paid these debts off and have relatively little debt at all.

Key Terms

net saving	intertemporal choice
present discounted value	marginal rate of substitution
total lifetime resources (*TLR*)	(*MRS*)
annuity value	substitution effect
permanent income	income effect
life-cycle permanent-income	forced saving
(LCPI) theory	inflation premium

Questions and Problems

1. What is the discounted present value of $1000 in today's dollars available ten years from now, if savings yield 3 percent per year over and above inflation?

2. Estimate the discounted present value of your lifetime income.

3. Of the three assumptions made about tastes by Fisher, by Friedman, and by Modigliani and Brumberg, which best describes your own attitude to spreading out your lifetime total resources?

4. To appreciate your own marginal rate of time preference, answer the following question: If you are offered five days of free skiing this year or X days next year, how many days would X have to be for you to be indifferent between the two alternatives? $100(X - 5)/5$ is a rough measure of your marginal rate of time preference in percent per year. What is X for you? Calculate your marginal rate of time preference in percent per year when you have chosen X.

5. What effect does a greater marginal rate of time preference (at each income level) have on the indifference map in a Fisher diagram?

6. Illustrate on a Fisher diagram the effect of a lottery winning. Is this permanent or transitory income?

7. What difference would it make to a Fisher diagram if borrowing rates were greater than lending rates?

8. If young families have the greatest need to buy new durable assets, why is their wealth not higher than that of older families?

Suggestions for Further Reading

Fisher, Irving. *The Role of Interest*. New York: Macmillan, 1907.

Friedman, Milton. *A Theory of the Consumption Function*. New York: National Bureau of Economic Research, 1955.

McMillan, Alexander. *An Introduction to Canadian Financial Markets: An Analytical Approach*. Scarborough, Ont.: Prentice-Hall Canada, 1989.

Modigliani, Franco, and Richard Brumberg. "Utility Analysis and the Consumption Function: An Interpretation of Cross-section Data," in K.K. Kurihara, ed. *Post-Keynesian Economics*. New Brunswick, N.J.: Rutgers University Press, 1954.

Neave, G. *Canada's Financial System*. Toronto: Wiley, 1981 or later edition.

Sarpkaya, S. *The Money Market in Canada*. Toronto: Butterworths, 1980.

Shearer, Ronald A., John Chant, and David Bond. *The Economics of the Canadian Financial System*, 2nd ed. Scarborough, Ont.: Prentice-Hall Canada, 1984.

Chapter eight

Non-Household Lending and Borrowing

This chapter continues our explanation of the borrowing and lending behaviour described in Chapters 5 and 6. In this chapter, we deal with borrowers and lenders other than households—non-financial or business firms, financial firms (referred to, for some reason, as financial *institutions*), and governments. Non-household groups account for most of the activity in financial markets and virtually all the activity in wholesale financial markets.

Section 1 uses two models to explain the borrowing and lending choices made by businesses. The first is a flow model of profit maximization carried over from introductory economics. The second model is a more sophisticated version which focuses more directly on firms' balance sheets. Section 2 extends the analysis to apply to financial institutions. Section 3 discusses the much less tractable case of governments. Section 4 briefly reintroduces the savings–investment identity from Chapter 4 as a constraint on the total borrowing and lending of all groups in the economy. Throughout the chapter, we watch how borrowers and lenders curves behave in the financial markets frequented by each non-household group. Chapters 5 and 6 described financial markets, so the level of institutional detail in this chapter is kept to a minimum. A discussion of risk factors is postponed until the next chapter.

You should learn in this chapter:

1. the simple Keynesian model of investment choice and how it relates to borrowers and lenders curves;

2. Tobin's q model of asset and debt choice;

3. the concept of leverage in balance sheets;

4. the interaction of borrowers and lenders curves for financial institutions;

5. how financial institutions help to transmit shocks between financial markets;

6. how the position of governments as borrowers differs from those of firms and households;

7. how the savings–investment identity constrains activity in financial markets.

SECTION 1

Borrower behaviour of business firms

Household behaviour was predicted in the last chapter by a model in which households maximize utility over a natural lifetime. Business firms' behaviour can be explained by models in which they maximize profits rather than utility, but firms have no obvious counterpart to the finite natural lifetime of a household. In principle, firms can exist forever. The Hudson's Bay Company has already done business for more than three hundred years. How far ahead do they plan? Economists have adopted two approaches to the choice of a time horizon. In the first approach, firms are assumed to maximize profits one year at a time (on the assumption that what is good for this year can be repeated for all following years). In the second approach, firms are assumed to take a longer view.

Model 1: Marginal efficiency of investment (MEI) theory

In trying to explain investment spending behaviour in *The General Theory of Employment, Interest and Money*, Keynes started from the traditional assumption of all microeconomics that firms try to maximize profits in any year. As seen from financial markets, each firm's problem is to find the levels of assets and debt that will maximize profit. The firm is constrained in its choices by two facts. First, its savings level cannot be adjusted much in the short run, so buying extra assets implies extra borrowing as well. Second, the firm has only a finite list of new assets it knows well enough to consider buying; assets the firm does not know much about are too uncertain, and it is generally expensive to find out all the firm needs to know about possible investments in new types of assets.

If the firm ranks all of its potential purchases of new assets in order of the yield it can expect per dollar spent on them, and if the firm's cost of funds is constant (which is plausible if the firm is a small borrower in a large loan market), then the firm's situation is shown in Figure 8–1. The downward-sloping line in the graph is familiar as the firm's **marginal efficiency of investment (MEI)** line from Keynesian macroeconomics. The cost of funds schedule for the firm is a horizontal line drawn at the *loan market rate of interest* (r_0).

A profit-maximizing firm faced with the choices in Figure 8–1 will keep on adding new assets and new debts to its balance sheet as long as each new asset yields more than the cost of funds. Each firm will therefore choose the point in Figure 8–1 where the MEI line intersects the firm's cost of funds schedule.

The effects of the activity in the graph of Figure 8–1 are shown in the balance sheet. On the asset side, the firm's balance sheet will have the firm's

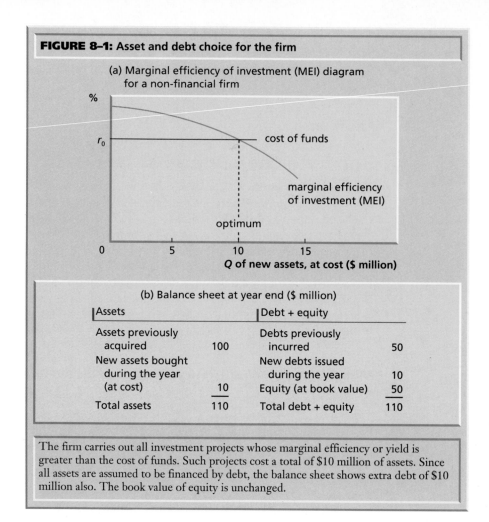

FIGURE 8–1: Asset and debt choice for the firm

(a) Marginal efficiency of investment (MEI) diagram
     for a non-financial firm

%

r_0 — cost of funds

marginal efficiency
of investment (MEI)

optimum

0   5   10   15

Q of new assets, at cost ($ million)

(b) Balance sheet at year end ($ million)

Assets		Debt + equity	
Assets previously acquired	100	Debts previously incurred	50
New assets bought during the year (at cost)	10	New debts issued during the year	10
		Equity (at book value)	50
Total assets	110	Total debt + equity	110

The firm carries out all investment projects whose marginal efficiency or yield is greater than the cost of funds. Such projects cost a total of $10 million of assets. Since all assets are assumed to be financed by debt, the balance sheet shows extra debt of $10 million also. The book value of equity is unchanged.

previously acquired assets plus the $10 million-worth of new assets bought during the year, shown in Figure 8–1. The debt side of the balance sheet will have previously incurred debts plus new debt of $10 million incurred during the year to finance the extra assets. Here it is assumed for simplicity that all new assets are financed by extra debt.

This elementary view of the firm's investment behaviour brings out the most important characteristic of a business firm's debt: it is tied to and derived from purchases of assets. Firms rarely consider borrowing unless they are buying some asset or other.

Further, the interest cost attached to new debts is usually paid from the return the firms receive from the assets that those debts help to finance. As a result, firms try to issue debts to match the payment pattern provided by their assets; not to do so is to invite a string of headaches in cash flow management

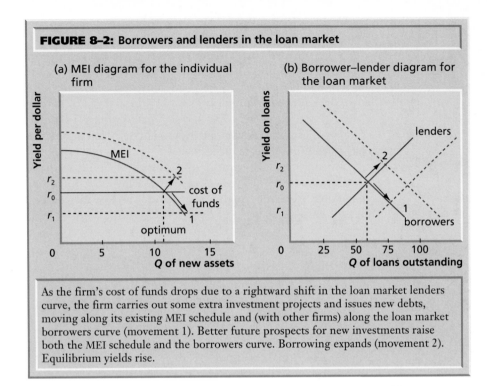

FIGURE 8–2: Borrowers and lenders in the loan market

(a) MEI diagram for the individual firm

(b) Borrower–lender diagram for the loan market

As the firm's cost of funds drops due to a rightward shift in the loan market lenders curve, the firm carries out some extra investment projects and issues new debts, moving along its existing MEI schedule and (with other firms) along the loan market borrowers curve (movement 1). Better future prospects for new investments raise both the MEI schedule and the borrowers curve. Borrowing expands (movement 2). Equilibrium yields rise.

and perhaps even bankruptcy. The assets to be bought, therefore, determine not only the amount of debt to be issued, but also the type. Long-term assets are usually financed by long-term debts and short-term assets by short-term debts. Assets with fixed yields are usually financed with fixed-yield debts. Assets that have highly uncertain yields, such as potential ore deposits, can only be financed safely with flexible-yield debts like preferred shares or even common shares. We will return to this idea of matching debts to assets in the next chapter when we deal with risk more thoroughly.

What is implied by the marginal efficiency of investment model for the behaviour of business firms as borrowers and lenders? Since this section is devoted to non-financial firms, we will assume that the assets bought are real assets. The explanation of firms' behaviour when they borrow to finance their real assets is explained in Figure 8–2. Figure 8–2(a) is the MEI curve diagram from Figure 8–1(a). Figure 8–2(b) is a basic supply and demand diagram, such as economists use for elementary market analysis, adapted somewhat to fit the special circumstances of financial markets. It is called a **borrower–lender diagram**, and is defined and explained in the box on pp. 132–133.

For simplicity, in Figure 8–2(b) the various debts of non-financial firms are all lumped together as loans, demanded and supplied in a single large loan market. Lenders in this diagram are banks and other financial institutions at home and abroad. Borrowers in the diagram are the non-financial firms facing the MEI curves of Figure 8−2(a).

In Figure 8−2, consider first a drop in the interest rate on loans, caused by greater lender enthusiasm for some reason. Firms move along their individual MEI curve in (a), and move down the borrowers curve in (b). In the loan market in (b), the lenders curve shifts outward to the right. The equilibrium interest rate and the cost of funds schedule for each firm drops to r_1. Each firm invests more along its MEI curve (movement 1 in a) and non-financial firms collectively issue more debt along their borrowers curve (movement 1 in b).

Second, consider instead an outbreak of optimism in the business world about future sales growth. Expected yields per dollar on new assets rise (remember, expected yields reflect emotions like fear and optimism; they are not just determined by some cold calculator program). In Figure 8−2(a) the MEI

The Borrower−Lender Diagram

Each financial market has a demand side and a supply side. Using the bond market as an example, demanders are those who wish to hold bonds in their collection of assets. They are the lenders, and their demand behaviour generates the lenders curve in the borrower−lender diagram. Suppliers are those willing to issue or to leave outstanding the bonds with which they borrow. They are the borrowers, and their behaviour generates the borrowers curve.

The past and current behaviour of borrowers and lenders in the bond market determines the quantity of bonds currently outstanding. This quantity is measured along the horizontal axis of the borrower−lender diagram for the bond market. Note that this is not the flow of new borrowing in any year, but the total stock of bonds outstanding from both current and all past borrowing.

The behaviour of lenders and borrowers in any asset market is usually influenced strongly by the yield expected on the asset itself—in this case, by the yield expected on bonds. The bond yield is measured on the vertical axis of the borrower−lender diagram for the bond market. Lenders can be expected to lend more in the bond market as bond yields rise, assuming that all other yields in other financial markets stay constant, so the lenders curve has a positive slope. Borrowers are deterred from borrowing in the bond market when bond yields rise, assuming that all other yields stay constant, so the borrowers curve slopes downward.

The intersection of borrowers and lenders curves in the market for any asset determines the equilibrium yield and quantity of that asset outstanding. In financial markets yields are flexible enough to adjust quickly to equilibrium levels. We can therefore interpret actually observed yields curve is shifted upward by the amount of extra yield that optimism has added. Firms now want to invest and borrow more at each cost of funds, so the borrowers curve in (b) shifts outward to the right. Firms' extra borrowing is movement 2 in the loan market; the equilibrium loan yield is driven up to r_2. In the MEI diagram, the horizontal cost of funds schedule for the single firm is shifted up to r_2 as well, and the firm settles at position 2 on its new, more optimistic MEI curve.

The marginal efficiency of investment theory is a useful starting point for considering the borrowing of business firms. It brings out the intimate connection between businesses' borrowing and their real investment activity. The same swings of mood that make real investment spending so volatile also make business firms' borrowing behaviour volatile. The MEI model does not show the impact of businesses' borrowing and investment on shareholders' equity, however, which the second model emphasizes.

and quantities as reflecting the intersection of borrowers and lenders curves at the date of each observation. Figure 8–3 illustrates such an equilibrium for the bond market.

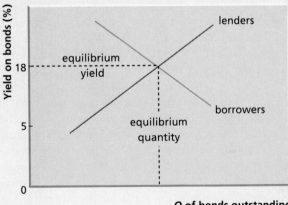

FIGURE 8–3: Borrower–lender diagram for the bond market

Factors that cause changes in borrowing or lending, without any change in the bond yield cause horizontal shifts of the borrowers and lenders curves. For instance, higher yields on shares will cause many lenders to switch to shares, shifting the bond market lenders curve to the left; it might also cause borrowers to switch to more bond financing at any given bond yield, shifting the borrowers curve to the right.

Model 2: Tobin's *q* theory

James Tobin of Yale University has developed an alternative version of Keynes's MEI theory with a longer-term perspective. He assumes that managers of business firms try to maximize the value of shareholders' equity, rather than just current profits.[1]

Equity is the difference between assets and debts. This general definition gives rise to a multitude of specific measures of equity, one for each convention in valuing assets and debts. In public accounting statements, assets are conventionally valued at historical cost less depreciation, and debts are recorded at face value. The public accounting values are usually referred to as *book values*.

Owners care more about the *market value of equity*, and generally they see to it that managers care about it as well. The market value of equity is defined as the market value of assets less all debts, though it is more easily measured for firms whose shares are widely traded as the product of shares outstanding multiplied by the current market price per share in the stock market. The market value of equity is assumed by economists to be the market's valuation of all expected returns to shareholders — that is, the *present discounted value of current and future profits* of the firm.

The firm's problem in Tobin's theory is to find the size of assets and debts that will maximize the market value of equity. The firm is subject to the same constraints as in Keynes's MEI theory: a finite list of assets about which the firm is well-informed and the requirement that extra assets be financed by issuing extra debt. The process of buying an extra asset changes three entries on a firm's balance sheet when assets are recorded at market value. First, assets rise by the *market* value of the new asset bought. The asset's market value is the present discounted value of its expected income stream. Debts rise by the amount actually paid to build the new asset, that is, by the new asset's *cost*. The market value of equity rises by the difference between the market value and the cost of the new asset.[2]

Equity-maximizing firms keep building assets and issuing debts as long as each new asset acquisition adds something to the market value of equity. Only when the market value of the last asset built just equals its cost does the firm stop acquiring new assets. An alternative way of expressing this result is in terms of the ratio called **Tobin's** *q*: the ratio of market value to cost. The equity-maximizing firm will add assets as long as their *q* ratio is greater than 1.0. The optimal balance sheet is one where $q = 1.0$ for the last asset.

---

[1] Since shareholders' equity reflects all expected future profits, maximizing equity has the same implications as maximizing long-run profits. Tobin's *q* theory first appeared in "A General Equilibrium Approach to Monetary Theory," *Journal of Money, Credit, and Banking* 1 (1969), 15–29.

[2] The book value of equity would not change in this case, because the extra asset would be recorded at cost of construction rather than at market value. Almost all formal accounting statements are at book values.

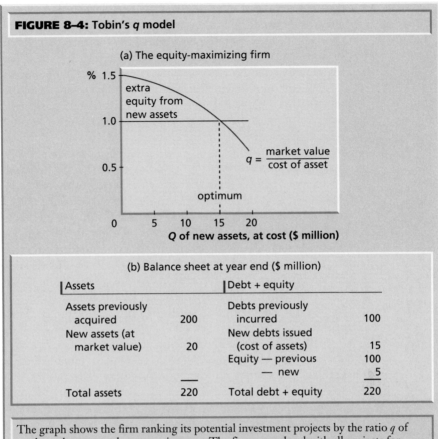

FIGURE 8–4: Tobin's *q* model

(a) The equity-maximizing firm

extra equity from new assets

$q = \dfrac{\text{market value}}{\text{cost of asset}}$

optimum

Q of new assets, at cost ($ million)

(b) Balance sheet at year end ($ million)

Assets		Debt + equity	
Assets previously acquired	200	Debts previously incurred	100
New assets (at market value)	20	New debts issued (cost of assets)	15
		Equity — previous	100
		— new	5
Total assets	220	Total debt + equity	220

The graph shows the firm ranking its potential investment projects by the ratio *q* of market value to actual construction cost. The firm goes ahead with all projects for which the market value exceeds construction costs—that is, for which *q* is greater than 1.0. The firm's equity rises by the difference of $5 million between the market value of $20 million and the cost of $15 million for its new assets.

The individual firm's situation in Tobin's theory is described in Figure 8–4. The firm is assumed to have ranked possible new asset purchases in order of *q*. The equity-maximizing firm invests or buys new assets along the *q* schedule until the *q* ratio reaches 1.0. Each dollar of new asset bought adds to the market value of the firm's equity the vertical distance between its *q* schedule and the horizontal line at *q* = 1.0. The extra market value of equity available from new assets is the triangle or wedge between the *q* schedule and the horizontal line at *q* = 1.0. The firm's balance sheet, at its new optimum level of assets and debts, is shown in Figure 8–4(b). On the asset side are the firm's previously acquired assets plus $20 million of new assets bought, all listed *at market value*. On the debt side are the debts previously incurred plus the new debt issued to finance the $15 million *cost* of the new assets. The equity section of the balance sheet shows the previous equity level plus the difference of $5 million between the market value of new assets added and the amount of new debt issued.

The borrower behaviour implied by Tobin's q theory is not much different from that of MEI theory, but it is couched in terms of stock market activity rather than loan market borrowing. First, consider a drop in loan rates. Firms will still raise the amount of debt outstanding if the loan rate drops (moving down along the borrowers curve in Figure 8–2(b). Lower loan rates enter Tobin's theory not as a cost of funds, but in the form of lower discount rates for discounting future asset returns. At lower discount rates, asset market values rise. The q schedule in Figure 8–4 is shifted up. With a higher q schedule, the firm in Figure 8–4 maximizes its equity value by spending more than $15 million on new assets.

Second, consider an increase in expected asset yields. Firms will raise the amount of debt outstanding if expected asset returns rise. Higher expected asset returns raise the market value of assets and shift the q schedule upwards. Firms want to buy more assets and issue more debt at the previous loan rate. In the borrower–lender diagram, the borrowers curve shifts outward to the right. Since the lenders curve is upward-sloping and does not shift, the equilibrium loan rate rises a bit. Some of the borrowers' enthusiasm is dampened: higher loan rates mean lower market values of assets, a fact that shifts the q schedule down *part of the way* toward its original position. The equilibrium is still at a higher quantity of assets and debts than before.

Tobin's theory allows stock market moods to affect firms' borrowing and lending. If a bullish stock market decides to value asset returns more highly without any change in loan rate or profit expectations, then the q schedule will shift upwards. Firms will add assets and debts. The borrowers curve in Figure 8–2(b) will shift to the right. Tobin's theory is the only explanation of investment spending that allows a role for swings in stock market valuation. The box on page 137 explains how stock market moods influence not only real investment spending, but also the frequency of bids to take over existing firms.

Leverage and limits to business financing

If firms can issue new debts without limit to buy whatever assets they think sufficiently profitable, then a firm's size seems to depend only on its owners' optimism about the profitability of new assets. Firms with optimistic managers would buy many assets and grow big; firms with pessimistic managers would buy few and stay small. In practice, optimistic firms have a further constraint on their borrowing: lender resistance.

Lenders generally insist that borrowers keep the ratio of assets to equity — known as the **leverage ratio** — within reasonable limits. Equity is seen by lenders as the cushion that separates a firm from bankruptcy in case the value of its assets drops (see Figure 8–6). That perception creates a **leverage constraint** for optimistic prospective borrowers.

Lenders see equity as the firm's own stake in the firm's projects, what the firm has to lose by not being careful in its use of funds. The leverage ratio is then

Expansion by Takeover
Versus
Expansion by New Investment

Tobin's q theory has implications for the volume of takeover activity in stock markets. Firms are assumed to want to expand output capacity by the cheapest route. One route is to pay the cost of new capacity by building new plants and buying new equipment. A second route is to pay the market value of existing capacity by buying up the shares of a company that owns an existing plant. If the stock market value of the company owning an existing plant is below the plant's replacement cost (that is, if Tobin's q is less than 1.0 for that asset), a takeover bid for that company's shares will be a cheaper route to extra capacity than building a new plant from scratch. If share values are low, therefore, expect aggressive firms to expand through takeovers. If share values are high, expect them to expand instead through new investment spending. Figure 8–5 shows this pattern at work in the United States since 1961.

FIGURE 8–5: Mergers and acquisitions versus Tobin's q (1970 = 100)

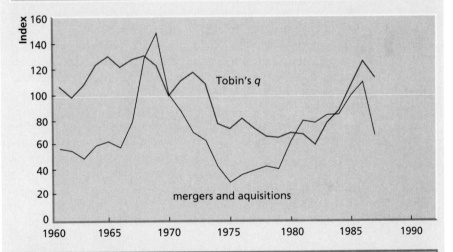

Note: Tobin's q is measured as the ratio of Standard & Poor's composite stock price index to the investment spending price deflator. Mergers and acquisitions are added together to create one number. Both series are presented as indices, indexed so that 1970 = 100.

Sources: Economic Report of the President; Statistical Abstract of the United States, various issues; *Mergers and Aquisitions: The Journal of Corporate Venture,* various issues.

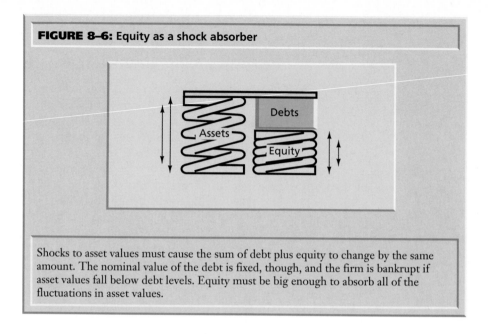

FIGURE 8–6: Equity as a shock absorber

Shocks to asset values must cause the sum of debt plus equity to change by the same amount. The nominal value of the debt is fixed, though, and the firm is bankrupt if asset values fall below debt levels. Equity must be big enough to absorb all of the fluctuations in asset values.

an (inverse) index of how careful and prudent the firm is likely to be.[3] For lenders to feel secure, a borrowing firm's leverage ratio must not be too large. Owners of firms able to identify a long list of clearly profitable projects will not be able to borrow enough to take advantage of all of them. Massive borrowing would raise the asset:equity ratio to too high a level. Lenders would balk at providing funds. Further expansion would therefore call for an injection of new equity capital into the firm.

Firms can raise new equity by increasing saving or by issuing new shares. Both sources of new equity may be closed or have high costs in the short run. For instance, Figure 8–7 suggests that firms in Canada can increase savings only by increasing profits. In Figure 8–7, gross income is defined as profit after tax plus capital consumption allowances. Capital consumption allowances rise over time, mechanically, with the depreciable capital stock of corporations. If gross income is to be increased in the short run, it must be through increases in profit after tax. Yet well-run firms will already have exploited all existing means of raising profit after tax. Saving can still be increased in the short run if dividend payments to shareholders can be lowered. The steady rise in dividends shown in Figure 8–7, with only a slight pause in the savage recession of 1981–82 when profit after tax

---

[3] Shareholders of limited-liability firms face asymmetrical risks, especially where shareholders' equity is small. Shareholders of a firm taking large risks will benefit fully from large gains but will suffer only the part of any loss that is absorbed by equity; losses beyond that are borne instead by creditors.

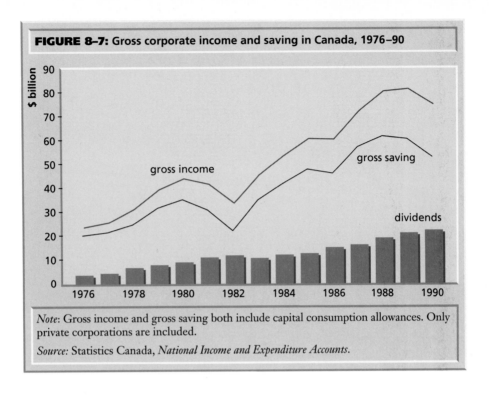

FIGURE 8–7: Gross corporate income and saving in Canada, 1976–90

Note: Gross income and gross saving both include capital consumption allowances. Only private corporations are included.

Source: Statistics Canada, *National Income and Expenditure Accounts.*

was actually negative, shows that firms are very reluctant to lower dividends.[4] So in the short run, firms cannot raise more new equity simply by increasing gross saving.

If corporate saving cannot be increased easily in the short run, that leaves the issue of new shares as the only other source of new equity. Issuing new shares to new owners reduces the control that existing owners have over the firm and dilutes their share of returns from new assets. The issue of new shares is like selling part of the firm. For owners who want their firm to grow and who also want the firm to stay theirs, issuing new shares is the last resort rather than the first.

In the short run, therefore, the more optimistic firms will find their asset purchases and debt issues limited by their own equity and savings flow. Paradoxically, such firms will borrow more if their current profit and saving rise, because current saving eases their leverage constraint a bit. More pessimistic

---

[4]A school of macroeconomists known as post-Keynesians disagree with this proposition. They argue that profits can easily be raised by oligopolistic firms. In fact, some argue that prices are set by such firms at whatever level is needed to provide equity funding for new investment projects. Instead of business saving being fixed in the short run, it adjusts to match investment plans.

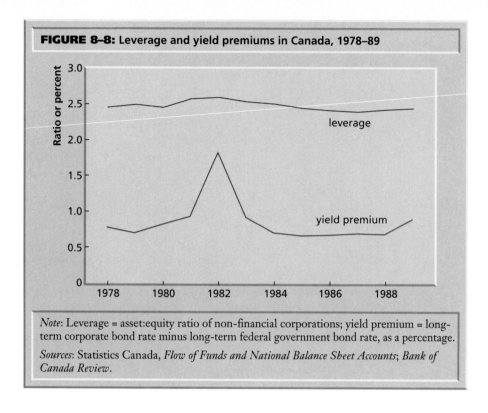

FIGURE 8–8: Leverage and yield premiums in Canada, 1978–89

Note: Leverage = asset:equity ratio of non-financial corporations; yield premium = long-term corporate bond rate minus long-term federal government bond rate, as a percentage.

Sources: Statistics Canada, *Flow of Funds and National Balance Sheet Accounts*; *Bank of Canada Review*.

firms would use greater current profit and saving to reduce borrowing. It is not clear what the net outcome would be for all firms collectively.

Firms may not find themselves cut off from funds abruptly as their leverage ratios rise. Instead they find their new debt issues classified by bond rating agencies at a lower and lower credit rating: from Baa to Ba to B, and still lower. Lenders will sometimes buy debts with lower credit ratings, but only at higher interest rates. Only where rating agencies classify a new issue as speculative do funds for new issues usually dry up entirely. Firms expanding their leverage ratios therefore face a rising cost of funds as they move from borrowing in the Baa market to borrowing in the B market. Figure 8–8 shows the cost of extra leverage to firms over the period 1978–88. As firms raised their leverage by extra borrowing in 1981–82, the yield premium of long-term corporate bonds over long-term federal government bonds soared from 0.8 percent to 1.8 percent (from 80 basis points to 180 basis points, in financial jargon). Since then, decreases in the leverage ratio have been rewarded by lenders with a drop in the yield premium to below even the levels of the late 1970s.

▣ Financial institutions

The behaviour of financial institutions, like that of business firms, can be explained with the MEI theory (maximizing the annual flow of profits) or with Tobin's q theory (maximizing the value of equity). In this section we will apply just the MEI theory: we will be assuming that financial institutions try to maximize annual profits and that they do so by investing in all assets with MEI above the cost of funds.

The essential difference between modelling financial institutions and business firms is that financial institutions buy financial rather than physical assets with the debts they issue. As a result, financial institutions are part of borrowers and lenders curves at the same time. They lend in the markets where they buy financial assets, and they borrow in the markets where they issue new debts of various sorts. For a bank, therefore, marginal efficiency of assets means yield on loans and cost of funds means the interest and operating costs payable on deposits. For other financial institutions, the MEI approach applies in roughly the same way but with different types of assets and debts.

Figure 8–9 shows an MEI-type diagram for a small near-bank, Faithful Trust Company, which makes loans and borrows in the term-deposit market. Figure 8–9 differs from the graph in Figure 8–1 in two ways. First, the horizontal cost of funds schedule of Figure 8–1 is replaced by a horizontal cost of term deposits. Second, the downward-sloping MEI curve of Figure 8–1 becomes a downward-sloping schedule of net yields on new loans (net of operating costs).[5] The horizontal axis measures the quantity of new assets, which now reflects, essentially, new loans made by Faithful. Where Faithful's equity is fixed, as it is in the short run, extra new loans made require extra new deposits to have been issued in an amount equal to the loans.

Faithful maximizes profits by taking on new loans to the point where their net yields just cover term deposit rates. Faithful stops new lending where the two schedules intersect in Figure 8–9.

The single firm in Figure 8–9 is representative of financial institutions as a whole if financial markets are competitive. The collective behaviour of financial institutions in deposit and loan markets is shown in Figure 8–10. As borrowers in deposit markets, banks and near-banks would borrow more when the cost of term deposits falls (as might happen, for instance, if households came to see deposits as more attractive at a given yield). Banks and near-banks move farther down their individual net yield curves for loans in Figure 8–9, and their collective borrowers

---

[5] Since most loans are repaid within a short period, Faithful's new loans during the year will account for most of its total assets. Faithful's loan schedule slopes downwards even though it is a small lender in a big loan market, because with limited information, Faithful has only a finite list of potential loans it knows well enough to consider seriously. Financial institutions that start making loans in areas they do not know well quickly run into large default losses.

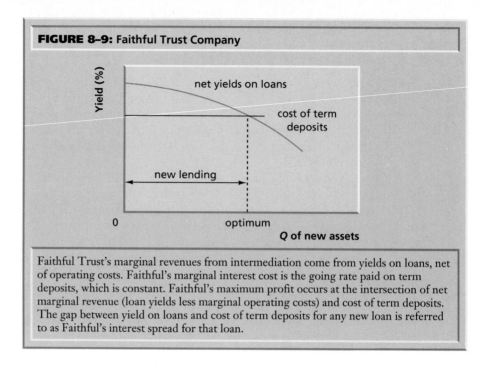

FIGURE 8–9: Faithful Trust Company

Faithful Trust's marginal revenues from intermediation come from yields on loans, net of operating costs. Faithful's marginal interest cost is the going rate paid on term deposits, which is constant. Faithful's maximum profit occurs at the intersection of net marginal revenue (loan yields less marginal operating costs) and cost of term deposits. The gap between yield on loans and cost of term deposits for any new loan is referred to as Faithful's interest spread for that loan.

curve in Figure 8–10(a). They borrow more also when loan yields rise; they move farther along their individual cost of term deposits schedule in Figure 8–9 and farther up their collective lenders schedule in Figure 8–10(a).

As lenders in the loan market, banks and near-banks lend more as their cost of term deposits falls; they move down their individual net yield curves in Figure 8–9 and their collective lenders curve shifts outward to the right in the loan market of Figure 8–10(b). They also lend more as loan yields rise (perhaps due to a burst of borrower enthusiasm in the loan market); they move farther along their individual cost of term deposits schedules in Figure 8–9 and their collective lenders curve in Figure 8–10(b).

The two parts of Figure 8–10 introduce a new concept: the **spread**. The spread is the gap between the average yield on assets and the average cost of debt. If all operating costs are either netted out of asset yields or added into the costs of debt, the spread is the same as the profit per dollar of assets. In that case, spread multiplied by total assets equals total profit. If operating costs are not netted out, the measure is a **gross spread**. Figure 8–10 shows a gross spread between equilibrium loan yield and equilibrium term deposit cost. The box on pp. 144–145 explains how spreads will tend to be squeezed by competition, and how that squeezing will force surviving firms to keep their leverage ratios high. Chapter 10 explains in much more detail the factors that determine the size of these spreads.

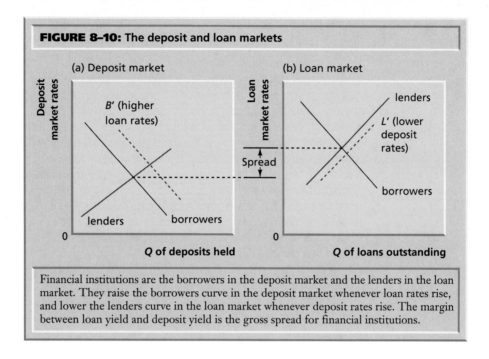

FIGURE 8–10: The deposit and loan markets

(a) Deposit market

Deposit market rates

B' (higher loan rates)

lenders   borrowers

0   Q of deposits held

(b) Loan market

Loan market rates

lenders

L' (lower deposit rates)

Spread

borrowers

0   Q of loans outstanding

Financial institutions are the borrowers in the deposit market and the lenders in the loan market. They raise the borrowers curve in the deposit market whenever loan rates rise, and lower the lenders curve in the loan market whenever deposit rates rise. The margin between loan yield and deposit yield is the gross spread for financial institutions.

Limits on expansion

Like business firms, financial institutions are also subject to constraints from lenders. Lenders who buy the term deposits and floating-rate notes and other debts issued by financial institutions want to be sure of repayment. Lenders to financial institutions want the institutions to have a significant stake in selecting and then monitoring their assets with care. Lenders to financial institutions therefore insist that financial institutions keep their leverage ratios within prudent limits. Once at that limit, financial institutions wishing to expand must match further borrowing with further equity contribution.

The leverage constraint adds another factor to influence the borrowers and lenders curves of Figure 8–10. Aggressive financial institutions who reach their leverage limit will buy more loans and issue more deposits as their current profits and savings rise; that is, with extra current profit the lenders curve in Figure 8–10(a) and the borrowers curve in Figure 8–10(b) will both shift outwards to the right. Any increase in acceptable limits for leverage ratios will have the same effect.

Adding equity presents the same problems for financial institutions as for non-financial firms: the only flexible source of new equity in the short run is to sell more shares to new owners, which dilutes the control that existing owners can exercise. However, leverage ratios are very much bigger for financial institutions than for non-financial firms, as Figure 8–12 shows. The result is that a small increase in equity supports a large increase in assets.

Competition, Spreads, and Leverage Ratios

It is easy to show with borrower–lender diagrams how competition squeezes spreads and forces financial institutions to keep their leverage ratios high. The gross spread between equilibrium deposit rates and equilibrium loan rates must be enough to cover operating costs of financial institutions and leave a normal return on equity. Figure 8–11 shows such a spread. The amount of spread per dollar of loans that is needed to provide a normal return per dollar of equity must fall as the leverage ratio rises. As the leverage ratio rises, financial institutions have less equity per dollar of loans, so any given profit per dollar of loans means a larger profit margin per dollar of equity. If new financial institutions enter deposit and loan markets with less equity per dollar of deposits than existing firms (that is, with higher leverage ratios), they will require less spread per dollar of loans to provide the same, normal return to equity.

Entry of new financial institutions drives deposit rates up and loan rates down. Spreads are narrowed. Existing firms with lower leverage ratios will find themselves with too little spread to provide normal returns to shareholders. Either they must move into different markets, or they must raise their leverage ratio so that a lower spread per dollar of assets still provides the same return per dollar of equity.

For example, the entry of chartered banks to the higher-quality consumer loan markets in the 1960s squeezed out consumer loan companies.

FIGURE 8–11: Loan and deposit markets

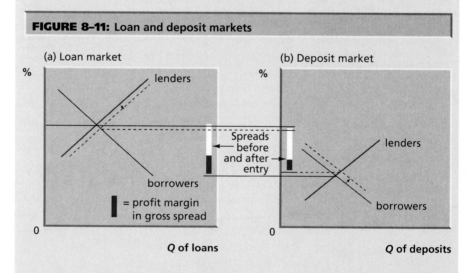

The entry of banks to this market narrowed the spreads available to all consumer lenders. Banks had leverage ratios of up to 20, so they could still prosper with small spreads. Consumer loan companies had leverage ratios of under 10, so they could not. Similarly, the entry of foreign bank subsidiaries into Canadian business loan markets in the 1970s narrowed the spread for large Canadian banks; the large banks responded by raising their own leverage ratios. Finally, the removal of international financial barriers in the 1980s has made competition worldwide in some markets and forced spreads to narrow in all wholesale markets.

Financial institutions as conductors of financial shocks

Financial institutions are both absorbers and conductors of financial disturbances. They smooth loan default shocks over many loans by pooling loan default risks, as you will see in the next chapter. But they faithfully transmit disturbances in demand and supply from the markets in which they lend to the markets in which they borrow, and vice versa. For instance, consider what follows an outbreak of optimism among business firms about future sales prospects. Optimism raises the returns expected by business firms on new plant and equipment. In terms of Tobin's q theory, optimism raises the expected market value of some new plant and equipment above its cost; q rises above 1.0. Firms want to borrow more than before at each possible interest rate on loans; the borrowers curve shifts outward to the right in the loan market diagram in Figure 8–10(b). Loan rates start to rise.

As financial institutions see loan rates rising, they become more eager to lend (they are just moving along their lenders curve in Figure 8–10(b). In order to lend, however, financial institutions must also borrow. Their desire to borrow more at given interest rates on deposits shifts the borrowers curve in the deposit market outward to the right, in Figure 8–10(a). Deposit rates start to rise. Financial institutions have transmitted a borrower or demand shock from the loan market to the deposit market.

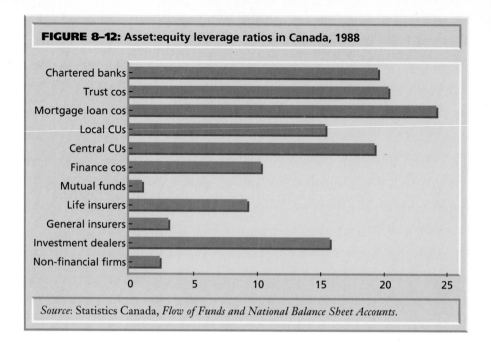

FIGURE 8–12: Asset:equity leverage ratios in Canada, 1988

Source: Statistics Canada, *Flow of Funds and National Balance Sheet Accounts.*

SECTION 3

Governments

Governments are different from other sectors. In particular, it is not easy to set up a simple objective for governments, from which predictions about their behaviour can be derived. Neither profit nor equity can be used. Social welfare is the usual objective attributed to governments, but it can rarely be defined precisely enough to be useful for economic analysis.

Explaining government lending and borrowing is therefore difficult. It is made worse by the extra range of options open to governments. Like firms, governments can borrow to finance long-lived assets such as airports, roads, and hospitals.[6] Governments can also borrow for pure consumption, as the medical student Casey did in the previous chapter. For instance, governments can issue bonds to finance extra transfer payments to the elderly or extra medical coverage for everyone.

Governments in developed economies have an infinite lifetime and a relatively stable income (derived from taxes on millions of different taxpayers).

---

[6] Much government debt is in fact for this purpose. The national balance sheet, for instance, records $180 billion of debts outstanding for provincial and local governments, but $262 billion of physical assets (excluding land) to show for it. The federal government, on the other hand, has only $38 billion of physical assets to show for a debt ten times as large.

Printing Money

There is a big formal distinction between national governments and other levels of government. National governments can print the paper money in which their domestic debts are repaid. In principle, this allows national governments to borrow without limit, whereas lower-level governments cannot borrow beyond the limits of their tax base. For domestic borrowing this distinction is important. For developed industrial countries in today's world, however, extra borrowing is not generally done at home. At the margin, governments are tapping the savings of foreigners through the capital inflow. Extra debt must therefore be repaid eventually in foreign currency, which the government cannot print. Only the United States, which prints the currency used most widely for foreign payments, can use the power of the printing press to help it out in foreign borrowing.

Both features make governments very creditworthy in financial markets. Governments can therefore borrow for very long terms in any part of the financial world, without collateral. They are not tied to borrowing for only as long as the lifetime of the assets being financed. Governments can extend the term of any borrowing by merely borrowing again to repay bonds at maturity. This is known as refinancing debt.

Governments are subject to some constraints, but relatively mild ones. Governments cannot issue equity shares in themselves. Governments are subject to a sort of leverage limit as well. Instead of the ratio of assets to equity, lenders to governments look at the ratio of debt to the government's tax base (its income source). Too high a debt-to-income ratio suggests the government may have difficulty persuading taxpayers to service the debt later on. Even this ratio allows governments to add to their debt each year in the same proportion as (nominal) national income grows; that is, if national income grows at 7 percent per year and the federal debt is $400 billion, debt can grow by $28 billion without increasing the debt-to-income ratio at all.

Extra borrowing options allow governments to reallocate spending from one *generation* to the next. Extra consumption spending financed now by long-term borrowing that will be refinanced and therefore serviced by taxpayers not yet born is a transfer of spending power to our generation from our grandchildren. Indeed, it may be a transfer from our grandchildren's grandchildren; refinancing of debt has no clear time limit. Inter-generational transfers raise a host of moral questions in a democracy, since future generations have no say in the decisions of the current generation. The only choice left to future generations is whether to pay or default on the debts we bequeath them. In the continuing Third World debt crisis, many of those voters who are now asked to pay for borrowing done by governments in the 1970s are voting to default instead.

There is one cyclical feature of government debt that is akin to the life cycle of households. Government tax revenue is tied to national income, which can be

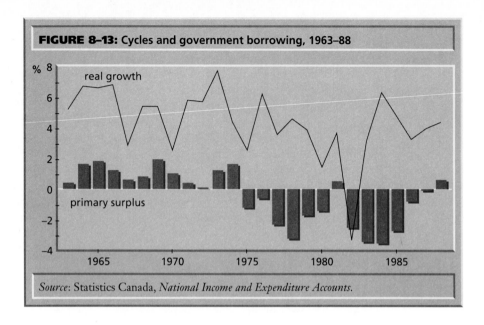

FIGURE 8–13: Cycles and government borrowing, 1963–88

Source: Statistics Canada, *National Income and Expenditure Accounts.*

thought of as the government's tax base. National income fluctuates with the business cycle. The public does not want the flow of government services to fluctuate with national income; for some services, such as unemployment relief, we want fluctuation counter to that of national income. In order to reallocate its revenue flow to finance its spending pattern, the government must adopt a cyclical pattern in its budgeting: it must issue more debt in the lean years, to be repaid out of extra tax revenue in the fat years. Figure 8–13 shows cyclical budgeting at work for the federal government since 1963. Whenever the growth rate of real GDP drops, the government's *primary surplus* falls as well. The primary surplus is the federal government surplus measured without interest payments on the federal debt.

Governments are of course the borrowers in government bond markets. Their behaviour determines the shape and location of borrowers curves in those markets. For instance, new government borrowing shifts the borrowers curve outward to the right in the government bond market. Cyclical budgeting causes that borrowers curve to shift outward faster in recessions and slower in booms. Other than that, governments as borrowers are relatively insensitive to the factors that influence other borrowers. Governments' borrowers curves are close to vertical. In fact, governments' borrowers curves may even be positively sloping: as loan rates rise, governments facing higher interest costs will sometimes borrow more rather than less just to cover the interest expense. The sharp increase in interest rates in 1988–89, for instance, caused the Canadian government to *increase* its deficit for 1989–90 (to borrow more) when it had previously planned to lower the deficit.

Questions and Problems

1. What causes the marginal efficiency of investment curve to slope downward, either for a firm or for the economy as a whole? Aren't there enough viable investment projects to make this curve essentially flat over a huge range?

2. Both the MEI theory and Tobin's q theory yield lists of factors affecting demand for real assets. How do those lists differ?

3. Why do you think firms keep their flow of dividends so much more stable than their flow of income, as shown in Figure 8–7? Relate your answer to borrowers and lenders curves in the stock market.

4. In Figure 8–9 Faithful Trust Company has a downward-sloping loan yield curve and a flat term deposit cost curve. Does that mean Faithful has some market power in the loan market but none in the term deposit market?

5. Why does leverage matter to financial institutions?

6. In 1985 two small regional banks failed, causing a loss of confidence in small regional deposit-taking institutions generally. Explain with borrower and lender diagrams how this shock would be transmitted by deposit-takers from their debt markets to their asset markets.

7. At one point in the 1980s, the book value of loans outstanding to developing countries from Canadian chartered banks was up to 2.5 times the banks' collective equity. At the time, the market values of such loans were about 40 percent of their book value. Was the equity of Canadian banks sufficient to absorb fluctuations in the market value of bank assets? Discuss.

Suggestions for Further Reading

Fisher, Irving. *The Role of Interest*. New York: Macmillan, 1907.

Hirshleifer, Jack. "On the Theory of Optimal Investment." *Journal of Political Economy*, August 1958.

McMillan, Alexander. *An Introduction to Canadian Financial Markets: An Analytical Approach* (Scarborough, Ont.: Prentice-Hall Canada, 1989)

Neave, G. *Canada's Financial System*. Toronto: Wiley, 1981 or later edition.

Tobin, James. "A General Equilibrium Approach to Monetary Theory." *Journal of Money, Credit, and Banking*, 1 (1969), 15–29.

Chapter nine

Risk and Hedging

> ... in this world, nothing is certain but death and taxes.
>
> — *Benjamin Franklin, 1789*

The financial system specializes in helping borrowers and lenders manage their risk. The sophisticated way in which the financial system handles risk accounts for much of what is distinctive about the financial system. Differences in risk characteristics explain most of why one asset is bought at high prices while another asset is a "dog" even at low prices.

This chapter explains risk. It does so in several parts. Not all parts will be of interest to all readers, so here is a reader's guide. Section 1 defines risk as uncertainty of future yields on one's wealth, and explains the sources of risk in non-technical terms. Section 2 measures risk by the variance of possible yields on wealth. Section 3 uses this definition of risk to develop the two most basic insights of the theory of asset choices under risk (known as *portfolio theory*).

For those who want to know more about portfolio theory, section 4 uses a well-known indifference curve diagram to develop it further. Section 5 presents a version of portfolio choice theory very popular in finance theory; this version is less general than the version of portfolio theory explained in section 4, but it is able to generate much more specific predictions. Section 6 discusses how borrowers and lenders can manage the risks that cannot be removed just by diversification of lending across different assets. It discusses the use of hedging and matching strategies as part of risk management.

Two appendices contain technical extensions of portfolio theory. Appendix 9–1 formally derives the property of risk aversion that is simply assumed in section 3. Appendix 9–2 extends the discussion of section 4 to consider situations where asset yields fluctuate in patterns that are more complex than those assumed in section 4.

You should learn in this chapter:

1. the sources of fluctuations in yields on individual assets;

2. the concept of variance of portfolio yields as a measure of risk;

3. how diversification of assets can remove unsystematic risk;

4. how systematic risk of an asset adds to portfolio risk and therefore affects lenders curves for individual assets;

5. why all lenders will have roughly the same degree of risk aversion at the margin;

6. how the assumptions of systematic risk and a single degree of risk aversion at the margin can be used to determine the entire set of market prices of individual assets;

7. how hedging and matching strategies are used to offset risks that cannot be removed by diversification.

SECTION 1

Nature and sources of risk

In this chapter, the terms *risk* and *uncertainty* are synonymous. Both refer to not knowing which of different possible outcomes will actually occur at various future dates — for example, which of many possible resale prices will be obtained when a block of shares is sold in a year's time.

The risk that matters is the risk of not getting the future yields we expect. We care more about whether our assets provide good yields than we do about their other features. Furthermore, the yield that matters to rational lenders like Sarah Brown and Rick Stagger of Chapter 7 is the average yield they will realize per dollar on their whole portfolio of assets. This important average yield is called the **portfolio yield**. Yields on individual assets matter only because they contribute to the portfolio yield. It is the portfolio yield on each household's asset portfolio that determines whether or not the parents will be able to retire early on a sunny beach. It is the portfolio yield on Faithful Trust's asset portfolio that determines whether Faithful will have any income left over after paying interest on deposits to pay dividends to shareholders.

A portfolio yield is an average of all the yields on individual assets in the portfolio. A portfolio yield is therefore uncertain only because yields on individual assets are uncertain. Yields on individual asset yields are uncertain because they are exposed to one or more sources of risk, which can be classified into the categories of credit risk, income risk, market risk, and inflation risk.

Credit risk

Credit risk arises whenever borrowers promise to make specific payments as part of loan agreements. **Credit risk** is the risk that borrowers will not make those payments. Instead borrowers may default totally, they may pay only part of what was promised, or they may pay later than promised. Borrowers may be unwilling to repay, or they may be unable to repay because of some unexpected setback. In either case the lender will realize a lower yield than the borrower originally promised.

It is credit risk that is reflected in credit ratings of debt issues by Moody's and by Standard & Poor's and other rating agencies. These ratings range from investment grade (all A grades and the top B grades) to various classes of "junk" securities (the C and D grades; D stands for default). The box provides an example of ratings of securities of national governments by both major rating agencies, for ratings down to the B level.

How countries rate

MOODY'S and STANDARD & POOR'S

MOODY'S	S & P'S
AAA	
Austria, Canada, Finland, France, W.Germany, Japan, Netherlands, Sweden, Switzerland, Britain, U.S.A.	
AAA	**AAA**
Italy, Luxembourg	Norway
AA1	**AA+**
Belgium, Denmark Norway	Belgium Italy
AA2	**AA**
Australia, Spain	Australia, Spain, New Zealand, Singapore, Taiwan, Denmark
AA3	**AA−**
Ireland, New Zealand, Singapore	Ireland
A1	**A+**
Portugal	S. Korea
A2	**A**
S. Korea, Iceland, India, Thailand	Portugal, Iceland, Hong Kong
A3	**A−**
Hong Kong	Malaysia, Thailand
BAA1	**BBB+**
China, Malaysia	---
BAA2	**BBB**
Hungary	Greece
BAA3	**BBB−**
---	Israel
BA	**BB**
Venezuela (2)	---
B	**B**
Brazil (2), Argentina (3)	Venezuela (+)

Source: The Financial Post March 5, 1990, p. 3.

Income risk

Stocks, mutual funds, pension funds, most insurance policies, notice deposits at banks, many deposits at credit unions, and renegotiable mortgages all offer streams of income payments that are not fixed. The terms of each of these assets allow the issuer to vary the amount of income payment from time to time in specified ways. Allowable variations in the income payments on an asset (that is, variations not caused by default) cause variations in the asset's yield that are called **income risk**. Different assets have quite different kinds of income risk, since different income streams vary in quite different ways. The stream of income may fluctuate with company profits, with prevailing yields on new bonds, with the level of exchange rates (for all assets denominated in foreign currencies), or even with the level of the consumer price index.

Market risk

Yields on many assets reflect the difference between the known current asset price and an unknown market resale price at some point in the future. Variations in an asset's yield due to variations in a future market price are called **market risk**. Section 4 of Chapter 5 has explained how future resale prices can matter to yields. Market risk does not affect fixed-term assets that will be held until maturity and then redeemed at full face value in domestic currency; their yields to maturity do not depend on future market values. All other assets, including stocks, houses,

> ## Credit Risk and Market Risk in New England
>
> In September 1989, the Bank of New England issued $200 million in bonds. In December 1989, it released the information that many of its large portfolio of property loans were unlikely to be repaid. This is an example of credit risk. By January 30, 1990, the bank's own bonds were bid at $15 (per $100 of face value) and offered at $25. This is an example of market risk, at least for all lenders who plan to hold these bonds for less than full term.

land, and foreign currency, must eventually be resold in a secondary market; therefore, they are all subject to market risk.

An important kind of market risk in the Canadian economy is **foreign exchange risk**. Many assets held by Canadians are denominated in foreign currencies, so their yield to a Canadian lender depends on the market price of foreign currency when the assets are redeemed or resold. Small variations in the exchange rate can cause a lot of foreign exchange risk in asset yields. For example, a 90-day U.S. treasury bill bought for U.S.$980 will yield 8 percent per year (2 percent per quarter) if the exchange rate does not change, but 0 percent if the market price of the U.S. dollar drops by 2 percent over the 90 days.

Inflation risk

All real yields are subject to inflation risk. **Real yield** is defined as nominal yield less the expected inflation rate. Whenever the expected inflation rate varies and nominal yields do not, every asset's real yield varies in the opposite direction. All variations in real yields caused by variations in expected inflation are called **inflation risk**. For instance, with inflation of 4 percent per year, a nominal yield of 10 percent means a real yield of 6 percent. With inflation of 7 percent, the same nominal yield of 10 percent provides a real yield of only 3 percent.

Inflation risk is very important for long-term, fixed-income assets such as pension annuities. A $1000 pension starting at age 65, for example, will still buy $1000 worth of goods at today's prices at age 75 if there is no inflation, but only $508 worth of goods if inflation averages 7 percent per year over the ten-year period, and only $386 worth of goods if inflation averages 10 percent per year. Those are large differences for someone planning to live on a fixed pension income.

Despite its importance, inflation risk plays little part in our analysis of financial markets. Inflation risk has little effect on relative yields because annual yields on almost all assets are affected more or less equally. For most financial analysis, it is only relative yields that matter, so we pay little attention to inflation risk in the rest of this chapter.

Identifying different categories of risk can help us recognize more of the factors causing uncertainty of yields. Remember, however, that what matters to lenders is the total risk to which they are exposed, regardless of whether it is mostly credit risk, or mostly income risk, or equal amounts of all the risks above.

Definition and measurement of risk

The definition of risk used in this chapter is from the Tobin–Markowitz approach to financial-market analysis.[1] The **Tobin–Markowitz approach** is based on the assumption that investors can estimate more or less crudely the risks associated with various assets they are considering. In particular, lenders are assumed to behave as though they had some idea of both the range and the relative probabilities of possible future yields. This knowledge is assumed both for the asset portfolio as a whole and for individual assets making up that portfolio. It may seem that that is attributing too much knowledge to financial-market participants, but pension fund managers and other wholesale investors have at least that much information about any financial asset that really interests them. Brokerage firms' research departments also work constantly to provide clients with information about individual financial assets.

Information about possible outcomes and the relative probabilities of each make up a **probability distribution**. Two probability distributions are illustrated in Figure 9–1, one for portfolio yield outcomes and also a more familiar one for future course grade outcomes. In a probability distribution, uncertainty is reflected in the distribution's *width*. This corresponds to what most people recognize intuitively as risk. For instance, in considering potential grades from two courses, the first with possible grades ranging only from C+ to B+ and the second with possible grades ranging from F to A+, most people would call the first course less risky than the second. The first course has a narrower probability distribution. The same logic applies to yields. A portfolio whose possible yields range from 5 to 15 percent is less risky than one whose possible yields range from −10 to +30 percent. The least risky portfolio is one whose yield has a probability distribution with zero width: only one yield would be possible, and its probability would be 1.0.

The Tobin–Markowitz approach measures risk not by the range of a probability distribution, but by either the variance or the standard deviation of the probability distribution. The **variance** is the weighted average squared deviation of yields from the midpoint of the probability distribution. In calculating the variance, each deviation from the midpoint is squared so that negative deviations will not cancel out positive deviations. Then each squared deviation is weighted by its relative probability so that improbable outcomes get

---

[1]James Tobin, "Liquidity Preference as Behavior Towards Risk," *Review of Economic Studies*, 1958, 65–86; Harry Markowitz, *Portfolio Selection: Efficient Diversification of Investments* (New Haven, Conn.: Yale University Press, for the Cowles Foundation, 1959).

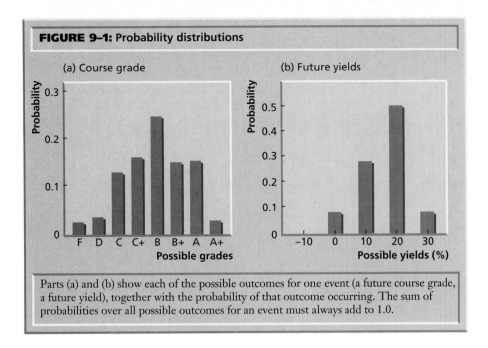

FIGURE 9-1: Probability distributions

(a) Course grade

(b) Future yields

Parts (a) and (b) show each of the possible outcomes for one event (a future course grade, a future yield), together with the probability of that outcome occurring. The sum of probabilities over all possible outcomes for an event must always add to 1.0.

little weight. The **standard deviation** is the positive square root of the variance; it has almost the same properties as the variance. A higher standard deviation or variance around the midpoint of a distribution means a wider probability distribution and measures a higher level of risk exposure. The midpoint of the probability distribution is measured as the **expected yield**; it is a weighted average of possible yields, with relative probabilities serving as weights.

The formula for calculating a variance from a probability distribution with n possible outcomes is

$$V = \sum_{i=1}^{n} prob_i(r_i - E)^2,$$

where V is the variance, E is the expected yield, r_i is the ith possible yield, $prob_i$ is its probability of occurring in the future. $\sum$ is the algebraic summation symbol meaning "sum of all following terms, for all pairs of probabilities and yields from $i = 1$ to $i = n$." In the preceding equation, the sum of all probabilities must add up to exactly 1.0, by definition of a probability distribution.[2] The formula for expected yield (E) of a probability distribution is (dropping the subscripts on the summation symbol, for simplicity):

$$E = \sum prob_i r_i.$$

---

[2] It is because the probabilities add up to 1.0 that V is a *weighted average* squared deviation, rather than just a combination of squared deviations.

The formula for the standard deviation is:

$$S = \sqrt{V}.$$

As an example, consider a simple probability distribution of future yields for a portfolio that could yield either 20 percent or 10 percent, with 60:40 odds. The expected yield in percentage points is

$$E = 0.60(20) + 0.40(10) = 16 \text{ percent.}$$

The variance is

$$V = 0.60(20 - 16)^2 + 0.40(10 - 16)^2 = 24 \text{ (percent squared).}$$

The standard deviation is

$$S = \sqrt{24} = 4.9 \text{ percent.}$$

Another more extreme but important example is of a **risk-free asset**, one whose probability distribution of possible yields has only one possible outcome with probability 1.0. Such a probability distribution has a variance and a standard deviation of zero.

Variance and standard deviation can be used interchangeably as measures of risk, since one is simply the positive square root of the other. Which one to use is simply a matter of convenience. Variance is easier to calculate, but standard deviation has the advantage of being in the same units as yield; that makes it intuitively easier to grasp and to apply in practice.

SECTION 3

Variance, diversification, and systematic risk

Lenders can be assumed to be *risk-averse*; that is, other things being equal, lenders would prefer a smaller risk of their portfolio yield.[3] The risk of a lender's portfolio yield depends on the risk characteristics of the individual assets which make up that lender's portfolio. It follows that risk-averse lenders will value more highly those assets whose risk characteristics do not add much to the risk of portfolio yield. In this section we find out what those risk characteristics are.

---

[3] Risk aversion does not imply that lenders never take risks. Far from it. Risk averters are always taking risks, but they take those risks only because other things are *not* equal: because the choices involving greater risk also offer a more than compensating amount of extra expected yield.

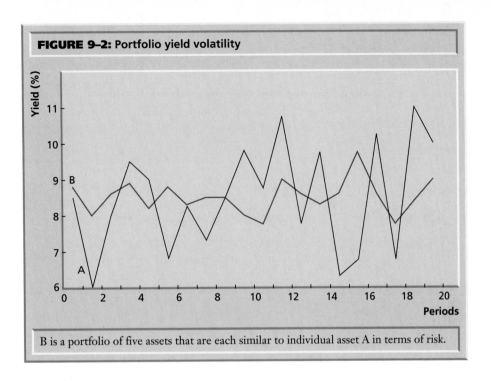

FIGURE 9–2: Portfolio yield volatility

B is a portfolio of five assets that are each similar to individual asset A in terms of risk.

Diversification

The fundamental insight of the Tobin–Markowitz approach is that **diversification** reduces portfolio risk, even if one diversifies by adding assets whose yields have high variances by themselves. A constructed example of diversification is shown in Figure 9–2. Six asset yields were generated over 20 periods by a random number generator. Each yield series starts at the same level in period 0 and has the same variance, but each varies with complete independence from all of the others. The assets are put into two portfolios A and B: portfolio A consists of just the first asset by itself; portfolio B consists of equal shares of each of the other five assets. Figure 9–2 shows the time path of portfolio yields for the two portfolios. The variation in the yield for the undiversified portfolio A is over twice as wide as the that for the diversified portfolio B. Yields for portfolio B are more stable (less risky) because the independent fluctuations of yields on the separate assets in portfolio B offset each other to a large extent. That is, diversification reduces risk where asset yields move independently.

What diversification implies about demand for individual assets can be seen most easily by extending diversification to its limit. If a portfolio can be diversified among an infinite number of assets whose yields move independently, all portfolio risk will be diversified away. That is, the variance of portfolio yield will be reduced to zero. If portfolio risk is zero, then the variances of yields on individual assets cannot be contributing anything to portfolio risk, so the variances of individual assets cannot matter to lenders; they will shrug it off as being irrelevant.

In practice, it is not possible to diversify among an infinite number of assets. However, institutional investors like mutual funds, pension funds, banks, finance companies, and trust companies can spread their asset portfolio over dozens or hundreds of different assets and reap well over 90 percent of the risk reduction available from diversification. Figure 9–2 shows that even diversifying over only five independent assets reduces portfolio risk by more than half.

The formula relating variance of individual assets to variance of a portfolio diversified across n independent assets is

$$V = \sum X_i^2 V_i$$

where V is the portfolio variance, V_i is the variance of the ith individual asset, and X_i is the portfolio share of the ith asset. Where V_i are all identical, and portfolio shares X_i are also identical, the formula simplifies to

$$V = (1/n) V_i$$

and the standard deviation becomes

$$S = \sqrt{(1/n)}\, S_i.$$

It is easy to calculate values of S with such a simple formula to see how fast portfolio risk falls with diversification. For portfolio B in Figure 9–2, for example, where n is 5, $\sqrt{(1/n)} = \sqrt{(1/5)} = 0.45$, so the standard deviation of the portfolio yield is only 45 percent of that of yields on individual assets. That is what Figure 9–2 shows.

Systematic risk

Unfortunately, the real world does not fit the key assumption of the special case illustrated in Figure 9–2. In the real world it is not possible to diversify away risk quite so easily because in the real world it is not possible to find many assets whose yields move as independently as the artificial yields used in Figure 9–2. Instead, most asset yields move together over time because they are all responding to many of the same common factors. Fiscal and monetary policy stimuli, for instance, push almost all asset yields in the same direction at once, so that the yield fluctuations of individual assets due to monetary and fiscal policy will not be independent. The globalization of financial markets has increased the extent to which shocks in the world's central financial markets (London, New York, and Tokyo) are transmitted immediately to all other financial markets. As a result, asset yields even in different countries like Canada, Australia, and South Korea tend to move together more than before financial markets became global.

Where yields on different assets move together most of the time, the diversification of a portfolio across different assets does not greatly reduce the variance of portfolio yield. At the extreme, where one diversifies over assets whose yields all move together all the time, diversification does not reduce the variance of average portfolio yield at all. In everyday language, this is the case of putting eggs in many different baskets, but carrying all the baskets together; one trip-up still breaks all the eggs because all the baskets fall together. In such a case, the variance of portfolio yield is just the average variance of individual asset yields. The formula is:[4]

$$V = \sum X_i V_i.$$

The analysis will be greatly simplified if we assume that all asset yield fluctuations are of one of the two extreme types considered so far: either entirely in unison with movements of other asset yields, or entirely independent of movements in other asset yields.[5] The asset yield fluctuations that are in unison with all other assets are known as the **systematic risk** of the asset. They give rise to systematic risk of the portfolio. The asset yield fluctuations that are entirely independent of movements of other asset yields are known as the **unsystematic risk** of the asset. They give rise to the unsystematic risk of the portfolio.

Systematic risk is caused by factors that are assumed to be system-wide, and that therefore affect all assets together. Systematic risks of individual assets cannot be cancelled out at all by diversification, because all asset yields move in the same direction when the cause is system-wide. Systematic risk is definitely a marketing handicap for an asset. Before lenders will take on more of an asset with a lot of systematic risk, they must be offered some compensating bribe such as extra expected yield.

At the other extreme, the unsystematic risk of an asset is caused by factors that affect only the one asset rather than the system as a whole. The personality of the Bank of Montreal's president, the product profile of General Motors, the vagaries of an ore vein in the Hemlo gold mine — these are unsystematic factors. The unsystematic risk of an asset can be cancelled out in a portfolio by offsetting fluctuations of yields on other assets, so the unsystematic risk of an asset does not add much, if at all, to portfolio risk. If unsystematic risk does not add to portfolio risk, then lenders do not care much about it, and unsystematic risk is therefore not a marketing handicap for someone selling the asset.

Three general principles emerge from the concepts introduced in this section:

1. Diversification pays as long as the yields from different assets do not move entirely in unison, so that lenders can offset negative swings in some yields with positive swings in others;

---

[4] This looks very similar to the formula for variance where asset yields move independently, but in this formula the portfolio share coefficients X_i are not squared. Since all X_i are fractions less than 1, squaring them greatly reduces their value. For instance, if $X_i = 0.2$, $X_i^2 = 0.04$.

[5] In the real world, asset yields can be in unison with only some other assets but not all, and some asset yields can move opposite to other asset yields. This more general situation is analyzed with more complex tools in Appendix 9–2.

2. Only the systematic part of an asset's risk contributes significantly to risk of a diversified portfolio;

3. Unsystematic risk does not matter much to lenders who can diversify.

It follows from these principles that the lenders curve for an individual asset should be quite sensitive to differences in the systematic risk of that asset relative to other assets, and that the lenders curves should not be sensitive to differences in unsystematic risk.

SECTION 4

Attitude to risk: the mean-variance model

Economists explain the asset choices made by risk-averse lenders with the **mean-variance model** developed by James Tobin and Harry Markowitz in the 1950s. This model applies directly to choices among different portfolios, but it indirectly explains choices of different assets to put into a portfolio. The indirect explanation of demand for individual assets is provided in section 5 and in Appendix 9–1. This section uses the Tobin–Markowitz model to explain how much lenders care about adding risk to their portfolio.

The Tobin–Markowitz approach to investor or lender choice under risk argues that lenders choose among portfolios on the basis of only two aspects of portfolio performance: *mean*, or expected yield (E), and risk, measured by portfolio *variance* (V) or standard deviation (S). The argument that only the mean yield (E) and risk (V or S) matter is well-grounded in microeconomic theory of choice under uncertainty if either of two assumptions holds (Appendix 9–1 contains the derivation). The first assumption is that probability distributions facing lenders on different portfolios are approximately "normal" in shape. The alternative assumption is that lenders have utility functions that rise quadratically with yield or with wealth.

If lenders choose among asset portfolios solely on the basis of the means and risks they offer, their choice can be explained and illustrated with the standard two-dimensional microeconomic apparatus of feasible set and indifference curves. These make up what is called the **portfolio choice diagram**. The slope of lenders' indifference curves at their chosen point in the feasible set measures how much lenders care about taking on extra portfolio risk.

The feasible set

Consider a rational lender, called Carmen Miranda. Carmen can choose combinations of risk-free and risky assets to make up her asset portfolio. Here, a risky asset is simply an asset whose yield has positive standard deviation; the risk could be systematic or unsystematic or a mixture of both. Risk-free assets can include short-term government bonds or treasury bills, government-insured term deposits, or even currency. In choosing among risk-free assets, Carmen

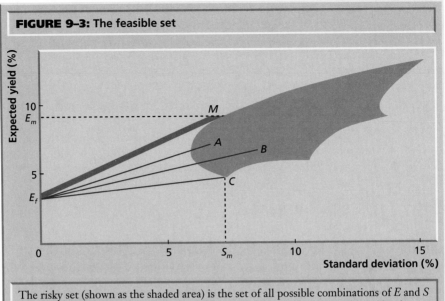

FIGURE 9–3: The feasible set

The risky set (shown as the shaded area) is the set of all possible combinations of E and S that can be achieved with combinations of risky assets. E_f is the point achieved by the risk-free asset. Points on straight lines between E_f and points in the risky set (for instance, on the lines $E_f C$ or $E_f A$) are achieved by combinations of the risk-free asset and a risky portfolio such as C or A. The risky portfolio M is the portfolio providing the steepest line to the risky set. Points on the line $E_f M$ are achieved by combinations of the risk-free asset and the risky portfolio M.

will hold the one that offers her the highest yield net of transactions costs; since all risk-free assets have the same zero risk, there would be no point in forgoing expected yield by holding a relatively low-yield, risk-free asset. Let her chosen risk-free asset have an expected yield E_f. Carmen estimates that each risky asset i has an expected yield E_i and standard deviation S_i. For each portfolio, Carmen can use the information on individual asset yields and standard deviations to calculate the portfolio's E and S (the calculation of a portfolio's standard deviation from individual assets is explained in section 5 and Appendix 9–2). Each portfolio's E and S can be plotted as a point in Figure 9–3. The set of such points for all possible portfolios makes up Carmen's feasible set of portfolio E and S characteristics.

The **feasible set** consists of three overlapping parts. The first part is the set of E and S combinations for portfolios consisting only of risky assets. In Figure 9–3, this part is called the risky set. The second part of the feasible set consists of the E and S for a portfolio consisting of only the risk-free asset. This second part of the feasible set is a point on the vertical axis in Figure 9–3, with $E = E_f$ and $S = 0$.

The third part of the feasible set consists of combinations of the risk-free asset and various collections of risky assets. It is a characteristic of combinations involving a risk-free asset and a collection of risky assets that the combined expected outcomes S and E lie along a straight line between the outcomes for each part separately.[6]

If the collection of risky assets used is that producing the pair of outcomes M in Figure 9–3, the combined expected outcomes lie along the straight line between E_f and M. Portfolios with a lot of M and little of the risk-free asset will have outcomes close to M. Portfolios with a lot of the risk-free asset will have outcomes close to E_f. Figure 9–3 includes some other examples of such lines; they join the risk-free asset with risky collections A, B, and C.

Efficient frontier

Risk-averse lenders see S as bad and E as good in Figure 9–3. They want to get as close to the top left edge of Figure 9–3 as they can. All risk-averse lenders will therefore choose some point on the top left edge of the feasible set, known as the **efficient set**. Different lenders will choose different points along the efficient set, but no lender will choose a point not on the set: lenders can always find a point on the efficient set that is better than any point not on it.

The portfolio choice diagram shows that the efficient set will be the line $E_f M$, consisting of combinations of the risk-free asset and one particular risky collection. The risky asset collections A, B, and C in Figure 9–3 are all inferior to M since all combinations of the risk-free asset with A, B, or C lie further away from the top left edge of the diagram than some combination of the risk-free asset with M. M is called the efficient risky portfolio.

Note that the choice of M as the proper collection of risky assets does not depend on how risk-averse lenders are. Our rational lender Carmen will want some point on the line $E_f M$ in Figure 9–3, so she will choose risky assets in the proportions of portfolio M to the extent that she chooses any risky assets at all. Carmen's degree of risk aversion will only determine what share of her portfolio is in the collection M and how much in risk-free assets. That is, the optimal proportions in which to hold risky assets are independent of lenders' tastes.

---

[6] The algebra is as follows. Let X_s, E_s, and S_s be the portfolio share, expected yield, and standard deviation of the group of risky assets in the portfolio, respectively. Portfolio E and S are determined as:

$$S = X_s S_s$$
$$E = E_f + X_s(E_s - E_f).$$

Substituting for X_s from the first equation into the second, we can get the equation for the line joining the possible pairs of E and S. That equation is

$$E = E_f + [(E_s - E_f)/S_s]S,$$

which is a straight line with slope $(E_s - E_f)/S_s$.

The optimal proportions in which to hold risky assets depend only on the yield on the risk-free asset, and on the information used to generate the risky feasible set. All lenders will use more or less the same risk-free asset yield in their calculations. It is also plausible and useful to assume that all lenders use more or less the same information to estimate yields and risks of risky assets. After all, the large investment fund managers all listen to the same news, read the same newspapers, and receive the same brokers' newsletters each month. It follows that all lenders will face roughly the same feasible risky set and all lenders will identify the same risky collection M as their optimal risky collection.

However, if each lender wants to hold risky assets in the same proportions as all other lenders, then the proportions of risky assets in each individual portfolio must be the same as the proportions of risky assets demanded in total over all portfolios. The latter must be the same as the proportions of risky assets in existence. For example, if there were some risky asset that lenders wanted to hold in smaller proportions than existed in total, there would be excess supply of the asset in its financial market. The asset's price would fall. The fall in price would both lower the asset's share in the total value of all existing risky assets and also (by raising the asset's expected yield) increase the demand for it by lenders. A portfolio of risky assets in which each asset has the same share that it has in total risky assets in the financial system is known as a market portfolio.[7]

Optimal portfolio choice and attitude to risk

For the final step in Carmen's optimal portfolio choice we need to add in her indifference curves. This is done in Figure 9–4. Since she regards portfolio risk S as bad, Carmen's indifference curves slope upward to the right. She insists on more E to compensate her for exposure to more S. Typically, she would feel more strongly about extra risk as her level of S rises, so her indifference curves are convex from below.

Carmen chooses from the efficient set the point lying on her highest indifference curve. This is the point of tangency A in Figure 9–4. At point A Carmen has roughly 60 percent of the portfolio in the risky collection M, and 40 percent in the risk-free asset. Different lenders more risk averse than Carmen would have steeper indifference curves, which would generate points of tangency closer to E_f. Those less risk averse would have flatter indifference curves and points of tangency closer to M.

The slope of her indifference curve at point A tells us how Carmen feels about taking on extra risk. For Carmen to take on extra portfolio risk willingly, starting from point A, she would have to be offered at least as much extra expected portfolio yield as would keep her on the indifference curve I_1. That implies a ratio of extra expected yield to extra risk equal to the slope of her indifference curve.

---

[7] The market portfolio can be thought of as equivalent to the basket of stocks making up the TSE 300 or the S&P 500, although there is much more to a complete market portfolio than just stocks.

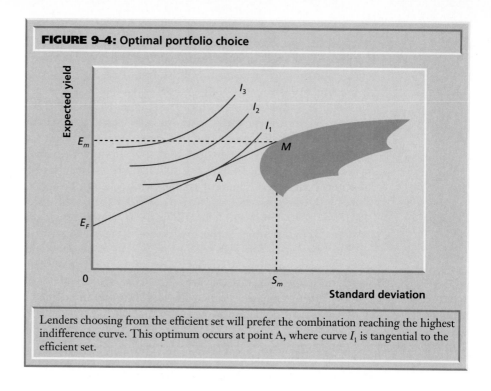

FIGURE 9–4: Optimal portfolio choice

Lenders choosing from the efficient set will prefer the combination reaching the highest indifference curve. This optimum occurs at point A, where curve I_1 is tangential to the efficient set.

Since her indifference curve is tangent to her efficient set at A, the ratio of extra expected yield to extra risk that Carmen will insist upon is also the slope of the efficient set. In Figure 9–4 this is

$$(E_m - E_f)/S_m,$$

where E_f is the known risk-free yield, and E_m and S_m are the expected yield and the standard deviation of Carmen's optimal collection of risky assets. The ratio $(E_m - E_f)/S_m$ is often called the price of extra risk.

   If all lenders like Carmen have the same efficient set, as was discussed above, they will have the same optimal collection of risky assets (M), and the collection's expected yield and risk will be that of the market portfolio. When all lenders have the same values of E_m, E_f, and S_m, and when the values of E_m and S_m are easily observable from past behaviour of the market portfolio, the price of risk is the same for all lenders, and is also easily observable. There will be one market-wide price of extra risk even though different lenders choose quite different proportions of risk-free and risky assets. The actual market price of risk in the real world that is implied by the Tobin–Markowitz theory can be estimated roughly from the gap between the yield on the market portfolio of stocks and the yield on government bonds. Over long periods in the United States, the gap $E_m - E_f$ has been around 6 percent. This has been the price lenders have exacted for bearing the amount of portfolio risk S_m in Figure 9–4.

SECTION 5

◼ The capital asset pricing model

We have seen that risk can be measured as the variance or standard deviation of average portfolio yield. Only the systematic risk of individual assets adds to portfolio risk; non-systematic risk does not matter much to lenders who can diversify. Lenders will insist on compensation for extra portfolio risk at the rate given by the slope of the efficient set, $(E_m - E_f)/S_m$. What remains to be seen is how the systematic risk of individual assets adds to portfolio risk. The **capital asset pricing model** (CAPM, for short) is the model most often used by finance theorists to provide this analysis. The CAPM builds on the simplifying division of risk into purely systematic and purely unsystematic components, the division introduced in section 3 above.

In the CAPM, the systematic component of each asset's yield moves together with the average yield on the market portfolio, and the unsystematic component is independent. Both are reflected in the **characteristic equations** that explain each asset's yield:

$$r_{it} = \alpha_i + \beta_i r_{mt} + u_{it}$$

for all assets $i = 1, \ldots, n$ and all periods $t = 1, \ldots, T$, where r_{it} is the yield on the ith the asset in the tth period, r_{mt} is the market portfolio yield in the same tth period, u_{it} is the unsystematic portion of the asset's yield in the tth period, and α_i and β_i are coefficients that are constant for all periods. The unsystematic component of r_{it} is u_{it}, and the systematic component is $\alpha_i + \beta_i r_{mt}$. For example, the characteristic equation for Faithful Trust stock for 1990 might be

$$r_{FT,90} = 0.5 + 1.3 r_{m,90} - 1.5,$$

so that if the market portfolio yield was 10 percent in 1990, Faithful Trust's yield must have been $0.5 + 1.3(10) - 1.5 = 12$ percent. The coefficients α_i and β_i can be found statistically by plotting a scatter diagram of pairs of r_i and r_m that have occurred in the recent past, and by then drawing a regression line through the centre of the scatter. Figure 9–5 is an example of such a diagram. The coefficient β_i is the slope of the line. Known as the asset's **beta**, it measures the asset's volatility relative to the market portfolio. A beta greater than 1.0 implies an asset yield that is more volatile than the market yield; an increase of 1 percentage point (100 basis points) in r_m is accompanied by an increase of more than 100 basis points in r_i. A beta less than 1.0 implies an asset yield that is less volatile than the market yield.

The variance of the asset yield r_i is the sum of the variances of the systematic and unsystematic components. Since the systematic component of r_i is tied directly to the market yield, the variance of the systematic component is a multiple of the variance of the market portfolio. That multiple is the square of the asset's beta coefficient. Algebraically,

$$V_i = V_{si} + V_{ui}$$
$$= \beta_i^2 V_m + V_{ui},$$

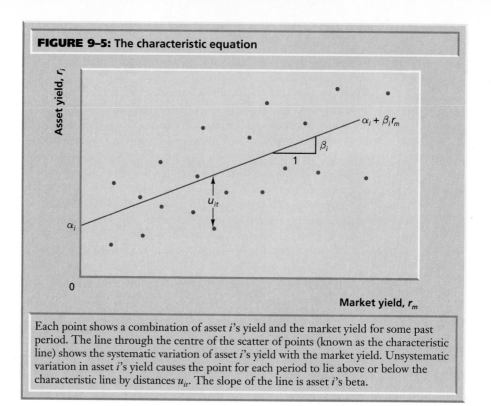

FIGURE 9–5: The characteristic equation

Each point shows a combination of asset i's yield and the market yield for some past period. The line through the centre of the scatter of points (known as the characteristic line) shows the systematic variation of asset i's yield with the market yield. Unsystematic variation in asset i's yield causes the point for each period to lie above or below the characteristic line by distances u_{it}. The slope of the line is asset i's beta.

where V_i is the variance of the yield on asset i, V_{si} is the variance of the systematic component, V_{ui} is the variance of the unsystematic component, V_m is the variance of the market portfolio's yield, and β_i is the asset's beta from its characteristic equation.

When assets are combined into portfolios, the expected portfolio yield (E_p) is

$$E_p = \sum X_i E_i,$$

where X_i is the portfolio share of asset i. Adding more of asset i to the portfolio to replace asset j (raising asset i's portfolio share X_i and lowering asset j's portfolio share X_j to make room) adds to the expected portfolio yield at the rate $E_i - E_j$ per unit of extra X. If asset j is the risk-free asset, then adding more of asset i raises expected portfolio yield at the rate $E_i - E_f$. For instance, a portfolio share increase of 0.01 (1 percent) in a stock yielding 15 percent, financed by a decrease of 0.01 in the share of a risk-free savings deposit yielding 8 percent, would raise the portfolio yield at a rate of $(15 - 8) = 7$ percent per unit change in X_i, and $7(0.01) = 0.07$ percent in total.

When assets are combined into diversified portfolios, the unsystematic part of each asset's risk is diversified away and can henceforth be ignored. The systematic parts are not diversified away at all, so portfolio risk is a weighted average of the systematic risks of individual assets in the portfolio, with weights equal to portfolio shares X_i. For convenience we use the standard deviation as the measure of risk, so the equation for portfolio risk (S_p) is

$$S_p = \sum X_i S_{si},$$

where $S_{si} = \sqrt{V_{si}}$ is the standard deviation of the systematic risk of asset i. Since $V_{si} = \beta_i^2 V_m$ and $S_m = \sqrt{V_m}$, where S_m is the standard deviation of the market portfolio,

$$S_{si} = \beta_i S_m$$

and the equation for portfolio risk becomes

$$S_p = \sum X_i \beta_i S_m.$$

It follows from this equation that as more of asset i is added to replace asset j (raising X_i and lowering X_j), portfolio risk S_p changes at the rate $(\beta_i - \beta_j) S_m$ per unit of extra X_i. If asset i has greater systematic risk than asset j, and therefore a greater beta, then the portfolio risk will rise as asset i replaces asset j. In general, assets will raise portfolio risk to the extent that they have greater systematic risk than that of the asset they replace. If the asset replaced is the risk-free asset, whose beta coefficient is zero, portfolio risk will rise at the rate $\beta_i S_m$.

To see how this would work in practice, consider a risk-free savings deposit with beta coefficient of zero, a share (s) with beta coefficient $\beta_s = 1$, and a stock option (o) with beta coefficient $\beta_o = 5$. Let the market portfolio have a risk S_m of 6 percent. Shifting 1 percent of the portfolio from savings deposit to shares adds to portfolio risk by $(1 - 0) * 6 * 0.01 = 0.06$ percent. Shifting 10 percent of the portfolio from shares to options adds to portfolio risk by $(5 - 1) * 6 * 0.1 = 2.4$ percent.

The conclusions reached in the previous paragraphs can be put together to establish the risk premium that any one asset must provide if it is to be attractive to lenders. Adding an extra asset i to the portfolio to replace the risk-free asset adds to expected yield at the rate $(E_i - E_f)$ and to portfolio risk at the rate $\beta_i S_m$. The price of one unit of extra portfolio risk is $(E_m - E_f)/S_m$ percentage points of extra expected yield, the slope of the efficient set. The price of adding $\beta_i S_m$ units of extra portfolio risk is therefore $\beta_i S_m (E_m - E_f)/S_m = \beta_i (E_m - E_f)$ of extra yield. For asset i to be accepted by lenders, the minimum that it must add to portfolio yield is the market price of its extra risk. That is,

$$E_i - E_f = \beta_i (E_m - E_f)$$

or

$$E_i = E_f + \beta_i (E_m - E_f).$$

If the asset's expected yield premium over that of the risk-free asset is less than the necessary risk premium $\beta_i (E_m - E_f)$, lenders will not buy the asset.

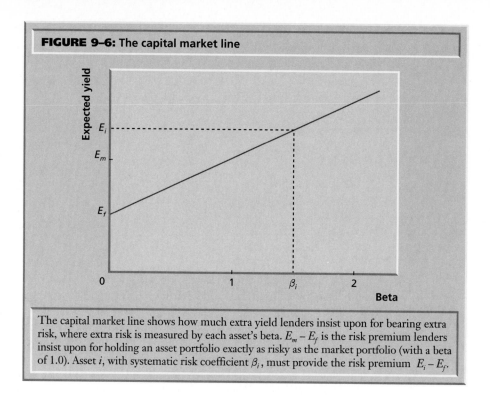

FIGURE 9–6: The capital market line

The capital market line shows how much extra yield lenders insist upon for bearing extra risk, where extra risk is measured by each asset's beta. $E_m - E_f$ is the risk premium lenders insist upon for holding an asset portfolio exactly as risky as the market portfolio (with a beta of 1.0). Asset i, with systematic risk coefficient β_i, must provide the risk premium $E_i - E_f$.

In the equation above, the terms E_f and E_m are constant for all assets. The only terms peculiar to the individual asset i are its own expected yield E_i and its beta coefficient β_i. The equation in fact relates the expected yield E_i of each asset to its beta coefficient β_i. The relationship is linear, as shown in Figure 9–6. It is known as the **capital market line**. Thanks to simplifying assumptions, the CAPM has reduced the determination of an asset's expected yield to depending only on two market-wide constants (the risk-free yield E_f and the market portfolio yield E_m) and the asset's own beta coefficient. Such a simplification is a real achievement.

In Figure 9–6, the CAPM predicts that assets with low betas can provide expected yields only slightly above the risk-free rate. Assets whose yields are twice as volatile as the market portfolio must provide yields twice as far above the risk-free rate as the market portfolio.

CAPM and borrower–lender curves

The CAPM is a powerful theory. With the help of several restrictive assumptions it has predicted relative yields on all individual assets on the basis of an easily observable characteristic, the asset's beta coefficient. Estimated betas are published for various stocks and the estimates are updated regularly. Here we will

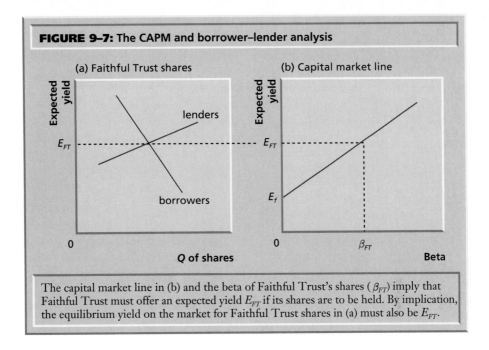

FIGURE 9–7: The CAPM and borrower–lender analysis

The capital market line in (b) and the beta of Faithful Trust's shares (β_{FT}) imply that Faithful Trust must offer an expected yield E_{FT} if its shares are to be held. By implication, the equilibrium yield on the market for Faithful Trust shares in (a) must also be E_{FT}.

put the CAPM's predictions into perspective by relating them to the borrower–lender curves used in Chapter 8.

The vertical axis of a borrower–lender diagram measures yield in the financial market being analyzed. When asset yields are uncertain, there are many possible yields on any one asset. By convention, the vertical axis will measure expected yield.[8]

The CAPM shows that lenders will not be in equilibrium (that is, they will not willingly hold the existing quantity of each asset) unless each asset provides an expected yield high enough to compensate for its beta or systematic risk. The expected yield required for Faithful Trust's stock, for instance, can be read off the capital market line directly above Faithful Trust's beta level β_{FT} in Figure 9–7(b). If E_{FT} is to be an equilibrium level, then the borrowers and lenders curves of (a) must intersect at that height.

If Faithful Trust shifts its borrowers curve to the right for some reason and wants lenders to hold more of its shares, the lenders must be persuaded to make more room in their portfolios — that is, to change their efficient risky portfolio (M in Figure 9–3). What will persuade lenders is the higher expected yield on Faithful Trust shares. Only if Faithful Trust increases its risk premium will it also increase the desired proportion of its shares in lenders' portfolios. This is the logic that causes lenders curves to slope upward for individual assets.

---

[8] In some cases such as bond and deposit markets the promised yield to maturity is used instead, probably because it is so visible compared to the expected yield.

The Evidence from Takeover Bids

The slope of lenders curves for an individual asset can be surmised from the premium that bidders must pay if they want to buy large percentages of the shares of any one company. In the United States over the last two decades, takeover bidders have paid premiums of between 35 and 50 percent over the previous market price for the companies they have taken over. The reason is that some lenders are being asked to depart significantly from what they regard as their efficient risky portfolios. To do so they require significantly higher expected yield in the form of higher resale prices for their shares.

The logic just discussed does not explain much of an upward slope for lenders curves, however. Faithful Trust is tiny compared with the stock of wealth in financial markets that must be placed in financial assets of some sort. It would seem that only a tiny amount of extra risk premium in expected yield would be needed to attract enough extra lenders to finance even a large new issue of Faithful Trust's shares. The lenders curve in Figure 9–7(a) could be expected to be very flat in a CAPM world.

In the real world, lenders curves are quite steep for individual assets. The reason lies in information costs. Faithful Trust is indeed small relative to the total lenders group, but not relative to the few lenders that know Faithful Trust well. Those few lenders cannot absorb many extra Faithful Trust shares without changing the composition of their portfolios considerably, so those few lenders would accept more Faithful Trust shares only if they were offered significantly more expected yield. New lenders can be found, but they regard Faithful Trust as more uncertain (with a higher beta, in CAPM terms) precisely because they are not as well informed. For them, β_{FT} lies farther along the capital market line in Figure 9–7 than it does for existing, better-informed holders of Faithful's shares. Their extra uncertainty means they insist on higher expected yield from Faithful Trust. So the lenders curve facing even small individual borrowers like Faithful Trust does have a significant upward slope.

Lenders curves will be shifted by changes in risk factors: either a change in betas, or a change in the risk of the market portfolio, or even a change in lenders' degree of risk aversion will cause shifts of one or more lenders curves. By contrast, changes in the unsystematic risk of any asset will have relatively little effect on lenders curves. Higher systematic risk for an asset shifts its lenders curve to the left. Higher systematic risk for all risky assets or a higher market price of risk (such as might have occurred after the October 1987 stock market crash) would cause all lenders curves for risky assets to shift to the left. Lenders curves for the risk-free asset would shift to the right by the same total amount. Yields in all risky markets would increase (prices would tumble) until once again lenders were willing to hold all the risky assets outstanding.

SECTION 6

▣ Matching and hedging

Once lenders have diversified away unsystematic risk, they are still left with the systematic risk. And there is plenty of systematic risk. Not only do many financial assets have a lot of risk by themselves, but they have most of it in common. As economies become more tied together, both internally and with each other, the proportion of risk that is systematic will probably increase even for internationally diversified portfolios. For example, the two graphs in Figure 9–8 show how stock market price indexes in four continents have varied around their trends, for six years in the 1960s and five years in the 1980s. The deviations in the 1980s are much less independent than those in the 1960s.[9]

The answer to systematic risk has been hedging and matching. Hedging and hedging markets were discussed in Chapter 6. Both hedging and matching aim directly at lowering portfolio risk by rearranging the probability distributions to remove some of the more extreme possibilities. This section examines how these strategies affect risk and lenders' behaviour.

Hedging

Hedging financial risks can be done through futures contracts, options, and insurance. In each case, the probability distribution that would exist without hedging is converted to a different, less risky distribution by adding a hedge. For instance, the yield on a future investment in treasury bills is uncertain until the T-bills are actually bought. By buying a treasury bill futures contract, the lender can guarantee in advance what the future T-bill yield will be.

Insurance can also be used as a hedge. The yields on many real investment projects can depend critically on the health of key personnel, especially in small companies. The illness or death of these people would cause turmoil and very low yields for the company. The low yields can be improved by buying life and health insurance on the lives and health of key personnel. In case of death or illness, the payoff of insurance benefits improves the probability distribution of yields facing the company.

Options provide another tool that can be used for hedging. Consider an investment in common shares that will have to be resold at the end of the lender's holding period. The range of possible future resale prices of the shares may be from $1 to $20. Lenders can narrow the range by buying a put option on the shares with a strike price of, say, $7; with the put option in their hands, they are certain they will be able to sell their shares for at least $7. Figure 9–9 shows what the put option does to a probability distribution. After a put option is bought with

---

[9] The correlation coefficient measures how closely any two variables move together. The average of the six pairwise correlation coefficients in Figure 9–8 rose from 0.10 in (a) for the 1960s, to 0.37 in (b) for the 1980s.

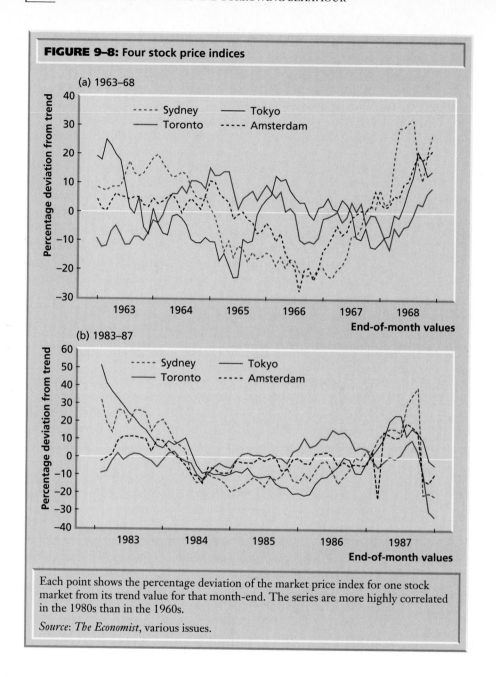

FIGURE 9–8: Four stock price indices

(a) 1963–68

(b) 1983–87

Each point shows the percentage deviation of the market price index for one stock market from its trend value for that month-end. The series are more highly correlated in the 1980s than in the 1960s.

Source: The Economist, various issues.

a strike price of $7, all of the resale prices below $7 are no longer possible. All of the probabilities previously attached to those low prices are now attached to $7. The resulting probability distribution (shown as the shaded bars) is much narrower.

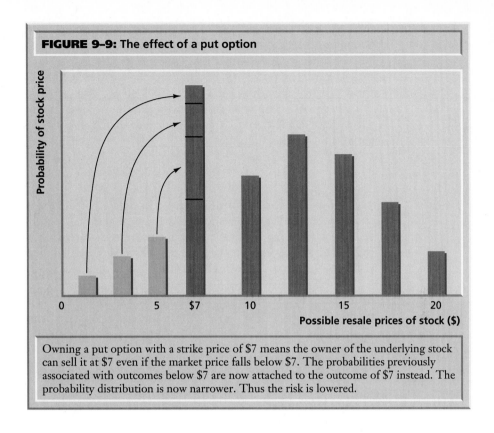

FIGURE 9–9: The effect of a put option

Probability of stock price (y-axis)

Possible resale prices of stock ($) (x-axis)

0   5 $7   10   15   20

Owning a put option with a strike price of $7 means the owner of the underlying stock can sell it at $7 even if the market price falls below $7. The probabilities previously associated with outcomes below $7 are now attached to the outcome of $7 instead. The probability distribution is now narrower. Thus the risk is lowered.

Hedging will rarely allow lenders to remove all risk. Even a futures contract that fixes a future price exactly will be removing only one source of yield fluctuations as a rule. Most investments face risks from more than one source. Not all of them can be hedged.

Leverage and matching

Many investments in financial markets have their risks magnified by debt financing. When lenders finance asset purchases partly with their own equity and partly with borrowed funds, the yield on their equity is no longer the same as the yield on the asset. The yield on equity reflects (a) the asset yield, for the part of the asset bought with equity *plus* (b) the spread between asset yield and debt cost for the part of the asset bought with debt. The equation for equity yield (r_e) is

$$r_e = r_a + (L-1)(r_a - r_d),$$

where L is the leverage ratio of assets to equity, r_a and r_d are the yields on assets and debts, respectively, and $r_a - r_d$ is the interest spread net of operating costs.[10]

For the deposit-taking intermediaries, Figure 8–8 showed that the leverage ratios average around 20. A one-unit change in the interest spread $r_a - r_d$ therefore has an effect on equity yield about nineteen times as large. The importance of leverage to risk is made even more dramatic in the formulae for variance of equity yield. If asset and debt yields fluctuate independently, the variance of yield on equity is

$$V_e = L^2 V_a + (L-1)^2 V_d,$$

where L is the leverage ratio, and V_a, V_d, and V_e are the variances of yield on assets, debts, and equity, respectively. If leverage is 20, L^2 is 400 and $(L-1)^2$ is 361; equity risk V_e in the case of independent asset and liability risks is enormous relative to V_a and V_d. Even if debt costs are fixed so that V_d becomes zero, equity risk V_e will still be a huge multiple (L^2) of the asset risk V_a.

On the other hand, if debt costs per dollar can be arranged to match fluctuations in asset yields exactly, point for point, equity risk can be cut down to merely

$$V_e = V_a.$$

Here the equity risk is no greater than that of the asset being bought, regardless of the leverage ratio reached in financing it. With exactly matching yields, the spread between asset yield and debt cost is fixed, so there is no variation in spread to contribute to equity risk. The only remaining risk comes from putting some of lenders' own funds into the asset in the form of equity, with risk V_a. The levered portion of the asset purchase does not add to risk at all if it can be perfectly matched.

Matching can be difficult in some cases, but the growth of interest rate and currency swaps is making it easier each year. Levered lenders match by tying their debt costs to the same factors that influence their asset yields. If the asset earns its income in Swiss francs, then the debt will either be issued in Swiss francs to start with, or swapped into Swiss francs after issue. If the assets are a block of five-year mortgage loans, matched debt would be issued for the same term. If the assets are a block of floating-rate loans, debts such as term deposits will either be issued with floating rates (in the Eurodollar market) or issued with fixed rates and then swapped into floating rates. Some assets have risks that cannot be fully matched by issuing any form of debt. For example, if the asset is a mine under

---

[10] The equation for r_e is derived from the equation for profits, which are the product of r_e and total equity:

$$r_e E = r_a A - r_d D,$$

where E is equity, A is assets, and D is debts, and where operating costs are either netted out from the asset yield r_a, or are included in the debt cost r_d. Dividing both sides of this equation by E, and recognizing that the ratio $D/E = L - 1$ because of the balance sheet identity that $A = D + E$, we can rearrange to obtain the equation in the text.

development, with highly uncertain prospects, even a preferred share's yield will not fluctuate exactly with the yield on the mine.

Households have a slightly different matching problem to keep their risks down. Debts incurred for the sort of assets that households buy are typically repaid out of household labour income rather than from asset income. Houses and land, the major household assets, do not generate cash income. Households are concerned that their labour income after debt costs, their discretionary income, not fluctuate too much. Households reduce risk to their discretionary income each year by matching their debt costs to their household incomes. Those with steady incomes match by issuing debts with level, blended payments over time: the standard mortgage loan arrangement. Those with more variable income want at least to be able to make larger payments if and when their income jumps. Some of them will match more closely by issuing demand loans, where the timing of all repayments above a low minimum is left to the borrower.

Matching and hedging can be combined by large-scale lenders. If the closest matching debt still does not match asset risk closely enough, either the debt or the asset yield pattern can often be modified by buying or selling (writing) one or more options.

The fact that hedging can remove some risks entirely affects the shape of lenders curves in some markets by making some risky assets potentially perfect substitutes (after hedging) with other, risk-free assets. For example, when U.S. lenders can remove the foreign exchange risk of a Canadian-dollar treasury bill by hedging with a forward exchange contract at an annual cost of, say, 0.8 percent, they will regard the combination of Canadian treasury bills plus the hedge as perfect substitutes for U.S. treasury bills. Whenever the Canadian treasury bill rate rises above the U.S. treasury bill rate by more than 0.8 percent, these lenders will swarm into the Canadian treasury bill market and the market for forward exchange contracts. The effect of such swarming of lenders is to make the lenders curve for Canadian treasury bills quite flat at the yield that just matches the U.S. treasury bill rate plus the annual per-dollar cost of the hedge.

The example of Canadian and U.S. treasury bills is one of many, involving many different pairs of assets. Figure 9–10 illustrates the general case. For a given safe yield on risk-free assets, lenders will buy few risky assets at small yield premiums: only lenders who are nearly risk-neutral are interested at that point. As the risky asset offers a larger expected yield premium, more lenders become willing to take on the extra risk. Once the risk premium exceeds the cost of hedging, all lenders who demand perfect safety are now potential lenders because they can get perfect safety at a higher yield than on the risk-free asset by buying the risky asset together with the hedge. The influx of lenders at that level of the risk premium is large enough to make the lenders curve horizontal over most of its range. When the lenders curve is horizontal over most of its range, the height of the lenders curve effectively determines the equilibrium yield, and the position of the borrowers curve determines the equilibrium quantity.

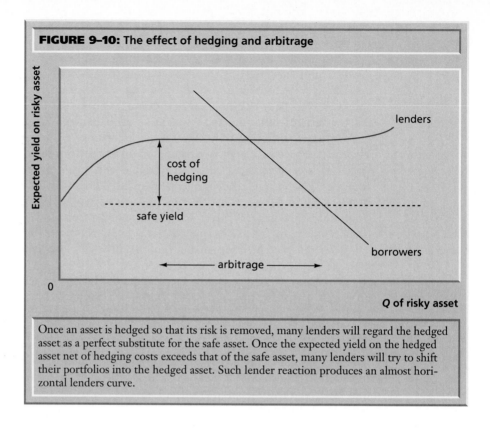

FIGURE 9–10: The effect of hedging and arbitrage

Once an asset is hedged so that its risk is removed, many lenders will regard the hedged asset as a perfect substitute for the safe asset. Once the expected yield on the hedged asset net of hedging costs exceeds that of the safe asset, many lenders will try to shift their portfolios into the hedged asset. Such lender reaction produces an almost horizontal lenders curve.

SECTION 7

Summary

Yields on assets are uncertain or risky because of credit risk, market risk, income risk, and (for real yields) inflation risk. It is assumed that lenders know enough about the future to specify a rough probability distribution of possible future yields. Using that assumption, the Tobin–Markowitz definition of risk is the variance or standard deviation, both equivalent measures of the width of such probability distributions.

It follows from the behaviour of variances that portfolio risk can be reduced simply by diversifying the portfolio over more different assets. Such diversification could eliminate unsystematic risk entirely, but will have no effect on systematic risk.

Attitudes to risk can be predicted by the Tobin–Markowitz approach from actual market data. Each lender has a feasible set of yield and risk outcomes from available portfolio combinations. The boundary of the feasible set will be a straight line if a risk-free asset is available. In equilibrium, all lenders will reach a point of tangency of their highest accessible indifference curve and the boundary of the feasible set. Lenders' attitudes to risk can then be measured as the slope of the boundary of the feasible set, which is not only constant but may well be the same for all lenders.

Relative systematic risk can be captured in the beta of each asset. The capital asset pricing model relates each asset's beta to the market-wide price of risk to come up with an appropriate risk premium to use for each asset in deriving its market-clearing price.

Systematic risks can be removed in many cases by either matching assets against debts or by adding options of some sort to the portfolio. In both cases one risk is cancelled by another similar but opposite risk.

Key Terms

portfolio yield	diversification
credit risk	systematic risk
income risk	unsystematic risk
market risk	mean-variance model
foreign exchange risk	portfolio choice diagram
real yield	feasible set
inflation risk	efficient set
Tobin–Markowitz theory	capital asset pricing model
probability distribution	(CAPM)
variance	characteristic equation
standard deviation	beta
expected yield	capital market line
risk-free asset	

Questions and Problems

1. Of the various sources of risk described in section 1, is it likely that any two types will tend to cause fluctuations in asset yields in opposite directions? Which two?

2. A $100 bill has various possible real values in the year 2010 that depend on the rate of price inflation between now and then. Identify a crude probability distribution for those real values by picking a high, low, and medium estimate, and then assigning probabilities to each. Draw your probability distribution as in Figure 9–1.

3. Calculate the mean, variance, and standard deviation of the distribution you have identified in question 2.

4. Draw the probable shape of the probability distribution of default losses on a typical loan and on a government-guaranteed loan.

5. What would a risk seeker's indifference curves look like on a portfolio choice diagram such as Figure 9–4?

6. Why is the efficient set the only relevant part of the feasible set?

7. Is the uncertainty of yield on a business insurance policy likely to be systematic, unsystematic, or something else such as " anti-systematic"? Would you classify the uncertainty of other possible hedges the same way? Explain.

8. Why is the efficient frontier likely to be the same for everyone, or is it?

9. Is demand for lottery tickets consistent with the theory of rational asset choice by risk-averse individuals?

10. Does doubling of leverage double risk? What difference does the degree of matching make to your answer?

Suggestions for Further Reading

Markowitz, Harry. *Portfolio Selection: Efficient Diversification of Investments.* New Haven, Conn.: Yale University Press for the Cowles Foundation, 1959.

Mossin, Jan. *The Theory of Financial Markets.* Englewood Cliffs, N.J.: Prentice-Hall, 1973.

Sharpe, William E. "A Simplified Model for Portfolio Analysis." *Management Science*, 1963, 277–93.

———. *Portfolio Theory and Capital Markets.* New York: McGraw-Hill, 1970.

Tobin, James. "Liquidity Preference as Behavior Towards Risk." *Review of Economic Studies*, 1958, 65–86.

Van Horne, James C. *Financial Market Rates and Flows*, 2nd ed. Englewood Cliffs, N.J.: Prentice-Hall, 1984.

Most major brokerage houses also have free brochures available that explain the workings of futures and options markets.

APPENDIX 9–1

Expected utility and attitudes toward risk

In the chapter, risk aversion has simply been assumed. In this appendix, it is derived from more basic assumptions.

Expected utility maximization

Under certainty, rational individuals are defined as those who act so as to maximize utility. Under uncertainty, rationality is usually defined as acting so as to maximize *expected* utility. Expected utility is the probability-weighted average of the possible utilities that might result from any one action. If U_i is the level of

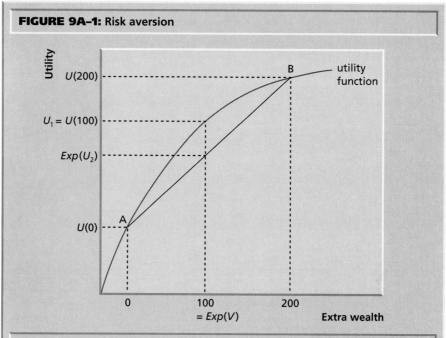

FIGURE 9A–1: Risk aversion

The utility of a 100-dollar bill, U_1, is the height of the utility function above the extra wealth level of 100. The expected utility of the gamble, $Exp(U_2)$, that offers an equal chance of $200 or zero, is the height of the midpoint of a straight line joining the two points on the utility function above $200 and zero. The expected utility is also the point on the vertical axis midway between $U(0)$ and $U(200)$. The gamble has a smaller expected utility than the 100-dollar bill because the utility function is concave from below—that is, because the marginal utility of wealth declines as wealth rises.

utility attached to a possible outcome i, $prob_i$ is its probability of occurring, and there are n possible outcomes, then the expected utility, $Exp(U)$, is

$$Exp(U) = \sum prob_i U_i.$$

Now consider a choice between a 100-dollar bill and a simple gamble that will pay off a value (V) of $200 if you win and nothing if you do not. Let the gamble have one chance in two of winning. The expected value of the gamble, $Exp(V)$, is the same as for the 100-dollar bill:

$$Exp(V) = 0.5(\$200) + 0.5(\$0) = \$100.$$

Which is the best choice? The only difference between the gamble and the 100-dollar bill is that the gamble has greater risk, so a preference for the 100-dollar bill must imply aversion to risk. Rational preference for the 100-dollar bill turns out to depend only on whether marginal utility of wealth rises or falls as wealth levels rise.

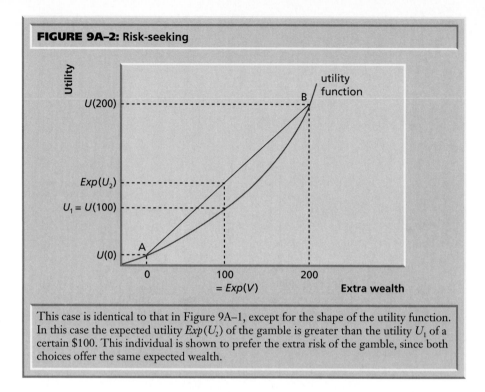

FIGURE 9A–2: Risk-seeking

This case is identical to that in Figure 9A–1, except for the shape of the utility function. In this case the expected utility $Exp(U_2)$ of the gamble is greater than the utility U_1 of a certain \$100. This individual is shown to prefer the extra risk of the gamble, since both choices offer the same expected wealth.

Figure 9A–1 shows the ingredients of the choice discussed above, together with the relevant part of the utility function of an individual whose marginal utility of wealth declines as wealth rises. The possible outcomes for each option are given on the horizontal axis as different possible amounts of extra wealth (\$0 and \$200 for the gamble, \$100 for the 100-dollar bill). The utility levels associated with each possible level of extra wealth are given on the vertical axis. The expected *utility* level of the gamble, $Exp(U_2)$, is the point midway between $U(200)$ and $U(0)$ on the vertical axis. $Exp(U_2)$ can also be found as the midpoint of a straight line between A and B on the utility function, or as the point on that straight line directly above the expected value of the gamble. For this lender, the expected utility of the gamble $Exp(U_2)$ is less than the utility U_1 of the certain \$100. This lender avoids the gamble and must therefore be risk-averse.

Risk-seeking

In Figure 9A–2 the same exercise is carried out for another lender whose marginal utility of wealth increases as wealth rises. The same two alternatives are shown. In this case the expected utility of the gamble is greater than that of the certain \$100. This individual is a risk seeker.

Many other situations can be illustrated on this diagram, but the most important conclusion is the one we have already reached: to be risk-averse, it is sufficient (a) to follow an expected utility rule in making choices under uncertainty, and (b) to have declining marginal utility of wealth or yield.

A measure of risk aversion

A lender's degree of risk aversion can be measured by the sharpness of curvature of the utility function, which is determined by how quickly the marginal utility of wealth falls as wealth rises. This can be measured by the ratio of (a) the rate of change of the marginal utility of wealth (the second derivative of the utility function, U'') to (b) the marginal utility of wealth (the first derivative of the utility function, U'). A commonly used measure of risk aversion is $-U''/U'$, with the minus sign added to convert the ratio to a positive number. The higher this ratio, the more risk-averse is the individual.

Quadratic utility functions and mean-variance theory

Expected utility theory can be shown to predict the same choices as the simpler Tobin–Markowitz or mean-variance theory if the utility function takes a particular shape over the relevant range of wealth levels. The particular shape of utility function is quadratic, as in

$$U = a + bW + cW^2.$$

If this function is substituted in the expression for expected utility, we obtain

$$Exp(U) = \sum prob_i(a + bW_i + cW_i^2)$$
$$= a + b \sum prob_i W_i + c \sum prob_i W_i^2.$$

$\sum prob_i W_i$ is expected wealth, $Exp(W)$, by definition. This can be written

$$Exp(U) = a + b\, Exp(W) + c \sum prob_i\{[W_i - Exp(W)] + Exp(W)\}^2.$$

The squared expression can be multiplied out and evaluated. One of its terms is $\sum prob_i\{[W_i - Exp(W)]Exp(W)\}$, which is zero. That leaves

$$Exp(U) = a + b\, Exp(W) + c \sum prob_i[W_i - Exp(W)]^2 + c\, Exp(W)^2.$$

In the third term above on the right-hand side, $\sum prob_i[W_i - Exp(W)]^2$ is the variance of wealth, $Var(W)$, so that

$$Exp(U) = a + b\, Exp(W) + c\, Var(W) + c\, Exp(W)^2.$$

This expression involves only the mean $Exp(W)$ and the variance $Var(W)$ of the probability distribution of future wealth levels. Nothing else matters. Q.E.D.

APPENDIX 9–2

Risk behaviour in the general case

In order to simplify the analysis of risk, the chapter restricts fluctuations in asset yields to be either totally systematic or totally unsystematic. In reality, the range of choices is much wider. The yield of an asset can move together with other asset yields and not others, and it can even move partly opposite to other yields. This appendix presents a more general approach to risk analysis that allows a wider range of relationships among asset yields.

Portfolio variance

The variance of yield on a portfolio consisting of only two assets is

$$V = X_1^2 V_1 + X_2^2 V_2 + 2 X_1 X_2 COV_{12},$$

where X_i is the portfolio share of the ith asset, V refers to variance, and COV_{12} is the covariance of yields on assets 1 and 2. Covariance is a weighted average product of deviations of yields of each asset from their respective means, with probabilities serving as weights. Where the joint probability distribution of yields on the two assets is known, the covariance is found as

$$COV_{12} = \sum prob_k(r_{ik} - E_i)(r_{jk} - E_j).$$

The covariance will be positive if the two assets' yields, r, tend to be above or below their means, E, together, negative if they tend to be on opposite sides of their means, and zero if they vary independently. A closely related concept that is often used in discussion instead of the covariance is the correlation coefficient. The correlation coefficient ρ_{12} is a standardized version of the covariance, in which deviations of each asset yield from its mean are divided by the asset's own standard deviation. The covariance is related to ρ as follows:

$$COV_{12} = \rho_{12} \sqrt{V_1} \sqrt{V_2}$$

The correlation coefficient must have the same sign as the covariance, but the correlation coefficient must also vary only between -1 and $+1$. ρ_{12} will be $+1$ if two asset yields move together linearly, -1 if they move opposite to each other linearly, and zero if the two yields vary independently.

It may help to put this approach to portfolio variance into context if you note that in the special case where covariance and correlation coefficient are zero, the formula for portfolio variance is identical to that in the chapter for the case of totally unsystematic risk. It will also help to make our analysis of the simple two-asset portfolio more general if you think of asset 1 always as the particular asset that we are trying to analyze, and of asset 2 as all other assets pooled together, for simplicity, into a single asset much like a mutual fund share.

Diversification and marginal risk

The formula for portfolio variance can be analyzed to determine just how portfolio risk is affected by adding more of asset 1. Since X_1 and X_2 must add up to 1, we can substitute $1 - X_1$ for X_2 to obtain

$$V = X_1^2 V_1 + (1 - X_1)^2 V_2 + 2X_1(1 - X_1)COV_{12}.$$

The effect on portfolio variance of adding a little bit of asset 1 is asset 1's marginal risk, which can be found as the partial derivative of V with respect to X_1:

$$dV/dX_1 = 2(COV_{12} - V_2) + 2X_1(V_1 + V_2 - 2COV_{12}).$$

This is a difficult expression to contemplate. However, consider the case where asset 1 is a new asset, so that the portfolio share X_1 is zero to start with. The second term on the right-hand side disappears, leaving us with the much simpler expression

$$dV/dX_1 = 2(COV_{12} - V_2).$$

Note that for this case, marginal risk does not involve V_1 directly. The only part of the risk of asset 1 that matters in the equation for marginal risk is the part that appears in COV_{12}. That is, the risk that matters for an asset is not its variance, but its covariance with other assets. This is the counterpart to saying in the CAPM approach that only the systematic risk of an asset matters to portfolio risk.

Also, note that if asset 1's yield varies independently, so that COV_{12} is zero, then marginal risk is negative: that is, adding asset 1 reduces portfolio risk. This is the general result of diversification. The benefit of diversification depends on the difference between COV_{12} and V_2, which can be interpreted as meaning the extent of systematic risk in the new asset. In the case where all assets have identical variances and all move together, COV_{12} will equal V_2 and there will be no gain at all from diversification.

Finally, note a possibility akin to an asset having a negative beta. An asset has negative covariance if its yield tends to move opposite to other financial market yields. Such is the case for yields on insurance policies and the other hedges discussed in section 6 of this chapter. An asset with negative covariance will have sharply negative marginal risk to start with; $COV_{12} - V_2$ will be negative because of both terms.

As an example involving negative covariance, let asset 1 be an insurance policy against fire and theft, to be added to an asset 2 made up of normal business assets. Insurance policies are as risky as lottery tickets: a policy may pay off handsomely if there is a claim, but the chances are slim. If there is no claim, the policy will be a total loss, yielding -100 percent on the premium paid. However, the policy is likely to pay off precisely when the other assets have abysmal yields (the other assets will yield -100 percent if they are stolen, possibly only -50 percent if they are half destroyed by fire). The insurance policy has a large negative covariance with other yields. The result of adding the insurance policy to the portfolio is that two extreme but unlikely downward fluctuations in yields on asset 2 are offset. The remaining probability distribution is narrower; the level of risk is significantly reduced.

PART THREE

Financial Intermediation

Chapter ten

Financial Intermediation and Deposit Expansion

So far in this book financial intermediaries have been treated as borrowers and lenders much like all other borrowers and lenders in the economy. The only distinction that has been made between financial intermediaries and business firms such as automakers or fast-food chains is that financial intermediaries buy mainly financial assets, whereas business firms buy mainly real assets. This chapter looks more closely at the functions of financial intermediaries.

The chapter starts with a fairly simple model of a financial intermediary. In section 1 we ask why financial intermediaries exist; why do individuals, for instance, not lend directly to commercial borrowers, rather than lending to them indirectly through financial intermediaries? Section 2 asks how financial intermediaries are able to borrow for less than they lend—why do they have positive spreads? Section 3 asks what difference it makes that banks issue not just any financial assets, but the very assets we use as money. Finally, in section 4, we discuss the effects of government regulation on financial intermediaries.

This chapter is designed to bring out essential ideas that apply to many different types of intermediary. The chapter therefore does not provide much institutional detail about individual types of intermediation. A more descriptive analysis of specific intermediary groups in Canada is provided in Chapters 11–13.

You should learn in this chapter:

1. the effect of transactions costs and information costs on the type of financial intermediation;
2. the nature of equilibrium for financial intermediaries;
3. sources of positive spread for intermediaries;
4. why and how the bank deposit expansion process works;

5. how the bank deposit expansion process will be affected by the removal of cash reserve requirements;

6. how various regulatory requirements affect intermediaries.

SECTION 1

▦ Sources and types of intermediation

It is a fact, bemoaned by some, that we earn less per dollar on our savings deposits than banks earn when they re-lend those same dollars in unsecured commercial and consumer loans. Why do we not choose to lend out those funds ourselves in commercial and consumer loans, and so earn the banks' higher asset yields ourselves? The answer lies in transactions and information costs.[1]

Transactions costs

Most **transactions costs** are incurred in changing the registered ownership of assets. Financial transactions costs are often fixed, or at least they vary less than proportionally with the dollar amount being transacted. Brokerage expenses of trading financial assets, for example, are lower per dollar for large transactions than for small. Mutual funds and pension funds have sprung up to exploit just this technical advantage of large-scale activity; they issue shares and trust units whose net yields, after brokerage and management costs, are slightly lower than yields earned on the funds' assets themselves but better than individuals could achieve by diversifying on their own. Transactions cost advantages do not explain the main features of other types of **intermediation** such as banking and insurance, however.

Information costs

Information is the lifeblood of the financial system, but it is expensive. Different kinds of **information costs** give rise to different kinds of intermediation. Here we consider three kinds of information.

The first kind of information is about the future prospects of widely traded assets such as stocks and bonds. Suppose that Lesage has collected such information and has processed it with some techniques to produce investment advice.[2] Many lenders value such information and will pay for it. Lesage can

---

[1] This section draws on John Chant, *Regulation of Financial Institutions: A Functional Analysis* (Ottawa: Bank of Canada Technical Report 45, January 1987), chapter 1.

[2] Lesage is likely to use as his technique either fundamental analysis or technical analysis. *Fundamental analysis* predicts future financial asset yields from information about issuers' circumstances, such as input costs and market shares. *Technical analysis* predicts yields only on the basis of the pattern of prices to date.

earn income from his information (a) by selling the information and investment advice directly, either personally as an investment adviser or more impersonally by issuing a market letter to subscribers, or (b) by setting up an asset-trading intermediary (a brokerage firm) to earn brokerage commissions on trades suggested by his information, or (c) by offering to use his information to make asset-selection decisions on behalf of investors for a portfolio management fee. Thus Lesage could set up as an investment counsellor, as the author of a market letter, as a brokerage firm, or as an asset portfolio manager for mutual or pension funds.

The second kind of information is about the future prospects of assets that are not widely traded, such as business or personal loans, venture capital stock, junk bonds, or financial leases. Suppose Lesage has such information. Lesage may find it difficult to sell this information because buyers cannot easily check its quality. In order to be more confident that Lesage has high-quality information, buyers may insist that he have some financial stake in the quality of his advice — that he suffer financially in the event his advice turns out to be wrong. For instance, Lesage can use his information to manage his own as well as customers' funds, as is frequently done by founders of venture capital companies. Or Lesage can reassure buyers about the quality of his information by agreeing to base his management fee on the performance of the assets being recommended, or by guaranteeing returns to clients in some way. One way of guaranteeing returns to clients is to issue fixed-income claims to them, such as term deposits, rather than claims such as shares, whose earnings can easily fall. Another way for Lesage to provide guarantees to wary lenders is to set up a limited partnership arrangement in which he, as general partner, offers initial guarantees on cash flow to all the other limited partners.

A third kind of information is about the *current status* of non-traded assets such as loans. Where it is difficult to detect the current situation (for example, whether a bank has many or just a few bad loans on its books), there are substantial ongoing monitoring costs over and above the initial screening costs of selecting an asset portfolio. In order to avoid large monitoring costs for assets they buy, Lesage's customers will prefer to buy simple kinds of claims such as fixed-yield deposits; lenders can easily keep track of the value of funds left in deposits, whereas they could not keep track as easily if instead they held a share of a portfolio of personal loans. If Lesage's firm is set up so that Lesage collects any residual income from high-quality monitoring and suffers large losses from low-quality monitoring, depositors are also more likely to have faith in the quality of his monitoring and therefore in his deposit guarantees. Most deposit-taking intermediaries are examples of intermediation driven by the difficulty of monitoring the current status of non-traded loans.

Model of a deposit-taking intermediary

A model of financial intermediation is easy to build and analyze with the assumptions that we have made about the role of information. For example, take a deposit-taking intermediary called Faithful Trust. It is a firm owned by shareholders. Faithful's managers are under instructions from the board of directors to choose the firm's asset mix, debt mix, and level of total assets and debts so as to maximize the market value of shareholders' equity. The market value of shareholders' equity is the present discounted value of Faithful's current and expected future profits. Assume for simplicity that future profits are expected to be the same as current profits. The equity value (EQ) is then

$$EQ = Profit/r,$$

where r is the discount rate (in fractional form). Faithful's discount rate can be taken as fixed by Faithful's managers.[3] They therefore maximize equity by maximizing short-run profit. Profit is the difference between Faithful's revenue from assets and its debt costs. Let $r_a A$ be revenue from assets net of monitoring costs, where r_a is the average yield per dollar of assets, and A is average assets for the year. Let $r_d D$ be debt costs including all operating costs of servicing deposits, where r_d is average debt cost per dollar and D is average debts for the year. That is,

$$Profit = r_a A - r_d D.$$

Faithful's potential profit is constrained by the costs of information about its loan customers' affairs, and by the risk aversion of its depositors. Loan information costs are lowest for loans to a core of regular customers whose management Faithful has come to know and trust. As Faithful expands its lending beyond this core of customers, either its screening and monitoring costs will start to rise, or its default rate will rise, or both. Asset yields net of monitoring costs and default losses will therefore tend to fall as Faithful's volume of assets increases.

On the debt side of its balance sheet, Faithful's depositors realize that as Faithful increases its leverage by issuing more deposits, its equity provides a smaller and smaller cushion, per dollar of deposits, against the risk of bankruptcy. Some depositors also realize that as Faithful expands its lending, it will be dealing with a growing proportion of doubtful loan prospects. Faithful's lenders will react to the intermediary's higher leverage by insisting on a higher expected yield as the price of continuing to hold Faithful's deposits.[4] Only lenders locked into fixed-yield and fixed-term deposits will continue to lend to Faithful at the previous, lower yields, until their fixed term is up, at which point even these lenders will insist on higher expected yields. Faithful's marginal debt cost schedule therefore slopes upward with extra debt issues.

---

[3] The rate r at which future profits are discounted includes the risk premium appropriate for Faithful's beta. Once Faithful's beta has been determined by the managers' choices of leverage and an asset-and-debt mix, Faithful's risk premium can be read off the capital market line (see Figure 9–6 or 9–7(b)).

[4] Deposits up to $60 000 are insured against default by the Canada Deposit Insurance Corporation (CDIC). The effect is that debt costs are not sensitive to leverage for individual deposits under this amount. See Chapter 15, section 2, for further discussion of the effect of the CDIC on risk-taking by intermediaries.

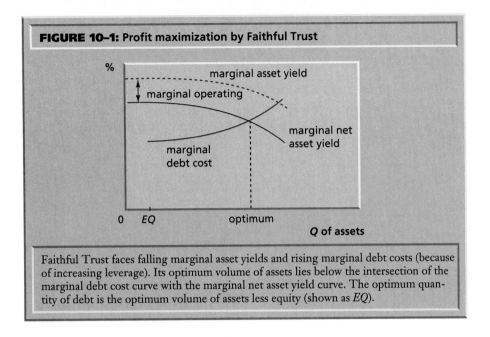

FIGURE 10-1: Profit maximization by Faithful Trust

Faithful Trust faces falling marginal asset yields and rising marginal debt costs (because of increasing leverage). Its optimum volume of assets lies below the intersection of the marginal debt cost curve with the marginal net asset yield curve. The optimum quantity of debt is the optimum volume of assets less equity (shown as *EQ*).

Faithful's falling marginal asset yield schedule and rising marginal debt cost schedule are shown in Figure 10–1. The marginal debt cost schedule starts only above the point *EQ*, since assets totalling less than that are financed entirely out of equity (with no debt at all). Marginal operating costs are subtracted from marginal asset yields to leave marginal net asset yields. The profit-maximizing level of total assets, measured along the horizontal axis, is below the intersection of marginal net asset yield and marginal debt cost. The profit-maximizing level of debts to finance that level of assets is the value of total assets less the part financed by Faithful's equity (shown as the distance from the origin to *EQ*).[5] The extra annual profit to be made by levered asset purchases is the area between the marginal debt cost schedule and the marginal net asset yield schedule.

Faithful's managers not only maximize expected profits per year, but they also take several steps to keep risk down. The firm's asset portfolio will be diversified widely to eliminate almost all unsystematic risk. Many intermediaries operate on a sufficiently large scale that it is easy to spread the portfolio over hundreds of different loans even when individual loans are in wholesale amounts. Faithful's managers will reduce or offset systematic risk where they can, either by

---

[5] Whenever Faithful raises its leverage ratio significantly, the volatility of its profit stream will increase, as described in Chapter 9, section 6. To the extent that the extra volatility of its equity yield is systematic, Faithful's lenders will insist on a higher expected yield on Faithful's shares and therefore will discount its expected future profits more heavily. This by itself will reduce the market value of Faithful's equity. For small changes in leverage this effect is not likely to be noticeable.

Scoundrels and Non-price Credit Rationing

Being a loan officer is not all gravy. Loan officers are well aware that a small share of loan applicants are scoundrels who have no intention of repaying either in full or on time. Another small share are honest but incompetent. A great deal of time and effort goes into trying to weed out those applicants. Nevertheless, some do get through. And the more poor applicants there are, the more will get through.

Since one complete default cancels out the profit on more than 100 good loans, prudent intermediaries go to great lengths to avoid anything that would raise the share of scoundrels and incompetents among their loan applicants. One solution that can sometimes increase net asset yields is **non-price credit rationing**. This term describes the situation when an intermediary rations its scarce credit among loan applicants by some other means than charging the market-clearing interest rate on loans. Higher loan rates, after all, only discourage those who seriously intend to repay interest and principal; scoundrels and incurable optimists are not deterred at all. Higher loan rates therefore imply a lower average quality of loan applications, which in turn implies higher loan losses and higher applicant screening costs.

FIGURE 10–2: Credit rationing

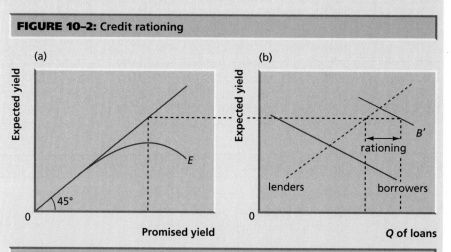

Source: Joseph Stiglitz and Andrew Weiss, "Credit Rationing in Markets with Asymmetric Information," *American Economic Review*, June 1981, 393–410. See also Dwight Jaffee and Thomas Russell, "Information, Uncertainty and Credit Rationing," *Quarterly Journal of Economics*, November 1976, 651–666.

Schedule *E* in Figure 10–2(a) illustrates the effect of higher promised loan rates on expected loan yield. The horizontal axis measures the *promised* loan yield, the vertical axis the *expected* loan yield to intermediaries. As the expected loan yield falls below the promised yield, schedule E falls below the 45° line. This happens because of higher expected loan losses and the greater cost of screening applicants. E eventually reaches a maximum at some finite promised loan rate as loan losses and screening costs grow. If a surge in loan demands in part (b) were to push the market-clearing promised loan rate above the rate that maximizes E, lenders would stop short of the market-clearing level and ration credit by some means other than loan rates.

choosing matching terms of deposits or by hedging with interest rate swaps and futures contracts, as discussed in Chapter 9, section 6. The choices of assets and debts that Faithful makes to keep its risks down will influence the marginal asset yield and marginal debt cost schedules in Figure 10–1, so Faithful's managers must consider the impacts of their choices on both risk and expected profit at the same time.

Faithful's lending and borrowing behaviour depends on all the ingredients of the optimal decisions above. The effects of factors affecting marginal operating costs, marginal asset yields, and marginal debt costs can all be seen by allowing exogenous factors to cause shifts in each of those three parts of Figure 10–1. Section 4 of this chapter provides some examples of such an analysis in looking at the effects of different types of regulation of financial intermediaries.

Long-run equilibrium

In the long run, the efforts of Faithful and its rivals will bring about a competitive equilibrium in which Faithful's margin of expected profit just compensates its shareholders for yields they might have gained by holding other assets of similar systematic risk. More profit than that will attract more competitors. Less profit than that will cause some existing competitors to move into other markets. The mergers, acquisitions, new product launchings, and occasional bankruptcies and closures announced in the financial press are the forces that push toward this long-run equilibrium state.

SECTION 2

▣ Sources of positive spread

In the above analysis, Faithful Trust's shareholders earn a profit only if Faithful can issue its deposits at much lower yields than those it receives on its loans; that is, if it has a **positive spread**. But why do intermediaries have positive spreads? Why is it that banks, for instance, can issue chequing deposits that pay no interest, and yet can lend out at the prime rate? At first sight, such transactions seem

Reprinted with permission: Tribune Company Syndicate, Inc.

both immensely profitable for banks, and foolish for their depositors. Why do individuals not lend their saving directly to business borrowers at the prime loan rate, instead of lending it indirectly through a financial intermediary for what is often less than half the yield? There are several answers to these questions, although not all of them may be relevant for any one financial intermediary.

In the following we discuss the factors that help intermediaries to generate positive spreads: transmutation of assets, pooling of risks, provision of services, and economies of scale and of scope.

Transmutation of assets

One source of positive spreads is that most financial intermediation involves more than simply passing funds from primary lenders to primary borrowers. The process of intermediation usually changes or "transmutes" the assets involved. Intermediaries issue debts that are different from the assets they buy in several ways. Each difference or **transmutation of assets** is calculated to appeal to a particular group of investors. Each time an intermediary "improves" the debts it issues, it can expect lenders to buy its debts at a lower yield. If its improvements are important to lenders, yet inexpensive for the intermediary, it will be left with a positive spread large enough to leave a big profit margin, at least in the short run.

There are many ways in which intermediaries transmute assets. These are listed below, with examples from the Canadian financial system.

1. Intermediaries can issue debts that are more marketable than the assets they buy. Finance companies, for instance, issue large-denomination, standardized sales finance paper that is easily marketable in the wholesale money market; finance companies buy individual consumer installment loans secured by new or used cars, boats, and appliances of all kinds. Until recently, individual consumer installment loans were not marketable at all.[6] As another example,

---

[6] Packages of consumer installment loans are now being marketed in the form of *asset-backed securities*. These are discussed in Chapters 6 and 12.

banks issue highly marketable bearer term deposit notes, and buy much less marketable unsecured demand loan notes.

2. Intermediaries can issue debts with much less uncertainty than that of the assets they buy. For instance, banks and near-banks issue deposits with yields fixed for terms of up to five years, and with a government guarantee against default loss. They buy unsecured loan notes and mortgage loans whose yields are not as fixed, and which will pay off as promised only if things go well for the borrower.

3. Intermediaries can issue debts that are redeemable whenever lenders want, while they buy assets that are redeemable whenever borrowers want. Bank deposits (even fixed-term deposits) can all be redeemed on demand by depositors, despite the legal fiction that banks can require notice for all but chequing accounts. Bank loans, however, cannot be redeemed by the bank before maturity unless the loan customers agree, despite the legal fiction that demand loans can be called at the discretion of the bank.[7]

4. Intermediaries can issue debts whose repayment patterns suit lenders, while buying assets whose repayment patterns suit borrowers. Life insurers and finance companies both provide examples. Life insurers issue life annuities that pay a fixed amount for the life of the lender—a very convenient arrangement for the retired. Life insurers buy mortgages whose level blended payments of principal and interest are designed to suit individual borrowers with level incomes. Life insurers also buy corporate preferred shares whose dividend payments drop in hard times to suit the issuing company. Finance companies issue wholesale financial paper sold on a discount basis that is convenient to money-market investors. Finance companies buy consumer loans whose patterns of repayment by equal installments suit individual consumer borrowers.

5. Intermediaries can issue debts whose terms are markedly different from those of the assets they buy. The most dramatic example is that of banks that issue demand deposits (repayable at any moment) and buy mortgages or government bonds whose repayments are spread over 20 years.

6. Intermediaries can issue debts denominated in one currency and buy assets denominated in another. For example, banks can issue Canadian dollar deposits and use the proceeds to finance U.S. dollar loans. With the growth of international financial markets, any pair of currencies could be used for this intermediation.

7. Intermediaries can issue small-denomination (retail) debts and buy large-denomination (wholesale) assets, or vice versa. Banks issue retail deposits to individuals, and make million-dollar loans to business customers. Finance companies, on the other hand, issue wholesale financial paper in million-

---

[7] Any bank that actually called a demand loan would automatically forfeit any chance of future business with that loan customer. Demand loans are therefore called only when loan customers are hours away from bankruptcy.

dollar lumps in money markets in order to buy retail consumer installment loans.

Risk pooling

Almost all of the transmutations listed above could get an intermediary into big trouble. For instance, what if a bank loan turns sour, while the bank is committed to continue paying interest on the deposits that financed that loan? What if a life insurer finds its annuitant living on to collect annuity payments longer than expected, while the company whose preferred shares it has bought fails to earn enough profit to pay dividends?

Some intermediaries do get into big trouble, but not many. What usually saves the others is **risk pooling**: they pool together many risks by operating on a large scale, and so they can diversify away almost all of the unsystematic component. What is risky about an individual loan (the risk that the borrower will be unable or unwilling to repay on time) is often unsystematic; when many loans are pooled in a large loan portfolio, the averaging of results of many loans cancels out almost all of the unsystematic risk.

Risk pooling works because intermediaries' debts are almost all *generalized claims* on the entire asset portfolio rather than specialized claims on particular assets. For instance, if I hold 0.1 percent of the total shares of a bank, I can claim 0.1 percent of the profit (or loss) from *all* of the bank's intermediation — not just from a specific 0.1 percent of it such as from a particular loan. Similarly, bank depositors claim their interest payments from the bank's total revenue from all sources, not just from particular assets of the same currency or maturity date.

Risk pooling eliminates not only unsystematic default risk in the loan portfolio, but also the unsystematic **liquidity risk** that deposits might be redeemed earlier than expected. If too many deposits are redeemed earlier than expected, an intermediary will find itself illiquid and will be forced to sell off assets or to borrow large amounts on very short notice; either solution is likely to be expensive for the intermediary. For any one withdrawable deposit, a bank must be highly uncertain about when that deposit will be withdrawn, and therefore about when liquid reserves will be needed for it. For all of a bank's depositors collectively a bank is much less uncertain. Much of the variability of individual depositors' behaviour cancels out, leaving total deposit redemptions relatively stable and predictable.[8] As another example, life insurers are very uncertain about how long any one individual annuitant will live to collect his or her annuity payments. When life insurers are diversified over a large pool of annuitants, the insurers are much less uncertain about the possible total outflows of annuity payments they will have to finance.

Risk pooling will not eliminate all the dangers for financial intermediaries, however. Systematic risks remain. Some of these are removed by hedging. For

---

[8] The exception that keeps bankers awake some nights is the case of a bank run, where all depositors want to redeem early. Such uncertainty is systematic. Systematic risk cannot be removed by diversification.

example, a bank may have borrowed in Swiss francs to lend in U.S. dollars; it will generally hedge its foreign exchange risk by swapping its Swiss franc interest obligations for U.S. dollar interest obligations. For example, an intermediary may have loaned out at floating rates and borrowed at fixed rates; it will generally swap its fixed-rate obligation for a floating-rate obligation. An intermediary holding long-term assets financed with short-term debts may be able to protect itself against unexpected capital loss on its long-term assets if it can sell futures contracts on the long-term assets.

What systematic risk is not removed by hedging is left for the shareholders to bear. If shareholders' equity is not large enough to absorb it all, bankruptcy will occur and the remainder will be borne by creditors.

Provision of services

Financial intermediaries generate a large part of their positive spread by providing services of various sorts to customers. Some of these **customer services** are independent of intermediaries' lending and borrowing; for example, they may provide safety deposit boxes inside bank vaults, or may arrange for magnetic tape transfers to handle a customer firm's payroll transactions. Such services are usually charged for separately and have little to do with intermediation *per se* other than that they reduce the interest spread required on intermediation to cover overhead costs. Many customer services are provided free as part of lending to or borrowing from the intermediary. For example, intermediaries often provide a range of advisory services to loan customers to help them budget, plan, or forecast. Retail deposit-taking intermediaries have automated teller networks and staffed branch networks to look after redemptions and deposits, and provide tax or accounting records for customers. All intermediaries issuing transferable deposits in Canada provide cheque-clearing services through the Canadian Payments Association. All of these free services appeal to either lenders or borrowers, or both. Because of the appeal of the free services, borrowers and lenders agree to higher loan rates and lower deposit rates than they otherwise would, so the intermediary makes a wider interest spread.

The source of profits: economies of scale and scope

All of the special features that intermediaries arrange to make their debts more attractive than their assets will generate a profit only if those features can be added at lower cost than banks' customers would incur in doing the same thing themselves. Otherwise the intermediary will at best only cover its costs. For instance, if an individual could eliminate the default risk of a small business loan by buying a loan guarantee, the combination of small business loan plus loan guarantee would be a very close substitute for an illiquid term deposit of the same term to maturity at a trust company. The individual would therefore not accept any yield on an illiquid term deposit that was lower than the small business loan yield less the cost per dollar of the loan guarantee. As another example, if a large firm can tap the savings of many retail investors at a cost of X by issuing and distributing its own securities to individuals in retail-size chunks, then X is the maximum it will pay some intermediary for the service of pooling retail savings into large blocks.

Size provides intermediaries with much of their advantage and profit. It is size that allows intermediaries to diversify away unsystematic risk, even when individual loans may be in units as large as hundreds of millions of dollars. Bigger institutions have an advantage over smaller institutions in risk pooling of all sorts. The major benefits of risk pooling are available with quite low levels of diversification (see Figure 9–2), but often an intermediary must be quite large in order to have access to many different (that is, unsystematically varying) kinds of loan customer.

Size provides intermediaries with an advantage in monitoring loans. Much of the information gathering that must be done to keep track of loan customers' affairs involves keeping informed about the industries in which loan customers operate. The cost of such information gathering is a fixed cost that does not vary much with loan size or even with the number of customers in an industry. That cost can be spread more thinly, over a larger volume of loans, by large intermediaries with many customers in an industry or region. Large intermediaries can therefore operate with smaller operating costs per dollar of loan assets than small intermediaries. That is, large intermediaries have **economies of scale**. If larger intermediaries choose to spend the same amount on information gathering as smaller firms, per dollar of loan assets, the larger firms will have more information per loan. This also keeps loan losses down relative to those of their smaller competitors. Either way, the larger institutions have a competitive advantage over smaller firms and individuals.

Size can give bargaining advantages as well. For instance, insurance companies large enough to buy up entire issues of new bonds in private placements are able to get better terms because such private placements are cheaper to arrange for the issuer.

It is part of the conventional wisdom that the wider the range of assets and liabilities in which a firm deals and the wider the range of services it offers, the greater is the convenience for its customers. These advantages are known as **economies of scope**. An effort to exploit economies of scope has taken shape in the "one-stop shopping centre" concept of a financial institution. The Desjardins Caisses Populaires have long had the legal powers to provide a broad range of financial services and products to customers. Their experience with such outlets in Montreal and Quebec City has been that the general public do not value the extra convenience much, if at all; the volume of business done by branch outlets set up as one-stop financial shopping centres was nowhere near the vigorous level that was expected.

SECTION 3

The special case of banks: deposit expansion models

For some purposes we can make do with a much simpler model of financial intermediation than that developed for Faithful Trust in section 1. The simpler model is the mechanical model of deposit expansion. **Deposit expansion models** can be used to predict total assets and debts for the specific group of intermediaries that issue debts used as money — that is, to predict the quantity of money that will be issued. The quantity of money is often the only aspect of financial intermediation used in macroeconomic analysis, so deposit expansion models are widely used in macroeconomics instead of the richer and more general model developed in section 1.

Deposit expansion models are based on two features of money-issuing intermediaries that differentiate them from other intermediaries. The first is that money-issuing intermediaries are subject to a cash reserve constraint. The second is that money-issuing intermediaries as a group do not have to worry about marketing their debts in quite the same way that life insurers, for example, must worry about marketing life insurance; money cannot be refused by lenders as a group once it has been created, although each individual lender can easily buy something to pass the money off to someone else.

Banks as a special case

The economic logic of deposit expansion models was first made clear by James Tobin in an article that related the special case of banks to the more general case of intermediaries.[9] The key feature used in this demonstration is the cash reserve constraint.

The **cash reserve constraint** arises from (a) the requirement in federal financial legislation that members of the Canadian Payments Association keep settlement balances on deposit with the Bank of Canada to cover possible cheque-clearing losses, and (b) the requirement by depositors that firms issuing demand deposits be ready to redeem deposits in currency on demand (especially at automated teller machines).[10] The total of all settlement balances and currency held by deposit-takers is their cash reserve. The total of **cash reserve assets** in existence is under the direct control of the Bank of Canada, since both types of cash reserve asset are debts issued by the Bank of Canada. Deposit-takers are

---

[9] James Tobin, in "Commercial Banks as Creators of Money," in Deane Carson, ed., *Banking and Monetary Studies* (Homewood, Ill.: Irwin, 1963).

[10] Chapter 2, section 4, explains the cheque-clearing process. Section 3 of that chapter defines the money supply. Smaller members of the Canadian Payments Association do not hold balances with the Bank of Canada directly, but instead clear their cheques through other, larger members.

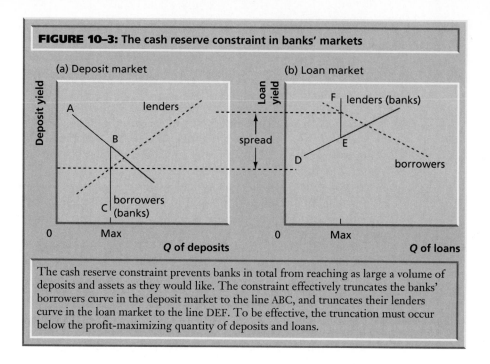

FIGURE 10–3: The cash reserve constraint in banks' markets

(a) Deposit market

(b) Loan market

The cash reserve constraint prevents banks in total from reaching as large a volume of deposits and assets as they would like. The constraint effectively truncates the banks' borrowers curve in the deposit market to the line ABC, and truncates their lenders curve in the loan market to the line DEF. To be effective, the truncation must occur below the profit-maximizing quantity of deposits and loans.

therefore constrained collectively by the Bank of Canada in the quantity of cash reserves they can hold. The 1980 Bank Act also set legal minimum holdings of cash reserves for chartered banks, equal to specified proportions of various types of deposits outstanding. The legal minimum cash reserve requirement is to be phased out in the Bank Act revision introduced in Parliament in 1991, but banks' own requirements will remain almost as large as the legal minima being removed.

For more convenient reference in what follows, the deposit-taking inter-mediaries subject to the cash reserve constraint will be called simply banks. The scarcity of cash reserves imposes an additional constraint on banks, over and above the constraints of profit maximization illustrated for the case of Faithful Trust in section 1. Since banks cannot collectively acquire more cash reserve assets, there is a limit to the total volume of deposits that banks will issue, and therefore to the quantity of loans that banks will buy. If the Bank of Canada restricts the quantity of cash reserve assets sufficiently, the banks will be stopped short of issuing as large a total of deposits as would otherwise maximize their profits.

Figure 10–3 shows the cash reserve constraint as imposing a maximum quantity on the two curves that reflect banks' behaviour in financial markets: the borrowers curve in the deposit market, and the lenders curve in the loan market. These two maximum points are labelled *Max* in Figure 10–3. They are explained by the deposit expansion models developed in the next subsection.

The significance of Figure 10–3 is that the quantity of deposits outstanding depends only on the location of *Max* on the horizontal axis — that is, on the quantity of reserve assets made available. Nothing else matters. Furthermore, the relationship between total deposits and total cash reserves available is quite mechanical. Total deposits are not affected by relative yields on assets and debts, by investors' degree of risk aversion, or by any of the other factors that play a role in the Faithful Trust model of section 1. Upward and downward shifts of lenders and borrowers curves over a wide range will make no difference to total deposits issued. Figure 10–3 shows that the cash reserve constraint will continue to determine the quantity of deposits as long as the Bank of Canada keeps total cash reserve assets below what the banks would need at the unconstrained, profit-maximizing level of deposits.[11]

The deposit expansion process

Deposit expansion models relate changes in the quantity of cash reserves to the quantity of deposits or money. The model reflects both the cash reserve constraint and the fact that, collectively, banks can lend by issuing the very asset (a demand deposit) that all borrowers want. All other intermediaries must first acquire demand deposits before they can make loans. As we will see in the rest of this section, the huge collective advantage this gives banks as a group is not likely to be perceived as such by any one individual bank. Although each bank can issue its own chequing account balance to make a loan, there is little chance that money newly created to make a loan will continue to be held in the bank that created it; individual banks therefore do not see themselves as having any "licence to print money." This proposition is more easily understood by looking in more detail at the deposit expansion process.

Simple deposit expansion: Case 1

Assume that each bank has a very simple balance sheet structure (the real balance sheet structure will be described in Chapter 11). Let each bank hold loans and cash reserves as assets, issue demand deposits as liabilities, and have fixed equity. Cash reserve assets earn no interest, but must be kept at least equal to 10 percent of deposits either by law or because past practice has shown this to be the minimum prudent level. Cash reserve assets consist of Bank of Canada deposits. The money supply consists entirely of banks' demand deposits; there are no notes in this simple case. Loan applications are always available at loan yields that exceed the servicing cost of deposits. If there are $20 billion of Bank of Canada deposits in existence, and Typical Bank has 10 percent of banking markets, the banking system will look as in Table 10–1.

---

[11] The unconstrained level of deposits is that below the intersection of borrowers and lenders curves in the deposit market when there is no constraint.

TABLE 10–1: Bank balance sheets ($ billion)

Typical Bank				All banks			
Assets		Debt + equity		Assets		Debt + equity	
B of C deposits	2	Deposits	20	B of C deposits	20	Deposits	200
Loans	19	Equity	1	Loans	190	Equity	10
Total	21	Total	21	Total	210	Total	210

B of C deposits = cash reserve assets (Bank of Canada deposits and vault cash).

Typical Bank and all banks collectively will have deposits exactly equal to 10 times the reserve assets available; in other words, reserve assets will always be 10 percent of total deposits. Loans will always be equal to deposits plus equity, less cash reserve assets held.

Now suppose that a $100 million cheque on the Bank of Canada (B of C) is deposited in Typical by one of its customers, who got it by selling a large bond to the B of C. Typical presents the cheque to the B of C for settlement, at which point it is converted to an increase in Typical's B of C deposit. We will now follow through the stages of deposit expansion that the injection of extra reserves starts off.

Stage 1: Typical begins stage 1 with extra deposits of $100 million and extra reserves of $100 million. $90 million of those extra reserves are excess, so Typical invests $90 million in loans. Typical does not hand over $90 million of B of C deposits to its loan customer; that would not be convenient for the loan customer, and besides, individuals cannot hold deposits in the B of C. Instead, Typical adds $90 million to the loan customer's demand deposit. The loan customer promptly writes cheques for the entire $90 million to pay for a (small) takeover bid. When the cheques are deposited in some other bank and cleared, both the loan customer's deposit and Typical's cash reserves fall by $90 million. Typical is left happy at the end of stage 1 with $100 million more in deposits, the required $10 million more in reserves, and $90 million more in interest-earning loans. Typical's stock price rises a few points, and the board of directors votes Typical's managers a bonus.

Stage 2: The cheques written on Typical for the $90 million takeover bid are all redeposited by the recipients; there is nothing else to do with them. Let us assume for simplicity that all the cheques are redeposited in Standard Bank. After the cheques have been cleared, Standard starts stage 2 with $90 million more in customers' deposits and $90 million more in cash reserves. Standard realizes that it needs only $9 million of reserves to meet its cash reserve requirement, and the remaining $81 million is loaned out to an eager loan customer to spend on election advertising. The loan customer's account is written up by $81 million and a loan of $81 million is added to Standard's total loans. The loan customer proceeds to write cheques for $81 million to assorted media firms. When the cheques are deposited in some other bank and cleared, both the loan customer's deposit and Standard's reserves fall by $81 million. Standard is left happy at the end of stage 2 with $90 million more in deposits, the required $9 million more in reserves, and $81 million more in interest-earning loans. Standard's stock rises a bit too.

Stage 3, etc.: Stage 3 is a repeat of stages 1 and 2, with the scale of transactions reduced by 10 percent relative to stage 2. Only $81 million is deposited. Only $8.1 million is needed as extra required reserves. Only $72.9 million is available as excess reserves to lend out. Only $72.9 million gets redeposited to start stage 4. The process continues through many stages until the amounts become negligible. The end comes when enough extra deposits have been created (by writing up loans, spending them, and having the proceeds redeposited by recipients) so that all of the extra reserves available are required reserves, and there are no excess reserves.

The final state must be one in which deposits have risen by ten times the increase in reserves. Since deposits are the only form of money, the money supply has also risen by ten times the increase in reserves. Alternatively, the total increase in deposits must be the sum of the series of deposit increases at each stage, namely (in millions):

$$\$100 + \$90 + \$81 + \$72.9 + \ldots$$

This series of extra deposits is a geometric series:

$$\$100(1 + 0.9 + 0.9^2 + 0.9^3 + 0.9^4 + \ldots + 0.9^n),$$

where n is the (very large) number of stages allowed. The sum of this geometric series for large n is (in millions)

$$\$100[1/(1 - 0.9)],$$

or ten times the increase in reserves.

Throughout the stages of this process, each bank sees itself as simply lending out part of the funds that have been deposited with it. *True*. Also each bank regards the deposit it creates while making a loan as just a will o' the wisp that disappears again as soon as the loan customer can spend it. *Not true*: the newly created deposit does not disappear, it merely shifts to another bank.

Bank deposit expansion with currency drain: Case 2

The simple bank deposit expansion is *too* simple, however. Here we expand the model to allow for currency as well as deposits. Currency and B of C deposits serve equally as reserves; they are collectively known as the *monetary base* or (because they support many dollars of demand deposits) **high-powered money**. In this case we add a **currency drain** : we assume the public always wants to hold

$2 of currency for every $3 of deposits[12] — that is, the desired currency:deposit ratio is 0.67. Other than that, the model is kept as above in the simple case. Assume again that the banks collectively have reserves of $20 billion, so they start in the same situation as in Figure 10–2 above. Assume again that the B of C creates $100 million of extra reserves, and we will briefly trace through the first two stages of deposit expansion to see what difference a currency drain makes.

Stage 1: A $100 million cheque on the B of C is presented to Typical Bank by one of its customers. The customer wishes to keep $40 million in the form of currency and to deposit the remaining $60 million, keeping the proportions of currency to deposits at 2:3. Typical obliges by adding $60 million to the customer's demand deposit account and handing over $40 million in currency (in large bills, presumably with armed escort). Typical's reserves are increased by $100 million when the cheque clears. Typical therefore has extra deposits of $60 million and extra reserves of $60 million. Required reserves rise by $6 million. $54 million are excess reserves, which are promptly loaned out and spent by the loan customer as in the simple case. When the loan customer's cheques are deposited in some other bank (Standard Bank again) and then cleared, both the loan customer's deposit and Typical's reserves fall by $54 million. Typical is still ahead by $60 million of deposits and $54 million of interest-earning loans. Typical's stock rises in the market, but not as much as in case 1. Typical's managers get a small bonus.

Stage 2: The $54 million of cheques written on Typical are presented to Standard Bank. Standard's customers want to take 40 percent in cash ($21.6 million) and deposit the remaining 60 percent ($32.4 million). Standard obliges by adding $32.4 million to its customers' deposits, and records the same amount as added to its reserves when the cheques have cleared ($54 million less currency payouts of $21.6 million). Standard realizes that it needs only $3.24 million of reserves to meet its cash reserve requirement. The remaining $29.16 million is loaned out and is promptly spent by the loan customers. When the loan customers' cheques have cleared, Standard is still ahead by $32.4 million of deposits and $29.16 million of interest-earning loans.

In later stages the process is repeated, but the scale declines much more rapidly. In stage 3, for instance, the deposit is only $17.5 million instead of the $72.9 million of case 1 above. The end comes when enough extra deposits have been created that all of the $100 million additional high-powered money is absorbed in either extra currency demand or extra required reserve holdings; excess cash reserves are zero. The total increase in deposits must be the sum of the series of deposit increases at each stage:

$$\$60 \text{ million} + \$32.4 \text{ million} + \$17.5 \text{ million} + \ldots$$

---

[12] Think of this ratio as driven by the ratio of transactions made with cash to transactions paid for by cheque. Such a ratio is likely to be quite stable; 2:3 is roughly the ratio currently observed in Canada, as shown in Figure 2–3.

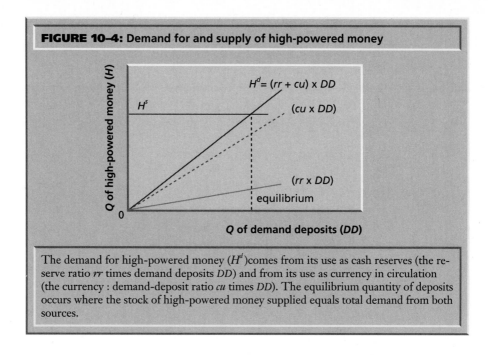

FIGURE 10–4: Demand for and supply of high-powered money

The demand for high-powered money (H^d) comes from its use as cash reserves (the reserve ratio *rr* times demand deposits *DD*) and from its use as currency in circulation (the currency : demand-deposit ratio *cu* times *DD*). The equilibrium quantity of deposits occurs where the stock of high-powered money supplied equals total demand from both sources.

which can be written as the geometric series (in millions):

$$100(0.6)(1 + 0.54 + 0.54^2 + \cdots + 0.54^n),$$

which for many stages (that is, large values of *n*) approaches

$$\$100(0.6)[1/(1 - 0.54)].$$

Currency is always two-thirds of deposits, so the total increase in currency *and* deposits is

$$(1 + 0.67)\$100(0.6)[1/(1 - 0.54)]$$

$$= \$100[1/(1 - 0.54)]$$

$$= \$100 \, \text{million}(2.174).$$

The bank deposit expansion process is much smaller in case 2. The reason is that case 2 adds another use of high-powered money: currency in circulation. More high-powered money gets absorbed in each round of deposit expansion.

The deposit expansion process must be followed through stage by stage if its economic and financial logic is to be understood. Once that understanding is achieved, however, it is much easier to analyze bank deposit expansion with the aid of Figure 10–4. This figure matches up the stock of high-powered money with the demand for it for cash reserves and currency holdings.

The supply of high-powered money H^s is given by the horizontal line at whatever level the B of C decides; high-powered money is exogenous in this discussion. The demand for high-powered money (H^d) is equal to required reserve holdings in case 1. In case 2, H^d includes both required reserve holdings and currency holdings of the public. There are no other uses for high-powered money. The demand for required reserves rises at the rate rr as outstanding demand deposits rise. Public demand for currency holdings (if any) rises at a rate given by the currency:demand-deposit ratio cu. The total demand for high-powered money in case 2 is the vertical sum of both types of demand:

$$H^d = (rr + cu)\, DD,$$

where DD is the quantity of demand deposits.

Equilibrium for reserve assets, deposits, and currency holdings occurs at the intersection of demand and supply in Figure 10–4. It can be deduced geometrically from Figure 10–4 or from the algebra ($H^s = H^d$) that total demand deposits in case 2 will be the supply of reserve assets divided by the slope of the total demand for reserves line:

$$DD = H^s/(rr + cu).$$

Currency demand is the fraction cu of demand deposits. Currency plus demand deposits make up the money supply M:

$$M = H^s(1 + cu)/(rr + cu).$$

With the values of cu and rr from case 2,

$$M = H^s(1 + 0.667)/(0.1 + 0.667)$$
$$= H^s 2.17$$

as in the numerical illustration above.

With Figure 10–4 it is easy to extend our discussion to a much more realistic case in which the public also holds time deposits in banks.[13] Suppose each bank issues time deposits as the public demands them, because time deposits have a fixed interest rate low enough to be profitable for banks. The public demands $\$t$ of time deposits per $\$1$ of demand deposits. Let time deposits have a required cash reserve ratio rr_t. These changes can be added onto Figure 10–4 by adding a new component to H^d: the demand for cash reserves against time deposits. The demand for cash reserves against time deposits would have a slope of $t\, rr_t$; $\$rr_t$ per dollar of time deposits, and $\$t$ dollars of time deposits per dollar of demand deposits. The revised total demand for high-powered money would be

$$H^{d'} = (rr + cu + t\, rr_t)\, DD.$$

---

[13] Time deposits include all deposits not repayable on demand. Savings, notice, and term deposits are all time deposits.

For any supply of high-powered money the equilibrium quantity of demand deposits would be

$$DD = H^s/(rr + cu + t\,rr_t).$$

Any change in high-powered money would bring about an increase in demand deposits of $1/(rr + cu + t\,rr_t)$ times as much. Currency holdings would rise by the fraction cu and time deposits by the multiple t of the rise in demand deposits.

Zero cash reserve requirements and deposit expansion

It is easy to analyze changes in reserve requirements with the model of Figure 10–4: they change the values of rr and rr_t in Figure 10–4 and in the algebra of this section. Suppose the legal cash reserve requirement for both time and demand deposits is dropped to zero, as is planned in the current Bank Act revision. This would mean replacing the legal level of rr with that presumably lower level that banks find prudent. In the more realistic model of case 2, such a decrease in the effective reserve requirement has a relatively small effect on the total demand for high-powered money.

Abolishing the cash reserve requirement entirely would set rr at zero. The total demand for high-powered money would then be only the demand for currency holdings, which rises at the rate cu. Total deposits become the multiple $1/cu$ times the stock of high-powered money. Currency holdings and time deposits are still the fraction cu and the multiple t of demand deposits.

Note as an empirical matter that if cu is around 0.667, it does not make much difference whether rr is 0.10 or 0, or whether rr_t is 0.02 or 0. The size of the bank deposit expansion multiplier is dominated by cu anyway. $1/cu = 1.5$, while $1/(cu + rr) = 1.3$ and (if t is as large as 3) $1/(cu + rr + t\,rr_t) = 1.21$. What may be more important than a change in the *level* of the deposit expansion multiplier is a change in its *stability*. The simple deposit expansion model cannot help us with that question.

SECTION 4

▣ Regulations and financial intermediation

Regulation of financial intermediaries was a hot topic during the second half of the 1980s. This section shows what impact each major type of regulation can be expected to have on intermediaries, using the model of Faithful Trust summarized in Figure 10–1.

One of the more visible types of regulation requires intermediaries to report frequently on their assets, debts, and flows of funds. The purposes of reporting requirements are to ensure that investors can inform themselves about the affairs of all firms soliciting their funds, and to allow government regulators to see whether other regulations are being followed. Reporting requirements have two effects on Faithful Trust. First, Faithful incurs some accounting costs in assembling the reports. It is quite likely that the accounting costs are almost all in the nature of fixed rather than variable costs, so Faithful's marginal operating costs would not be affected. However, Faithful and its rivals will need a larger spread in equilibrium to cover their fixed costs. Second, Faithful benefits from having its accounts made public (assuming Faithful is not violating any regulations). Faithful's depositors will be less worried about unsafe practices by Faithful's managers if they believe that any such practices will be quickly revealed in regular reports. "Depositors being less worried" implies lower debt costs for Faithful. On the other hand, depositors can also check Faithful's leverage ratio more easily, so depositors will be more quickly sensitive to increases in leverage; that could make the slope of the marginal debt cost curve steeper in the short run.

A second type of regulation takes the form of limitations on asset proportions. Such regulation either constrains Faithful to hold more liquid assets than it would otherwise like (such as cash reserve assets or government bonds), or else prohibits Faithful from holding as many risky assets as it would like (such as shares of new companies or unsecured commercial loans). An immediate and obvious effect of holding more liquid assets and less risky assets is to lower the marginal asset yield schedule in Figure 10–1. That makes Faithful's shareholders worse off. However, there is a second effect on debt costs. If depositors believe the regulations are being followed, they worry less about default risk on their deposits. They therefore accept lower deposit interest rates, and Faithful's marginal debt cost schedule also drops. Faithful's shareholders also worry less about bankruptcy when the asset portfolio is safer, so they do not insist on as large a risk premium on Faithful's shares. This generally raises the market value of Faithful's shares.

Regulators set maximum leverage ratios by laying down minimum **capital ratios** (ratios of equity capital to either total assets or total liabilities). In the short run, with fixed equity capital, minimum capital ratios put a maximum quota on Faithful's total assets and total deposits outstanding. Faithful's demand for loans and supply of deposits is truncated at the maximum quota point. If capital ratios are raised, the lenders curves and borrowers curves generated by intermediaries are shifted to the left in the loan and deposit markets, respectively. This increases interest spreads between loan and deposit yields. A wider interest spread is needed when capital ratios are raised, because Faithful must make its profit with fewer dollars of assets per dollar of equity. Faithful needs a larger interest spread per dollar of assets to provide the same return on equity. The good news for Faithful is on its debt costs: lower leverage ratios comfort depositors by lowering the risk of bankruptcy. Debt costs fall and interest spreads may widen further.

Deposit insurance by the Canada Deposit Insurance Corporation is a form of government intervention, rather than a form of regulation by itself, but it has powerful effects on Faithful Trust's situation. Deposit insurance guarantees intermediaries' retail deposits against default losses. In return, intermediaries pay an annual insurance premium at a flat rate per dollar of insured deposits. The deposit insurance premium that Faithful pays for its deposit insurance increases Faithful's marginal operating costs in Figure 10–1 by a constant amount. The introduction of deposit insurance lowers the default risk of guaranteed deposits to zero (for the depositor, that is, not for the taxpayer supporting the Canada Deposit Insurance Corporation). The *promised* yield on guaranteed deposits can drop by the amount of previously expected default loss, without lowering the *expected* yield to the depositor below what it was before deposit insurance. Lenders in the deposit market will accept lower promised deposit yields with deposit insurance, so Faithful's marginal interest cost schedule falls in Figure 10–1. What the net effect is on Faithful's profit depends on whether Faithful's marginal interest cost falls by more than its deposit insurance premium. That in turn depends on whether Faithful's default risk is perceived to be above or below the industry average for all deposit-takers; it is the above-average risks that stand to benefit most from deposit insurance at a flat-rate premium.

A final, contentious form of regulation concerns the ownership of intermediaries. Ownership is restricted both to prevent too great a concentration of power in financial markets, and also to ward off serious conflict of interest situations. Such a situation would arise if, for example, a commercial firm owned a bank and had conflicting interests as both (a) the bank's shareholder, and (b) the bank's loan customer. One effect of any restriction preventing some group from buying a particular stock is to lower the stock's price somewhat; the lenders curve in the market for that stock is shifted to the left. Another effect is on the expectations of the remaining shareholders; with a lower probability of conflict of interest they may expect management to pursue shareholders' interests more single-mindedly, and therefore shareholders might expect higher profits. That would shift the lenders curve out to the right again. If any of this made a difference to depositors, debt costs could fall as well.

In this section we have highlighted the effects of imposing each type of regulation. We have not traced through all of the subsequent effects in all cases. In general, Faithful will expand if its marginal net asset yield schedule rises relative to its marginal debt cost schedule. Faithful's expansion and that of all other firms similarly affected will push Faithful's asset yields down and its debt costs up. The end result will once again be equality of marginal net asset yields and marginal debt costs, but with Faithful operating on a larger scale and some other type of intermediary operating on a smaller scale.

SECTION 5

▢ Summary

Most financial intermediaries can be analyzed as profit-making firms, using an approach not too different from that generally used in microeconomic theory. Each intermediary operates in a part of the financial system where it has acquired enough information to understand its asset risks and to find suitable sources of funding. Managers of intermediaries try to keep risks in check, for any scale of operation, by a combination of diversification, matching, and hedging. Given the risk level that remains for each scale of operation, profit-maximizing managers choose their scales of operation so that marginal net asset yields just offset marginal debt costs.

Positive spreads are necessary to cover intermediaries' costs of operation and to leave a normal profit margin for shareholders. Intermediaries increase their spreads by adding features to their debts that will appeal to lenders. These features include customer services provided by specialized staff, such as tellers or financial advisers or cheque-clearing personnel. Other features include such properties of asset yields as safety from default risk, liquidity, or having the payment pattern suited to lenders' individual needs. The general process of buying assets with one set of properties and issuing debts with a quite different set is known as the transmutation of assets. Most transmutation of assets is made possible by diversification or risk pooling. Some of it is accounted for by economies of scale, especially in the gathering of information.

Intermediaries issuing chequing deposits (that is, banks and other members of the Canadian Payments Association) are special in that they collectively issue the money they lend, and the amount of money they issue is constrained by the government through cash reserve requirements. Changes in demand deposits can be modelled as being mechanically determined by changes in high-powered money, in deposit expansion models. Bank deposit expansion multipliers that relate deposits to cash reserves are most heavily determined in practice by the public's desired currency to deposit ratio.

The effect of regulation of financial intermediaries on a typical institution can be analyzed by looking at how each regulation influences (a) marginal asset yields, (b) marginal operating costs, (c) marginal debt costs, and (d) the spread needed for long-run equilibrium. Many of the biggest impacts of regulations come from changes in systematic risks perceived by lenders, which cause changes in intermediaries' debt costs.

Key Terms

transactions costs	economies of scope
intermediation	deposit expansion models
information costs	cash reserve constraint
non-price credit rationing	cash reserve assets
positive spread	high-powered money
transmutation of assets	currency drain
risk pooling	regulation of financial
liquidity risk	intermediaries
customer services	capital ratios
economies of scale	

Questions and Problems

1. Credit union depositors essentially share in the profits of credit unions through the bonus interest paid at year end to return profits to members. Given the information costs associated with credit union lending, is this practice consistent with what the theory of section 1 recommends for prudent depositors? If not, what are the likely consequences of any inconsistency?

2. What steps would you take, and what information would you want to acquire, if you were a bank loan officer responsible for weeding out the scoundrels from other loan applicants?

3. In what ways, if any, is the transmutation of assets by financial intermediaries different from the normal transformation of inputs into different outputs by any producing firm?

4. Do you think the banks are likely to keep stable cash reserve ratios if the cash reserve requirement is abolished? Why or why not?

5. Why do we have mechanical deposit expansion models for bank deposits, but no similar models to predict total insurance or total mutual fund shares outstanding?

6. Do regulations of financial intermediaries always reduce intermediary profits? If not, which types of regulation might not?

Suggestions for Further Reading

Bodie, Zvi. "Pensions as Retirement Income Assurance." *Journal of Economic Literature*, March 1990, 28–49.

Chant, John. *Regulation of Financial Institutions: A Functional Analysis*. Ottawa: Bank of Canada Technical Report 45, January 1987.

Jaffee, Dwight, and Thomas Russell. "Information, Uncertainty and Credit Rationing." *Quarterly Journal of Economics*, November 1976, 651–666.

Stiglitz, Joseph, and Andrew Weiss. "Credit Rationing in Markets with Asymmetric Information." *American Economic Review*, June 1981, 393–410.

Tobin, James. "Commercial Banks as Creators of Money." In Deane Carson, ed. *Banking and Monetary Studies*. Homewood, Ill.: Irwin, 1963.

Chapter eleven

Chartered Banking

This chapter applies the logic of financial intermediation in the specific circumstances of Canada's chartered banks, in order to explain their behaviour in much greater detail than was possible in Chapter 10.

Section 1 discusses different approaches to defining "banking." Section 2 describes the fast-changing legal structure within which banks in Canada must operate. Section 3 describes the different kinds of bank intermediation in three steps. The first is to describe the mix of assets and liabilities held by banks. The second is to recognize the main kinds of transmutation of assets that occur in banking. The third is to summarize the net effect for shareholders by looking at one bank's income statement. Finally, section 4 discusses how banks manage the risks raised by their intermediation.

You should learn in this chapter:

1. the different approaches to defining "banking";
2. the legal background of chartered banks in Canada;
3. the types of assets and debts that banks buy and issue;
4. the types of asset transmutation carried out by banks;
5. how banks manage their risks by diversification, matching, and hedging.

SECTION 1

■ Definitions of banking

The term banking is used much more loosely in financial discussions than it is in everyday language. Those outside the financial sector almost always think of banking as referring to the activities of chartered banks. Chartered banks are an easily recognizable group of institutions reported on frequently in the daily press; each has a charter that explicitly identifies it as a bank; only a chartered bank can have the word "bank" somewhere in its name, and all but four chartered banks make use of that privilege. As a result, most of us conceive of banking as "whatever chartered banks do." However, there are three other conceptions of banking that are also used frequently in financial discussions: commercial banking, merchant banking, and investment banking.[1] The last two usually refer to activities undertaken in Canada by institutions that are *not* chartered banks. It is confusing. A brief tour of all four conceptions of banking is in order.

Commercial banking

Pure **commercial banking** means issuing highly liquid liabilities and buying only short-term loans that are used by the borrowers to finance trade flows. The highly liquid liabilities of the earliest commercial banks were banknotes. In this century banknotes have been replaced by demand deposits and some very liquid notice deposits. Commercial bank loans are generally unsecured by any other financial asset of the borrower, and used to finance the purchase of inventories by merchants; they are also self-liquidating in that the later resale of the inventories to customers generates the cash flow that merchants use to repay the loan and interest.

Commercial banking is the simple prototype of banking used in most economic discussions. For instance, our discussion of the bank deposit expansion model in Chapter 10 was all about the issue of demand deposits by banks engaged in commercial banking.

Almost all of the commercial banking in Canada is done by chartered banks. Credit unions and some trust companies also issue demand deposits and do a modest amount of commercial lending, but the vast bulk of both is done by chartered banks. As we will see, however, chartered banks do not stop there.

Merchant banking

Merchant banking looks after a variety of financial needs not met by commercial banking. Institutions serving as merchant banks underwrite new issues of securities for firms and governments. Often they will buy some of the firm's or government's securities themselves. They provide brokerage services to help others trade securities in secondary markets. They offer advice and support to firms in mergers and acquisitions. They manage asset portfolios on behalf of

---

[1] Sometimes in public discussions the term "banking" is used to mean no more than lending or borrowing. For instance, mortgage lending by intermediaries is often referred to as "mortgage banking." Lending by deposit-takers that is financed through savings deposits is often referred to as "savings banking." Also, in public discussions the terms merchant banking and investment banking are sometimes used interchangeably.

Source: *The Economist*, December 9, 1989, p. 52. © 1989, David Simonds/The Economist Newspaper Ltd. Reprinted with permission.

clients. And they help firms manage their short-term debts. Managing short-term debts includes such activities as lending for short periods to finance fleets of vehicles, for example, or lending to finance construction loans while long-term mortgage financing is being arranged, or collecting short-term accounts receivable on behalf of a client firm (the activity known as *factoring*).

Several different groups of intermediaries provide some merchant banking services, but few provide all of them. Investment dealers provide almost the whole range of merchant banking services except factoring and making short-term loans. Domestically owned chartered banks provide short-term loans and brokerage services. Some foreign-owned chartered banks provide only merchant banking loans. Foreign exchange dealers provide specialized brokerage in a few highly liquid foreign currency assets. Finance companies help client firms manage short-term debts by factoring, by buying short-term accounts receivable from the client at a discount (an activity known as the *acceptance* business), and by financial leasing. Trust companies and specialized mutual fund management companies provide portfolio management services. As you can see, the label "merchant bank" applies in different ways to a wide range of financial intermediaries in Canada, and almost all of the institutions that perform merchant banking functions are usually called something other than a merchant bank.

Source: *The Economist*, December 9, 1989, p. 54. © 1989, David Simonds/The Economist Newspaper Ltd. Reprinted with permission.

Investment banking

Investment banking involves longer-term, less liquid loans to firms. Usually the loans are to finance start-ups of firms or projects, or to finance turnarounds of unprofitable companies, or to finance mergers and acquisitions. Such loans are not self-liquidating; they expose the lender to significantly higher risk. Investment banks both arrange such lending and also lend themselves. Investment bankers arranging a leveraged buyout (the purchase of the controlling interest in a firm with mainly borrowed funds) for a client are likely to buy up 20 percent or so of the debts issued by the client to finance that buyout. There is no typical debt issued by investment banks to finance their investments, but it must be either longer-term debt or equity since investment banks' assets are not liquid.

Investment banking in Canada is conducted by venture capital companies (themselves owned by a wide variety of other intermediaries including chartered banks), by investment dealers, and by subsidiaries of financial holding companies such as Trilon Financial Corporation and Power Financial. At 22 years of age, Hees International is by far the oldest of these subsidiary firms.

Chartered banking

Chartered banking is defined by the firms engaged in it, rather than by the kind of activity engaged in. **Chartered banking** is whatever chartered banks do. A chartered bank is any institution to which the government has issued a **bank charter** under the current federal Bank Act. A bank charter is simply a license to operate as a bank, subject to the restrictions of the Bank Act. All chartered banks are listed as such in one of the two schedules attached to the most recent revision of the federal Bank Act.

As a definition of banking, chartered banking has the advantage that the firms involved can be precisely identified. It has the disadvantage that the kind of intermediation involved is hardly defined at all. Chartered banks engage in much the same types of intermediation as several other intermediaries, and the degree of overlap increases each year.[2] Nevertheless, chartered banking is the common, everyday conception of the word "banking," and it is the one we use in the rest of this chapter.

SECTION 2

The legal structure of chartered banking in Canada

All banks in Canada are chartered under the federal Bank Act; there are no provincial banks.[3] Charters are available either by special Act of Parliament, or since 1980 by the far simpler route of obtaining letters patent from the Minister of Finance. Since the 1980 Bank Act revision, two kinds of federal charters have been available: the original kind, now known as **schedule I,** and the newer **schedule II charters**. For schedule I charters, banks must be widely held and domestically owned. Widely held means having no individual or group of associated shareholders owning more than 10 percent of any class of shares. Domestically owned means having no more than 25 percent of the shares owned by non-residents (excluding U.S. residents, under an exemption granted by the Free Trade Agreement). Schedule II banks need be neither widely held nor domestically owned. There are now eight operating schedule I banks and 57 operating schedule II banks. All but one of the schedule II banks are subsidiaries of foreign banks, though after the new Bank Act is passed in 1991 or 1992, widely held non-bank financial institutions such as policyholder-owned mutual insurance companies and loan companies will also be able to establish schedule II bank subsidiaries.

---

[2] The government's own summary of its proposed revisions of financial legislation in the fall of 1990 says explicitly: "To enhance competition and thereby strengthen institutions, it is proposed that banks and federally incorporated trust, loan and insurance companies generally have the opportunity to offer a similar range of services and compete in markets that were not previously open to them." Hon. Gilles Loiselle, *Reform of Federal Financial Institutions Legislation: Overview of Legislative Proposals* (Ottawa: Finance Canada, Fall 1990), p.3.

[3] The Alberta treasury branch system operates in Alberta as a (provincial-government-owned) bank, but without the word "bank" in its name and outside the Bank Act. This example shows how the chartered bank definition of banking is one of form rather than substance.

TABLE 11–1: Bank charters in Canada, 1792–1990

	1792– 1866	1867– 1929	1930– 1967	1968– 1980	1981– 1982	1983– 1990
Entry of banks						
Banks chartered	80	76	3	5	58	12
less charters not used	22	38	1	0	0	0
entry of new banks	58	38	2	5	58	12
Mergers with other banks	2	34	4	3	0	6
Exit of banks						
failed or wound up	21	28	0	0	0	10
Active at end of period	35	11	9	11	69	65

Note: B.C. Bancorp and Continental Bank, still formally in existence in 1990, are classified in this table as being wound up.

Source: For data up to 1978, S. Sarpkaya, *Canadian Banker and ICB Review*, October and December 1978. Since then, *The Canada Gazette*.

Table 11–1 summarizes the eventful history of bank chartering in Canada since 1792. The number of banks grew to over five dozen by 1900. Then a wave of bank mergers and some failures reduced the number of banks to nine in 1967. In the 1970s more than 60 foreign banks set up operations in Canada, and the revision of the Bank Act in 1980 forced these banks to seek federal charters in 1981–82 and after. Since 1985 the number of active banks has resumed its downward trend again. Two small western banks failed in 1985. Four other medium-size banks (two of them also western-based) were so undermined by the ensuing loss of confidence in small regional banks that they were forced to merge with stronger foreign banks. Two tiny western banks have since merged into one still tiny western bank. The only significant domestic entrant to chartered banking, Laurentian Bank, is a new entrant in name only. It was already in banking before 1980 as the last remaining Quebec Savings Bank. The number of domestic banks is now down to eight, its lowest total ever.

Bank charters convey some special rights and some restrictions. The list of special rights is much shorter than the list of restrictions.

Bank Act rights and privileges

A bank charter enables an intermediary to call itself a bank. This can bring significant advantages in the form of lower debt costs where the lending public believes banks to be safer than similar institutions operating under other names like trust company.[4]

---

[4]Canada Trustco has been trying to become a chartered bank for years, mainly for this reason. Canada Trustco depends heavily on retail deposits, and therefore on the retail lending public's expectations. Wholesale depositors might be expected to be more rational and less swayed by the word "bank," especially after the difficulty experienced by small banks in 1985–87.

A bank charter also enables an intermediary to make unsecured business and personal loans without limit (but see below for the limit on each individual loan). Unsecured loans are non-mortgage loans that do not have marketable securities as collateral. By contrast, trust and mortgage loan and insurance companies were not allowed before 1992 to make unsecured loans above 7 percent of total assets.[5]

Those are the only two special rights conveyed by a bank charter. As we shall see, other intermediaries can issue all the liabilities banks can issue and buy all the other assets banks can buy. As Canada Trustco and the Alberta treasury branches have demonstrated, non-banks can be banks in all but name. [6]

Bank Act restrictions

Schedule I banks must be widely held and domestically owned, as defined above. Schedule II banks can have both concentrated ownership and complete foreign ownership, but they are subject to two extra limitations relative to schedule I banks. First, schedule II banks' assets cannot exceed 20 times the equity capital authorized by the Minister of Finance in their letters patent. Second, the maximum equity capital allowed for any schedule II bank is $750 million —roughly one-fifth of the average equity of the biggest six domestic banks. In addition, a Canadian-owned schedule II bank must convert to a schedule I bank within ten years of getting its charter.

Foreign, non-U.S.-owned banks are also currently subject to an aggregate market share limitation: their aggregate authorized capital will be set by the Minister of Finance such that their total Canadian assets do not exceed 12 percent of total Canadian assets of all banks in Canada. U.S.-owned chartered banks have been exempted from this ceiling as part of the Free Trade Agreement; European-owned chartered banks may well become exempted in the future to ensure reciprocal rights for Canadian-owned banks in the European financial system. The market share of foreign-owned schedule II banks is not near the limit, so this is not yet an important restriction on schedule II banks.

The following restrictions apply to both schedule I and schedule II banks:

1. they are subject to cash reserve and secondary reserve requirements against deposits, though the former are to be phased out within two years of the new Bank Act's passage in 1991 or 1992 and the latter will be abolished immediately;

2. they are subject to supervision by the Superintendent of Financial Institutions (formerly the Inspector General of Banks), and must report each week to the Bank of Canada;

3. they issue deposits that are insured by the Canada Deposit Insurance Corporation (CDIC) up to $60 000 per depositor, and so they are subject

---

[5] This limit is to be abolished in the federal financial legislation introduced in 1991.

[6] Canada Trustco has the fourth largest total of personal deposits in Canada, well ahead of Toronto Dominion Bank and the Bank of Nova Scotia.

to whatever restrictions the CDIC imposes in exchange for its insurance coverage;

4. they can issue debentures as well as deposits, but the debentures must have terms longer than five years at issue, and total debentures outstanding must not exceed half of the bank's equity;

5. they are not allowed to lend to any one customer an amount greater than half of the bank's equity; [7]

6. they are prohibited from acquiring more than 10 percent ownership of non-financial companies;

7. like other federally incorporated deposit-taking institutions, they will be restricted in their holdings of real estate and common shares (other than those of subsidiaries) to 70 percent of their equity for each type of asset and 100 percent of their equity for both combined;

8. they are subject to overall limits on leverage (the ratio of assets to equity). Until 1992, the large schedule I banks have a maximum leverage ratio of 30 rather than the schedule II maximum of 20. After 1992 the maximum leverage ratio of both groups will also be subject to the limits imposed in the Basle Agreement on bank capital adequacy: this international agreement sets maximum ratios of (a) a risk-weighted measure of assets plus some other risk exposures to (b) two different measures of equity capital.

The powers of chartered banks

Domestically owned chartered banks carry on a huge foreign business abroad through their subsidiaries. The Bank Act places no restrictions on the activities of foreign subsidiaries. Within Canada, chartered banks can engage in a wide range of financial activities either directly or more usually through wholly owned subsidiaries. Financial leasing, underwriting and brokerage of securities, factoring of accounts receivable, and venture capital lending have all been possible through subsidiaries. Under the new Bank Act introduced in 1991, banks can buy or form subsidiary trust companies, insurance companies (life or property and casualty), portfolio management corporations, and real estate firms. Banks will not, however, be allowed to own car-leasing subsidiaries or to arrange the sale or servicing of insurance products directly from their branches. The lobbying efforts of car-leasing firms and life insurance sales organizations succeeded in keeping banks out of these two markets for the time being.

In the past, banks were subject to many more restrictions on the type of assets they could hold. The restrictions were designed to keep them mainly in the business of commercial loans and to keep them out of term loans, personal loans, and mortgages. The theory was that banks should lend only on security of

---

[7] We mentioned in Chapter 5 that banks have started to develop a secondary market in which to resell parts of their commercial loans. Secondary loan sales are used partly to enable banks to continue lending to their biggest customers without violating the limit on loans to individual customers.

goods in process or in transport, whose sale would automatically provide funds for loan repayment. That is, chartered banking was to be purely commercial banking as defined in section 1. Restrictions on the banks' asset mix have been steadily relaxed, starting in 1954. Almost all that remains is that the core of chartered-bank activity is still domestic commercial lending. When the new Bank Act allows banks to promote goods and services to their credit-card customers, banks will even be straying outside the financial system into a mail-order form of retail trade.

SECTION 3

Bank intermediation

The previous section described the powers of the chartered banks; this section describes the uses banks have made of those powers, the kinds of intermediation in which banks actually engage. We start with a look at the balance sheet of the whole banking sector. Then we identify the different forms of transmutation of assets that banks use to generate their positive spreads. Finally, we look at a profit and loss statement of one of the large domestic banks to see how successful the transmutation of assets has been. We do not discuss the risks of bank intermediation until section 4.

Bank assets

The asset proportions of the chartered banks have changed quite dramatically over the last three decades, even though some elements of banking seem unchanged. Table 11–2 shows a fairly broad breakdown of bank assets as of early 1991, late 1982, and late 1960.

Several features of bank activity stand out from Table 11–2. One is the large share of foreign currency loans and other assets in the total, even though that share has declined sharply since 1982. We mentioned the idea in Chapters 5 and 6 that Canada's financial system is now well tied into the international financial system; Canadian banks provide much of the linkage through their foreign currency business.

The dominant type of asset on banks' balance sheets is the loan, whether an unsecured loan or a mortgage loan secured by a mortgage on real estate or a loan secured by financial assets, whether in Canadian dollars or foreign currency. Loans account for almost three-quarters of bank assets.

Within the category of loans there have been some shifts during the 1980s: mortgage loans have grown in importance, whereas foreign currency loans have shrunk. Most of the mortgage lending is done through the banks' mortgage loan company subsidiaries. Much of the international borrowing that was done through banks in 1982 is now either not done at all (for instance, by troubled Third World debtors) or is done directly (by larger corporations) by issuing securitized, resalable loans directly to non-financial lenders.

TABLE 11-2: Chartered bank assets

	April 1991 (percent)	September 1982 (percent)	December 1960 (percent)
Canadian-dollar assets			
Cash reserve assets	0.8	1.7	5.9
Secondary reserve assets	3.9	2.4	6.7
Other liquid assets			
Government of Canada bonds	1.0	0.4	12.3
Other money market assets	0.2	0.3	0.7
Total liquid assets	5.9	4.8	25.6
Business and consumer loans	29.5	34.2	37.8
Mortgage loans	18.4	8.5	5.7
Leasing contracts	0.5	0.7	0.0
Other bonds and shares	3.2	2.7	5.9
Other assets	3.7	3.0	7.1
Total Canadian-dollar assets	61.3	53.9	82.1
Customers' acceptance liabilities	7.0	3.6	1.5
Foreign currency assets			
Call and other loans	20.9	28.1	9.6
Securities	3.2	1.8	3.3
Deposits with other banks	5.7	10.3	3.1
Other foreign currency assets	1.9	2.2	0.1
Total foreign currency assets	31.6	42.4	16.1
Total assets	100.0	100.0	100.0

Notes: Total assets were $610 billion in April 1991.

Source: Bank of Canada Review, Tables C3 and C11.

The banks' balance sheets of 1991 are not much affected by the purchase of investment dealers as banks' subsidiaries in 1987 and 1988 after first Quebec and then federal law was changed to allow such ownership by banks. Holdings of liquid assets (treasury bills, Canada bonds, short-term paper, bankers' acceptances) are only a bit larger in 1991 than in 1982 even though the 1991 figures include most of the assets held by Canada's investment dealers.

Some of the broad asset categories in Table 11–2 require description or special comment. Definitions of other terms are to be found in the glossary or in Chapter 6.

Cash reserve assets consist of coin and Bank of Canada notes and deposits in the Bank of Canada. All but a trivial fraction of cash reserve assets are held because they are required by the 1980 Bank Act, rather than by choice. The 1980 Bank Act requirement is as follows: on average over each two-week period in each month, cash reserve assets must be kept at least equal to 10 percent of demand deposits, plus 2 percent of the first $0.5 billion of notice deposits and *reservable* term deposits, plus 3 percent of any remaining notice and reservable term deposits, plus 3 percent of foreign currency deposits of Canadian residents held with banks in Canada. Reservable term deposits are those with an original term to maturity of one year or less. Term deposits of over one year to maturity at the time of issue have a zero percent cash reserve requirement, as do foreign currency deposits of non-residents, whether held in Canada or not. As Table 11–2 shows, banks have already squeezed their average cash reserve requirements down almost to zero. The cash reserve requirement will disappear entirely two years after the new Bank Act is passed, but banks will still need to hold substantial amounts of cash in their automated teller machine networks. Chapter 21 discusses cash reserve behaviour more fully.

Secondary reserve assets are treasury bills, day loans to money market dealers, and any excess cash reserves over and above the cash reserve requirement. The vast bulk of secondary reserve assets are treasury bills. Some are held by investment dealer subsidiaries. The secondary reserve requirement is that direct bank holdings of secondary reserve assets plus any excess cash reserves over and above the cash reserve requirement must equal at least 4 percent of total Canadian-dollar deposit liabilities. The secondary reserve requirement can be changed by the Bank of Canada, but has deliberately been kept at non-restrictive levels since the mid-1970s. This requirement will be abolished with the new Bank Act.

Other money market assets are held mainly by investment dealer subsidiaries. Most of them take the form of provincial treasury bills, commercial and sales finance paper, bankers' acceptances, and bearer term deposit notes.

Business loans and some personal loans are made under lines of credit that allow the borrower to borrow and repay at the *borrower's* discretion (within the limits of the line of credit ceiling and some minimum total repayment per year). Line of credit arrangements leave the bank with little control over the timing of cash flows to and from individual loan customers.

Leasing contracts refer to the present discounted value of future payments receivable on holdings of financial leases. Financial leases are held in leasing subsidiaries.

Customers' acceptance liability: banks are liable for the amount of bankers' acceptances they have "accepted" (that is, guaranteed), in the event that the issuers default. If an issuer defaults on an acceptance so that the accepting bank has to pay, the bank automatically has a claim on the issuing customer for the full amount the bank has paid. It is that claim that appears here. Banks expect very few acceptances to be defaulted, so both the banks' and customers' acceptance liabilities are very low-probability contingent liabilities.

Foreign currency call loans are mainly loans to stockbrokers and investment dealers in New York. The Canadian banks have been making such loans throughout this century. Foreign currency call loans are now a very small part of "call and other loans," however. Other foreign currency loans are almost all wholesale loans made in international markets. Canadian banks do have a modest foreign retail banking business in the Caribbean and in Latin America, but this is dwarfed by the wholesale international business. Some of the international business can be done in Canada, such as when a domestic firm like Bombardier decides to finance some of its foreign activity by borrowing in foreign rather than domestic currency.

Foreign currency deposits of other banks are almost all wholesale term deposits invested in large international banks.

Liabilities and equity

The liability portfolio of the chartered banks is shown in Table 11–3 for the same years as Table 11–2.

A comparison of 1960 with either 1982 or 1991 reveals quite startling changes in the kinds of liabilities that banks use. In 1960 over 70 percent of bank assets were financed by issuing either demand deposits or notice deposits, all redeemable effectively on demand. [8] By 1982 this percentage had shrunk to only 21 percent, recovering to 26 percent in 1991. Demand deposits had become a particularly small share by 1991. Banks have greatly lengthened the average term and decreased the average liquidity of their liabilities over the last three decades.

Apart from acceptance liabilities, which we have already discussed under the same heading in the assets section, banks borrow almost entirely through the issue of deposits. They issue foreign currency deposits in more or less the same volume as they buy foreign currency assets; both had lower shares in 1991 than in 1982, but both are very much bigger than in 1960. As international financial markets have grown from being largely an interbank market, the relative importance of deposits issued directly to non-banks has risen.

Only a few of the liability categories require special comment.

Government of Canada deposits are partly demand deposits that receive interest. Balances over about $1 billion are put into short-term term deposits. The interest rates on both demand and term deposits are determined by frequent auctions.

Other demand deposits include not only personal and business chequing accounts, but also deposits of other banks. Deposits of other banks are partly correspondent deposits of foreign banks and partly interbank deposits of Canadian banks.

---

[8] Government of Canada deposits are partly demand deposits. Foreign currency deposits are almost all term deposits.

TABLE 11–3: Chartered banks' liabilities and equity

	April 1991 (percent)	September 1982 (percent)	December 1960 (percent)
Canadian-dollar liabilities			
Government of Canada deposits	0.4	0.5	3.0
Other demand deposits			
personal chequing	1.0	1.0	26.4
non-personal (business)	2.7	3.6	
Personal savings deposits			
chequable notice deposits	5.5	1.8	42.6
non-chequable notice deposits	12.8	12.9	0
fixed term deposits	16.3	12.6	0
Total personal deposits	38.7	27.3	42.6
Non-personal deposits			
notice	3.8	1.3	3.4
fixed term	7.1	12.7	
Bank of Canada advances	0.1	0	0
Debentures	0.8	0.7	0
Other Canadian-dollar liabilities	3.9	2.0	0.5
Total Canadian-dollar liabilities	54.4	49.1	74.9
Acceptance liabilities	7.0	3.6	1.5
Foreign currency liabilities			
Deposits held by banks	10.6	23.1	3.8
Deposits held by others	18.5	17.4	4.0
Other liabilities	4.1	3.1	7.8
Total foreign currency liabilities	33.3	43.7	15.6
Total liabilities	94.7	96.3	94.1
Shareholders' equity	5.3	3.6	5.9
Total liabilities and equity	100.0	100.0	100.0

Notes: Total liabilities and equity is $610 billion for April 1991.

Source: Bank of Canada Review, Tables C4 and C11.

Correspondent deposits are used by foreign banks to help their customers make payments in Canada. [9] Interbank deposits are a means of borrowing and lending domestic cash reserves.

---

[9] The Royal Bank and the Westdeutsche Landesbank, for instance, hold correspondent deposits in each other so that each can write bank drafts in the other's currency. Such bank drafts are widely used as a means of international payments by firms and individuals.

Personal savings deposits were available in only the one form until after the 1967 Bank Act revision: low-yield, chequable notice deposits. Now there are many different forms, some tailored to meet the needs of special groups like seniors. Many of the personal fixed-term deposits are held in Registered Retirement Savings Plans (RRSPs), a form of tax-sheltered arrangement whose tax provisions limit depositors' ability to switch funds between assets.

Bank of Canada advances are loans to provide banks with extra cash reserves to meet the cash reserve requirement. In 1985–88 much of this item represented longer-term, lender-of-last-resort financing of the smaller banks that were failing in those years. What is now remarkable about Bank of Canada advances is that the balance, though small, is consistently positive. Banks are now making fairly routine use of Bank of Canada advances for cash reserve management. Before 1980 such advances were rarely used.

Debentures are limited under the Bank Act, as discussed in section 2. Debentures are a subordinated form of debt, which means that in event of bankruptcy they are paid off only after deposits. Debentures qualify as supplementary capital for purposes of meeting capital adequacy guidelines under the Basle Agreement. Debentures must have a term to maturity of at least five years at the time of issue, but the passage of time can make them just as short-term as term deposits.

Foreign currency deposits are almost all fixed-term wholesale deposits. The others represent the small retail business that a few Canadian banks have in the Caribbean and Latin America.

Shareholders' equity consists of amounts raised by share issues (of common or preferred shares), plus all retained earnings since the bank began operation, plus any general contingency reserve that is not set up against specific, anticipated loan losses. [10]

Types of transmutation

Section 2 of Chapter 10 listed the ways in which intermediaries can make their liabilities more attractive than their assets to lenders, in order to generate a positive interest spread. The process is known as transmutation of assets. Here we identify the main kinds of transmutation of assets used by chartered banks.

In their foreign currency business, banks issue fixed-term deposits that are more marketable than their international loans. Banks' foreign currency deposits have lower credit risk, shorter terms, and more standardized wholesale amounts than their foreign currency loans. The differences are slight for securitized loans of large, well-known international firms, but the differences are huge for loans to

---

[10] Reserves set up against *specific* loans are regarded as expected loan losses; they are properly deducted from the book value of loans on the asset side of the balance sheet. *General* provisions for loan losses do not usually reflect expected loan losses, but merely act as a prudent cushion in case extra losses do occur. Such a cushion belongs in equity.

Market Prices for Developing Country Debt, September 1989
(percent of face value)

Argentina	17	Peru	6
Brazil	31	Philippines	50
Chile	65	Poland	38
Colombia	68	Venezuela	42
Ecuador	16	Yugoslavia	42
Mexico	43		

Source: Shearson Lehman Hutton, Inc.

Third World governments. As evidence of the credit risk of Third World loans, the box above shows how expected default losses have depressed market prices of bank loans to a few Third World countries.

The banks' lending business both in Canada and abroad relies heavily on buying assets with significant credit risk, and issuing deposits that are expected to have almost none. Some of the credit risk is systematic and therefore would matter even to diversified investors. The credit risk of domestic retail deposits is effectively eliminated by deposit insurance on the first $60 000 of any deposit.

Banks have engineered a huge difference in liquidity between their domestic deposits and their domestic loan assets. Demand deposits are of course fully liquid. Notice deposits have been made almost as liquid by banks' waiving of the notice requirement. That waiver is not explicit, but all Canadians take it for granted. Finally, almost all term deposits issued directly by chartered banks (but not those issued by their mortgage loan subsidiaries) are redeemable before maturity at some interest penalty; only deposits in the banks' mortgage loan subsidiaries are locked in to maturity.

The loan assets financed by the banks' liquid deposits, in contrast, are left very illiquid indeed. The standard business demand loan, made under a line of credit arrangement, will not be called by the bank unless the customer is just hours from bankruptcy. Under all other circumstances the bank will be repaid when the borrower chooses. Indeed, the borrower is free to *increase* the loan amount rather than repay it if there is still room in the borrower's line of credit. Many personal loans are now made under similar arrangements.[11]

Domestic bank loans and mortgages are arranged with payment patterns to suit borrowers' income streams. Demand loans are the best example: each borrower can repay at whatever time best fits his or her income stream. Mortgage loans are also adjusted to suit borrowers, in that the blended payments of principal and interest are kept level over the term of the loan. Level payments do not suit everyone, but they do suit those earning fairly regular salaries.

---

[11] Including the one to buy the computer used to prepare this book.

TABLE 11–4: Interest rate spreads of the Toronto Dominion Bank, 1990 (percent)

1. Foreign currency loans		10.58
Foreign currency term deposits		9.67
Spread	0.91	
2. Personal loans and residential mortgages		12.46
Domestic savings deposits		9.58
Spread	2.88	
3. Other domestic loans		12.98
Domestic term deposits		10.24
Spread	2.74	

Source: Toronto Dominion Bank, *135th Annual Report, 1990* (Toronto: Toronto Dominion Bank, 1990).

Banks make fairly little use of cross-currency intermediation. Almost all of their foreign currency assets are matched with foreign currency deposits.

Banks buy loan assets in large amounts to suit large corporate borrowers, and issue deposits in relatively small amounts to suit household lenders. Even the biggest wholesale deposits are not nearly as big as the biggest loans.

The effect of transmutation of assets is to generate and widen a spread between asset yields and deposit costs. Table 11–4 shows the **interest rate spreads** reported by one of the more successful banks, the Toronto Dominion Bank.

As might be expected from the different types of transmutation used, the margin for foreign currency banking is very much smaller than for domestic business. Banks have arranged much smaller differences between their foreign currency assets and foreign currency deposits, so depositors will not accept a much smaller yield on foreign currency deposits.

Bank income and expenses

Bank profit reflects the spreads that banks have been able to generate through transmutation of assets, the costs they incur to monitor assets and service deposits, and any other income they are able to generate. The income from fees for performing financial services, for instance, now amounts to well over 1 percent of total assets.

One other source of income for banks is from what can be called **pure risk intermediation**. Increasingly through the 1980s banks took over risks for customers through forward-rate agreements, interest rate and currency swaps, and forward exchange agreements—the hedging instruments described in Chapter 6. Banks also absorb risk for others through guaranteeing bankers' acceptances, through issuing letters of credit, and occasionally through guarantees of preferred share issues or blocks of residential mortgage loans.

Of these types of pure risk intermediation, only guarantees of bankers' acceptances show up at all on bank balance sheets. However, all of a bank's pure risk absorption contributes to its income in fees and (possibly) trading profits.

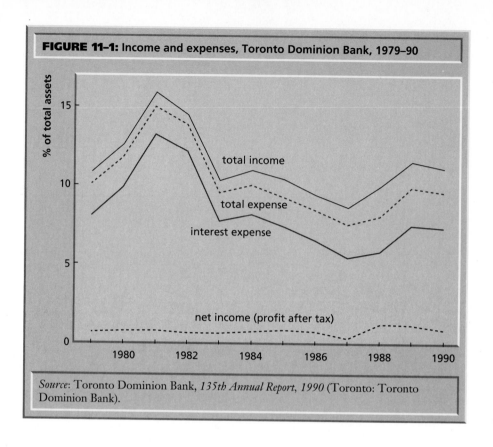

FIGURE 11–1: Income and expenses, Toronto Dominion Bank, 1979–90

Source: Toronto Dominion Bank, *135th Annual Report, 1990* (Toronto: Toronto Dominion Bank).

For the large banks this type of business is becoming important. For instance, at the end of its 1990 year, the Toronto Dominion Bank had commitments outstanding under interest rate and foreign exchange contracts (especially the latter) whose notional principal value was over three times as large as the bank's total reported assets.

Figure 11–1 shows the "bottom line" for bank intermediation. Since the variation in profit is as much of interest as the level of profit, Figure 11–1 shows the profit for an individual bank rather than a combined (and therefore smoothed) total for all banks. The amounts in Figure 11–1 have been expressed as percentages of total assets so that they can be more easily related to the logic of intermediation presented in Figure 10–1.

The after-tax net income or profit margin looks small relative to total assets, but relative to equity it is much healthier. For instance, the 1990 profit margin of 0.89 percent of assets translates into a yield on common shareholders' equity 14.2 times as big, since the leverage ratio for the Toronto Dominion Bank was 14.2 in 1990. That gives 12.6 percent on equity after tax. In 1987, when a large loan loss expense was charged against Third World loans, the profit was only 0.27 percent on assets and 4.4 percent on equity. That is the down side of leverage.

SECTION 4

Management of banking risks

The previous section has explained the asset transmutations used by banks to get a positive *expected* interest spread. That is not the end of the story, however. Banks must also manage their assets and liabilities so that their *actual* interest spreads do not vary much around the expected level. As explained in Chapter 9, intermediaries with leverage ratios as large as 20 will have enormous volatility of equity yield if their interest spread is not kept stable. Deposit-taking intermediaries depend heavily on depositor confidence, which will be undermined if the firm suffers even a short string of large losses, so banks cannot afford to have volatile interest spreads even if the expected spread is large.

This section explains banks' efforts to reduce credit risk and liquidity risk, and to use matching and hedging strategies to offset much of the credit and liquidity risk that remains. It also explains the new rules that bank regulators use for minimum equity capital, to see that any remaining risk is borne mainly by shareholders rather than depositors.

Credit risk

A bank's yield on any one loan can vary all the way down to -100 percent if the borrower defaults. If even a few large loans default together, a bank's equity can be seriously impaired. Once this becomes common knowledge, depositor confidence is undermined and bankruptcy may well follow. The Canadian Commercial Bank folded in 1985 for just this reason; a short time later Northland Bank followed. Both had large amounts of loans in western Canada that suffered heavily when the energy sector slumped in the early 1980s.

Credit or **default risk** can be systematic and unsystematic. Unsystematic default risk can be diversified away, whereas systematic default risk cannot. Most unsystematic default risk reflects features of individual borrowers: their background, competence, drive, morals and business sense. Some unsystematic risk reflects factors peculiar to an individual product or sector.

Banks attempt to stabilize unsystematic default losses on loans by diversifying across thousands of different borrowers, in dozens of different sectors and even in dozens of different countries. In this the big chartered banks have the advantage of being spread over almost all of Canada and into international markets. The smaller chartered banks that folded or merged in 1985–88 were restricted to particular regions, and poorly diversified regions at that. Figure 11–2 shows loan loss rates by region for the Royal Bank, Canada's largest bank, for 1984–90. It is clear from Figure 11–2 that any bank restricted to Alberta, or even to the three western provinces, would have had great difficulty in the period 1984–87 even if it had tried hard to be prudent.

Note, however, that bankruptcy does not follow automatically for large banks. It is appropriate to quote one of the banks' competitors on this point:

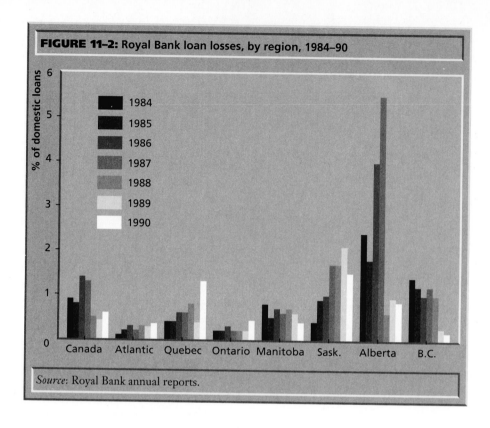

FIGURE 11–2: Royal Bank loan losses, by region, 1984–90

Source: Royal Bank annual reports.

But what about the larger banks? In 1982 they held less-developed country (LDC) loans equal to twice their capital at a time when the market value of their LDC debt was trading for less than 40 cents on the dollar. Our whole banking system was then insolvent. However, the government accommodated the banks by ignoring the market discrepancy until they worked themselves out of the difficult ... loans that caused them problems...[12]

In addition to diversifying to reduce the variability of loan default losses, prudent banks also attempt to reduce expected default losses by a variety of measures. The first is to screen applicants to weed out those who do not sound responsible, or who have little personal stake in the project being financed. The second is to monitor the affairs of loan customers in order to recognize trouble before it becomes a crisis, and then to arrange for help in the early stages. For personal loans, banks attempt to protect themselves by such means as taking out life insurance on consumer borrowers for the amount borrowed, or insisting on collateral. Small business loans are often protected by adding personal guarantees of owners.

---

[12] H.N.R. Jackman, *The Financial Post*, 18 June 1990, p.8.

Credit Ratings of Senior Debt of Top U.S. Banks		
	1982	1990
AAA	4	1
AA+	4	1
AA		2
AA–	1	1
A		3
A–		1
BBB+		1
BBB		1

Source: Standard & Poor.

Systematic risk cannot be diversified away. We have already noted that in the 1980s the world became more integrated, which means that its economies had more disturbances in common than before. For banks, this has meant that sectoral and international diversification is less effective than before in reducing default risks. The banks' collective nightmare with Third World debts is an example that they will be slow to forget. Even banks spread over many less developed countries' debts were no further ahead: all non-oil primary producing countries ran into the same difficulties following massive oil price increases in 1974 and 1979, and all developing countries alike ran afoul of the developed countries' recession of 1981–82. As late as 1989 the big domestic banks were still using over half their profits to get their loan loss reserves on Third World debts up to the 35–45 percent range required by the Superintendent of Financial Institutions.[13] The decline in U.S. banks' credit ratings, shown in the box above, suggests that the top U.S. banks did no better than those in Canada.

The Third World debt fiasco, the massive bankruptcy of savings and loan institutions in the United States after equally massive overinvestment in real estate development, and current high levels of lending exposure to large firms for highly leveraged takeover bids suggests that bank lending is subject to swings of imprudent euphoria just like speculation in the stock market. Why? One perceptive journalist explained, in discussing U.S. banks' exposure to highly leveraged takeover loans, "for the same reasons that drive every credit boom: high interest margins, lavish transaction fees and the 'security' of asset backing." He noted about the latest wave of bank lending, for highly leveraged takeover bids: "Bank lending to highly leveraged transactions may well seem

---

[13] *Annual Report* of the Superintendent of Financial Institutions for 1989, p. 11. Actual reserves were 43 percent on loans from a group of 38 designated less-developed countries in financial trouble. These loans still amounted to 56 percent of total bank equity.

adequately secured, but so did their lending to supertanker fleets, Texas real estate developers, and Third World governments."[14]

Liquidity risk

There are two sources of **liquidity risk**: large withdrawals or redemptions of deposits, and large drawdowns of lines of credit by borrowers. Recall from the discussion of bank deposit expansion in Chapter 10 that new bank lending causes the lending bank to lose cash reserves as soon as loan proceeds have been spent and the cheques have cleared. If either large withdrawals or large loan drawdowns occur, a bank would need access to large amounts of cash reserve assets.

Banks protect themselves against liquidity risk in two ways. First, they reduce the chances of large withdrawals and large loan drawdowns, and then they arrange access to large amounts of cash reserves in case extra liquidity is needed.

Diversifying sources of funds and loans greatly reduces the chances that many deposits will be withdrawn and many lines of credit drawn down all at the same time. Unsystematic fluctuations in deposit withdrawals and in loan drawdowns are largely cancelled out by diversification. What is left is either the predictable systematic fluctuations such as extra cash needs around Christmas, or unpredictable fluctuations caused by common factors such as higher yields offered by competitors. Such systematic fluctuations are not cancelled out by diversification.

One large systematic liquidity risk is removed for banks by the Bank of Canada. Each fall the federal government issues billions of dollars of Canada Savings Bonds by announcing a rate well in advance and then waiting to see how much demand there is. Most of this demand comes at the expense of term deposits, usually those in banks. A huge withdrawal from banks would occur each fall if the Bank of Canada did not compensate by shifting the federal government's deposit balances in the opposite direction.[15]

Some reserve shortages do occur, however, even though banks diversify deposits and loans. To meet these reserve shortages, banks hold stocks of liquid assets. Banks do not hold excess cash reserves in any significant amount, since excess cash reserves earn no interest. They do hold excess secondary reserves (that is, day loans and treasury bills) and special call loans, all of which can be called or sold to add cash reserves quickly. Federal government bonds are nearly as liquid. On the liability side, banks can raise their term deposit rates and attract wholesale term deposits to replace deposits withdrawn. Reserves can be borrowed with an interbank deposit if another bank has excess cash reserves to lend.[16] If

---

[14] Anatole Kaletsky, *The Financial Post*, 25 September 1989, p.4.

[15] The deposit funds are auctioned among clearing members of the Canadian Payments Association (CPA). Other institutions therefore do not benefit even though they lose deposit business to Canada Savings Bonds.

[16] In the U.S. and the U.K. there are well-developed markets for overnight borrowing and lending of excess cash reserve assets, which solve the liquidity risk problem for many

all else fails, banks can automatically borrow from the Bank of Canada. Advances from the Bank of Canada bear the Bank Rate, 25 basis points above the treasury bill yield.

Matching asset and debt yield fluctuations

Diversification cannot cancel out systematic risk in asset yields, nor systematic fluctuations in deposit withdrawals and in loan drawdowns. Banks are stuck with them; all banks can do is try to prevent such fluctuations from endangering their interest spreads. For instance, the Toronto Dominion Bank's net income, shown as the bottom curve in Figure 11–1, can be held stable even if asset yields fluctuate wildly, as long as the bank's debt costs vary in step with asset yields. Figure 11–1 shows that, by and large, that is what has happened.

In thinking about **matching asset and debt yields**, banks differentiate between floating-rate instruments and fixed-rate instruments. Floating-rate assets and debts have yields that are tied to some benchmark rate: for domestic floating-rate loans it is the prime rate; for both international loans and deposits it is usually the London interbank offer rate (LIBOR). When the benchmark yield moves up and down with market forces, so do yields on all new *and existing* floating-rate assets tied to it. The yields of fixed-rate assets and debts are fixed for some period at time of issue — either for the whole period to maturity or for some lesser period at the end of which the rate will be renegotiated. Existing fixed-rate assets can therefore change their yields in response to market forces only after enough time has passed to bring around maturity or the renegotiation date for that asset.

Banks interested in matching fluctuations in asset and debt yields must match floating-rate assets with floating-rate debts. They must match fixed-rate assets with fixed-rate debts having the same fixed-rate period. For example, most business loans and notice deposits have floating rates. Yields on foreign currency loans and foreign currency term deposits are generally both tied to LIBOR. One-year mortgage loans and one-year term deposits both have fixed yields that are adjusted equally slowly to new market yields (they are said to be equally rate-sensitive). By contrast, financing business loans with personal term deposits is financing a floating-rate asset with a fixed-rate liability; this is not matching asset yield patterns with similar debt yield patterns. Nor is the investment pattern reported in the box for Japanese banks, which had been borrowing short-term to lend long-term in the belief that there was a reliable positive spread to be made from that kind of intermediation.

Table 11–5 shows what interest rate matching the Toronto Dominion Bank was able to report to its shareholders for 1990. Matching was not exact, but it was fairly close. Certainly it is now much closer than any bank arranged in the 1960s when Canadian banks were more narrowly focused on commercial banking.

---

banks. This is called the federal funds market in the U.S. Settlement is the same day in the federal funds market, whereas it is only the next day for Canadian interbank deposits.

Another means Canadian banks have used to improve their matching of interest rate adjustments is to shift business away from the banks proper and into mortgage loan subsidiaries. Bank term deposits are generally redeemable before maturity with an interest penalty, so the banks cannot be sure of an interest rate match when they finance a five-year mortgage loan with a five-year deposit. If rates on new deposits and mortgages were to rise considerably, the deposit would be redeemed despite the interest penalty and rolled over to a higher rate. The mortgage borrower would continue to pay at the old rate. The bank would be stuck for the remaining term of the mortgage with a spread too small to cover costs, and possibly even a negative spread. Better to rely instead on the non-withdrawable deposits issued by their mortgage loan company subsidiaries. Mortgage loan company deposit rates have to be a little higher than bank deposit rates because of the lower liquidity, but the smaller expected spread is accompanied by much less risk. Banks find the reduced risk exposure more than sufficient compensation.[17]

There still remains some degree of mismatching, which becomes visible when yields rise and fall. When prevailing interest rates rise, all business and personal demand loan rates rise immediately. Notice deposit yields rise, but not all the term deposit yields. Term deposit yields rise only as each deposit reaches maturity. For a while, therefore, the banks' yield spread widens. On a downturn, exactly the opposite happens, and bank yield spreads are squeezed. The squeeze can be prolonged if the public speculates on future interest rate changes by taking out only short-term deposits when they expect yields to rise, and only long-term deposits

---

FINANCE

Japanese interest rates

Topsy turvy

TOKYO

THE good old days in Japan, when bankers could still borrow short and lend long, have vanished and are unlikely to return for some time. Last May, with inflation on the prowl again, the Bank of Japan brought its nine-year spell of easy money to an abrupt and inconsiderate end by raising Japan's discount rate to 3¼%, from a postwar low of 2½%. It then raised the rate again in October, to 3¾%. Tight money has inverted Japan's yield curve, pushing short-term rates above those on long-term government bonds. The damaging effect on Japanese banks is already beginning to show. The central bank is becoming quite twitchy about it.

Japanese banks raise their cash by issuing money-market instruments—such as call money, discount bills and *gensaki* bonds (bonds sold with a repurchase agreement). In recent years they have made a nice turn by investing the cash in the long-term market. A yield curve that stayed inverted for more than a couple of quarters could wreak havoc on banks' profitability.

Early signs, in the form of banks' results for the six months to September, have confirmed this. The profitability of Japan's 13 national commercial banks slipped by more than 6% over this period. Analysts estimate that the banks' underlying operating profits could be down by 25-30% for the whole financial year.

Source: The Economist, December 16, 1989, p. 80. © 1989, The Economist Newspaper Ltd. Reprinted with permission.

---

[17] As another step to improve the matching of mortgage yields and term deposit costs, many of the banks have recently made their mortgage loans closed — not repayable even with an interest penalty — for a larger portion of the loan period (such as four years for a five-year mortgage).

TABLE 11–5: Interest rate sensitivity of Toronto Dominion Bank at year end 1989 and 1990 (percent of total assets)

	Net exposure (assets − liabilities)	
	1989	1990
Floating-rate and less than 1 month	−3.49	−6.91
1–3 months	−0.20	5.26
3–12 months	3.98	2.18
over 1 year	10.11	8.22
Non-interest-sensitive		−8.76

Source: Toronto Dominion Bank, *Annual Reports, 1989 and 1990* (Toronto: Toronto Dominion Bank).

when they expect yields to fall. Figure 11–3, from the 1981 annual report of the Royal Bank to its shareholders, illustrates the effect of interest rate changes on bank margins. The Royal's spread widened as the general level of yields rose and temporarily disappeared while yields were falling.

Matching currencies

Banks could endanger their interest spreads quite easily if their assets were denominated in a different currency than their liabilities. Tables 11–2 and 11–3 show foreign currency assets of Canadian chartered banks in 1991 to be 31.6 percent of total assets, while foreign currency debts were 33.3 percent. Net foreign currency liabilities were only 1.7 percent of total assets. Within foreign currencies also there was fairly close matching.

Nevertheless, the mismatching that remains is still big enough to do damage. A 10 percent appreciation of foreign currency would raise net foreign currency liabilities and lower equity by 0.17 percent of total assets; a glance at the profit margins of the Toronto Dominion Bank in Figure 11–1 shows that this would have a large impact on profits. Currency matching is not as close as it could be.

Hedging

Some risks that have not been diversified away or matched can be eliminated by **hedging**. These are risks generated by changes in interest rates, exchange rates, and stock market prices. Financial hedges have sprung up to protect against all of these. Banks can easily protect themselves against foreign exchange risk exposure on their net foreign currency liability of $9684 million by entering foreign exchange contracts to buy those same currencies forward at the maturity dates of their deposit liabilities. Most banks have done so.

Similarly, banks can hedge any difference in timing of yield changes between their assets and their liabilities by using forward-rate agreements or interest rate swaps, or any variant of interest rate options. Banks do a large volume of hedging

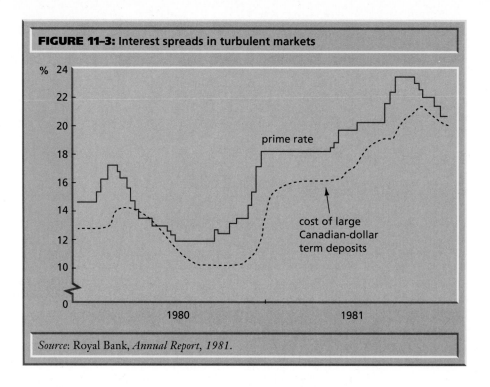

FIGURE 11–3: Interest spreads in turbulent markets

Source: Royal Bank, *Annual Report, 1981.*

business for clients (for fees) as an intermediary between offsetting contracting parties; it is therefore easy for banks to undertake some of that business to hedge their own portfolios as well. To provide an example of the scale of bank hedging activity, Table 11–6 reports the Toronto Dominion Bank's activity in hedging markets for 1990. Total balance sheet assets are shown for comparison. The total of off-balance-sheet commitments is now enormous. Forward contracts alone are for amounts twice as large as total bank assets.

Capital adequacy

Even with diversification, matching, and hedging, banks cannot avoid all risk. Bank leverage is such that any remaining risks are likely to have dramatic effects on equity yield. The larger risks can cause bankruptcy.

It is not just the shareholders of a bank who bear this risk. If loan losses exceed equity values, the whole bank folds and depositors may lose some of their interest and principal. The failure of a large bank would also reduce public confidence in the entire financial system. Such confidence is fundamental to any sensible planning of lifetime consumption plans by households. Regulators therefore interfere in the normal conduct of banking to reduce the chances of bankruptcy still further than shareholders themselves might prefer. They do so through regulations on **capital adequacy**.

TABLE 11–6: Off-balance-sheet commitments of Toronto Dominion Bank, 1990 ($ million)

Commitments to extend credit (including acceptances)	43 007
Note issuance facilities or revolving underwriting agreements	803
Financial futures and future rate agreements	20 727
Forward contracts	136 688
Interest and currency options	12 728
Interest and currency swaps	46 347
Total off-balance-sheet commitments	260 300
Total balance sheet assets	66 900

Source: Toronto Dominion Bank, *135th Annual Report, 1990* (Toronto: Toronto Dominion Bank).

Banks in Canada are subject to new guidelines for capital adequacy starting in 1992. These guidelines have been drawn up by the Bank for International Settlements and adopted by the Canadian Superintendent of Financial Institutions in what is called the Basle Agreement. Core equity capital will have to be at least 4 percent of risk-adjusted assets. Core plus supplementary capital will have to reach at least 8 percent of risk-adjusted assets. Core capital is basically shareholders' equity excluding preferred shares. Supplementary capital is core capital plus preferred shares, debentures, and general reserves against losses. Risk-adjusted assets is a total of assets and off-balance-sheet commitments, weighted to reflect relative default risks.[18] By late 1991, Canadian banks had already met the 4 percent core capital standard, and had almost met the 8 percent supplementary standard. Table 11–3 has shown that banks significantly increased their equity–capital ratio between 1982 and 1991, from 3.6 percent to 5.3 percent (partly because of prodding by bank regulators).

SECTION 5

Summary

Banking can be defined in several ways. Commercial banking, merchant banking, and investment banking each refer to a different type of intermediation, distinguished by the kind of assets bought and the kind of financial services rendered. Chartered banking is the term most commonly used because it offers a clear definition of banks: all those with legal charters to call themselves banks.

---

[18] For instance, government bonds and guaranteed loans have a weight of zero. Unsecured loans count in full. Mortgage loans have a weight of 50 percent. Securities have weights of 10 or 20 percent, or sometimes 50 percent. For further details, see Peter Martin, *Inside the Bank of Canada's Weekly Financial Statement* (Vancouver: Fraser Institute, 1989), pp.108–9.

Chartered banks engage in a wide variety of types of intermediation, almost all of which are also engaged in to some extent by non-banks. Bank charters convey some specific restrictions, but few specific, exclusive rights.

Bank assets are dominated by loans. Bank liabilities are dominated by term deposits. Demand deposits make up only a small share of the total. Foreign currency assets are large but are declining as a share of total business.

Banks use several different kinds of transmutation of assets to generate their positive interest spread. Within Canada the banks arrange for deposits to be more liquid, more convenient, and mostly risk-free; the banks buy loans with high risk, low liquidity and unpredictable repayment terms. Domestic spreads are wide. Banks also increase their spread by providing a wide range of financial services.

Chartered banks keep their interest spreads relatively stable by managing risks in several ways. Default risk differences between bank assets and liabilities are managed mainly through diversification across individuals, sectors, regions, and even countries. Much systematic risk remains, however.

Liquidity risk from deposit withdrawals and line of credit drawdowns are managed by diversifying across thousands of customers and sectors, by keeping reserves of liquid assets to be sold off, and by borrowing from the Bank of Canada if necessary.

The remaining risks to shareholders from asset yield fluctuations are neutralized in part by matching assets with deposits whose yields fluctuate in the same pattern. Asset yield variations that cannot be matched in this way can sometimes be hedged with forward-rate agreements or interest rate swaps. What remains after that must be borne by shareholders.

Key Terms

commercial banking	pure risk intermediation
merchant banking	credit or default risk
investment banking	liquidity risk
chartered banking	matching asset and debt yields
bank charter	matching currencies
schedule I and II bank charters	hedging
interest rate spreads	capital adequacy

Questions and Problems

1. Is chartered banking likely to be a useful conception of "banking" by the year 2000? Why or why not?

2. Which types of asset transmutation do the banks rely on most in their banking business?

3. Why has diversification of bank lending business across millions of borrowers (some in other countries) not succeeded in completely stabilizing loan loss rates?

4. What is the significance of lines of credit for bank asset management?

5. Why are banks unable to change their average asset yield at the same rate as their average deposit cost? Does this lag serve to increase bank profits when interest rates are rising, or when they are falling?

6. What is the significance of tying foreign currency loan rates to LIBOR?

7. Will an increase in cash reserves (caused by monetary policy) always lead to the same pattern of changes in bank loan rates and deposit rates? Explain.

8. Where can banks get extra cash reserve assets?

Suggestions for Further Reading

Binhammer, H.H. *Money, Banking and the Canadian Financial System*, 5th ed. Toronto: Methuen, 1988.

Martin, Peter. *Inside the Bank of Canada's Weekly Financial Statistics: A Technical Guide*. Vancouver: Fraser Institute, 1989.

Neufeld, E.P. *The Financial System of Canada*. Toronto: Macmillan, 1972.

Superintendent of Financial Institutions. *Annual Report*. Ottawa: Supply and Services.

Chapter twelve

Near-Bank Deposit-Takers

This chapter explains intermediation by near banks. Near banks compete with banks in deposit markets and in household lending. The near-bank groups are credit unions and their francophone counterparts, the caisses populaires, trust companies, mortgage loan companies, and two provincial government savings institutions. Finance companies used to be classed as near banks because of the competition that they offered in consumer loan markets, but they have been squeezed out of most of the market and have turned more to business financing. Since finance companies have never issued deposits, they are dealt with separately in Chapter 13.

Section 1 describes the legal structure within which near banks operate. Section 2 describes the intermediation activities of near banks and explains how each earns its positive spread. Finally, section 3 looks at how near banks manage the various risks of near-bank intermediation.

You should learn in this chapter:

1. the legal background of each type of near bank;
2. the kinds of assets and liabilities used by near banks;
3. the kinds of risk problem experienced by near banks;
4. how near-bank risks are handled.

SECTION 1

▣ The legal structure of near banks

Near banks are governed by a mosaic of federal and provincial laws that provide rights and obligations. In this section we will concentrate on those parts of the mosaic that distinguish each type of near bank from other types and from banks. The issue of whether the mosaic of laws governing near banks is appropriate for them or for the financial system as a whole is dealt with more thoroughly in Chapter 15. We start with credit unions and caisses populaires, and then discuss trust companies, mortgage loan companies, and provincial savings institutions.

Credit unions and caisses populaires

Credit unions and **caisses populaires** are provincial, co-operative savings and lending associations that are owned by their member depositors and borrowers. There are now some 4000 branches and offices (compared with about 7000 bank branches). Credit unions or caisses populaires (known as locals) were started in 1900 in Quebec by Alphonse Desjardins, whose name is still given to the Quebec movement. Most intermediation is done by locals. **Central credit unions** or **caisses centrales** (known as centrals) have been set up in each province by the locals to perform cheque clearing, inspection, and some central banking services for member locals. The Desjardins movement is so strong in Quebec that there are 11 centrals operating under the umbrella of the Desjardins Group. The Canadian Co-operative Credit Society (CCCS) serves as a national central for the provincial credit union centrals outside Quebec.[1] As an indicator of the strength of the caisse populaire movement in Quebec, over 70 percent of the population were members of a caisse in 1989.[2] Outside Quebec credit union membership averaged only 22 percent of the population, though proportions are much higher in western Canada. Credit unions and caisses populaires grew very rapidly in the 1970s but much less so in the 1980s; membership as a percentage of total population grew from 24.7 percent in 1970 to 40.1 percent in 1980, but fell back to only 34.6 percent in 1990.

Credit unions operate almost entirely within one province, and are therefore subject to only one set of provincial laws and regulations. Locals are limited in size by the nature of the organization, and by their objective: they are co-operatives owned by their members, and their objective is to enable members to manage their own financial affairs. In recent years there has been a shift toward more professional management, and many weak locals have merged with stronger ones, but credit unions and caisses are still small in scale. In 1988 the average credit union membership was only 3300 members. The only really large credit union, the Vancouver City Savings Credit Union, is almost three times larger than the next largest credit union in both membership and assets. Its total assets ($1.7 billion in 1988) were still less than 2 percent of the total assets of the Royal Bank.

Local credit unions and caisses get around some of the disadvantages of their small size by pooling resources in their centrals. The centrals have

---

[1] The CCCS and the Caisse Centrale Desjardins have become clearing members of the Canadian Payments Association, to clear cheques on behalf of their locals.

[2] Statistics Canada, *Credit Unions, Fourth Quarter 1990* (Ottawa: Supply and Services, 1990).

established their own trust company and insurance company subsidiaries, as well as automated teller networks. As a result of more permissive legislation, the Quebec caisses were the first financial institutions to pioneer the "financial shopping centre" concept by offering loans, deposits, trust services, brokerage services, and insurance products under the same roof.

There are few legal restrictions on the activities of credit unions and caisses (though Ontario does limit commercial lending in its credit unions to 15 percent of assets). As unrestricted, deposit-taking intermediaries, the credit unions are well described as "co-op banks."

Trust companies

There are about 100 federally and provincially chartered **trust companies** in Canada. Most business is done by the 30 federally registered firms; the most important provinces for trust company registration are Ontario and Quebec. Quebec's trust company legislation has been the most permissive since the mid-1980s, though the new federal Trust and Loan Companies Act, introduced to Parliament in late 1990, makes federal legislation almost as permissive.

Trust companies started in the 1880s as corporate trustees to manage others' money under provisions of estate, trust, and agency (ETA) business. Trust companies became financial intermediaries in the 1920s by starting to borrow in their own name, and as a group they now have $1 of their own debts and assets for every $2 of ETA funds. Corporate trustee business is now the only special privilege reserved to trust companies. Even that will effectively be opened up to other intermediaries when new federal legislation allows banks and loan companies and insurance companies to own trust company subsidiaries, as expected in 1991 or 1992. Most trust companies do only a small amount of ETA business. Many do their ETA business as transfer agents for corporations (to handle share registration and payment of corporate dividends or interest) and as custodians of securities for trust funds, pension funds, and mutual funds.

Federal legislation limits trust companies in a few ways. Assets of trust companies must not exceed 20 times equity capital. Each mortgage loan made by a trust company can only be for 75 percent or less of the value of the real estate being mortgaged. A modest limit on domestic ownership of trust companies is being introduced in the new federal act of late 1990: at least 35 percent of voting shares will have to be widely held, so concentrated ownership will be limited to 65 percent. Foreign ownership is restricted as for schedule I banks (to 25 percent in total, with no single owner having more than 10 percent), though U.S. residents are exempt from this provision under the Free Trade Agreement. A previous ban on insurance and a ceiling on holdings of unsecured loans are both to be removed. The new federal legislation will allow (federally registered) trust companies to own insurance companies, and to invest an unlimited amount of their assets in unsecured loans, but holdings of real estate and common shares will be limited to 70 percent of the trust company's equity for each or 100 percent for both combined (as for banks).

The proposed restrictions on ownership are the outcome of a decade during which almost all of the widely held trust companies acquired controlling shareholders; some of the controlling shareholders also have significant non-financial interests (for instance, Imasco, Power Corporation, the Edper Group, Bell Canada). This change has raised the issue of self-dealing (lending to oneself) and of conflict of interest in using depositors' funds. The temptation to self-dealing and to conflict of interest is to be reduced by the provision that at least 35 percent of shares be widely held for large trust companies (that is, those with more than $750 million of equity). Companies with that large a proportion of tradable shares must release financial information promptly to securities regulators, and are also likely to be monitored and reported on frequently by private security analysts. These mechanisms, it is hoped, will persuade majority owners of trust companies that any giving in to temptation will be detected quickly and punished by reactions of lenders and the stock market.

Mortgage loan companies

Mortgage loan companies originated as terminating (that is, self-liquidating) co-operative building societies, in which members pooled their savings so that each member in turn could borrow to build a house. These building societies flourished in the nineteenth century, at a time when there were few other sources of long-term funds. Now building societies are permanent rather than terminating, and privately owned rather than co-operative, and they are called mortgage loan companies.[3] There are 30 federally registered mortgage loan companies, as well as many provincially chartered companies. Their powers and restrictions are now and will be in the future almost the same as for trust companies, except they are not allowed to act as corporate trustees. No type of intermediation business is restricted exclusively to mortgage loan companies, though there was in the past.[4]

There is no ownership restriction for mortgage loan companies. Banks bought up or set up their own mortgage loan subsidiaries in the 1970s and 1980s, and by 1988, 90 percent of mortgage loan company assets were held by these large but "captive" firms. Many others are owned or controlled by other financial institutions such as trust companies, the Ontario Credit Union League, and groups of pension funds. The intermediation of the mortgage loan subsidiaries of banks has already been included in chartered bank intermediation in Chapter 11, since all bank data are presented on a consolidated basis. Since the mortgage loan companies not owned by banks are relatively unimportant, we will follow the Bank of Canada's lead and lump the accounts of these mortgage loan companies

---

[3] The name building society is still used in the United Kingdom, the birthplace of this type of financial institution.

[4] The right to issue debentures was important before 1914, because it gave the mortgage loan companies access to the important London capital market — access that other intermediaries did not have.

together with those of trust companies. Both types of firm conduct much the same kind of intermediation.

Provincial savings institutions

The **Alberta treasury branch** (ATB) system was set up in 1938 by the Alberta government, which still owns it. ATBs intermediate within Alberta just like a bank, but without being subject to federal Bank Act regulations. The ATB system keeps small reserve balances with the Bank of Canada, but only because it is a clearing member of the Canadian Payments Association. The ATB system is not large by the standards of nationwide banks, but it is a significant and vigorous competitor in the Alberta financial system.

The **Province of Ontario savings office system** (POSO) is a captive intermediary owned by and lending exclusively to the Ontario government. POSO issues deposits to the public, but all funds raised are loaned to the government so directly that POSO's deposits and withdrawals are paid into and taken out of the government's consolidated revenue account just like tax receipts and government expenditures. When POSO was set up in 1920, it loaned out its deposits to farmers, but now it lends only to the government of Ontario. POSO is a small and not very vigorous competitor in Ontario's deposit markets; its deposit totals match those of a single large credit union.

SECTION 2

▣ Near-bank intermediation

In this section the intermediation activities of the near banks are first compared with those of the chartered banks. The differences show up in comparison of their asset and liability proportions. Then the forms of asset transmutation are discussed, and finally the interest spreads and profit margins of the near banks.

Assets and liabilities

The forms of near-bank intermediation are reflected in the balance sheets of near-bank deposit-taking firms. These balance sheets are shown in Table 12–1 for credit unions and caisses populaires (both locals and centrals), and for trust companies and non-bank mortgage loan companies. For comparison, the balance sheet proportions of Canadian-dollar business of chartered banks are also included.

Several features of near-bank intermediation stand out in Table 12–1. First, the near banks do very little foreign currency business. The reason is that the federal government levies a 15 percent withholding tax on all interest paid on foreign currency deposits, except those issued by chartered banks. Credit unions might not want to get into foreign business anyway, but trust companies deal with

TABLE 12–1: Near-bank balance sheets, third quarter 1990

	Credit unions and caisses populares		Trust and non-bank mortgage loan companies	Chartered banks (C$ business only)
	Locals	Centrals		
Assets (% of total assets)				
Cash and chequing deposits	8.1	2.0	1.0	1.5
Term deposits	9.0	12.1	0.8	1.5
Money market assets				
treasury bills		12.0	4.7	4.4
other	0.5	30.4	0.7	0.9
Total liquid assets	17.6	56.6	7.2	8.3
Bonds				
federal	0.2	1.9	0.7	0.9
other government	0.3	0.6	0.5	0.4
corporate	0.6	2.4	1.1	1.0
Total bonds	1.4	5.0	2.3	2.3
Loans				
personal	16.0	0.0	6.1	19.5
business	11.5	10.3	4.4	28.8
locals		16.1		0.0
Total loans	28.1	29.7	10.8	48.8
Mortgages				
residential	43.2	0.9	53.5	31.5
non-residential	5.5	1.7	11.0	2.0
Total mortgages	48.7	2.6	64.4	33.6
Shares (including subsidiaries)	1.2	0.8	5.9	2.6
Other assets	3.0	5.3	9.5	4.5
Total assets	100.0	100.0	100.0	100.0
($ million)	$71 161	$17 908	$128 053	$309 228
Liabilities and Equity				
Deposits				
chequable	14.2	48.8	8.7	17.2
other notice	22.3	0.0	12.1	31.5
term	50.0	41.0	68.3	35.0
Total deposits	86.6	89.8	89.1	83.7
Loans and notes	3.4	2.7	3.8	0.0
Other liabilities	3.8	2.4	2.0	10.7
Total liabilities	93.8	95.0	94.9	94.4
Shareholders' equity	6.2	5.0	5.1	

Notes: Bank data exclude banks' acceptance business, which appears in Table 11–2. Shareholders' equity of banks cannot be separated into domestic and foreign currency parts. Trust company data exclude ETA business.

Sources: Statistics Canada, *Financial Institutions*; Bank of Canada Review.

increasingly sophisticated households and would certainly want to. The trustee business of trust companies already involves them in foreign markets extensively.

Second, the credit union centrals are clearly a special case. Centrals have been established to serve as a form of central bank for local credit unions. Deposits in centrals are the main source of liquidity for locals (note that locals do not hold money market assets). Since locals are quite likely to have systematic as well as unsystematic fluctuations in net withdrawals, the centrals must remain very liquid. Table 12–1 shows that centrals are indeed much more liquid than banks. Surprisingly, locals are also more liquid than banks; the first three most liquid asset categories account for 17 percent of locals' assets, compared with only 7 percent for the Canadian-dollar business of chartered banks.

Third, credit union locals and trust companies do less chequing account and more term deposit business than chartered banks. Almost one-quarter of the trust company deposits are tax shelter deposits (held in registered retirement savings plans and the like); the regulations governing tax shelters have the two effects of raising after-tax yields and of lowering liquidity for depositors. Trust company retail deposits are insured by the Canada Deposit Insurance Corporation, as are bank deposits. Credit union deposits are insured instead by provincial stabilization funds set up by the credit unions themselves; the stabilization funds have varying amounts of backing from provincial governments.

The main lending business of credit unions and trust companies is to lend to households in the form of mortgage loans. The credit unions do a significant amount of unsecured lending in consumer and small business loans. The credit union centrals also do some business lending (mainly to other co-ops) with deposit funds raised from locals. Trust companies have done almost no unsecured lending in the past. Almost all of the loans shown for trust companies in Table 12–1 are secured loans with securities as collateral. The new financial legislation introduced in 1991 will allow trust and mortgage loan companies to do as much unsecured consumer lending as they like, and all but the smaller firms will also be unlimited in commercial lending. So far, however, few trust companies have used much of even the limited powers they now have to make unsecured loans.

Finally, both credit unions and trust companies operate with close to the same leverage as chartered banks.

Types of transmutation of assets

Both credit unions and trust companies rely mainly on differences in default risk between their assets and liabilities. Mortgage loans and the credit unions' unsecured loans have much higher credit risk than the notice and term deposits issued by near banks. Only one-quarter of the mortgage loans made by trust companies are insured against default by the Canada Mortgage and Housing Corporation, and almost none of those made by credit unions.

There is a difference in the marketability of assets and liabilities of trust companies, but in the wrong direction for generating positive spreads. Trust companies hold about 10 percent of their assets in bonds and shares that can be resold on secondary markets. Trust company mortgage loans can also be resold on the secondary mortgage market, in the slightly transmuted form of mortgage-backed securities. Trust company term deposit liabilities, on the other hand, can not be resold and are not redeemable before maturity.

Credit unions and trust companies rely on large differences in liquidity in their unsecured lending business. Chequing and notice deposits are very liquid; unsecured loans are not liquid at all. For the more important mortgage lending business, however, there is very little difference in liquidity between assets bought and liabilities issued. Mortgage loans can be repaid before maturity at credit unions (they are called "open" mortgages), but generally not at trust companies. Term deposits are generally not redeemable before maturity. For mortgage lending financed by term deposits, therefore, the near banks are financing an illiquid asset with an illiquid liability. There is not much transmutation of liquidity to generate a positive spread.

Credit unions and trust companies take advantage of different terms to maturity for assets and liabilities when they use notice deposits to finance loans; the notice deposits have much shorter terms than the loans. In the rest of their business, demand deposits are more or less matched with liquid assets and term deposits with mortgages of the same term to maturity.

Both trust companies and credit unions provide extra services for fee income. Trust companies provide services as corporate trustees in handling estates, trusts, and agency business. Several trust companies have real estate subsidiaries that earn important real estate sales commissions. Both trust companies and credit unions provide standard depositor services in their retail branches (money orders and the like). Credit union centrals perform a wide variety of financial services for local credit unions, from auditing to management consulting. Credit unions (locals and centrals) provide members with a range of social benefits and financial management training experience; they could generally be run more efficiently with specialized employees, but it is part of their objective to involve unspecialized, unpaid members in managing the credit unions' affairs.

Spreads and profit margins

Table 12–2 shows the **interest spreads**, fee income, costs, and profits for the near banks, compared with those of the chartered banks. Interest spreads reflect the extent of transmutation of assets: local credit unions have wide interest spreads, while those of central credit unions are narrow. Trust companies, whose loans are almost all secured, have smaller spreads than local credit unions and schedule I banks, whose loans are often unsecured. Trust company spreads are also somewhat narrower than the spread of 2.74 percent reported for the Toronto Dominion Bank between domestic loans and term deposits (see Table 11–4). Trust companies make up for their relatively smaller spreads by the large fee income earned from trustee services, real estate commissions, and depositor services. Credit union centrals earn large fee income from services provided to locals; locals have tiny net fee income because of what they pay to centrals.

TABLE 12–2: Spreads and profit margins, third quarter 1990
(percent of total assets, at annual rates)

	Credit unions		Trust and non-bank mortgage loan companies	Chartered banks	
	Locals	Centrals		Schedule I	Schedule II
Interest income	12.2	12.0	11.5	9.7	6.9
less					
Interest expense	8.6	11.0	9.9	7.1	6.4
equals					
Interest spread:	3.6	1.0	1.6	2.6	0.5
that plus					
Net fee income	−0.0	1.7	1.0	1.0	0.7
equals					
Gross spread:	3.6	2.7	2.6	3.7	1.2
that less					
Expenses					
Salaries	1.5	1.1	1.1	1.6	0.5
Other expenses	1.0	1.1	1.1	1.1	0.2
Taxes	0.1	0.1	0.1	0.3	0.1
equals					
Profit after tax	0.9	0.4	0.3	0.7	0.4
as % of equity	15.3	8.9	5.5	10.5	6.5

Sources: Statistics Canada, *Financial Institutions*; *The Canada Gazette.*

A striking and contentious feature of Table 12–2 is the low rate of tax paid per dollar of profits for credit unions compared to that for its competitors. A credit union's profit is treated as though it were merely an extra capital contribution by member depositors and lenders, rather than net income. Credit unions can even use it to pay dividends (rather than to build up equity) without paying tax. Credit unions can therefore achieve the same **profit margins** after tax with smaller before-tax profit margins than their rivals.

Credit unions have large expenses relative to the other institutions shown in Table 12–2. Some of this reflects the extra cost of unsecured lending and of chequing deposit business. Some of it reflects the small size of the average credit union: a credit union local has only a small asset base over which to spread the many fixed costs of intermediation.

Table 12–2 shows trust company spreads to be comparable with those of the foreign banks in Canada. Trust company spreads are somewhat wider because trust companies have more retail business than the foreign banks. Trust company expenses are almost twice as high, however, so their profit margins are positive only because of their large fee income. Trust companies also receive income from capital gains realized on their marketable assets (bonds, stocks, and even mortgages). On average over the years 1985–88, capital gains added 23 percent to after-tax income.[5]

SECTION 3

Risk Management

In this section we examine how the near banks manage the risks raised by their intermediation. Credit risks and liquidity risks are largely cancelled out. Remaining risks are partly offset by matching. What is left must be absorbed by equity capital, so near banks must keep an adequate equity capital cushion.

Credit risk

Near banks take the same sort of steps as banks to reduce the chances of default on individual loans. They arrange life insurance on loans, a practice introduced into loan markets by the credit unions. They rely on fixed-installment loans for consumers, in order to match repayment schedules more closely with consumers' incomes and to make repayment easier. They insist upon high collateral values for mortgages. They arrange mortgage default insurance with either the Canada Mortgage and Housing Corporation (a federal Crown corporation) or with the privately owned Mortgage Insurance Corporation of Canada. Finally, their loan officers and credit committees screen loan requests.

Trust companies have so far avoided unsecured lending; they have been permitted to make unsecured loans under a "basket clause" in their legislation that allows limited amounts of otherwise forbidden investments such as unsecured loans, but the trust companies have taken little advantage of even that limited power. They have insisted on having their loans secured by real estate or by securities (that is, they have made only mortgage or collateral loans). It will be interesting to see whether trust companies make much use of the expanded powers of unsecured lending to be granted them in the new Trust and Loan Companies Act introduced to parliament in late 1990. Significant conflict of interest problems can arise if a trust company puts trust funds into securities issued by a firm that is also an unsecured borrowing customer of the trust company; there is great temptation to serve shareholders' interest rather than the interests of the trust beneficiaries.

One should not exaggerate the security of loans secured by real estate, especially commercial real estate. Mortgage loans to finance property being held for resale are often riskier than the standard, unsecured, commercial loan in that there is no automatic source of funds to repay the loan. If, as sometimes

---

[5] Trust companies can expect to make capital gains on bonds only during periods of falling interest rates, so this is not a reliable source of income even over long periods. During 1985–86 gains were large, but during 1988 they were negative.

happens, the property market dries up and the property cannot be resold at the appointed time, the borrower often cannot repay. In such a situation property values are quite likely to fall below the level needed to repay the mortgage principal. Lenders can be left with large losses on what were initially more than fully secured loans. A large part of the enormous woes of the U.S. savings and loan sector is due to lending of this sort. The two cartoons on pages 216 and 217 capture this situation well.

Credit union locals have a special credit risk problem. Local credit unions cannot diversify because they are small: in 1988 the average membership was only 3300, all in the same locality and often deriving their incomes from the same basic source. Credit unions in towns are at a greater disadvantage in this respect than credit unions in larger cities. Business and personal loans in even a medium-size town are bound to have highly correlated default risks, which even the tightest screening by credit committees cannot remove. Most credit union locals therefore avoid the larger-volume business credit entirely; the risks are too systematic for purely local financial institutions.

The caisses d'entraide (a type of caisse populaire in southern Quebec) ignored this logic. They concentrated on business loans to members. In 1980–81 a series of defaults on business loans caused large losses. Those defaults would not have been serious wounds for a medium-size bank spread over many different centres, but they were mortal for small, local caisses d'entraide.

Credit unions concentrate on personal consumer and mortgage lending where they do have an advantage, instead of business lending where they are at a disadvantage. The credit unions' advantage is in greater willingness of members to repay loans, and therefore in lower loan losses than banks and finance companies experience in household lending. Credit union loans are made only to members, and always using the funds of other members, all from the same locality. There is some extra moral pressure on such borrowers not to default on their neighbours, especially in small towns.

The credit union movement can still handle larger-scale or riskier types of financing through the centrals. Such financing is equivalent to having all the member locals syndicate a loan (that is, lending as a group or syndicate), with the central acting as lead manager of the syndicate. The locals own the central and are almost its only source of funds, so lending by the central is done with the collective funds of the locals. The Caisse Centrale Desjardins du Québec actively plays the role of collective lender for the caisses populaires in Quebec. Provincial centrals in provinces smaller than Quebec still have a problem of arranging enough diversification.

Figure 12–1 shows the loan loss provisions for credit unions and trust companies in comparison to those for domestic loans of the Royal Bank (from Figure 11–2). Locals and especially trust companies have small loan losses. The extra security that trust companies insist upon does pay off in lower loan loss rates (at least in years of rapid growth like the mid-1980s). The low loan losses of credit union locals probably reflect their advantage as local institutions that know their members and with which borrowers identify. The high loan losses of

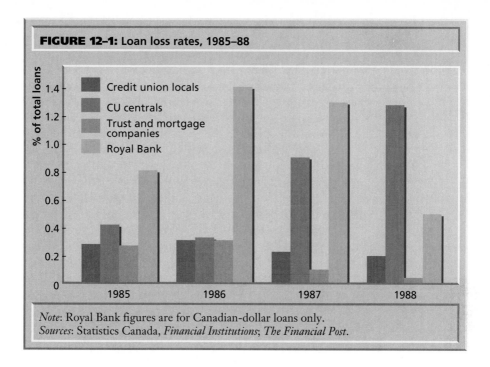

FIGURE 12–1: Loan loss rates, 1985–88

Note: Royal Bank figures are for Canadian-dollar loans only.
Sources: Statistics Canada, *Financial Institutions*; *The Financial Post*.

central credit unions reflect the failure rate of local credit unions; as Table 12–1 shows, the majority of loans made by centrals are to member locals.

It will help to set the loan losses of Figure 12–1 in perspective if we look at some other loan loss figures over longer periods of time. Under the Farm Improvement Loans Act (since 1945) and the Fisheries Improvements Loans Act (since 1955) the government has paid out claims of private lenders for loan defaults amounting to 0.15 and 0.19 percent, respectively, of the total amount loaned since the start of each program. Under the Small Business Loans Act (since 1961) the government has paid out default-loss claims amounting to 0.42 percent of amounts loaned.

However, under the Small Loans Act governing consumer borrowing, the registered lenders reported a bad-debt loss in 1979 of 3.3 percent on small loans (under $1500) and 3.8 percent on other loans. These percentage loss rates are higher than in earlier years, but even in 1969 they were 1.8 percent and 1.0 percent, respectively. By comparison, the loan loss rates shown in Figure 12–1 look very good.

Liquidity risk

Credit unions and trust companies are subject to liquidity risk from cheque-clearing losses on chequable deposits; from net withdrawals of notice deposits; and from surges of drawdowns of mortgage loan commitments, net of mortgage loan repayments. Mortgage borrowers planning to buy a house will normally seek a commitment from the lender six months or more before actually borrowing money on a mortgage loan, and the lender must come through once that commitment has been made. Once large trust companies have made public their term-deposit and mortgage-loan rates, they are implicitly committed to accept whatever creditworthy business comes through their doors. Where mortgage lending business is referred to them by their subsidiary real estate sales divisions, the commitment is even stronger. For such precommitted mortgage loans, it is the borrowers who decide when and by how much to draw down the agreed mortgage loan amount.

Credit union centrals make the equivalent of line of credit loans in serving as lender of last resort to member locals. Centrals must have funds available when members call on them in order to be reliable lenders of last resort.

There are three main ways in which liquidity risk can be reduced. The first is to diversify across many different depositors and mortgage borrowers. The small size of credit unions makes this difficult for them. Trust companies have less difficulty because most trust company business is with large firms operating nationwide.

The second solution is to hold large stocks of liquid assets that can be sold off quickly to meet sudden cash needs. Credit unions rely heavily on this solution, trust companies much less so. Credit union locals hold much larger stocks of liquid assets than banks or trust companies to make up for their lack of diversification. Credit union centrals, with half of their liabilities in the form of chequing deposits used by member credit unions to handle all their withdrawals and clearing losses, hold huge liquid asset balances. Only the Bank of Canada holds a comparably liquid asset portfolio.

Trust companies' holdings of cash and chequing deposits are small, but only slightly smaller than those of chartered banks. Since trust companies are not subject to any cash reserve requirement, their entire holdings of cash reserves are available to solve liquidity crises. In fact, their cash reserves are many times larger than the excess cash kept on hand by banks. Most of this is accounted for by the currency needed for automated teller networks.

The third solution to liquidity risk is to make arrangements to borrow from other institutions in time of need. Credit union locals set up the centrals for just this reason. The centrals' loans to locals amount to one-quarter of the centrals' assets, and 6 percent of the locals' deposit liabilities.

Matching and hedging

The solution to those systematic risks that remain after diversification is to offset asset risks with **matching** liability risks. Figure 12–2 compares the main portfolio proportions of credit union locals, trust companies, and banks to show the main patterns of matching. The share of mortgages rises as we move from banks to credit union locals to trust companies in Figure 12–2, and so does the share of term deposits. Mortgages are assets with five years or less to maturity; so are term deposits. The share of loans falls as we move from banks to credit union

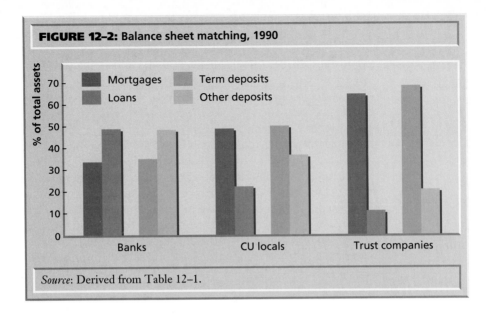

FIGURE 12–2: Balance sheet matching, 1990

Source: Derived from Table 12–1.

locals to trust companies; so does the share of notice deposits. Loans are generally shorter-term assets, mostly to be paid off in a year or two. Notice deposits are balances to be withdrawn at will, but generally not for some months or even years after deposit. All three institutions in Figure 12–2 are roughly matching terms of assets and debts.

Credit unions have protected themselves by yet another kind of matching that only co-operatives can use. Credit unions issue many of their mortgages at floating rates, and then tie the rates to their cost of funds by special year-end dividends. At the end of each financial year credit unions can adjust both deposit yields and loan rates, by paying either a bonus to depositors or an interest rebate to borrowers. Changes in annual dividends can complete the matching process for credit unions as long as the previous dividend was big enough; the dividend can never be negative.

Near banks could also reduce some risks by hedging with options contracts, but so far this is uncommon.

Capital adequacy

The risks remaining after diversification and matching are borne by shareholders, and (if that is not enough) by depositors or deposit insurers. Credit union deposits are insured by provincial stabilization funds; retail deposits of trust companies are insured just like bank deposits, by the Canada Deposit Insurance Corporation.

In order to protect depositors and the CDIC, trust companies are required to satisfy **capital adequacy** restrictions by having equity capital of at least 5 percent of total assets.[6] Table 12–1 shows they have that and little more. Credit unions do not have minimum capital requirements, since the owners are the depositors and borrowers, but they have built up equity levels higher than those of trust companies. Being a small, undiversified credit union is still a risky proposition. Many individual credit unions fail each year despite prudence and caution on their part and considerable help from their centrals. Centrals' high loan loss rates shown in Figure 12–1 suggest the size of this problem. The bankruptcy or closure of any large local firm, the collapse of world market prices for a local product, or a crop failure, are often enough to sink the local credit union as well.

Trust companies are now almost all closely held, which means that there is a controlling shareholder who can put up extra equity in the event of financial pitfalls. Depositors do not always get more protection when there is a controlling shareholder, however. In mid-1983, for instance, Fidelity Trust sank because it had loaned too much to its controlling shareholder in the form real estate loans to its owner's company, Patrician Land Corporation. This is an example of the dangers of self-dealing that can arise in using an intermediary's funds.

SECTION   4

▣ Summary

Near banks consist of credit unions (locals and centrals), trust companies, mortgage loan companies, and two provincial savings institutions. This chapter discusses only the first two groups, since the larger mortgage loan companies are mostly captive subsidiaries of banks and are consolidated with their parent banks in reporting bank assets.

Both near-bank groups are or have been limited. Credit unions are limited by their structure as essentially autonomous local co-op banks. Trust companies have been limited by legislation that has prevented them from entering into unsecured lending in a significant way; that has been the price for their exclusive privilege of providing corporate trustee services.

Both near-bank groups are predominantly mortgage lenders, financing residential mortgages by issuing term deposits for similar terms. Credit unions also do a significant amount of unsecured consumer and business lending. Credit union centrals lead a specialized existence as central bankers for member credit union locals; most provide a variety of financial services to their members, and serve as bankers for large co-operative organizations.

Near banks maintain their positive spreads mainly through buying risky loans and issuing guaranteed deposits. Unfortunately, credit unions are not large

---

[6] The maximum leverage ratio was raised from 5 in 1914 to 7 in 1931, 10 in 1947, 12.5 in 1958, and 15 in 1965 before being raised to its current level of 20 in 1970. Jack Mintz, *The Measure of Rates of Return in Canadian Banking* (Ottawa: Economic Council of Canada, 1979), 39.

enough to diversify away even their unsystematic credit risk. Membership is so locally concentrated that a lot of credit risk is systematic: all borrowers are subject to the same economic forces, particularly if all those borrowers live in the same town.

Key Terms

credit unions
caisses populaires
central credit unions
caisses centrales
trust companies
mortgage loan companies
Alberta treasury branches

Province of Ontario savings office system (POSO)
interest spreads
profit margins
matching
capital adequacy

Questions and Problems

1. What legal barriers are there to prevent trust companies from competing with banks?

2. How different is the consolidated asset portfolio of all near banks together from that of the chartered banks? The liability portfolio?

3. If near banks compete with banks, can the banks be described as an oligopoly?

4. What is the point of a near bank's arranging for life insurance on all personal loans?

5. What sort of liquidity problems do near banks have? Do banks have the same liquidity problems?

6. Why does a mortgage loan company have a matching problem even when it finances a five-year mortgage with issue of five-year term deposits?

7. Do the actions of near banks cause interest rates in different markets to be held in a more stable structure, or do they cause greater volatility of relative yields? Explain.

8. If the purpose of monetary policy actions is to influence the level of demand for real goods and services by bringing about changes in interest rates, is the presence of near banks a help or a hindrance?

Suggestions for Further Reading

Binhammer, H.H. *Money, Banking and the Canadian Financial System*, 5th ed. Toronto: Methuen, 1988.

Economic Council of Canada. *A Framework for Financial Regulation*. Ottawa: Supply and Services, 1987.

——. *A New Frontier: Globalization and Canada's Financial Markets*. Ottawa: Supply and Services, 1989.

Finance Canada. *New Directions for the Financial Sector*. Ottawa: Supply and Services, 1986.

Neufeld, E.P. *The Financial System of Canada*. Toronto: Macmillan, 1972.

Shearer, Ronald A., John Chant, and David Bond. *The Economics of the Canadian Financial System*, 2nd ed. Scarborough, Ont.: Prentice-Hall Canada, 1984.

Statistics Canada. *Financial Institutions*. Ottawa: Supply and Services, most recent issue.

Superintendent of Financial Institutions. *Annual Report*. Ottawa: Supply and Services.

Chapter thirteen

Other Financial Intermediaries

Compared to the banks and near banks, the group of intermediaries discussed in this chapter are much less homogeneous. Other financial intermediaries includes finance companies, investment dealers, insurance companies, mutual funds, and pension funds. The different types have little in common. Some look only remotely like financial intermediaries. The most important common feature of this group of intermediaries is that its members generally hold larger proportions of long-term assets than banks and near banks.

This chapter is organized the same way as Chapters 11 and 12. Section 1 describes the legal structure of each type of intermediary. Section 2 looks at balance sheets and income statements to show the kinds of intermediation practiced by each group of institutions. Section 3 discusses problems of risk management.

You should learn in this chapter:

1. the legal background of financial intermediaries outside banking and near banking;
2. the kinds of assets and liabilities used by these financial intermediaries;
3. the kinds of risk problem raised by their intermediation;
4. how those risk problems are handled.

SECTION 1

Description and legal structure

Finance companies

The group of **finance companies** includes dozens of firms much more similar in their borrowing than in their lending. Some of them operate under specific legislation for their type of intermediation, but most just operate under standard business corporation acts.[1]   Most operate under provincial legislation. Their legislation is restrictive in only a few cases; finance companies can even issue deposits, though so far none have done so.

The first type of finance company is the *consumer loan company*. These make loans directly to households for consumption purposes. The loans are generally secured either by a lien (a right to seize in event of default) on the goods purchased (known as a *chattel mortgage*), or by a second or even third mortgage on the borrower's home.[2]

The second type of finance company consists of *sales finance* and *acceptance companies*. These companies buy short-term loans or accounts receivable from retail stores and from suppliers of business inventories and equipment. Most of the loans are made by retailers to help customers finance consumer appliances like cars and TV sets, others to help business firms finance their inventories or new equipment. As a rule, the loans are secured by a lien on the goods purchased. Many acceptance companies are wholly owned subsidiaries of appliance or equipment manufacturers such as General Motors, Ford, and Chrysler.[3]   Some acceptance companies also make short-term loans to finance construction until longer-term mortgage financing is arranged; these are known as *bridge loans*.

The third type of finance company is a *financial leasing company*. As the name implies, these companies invest in financial leases to help firms finance large equipment items such as aircraft, ships, or fleets of trucks. Financial leases have been described in Chapter 6. In all financial respects the business of financial leasing is much like lending for medium terms to finance outright purchases of equipment. Many financial leasing companies are wholly owned subsidiaries of banks and trust companies.

---

[1] For instance, venture capital corporations are often chartered under special provincial acts that provide favourable tax treatment.

[2] In event of default by a borrower, a second-mortgage holder can claim only the remainder of the mortgaged property's value after settling the first mortgagor's claim, so a second mortgage provides less security than a first mortgage. As a result, second-mortgage loans have higher interest rates and shorter repayment schedules than first mortgages.

[3] Sales finance companies owned by large retailers or manufacturers are different from others in two ways. First, they have guaranteed, non-competitive access to consumer loans originated by the parent firm or its dealers. Second, terms and conditions of the loans they buy from parent firms may even have negative spreads for the subsidiary; the loans are made by parent firms as just one part of the parent company's overall sales strategy.

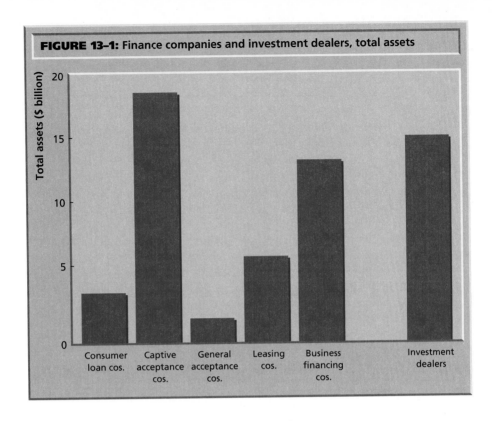

FIGURE 13-1: Finance companies and investment dealers, total assets

The fourth type is a *business financing company*. This category includes those merchant banks (see Chapter 11, section 1, for a definition of merchant banking) that are not accounted for in other categories of financial intermediary. Business financing companies invest in a wide variety of business loans and securities, generally for longer terms than are common for acceptance companies. Venture capital corporations are a special class of these firms specializing in lending for new start-ups.

Figure 13–1 shows the relative sizes of different groups of finance company. The captive acceptance companies dominate in total assets, but all groups are of significant size.

Investment dealers

There are about 100 **investment dealers** in Canada. They are important to the financial system, though not in terms of total assets. Total assets of investment dealers, shown in Figure 13–1 along with those of finance companies, are less than total assets of just the captive acceptance companies.

Initially investment dealers were all small, independent firms, but as securities markets have become global rather than national, that has changed. The sector was opened up to all comers in 1987 and 1988 as a result of

Quebec's initiative. Now many of the largest domestic investment dealers have become subsidiaries of banks, and huge foreign firms have set up Canadian subsidiaries.[4] Investment dealers operate under provincial securities legislation when they underwrite stock and bond issues and make secondary markets for such assets. There is no national securities legislation. Each province supervises the performance of securities markets, and therefore of investment dealers, through its own securities commission; of these, the Ontario Securities Commission is by far the most important.[5]

Investment dealers' legislation is restrictive only in disclosure requirements. Detailed regulations specify exactly the information that must be presented to potential lenders when new securities are issued through investment dealers. Other than those provisions, investment dealers are allowed wide powers of borrowing and investment. Investment dealers are not formally allowed to issue deposits, but many issue "cash management accounts," which are very similar. Investment dealers are not allowed to make unsecured personal loans, but they regularly lend to personal clients through margin loans; these are loans secured by stocks or other securities held by personal clients. Investment dealers that operate as jobbers in the money market (see Chapter 6) even have special access to Bank of Canada credit through purchase and resale agreements, a privileged arrangement not available to any other intermediaries.

Insurance companies

The insurance sector of the financial system is both technically and administratively complex. This legal background section on insurance companies will therefore be longer than the legal background section for other intermediaries.

Private **insurance companies** are divided into life insurance and general (property and casualty) insurance, each regulated under a separate act. There are almost 200 life insurers, over 350 general insurers, and none are allowed to be both at once. Some are domestic, some are branches of foreign firms; about 80 percent of life insurance business, and 68 percent of general insurance, is carried by Canadian companies. Most, but by no means all, insurance companies are federally chartered. Entry and exit is easy and frequent. Of all the markets for individual types of insurance, the only one that is concentrated (by the usual measure of large market shares for the four largest firms, given in Table 1–1) is the market for basic automobile insurance; this market is a state monopoly in four provinces (British Columbia, Saskatchewan, Manitoba, and Quebec). All the other markets have many suppliers.

Until the current round of revisions, insurance legislation has restricted competition by insurers in several ways. However, insurers have found ways

---

[4] Intermediation by investment dealer subsidiaries of chartered banks is included in the figures presented for banks in Chapter 11.

[5] There has been discussion of setting up a national securities commission in addition to the existing provincial securities commissions, but nothing has come of it as of early 1991. Provincial securities laws are far from uniform.

around the restrictions that they find most inconvenient. Insurers have not been allowed to make unsecured commercial loans, but they make many commercial loans secured by property mortgages. In the new federal legislation, all but the smallest insurance companies will be allowed into commercial lending. Until now, insurers have not been allowed to make personal loans, but they make "policy loans" to clients, secured by life insurance cash values; and even this restriction will be removed in the new federal act. Insurers cannot solicit funds for deposits, but they solicit funds for "short-term deferred annuities" whose features are almost identical.

Federal legislation provides that only life insurance companies can issue and distribute life insurance and life annuities, with a few exceptions.[6] The proposed insurance acts will allow banks and trust companies to buy up insurance companies as subsidiaries, but will not allow them to offer the subsidiaries' insurance and annuity policies through regular bank or trust company branches. All life insurance companies must conform to quite specific regulations on the valuation of their insurance liabilities (to ensure that overly optimistic assumptions are not used to hide financial problems from creditors). There have been restrictions on the asset mix permitted to insurance companies, though these are to be greatly relaxed in the new act. After the relaxation, insurers will be able to hold real estate and common stocks only up to 70 percent of the insurer's capital for each, and 100 percent for both combined.[7] Insurance companies cannot hold shares accounting for more than 10 percent of the votes or 25 percent of the shareholders' equity of companies in an unrelated business.

Provincial legislation generally differs little from federal legislation. Quebec, however, has given its insurance companies far wider investment powers than other provinces, in an attempt to develop a strong, integrated financial system in the province. The Laurentian Group (which owns the Laurentian Bank), for instance, has an insurance company (La Laurentienne) at its core. It remains to be seen how far the other provinces will follow Quebec's lead.

There is no limit on who can own insurance companies, other than a requirement that no insurance company be owned directly by a commercial firm. Under their new federal legislation, even banks and trust companies will be able to own insurance company subsidiaries. Many insurance companies are wholly owned subsidiaries of financial firms such as credit union centrals or financial holding companies such as Power Corporation, that have extensive non-financial interests.

Roughly half of all life insurance coverage in Canada is provided by **mutual companies**. These are companies owned by their policyholders rather than

---

[6] Banks and near banks routinely sell some life insurance coverage as part of "insured" mortgage loans; the life insurance is actually provided by an insurance company, not by the bank or near bank.

[7] This restriction was put into insurance acts only after Sun Life found itself in difficulties in the 1930s. Since then, no company has had even close to 25 per cent of its assets in stocks, so the restriction does not constrain insurers much.

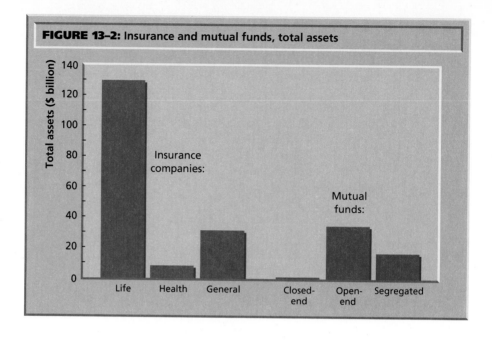

FIGURE 13–2: Insurance and mutual funds, total assets

by shareholders.[8] Even the shareholder-owned insurance companies have a strong mutual flavour because almost all Canadian life insurance business is participating: holders of participating policies are entitled by law to the lion's share of profits from intermediation and underwriting for their business; they are also entitled to elect a specific number of members of the company's board of directors.[9]

Figure 13–2 shows the relative sizes of the groups of insurance companies. Life insurance assets are on the same scale as those of trust companies, which is almost half as large as the domestic assets of the chartered banks.

Mutual funds

Mutual funds (sometimes also called investment funds) are pools of assets owned by a single class of shareholders. Mutual funds are run by management

---

[8] Some firms like Mutual Life were established as mutuals right from the start. Others like Sun Life (the biggest) were converted to mutuals between 1958 and 1965 to escape the threat of foreign takeovers.

[9] Dividends on participating policies are treated as a rebate of excess premium, rather than as a distribution of taxable profits (recall that dividends to credit union members are treated the same way). For group policies there is a similar provision called an *experience refund*. In practice, policyholder dividends actually paid or credited are kept quite stable; what changes instead as profits fluctuate is a separate account called "provision for policy-holder dividends," a liability to policyholders much like the policy reserve.

companies, for management fees that are tied to volume of the fund. Better-performing funds grow more rapidly, so the managers' return is also tied to performance, indirectly. Mutual funds are sold either by the management company's own sales staff (Investors Group is the biggest example of this type) or at arm's length through investment dealers and other financial institutions. Most mutual funds are formally trusts (issuing trust units rather than shares), but some are separate corporations.

There are several distinct classes of mutual funds: *open-end, closed-end*, and *segregated funds*. Figure 13–2 shows their relative sizes.

Open-end mutual funds are open-end in that the manager of the fund stands ready to take in extra funds or to redeem existing shares at any time. Shares are issued and redeemed at the share's *net asset value* as of the date of issue or redemption. Net asset value is found by taking the market value of all assets in the entire pool, subtracting any liabilities, and then dividing by the number of shares outstanding.

Closed-end funds are a small but distinct group of mutual funds. Shares of closed-end funds are not issued or redeemed by the management company at the discretion of the lender. Instead, closed-end fund shares must be bought and sold on the secondary stock market just like any other corporation share, for whatever the market will bear. Closed-end funds that invest in large blocks of shares are quite similar to holding companies, in that both hold shares of other companies but do not actively manage those other companies. In fact, the two types of firm are so similar that it is hard to draw the line between them.

Segregated funds are mutual funds managed by life insurance companies. They are essentially open-end mutual funds with some extra life insurance features attached. Their main life insurance feature is that they can be redeemed either in cash or in extra insurance protection or in a life annuity.[10] Management of segregated funds by life insurers is supervised by the Superintendent of Financial Institutions (federal or provincial) as part of supervision of life insurance companies.

Mutual funds have few restrictions. As a result, mutual funds vary enormously in the type of assets held. The main categories are those concentrating on equities (shares), on bonds and money market assets (referred to as income funds), and on mortgages. Equity funds are by far the biggest group. An important distinction among mutual funds arises from tax law: only those predominantly invested in Canadian assets are eligible investments for registered retirement savings plans (RRSPs) and other investment plans set up to shelter households from income tax. After-tax yields are much higher when yields are sheltered from income tax, so households lend far more to mutual funds that are eligible as RRSPs than to those that are not.

---

[10] The name "segregated funds" derives from the fact that life insurers must keep such insurance business segregated from all other business.

Pension funds

Pension funds are already huge and are growing rapidly. They are all tax-sheltered arrangements for accumulating retirement income, so their structure is heavily influenced by current federal tax law provisions. The tax shelter provided is basically as follows:

1. contributions can be deducted from taxable income in the year of contribution;
2. income earned on contributions is not taxed as it is earned; but
3. both contributions and accumulated earnings are taxed at full personal tax rates as they are withdrawn (usually as a pension).

For typical investors whose income tax rates in retirement are lower or at most equal to those in their contributing years, the tax shelter above can double their after-tax yield relative to a normal investment program.

Both provincial and federal governments regulate pension funds. Generally, each pension fund is regulated by the same jurisdiction that incorporated its sponsoring employer. Federal tax laws apply to all pension funds whether federally or provincially regulated.

Figure 13–3 shows the different groups of pension funds and their relative sizes. The first two groups involve very few but very large pension plans; the other two groups contain all of the private-sector pension plans. All groups have grown from almost nothing in the mid-1960s; collectively, the assets of pension plans now match the Canadian-dollar assets of the chartered banks.

The three largest pension funds are special in several ways. The *Canada Pension Plan* and the *Quebec Pension Plan* are mandatory and pay-as-you-go. Contributions must be made by all employees and employers in proportion to their incomes (up to a fairly low ceiling), at a single rate that applies to everyone; it is similar to a wage tax. Benefits are tied to total lifetime contributions and pre-retirement income level, but not to the value of accumulated contributions. Accumulated contributions under the Canada Pension Plan are loaned out in special non-marketable bonds issued by provincial governments. Benefits are paid by the federal government out of general revenue. In **pay-as-you-go pension plans**, there is no requirement that either individual or total benefits paid out be restricted to the value of investments accumulated. Quebec Pension Plan arrangements are similar except that contributions are invested by the provincially owned Caisse de Dépôt et Placement in assorted Quebec ventures, both private and public.

The third large pension plan illustrated in Figure 13–3 is the one for the federal *civil service*, the armed forces, and some federal Crown corporations. It is similar to the Canada Pension Plan except that (a) contributions and pensions payable are very much bigger, and (b) contributions are loaned directly to the federal government by being put right into the government's general revenue. No specially earmarked assets are accumulated to pay the pensions at retirement. Instead the government has a liability to pay all future civil service pensions, a liability that actuaries periodically re-estimate for the government. The federal

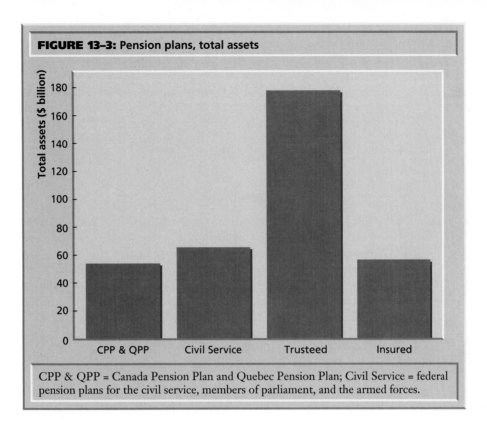

FIGURE 13–3: Pension plans, total assets

CPP & QPP = Canada Pension Plan and Quebec Pension Plan; Civil Service = federal pension plans for the civil service, members of parliament, and the armed forces.

civil service pension plan is a pure pay-as-you-go plan. Some provincial civil service pension plans are also of this sort.

Pension plans other than the three just discussed above are collectively referred to as *registered pension plans* (because they are registered with the government to benefit from the special tax shelter mentioned above). Registered pension plans cannot be pay-as-you-go but must be funded. A **funded pension plan** is one for which enough assets have been accumulated to pay off expected future pension commitments. Assets accumulate in pension plans either as contributors deposit pension plan contributions with an insurance company (in what are then called *insured plans, deposit administration plans*, or *group annuities*) or as contributors save their contributions with a trustee, (in *trusteed plans*). The trust agreement that lays out the terms of a trusteed plan is administered either by a trust company or by a committee of individual trustees chosen by the contributors. The trusteed plans generate the largest block of funds in Figure 13–3, and tend to be larger individually than the insured plans. There are no separate figures on intermediation via insured plans, because that business is mixed together in insurance companies' balance sheets with all other life insurance business.

Registered pension funds are supervised by provincial pension commissions. The management of insured plans by insurance companies is supervised as part of regular supervision of life insurance companies. The federal government influences both groups of pension funds indirectly through its Pension Benefits Standards Act, as well as through the provisions of the Income Tax Act, which specify eligibility conditions for the important federal tax shelter. One important eligibility condition has been that no more than 10 percent of assets be foreign; this restriction is onerous: it both lowers yield and raises risk for pension plan contributors.[11]

Individual pension plans?

Just as group pension plans are trust arrangements to manage accumulated savings in the name of groups of contributors, so there are individual trust arrangements to do the same for individual contributors. The most important such arrangements are registered retirement savings plans (RRSPs). Under the rules of RRSPs, individuals contribute funds to a trustee, who follows the contributor's wishes in investing the funds. There are limits on uses of RRSP funds, as there are on investment of registered pension plan funds. In exchange for these limits, contributors benefit by getting the same special tax status accorded to contributions to group pension plans.

We will not spend time on RRSPs in this chapter because they are not by themselves a separate class of intermediation. While the trustees of a pension plan have substantial discretion in investing contributions to a pension plan, and so are worth treating as a type of intermediary, the trustees of an RRSP have a much more superficial role: they serve only to keep the funds contributed at arm's length from the contributor, to ensure that he or she does not spend them before retirement without forfeiting the special tax shelter benefits.

Such trusteeship does not involve significant intermediation by itself, though many of the funds put into RRSPs go into banks and other intermediaries right after being given to the trustee. To the extent that individuals buy bank deposits as part of their RRSP strategy, the flow of funds involved is part of bank intermediation. To the extent that individuals buy trust company deposits or mutual fund shares instead, their transactions are part of intermediation by trust companies and mutual funds. To the extent that individuals buy shares or bonds of business firms directly, there is no intermediation involved at all.

---

[11] George Pink, "Government restriction on foreign investment by pension funds: an empirical evaluation," *Canadian Public Policy*, September 1989, 300–312.

SECTION 2

Types of intermediation

In this section we look at the asset and liability proportions of the financial intermediaries described in section 1, to see what kinds of intermediation each carries on. We identify the types of asset transmutation involved, and then look at the interest spreads and profit margins which that asset transmutation makes possible.

Balance sheet proportions

Most of the differences in legal structure and purposes of the intermediaries discussed above are reflected in Table 13–1, which shows their assets and liabilities.

Finance companies do not do significant foreign business. Their assets seem well spread over loans and leases, but individual companies are more specialized than the group figures suggest.

Investment dealers have by far the most short-term assets and an even larger proportion of short-term debts. Their loan assets are all collateral "margin" loans made to clients to swell the volume of securities trading and commission income. Clients buy the securities on margin by borrowing the remainder of the purchase price from the investment dealer. The loan liabilities issued by investment dealers are all regarded as very liquid money market assets for their creditors; these loans consist of day- to-day loans from banks, call loans from banks and others, and cash management accounts of clients. These liabilities are much shorter-term than the liabilities shown in Table 13–1 for other groups.

Mutual funds have about 11 percent of their assets in foreign shares. These are of course held by the equity funds, some of which specialize in foreign shares. Mutual fund liabilities are almost all to owners; they make very little use of leverage. Insurers' assets and liabilities are mainly long-term. The mix of their liabilities does not show up clearly in Table 13–1 because their liabilities to policyholders (called policy reserves) are not broken out by type of policy.

Policy reserves of insurers amount to a liability provision for unpaid claims arising from insurance protection already in force. For simple, current insurance business like fire insurance, the policy reserve is essentially the expected number of fires in the next year among the insured properties, multiplied by the average expected amount of insured damage per fire. For longer-term insurance business such as life insurance or life annuities, the calculation is more complicated; claims can occur anywhere from the present to 80 years in the future. Possible claims at each possible date must therefore be discounted for the effect of time as well as the probability of occurrence. The policy reserve for annuity business, for instance, is the expected, discounted present value of annuity benefits to be paid out, less the expected, discounted present value of any annuity premiums still to be received under existing annuity contracts.

TABLE 13–1: Balance sheet proportions

	Finance companies	Investment dealers	Mutual funds	Insurers	Trusteed pension funds
Assets					
	(percent of total assets)				
Cash and demand deposits	0.3	3.3	1.6	0.8	
Term deposits	0.0	0.0	0.7	0.7	
Canada treasury bills		16.7	8.4	1.8	
Other liquid assets	0.0	24.4	6.6	2.6	
Total liquid assets	0.3	44.4	17.2	6.0	14
Loans: household	41.6 ⎱	36.4		2.0	
business	28.7 ⎰				
Mortgages: residential	4.5		6.1	10.5 ⎱	4.7
other	3.4		1.9	19.0 ⎰	
Financial leases	5.4				
Bonds	0.0	11.2	22.4	35.9	45.9
Shares (including subsidiaries)	3.6	2.7	47.5	10.8	27.8
Other assets	1.0	5.3	4.9	15.9	7.4
Total assets ($ million)	24 030	15 259	53 107	152 983	157 01
Liabilities					
Deposits				2.9	
Loans: banks	1.1	7.3	0.2	0.5	
other lenders		11.3			
Short-term paper	40.1	4.4			
Short-term credits	2.8	53.1	1.0	2.2	
Total short-term	44.0	76.1	1.2	5.6	
Policy reserves				70.5	
Bonds and long-term notes	37.3			0.7	
Subordinated loans and loans from parents	7.8	16.9		0.5	
Preferred shares	0.6	1.4	0.4	0.0	
Common equity	10.1	4.6	98.3	18.7	99.7

Sources: Statistics Canada, *Financial Institutions*; *Trusteed Pension Plans: Financial Statistics.*

The insurers' deposit liabilities shown in Table 13–1 are proceeds of maturing policies (including dividends paid on some policies) that policyholders have left to accumulate in the company instead of taking them out in cash to invest elsewhere. Funds that insurers take in for short-term deferred annuity liabilities, which are the equivalent of term deposits, are not shown separately; they are included in the policy reserves total.

The extent of foreign business of insurers does not show explicitly in Table 13–1. For the Canadian life insurers (excluding branches of foreign firms), foreign insurance business is 44 percent of domestic business.

Types of asset transmutation

Of all the intermediaries discussed in this chapter, finance companies are the most similar to banks and near banks; the others are quite different. Finance companies take in consumer and business credits with high default risk, and issue money market liabilities with very little default risk. Most finance companies also profit from term differences: the average term to maturity of money market paper is shorter than that of the average consumer installment loan.[12] Finally, finance company assets are less marketable and less liquid than their liabilities. The spread of securitization from mortgage loans to consumer installment loans and trade credits will reduce the liquidity difference somewhat in the near future.

Investment dealers are intermediaries only as a by-product of being traders in financial assets. They hold assets and issue debts only as needed to generate commission income from buying and selling for clients. True, they make trading profits (and losses) for themselves, but that is not the core of their business. When trading volumes fall, as after the October 1987 stock market crash, investment dealers fall on hard times. Since the core of their business is not intermediation, investment dealers are not much concerned about their transmutation of assets.

Indeed, transmutation of assets by investment dealers looks to be the kind that generates *negative* spreads. The assets they hold in (see Table 13–1) are generally more liquid, more marketable, and even shorter-term than the debts they issue. The only profitable transmutation is in buying margin loans of individual retail clients (with significant default risk despite the collateral), and using their own, less risky credit to finance it. Otherwise, one should expect interest spreads of investment dealers to be negative.

Mutual funds provide a pure example of risk pooling. Mutual fund shares or units are direct, undifferentiated claims on the whole underlying pool of assets. The only difference between assets and liabilities of mutual funds is that mutual fund shares, being diversified, must have less unsystematic risk than individual mutual fund assets. Mutual funds make no significant use of leverage. They also provide few services other than whatever skill and information gathering goes into the selection of the assets in each mutual fund.

Insurers intermediate by issuing liabilities (insurance and annuity policies) with payment patterns customized to suit creditors, and buying assets better suited to borrowers' needs. Annuity policies pay benefits as long as the insured person lives. Disaster insurance policies pay off just when disaster strikes. By contrast, regular stocks and bonds do not pay off nearly as conveniently for

---

[12] This was especially true of sales finance paper to finance car purchases. General Motors Acceptance Corporation reduced the term mismatch in the United States by creating medium-term notes in 1978. The instrument spread outside the United States in the 1980s.

their holders. Insurance company liabilities can cancel out (hedge) the financial risks caused by such non-diversifiable events as fire, theft, death, or longevity.[13] Creditors value the properties of such hedging assets sufficiently to hold them despite very low expected yields.

Life insurers' policy and annuity liabilities are generally longer-term and less liquid than their mortgage and bond assets. To counteract the effect this reverse transmutation would normally have on spreads, insurers allow policies to be redeemed before maturity, and they also provide automatic collateral loans against the asset value of customers' policies.

Trusteed pension funds intermediate in either of two ways. Some pension funds are part of what are called *money-purchase* pension plans; others belong to *defined-benefit* plans. For money-purchase plans, members are entitled at retirement only to whatever pension annuity the current market value of the pension fund will buy—no more, no less. For members of money-purchase pension plans, the pension fund is simply another kind of mutual fund with better tax treatment and more restricted withdrawal provisions.

For defined-benefit plans, the pension plan promises members defined, guaranteed pension annuities that do not depend on what the pension fund earns on its assets. Such liabilities have much less risk (systematic and unsystematic) than the assets in the pension fund. Some defined-benefit plans even offer indexation to protect against most inflation risk. Defined benefit plans therefore more closely resemble a form of bond than a mutual fund.

Spreads and profit margins

Spreads and profit margins, shown in Table 13–2, show the effects of each intermediary group's kind of asset transmutation.

For mutual and pension funds there are almost no costs. Asset yields pass through to shareholders with little transmutation other than pooling. The two significant expenses for mutual funds are management fees (0.72 percent of assets) and brokerage expenses (0.20 percent).

Investment dealers lie at the opposite end of the spectrum. Dealers receive huge fee income from brokerage and underwriting services. As Table 13–2 shows, however, their huge fee income was more than matched by huge salary and other expenses. Those expenses are incurred to operate various financial markets. The money market, the bond market, and the over-the-counter stock market are entirely run out of dealers' offices, while much of the work of the formal exchanges is performed in dealers' offices.

Finance companies generate much larger interest spreads between asset yields and debt costs than any of the banks or near banks (see Table 12–2 for comparison). Also, their profit after tax is almost twice as large as that of the banks. However, finance companies' leverage is only half as large, so their return on equity is only the same as for banks rather than twice as large.

---

[13] The financial risk posed by longevity is of outlasting one's resources.

TABLE 13–2: Spreads and profit margins, 1990 (cents per dollar of total assets)

	Finance companies	Investment dealers	Mutual funds	Insurers	Trusteed pension funds
Asset income	16.26	8.36	7.05	9.24	9.59
Gross underwriting margin				5.34	
Net fee income	0.00	11.35	−0.72	0.38	− 0.17
Total revenue	16.26	20.53	6.33	14.96	9.42
Interest expenses	11.25	6.89	0.01	0.47	0
Policy dividends				1.00	
Addition to reserves				5.58	
Gross spread	5.01	13.63	6.32	8.85	9.42
Salary expense	0.87	8.94	0.02	3.83	0
Other expense	2.08	5.50	0.38	2.43	0.07
including premium tax:				0.36	
Income taxes	0.63	0.45	0.12	0.44	0
Profit after tax	1.43	−1.26	5.80	1.21	9.35
Total assets ($ billion)	24.0	15.3	53.1	152.1	143.4

Sources: Rearranged from Statistics Canada, *Financial Institutions*, and *Trusteed Pension Plans: Financial Statistics.*

Insurance companies' accounts are difficult to follow because the two elements of underwriting and investment intermediation are mixed together, as explained in Figure 13–4. In Table 13–2 we must be content with a single, combined account for both elements. Table 13–2 shows the insurance group to have a very large gross spread before expenses, but such large expenses as to leave only a normal profit after tax. Within the insurance group, the life insurers have the smallest spreads (3.6 percent) and the smallest profit after tax (0.25 percent). Note that over half of domestic life insurance business is done by mutual companies, which have no shareholders to complain about low returns on equity.

SECTION 3

◻ Risk management

The group of intermediaries discussed in this chapter are exposed to a different set of risks from those of banks and near banks. Liquidity risk is less important for long-term intermediaries, while market risks are more important. Default risk is important only for the finance companies; the others lend little in the way of unsecured loans.

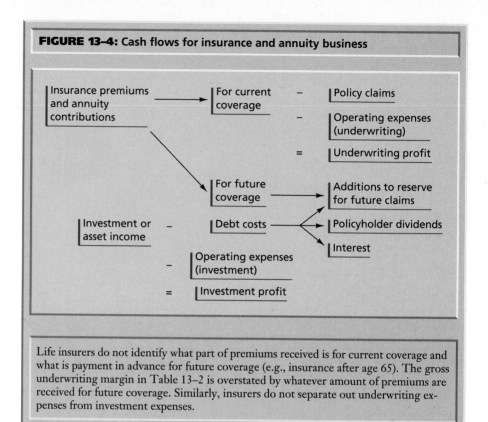

FIGURE 13–4: Cash flows for insurance and annuity business

Life insurers do not identify what part of premiums received is for current coverage and what is payment in advance for future coverage (e.g., insurance after age 65). The gross underwriting margin in Table 13–2 is overstated by whatever amount of premiums are received for future coverage. Similarly, insurers do not separate out underwriting expenses from investment expenses.

Credit risk

The finance companies have a credit risk problem with their short-term, retail lending. Even though the loans are secured by consumer durables or business inventory, defaults will cause low or negative yields. Over the period 1986–88 the finance companies averaged loan loss provisions of 0.77 percent on their loans (short-term and mortgage), a level comparable with those of the chartered banks but well above those of trust companies. Finance companies that are captive financiers of consumer durable manufacturers or retailers have little choice about the loans they accept, since their lending is only part of a wider sales strategy by the parent firm.

There is some risk attached to mortgage lending, and therefore a default risk problem for life insurance companies in particular. Their answer is to diversify across all regions of the country (and abroad), to seek government insurance if available, and to arrange at least one-third greater market value of the real estate collateral (at time of lending) than the principal value of the mortgage loan.[14] However, even that is not enough in areas that experience severe recession; real estate values in such areas can quickly fall below mortgage principal amounts, leaving the lenders at least partially unsecured, while borrowers may well be unable to pay despite their best intentions. The most volatile price swings, and therefore the largest credit risks, tend to occur in commercial real estate developments. The largest mortgage lenders by far for commercial real estate developments are life insurance companies.

Market risk

Holders of long-term assets are much more exposed to risk of market price swings than holders of short-term assets, because prices of long-term assets respond much more vigorously to interest rate changes than do prices of short-term assets.[15] Stocks, real estate, and long-term bonds can therefore present intermediaries with important market price risks. Finance companies hold some stocks, often of new ventures whose stock has a thin market at best. But mutual funds, pension funds, and insurers are the most exposed.

Investment dealers are exposed to market risk as underwriters. They hold underwritten securities only for short periods between issue and distribution to others, but even small price changes in that interval mean large changes in profitability. Diversification is not possible: there are not that many underwriting deals done each week. Nor would it be of much use, because the risk of bond or preferred share price fluctuations is mostly systematic. Hedging in financial futures markets is part of the answer. Investment dealers used to be more protected from market risks when they could underwrite on a "best efforts" basis. Market price fluctuations on "best efforts" underwritings were passed on to the issuer. Nowadays, however, competition has forced dealers more into *bought deals*, where they do make a commitment on price to the issuer.

Mutual fund managers worry about market price risk only when it causes shareholders to redeem their shares and move elsewhere. As long as other long-term assets (especially other mutual funds) suffer similarly, mutual fund shareholders are likely to bear the risk stoically without inconveniencing mutual fund managers. All market price risks not diversified away are passed on directly to shareholders, who in turn (in most cases) diversify the risks further by combining their mutual fund shares with other assets. Pension fund managers need worry even less about market price risk, since tax law makes frequent

---

[14] That is, the mortgage loan is not made for more than 75 percent of the value of the real estate used as collateral.

[15] Short-term yields are about twice as volatile as long-term yields, but changes in short-term yields have much less effect on short-term bond prices than long-term yield changes do on long-term bond prices, so long-term bond prices are still much more volatile.

shifting between pension funds more difficult than between mutual funds.[16]

Insurance companies cannot fully protect themselves against market price risk by diversification; market prices of mortgages and bonds and preferred shares all move together — that is, too systematically. What protects insurance companies is that they hold their assets for very long terms, usually to maturity. They very seldom need to sell off bonds in the secondary market to raise cash. The reason is that their inflow of premiums from new and existing business almost always exceeds their outflow for claims and benefits and policy redemptions; their net cash inflow is almost always positive. Since insurers generally hold their assets to maturity, they are allowed to record market price changes in their financial statements only with a long lag, if at all.[17]

Insurance company shareholders are also protected from market price risks (a) by the participating feature of most life insurance, which forces the insured policyholder to absorb some of market price losses in the form of a lower provision for policyholder dividends; (b) by hedging some risk exposure in financial futures markets; and (c) by keeping large surplus margins. Sun Life, a company that was ridiculously exposed to market risk in the 1930s, has by far the largest surplus margin.[18]

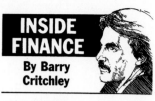

INSIDE FINANCE
By Barry Critchley

THE CHAPS at **Merrill Lynch Canada Inc.** and **ScotiaMcLeod Inc.** must be thankful they weren't members of the team underwriting the $515-million equity issue by **Laidlaw Transportation Ltd.** Equally, their rivals at **Burns Fry Ltd.** and **Wood Gundy Inc.** must be wondering about their decision to join the syndicate.

Since the financing was announced, Laidlaw's share price fell by up to $1¾, to $24⅜: At that price, the stock was $1⅜ below the issue price of $25.75.

With the total underwriting fee being 95¢ a share, the issue, at that price, is what the trade calls "under water." In the final two days of trading last week, Laidlaw rallied to reach $25⅛ at the close of business Friday: At that price, the dealers stand to make something. All the shares haven't been sold.

Source: The Financial Post November 27, 1989.

Liquidity risk

Finance companies and investment dealers have little problem with liquidity. Both groups have ready access to the wholesale money market for their paper, plus access to bank loans. Money market dealers have extra access to the Bank

---

[16] The risk for pension fund managers is that the trustees may decide to replace current fund managers with new ones as soon as fund performance turns sour.

[17] Life insurers are only required to include the following market price changes in the balance sheet: 10 percent of changes in market values of bonds and mortgages, once the gap between book and market values exceeds 1.5 percent; and less than one-third of changes in the market values of shares in the current and two preceding years. Only 7 percent of any difference between the book and market values of shares need be taken into income each year as (unrealized) capital gain or loss. Realized losses on bonds actually sold can be taken into income gradually over 20 years. This kind of lagged accounting was also allowed for chartered banks in the 1980s after their Third World loans turned sour.

[18] Sun Life held 58 percent of its assets in common stock on the eve of the Depression.

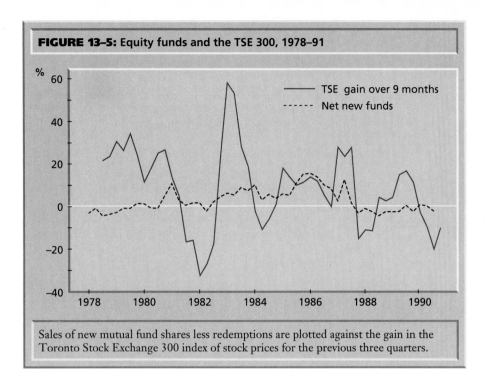

FIGURE 13–5: Equity funds and the TSE 300, 1978–91

Sales of new mutual fund shares less redemptions are plotted against the gain in the Toronto Stock Exchange 300 index of stock prices for the previous three quarters.

of Canada to meet liquidity needs. Finance companies are not subject to the sort of sudden, non-refusable demands for credit that banks are subject to when bank customers are borrowing under previously negotiated line of credit arrangements. Now that many of the large investment dealers have been bought by banks, those dealers also have more financial resources to call on in liquidity crises.

Managers of open-end mutual funds have a liquidity problem when many shareholders decide to redeem their shares. Equity-based mutual funds are especially vulnerable if lenders' net redemptions are tied to fluctuations in stock market prices, since all such redemptions would be systematic. Figure 13–5 shows net new funds (net sales less redemption of equity-based mutual funds) and quarterly changes in the Toronto Stock Exchange 300 index of Canadian stock prices. When the stock market index grows slowly or falls, as it did in 1987–90, redemptions of equity-based mutual fund shares outweigh new sales. In such circumstances mutual fund managers have a liquidity problem. That explains the large holdings of liquid assets shown in Table 13–1.

Pension funds have less of a liquidity problem than open-end mutual funds because pension plan shares cannot be redeemed as easily: only at retirement, or on change of employment.

Insurance companies have a greater liquidity risk problem than mutual funds, for several reasons. First, they are liable to pay death benefits on life insurance policies whenever policyholders die, and that is not closely predictable even for large companies. Second, permanent policies and annuity policies can be surrendered for their cash values. This is likely to occur whenever households fall on hard times, or whenever the yields offered by competing assets improve a lot. Payments of surrender values are often the largest type of cash outflow for life insurers, ahead of insurance claims. Demands for surrender values are also likely to vary systematically; many of the factors that cause policy surrenders are common to all households.

Insurance companies reduce their liquidity risk in two ways. One is to diversify their insurance business across types of policyholders, regions, and occupations. Insurance risks are by and large independent, so there is a big gain in the predictability of benefit payments. There is still significant variability left, however. To diversify more broadly, insurance companies can sell off blocks of policies to reinsurance companies and buy different insurance from them — for a fee.

The second way of reducing liquidity risk is to cut down policy redemptions (a) by offering policy loans at low rates (secured by the policy's own cash value), and (b) by levying a penalty on early surrenders, like the partial interest penalty on early surrender of fixed-term deposits at a bank. Some insurance companies also try to screen new business as agents bring it in, in order to reduce business likely to be surrendered, and they offer special "persistency" bonuses to agents for business not surrendered after the first few years.

Matching

A striking feature of the group of financial intermediaries discussed in this chapter is the degree of mismatching that they allow.

Finance companies have assets with relatively fixed yields for short to medium terms. The yields are adjusted infrequently, and usually in response to the parent firm's sales strategy rather than to the cost of funds for the finance company. Finance company liabilities are shorter-term, bearing interest at current or very recent money market rates. Spreads for finance companies therefore fluctuate with changing money market rates.

Investment dealers are much better matched: their credit to clients is at floating rates that can be adjusted to the cost of credit to dealers; their large holdings of money market assets are financed with money market loans, although the loans have shorter terms than the assets.

Mutual funds, money-purchase pension funds, and participating life insurance business have no matching problem at all, almost by definition. The first two have almost no liabilities at all. The third is fully mutual business for which almost all risks are passed on unchanged to policyholders.

Defined-benefit pension plans and non-participating insurance and annuity business (almost all annuity business is non-participating) have a serious mismatching problem. There is no asset that will match the mortality and longevity risks involved in life insurance intermediation. Longevity risks (of making annuity payments for longer than expected) are particularly large. When actuaries revise their estimates of longevity, the changes implied in defined-benefit pension obligations are large. Since provincial laws on pension plan funding require that shortfalls between pension fund assets and obligations be made up quickly, any change in expected longevity implies a big change in the financial position of the pension plan guarantor — either the employer or an insurer. To make matters worse, since 1989 Ontario has required such plans to raise pension benefits after retirement by at least 75 percent of any inflation that occurs after retirement. As we will see in Chapter 14, pension funds cannot match inflation risk either. Some pension funds will therefore shift out of defined-benefit plans that carry such risks, and into money-purchase plans that do not.

In response to their mismatching, both finance companies and insurers have kept their leverage low and their equity cushions large (see Table 13–1).

SECTION 4

◼ Summary

The financial intermediaries discussed in this chapter vary widely in organization and purpose. Few of them are straightforward, capitalist financial intermediaries like the stereotypical Faithful Trust of earlier chapters. Many finance companies are the captive sales financing arm of consumer durable or equipment manufacturers or of retail merchant chains. The *raison d'être* of investment dealers is not intermediation, but rather trading of securities for commission income; intermediation is merely a by-product. The majority of mutual funds and pension funds are trusts that manage funds for owner/creditors, rather than owning assets in their own names. Insurance companies are partly co-operative or mutual like credit unions, and conduct almost all of their life insurance business on a mutual basis.

Asset mixes reflect both the constraints and the purposes of each interme-diary. Finance companies look much like banks on the asset side, but they look much different on the liability side. Finance companies do not use deposits at all, but they use long-term bonds and notes and subordinated loans much more than do banks.

Investment dealers' assets and debts are mainly short-term. Mutual funds and pension funds and insurers invest for long terms in stocks, bonds, and mortgages. Insurers are by far the largest investors in non-residential mortgages to finance real estate developments of various sorts.

Income, expenses, spreads, and profit margins vary enormously among these institutions. At one extreme, mutual funds and pension funds have almost no expenses and no liabilities; at the other, investment dealers have huge expenses — and huge trading incomes to match them — from underwriting and brokerage.

The risks borne vary equally widely. Long-term intermediaries can generally expect greater market risk and lower liquidity risk than short-term intermediaries. Mutual and money-purchase pension funds do nothing to alleviate this risk; it passes right through to shareholders. Life insurers protect shareholders from risks on participating insurance business by passing it on to policyholders instead. For defined-benefit pension funds and non-participating insurance business, important risks remain from mortality and longevity risks — risks that cannot be hedged or matched and that cannot be fully diversified away by companies of the size available in this sector.

Key Terms

finance companies	closed-end funds
investment dealers	segregated funds
insurance companies	pay-as-you-go pension plans
mutual insurance companies	pension funds
mutual funds	funded pension plan
open-end funds	interest spreads

Questions and Problems

1. Which of the intermediaries in this chapter has the longest-term liabilities, and which the shortest?

2. What is participating insurance, and how does it affect yield and risk for life insurance company policyholders?

3. Who are the primary lenders and primary borrowers whose lending and borrowing is intermediated by the Canada Pension Plan and by the Quebec Pension Plan?

4. Why are there much looser restrictions on holdings of assets in segregated funds than for the rest of life insurance companies' asset portfolios?

5. Why is it that finance companies have much lower leverage ratios than the group of deposit-taking firms described in Chapter 12?

6. Are investment dealers simply service-producing firms, or are they true intermediaries?

7. If the demand for deferred pension benefits and life insurance is *not* sensitive to relative yields on financial assets, does it follow that pension funds and life insurance companies' demand for assets will also not be sensitive to relative yields? Explain.

8. How do life insurance companies and pension funds contribute to the transmission of monetary policy effects across financial markets? Do mutual funds contribute in the same way?

Suggestions for Further Reading

Bodie, Zvi. "Pensions as Retirement Income Assurance." *Journal of Economic Literature*, March 1990, 28–49.

Canadian Life Insurance Association. *Canadian Life Insurance Facts* (annual).

Chant, John. *Regulation of Financial Institutions: A Functional Analysis*. Ottawa: Bank of Canada Technical Report No. 45, January 1987.

Economic Council of Canada. *A Framework for Financial Regulation*. Ottawa: Supply and Services, 1987.

———. *A New Trend: Globalization and Canada's Financial Markets*. Ottawa: Supply and Services, 1990.

Finance Canada. *New Directions for the Financial Sector*. Ottawa: Supply and Services, 1986.

Neufeld, E.P. *The Financial System of Canada*. Toronto: Macmillan, 1972, Chapters 8 and 13.

Pedoe, A. and C.E. Jack. *Life Insurance, Annuities and Pensions*. Toronto: 1978 or later edition.

Statistics Canada. *Financial Institutions*. Ottawa: Supply and Services, most recent issue.

———. *Pension Plans in Canada*. CS74–401 (occasional).

———. *Trusteed Pension Plans Financial Statistics*. CS74–201 (annual).

Superintendent of Financial Institutions. *Annual Report*. Ottawa: Supply and Services.

PART FOUR

Financial Market Equilibrium

Chapter fourteen

General Equilibrium, Arbitrage, and Yield Structures

Parts Two and Three explained the logic of individual decisions in financial markets: those of lenders, borrowers, and intermediaries. Such individual decisions are gathered together in lender and borrower diagrams to explain responses of yields and quantities in individual financial markets. Together, all the borrower and lender diagrams provide an explanation of general equilibrium of the financial system.

General equilibrium is a fine concept—the major contribution of economics, many would argue—and it is as useful in financial analysis as elsewhere. However, general equilibrium models suffer from the defect that they are too general; so many yields and other variables affect each market's equilibrium yield in a general equilibrium model that such models are difficult to apply to real financial systems. Fortunately, we can explain the behaviour of yields in some parts of the financial system separately from the rest by using arbitrage models. Where arbitrage models can be applied, they explain yields much more simply than general equilibrium models. This chapter describes arbitrage models that have been applied to several parts of the financial system.

Section 1 describes the properties of a general equilibrium model. The speed with which general equilibrium is achieved is explained by the efficient markets hypothesis, which is also discussed in section 1. Section 2 presents the logic of all arbitrage models. Sections 3–5 present applications of arbitrage logic to the term structure of interest rates, to international yield differentials, and to the corporate financing problem (an application better known as the Modigliani–Miller hypothesis). Section 6 presents a new approach that decomposes actual financial instruments into a few basic components—a risk-free asset and one or more option contracts, and then predicts arbitrage between the actual financial instruments and the combinations of basic components to which they are equivalent. This arbitrage-based view has become more important as option markets themselves have become more important. Finally, section 6 briefly describes some other arbitrage models that have been used to explain other features of yields in financial markets.

You should learn in this chapter:

1. the nature of general equilibrium in financial markets;
2. the meaning and significance of informational efficiency;
3. how the presence of arbitrage between a few markets simplifies explanations of relative yields by generating stable yield structures for just those markets;
4. how arbitrage between bonds of different terms to maturity produces stable patterns of yields to maturity depending only on expectations of the future;
5. how arbitrage between assets denominated in different currencies produces equal yields by changing spot or forward exchange rates;
6. how the option-based view of financial markets helps to widen the range of application of arbitrage logic in understanding financial markets;
7. how arbitrage models fail when the arbitrage assumed is not in fact possible.

SECTION 1

■ General equilibrium in financial markets

This section starts by summarizing the ingredients in a general equilibrium model of the financial system and listing the equilibrium conditions that must be satisfied in general equilibrium. Next it discusses the linkages between financial markets that are implied by general equilibrium, and explains how those linkages occur in the Canadian financial system. Finally, this section discusses the speed of adjustment of financial markets, in particular the efficient markets hypothesis about the speed with which financial markets adjust to new information.

Equilibrium conditions in general equilibrium

General equilibrium in the financial system is achieved whenever yields are such that equilibrium conditions are satisfied in all individual financial markets. The equilibrium condition in any one financial market has already been explained: lenders must be willing to hold all the debts that borrowers have issued. The motives behind the behaviour of lenders and borrowers have been discussed under the headings of household, business firm, government, and financial intermediary behaviour in Chapters 7–10. To summarize those motives:

1. households participate as lenders mainly in order to accumulate wealth for retirement; they borrow mainly to purchase large assets, in order to spread the payment burden over more than one year;
2. firms buy assets and issue debts to raise the equity value of the firm (or profits; equity value and profits are closely related);

The Firm in Equilibrium

Two farmers got together and bought a truckload of watermelons, paying a dollar for each melon. They drove them to the market and sold them at the same price they had paid for them.

After counting up their money, they realized that they had the same amount of money they had started with.

"See?" said one to the other. "I told you we should have got a bigger truck!"

Source: Copyright, 1983, by Paul Collins. Distributed by Los Angeles Times Syndicate.

3. households and sometimes firms diversify their asset holdings in order to reduce unsystematic risk;

4. both households and firms take on extra systematic risk when there is enough extra expected yield to justify it;

5. financial intermediaries enter markets as borrowers or lenders when they see the chance of an interest spread that will cover costs and leave enough over to compensate for risk to their shareholders.

When general equilibrium is achieved, several conditions must be satisfied for all lenders and borrowers, both individually and collectively. These equilibrium conditions are:

1. For the economy as a whole, the flow of savings must equal the flow of investment. Another way of putting this is that the flow of borrowing must equal the flow of lending. This is **flow equilibrium**.

2. All lenders and borrowers and intermediaries must be satisfied with their levels of assets and debts, at least for the time being. This is **stock equilibrium**. Any lender at the optimal point on a portfolio choice diagram is in such a stock equilibrium. In other words, all assets held are held willingly.

3. In each asset portfolio, the lender must feel about an extra unit of each asset that the extra yield it would add to the portfolio just offsets the extra risk it would also add.

4. If all lenders operate with the same information, all must set the same price on systematic risk; in the terms of the capital asset pricing model of Chapter 9, all lenders must accept extra systematic risk in an asset only if comes with at least the extra yield implied by the slope of the capital market line.

5. Intermediaries must be operating at the volume of assets and debts where the expected marginal net asset yield (net of operating costs) just equals the expected marginal debt cost.

6. Entry into and exit from each financial market must leave any potential new intermediary with only a normal expected profit margin for that type of business.

Linkages in general equilibrium

The conditions for general equilibrium impose many linkages between financial markets. Lenders and borrowers are assumed to compare yields on different assets and to shift their lending and borrowing between financial markets whenever any one yield moves out of line with the general equilibrium pattern. The result is that disturbances in any one financial market have ripple effects on all other financial markets. For instance, monetary policy actions at first move yields out of line in the overnight money market. Then, as the process is described by the Bank of Canada, "movements in these rates in turn influence the whole spectrum of interest rates and rates of return on a wide variety of assets and liabilities and, through them, the exchange value of the Canadian dollar. The movements of the various rates of return and of the price of foreign exchange affect over time total spending in the economy."[1] As another example, shocks to the corporate junk-bond market will have a ripple effect on the market for bank term deposits. Some ripple effects will be small enough to ignore, but no financial market will be immune to shocks from elsewhere in the financial system. No financial market is an island. In today's world, no nation's financial system is an island either. Ripple effects travel right around the world.

The financial intermediaries discussed in Chapters 11–13 provide many of the linkages between markets in our financial system. Banks and near banks, for instance, link the various national and international deposit markets together by being willing to shift some of their borrowing when domestic deposit yields change relative to foreign deposit yields. Banks and near banks also link business and consumer loan markets by being willing to shift their lending to whichever type of loan has the higher marginal yields. Banks and near banks link loan markets with deposit markets by expanding both deposit issue and loan purchases whenever the spread grows between loan yields and deposit interest rates. Mutual funds, pension funds and life insurers link long-term asset markets at home and abroad. Individual firms and households provide some links between financial markets, but households are generally much less likely to shift their lending than are intermediaries run by full-time professional investment managers. In section 2 we will expand on how the links between financial markets work.

Speeds of response

In formal general equilibrium models, all yields are allowed to adjust to clear all markets. Such models say little or nothing about how long it will take for yields to

---

[1] John Crow, Governor of the Bank of Canada, *The Work of Monetary Policy*, Hansen Lecture at the University of Alberta, January 18, 1988.

complete that adjustment. Prices and yields in public auction-type markets such as the stock market or the foreign exchange market adjust much more quickly than do prices in less open, less informed, less competitive markets such as those for consumer loans or life insurance. The adjustment process takes enough time in many financial markets that yields on any particular day may not fully reflect equilibrium; they may still be in transit toward equilibrium.

The speed with which yields adjust in different markets is determined by the adjustment mechanism used and by the kind of participants in each particular financial market. Prices and yields adjust very quickly in auction markets whose major participants are professional, full-time traders. That category includes at least the money market, the bond market, futures markets, the foreign exchange market, and the stock market for all stocks listed on major stock exchanges. The market for a few common retirement annuities also belongs in this category. Whenever demand exceeds supply in these markets, the market price is driven up immediately.

The alternative to an auction market is one in which large lenders or borrowers (almost always intermediaries) post the yields at which they will make loans or accept deposits, and then accept whatever volume of loans or deposits are forthcoming from other participants in the market. **Posted yields** are usually adjusted only periodically—some daily, some weekly, some monthly. Posted markets include most markets in which intermediaries deal with households, such as markets for term deposits, savings deposits, insurance, most annuities, consumer and commercial loans, mortgages, and mutual fund shares. The intervals that intermediaries allow between postings of rates depend on how quickly customers respond to changes in relative yields. Households generally do not review their investment portfolios even monthly, so posted yields on household deposits and loans need not be changed more frequently than monthly unless competing, auction-market yields change dramatically.[2] Professional investment managers in business firms and intermediaries, on the other hand, review their investments full time. Banks therefore adjust their posted rates for wholesale money market deposits almost continuously.

The fact that some markets adjust slowly will not cause significant dislocation of financial flows if the majority adjust quickly, especially if that majority includes the markets that have the highest volume of lending and borrowing flows. This is the situation in Canada. Canada's public auction markets are the most visible, highest-turnover financial markets. Retail, posted-price markets such as for bank savings deposits take their lead from auction markets to adjust more slowly but in the same direction. Over a macroeconomically relevant period such as three months, yields can reach equilibrium in almost all markets even though over a period of a few days many will not.

---

[2] An exception is near the end of February each year, when the registered retirement savings plan campaign is in full swing; failure to adjust RRSP deposit yields into line with the competition at that point could cause large changes in financial flows. This is a temporary, tax-driven exception that proves the rule in all other circumstances.

The efficient markets hypothesis

The efficient markets hypothesis (EMH) predicts how quickly market participants will use new information, and how equilibrium prices will therefore move over time.[3] The EMH is applied and tested most often in the stock market, but it applies to all the financial auction markets mentioned above.

The focus of the EMH is on how market participants (let us call them agents) form their expectations of future market prices. Future market prices must be estimated to calculate an expected yield on any asset that must be resold at the end of the agent's planned holding period. Such assets will include all stocks, and many other assets whose term to maturity is longer than agents' planned holding periods. The EMH makes several specific assumptions about agents' expectations. The first is that lenders on average use all relevant information in forming their expectations. Second, the expectations that agents form are, on average, **rational expectations**. A rational expectation is defined as one that is consistent, on average, with the true underlying structure of the economy, so that rational expectations will be wrong only randomly and not persistently. Third, the EMH assumes that lenders act upon their expectations immediately. A fourth, implicit assumption about the markets to which the EMH is applied is that yields and prices can adjust immediately in order to clear markets. Markets that satisfy all the assumptions above are said to be *informationally efficient*, and are called **efficient markets.**

If agents on average use all relevant information and use it rationally, the market as a whole will not make persistent, systematic mistakes. If there were such mistakes — for instance, if the stock market were persistently to overreact initially to bad news — then agents forming rational expectations and observing this would come to expect prices to bounce back a little after slumping on bad news. Such agents would then profit greatly by buying stocks right after bad news and selling a day later. Their stock purchases would prevent stock prices falling too far right after bad news, eliminating the overreaction.

Since agents act on their expectations immediately in efficient markets, and since yields adjust immediately afterward, it follows that all price and yield changes in efficient markets must be caused by new information. Old information could cause changes in current prices only if it had been overlooked when it was released; since agents on average take all relevant information into account, by assumption, such old information could not have been overlooked. This result has two further implications. First, prices in efficient markets at the end of any day will properly reflect all information available during that day. Second, the pattern of changes in efficient market prices over time will reflect the pattern of release of new information; since new information is completely unpredictable, so is the pattern of changes in efficient market prices.

---

[3] For a fairly advanced survey of this topic, see Stephen F. LeRoy, "Efficient Capital Markets and Martingales," *Journal of Economic Literature*, December 1989, 1583–621. This section is based on LeRoy's survey.

This last implication of the EMH contradicts two widely held beliefs of stock market participants. First, the EMH predicts that future market price changes will be independent of past price changes. But chartists or technical analysts use patterns of past stock price movements to predict future stock price movements. The EMH says these chartists are misguided and doomed to disappointment. Second, future market price changes are independent of all other past information that many lenders consider, such as the firm's cost and profit history. Fundamental analysts use past information on a firm to assess its fundamental value and then buy or sell according to whether the market price is below or above that fundamental value. The EMH says that such past information has already had all of its effect on prices in the past; there is no further effect to be expected in the future. Fundamental analysts too are doomed to disappointment.

Tests of market efficiency generally support the EMH's claim that stock prices move unpredictably over time. The EMH is also supported by data showing that mutual fund managers with sophisticated stock-trading strategies seem to do no better on average than a simple non-trading strategy of buying and holding a broad sample of stocks. On the other hand, there are some stock price movements that are inconsistent with the EMH.[4] Also, despite the EMH's predictions of disappointment, lenders continue to spend large amounts in trading commissions and information costs in order to trade stocks actively on the basis of technical and fundamental analysis. Finally, research results trying to explain actual market price changes *ex post* by changes in information about fundamental factors (such as explaining changes in orange juice futures prices by changes in the weather in Florida) have found such factors to be relevant even though unimportant.

What should we assume as a first approximation about the market pricing process in financial markets? Market prices respond very quickly to new information, but apparently (a) not just to new information about fundamental factors, and (b) not always rationally. This first approximation will be recalled later, in Chapter 17, where the rational expectations assumption reappears in the context of agents expecting future inflation of prices of goods and services.

SECTION 2

■ The logic of arbitrage models

Even where it is supported empirically, general equilibrium modelling of a financial system has the drawback of being too general, of including too many variables to explain anything. Consider the list of factors that matter to individual borrower and lender decisions and therefore to general equilibrium: all lenders' degree of risk aversion; all marginal operating costs of relevant

---

[4]January yields are persistently much higher than in other months. So are yields on small companies, and yields of stocks that lost the most on the previous day's trading. The volatility of stock price movements is also twice as large as the EMH implies.

intermediaries; the relative systematic risks of all assets; the expected yields available on all potential new investment in real assets that might need financing; relative tax rates now and in the future; regulatory restrictions on investment or intermediation; current and expected future income over the next 20 years or so; the level of wealth inherited from the past; and, of course, current and expected future monetary policy. It is a long list.

Arbitrage models are much less general, but they require much less information. In the rest of this chapter we look at how arbitrage models can be used to predict relative yields. This section presents the central idea of all arbitrage models in the context of a simple diagram of borrowers and lenders in two markets. Sections 3–6 look at separate situations in the financial system where arbitrage models have been predicted to work.

The central idea of **arbitrage models** is that any two combinations of assets that have the same possible cash flows should have the same price and yield. The proof of arbitrage models is what gives them their name: if the two combinations have different yields, then lenders will issue or sell short the lower-yielding one and buy the higher-yielding one (that is, they will arbitrage) as long as the yield difference persists. Such arbitrage will force the two yields to be equal. Whenever such arbitrage pressure is believed to exist, therefore, one can predict the level of either yield exactly, simply by knowing the level of the other yield. Relative to general equilibrium models, this is simplicity itself.

Asset combinations do not have to be clones of each other for arbitrage theory to be useful. If unsystematic risk truly does not matter because it can be diversified away, as argued in Chapter 9, then any two stocks are identical for the purposes of arbitrage if they have the same systematic risk. That is, stocks of different firms in different industries will be considered identical if they both rise and fall with the same volatility in response to common, system-wide factors. They will both have the same price per dollar of expected returns, and the same expected yield. Their different but unsystematic risks will be as irrelevant to their yield as is the colour of an automobile to its price.

Arbitrage will keep yields equal for two assets in either of two situations. The first is if it is possible for arbitrageurs to issue or sell short one of the similar assets while buying the other. Such arbitrage is self-financing, so it can be undertaken on a large scale not limited by the liquid wealth of the arbitrageurs. Large-scale arbitrage may be needed to move market prices and yields quickly into line. The second situation is where there is a large pool of lenders ready to reallocate their funds whenever yields on identical alternatives differ by more than transactions costs. It is not necessary that *all* lenders be so willing to switch between markets, merely that many of them be willing to do so.

Putting the central idea of arbitrage models in the context of a simple borrower–lender diagram may help to simplify the explanation. In the general borrower–lender diagram such as that for corporate bonds shown in Figure 14–1(a), both borrowers and lenders curves are drawn with significant slope. In such diagrams the positions of both curves must be known to determine the market equilibrium yield on corporate bonds; that is, the equilibrium yield

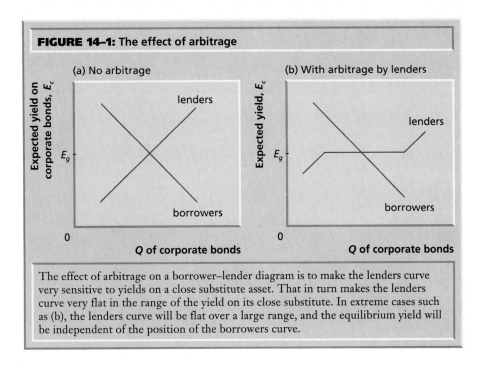

FIGURE 14–1: The effect of arbitrage

The effect of arbitrage on a borrower–lender diagram is to make the lenders curve very sensitive to yields on a close substitute asset. That in turn makes the lenders curve very flat in the range of the yield on its close substitute. In extreme cases such as (b), the lenders curve will be flat over a large range, and the equilibrium yield will be independent of the position of the borrowers curve.

depends on all factors that influence the position of either the borrowers or the lenders curve. This is the general equilibrium situation.

If there are arbitrageurs who consider corporate bonds as very similar to government bonds, their presence affects the shape of at least the lenders curve. For instance, in Figure 14–1(b) it is assumed that there are several large pension fund managers willing to shift their portfolios between corporate and government bonds whenever yields differ on the two assets. As soon as the corporate bond yield E_c rises above the expected government bond yield E_g these arbitraging lenders enter the corporate bond market on a large scale. Their willingness to lend on a large scale at just above E_g causes the lenders curve in Figure 14–1(b) to be much flatter than in (a), where such behaviour is assumed not to exist.

In the extreme case assumed in all arbitrage models, the existence of arbitrageurs causes the lenders curve to be essentially flat over a large range, as shown in Figure 14–1(b).

It is possible for arbitrage to be by borrowers rather than lenders. For instance, if banks were indifferent between borrowing with one-year and two-year deposits, the borrowers curve in the two-year deposit market would be very flat just below the yield on one-year deposits. Such a case is less likely than where arbitrage flattens lenders curves, however. As we have seen in Chapter 11, bankers are not indifferent about the proportions of deposits in different terms to maturity.

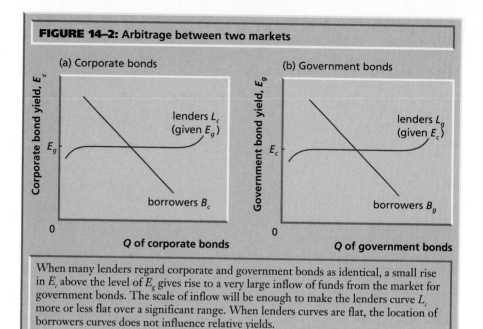

FIGURE 14–2: Arbitrage between two markets

(a) Corporate bonds

(b) Government bonds

When many lenders regard corporate and government bonds as identical, a small rise in E_c above the level of E_g gives rise to a very large inflow of funds from the market for government bonds. The scale of inflow will be enough to make the lenders curve L_c more or less flat over a significant range. When lenders curves are flat, the location of borrowers curves does not influence relative yields.

Figure 14–2 puts together borrower–lender diagrams for both of the markets between which arbitrageurs are assumed to be shifting funds. In Figure 14–2 the example used is corporate and government bonds, so that part (a) is a repeat of Figure 14–1(b). In later sections of this chapter, different pairs of markets are used.

If pension fund managers are assumed willing to shift out of government and into corporate bonds when the corporate bond yield E_c rises above the government bond yield E_g, this must cause lenders curves to be flat in both parts of Figure 14–2. Part (a) shows lenders to lend much more in the corporate bond market as soon as the corporate bond yield rises above the level of government bond yields. Part (b) shows the opposite side of the same coin: the same lenders lend much less in the government bond market as soon as E_g falls below the E_c. In each case there is a large lender reaction to a small change in relative yields, producing a flat portion of the lenders curve at the level of the close substitute's yield.

In Figure 14–2, any change in the level of the lenders curve L_g in the government bond market will not only change the government bond yield E_g, but it will also shift the corporate bond lenders curve L_c; L_c is drawn with a flat section whose level is entirely determined by the level of the substitute yield E_g. The result is that while many factors still move the lenders curve directly in either part of Figure 14–2, those factors will also move the lenders curve indirectly in the other market as well, by the same amount. The relationship between the two close substitute yields will not be affected at all. For instance, a large outward shift of the borrowers curve B_g caused by expansionary fiscal policy might raise E_g by, say, 2 percent; higher E_g raises L_c by 2 percent. Since L_c is flat, it raises the corporate bond yield E_c by 2 percent as well.

Arbitrage models will work in practice only if there is enough arbitrage to make either borrowers or lenders curves flat over the normal range of quantities. If such arbitrage is not possible for any reason, arbitrage models will not work.[5] The evidence of failure of an arbitrage model is that yields that are supposed to be tied together will vary independently over time in response to factors such as changes in asset supplies or changes in wealth. We will see such evidence in some of the applications that follow.

SECTION 3

◼ The term structure of interest rates

The best-known application of arbitrage theory in economics is to the **term structure of interest rates**.[6] The set of yields to which term structure theory has always been applied are those for marketable federal government bonds. Yields on short- and long-term government bonds are also good indicators of other short- and long-term yields in the financial system, so explaining the term structure of federal government bond yields is essentially the same as explaining the relationship between long- and short-term yields for other borrowers as well.

There are four theories explaining the term structure of interest rates: the pure expectations, segmented markets, liquidity preference, and preferred habitat theories. This section presents each view, then discusses the evidence, and finally shows what the supported theories imply about observable patterns of yield by maturity on government bonds.

Pure expectations theory

The starting point of term structure theory is an arbitrage proposition put forward in the 1930s by Irving Fisher, and later by Friedrich Lutz: the **pure expectations theory**.[7] Fisher and Lutz argued that there are large groups

---

[5] One reason could be that too few lenders see two assets as close substitutes. Another could be legal, tax, or regulatory barriers to the kind of lending strategy presumed by an arbitrage model.

[6] For a much more extensive survey of this area, see James C. Van Horne, *Financial Market Rates and Flows*, 2nd ed. (Englewood Cliffs, N.J.: Prentice-Hall, 1984). For a contrasting, general equilibrium approach to explaining interest rates, see John Cox, J.E. Ingersoll, and S.A. Ross, "A Theory of the Term Structure of Interest Rates," *Econometrica*, March 1985, 385–406.

[7] Irving Fisher, *The Theory of Interest* (New York: Macmillan, 1930); F.A. Lutz, "The Structure of Interest Rates," *Quarterly Journal of Economics*, November 1940, 36–63.

Geometric Versus Arithmetic Averages

Much discussion of average yields over more than one period makes use of the concept of a geometric average. An arithmetic average of n items is their sum divided by n. The geometric average of n items is the nth root of their product. For example, the geometric average of the two numbers 4 and 5 is $\sqrt{(4 * 5)} = \sqrt{20} = 4.472$, where the arithmetic average would be 4.5. The geometric average of the three numbers 3, 4, and 5 is $\sqrt[3]{(3 * 4 * 5)} = \sqrt[3]{60} = 3.915$. In general, geometric averages are fairly close to arithmetic averages.

of bond market lenders for whom short- and long-term bonds are perfect substitutes. Some of these lenders have long-term horizons but are quite willing to hold a long series of short-term bonds instead if the expected average yield is better than from holding a single long-term bond. Other arbitraging lenders have short-term horizons but are willing to buy long-term bonds instead (reselling them at their horizon date) if the expected yield from doing so is better than from holding short-term bonds to maturity. Both groups would shift between maturities in the bond market on a sufficient scale to generate equality of *holding period yields* in all maturities.

As a simple example illustrated in Figure 14–3, arbitrage by lenders with a two-year holding period would keep expected average annual yields equal on (a) a sequence of two one-year bonds, and (b) a single two-year bond. Where $E_{1,t}$ is the expected yield on a one-year bond held during year t, and R_n is the observed yield to maturity on an n-year bond, the Fisher–Lutz theory requires that both have the same average yield; that is,

$$1 + R_2 = \sqrt{(1 + R_1)(1 + E_{1,2})}.$$

In English, the annual yield to maturity on a two-year bond reflects a geometric average of current and expected future one-year yields over the next two years. For example, if R_1 is 0.10 (that is, 10 percent), and $E_{1,2}$ is 0.12, then R_2 must be such that

$$1 + R_2 = \sqrt{(1 + 0.10)(1 + 0.12)},$$

or

$$R_2 = \sqrt{1.232} - 1$$
$$= 0.11 \quad \text{or} \quad 11 \text{ percent per year.}$$

FIGURE 14–3: Two-year investment strategies

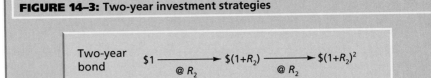

Investment in a two-year bond to maturity yields R_2 in each year. Investment in two one-year bonds yields R_1 in the first year, $E_{1,2}$ in the second year. The total yield over two years will be the same if there is enough arbitrage by lenders who regard the two strategies as of identical risk.

In general, arbitrage will cause the yield to maturity on an n-year bond to equal the geometric average of current and expected future one-year bond yields over the next n years.[8]

As a second example, arbitrage by lenders with one-year horizons will change the price and yield to maturity of 20-year bonds to bring about equality between the known one-year bond rate R_1 and the uncertain but expected one-year yield on a 20-year bond $E_{20,1}$. The expected one-year yield on a 20-year bond is the coupon yield plus the expected capital gain yield from buying at today's price and selling at next year's expected resale value. Where c is the known coupon yield (dollar coupon divided by current price) and (P_0) and $Exp(P_1)$ are the current and expected future prices of a 20-year bond, arbitrage in the Fisher–Lutz model ensures that

$$1 + R_1 = 1 + E_{20,1},$$

or

$$R_1 = E_{20,1} = c + [\,Exp(P_1) - P_0\,]/P_0.$$

If the coupon yield exceeds R_1, arbitrage will force P_0 up above the expected resale price $Exp(P_1)$ until there is enough expected capital loss to offset the extra coupon yield.

---

[8] The equivalent formula for the n-period case is

$$1 + R_n = \sqrt[n]{(1 + R_1)(1 + E_{1,2})(1 + E_{1,3}) \ldots (1 + E_{1,n})},$$

where all yields are in fractional rather than percentage form.

The pure expectation theory's first arbitrage condition implies that current long-term yields to maturity depend *only* on current short-term yields and expected future short-term yields, and *not* on such other general equilibrium factors as relative stocks of long- and short-term debt outstanding. The second arbitrage condition ties short-term yields to current and expected future long-term yields, but also with no role for relative supplies of long- and short-term debts outstanding.

Segmented markets theory

The opposite to the pure expectations theory is the idea that there is not much arbitrage between long- and short-term bonds. Such would be the case if lenders had relatively rigid preferences about the term of bonds they buy, independently of expected yields — that is, if the bond market as a whole had **segmented markets** for long- and short-term debts.[9] An easily observable implication is that long-term yields will depend on the supply of long-term debt, and will not depend on expected future short-term yields.

Liquidity preference theory

An extension of the pure expectations theory by J.R. Hicks, following a lead by Keynes, suggests that arbitraging lenders regard long- and short-term bonds as slightly different: they see long-term bonds as less liquid.[10] Hicks argued that arbitrageurs will still shift between long and short bonds, but only when lending in long-term bonds offers an extra margin of expected yield called a liquidity premium. In this **liquidity preference** version of term-structure theory, the equilibrium condition for one- and two-year bond yields becomes

$$1 + R_2 - LP_2 = \sqrt{(1 + R_1)(1 + E_{1,2})},$$

where LP_2 is the annual liquidity premium required on two-year bonds. For example, if LP_2 is 0.0033 (that is, 0.33 percent per annum), R_1 is 0.10, and $E_{1,2}$ is 0.12, then R_2 must satisfy the equation

$$1 + R_2 - 0.0033 = \sqrt{(1 + 0.10)(1 + 0.12)}$$

or

$$R_2 = 1.11 - 1 + 0.0033$$
$$= 0.1133, \text{ or } 11.33 \text{ percent.}$$

---

[9] John M. Culbertson is associated with this view. "The Term Structure of Interest Rates," *Quarterly Journal of Economics*, November 1957, 485–517.

[10] J.M. Keynes, *A Treatise on Money* (New York: Harcourt Press, 1930); J.R. Hicks, *Value and Capital*, 2nd ed. (London: Oxford University Press, 1946).

For the n-period case,

$$1 + R_n - LP_n = \sqrt[n]{(1 + R_1)(1 + E_{1,2})(1 + E_{1,3}) \ldots (1 + E_{1,n})},$$

where LP_n is the liquidity premium required per year on n-period bonds. According to Hicks, lenders would insist that higher liquidity premiums be paid on longer-term bonds, and the liquidity premiums would be constant over time. Hicks's arbitrage conditions imply that the long-term rates will change in response to exactly the same factors as in the pure expectations model.

Preferred habitat theory

Modigliani and Sutch have extended Hicks's liquidity preference theory to make the liquidity premiums dependent on relative supplies of long- and short-term bonds.[11] They argue that different lenders such as banks and pension funds have different **preferred habitats** in specific maturity segments of the bond market. What seems to each lender as risky or illiquid is lending in bonds of a term different from his or her preferred habitat. The required liquidity premiums for each lender therefore rise not with the gap between term to maturity and zero, but with the gap between term and preferred habitat. Short-term lenders regard long bonds as illiquid or risky, whereas long-term lenders regard short-term bonds as illiquid or risky. Lenders with medium-term preferred habitats regard both long and short-term bonds as riskier than medium-term bonds. Figure 14–4 shows the different liquidity premiums each group would insist upon before reallocating funds into bonds outside their preferred habitats.

The liquidity premium that is actually paid for bonds of any maturity depends on which groups of lenders must be enticed into it. That in turn depends on the relative supplies of each maturity. For example, a stock of debt that was almost all short-term could actually cause risk premiums to appear in short-term yields rather than in long-term yields; with little long-term debt available and lots of short-term debt to be held, long-term lenders would have to be enticed from their preferred habitats into short-term bonds by extra liquidity premiums.[12]

Evidence on the term structure

There is a vast amount of evidence from tests of the four theories of the term structure of interest rates. None of the evidence is conclusive, because all of the tests suffer from a weakness common in financial economics: in order to calculate yields for either long or short holding periods for different maturities of bonds,

[11] Franco Modigliani and Richard Sutch, "Innovations in Interest Rate Policy," *American Economic Review*, May 1966, 178–97; "Debt Management and the Term Structure of Interest Rates: An Empirical Analysis of Recent Experience," *Journal of Political Economy*, August 1967, 568–89.

[12] If all lenders in fact have short-term preferred habitats, the preferred habitat theory implies exactly the same behaviour as Hicks's liquidity preference theory.

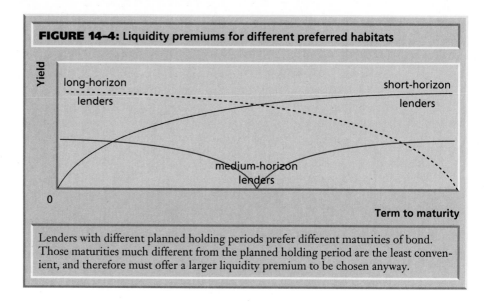

FIGURE 14–4: Liquidity premiums for different preferred habitats

Yield

long-horizon lenders

short-horizon lenders

medium-horizon lenders

0

Term to maturity

Lenders with different planned holding periods prefer different maturities of bond. Those maturities much different from the planned holding period are the least convenient, and therefore must offer a larger liquidity premium to be chosen anyway.

the researcher must find some way of approximating bondholders' expectations of future short- or long-term interest rates. There is no perfect way of doing this.[13]

The bulk of the test evidence points the same way, however, and thus makes up for some inconsistencies in individual test results.[14] The evidence suggests that:

1. Long-term yields are sensitive to current and expected future short-term yields. There is significant arbitrage between short-term and long-term bonds. The segmented market theory can be rejected.

2. There generally are liquidity premiums in holding-period yields on longer-term bonds, though it is not clear whether these premiums rise steadily with the length of term to maturity. In some studies, the liquidity premiums seem

---

[13] The existing methods are: (a) assuming perfect foresight, so that lenders in 1965 are assumed to expect for 1966 exactly what happened in 1966; (b) assuming that expectations, whatever their level, change only in response to past errors in expectations; (c) assuming that expectations of future short-term rates reflect extrapolation of recent trends but also regression toward more distant past levels regarded as normal; (d) assuming that changes in future expectations are caused only by new information received in this period, and not by old information already available from past periods; (e) borrowing implied expectations from financial futures markets, the earliest of which started up in Chicago in 1976; and (f) using expectations provided explicitly by questionnaire surveys of financial market professionals.

[14] For Canadian evidence, see Maureen E. Howe and John S. McCallum, "The Term Structure of Interest Rates in Canada: The Empirical Evidence," *Journal of Business Administration*, Fall 1980, 137–46.

to level off and stop rising after eight years or so. The pure expectations theory can be rejected as too extreme.

3. Relative supplies may make some difference to relative yields, but the effect is very small. Even when the Canadian government conducted a massive conversion of short- to long-term debt in the relatively undeveloped capital markets of 1958–60, it is not clear that the supply change had any impact.[15] Those who found supply effects found only small ones. It seems likely that supply effects are even smaller in today's more developed financial markets. If so, Hicks's liquidity preference model is a simple but adequate model of term structure behaviour.

Implications for observed yields to maturity

The liquidity preference model can be used in reverse to calculate the future short-term interest rates expected by lenders in bond markets. Such expected rates are otherwise unobservable. Recall the arbitrage result above for lenders with a two-year horizon:

$$1 + R_2 - LP_2 = \sqrt{(1 + R_1)(1 + E_{1,2})}.$$

In this equation R_2 and R_1 can be looked up in the (better) newspapers; LP_2 can be found from past evidence as long as liquidity premiums are stable. The equation can be solved for the value of $E_{1,2}$, the expected short-term interest rate for next year. Then the parallel equation for arbitrage by lenders with three-year horizons can be used (given R_1, R_3, LP_3 and the estimate of $E_{1,2}$) to calculate $E_{1,3}$, and so on for longer terms, one year at a time.

Different sets of observed yields by term to maturity (different term structures) imply different sets of expected future short-term rates. Just how different they can be is summarized as follows:

1. If all expected future short-term yields equal the current short-term yield R_1, and if liquidity premiums are as shown at the bottom of Figure 14–5, then the observed yield curve will rise just as fast as the liquidity premiums and no more. Yields excluding liquidity premiums will be constant at all terms to maturity. Yield curve A in Figure 14–5 illustrates this case. Applying the argument in reverse, an observed yield curve of shape A implies expected future short-term rates equal to the current short-term rate.

2. If future short-term yields are expected to be higher than R_1, then yields net of liquidity premiums will rise with term to maturity. Observed yields

[15] C.L. Barber and John S. McCallum, "The Term Structure of Interest Rates and the Maturity Composition of the Government Debt: The Canadian Case," *Canadian Journal of Economics*, November 1975, 606–9; Steven W. Dobson, "The Term Structure of Interest Rates and the Maturity Composition of the Government Debt: The Canadian Case," *Canadian Journal of Economics*, May 1973, 319–31; and L.N. Christofides, "Supply Variables in Term Structure Equations," *Canadian Journal of Economics*, May 1975, 276–81.

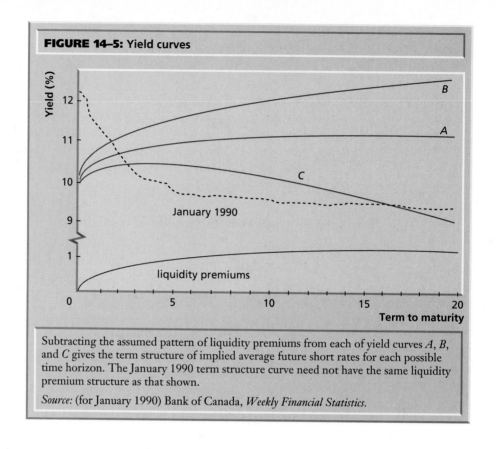

FIGURE 14–5: Yield curves

Subtracting the assumed pattern of liquidity premiums from each of yield curves *A*, *B*, and *C* gives the term structure of implied average future short rates for each possible time horizon. The January 1990 term structure curve need not have the same liquidity premium structure as that shown.

Source: (for January 1990) Bank of Canada, *Weekly Financial Statistics.*

including liquidity premiums will rise more steeply than yield curve *A*. Curve *B* shows this case.

3. If future short-term yields are expected to be lower than R_1, then yields net of liquidity premiums will fall with term to maturity. Observed yields including liquidity premiums will rise less steeply than curve *A* and may even fall if future short-term rates are sufficiently low. Curve *C* shows this case. The curve for January 1990 is a more extreme version of curve *C*; short-term rates were widely expected to decline abruptly over the rest of 1990 and 1991–92.

All sorts of combinations of the expectations above are possible. Each would produce a hybrid combination of the curves above.

Two properties of all yield curves should be mentioned. First, the currently observed long-term yields to maturity *already* contain the effects of predicted *future* changes in short-term yields. Analysts sometimes express this by saying that long-term yields "lead" short-term yields. Second, current long-term yields will change in the same direction as expected future short-term yields, but by less. A smaller response occurs because a long-term yield is an average of short-term yields; averages always change in the same direction as individual items when individual items change, but the average changes by less. For this reason, long-term yields are normally much less volatile than short-term yields. The two will move by equal amounts only if (as sometimes happens) current and all expected future short-term yields all change together. By analogy, when all items in an average rise by 5, the average rises by 5 as well.

SECTION 4

International yield differentials

Where lenders can choose between identical assets at home and abroad, arbitraging capital inflows and outflows should produce exactly equal yields for both options. Where alternative investments are only close to identical there may still be enough arbitrage to keep yields equal. Such arbitrage provides an important channel linking Canadian financial markets and the Canadian economy to the financial markets and economies of the rest of the world. It is important to know how this linkage works and how, if at all, it limits freedom of manoeuvre in the Canadian financial system. For instance, does it mean that the Bank of Canada cannot produce "made-in-Canada" interest rates, that its independence from New York is mere illusion?

International arbitrage comes in two forms: covered and uncovered. Each produces its own arbitrage condition. Covered arbitrage is the more straightforward; uncovered arbitrage is the more important.

Covered interest parity

Consider arbitrage by Canadian lenders between a 90-day (Canadian-dollar) treasury bill in Toronto yielding R_C percent and a 90-day (U.S.-dollar) treasury bill in New York yielding R_{US} percent. The two assets are not identical because the U.S.-dollar treasury bill pays off in U.S. dollars; it has foreign exchange risk for a Canadian lender. The foreign exchange risk can be removed by adding forward cover to the U.S.-dollar treasury bill (that is, adding a forward exchange contract to convert the U.S. dollars into Canadian dollars 90 days hence at today's forward exchange market price). Arbitrage will force yields to be the same for both choices when the cost of arranging forward cover is included. Specifically,

$$R_C = R_{US} - \text{cost of cover},$$

or

$$R_C - R_{US} = -\text{cost of cover}.$$

This arbitrage condition is known as **covered interest parity**. The cost of cover for a Canadian, who will be selling U.S. dollars in the forward exchange market, comes from the forward discount on the U.S. dollar, the amount by which the forward U.S. dollar price FWD is below the current or spot price S of the U.S. dollar.[16] The cost of cover is expressed in percentage annual form to match the

---

[16] There is also a tiny amount of brokerage commission, which is ignored here.

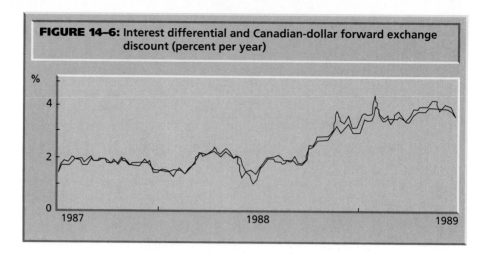

FIGURE 14–6: Interest differential and Canadian-dollar forward exchange discount (percent per year)

interest rate terms; that is, for our case,

$$R_C - R_{US} = -[100(360/90)(S - FWD)/S],$$

or, rearranging to remove one negative sign,

$$R_C - R_{US} = 100(360/90)(FWD - S)/S.$$

The role of the expression $(360/90)$ is to convert cost of cover to an annual basis; 100 converts the fractional discount into percentage form; R_C and R_{US} are already in percentage form. For instance, if R_C and R_{US} were 12 and 10 percent, respectively, the 90-day forward premium under the covered interest parity condition would have to be 2 percent per annum, or 0.5 percent for 90 days. If the spot U.S. dollar price S is C\$1.20, the forward price FWD must be C\$1.206, to produce the equation

$$12 - 10 = 100(360/90)(1.206 - 1.20)/1.20.$$

There are similar covered interest parity equations for all currencies and terms of investment. The evidence supporting covered interest parity is everywhere. The clearest example is provided each week by the Bank of Canada in charts of (a) the simple interest differential $R_C - R_{US}$ for 30-day prime corporate paper, and (b) the 30-day forward premium on the U.S. dollar. Figure 14–6 shows that the two series track each other very well over a recent two-year period; any gap is usually smaller than the tiny commission costs.

What can be inferred from Figure 14–6 is not that arbitrage ties R_C to R_{US}, but that it ties the forward premium on the U.S. dollar to the interest differential $R_C - R_{US}$. It is the cost of cover that adjusts first and fastest to satisfy the covered arbitrage condition. Some of the adjustment is made by a change in the forward exchange rate, some is made by a change in the spot exchange rate. If a covered interest advantage opens up for lending in the United States, for instance, Canadian lenders' buying of spot U.S. dollars and selling of forward U.S. dollar contracts quickly lowers the forward premium on the U.S. dollar and eliminates the covered interest advantage.

Uncovered interest parity

Without forward cover, Canadian and U.S. treasury bills are not perfect substitutes; one of them has foreign exchange risk. It is unlikely that such risk can be diversified away because there are not that many widely traded currencies. However, if foreign exchange risk is not much of a disincentive to many lenders, there will still be enough arbitrage to force equal yields to lenders in either Toronto or New York (or London, or Tokyo, etc.). Without forward cover a Canadian lending in New York would have to buy U.S. dollars at the current spot price S and sell them in the future at the uncertain future spot price F. The yield would be R_{US} plus any expected appreciation of the U.S. dollar over the investment period. Arbitrage will then cause

$$R_C = R_{US} + \text{expected appreciation of the U.S. dollar,}$$

where the appreciation is over the same term as the investment and is expressed in annual percentage terms. This condition is known as **uncovered interest parity**. Rearranging and substituting for expected appreciation gives

$$R_C - R_{US} = 100(360/90)[(Exp\{F\} - S)/S],$$

where Exp means expected. The uncovered and covered interest parity conditions are almost identical; the uncovered condition just uses the expected value of the uncertain future spot price F instead of the known forward price FWD.

Uncovered interest parity is not easy to test because expectations of appreciation are not observable. Many different proxies for such expectations have been used, including forward premiums from the forward exchange market, and the results support uncovered interest parity.[17] However, readers should be aware that none of the proxies for expected appreciation are good at predicting exchange rate changes; exchange rates have a great deal of unexplained volatility for the same reason that stock market prices do: both are determined in efficient markets.

Uncovered interest parity ties expected exchange rate appreciation to the known interest differential $R_C - R_{US}$. If expected appreciation is constrained close to zero, as under a fixed exchange rate system, then uncovered arbitrage ties

---

[17] Forward exchange rates are appropriate because forward and future exchange contracts are assets used by speculators to bet on foreign exchange rates; as such they should reflect speculators' expectations.

R_C to R_{US}. If exchange rates are flexible, as they have been since 1973, uncovered arbitrage only forces matching changes in $R_C - R_{US}$ and $F - S$. If R_C rises by 2 percent, arbitrage will force down the spot U.S. dollar price S, relative to its expected future value F, until 2 percent more appreciation is expected (at an annual rate). We will use this condition again in Chapter 20.

SECTION 5

Option theory

The **option theory approach** to financial markets has helped us see complex financial instruments as just combinations of risk-free assets and one or more put or call options (put and call options are described in Chapter 6). This insight has revealed many similarities between assets not previously compared, as this section will illustrate.[18] Once two financial instruments are regarded as similar, we can expect their yields to be equal because of arbitrage.[19] This section describes the basic arbitrage condition of option theory, and one application of that arbitrage condition to a classic theorem on the valuation of a firm's balance sheet.

Put–call parity in the option market

The basic arbitrage condition of options markets is most easily illustrated with options on shares of corporate stock. By combining options with a risk-free asset, we will construct a synthetic asset that duplicates exactly the possible future payoffs of a stock. Arbitrage then requires that the option prices be such as to provide equal yields on both the stock and the synthetic asset.

To construct the synthetic asset, let S be the current price and let S_f be the future price of some stock that, for convenience, pays no dividends. Let $C(K)$ be the current price of a call option with some strike price K (the call option entitles the holder to buy the stock for K before the option's expiry date). Let $P(K)$ be the price of a put option with the same strike price K (the put option entitles the holder to sell the stock for K before the option's expiry date). Let the expiry date of both put and call options be one period away. The synthetic asset is a portfolio put together by:

(a) buying a risk-free treasury bill that pays off K for certain at the expiry date (this costs $K/(1 + r)$, where r is the yield on this risk-free asset);

---

[18] It has also made it possible to design and price new and exotic instruments such as interest rate swaps with floors and caps and collars.

[19] Two articles in the Fall 1987 *Journal of Economic Perspectives* review much of option theory for non-specialists. Mark Rubinstein, "Derivative Assets Analysis," 73–94, and Hal Varian, "The Arbitrage Principle in Financial Economics," 55–72. For a more applied and less theoretical exposition, see Chapter 3 of *Recent Innovations in International Banking* (Bank for International Settlements, 1986).

(b) buying a call option on the stock at strike price K (this costs $C(K)$); and

(c) selling a put option at the same strike price K (this "costs" the negative amount $-P(K)$). The total cost of the synthetic asset is $K/(1+r) + C(K) - P(K)$.

Now consider the future values or payoffs that this synthetic asset could generate for its holder at the options' expiry date, as shown in Figure 14–7. This figure measures on its vertical axis the values that various assets will have to the asset holder at the expiry date of the option contracts. The horizontal axis shows possible market values of the stock, S_f, at that same expiry date. The value of the stock itself to the asset holder, for various possible values of S_f, can be read horizontally off the 45-degree line $0S$. The value of the treasury bill, whose value is K for all possible values of S_f, is shown by the horizontal line of height K. The payoffs of call and put options at expiry are more complex. The call option will be exercised if the future stock price S_f exceeds the strike price K, in which case the option will pay off $S_f - K$. If K exceeds S_f, the call option will be allowed to expire unexercised and will have value 0. The call option's payoff at expiry is shown as a horizontal line at 0 until $S_f = K$, and thereafter as an upward-sloping line with a slope of 45°.

The put option will be exercised by its holder (obligating the put option seller to purchase the stock at K) if S_f is lower than K. The put option will pay off $K - S_f$ for its holder, all at the expense of the put option seller; the put option seller has to buy the stock at K and resell it at S_f, and therefore loses $K - S_f$. If K is less than S_f, the put option will be allowed to expire unexercised and will have value 0. The put option's payoff at expiry is therefore shown as a 45° line rising to 0 at $S_f = K$, and as a horizontal line at zero for all values of S_f greater than K.

For each possible value of S_f, the payoffs of treasury bill and call option and sold put option add up to exactly S_f. In Figure 14–7 the vertical sum of ingredients of the synthetic asset at each level of S_f is always the same as that of the share of stock line $0S$. That is, the synthetic asset provides exactly the same set of possible payoffs as the stock itself. The synthetic asset and the underlying stock are perfect substitutes. Two assets that are perfect substitutes must by arbitrage have the same current market value; that is,

$$S = K/(1+r) + C(K) - P(K).$$

This is the **put–call parity condition**. It ties the value of put options to the value of call options, and ties the value of both to the value of whatever underlying asset is being optioned. The put–call parity condition holds for options on any asset and for any level of the strike price K.

Deviations of stock prices and of call and put options prices from the put–call parity condition give rise to immediate arbitrage flows. It is easy to construct the synthetic asset and easy to buy it and sell the stock whenever the synthetic asset is priced below the stock.

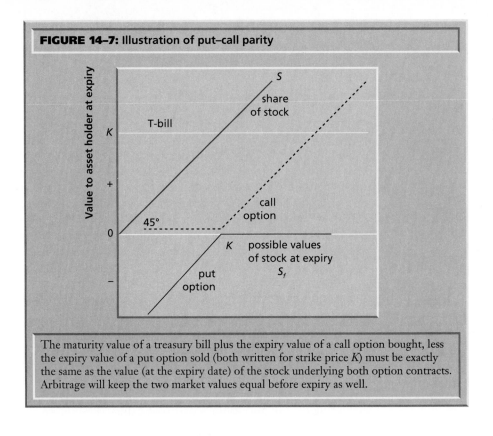

FIGURE 14–7: Illustration of put–call parity

The maturity value of a treasury bill plus the expiry value of a call option bought, less the expiry value of a put option sold (both written for strike price K) must be exactly the same as the value (at the expiry date) of the stock underlying both option contracts. Arbitrage will keep the two market values equal before expiry as well.

Put–call parity and the balance sheet: the Modigliani–Miller proposition

Put–call parity can be applied to an entire firm rather than just to its equity shares. The special case of put–call parity that emerges is better known as the **Modigliani–Miller (MM) proposition**. The MM proposition is a very early and influential use of arbitrage logic that preceded the development of option theory by 15 years.[20] It drastically changed the field of corporate finance by helping economists to see through legal differences between financial assets to the essential cash flow similarities underneath.

Let S now represent the current market value of the firm's entire stock of assets, rather than just the value of one share of its equity. Now imagine call and

---

[20] Franco Modigliani and Merton H. Miller. "The Cost of Capital, Corporate Finance, and the Theory of Investment," *American Economic Review*, June 1958, 261–77, and "Corporate Income Taxes and the Cost of Capital: A Correction," *American Economic Review*, June 1963, 433–42. The Modigliani–Miller propositions are reviewed and integrated with subsequent finance theory in a retrospective symposium by Miller, Modigliani, and others in *Journal of Economic Perspectives*, Fall 1988.

put options on the firm's whole asset portfolio, at a strike price K. Choose the strike price K to equal the redemption price of the firm's debt. The call option so defined generates the same payoffs as the firm's equity. To put it the other way around, the firm's equity can be seen as a special case of a call option. Equity shareholders are entitled to all the excess of future value of the assets (S_f) over the debts (K), should they decide to liquidate the firm. Thanks to limited liability, shareholders are not obliged to absorb any further losses should the asset value S_f turn out below K: they can just turn the assets over to the firm's creditors and walk away with zero.[21] This type of payoff is exactly what a call option provides. The value of the call option $C(K)$ must therefore be the market value of the firm's equity, and vice versa.

Another insight from this way of looking at the firm's balance sheet is that the current value of the firm's debt is not just the present discounted value of the future redemption amount K, that is, $K/(1 + r)$, as if K were certain, because bondholders cannot be certain of receiving K. If the future asset value S_f turns out to be below K, the shareholders walk away in bankruptcy and the bondholders receive only S_f rather than the full redemption price K. That is, the bondholders receive the promised K less a shortfall $K - S_f$ if $S_f < K$. Being obliged to absorb a shortfall like that is equivalent to having sold a put option on the firm's assets with strike price K. The total value to bondholders of the firm's debt is the present discounted value of the fixed redemption amount K (equivalent to the current value of a treasury bill paying K at maturity) less the value $P(K)$ of the put option.

The put–call parity condition applied to the entire firm says that the value of equity (a call option on the firm's assets) plus the value of debt (a treasury bill offering K, less the value of a put option on the firm's assets) must equal the market value of the firm's assets. Because that is true, the firm's annual revenue net of operating costs must provide the same average yield on the firm's debt plus equity as it does on the firm's assets, regardless of the proportion of debt to equity. This is the MM proposition. MM put it in the provocative form that the average cost of capital (the average yield required on the debt plus equity needed to finance any given asset total) is the same regardless of the proportions of debt and equity in the total.[22] The MM proposition ties equity yields and debt yields together in a way that had not been realized in 1958.

Modigliani and Miller's hypothesis can be extended to compare different firms. The value of debt plus equity should be identical for any two firms with similar assets, where similar is defined to mean having the same expected yield and the same systematic risk. If not, then arbitraging lenders can profit by buying

---

[21] This is the usual outcome of bankruptcy. In the case of Massey-Ferguson (now Varity Corporation), major shareholder Conrad Black did it without bankruptcy simply by cancelling his shares.

[22] It follows that almost all expert opinion concerning the cheapest mix of debt plus equity is a waste of time and money. There were many experts delivering such opinions in 1958 when Modigliani and Miller wrote their article.

up a fraction of the debt plus equity of the low-priced firm and selling short the same fraction of the debt plus equity of the high-priced firm. Such arbitrage would drive the prices of debt and equity of the two firms back into line.[23]

The MM proposition is not easy to test directly like the put–call parity condition applied just to stock, because the market value S of a firm's entire assets is seldom observable directly. Normally we measure the market value of a firm's assets indirectly by adding up the market values of its debt and equity, that is, by taking it for granted that the MM proposition holds exactly.

SECTION 6

Other arbitrage models

Arbitrage has been called upon in various other parts of the financial system to provide simple explanations of relative yields. Some of the hypothesized yield structures have been better supported than others. We look briefly at models of tax structure, of risk differentials, and at the differential between real and nominal yields.

Tax structure

The first model is of the structure of relative yields on assets whose yields are subject to different tax rates. This structure is called the **tax structure**. Lenders are predicted to care about yields after tax rather than yields before tax, so in equilibrium we would expect arbitrage to produce equal yields after tax on any two assets of similar systematic risk. Where yields on any two assets are subject to different tax rates, arbitrage will produce differences in before-tax yields to compensate for different tax rates. Where such differences have not yet appeared, arbitrageurs will buy the assets with relatively higher after-tax yields and shun or sell short those with lower after-tax yields; that pattern of purchases and sales will eventually produce the required difference in yields before tax.

An example will help explain this arbitrage condition. If R_s and R_b are before-tax yields on a share and a bond *of equal risk*, and their incomes are taxed at 25 and 50 percent, respectively, the yields on each after tax are $R_s(1 - 0.25)$ and $R_b(1 - 0.5)$, respectively. Arbitrage is expected to produce the condition:

$$R_b(1 - 0.5) = R_s(1 - 0.25).$$

---

[23] Modigliani and Miller originally relied on arbitrage only between firms that had more or less identical cash flows. Stephen Ross notes that where unsystematic risk is irrelevant to asset pricing, "identical" need mean only the same expected yield and systematic risk. "Comment on the Modigliani–Miller Propositions," *Journal of Economic Perspectives*, Fall 1988, 129.

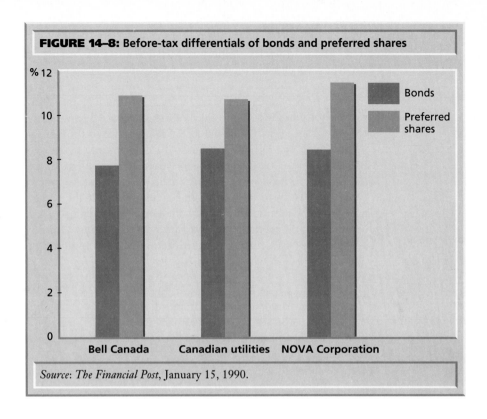

FIGURE 14–8: Before-tax differentials of bonds and preferred shares

Source: *The Financial Post*, January 15, 1990.

Rearranging this expression will give the implied ratio of yields before tax:

$$R_b/R_s = (1 - 0.25)/(1 - 0.5)$$
$$= 1.5.$$

That is, before-tax yields on bonds will have to be 1.5 times as large as yields on shares, simply to provide the same yield on each after tax.

In the real world of Canadian tax laws, share dividends are indeed taxed at much lower rates than bond interest, although the margin varies between households. Shares are also riskier than bonds. It is therefore difficult to predict any arbitrage condition as exact as in the example above. To illustrate the general result, however, Figure 14–8 shows bond and preferred stock yields of three high-grade utility firms. Preferred stocks are the least risky stocks, and utility companies are usually the least risky issuers of preferred stock. Bond yields are higher than preferred stock yields for all three companies, and by 41 percent for the least risky, Bell Canada. Figure 14–8 confirms the general arbitrage result, that low-taxed income streams will have lower before-tax yields than higher-taxed income streams. There are enough lenders who regard bonds and preferred shares of utilities as very close substitutes to bring about nearly the same after-tax yields on each.

Risk differentials

The second model considers differences in yields across assets that fall into different risk classifications. Corporate bonds are graded by rating agencies (such as Moody, Standard & Poor, or the Dominion Bond Rating Service) into risk categories with labels such as AAA, AA, A, BAA, BA, B, etc. These rating categories reflect both credit risk and market risk because to some extent the two risks go together; bonds with higher credit risk also have thinner, and therefore more volatile markets. Where risk levels differ, arbitrage by lenders will not allow all bond issuers to borrow at the same interest rate. What lenders' arbitrage might do is to force more or less constant margins between yields in different rating categories. If there were enough lenders who felt the same way about market risk, and who assessed credit risk the same way, then expected yields to maturity on bonds of different rating categories would always differ by the same amount. For instance, the arbitrage condition for AA- and A-rated bonds would be:

$$E_A = E_{AA} + mrp,$$

where mrp is the market risk premium in yields on A-rated bonds, and E_A and E_{AA} are the expected yields to maturity on A- and AA-rated bonds. The expected yield is the promised yield R less the expected default loss rate D. We can write the arbitrage condition as

$$R_A - D_A = R_{AA} - D_{AA} + mrp,$$

or, rearranging to isolate the observable differential in promised yields,

$$R_A - R_{AA} = D_A - D_{AA} + mrp.$$

Promised yields will differ by enough to offset extra default losses and extra market risk.

A look at the stability of actual differentials in promised yields to maturity will show how strong arbitrage pressure is between risk segments of bond markets. Figure 14–9 shows the range of three sets of interest differentials between promised yields to maturity over three years (1984–86) in the U.S. bond market. Arbitrage usually did keep utility yields above the more liquid government yields and it always kept BAA bond yields above AA yields, but the margins varied significantly. If this evidence is general, one can expect risk yield differentials but not constant ones. There are not quite enough lenders assessing and reacting the same way to market and credit risk to keep the differentials constant.

The Fisher effect

The third model is one where arbitrage hardly seems to take place at all, so the predictions based on an arbitrage condition fail miserably. The example is the so-called **Fisher effect** — the impact of expected inflation on nominal

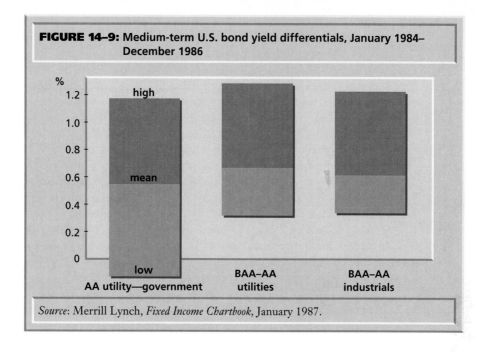

FIGURE 14–9: Medium-term U.S. bond yield differentials, January 1984–December 1986

Source: Merrill Lynch, *Fixed Income Chartbook*, January 1987.

interest rates.[24] The Fisher effect hypothesis in its simplest form is the arbitrage condition that an increase in expected inflation over the next year by x percent will cause nominal one-year yields to rise one for one, by exactly x percent.[25] The real yield will be unchanged. For instance, if expected inflation rises from 5 to 10 percent, then nominal interest rates previously at 8 percent should promptly move to 13 percent. The real yield would be 3 percent both before and after.

The rationale underlying arguments for the Fisher effect is one of arbitrage by both lenders and borrowers. If lenders have available and regard as close substitutes both bonds with fixed nominal income streams (call them "nominal bonds") and bonds with fixed real income streams (call them "indexed bonds"), they will shift lending between the two markets until each provides the same

---

[24]Named after Irving Fisher, who first expressed the idea back in 1896; "Appreciation and Interest," *Proceedings of the American Economics Association* (New York: Macmillan, 1896), 331–442. Fisher did not believe it likely, nor did he see much evidence around him (in 1930, at least) to support it. (See *The Theory of Interest* (New York: Macmillan, 1930), 43). His name has stuck to it nevertheless.

[25]To be exact, the extra nominal interest rate needed to offset the effect of x percent extra inflation is $x + rx$ percent, where r is the real interest rate in fractional form. For small values of r and x, the difference is not significant: $x + rx$ is approximately equal to x.

expected real yields;[26] that is, the nominal yield on nominal bonds will equal the real yield on indexed bonds plus an inflation premium equal to expected inflation.

The difficulty with the Fisher effect, seen as an arbitrage condition, is that indexed bonds are not available.[27] Neither is there any other inflation hedge that arbitrageurs could use to avoid the effects of higher expected inflation. For several reasons, including the effects of Canadian tax laws, even corporate profits and share prices are generally reduced by higher inflation rates. As a result, the arbitrage required for the Fisher effect cannot occur, and the Fisher effect result does not appear.[28] Some arbitrage will occur, but not enough. Individual lenders will stop shifting out of nominal bonds at the point where lower real yields on nominal bonds are just offset by whatever undesirable features their alternative has, such as extra market risk or lower liquidity. Nominal bond yields will rise by less than x percent.

In a study using U.S. inflation and interest-rate data from as far back as 1860, Lawrence Summers of Harvard University found virtually no relationship between inflation and nominal interest rates; what relationship there is exists only for the postwar years.[29] Other studies of the years since 1945, using a wide variety of approaches to estimate expected inflation, have estimated the inflation premiums in observed nominal yields to be smaller than expected inflation and much smaller than would maintain real yields constant after tax. In his survey of these results, James Pesando of the University of Toronto reports estimated response rates of inflation premiums to expected inflation from 0.46 to 1.04.[30]

SECTION   7

◻ Summary

The combined behaviour of all lenders and all borrowers in all financial markets produces a general equilibrium in the financial system. The evidence also suggests that equilibrium is reached very quickly in most of the large, wholesale

---

[26]Arbitrage would force expected real yields to be equal after tax, but this complication is ignored here.

[27]The Canada Mortgage and Housing Corporation (CMHC) has issued some indexed, mortgage-backed debt, but there is not enough of it to allow the scale of arbitrage needed to keep the Fisher effect satisfied.

[28]James Pesando of the University of Toronto noted this argument in 1977. *The Impact of Inflation on Financial Markets* (Montreal: C.D. Howe Research Institute, 1977), 23.

[29]"The Non-adjustment of Nominal Interest Rates: A Study of the Fisher Effect," in James Tobin, ed., *Macroeconomics: Prices and Quantities* (Washington, D.C.: Brookings Institution, 1983), 201–46.

[30]For a convenient summary of this research, see James Pesando, *Inflation and the Rates of Return on Bonds and Equities* (Economic Council of Canada Discussion Paper 148, January 1980).

auction markets such as the stock and bond and foreign exchange markets. Equilibrium is reached so quickly, in fact, that prices in these efficient markets change only with new, and therefore unpredictable information. Other markets adjust more slowly, especially those in which prices or yields are posted rather than set by auction. Most retail markets have posted yields.

The concept of general equilibrium is valuable because it brings out the linkages that exist between distant parts of the financial system. However, arbitrage between similar assets gives us a much easier method of generating predictions for particular parts of the financial system.

Arbitrage logic is used to explain the term structure of interest rates. If arbitrage by lenders forces holding period yields to be equal for bonds of different terms, then observed yields to maturity must fit particular yield curves determined by current and expected future interest rates.

Arbitrage between different national markets in our integrated world financial system should produce equal yields on similar assets such as treasury bills in different countries, after allowing for expected exchange rate appreciation or depreciation. Arbitrage has the effect of tying simple interest differentials to either cost of cover or expected exchange rate appreciation. In flexible exchange rate systems such as that in Canada, it is generally not the interest rates that adjust to maintain such arbitrage relationships.

Option theory has made it possible to replicate income flows of complex assets with synthetic combinations of options and other simple assets. Arbitrage then forces parity conditions that tie options values to market values of the more complex assets replicated. A special application of this argument is the Modigliani–Miller proposition that links debt, equity, and asset yields for firms.

Many other arbitrage relationships have been suggested in the financial system. Arbitrage maintains differentials in before-tax yields on assets with different personal tax rates, so as to provide more equal after-tax yields. Arbitrage maintains roughly constant differentials between promised yields on assets of different default and market risk. Arbitrage was predicted to add an inflation premium to nominal yields that would fully offset the effects of expected inflation, but in practice there has been no alternative asset that arbitrageurs could use for their arbitrage, so that arbitrage theory has not performed well.

Key Terms

general equilibrium	covered interest parity
flow equilibrium	uncovered interest parity
stock equilibrium	option theory approach
posted yields	put–call option
efficient markets	parity condition
arbitrage models	Modigliani–Miller (MM)
term structure of interest rates	proposition
pure expectations theory	tax structure of yields
segmented markets	risk differentials
liquidity preference	Fisher effect
preferred habitats	

Questions and Problems

1. Which of the equilibrium conditions in general equilibrium depends on free entry?

2. What are the three assumptions necessary for efficient markets? Which is the least realistic of these assumptions?

3. What does the efficient markets hypothesis imply about the value of technical and fundamental analysis provided by investment dealers?

4. If the yield on any one asset always bears a fixed relationship to the yield on some other asset, what is implied about the slopes of borrowers or lenders curves in that asset's market?

5. Why would banks have short-horizon preferred habitats in the bond market, while life insurers have long-horizon preferred habitats?

6. What pattern of expected future short-term yields would produce a U-shaped term structure of bond yields?

7. What attitude to risk is required to produce uncovered interest parity?

8. What is the adjustment mechanism that brings about covered interest parity?

9. How does the put–call parity condition link option market and stock market trading?

10. Why should one not expect the Fisher effect to hold nearly as closely as covered interest parity or put–call parity?

Suggestions for Further Reading

Bank for International Settlements. *Recent Innovations in International Banking*. Bank for International Settlements, 1986.

LeRoy, Stephen F. "Efficient Capital Markets and Martingales." *Journal of Economic Literature*, December 1989, 1583–621.

Miller, Merton H. "The Modigliani–Miller Propositions after Thirty Years." *Journal of Economic Perspectives*, Fall 1988, 99–121 and following comments.

Rubinstein, Mark. "Derivative Assets Analysis." *Journal of Economic Perspectives*, Fall 1987, 73–94.

Van Horne, James C. *Financial Market Rates and Flows*, 2nd ed. Englewood Cliffs, N.J.: Prentice-Hall, 1984.

Varian, Hal. "The Arbitrage Principle in Financial Economics." *Journal of Economic Perspectives*, Fall 1987, 55–72.

APPENDIX 14–1

Option pricing and stock market arbitrage

Since the sudden stock market crash of October 1987 there has been much discussion of the effect of arbitrage between options markets and stock markets. Options market trading has grown to be huge. Much of it is computer-driven, in that computer programs are used by most options traders to assess whether options prices are out of line with stock values by enough to create a profitable arbitrage opportunity. Such computer-driven trading has been alleged to be everything from reckless to harmless to positively stabilizing. This appendix provides a sketch of option pricing theory that is the basis for computer-driven options trading. The flavour of the arbitrage condition that should exist between the value of an option and the value of the underlying asset being optioned is easy to convey even though the mathematics of applying it is well beyond this book.

Start with the payoff at expiry for a simple call option with strike price K on, say, a market index such as the Standard & Poor's 500 share index. Let the index value be S at the expiry date of the option. For each possible value of S, the payoff from the option will be the greater of 0 or $S - K$.

Before expiry, the value of the option reflects the probability of S reaching values in excess of K (that is, generating positive payoffs) by the expiry date. In fact the value of the option can be thought of as the present value of each possible positive payoff, multiplied by its probability of occurrence at the expiry date. Probabilities of payoffs in turn depend on three factors. The probability of S exceeding K and therefore producing positive payoffs rises with

(a) the level of S now relative to K (it is easier for S to end up above K if it starts there);

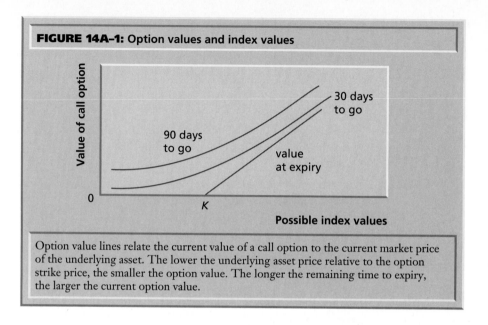

FIGURE 14A–1: Option values and index values

Option value lines relate the current value of a call option to the current market price of the underlying asset. The lower the underlying asset price relative to the option strike price, the smaller the option value. The longer the remaining time to expiry, the larger the current option value.

(b) the length of time to expiry (the longer the time left, the greater the chance of getting above K even from low current values);

(c) the greater the volatility of the index itself (really volatile indexes can "come from behind" even over short periods).

The current market values of options reflect these three factors plus the discount rate used for present value discounting. For specific assumptions about the volatility of optioned assets it is possible with complex mathematics to produce a matrix of what current option values should be in an efficient market for each time to expiry and each current price of the optioned asset. Figure 14A–1 shows sets of such option values for three different periods to expiry: 90 days, 30 days, and at the date of expiry (zero days). Option value lines fall as the expiry date gets closer, for a given underlying index value. Option values rise at an increasing rate with the underlying index value, for a given period to expiry.

The model above links prices in options markets to prices in stock markets. For those with confidence in all the assumptions of the arbitrage pricing model, seeing a lower stock option price than is predicted from the observed stock price is a signal to arbitrage by buying the stock option and selling the stock itself short. Such arbitrage causes option values to rise and stock values to fall, until they are back in line. Over time, the two move closely together. Any change in one market is quickly transmitted to the other.

Chapter fifteen

Government and the Financial System

So far we have discussed the financial system largely in terms of decisions of private lenders and borrowers, operating in markets that are started by private initiative. However, much of the structure of the current Canadian financial system is accounted for by government initiative and interference rather than by the private sector. In this chapter we take a comprehensive look at the involvement of governments in the financial system.

In order to help us understand the pattern of government activity in the financial system, section 1 presents two rival approaches — the social welfare approach and the rational politics approach — that explain how governments are likely to use their special powers to interfere with private activity. Section 2 describes the patterns of regulation that governments have chosen for the financial system. Section 3 discusses the problems associated with the current system of financial regulation. Section 4 discusses the range of financial intermediaries that have been set up by governments, and analyzes the effect of the government deposit insurance system in particular. Section 5 discusses how the pattern of taxes and subsidies influences private flows of funds in the financial system.

You should learn in this chapter:

1. how the social welfare approach and the rational politics approach predict different patterns of government activity;

2. the major types of government regulation used in the financial system, and how reliance on each type has changed over the last two decades;

3. the major problems still associated with the regulatory system in Canadian financial markets;

4. the types of intermediary that have been set up by governments, and whether these supplement or replace private intermediaries;

319

5. the impact of government deposit insurance on the rewards and sanctions for private risk-taking;

6. the main impacts of the tax system on savings and the pattern of investment.

SECTION 1

Two models of government behaviour

There are two approaches to understanding and predicting government behaviour: the social welfare approach, which assumes that government actions are designed to achieve goals of society as a whole; and the rational politics approach, which assumes that government actions are designed merely to ensure that the politicians in power are re-elected.

The social welfare approach

The **social welfare approach**[1] assumes that each government sets out to maximize some set of social objectives for the financial system. Such social objectives (see Chapter 4) include static efficiency, dynamic or allocative efficiency, equity across individuals and regions, and the stabilization of the economy. Many other objectives are often specified for the financial system, such as maintaining public confidence, keeping a high level of domestic ownership, and avoiding conflict of interest situations. These can usually be seen as intermediate objectives whose achievement promotes the more fundamental goals listed above.

Objectives for the financial system are met to a certain extent by the "invisible hand" described by Adam Smith — the forces of rivalry in competitive markets.[2] Governments have supplemented rivalry with other mechanisms in order to achieve goals that are not well met by the private sector: for example, the presence of a central bank together with cash reserve requirements for private-sector banks make stabilization policy more reliable; as another example, deposit insurance helps to reduce the contagion effects that can follow the failure of deposit-taking institutions and drag otherwise sound rivals down into bankruptcy. Regulations are also needed to counter the problems caused by asymmetric information: borrowers almost always know more about their ability to repay than lenders do, and borrowers who anticipate difficulty have an

---

[1] For a good example of this approach to financial regulatuion, see John Chant, *Regulation of Financial Institutions: A Functional Analysis* (Ottawa: Bank of Canada, January 1987).

[2] Ali Nathan and Edwin Neave found that the markets in which banks and trust and mortgage loan companies participated could be described as contestable, so that these firms operated as though they had little market power. "Competition and Contestability in Canada's Financial System: Empirical Results," *Canadian Journal of Economics*, August 1989, 576–94.

incentive not to reveal all they know. A better allocation of credit (that is, more dynamic efficiency) results when borrowers are forced to reveal more information to lenders. Where the private sector has left credit gaps, governments can set up public financial intermediaries and special loan schemes to fill those gaps, thereby increasing the equity with which the financial system as a whole treats Canadians. Governments can also create different rates of tax or subsidy for different types of asset income in order to channel private funds into uses for which there may be some social advantage not appreciated by private lenders, such as a more even distribution of economic activity across Canada.

In general, one would expect provincial governments to have roughly the same social goals, and therefore to choose much the same patterns of intervention in the financial system. However, different governments are subject to different constraints, and they may give different weights to particular goals. Quebec, for instance, feels that a strong, Quebecois-owned financial system is vital to the province's economic growth, and places more emphasis on the goal of domestic ownership than do other provinces. As another example, Ontario's financial sector is larger and more developed than that of any other province; Ontario is accordingly more concerned about ensuring prudent behaviour by intermediaries, and less concerned with attracting more intermediaries to develop its financial system, than is a province such as Alberta.

The rational politics approach

The **rational politics approach**,[3] on the other hand, assumes that politicians try to maximize their chances of (re-)election in order to enjoy the rewards of power; they do this by using the powers of government to benefit major supporters, and by avoiding any use of government power that would harm major supporters. Such concepts as social welfare, or society as a whole, are not relevant in the rational politics approach. The potential major supporters whose wishes matter in the rational politics approach would include groups with many votes (large groups), but also groups with money or other resources that could be used to sway many votes (wealthy groups). The powers of government could benefit major supporters either by changing regulations, or by providing financial services or subsidies at the taxpayer's expense.

The rational politics approach predicts a strong bias in how politicians will use government powers, for instance in setting up regulations. If any particular regulation affects some groups strongly and directly, those groups are most likely to lobby politicians actively — to make sure the politicians know that their group's support at election time depends on the fate of the regulation. On the other hand, groups that are only mildly affected by a regulation will tend not to lobby actively about it. Regulations that bring large benefits to at least one group, but which

---

[3] For a good exposition of this approach, see the original account by George Stigler, "A Theory of Economic Regulation," *Bell Journal of Economics*, 2, 1971, 3–21, or his *The Citizen and the State* (Chicago: University of Chicago Press, 1977). The approach is also known as the public choice approach.

do not impose large costs on any group, will tend to be lobbied for much more actively than they are lobbied against. Such regulations will be passed even if the total benefit is by any objective measure smaller than the total cost, just because the benefits are concentrated for a few and the costs are thinly spread over many. Conversely, regulations that have thinly spread benefits and concentrated costs will tend to be lobbied against more actively than they are supported; they will be avoided or removed.

In order to predict what regulations will appear in the financial system, the analyst who uses the rational politics approach needs to know which groups stand to gain and to lose large amounts from changes in regulation. The groups that stand to gain and lose large amounts from changing regulations in the financial system are usually groups of financial institutions rather than groups of households or business firms. The survival of financial institutions depends critically on how the financial system operates, while the survival of non-financial firms and households usually does not. One can therefore expect intermediaries to lobby actively for some regulations and against others, while other users of the financial system will not lobby much. The benefits that intermediaries will lobby for can come in several forms: straight subsidies, tax preferences, limits on the entry of competitors through licensing or charter restrictions, expansion of investment or borrowing powers, or even some sort of price-fixing arrangement. All of these benefits will increase the profits of existing firms. Where the benefits are given to intermediaries at public expense, the public is likely to protest vigorously only where the expense is concentrated or highly visible (such as a tax increase that is clearly traceable to tax preferences for the financial system).

Non-financial groups as well as intermediaries can seek benefits in the form of government action in the financial system. For example, exporters have sought government guarantees for their loans; consumer groups have persuaded governments to force intermediaries to disclose more explicitly their charges for financial services; and women's groups have fought what they see as discrimination by sex in the pricing of pension and insurance benefits. Groups that are large enough, such as the baby-boom generation at each of its stages, do not need to be highly organized to benefit from government. Political parties constantly try to attract the votes of such large blocks, and so will look for highly visible ways of changing financial regulations to their benefit (such as guarantees or subsidies for mortgage financing, when the baby-boom generation is old enough to be buying houses).

Differences between governments in financial regulation are thus to be expected because of the different financial constituencies of each government. Governments with few locally owned financial institutions will tend to promote consumer benefits at the expense of financial institutions, whereas governments with many local financial institutions will tend to keep more permissive financial regulations and let the consumers bear the extra risks that might result. For example, the caisses populaires are the predominant financial group in Quebec, and caisses populaires are allowed broader investment powers there than in any other province.

The rational politics approach is most useful for predicting government actions where there is no conflict between well-organized lobbies. Where there is such conflict, and the contesting groups are well matched, however, the choice of appropriate regulation will be decided by other criteria that might include how each choice would promote social welfare goals.

SECTION 2

▣ Financial regulation

Financial regulation in Canada is complex: it is done by 11 governments; it is done in different ways for most types of institution; and it is done through many different pieces of legislation enacted at various dates back to before World War II.[4] Both federal and provincial governments regulate many groups such as insurance, trust, and loan companies, pension funds, and finance companies. Only banks, investment dealers, and credit unions are regulated at only one level. Some groups such as financial holding companies and merchant or investment banks are hardly regulated at all. Until the latest round of revisions of federal financial laws that got underway in late 1990, only the Bank Act had automatic provision for revision every decade. All of the other financial acts were long overdue for revision by 1990.

Despite its complexity, the set of financial regulations consist mainly of two types. The first type of regulation forces those with special information to disclose it, so that all participants in a financial market can have equal access to information. The second type of regulation prohibits intermediaries from engaging in specific types of transactions.

Disclosure rules

Most **disclosure rules** apply to securities markets. The Ontario Securities Commission's rule is that all material facts must be released by whoever has them for any security offered or traded. Anyone in possession of material facts not released to the market (an insider, by definition) is forbidden to trade in securities whose price may be affected by such material facts. Regulators are constantly on

---

[4]A good description of the regulatory mix in the late 1980s is provided by the Economic Council of Canada, *A Framework for Financial Regulation* (Ottawa: Supply and Services, 1987). The pieces of federal legislation include the Bank Act, the Trust Companies Act, the Loan Companies Act, the Canadian and British Insurance Companies Act, the Foreign Insurance Companies Act, the Small Loans Act, the Investment Companies Act, the Pension Benefits Standards Act, the Interest Act, the Borrowers and Depositors Protection Act, the Competition Act, the Cooperative Credit Societies Act, and roughly parallel legislation in each province, plus provincial securities legislation. Many regulations are issued by provincial securities commissions or self-regulatory organizations such as the Toronto Stock Exchange or the Investment Dealers' Association.

the lookout for violations of insider trading rules.[5] There are some disclosure rules in retail deposit markets under Borrower and Depositor Protection Acts, but they are not nearly as stringent as those in securities markets.

Both the social welfare and the rational politics approaches are consistent with the disclosure rules we have in Canada. Disclosure rules increase social welfare by promoting equity in the financial system; every investor starts off with access to the same information. On the other hand, full disclosure also raises lenders' confidence and therefore attracts more of them to securities markets and raises the income of securities dealers. In the Vancouver stock exchange, which depends much more on speculative lending than does the Ontario securities market, lenders' confidence in the market is less important to brokers; as one would expect from the rational politics approach, the Vancouver exchange's disclosure requirements are less stringent than those in Ontario's securities markets.

Disclosure rules are much less common for financial intermediaries. As intermediaries are themselves borrowers, they prefer not to have full disclosure that might undermine lenders' confidence — especially as lenders' perceptions of difficulty in one intermediary can be contagious and cause difficulties in many other intermediaries. As one would expect from the rational politics approach, rules for public disclosure of intermediaries' affairs are therefore generally limited to posting of deposit yields and service charges, plus periodic reports of consolidated financial statements. Even those financial statements are reported to governments rather than to the public, and the governments report to the public only many months later.[6]

Less than full disclosure of intermediaries' material facts may also be consistent with the social welfare approach. Withholding or delaying the release of information about intermediaries to the public may be justified if it reduces the possibility of **contagion effects** (where the difficulties of one firm may undermine confidence in other, previously sound firms). Severe contagion effects can undermine confidence in the entire financial system, so it is worth some sacrifice of full information to avoid them. Under these circumstances regulators turn instead to prohibition in advance.

Prohibitive regulations

The purpose of **prohibitive regulations** is to close off avenues by which shareholders and their appointed managers can take advantage of less well informed creditors. The kind of prohibitions required are easier to understand if we pause to look at how shareholders and creditors share risks. We will use

---

[5] For example, when there was suspicion of insider trading by British Columbia premier Bennett in the mid-1980s, both British Columbia and Ontario investigated it, though the suspicions proved unfounded.

[6] Bank reports are published quickly in the *Canada Gazette*, but insurance company reports come out only with a two-year lag.

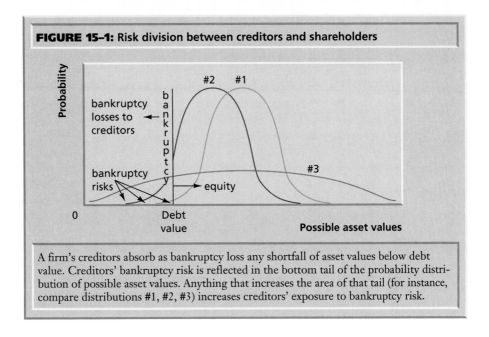

FIGURE 15–1: Risk division between creditors and shareholders

A firm's creditors absorb as bankruptcy loss any shortfall of asset values below debt value. Creditors' bankruptcy risk is reflected in the bottom tail of the probability distribution of possible asset values. Anything that increases the area of that tail (for instance, compare distributions #1, #2, #3) increases creditors' exposure to bankruptcy risk.

the idea of a probability distribution and the logic of the Modigliani–Miller proposition discussed in Chapter 14.

Figure 15–1 presents the possible balance sheet values of a financial intermediary (Faithful Trust again) looking one year ahead. Faithful's existing asset portfolio has a range of possible values at the end of next year, which reflect possible operating profits and possible capital gains or losses during the year. In the figure, future asset values are shown in the probability distribution labelled #1. The value of Faithful's existing debt commitments is certain from Faithful's point of view, so that value is a single point rather than a wide probability distribution. [7] The value of equity next year will be the value of assets less the value of debts, as long as the difference is positive. If asset values turn out to be below debts, Faithful goes bankrupt and it is the creditors who lose the shortfall of assets below debts; that is, the area of probability distribution #1 to the left of the debt value represents the creditors' bankruptcy risk. [8] The bigger that area, the bigger is the default risk exposure of Faithful's creditors.

Now consider some actions that Faithful's management might take to benefit shareholders. One is to pay large dividends to shareholders, in effect taking out some of Faithful's equity. The dividend payout would reduce each of the firm's possible asset values by the amount of the payout, so the probability

---

[7] Actually it is a vertical line with height 1.0, but it has no width.

[8] In Chapter 14 lenders' default or bankruptcy risk was shown to be equivalent to having sold a put option on the borrower's assets. The expected cost or payoff of the put option is proportional to the "bankruptcy risk" area of the probability distribution.

distribution of future asset values in Figure 15–1 would shift from position #1 to, say, position #2. Since the value of Faithful's debts has not changed, the bankruptcy risk area is increased. It now takes a smaller drop in asset values below their expected value to cause bankruptcy and impose losses on Faithful's creditors.

Creditors would not be happy with this action by Faithful's management, but they might not be able to detect it, let alone prevent it. For instance, Faithful's management may use a change in valuation methods to inflate the remaining asset values and cover up the lower equity. After all, the values of non-traded assets such as unsecured loans or real estate are partly a matter of opinion.

A second action that Faithful could take to increase equity at creditors' expense is to invest in riskier assets. In Figure 15–1 the probability distribution of asset values becomes wider, as illustrated by the change from distribution #1 to distribution #3. The bankruptcy risk area is likely to grow when the probability distribution widens, even if the new distribution #3 has an expected value above that of #1. If creditors know in advance about Faithful's new policy of taking on higher asset risk, they will insist on compensation for their extra bankruptcy risk; Faithful will have to give up profits to pay higher interest charges on its debts. If Faithful's management can cover up the change in risk exposure, creditors will end up bearing extra risk they are not paid for. By the time creditors discover their mistake it can be too late to recover. Over the past century, speculation in real estate has been the most common way in which intermediaries take unperceived risks with depositors' money.

A third action that Faithful's management might take on behalf of a controlling shareholder is to divert some of the firm's profits by offering cheap credit to other subsidiaries of the controlling shareholder, such as a real estate company or a merchant bank, or a car-leasing operation. Such self-dealing would impose extra bankruptcy risk on creditors in the same way that a large dividend payout would; the only difference is that minority shareholders would not benefit in this case. In practice it may be quite difficult to detect that self-dealing credits are in fact on better terms than an unrelated borrower would receive, so that creditors and even minority shareholders may not be able to protect themselves fully.

Regulators cannot prevent actions such as those above by forcing intermediaries to disclose all their material facts to the public, so regulators turn instead to mandatory inspection and prohibition. The inspections are carried out by Superintendents of Financial Institutions or their provincial equivalents, by external auditors, and by internal audit committees with special legal responsibilities. The prohibitions take many forms:

1. Deposit-taking institutions other than credit unions are prohibited from lowering their equity below a minimum ratio to total assets. Regulators in many countries became concerned about the **capital adequacy** of banks in particular in the 1980s; bank leverage in Canada, for example, had doubled between the mid-1960s and 1983. In 1988 the central bank governors of ten leading industrial economies signed the Basle Agreement on bank capital

adequacy, to enforce common international guidelines on this issue (see section 4 of Chapter 11 for details of the Basle Agreement).

2. Banks cannot own more than 10 percent of the voting shares or 25 percent of total equity of non-financial firms; neither can trust and loan companies and credit unions outside Quebec. There are almost no remaining **limits on ownership** of financial subsidiaries, however, including venture capital firms that take large equity positions in new firms.

3. The Bank Act requires that schedule I banks be widely held, and that new Canadian-owned banks become schedule I banks within ten years of being established. This is to prevent these banks from being controlled by one group of shareholders, who might then be tempted to profit at the expense of either depositors or minority shareholders. Schedule I banks are the only financial intermediaries prohibited from becoming closely held by controlling shareholders (other than credit unions and mutual insurance companies, for whom it is impossible). Almost all other financial intermediaries in Canada are now closely held, although that was generally not the case before 1970. The draft federal legislation for trust companies now specifies that even closely held companies must have at least 35 percent of their shares widely held.

4. Trust, loan, and insurance companies were until recently prohibited from investing much of their asset portfolio in assets with volatile values, such as unsecured loans, real estate, and stocks with volatile earnings. Before 1990 the combined upper limit for all three types of asset for federally registered trust and loan companies was 7 percent. The proposed limits in draft legislation as of early 1991 are now 70 percent of equity for real estate, 70 percent for common shares, 100 percent for both combined, and no limit at all for unsecured loans. [9]

5. Trust, loan, and insurance companies cannot invest in mortgage loans unless each is secured by real estate whose value at the time of investment is at least one-third again as large as the loan principal, or unless repayment of the loan is insured.

6. Various regulations also control the valuation procedures that must be used in assessing the value of assets. Intermediaries will be tempted, for instance, to improve the look of their financial reports by reporting unpaid interest as accrued income on the income statement and as an extra loan asset on the balance sheet, rather than by treating it as a signal to increase loan loss provisions at the expense of shareholders' equity. Some intermediaries have been tempted in the past to get real estate re-appraised at higher values in order to use it as security for larger mortgage loans. Regulations prescribe use of internal and external auditors and voluminous accounting standards in order to prevent firms from giving in to these temptations.

---

[9] Small companies will be limited in commercial lending, but not in consumer lending. Insurance companies' limits will be somewhat higher than for trust and loan companies.

The four-pillar system

Before 1987, there were regulatory barriers between some specific financial markets. Under what became known as the **four-pillar system**, four special intermediary functions were to be performed separately by four different groups of firms. Firms in one group were to remain independent of firms in other groups. The four functions were unsecured lending (done by banks and credit unions), corporate trusteeship (done by trust companies), securities underwriting and brokerage (done by investment dealers), and insurance (done by insurance companies, which were further split into separate life insurance and property and casualty insurance). Other functions, such as deposit-taking, were more widely shared. Firms in each pillar were not allowed to own or be owned by non-financial firms. Foreign ownership was likewise restricted or forbidden.

The four-pillar arrangement can be explained with social welfare arguments as a means of reducing the risks borne by creditors of the intermediaries in each pillar; it can be argued that any one intermediary cannot be expected to understand fully the risks of more than one or two of the functions. The four-pillar arrangement can also be explained in rational politics terms, as a set of entry barriers that reduced the contestability of all four financial markets to the benefit of existing firms. The rational politics view is supported by the fact that not only cross-ownership but even networking (offering the products of one firm from the branches of another) was forbidden. Networking does not expose lenders to the host institution to any extra risk at all, but it does upset existing competitive positions.[10]

Consistent with the rational politics view, the tightest restrictions of the four-pillar system were placed on the banks.[11] Credit unions, being small and not much of a competitive threat, had few restrictions. Banks, on the other hand, had expanded into consumer lending in the 1960s and quickly crowded out the consumer loan companies; other intermediaries did not want to see the banks do that in their markets. Even the small Canadian computer service companies managed to get regulations passed that prevented banks from using their excess computer capacity to service computer needs of non-financial companies.

---

[10] Even now that the four-pillar arrangement has been abolished, the prohibition on networking persists for insurance; other intermediaries which own insurance companies still may not offer insurance products out of their branches. This is a rational political response to a powerful lobby, the insurance agents.

[11] The four-pillar system was described by one seasoned and witty professional as "three very thin saplings and a giant oak" (Hal Jackman, quoted by Peter C. Newman in *The Financial Post 500*, Summer 1989, 35.

...The laws that keep American and Japanese banks out of investment banking and non-bank businesses are being eroded in both countries by piecemeal deregulation, inter-industry turf battles, and the willingness of regulators to turn a blind eye to transgressions of the letter of the law.

Source: "A Survey of International Banking," *The Economist*, April 7, 1990, p. 40.

Merging of pillars, crumbling of barriers

The four-pillar system is now almost completely dismantled. It has been made unworkable by a combination of foreign competition, financial innovation, and competition between regulators in different jurisdictions.

The four pillars were not completely separate even in 1970. For example, banks helped in the underwriting of a few (non-federal) government securities and in the distribution of corporate securities, though without soliciting business or offering advice. Banks sold some life insurance, in the form of credit insurance for amounts owed on mortgage loans. Life insurers and investment dealers made many loans to households, and even to some firms through policy loans and clients' margin loans, respectively. Credit union centrals owned their own trust and insurance companies. Trust companies were allowed to make some unsecured commercial and consumer loans.

By the end of the 1980s the pillars had been fused in many places. Financial innovation and the growth of international markets allowed firm after firm to get around restrictive regulations. Entry barriers crumbled or were routinely bypassed. The most dramatic crumbling occurred early on: dozens of foreign bank affiliates invaded the Canadian business loan market in the early 1970s, avoiding the reach of the Bank Act by the trivial adjustment of not including the word "bank" in their names. They were attracted by a large interest spread between loan yields and money market deposit yields. In the 1980s, large firms started to sell their loans abroad; medium-sized firms started to issue bankers' acceptances instead of taking out bank loans. Both developments opened up the wholesale loan market. Canadian borrowers issuing securities started to offer their securities in the international market, often through foreign securities dealers that were subsidiaries of Canadian banks; in the global securities market, separate Canadian securities dealers were too small to compete. For new hedging instruments such as interest rate options and financial futures, existing legislation had made no provision at all, so those markets have been invaded by banks at home and abroad.

Within Canada, intermediaries responded to these competitive pressures by finding ways around restrictive regulations. Stockbrokers got around the prohibition on issuing deposits by issuing cash management accounts. Life insurers got around the same prohibition by calling their term deposits "short-term deferred annuities." Some banks entered the general insurance business to the extent of offering policies of general insurance companies from their branches. Banks got around the Bank Act ceilings on their mortgage lending business by transferring excess mortgage loans to the books of subsidiary mortgage loan companies. Life insurers made creative use of holding company structures to issue bonds and preferred shares that would otherwise have been forbidden. Banks and trust companies blurred the lines between loan and securities markets by reselling loans and by repackaging mortgage pools to sell as mortgage-backed securities. Financial holding companies such as the Desjardins Group, Trilon, Laurentian Group, Traders Group, and Power Financial started to network the services of trust companies, life and general insurers, real estate firms, securities dealers, and even the Laurentian Bank. Large non-financial firms such as Edper Corporation, Power Corporation, and Bell Canada Enterprises started to buy into or form groups of financial service companies.

There are few remaining barriers to entry to Canadian financial markets. Life insurance companies may be owned by banks, though their policies may not be distributed from bank branches. Foreign ownership of financial firms is still limited for trust and loan companies, and to some extent for banks (for non-U.S. owners). The formation of the single market in Europe in 1992 will further speed up the opening of financial markets, since one of the principles of entry of Canadian firms to this large market is reciprocity — that Canada provides equal access for European firms to Canadian markets. The Free Trade Agreement with the United States has already had a similar effect.

Regulatory competition

The process of blurring pillars could not be stopped by any one regulator because, had any regulator tried, intermediaries would have shifted their head offices or registrations to a more congenial jurisdiction. Regulators in Quebec, Alberta, and British Columbia were in competition with each other and with Ontario and Ottawa to attract financial business out of Toronto to their cities. As an international example of such **regulatory competition**, international banking by U.S. banks grew so rapidly in the 1970s in unlikely but very permissive places like the Cayman Islands that even U.S. regulators had to relent. They allowed U.S. banks to carry on international business in designated international banking centres within the United States, under equally permissive regulation. By the 1980s, the leverage that individual jurisdictions had over institutions in wholesale markets was even less. Within Canada, Quebec started up a round of regulatory competition in 1985 when it permitted cross-ownership of trust, insurance, brokerage, and non-financial companies for provincially incorporated firms. When one of the big banks seized the opportunity to buy a Quebec investment dealer in early 1987, the federal government felt obliged to relax its own prohibition on banks owning investment dealer subsidiaries. The Ontario government removed ownership restrictions on its investment dealers in 1987 and 1988. By the end of 1987 all of the big banks had such subsidiaries. As a result, investment dealers have ceased to exist as a separate sector in much the same way that mortgage loan companies did before them.

By 1990 regulators in different countries had made a few attempts to halt the regulatory competition and stop the slide to ever more permissive regulation, the most significant being the Basle Agreement of 1988 on capital adequacy of banks. Regulators are working on a similar agreement for investment dealers.

SECTION 3

Problems of the regulatory system

The Canadian regulatory system still has several serious problems. The patchwork of federal and provincial regulations are far from uniform; they offer little protection of creditors against self-dealing by owners of intermediaries; they promote excessive risk-taking by some intermediaries; and they do not allow regulators to act quickly enough to protect creditors' interests. All of these problems undermine confidence in the Canadian financial system.

Lack of uniformity

In many financial markets in Canada, participating intermediaries are regulated by different jurisdictions (or sometimes no jurisdiction at all). The regulations are not uniform across provinces, or between provincial governments and the federal government. For example, trust companies chartered in Quebec have wider powers than those chartered in Ontario or Alberta. Business firms incorporated by Ontario face more expensive minimum pension requirements for their employees than business firms incorporated by Quebec.[12] Even the humble home mortgage has much less security in Alberta than in other provinces. Investment dealers in Vancouver are subject to fewer and lower standards than investment dealers elsewhere.

The old pattern in which provincial governments other than Ontario generally followed the lead of the federal government or of Ontario has gone. Many provinces—Quebec in particular—now think of their financial services sector as an important source of jobs and income, and a powerful engine of growth for small firms elsewhere in the economy. They are no longer willing to sit back when they can spur growth and attract relatively footloose financial firms by what seem like relatively small changes in financial regulations. Quebec, Ontario, Alberta, British Columbia and the federal government each has its own ideas about what powers financial firms should have and what restrictions are necessary.

Lack of uniformity in regulation of financial markets matters for three reasons. First, the variety of regulations imposes extra administrative costs for

---

[12] In particular, defined benefit pensions in Ontario must be indexed 75 percent to the inflation rate, while those in Quebec need not. This requirement adds significantly to both the cost and the risk of providing pension benefits to workers.

trust companies, for instance, who must observe the regulations of the province in which they operate as well as the regulations of the jurisdiction in which they are incorporated. Second, lenders are left more uncertain about the risks associated with lending to intermediaries. Where different trust companies, for example, have widely different powers and links with other firms, they also have widely different temptation to the kinds of excessive risk-taking discussed above in connection with Figure 15–1. Lenders can learn about differences in intermediary powers across provinces, but the extra information cost is no more desirable in this case than extra costs in any other context. [13]

Third, lack of coordination of regulations generates a drift of firms to the most permissive jurisdiction, which in turn lowers the average protection of creditors in the financial system. Lower protection of creditors must undermine confidence in the entire financial system, which interferes with the efficient flow of savings to the most productive investment.

Self-dealing

Figure 15–1 has already shown the risk to creditors that arises from **self-dealing** by controlling shareholders. The federal government's proposed revisions to financial legislation will in general ban non-arm's-length transactions between a financial institution and those in a position of influence over it, with some exceptions that will be supervised and screened by directors or by the Superintendent of Financial Institutions. There will be limits on loans made to directors or officers, or to companies owned by directors or officers. The federal government will also require that at least 35 percent of voting shares of large financial firms be widely held and publicly traded. The hope is that minority shareholders will be more likely to spot self-dealing than would creditors, and that having so many publicly traded shares would keep the company under the scrutiny of stock market analysts. These changes will greatly reduce the likelihood of self-dealing, though they will not eliminate it.

Where the controlling shareholder of an intermediary is a non-financial firm—and Canada now has several of those—the danger of self-dealing temptations is all the greater, since the controlling shareholder's non-financial business is automatically a potential loan customer of the intermediary. In 1980, for example, Campeau Corporation bid for a controlling interest in Royal Trust. The bid eventually failed, but before doing so it prompted widespread concern about a financial intermediary being controlled by a real estate developer. Real estate developers in particular are assumed to be always cash-hungry. The risk for Royal Trust lenders and trust owners would have been enormous if the bid had succeeded, as Campeau went on to bid billions of dollars for U.S. shopping chains and was then unable to service his debts. It should be noted that even the

---

[13] The push for uniform securities market regulation is coming from a private group called the Group of Thirty, rather than from a group of governments; not surprisingly the private groups are more concerned about cost pressures than are governments.

forthcoming federal legislation sets no limit on the amount that an intermediary could lend in mortgage loans to a controlling shareholder.

A conflict of interest with trust funds is most likely to arise when unsecured or poorly secured lending is combined with trustee activity. For instance, if Acme Ltd. is having difficulties making payments on an unsecured loan from Faithful Trust, then both Acme and Faithful Trust have a problem: Acme with possible bankruptcy, and Faithful with a possible loan loss. Both of their problems could be eased if Acme were to issue some preferred shares, for instance, and if Faithful were to use some of the trust funds that it controls to buy those preferred shares. Acme could then pay down its loan to Faithful. In this transaction, Faithful's shareholders benefit from recovery of unsecured loan funds, but only by transferring the risk of loss to the owners of the trust funds that Faithful Trust controls. Where Faithful Trust makes only secured loans like mortgages, shareholders would have less at stake in Acme's difficulties, and therefore Faithful's management would be less tempted to try to transfer the risk onto owners of trust funds.

Regulators are allowing far more conflict-of-interest situations to develop in the future by enlarging the unsecured lending powers of trust companies, and by allowing other intermediaries to buy or set up their own trust company subsidiaries. Shareholders' and management's incentives to profit at the expense of owners of trust funds are to be frustrated only by requiring that management of trust funds and unsecured lending go on in different sections of a company, with no sharing of information — as though there were a so-called Chinese wall between the sections. Chinese wall provisions are common in other countries such as the United States, where commercial banking and trustee activity are commonly carried on within the same firm. The senior executives of the firm, however, must know both about the trust funds' investments and also about any loan repayment difficulties of unsecured loan customers. Chinese walls cannot be expected to reach that high in the firm.

Excessive risk exposure

If shareholders can invest in increasingly risky assets and receive higher returns accordingly, and then pass on most or all of the risk to creditors without charge, they have an incentive to abuse creditors by excessive risk-taking. For instance, new hedging instruments allow financial intermediaries to take on large extra asset risks without those risks even showing on the balance sheet. Also, when a bank or trust company shifts to loans of more doubtful quality, the shift will not be visible in the firm's public reports, especially if management wishes to hide it. Neither depositors nor regulators may detect the worsening of asset quality until it is too late to recover depositors' funds. **Deposit insurance** insulates retail depositors from this risk exposure in almost all deposit-taking firms except insurance companies; only larger corporate depositors and holders of other liabilities are still at risk.

Some firms' managements fear the loss of reputation (and their jobs) enough to avoid such temptations. Widely held firms are more likely to fall into this camp, because the management's concern for continued employment will not be overridden by shareholders' concern for extra profits. Managements of closely held firms have controlling shareholders to please; they must be less reluctant to take risks unless shareholders also take the long view. Firms already in trouble for other reasons will be especially tempted: when it looks as though the firm may well founder anyway, bigger gambles with depositors' funds may appear to be the only option that has any chance of success.

It is hard to know how serious this risk of overexposure is. The massive exposure of big international banks to the risks of Third World debt after 1975, to the risks of property loans in the 1980s (in the United States and in Japan), and to loans to finance highly levered companies in the 1980s all suggest that even big, widely held banks are not immune to temptation. Simultaneous defaults by even a few large Third World debtors in the early 1980s would have left large banks insolvent around the world. It has not happened yet, but not because banks have been prudent.

Inadequate regulatory supervision

The supervisors of financial institutions have not been able to enforce the regulations that exist. Inevitably, there are few supervisors relative to the number of intermediaries being regulated, so that supervisors must rely heavily on the information provided by the firms being supervised. It is true that external auditors check management information each year, but auditors are hired by management rather than by the regulators. It is difficult to be sure that supervisors are being given accurate information.

Even where regulators have been provided with accurate information, it has been difficult to get them to act quickly enough in defence of creditors' interests. The last decade has shown many times in many provinces that supervisors detect abuses too late and governments act on them even later. Several examples follow. The Ontario government was seriously embarrassed when Re-Mor Investment Co. and its parent, the Astra Trust Co., failed in 1980 only shortly after Re-Mor had its licence renewed by the Ontario Registrar of Trust and Loan Companies, as a financially sound enterprise. In the early 1980s the Quebec government was equally embarrassed at the troubles of the caisses d'entraide movement (see Chapter 12), a group of small, local cooperative credit unions that went bankrupt making commercial loans. Since these incidents, governments have given their financial regulators much wider powers to act when they sense trouble in a financial institution. Nevertheless, in 1985 federal regulators were blamed for keeping Canadian Commercial Bank and Northland Bank going far too long before they collapsed. Similarly, in 1988 the Alberta and Saskatchewan governments were both castigated by the Principal Group inquiry for acting much too slowly to protect depositors in the Principal Group companies before they collapsed.

These cases are part of a long history of government embarrassment after the fact. More than two dozen financial firms have failed since 1980. Others like the caisses d'entraide have been saved from bankruptcy only by forced mergers with healthier institutions.

According to the social welfare approach, this failure by governments to act quickly enough is the result of insufficient resources being devoted to regulatory supervision of the financial system. The rational politics view is well put by Paul McCrossan, a member of parliament who has served on the Commons Finance Committee:

> Provincial governments, as illustrated in the inquiry into the Principal Group in Alberta, have often been more interested in the continuing employment opportunities in their provinces, and have put pressure on federal regulators to leave regional companies experiencing difficulty alone rather than clamp down early.
>
> There will always be a conflict between provincial employment concerns and federal regulatory concerns as long as the federal government picks up any losses through the CDIC.
>
> *The Financial Post*, 1989

SECTION 4

Government intermediation

Governments not only regulate the financial system, they also supplement it by setting up government loan schemes. There are over one hundred different government loan schemes in existence now, and more are born each year.[14] Government loan schemes are of two types: straightforward borrowing and relending of funds through government-owned intermediaries, and using the government's credit rating to guarantee specific types of loans made by privately owned intermediaries. Many of the major government-owned financial intermediaries were introduced in Chapter 5. Government intermediation accounted for $69 billion in 1990. Government loan guarantees amounted to $29 billion in 1980. Most guaranteed loan financing goes into housing; the rest is spread equally over the business sector, export financing, and farming.[15]

Government intermediaries

The following is a list of major financial intermediaries set up by the federal and provincial governments. In almost all cases these **government intermediaries**

---

[14]Neufeld reports that from 1867 to 1971 about 168 government financial intermediaries (including loan schemes) were established, of which about two-thirds remained in 1971. E.P. Neufeld, *The Financial System of Canada* (Toronto: Macmillan, 1972), 441. See also Economic Council of Canada, *Intervention and Efficiency* (Ottawa: Supply and Services, 1982).

[15]Economic Council of Canada, *Intervention and Efficiency*, 6.

can borrow in their own names or in those of their parent governments to raise funds.

1. The Bank of Canada exists to issue currency and deposits and thereby to control the monetary base of the economy. It also serves as lender of last resort to members of the Canadian Payments Association.

2. The Canada Deposit Insurance Corporation and Quebec's Régie de l'assurance-dépôts guarantee deposit liabilities of private intermediaries (up to a ceiling of $60 000 per depositor in any one institution). They also inspect the insured institutions. Credit unions have separate stabilization funds outside Quebec. The impact of government deposit insurance is analyzed more fully below.

3. The Canada and Quebec Pension Plans receive and lend out all of the individual and employer contributions to each pension plan, as discussed in Chapter 13. The Quebec investment body, the Caisse de Dépôt et Placement, has wide discretion in lending its funds and is an important lender in Quebec financial markets. Canada Pension Plan funds are put entirely in special non-marketable provincial bonds. In 1986 the Canada Pension Plan was changed to allow provinces not to pay even all the interest on their bonds, so the Canada Pension Plan's use of its funds can hardly be called lending.[16]

4. The Canada Mortgage and Housing Corporation lends its borrowed funds for specific types of housing construction, such as low-income townhouse development projects, and insures private mortgage loans on new houses for up to 90 percent of default losses.

5. The Export Development Corporation extends long- and medium-term credit to foreign customers to spur Canadian export sales, and insures short-term loans made by banks to export customers. Its insurance is said to cover "political risk" that private intermediaries would not be able to absorb.

6. The Federal Business Development Bank lends start-up and expansion money to new ventures that cannot find financing elsewhere. It also provides extensive management assistance. Venture capital lending is now very much bigger than when this intermediary was established.

7. The Farm Credit Corporation provides almost all of the long-term credit used by farmers.

8. The Alberta treasury branches operate as Alberta banks in all but name. The ATB system issues deposits and makes consumer and business loans.[17]

9. The Province of Ontario savings office issues deposits, and then "invests" the funds directly into the Ontario government's consolidated revenue fund.

10. The federal and provincial "superannuation accounts" are branches of government that were set up to accept pension contributions and to pay out

---

[16] For discussion of this change, see Bruce Kennedy, "Refining the CPP: the Cost of Acquiescence," *Canadian Public Policy*, March 1989, 34–42.

[17] See Chapter 12 for a discussion of the ATBs and of the POSO.

pension benefits for the civil service and the armed forces. Net contributions are invested directly into the governments' consolidated revenue funds.

11. The federal Department of Regional Industrial Expansion lends funds at attractive rates to firms that locate or expand in relatively depressed areas. These loans are often supplemented by other government grants.

The list could be extended much further, to cover lending by government intermediaries to almost every sector of the economy.

Loan guarantee schemes

The two largest **loan guarantee schemes** are deposit insurance and residential mortgage insurance for specific types of residential first mortgages under the National Housing Act ("NHA mortgages"). Mortgage loan guarantees by the Canada Mortgage and Housing Corporation (CMHC) have had a large influence on Canadian flows of funds. When in 1969 the CMHC approved insurance of residential mortgages with interest rates fixed only for a five-year term, trust and mortgage loan companies gained a new lease on life: the term to maturity of their main asset could now be matched much more closely with that of their main liability. Mortgage insurance is expensive for CMHC when interest rates rise, however. Figure 15–2 shows the default loss rates for 1982–88 for both CMHC's insured mortgages and for those insured by private corporations. The delayed impact of the very high interest rates and of the deep recession in 1981–82 is clear.

The federal government also has loan guarantee schemes for student loans, farm improvement loans, fisheries improvement loans, home improvement loans, and medium and small business loans. The conclusion of an Economic Council of Canada study of loan programs and guarantees was that "society as a whole has more to lose than to gain" from them.[18]

Government intermediation can be explained by either of the two approaches to government action. In the social welfare view, government intermediaries are set up to fill credit gaps left by the private sector. Credit gaps could occur, for instance, where the private perception of risk exaggerates the risk to society as a whole, or where private intermediaries ignore some non-financial consideration such as regional balance or the value of education. Deposit insurance, for instance, is justified as a way of removing the externality of unwarranted contagion effects (see below).

In the rational politics view, government intermediation is the response of government to whatever pressure group is served by the cheap credit that each loan scheme provides. Loan guarantee schemes in particular are not easily visible to outside groups, they are inexpensive to set up and administer, they do not

---

[18] J.M. Gagnon and B. Papillon, *Financial Risk, Rate of Return for Canadian Firms, and Implications for Government Intervention* (Ottawa: Supply and Services, 1984).

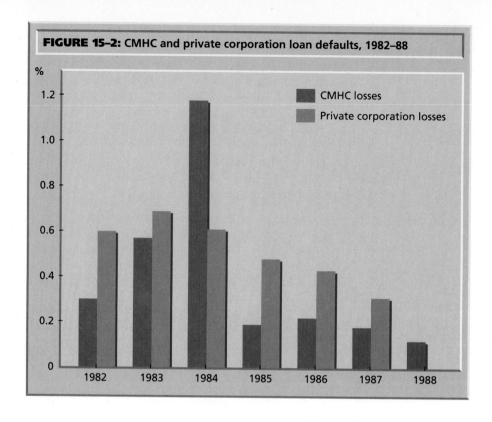

FIGURE 15-2: CMHC and private corporation loan defaults, 1982–88

appear in government budgets, and they leave room for private intermediation.[19]

The social welfare view of government intermediation is certainly correct for some institutions such as the Bank of Canada, the Department of Regional and Industrial Expansion, and the Canada Deposit Insurance Corporation. For others, many can be seen as filling credit gaps that existed 20 years ago, but which have since disappeared. For instance, the Farm Credit Corporation or the Federal Business Development Bank could not now be justified on the grounds that private intermediaries do not lend to farmers or new business firms, or that private intermediaries exaggerate the risks of such loans. Some government intermediaries have been allowed to wither, or have changed their role in response to the closing of credit gaps by private intermediaries. The Canada Development Corporation, which was set up to expand venture capital lending in the 1960s, was later sold off to private owners. The CMHC originally loaned to almost any household for new housing, but now restricts its mortgage lending to special types of project such as low-income housing.

---

[19]Although the U.S. government found out the hard way that loan guarantee schemes can bring huge costs later on. The Federal Savings and Loan Insurance Corporation accumulated losses of over $300 billion from insuring but not adequately supervising savings and loan companies in the late 1980s.

The CDIC and risk-taking

One government intermediary, the Canada Deposit Insurance Corporation, is now alleged to be compounding risk in the financial system rather than removing it. This requires some explanation.

Deposit insurance was introduced in 1967 in Canada to prevent contagion effects (where the failure of one intermediary automatically causes suspicion about other intermediaries). Any suspicion about the soundness of financial institutions can easily become self-fulfilling if it leads to a run on deposits. The introduction of deposit insurance as an antidote to contagion effects was seen as a useful bolster to confidence in Canada's financial system, and particularly to small and medium-size firms.[20] Banks argued that they did not need any such scheme because they had not lost a dollar of depositors' money even in the Great Depression. Nevertheless they were included in the deposit insurance scheme and, because of their dominance of the deposit markets, they paid the bulk of the premiums.[21]

The CDIC and its Quebec counterpart, the Régie de l'assurance-dépôts du Québec (RADQ) have succeeded in removing or greatly reducing contagion effects at the retail level. Even the failure of two western banks in 1985 did not cause retail depositors to withdraw funds from other banks (uninsured wholesale depositors were another story). However, the CDIC's flat-rate premium structure creates an incentive for intermediaries to take excessive risks.

This argument is easily demonstrated by reproducing a version of Figure 15–1. In Figure 15–3, probability distribution #1 refers to a relatively safe asset portfolio that exposes creditors to little bankruptcy risk. Distribution #2a refers to a riskier portfolio, bought under the assumption that the cost of credit is not affected by the extra risk exposure of lenders. The lenders' extra risk exposure is clear from the larger "bankruptcy risk" area under distribution #2a, to the left of the bankruptcy line. Distribution #2b refers to the same riskier asset portfolio, but assumes that lenders insist on higher yields as the price of taking on extra bankruptcy risk. Distribution #2b is to the left of distribution #2a by the present value of the extra yields that must be offered to depositors.

Comparing distributions #1 and #2a, management would quite probably choose to take the extra risk; the extra expected equity value would be worth the gamble. Comparing #1 and #2b they might well choose not to take the extra risk. In the real-world retail deposit market in Canada, intermediaries do not assume that insured depositors will insist on extra yields, because insured depositors are insulated from such risks. Nor do they assume that the CDIC will charge them higher insurance rates, because the CDIC does not yet have the legal authority to

---

[20] The contagion effects following the failure of a trust company and its mortgage loan affiliate in 1965 led to setting up the CDIC and the RADQ.

[21] Stigler notes that smaller firms are likely to have greater political influence over the form of regulations than they have economic power in their market. This case fits his theory exactly: the smaller firms were able to get the lion's share of the benefits of deposit insurance, while paying only the jackal's share of the premium costs.

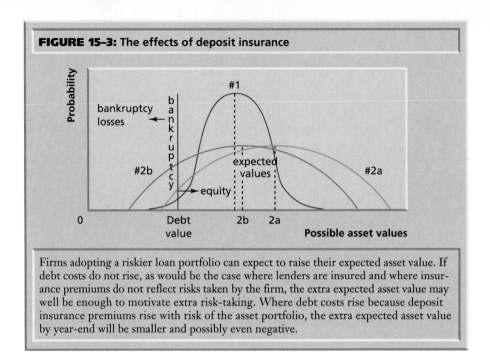

FIGURE 15–3: The effects of deposit insurance

Firms adopting a riskier loan portfolio can expect to raise their expected asset value. If debt costs do not rise, as would be the case where lenders are insured and where insurance premiums do not reflect risks taken by the firm, the extra expected asset value may well be enough to motivate extra risk-taking. Where debt costs rise because deposit insurance premiums rise with risk of the asset portfolio, the extra expected asset value by year-end will be smaller and possibly even negative.

do so. So firms with mainly insured deposits have an incentive to take more risks than they would if their deposits were not insured.[22]

One solution to this risk-taking incentive is for the CDIC to devise and impose risk-related premiums. Such premiums would offset the extra asset yield and equity value that attracts managements to riskier assets in the first place. Studies of deposit insurance in the mid-1980s concluded that it was impossible to devise measures of intermediary risk to which premiums could be related. These same studies also concluded, however, that the CDIC could collect information that would enable it to build an early-warning system to identify which firms needed closer monitoring.[23]

Another suggested solution is to rely on stock market pricing of intermediaries' stocks to provide early warning of problems. A study of 40 bank failures in the United States in the 1980s, however, concluded that stock market participants lagged behind specialized bank-rating agencies, and these in turn lagged behind regulators in detecting bank problems caused by loan losses. Regulators

---

[22] In government takeovers of insolvent savings and loan institutions in the United States in 1989, 60 percent showed evidence of criminal fraud. For bank failures the rate was 20 percent (*The Financial Post*, April 9, 1990, 7).

[23] For instance, Brian Smith and Robert W. White, "The Deposit Insurance System in Canada," *Canadian Public Policy*, December 1988, 333–46.

usually recognized the problems even before the banks' own management did so.[24]

The rational politics approach suggests that risk-related premiums will not be introduced, because smaller firms prefer the current arrangement and the opponents are not strong enough politically.[25] The Vancouver Stock Exchange provides an analogy: it has remained much less strictly regulated than the Toronto Stock Exchange for decades and will stay that way, simply because that suits the stockbrokerage firms in Vancouver.

SECTION 5

Taxes and subsidies

Governments try to steer financial flows in particular directions by means of special **taxes and subsidies** for particular kinds of income or activity. The important classes of income singled out for favoured tax treatment are capital gains and dividend income, and income from owner-occupied housing. Income from owner-occupied housing is received implicitly, in the form of rent that does not have to be paid or that is paid to oneself; it is entirely tax-free. Capital gains income (that is, income in the form of increases in the value of assets held) is not taxed at all for the first $100 000; it is taxed at less than personal rates after that, and only when the gain is finally realized through the sale of the asset rather than as soon as the gain occurs. Capital gains on principal residences (both houses and land) are completely tax-free. Recall that the bulk of government loan guarantees are for mortgage loans to finance housing as well. Governments have clearly been steering credit flows in the Canadian financial system towards improving the housing stock and raising residential land prices. The tax treatment of housing in Canada is not quite as generous as in the United States, where mortgage interest is deductible from income tax, but it is generous.[26]

Income from stocks is taxed at lower rates than income from bonds and deposits. Dividend income from stocks provides a dividend tax credit while interest income does not. Income from stocks is also received mainly in the form of capital gains, which are taxed at low rates, if at all. The effect of tax rates on relative before-tax yields was discussed in section 6 of Chapter 14.

---

[24] Richard Randall, "Can the Market Evaluate Asset Quality Exposure in Banks?" *New England Economic Review*, July–August 1989.

[25] This story might be different if the deposit insurer were privately administered, as in France, Japan, Switzerland, and Germany. A privately administered firm would not have the same incentives as a Crown corporation. Bank deposits in Canada were privately insured before 1967; credit union deposits are still privately insured.

[26] There used to be a further huge tax break for savings intended for housing investment, through Registered Home Ownership Savings Plans. Savings invested in RHOSPs were deductible on contribution, and not taxable on withdrawal if used for housing. This was similar to an arrangement still in place in the United Kingdom.

In the 1980s the Alberta and Quebec governments reinforced the tax advantage of stocks by offering large rebates of provincial personal income tax for investments in stock issued by provincial companies.

The tax treatment of intermediation varies widely among intermediaries, with dramatic effects on flows of funds. The biggest tax shelter for households is for funds contributed to either registered pension funds or RRSPs. Such contributions earn tax refunds at full personal tax rates, and the income from them is not taxable at all until contributions are withdrawn at retirement or after. Pension funds and assets in RRSPs are thereby given a huge competitive advantage over other assets; this favoured treatment can be contrasted with the 2 percent premium tax paid by insurance companies on life insurance premiums. Fortunately, the range of domestic assets eligible for inclusion in RRSPs is very wide, so tax-induced distortion of financial flows is kept fairly small. The most important distortions associated with retirement income tax shelter provisions are imposed (a) by the requirement of tax law that all household funds put into pension funds or RRSPs be rolled over before age 71 into one of a restricted list of annuities, and (b) by the provision that tax-sheltered mutual funds and pension funds must have no more than 10 percent of their portfolio in foreign assets. Professor George Pink of the University of Toronto has estimated that the restriction on foreign assets has served to reduce expected yields and to increase risk for pension plan contributors by an amount that would matter to any household. [27]

There are several other smaller-scale tax distortions in the financial system from tax shelters to favour investment in activities such as mining exploration, film-making, and the like. In the past there were more of these tax shelters, but the pressure of rising debt service payments in the federal budget has caused many tax preferences to be removed. Also, the government has found that its tax incentives tend to be overused. When a strong tax preference was extended for savings put into scientific research projects in the early 1980s, for example, the flood of money made available by households (with the help of investment dealers) swamped the government's monitoring ability and made a big dent in its revenue. Many abuses and much political embarrassment followed.

SECTION 6

Summary

Government activity can be seen as an attempt to steer the financial system to produce better outcomes of socially important goals. Alternatively, it can be seen as an attempt by politicians to attract the support of pressure groups for their

[27] George Pink, "Government Restriction on Foreign Investment by Pension Funds: An Empirical Evaluation," *Canadian Public Policy*, September 1989, 300–12.

own re-election. The pattern of Canadian government activity in the financial system can be explained in part by both theories.

Government regulations consist mainly of disclosure requirements for market participants, especially borrowers, and a set of rapidly changing restrictions on the behaviour of financial institutions. Both sets of regulations reflect the asymmetry of information in financial markets: disclosure rules attempt to correct the imbalance, whereas restrictions try to prevent the abuse of information by those who have an information advantage. To the extent that they are effective, both sets of regulations increase lenders' confidence in the financial system.

The very stringent disclosure rules that apply to securities markets can also be explained as intended to increase the volume of market trading, upon which securities dealers depend for their income. Similarly, in the past, restrictions on financial intermediaries acted as important barriers to entry to financial markets, keeping big banks in particular out of the markets of much smaller rivals. More recent regulatory changes and the forces of innovation have removed most of the barriers to entry to most financial markets.

The current regulatory system has several serious flaws, however. Regulation is by no means uniform across firms or across regions. The 11 provincial and federal governments do not agree on what is prudent for any one kind of intermediation. None of them has regulations that effectively counter management incentives to profit shareholders at the expense of lenders. Regulations are not enforced quickly or accurately enough to prevent frequent bankruptcies. The Canada Deposit Insurance Corporation and other deposit insurance arrangements have removed the danger of one bankruptcy escalating to become a general liquidity scare, but its pricing of insurance at a flat rate that is independent of risk exposure has encouraged excessive risk-taking and raised the frequency of individual bankruptcies.

Government intermediation supplements private intermediation in many areas and sectors. Many government intermediaries and loan schemes reflect credit gaps that existed in the past but which have since disappeared. Government tax preferences also steer financial flows by changing relative after-tax yields. Most of the tax preferences are part of the federal Income Tax Act, and many are large. They channel financial flows particularly into housing investment. The huge tax preferences for retirement saving have little effect on allocation of funds to investment because the preference is extended over a broad range of financial assets. Foreign assets are the main exclusions.

Key Terms

social welfare approach
rational politics approach
disclosure rules
contagion effects
prohibitive regulations
capital adequacy
limits on ownership
four-pillar system

regulatory competition
self-dealing
deposit insurance
regulatory lag
government intermediaries
loan guarantee schemes
taxes and subsidies

Questions and Problems

1. What are the objectives of government intervention in the financial system, and how are these objectives different from those for government intervention elsewhere in the economy?
2. How have you been the beneficiary or the victim of government intervention in the financial system?
3. Which problems of government regulation are not reduced or removed by allowing intermediaries into each others' jurisdictions?
4. Outline some of the consequences for financial markets if the CMHC were no longer to insure residential mortgages against default risk.
5. Outline some of the consequences for financial markets if the CDIC were no longer to insure depositors against the failure of deposit-taking institutions.

Suggestions for Further Reading

Economic Council of Canada. *A Framework for Financial Regulation*. Ottawa: Supply and Services, 1987.

——. *Intervention and Efficiency*. Ottawa: Supply and Services, 1982.

Neufeld, E.P. *The Financial System of Canada*. Toronto: Macmillan of Canada, 1972.

Schultz, Richard and Alan Alexandroff. *Economic Regulation and the Federal System*. Toronto: University of Toronto Press, for the MacDonald Commission, 1986.

Smith, Brian and Robert W. White. "The Deposit Insurance System in Canada." *Canadian Public Policy*, December 1988, 333–46.

Stigler, George. "A Theory of Economic Regulation." *Bell Journal of Economics*, 2, 1971, 3–21.

——. *The Citizen and the State*. Chicago: University of Chicago Press, 1977.

PART FIVE

Macroeconomics and Financial Markets

In previous parts we described and analyzed how the financial system channels funds from savers to investors, how it provides a payments mechanism, and how it allows households to make long-term financial plans for transferring income from early years to retirement. In Parts Five and Six we analyze how the financial system contributes to the social goals of stable levels of capacity utilization, of employment, of prices, and of output growth.

Before we can analyze how the financial system affects the stabilization of output and inflation, we must first have as a common starting point an explanation of how output and inflation rates are determined. Chapters 16–18 therefore briefly review the core of modern macroeconomic theory. The review has four distinguishable sections: aggregate demand, aggregate supply, equilibrium outcomes in short and long runs, and some theory of the dynamics of how we move from short run to long run. Where the financial system appears in this review we will treat it fairly crudely, as is usually done in intermediate-level macroeconomics. In Chapter 19 we return to consider the role of the financial system with more sophistication. The techniques used to explain the macroeconomic theory in Part Five are mostly diagrammatic, although simple algebra is also used in the explanation of aggregate demand.

Chapter sixteen

Aggregate Demand

This chapter provides a basic, no-frills review of the macroeconomic model of aggregate demand as it is presented in intermediate-level macroeconomics texts such as those by Wilton and Prescott, by Dornbusch, Fischer and Sparks, by Hall, Taylor and Rudin, and by some others.[1] The context throughout the chapter is a small, open economy, closely connected to the rest of the world in trade and in financial markets.

The macroeconomic model of aggregate demand explains the behaviour and interaction of three markets: the goods market, the asset or money market, and the foreign exchange market. Sections 1–3 explain in turn the goods, asset, and foreign exchange markets. Section 4 reviews the joint equilibrium of all three markets as a system and derives an aggregate demand curve.

You should learn in this chapter:

1. how aggregate demand behaves in a small open economy;

2. how equilibrium aggregate demand levels vary with levels of interest rates, as summarized in an IS curve;

3. how the range of equilibrium interest rates in asset markets vary with income levels, as summarized in an LM curve;

4. how the exchange rate adjusts to bring about equilibrium in the foreign exchange market;

---

[1] David A. Wilton and David M. Prescott, *Macroeconomics: Theory and Policy in Canada*, 2nd ed. (Don Mills, Ont.: Addison-Wesley, 1987); R. Dornbusch, S. Fischer, and G. Sparks, *Macroeconomics*, 3rd Canadian ed. (Toronto: McGraw-Hill Ryerson, 1989); Robert E. Hall, John H. Taylor, and Jeremy Rudin, *Macroeconomics*, 2nd Canadian ed. (Toronto: Norton, 1990).

5. how equilibrium levels of aggregate demand, interest rates, and exchange rates are simultaneously determined;

6. how equilibrium levels of aggregate demand respond to changes in the aggregate price level.

◫ The goods market

In macroeconomic models, **aggregate demand** for real goods and services (AD) corresponds to total spending on real gross domestic product (GDP), excluding any spending on additions to inventory that firms did not want to add (that is, extra unsold goods). Aggregate demand is the total of planned spending on final goods and services produced by Canadian residents in a year, measured in dollars of constant purchasing power (that is, in real terms).

The components of aggregate demand are the same as the components of real GDP: real consumption spending by households (C); real investment spending on new housing, inventories, and plant and equipment (I); real government spending (G); real export demand from foreigners (X); less the import content of all four categories of demand (M). Note that government spending as part of aggregate demand excludes transfer payments such as old-age pensions and unemployment-insurance benefits. Transfer payments by themselves are not a demand for goods and services, merely flows of income that recipients may use to finance such demand. Transfer payments are equivalent to negative taxes.

The behaviour of aggregate demand (AD) is the behaviour of the sum of its components, so we can start with the demand identity familiar from introductory economics:

$$AD = C + I + G + X - M. \tag{1}$$

We can lump the last two terms together and refer to $X - M$ jointly as net exports, which leaves only four components to explain: consumption, investment, government spending, and net exports. These are now explained in that order.

Consumption

In Chapter 7 we looked at the behaviour of consumption in the life-cycle or permanent-income hypothesis about savings behaviour. Here we take as a starting point the simple early Keynesian hypothesis that consumption spending depends linearly on current after-tax real income:[2]

$$C = a + b(Y - T), \tag{2}$$

---

[2] All algebraic slope coefficients are themselves positive in this chapter, so the sign of any relationship is given by the sign preceding its coefficient.

where C, Y, and T are real consumption spending, income, and taxes respectively, a is a constant intercept term, and the slope coefficient b is the marginal propensity to consume out of disposable income.[3] The life-cycle hypothesis suggests that both coefficients in Equation (2) are likely to be unstable over time. The intercept a will change with levels of wealth and with changes in the age structure of the population, the slope coefficient b will change as households come to see any change in income as more or less permanent, and both will change to some extent as different interest rates cause households to change their desired lifetime consumption paths. For this review of the basic model, however, we will keep Equation (2) as it stands.

Investment

Investment spending on new real assets was explained in Chapter 8 using the Keynesian marginal efficiency of investment theory, and then by Tobin's q theory. Investment spending is derived from the demand for real assets; investment spending is whatever is needed to close the gap between the total quantity of real assets currently demanded, and the total quantity in existence. The total quantity of real assets in existence is already fixed by the start of each year, by past investment levels. The level of current investment spending required to bring holdings of real assets up to the level demanded in the current year therefore depends on all of the factors that determine the level of real assets currently demanded: in particular, on relative yields on new real assets and on alternative financial assets, and the cost of credit to finance real assets. The financial system used in intermediate macroeconomics has only two financial assets (money and everything else, called debt + equity) and only one interest rate R (on debt + equity). The effect on investment of higher alternative yields on financial assets, and of higher financing costs on debts, are both reflected in the influence of R. The marginal efficiency of investment (the yield on new real assets) depends on business expectations; these are recognized as being volatile, but they are not explained directly.

The simple equation for investment spending (I) is therefore

$$I = I_a - eR, \tag{3}$$

where I_a is the intercept term, and e is a constant coefficient. I_a is the exogenous component of investment spending; it is expected to change with every change in business mood from optimism to pessimism, and with every change in technology.

---

[3] C is consumption spending, including any spending on durables regardless of whether the durables are in fact consumed during the current period. Also the income variable used is total income rather than just labour income as in the life-cycle model.

Government spending

The level of government spending on real goods and services reflects demand for the goods and services that government provides. Since those goods and services have to be paid for out of taxes, sooner or later, the demand for them must depend in some loose way on the economy's ability to pay taxes. The obvious measure of a nation's ability to pay taxes is the level of its real income, Y.

In practice, real income is not usually an important determinant of government spending in the short run. We therefore assume that government spending does not depend directly on income. Government spending will be left unexplained, an exogenous lump G that can be changed as needed for government stabilization policy.

Net exports

Net exports are total export demand by foreigners for Canadian goods and services, less Canadian demand for foreign goods and services. The export demand by foreigners is simply the share that Canadian producers receive of the rest of the world's aggregate demand. Total foreign aggregate demand is exogenous to Canada, but Canadian producers' share of it depends on our producers' competitive position. Similarly, imports are foreign producers' share of our aggregate demand, and therefore also depend on their competitive position.

The competitive position of Canadian producers is measured by the ratio of domestic to foreign prices, converted into a common currency.[4] Let P be the Canadian price level. Let the foreign price level be set at 1, to avoid an unnecessary extra symbol; the foreign price level is fixed in our analysis. Let π be the exchange rate (the price of the Canadian dollar in units of foreign currency; in 1990, for example, C\$1.00 = US\$0.81). Then the competitive position is measured by πP. Competitive position measured this way is also referred to as the **real exchange rate**. Higher levels of πP cause exports to fall and imports to rise.

The behaviour of net exports explained above can be summarized as

$$X - M = X_a - mY - s(\pi P), \qquad (4)$$

where X_a is the exogenous component of exports, m is the normal share of foreign producers in meeting Canadian aggregate demand, and the level of output Y is used as a measure of aggregate demand. In Equation (4), s reflects the combined response of both exports and imports to changes in competitive position.

---

[4] Strictly speaking, only the relative prices of tradable goods and services are relevant to the competitive position of Canadian producers. In this basic review we will assume that the prices of tradable goods move in unison with the aggregate price level.

Aggregate demand

Combining explanations for all of the component parts of aggregate demand gives an explanation of aggregate demand itself. Gathering together the simple linear equations used so far, and substituting them in the aggregate demand identity, gives

$$AD = C + I + G + X - M$$
$$= (a + b[Y - T]) + (I_a - eR) + G + (X_a - mY - s\pi P), \qquad (5)$$

where a, b, e, m, and s are constant coefficients, and the other variables are as defined above. The level of real taxes T can be explained simply as an exogenous lump T_0 and a portion dependent on the level of real income Y:

$$T = T_0 + tY,$$

where t is the marginal tax rate for the economy as a whole. The exogenous tax component T_0 will change with tax policies that change the tax structure or the basic tax-exemption limits, and the like. Substituting for T in Equation (5) gives

$$AD = a + b(1 - t)Y - bT_0 + I_a - eR + G + X_a - mY - s\pi P. \qquad (6)$$

If we rearrange this equation and group together all of the terms not depending on Y, we get the simpler expression

$$AD = AD_0 + b'Y, \qquad (7)$$

where the term AD_0 gathers together all of the terms that do not depend on Y:

$$AD_0 = a - bT_0 + I_a - eR + G + X_a - s\pi P, \qquad (8)$$

and

$$b' = b(1 - t) - m.$$

Equation (7) is shown in Figure 16–1 as the standard Keynesian cross aggregate spending schedule. The vertical intercept is AD_0, and the slope coefficient is b'. AD_0 depends on all its ingredients, such as R, π, and P. b' is the marginal propensity to spend on domestic goods and services out of extra national income.

Equilibrium aggregate demand and the IS curve

As elsewhere in economics, it is useful to focus on the equilibrium level: that is the level we are most likely either to observe or to move toward in practice. The **equilibrium level of aggregate demand** is the one that absorbs aggregate supply, so that inventories of output do not rise or fall. Aggregate supply is measured by real output, Y. The equilibrium condition is described by the line joining all points for which $AD = Y$, which is the the $45°$ line in Figure

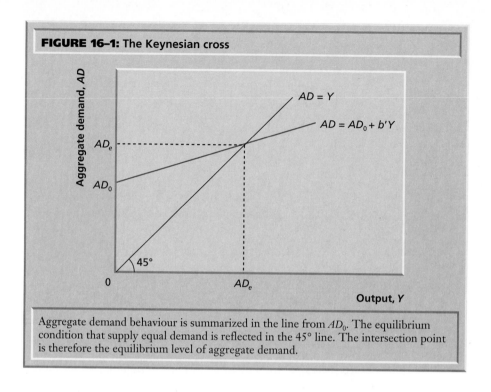

FIGURE 16–1: The Keynesian cross

Aggregate demand behaviour is summarized in the line from AD_0. The equilibrium condition that supply equal demand is reflected in the 45° line. The intersection point is therefore the equilibrium level of aggregate demand.

16–1. The equilibrium level of AD (AD_e) along the aggregate expenditure schedule in Figure 16–1 lies at its intersection with the 45° line. Algebraically, the equilibrium is found from Equation (7) by substituting AD for Y, to get

$$AD_e = AD_0/(1 - b').\qquad(9)$$

The factor $1/(1 - b')$ by which AD_0 is multiplied is the simplest aggregate demand multiplier, one that allows for changes in income but holds R, π, and P constant.

Equilibrium aggregate demand is sensitive to all ingredients of the intercept term AD_0. Equation (8) shows these to be a, T_0, I_a, R, G, X_a, π, and P. A change in any one will change AD_0 and therefore AD_e. Of this list of variables, the interest rate R attracts the most attention in macroeconomics. The sensitivity of AD_e to R is captured by a special curve called the **IS curve**, as follows.

Recall that higher levels of R reduce real investment demand. When real investment demand is reduced, the aggregate expenditure schedule is shifted downwards on a Keynesian cross diagram. In Figure 16–2(a), raising R from 8 to 10 to 12 percent, for instance, generates ever lower aggregate expenditure schedules. As the aggregate expenditure schedule falls, the equilibrium aggregate demand level AD_e also falls from AD_1 to AD_2 to AD_3. Figure 16–2(b) merely graphs the response of AD_e to R with R on the vertical axis. The IS curve in part (b) is the locus or line of equilibrium aggregate demand levels that will accompany

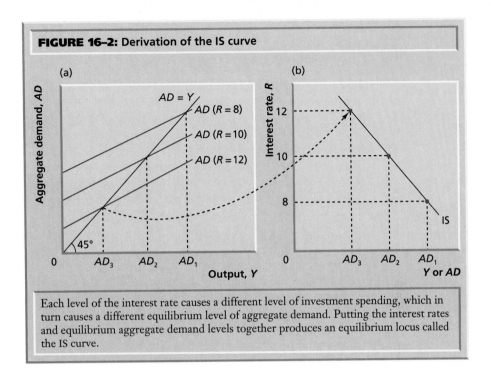

FIGURE 16–2: Derivation of the IS curve

Each level of the interest rate causes a different level of investment spending, which in turn causes a different equilibrium level of aggregate demand. Putting the interest rates and equilibrium aggregate demand levels together produces an equilibrium locus called the IS curve.

each possible level of R, holding all other variables like π and P constant. The meaning of equilibrium is as shown in Figure 16–1; that is, $AD = Y$.

Algebraically, the IS curve can be derived from Equation (9) by breaking AD_0 up into $AD_0' - eR$ and rearranging slightly:

$$AD_e = AD_0'/(1 - b') - (e/[1 - b'])R. \qquad (10)$$

The slope of the IS curve is the inverse of the coefficient of R in Equation (10); that is, $-(1 - b')/e$. The horizontal intercept is $AD_0'/(1 - b')$, which changes with any change in π or P or G or any other ingredient of AD_0'.

To complete our explanation of aggregate demand, we need to explain how the important variables R, π, and P in Equation (10) are themselves determined. We will leave P to the last, since it is determined jointly by aggregate demand and aggregate supply. R is determined as the equilibrium yield in asset markets, and π as the equilibrium price in the foreign exchange market. Asset market equilibrium is explained first.

SECTION 2

▣ The asset markets

This section briefly explains two approaches to the determination of equilibrium interest rates in asset markets. The first, classical approach is a simple extension of the approach to asset markets that is used in Parts Two to Four of this book. The second, Keynesian approach exploits a mathematical property called Walras' law to concentrate on just the market for money. The Keynesian approach is used to derive an explicit equilibrium condition that is then put together with the IS curve of section 1 to generate joint equilibrium in goods and asset markets. In Chapter 19 we will return to treat asset markets more completely.

The classical approach: borrowing and lending

The classical approach starts with the wealth constraint from the national balance sheet accounts from Chapter 5; each household or firm must hold its wealth in some form of assets, and total wealth for all sectors combined must equal exactly the existing stock of physical assets.[5] From one year to the next, the total wealth constraint implies that the change in total wealth (defined as net saving) must exactly equal the change in existing physical assets (defined as net investment). In asset markets, the flow of net saving appears as a flow of net, new lending at interest. The flow of net investment appears as a flow of net, new borrowing at interest. Both flows are assumed to be sensitive to the interest rate on lending and borrowing, R. In the long run, the interest rate adjusts to bring about an equilibrium in which *planned* investment equals *planned* saving.

In the short run there are two other ingredients that have come to dominate the modern, Keynesian explanation: the flow of savings from lenders to asset markets may be diverted into increases in holdings of money, and the flow of lending to finance net investment may be supplemented by increases in the money supply (as banks expand both their deposits and their loan portfolios). If some of the borrowers can borrow the money they need from banks that are expanding because of money creation, then the remaining borrowers can strike better terms (lower R) from the lenders whose funds come from saving. On the other hand, if some savers decide to plough their savings into building up money balances instead of the borrowers' debts, then the remaining savers will be able to strike better terms (higher R in this case) from borrowers. In the short run, therefore, classical theorists needed to explain what causes changes to both money demand and money supply, as well as to explain the flow of planned saving and planned investment.

---

[5] In calculating total wealth for all sectors combined, all financial assets held are cancelled out by exactly offsetting totals of financial liabilities outstanding. The discussion of the classical approach in this section is inspired by reading James C.W. Ahiakpor, "On Keynes's Misinterpretation of 'Capital' in the Classical Theory of Interest," *History of Political Economy* 22:3, 1990, 507–528.

The Keynesian approach and Walras' law

The modern, Keynesian approach starts with the wealth identity from the national balance sheet accounts, but uses it differently . The wealth identity required that total financial assets exactly equal total liabilities. Let all financial assets and liabilities be lumped together into only two markets — the market for money, and the market for everything else (which we will call debt + equity). Let the demand for money be L, measured in real terms.[6] Let the real supply of money be M_s/P where M_s is the nominal money supply. Let the demand for and supply of debt + equity be DE_d and DE_s, respectively. The wealth constraint requires that the total supply of these two assets exactly equal the total demand for them:

$$L + DE_d = M_s/P + DE_s.$$

It follows, as described by mathematical economist Leon Walras in **Walras' law** in the early nineteenth century, that both markets must be in equilibrium if either one of them is. That is, DE_d must also equal DE_s whenever L equals M_s/P. It will therefore be enough to ensure equilibrium in both markets if we merely establish equilibrium in either one. Keynesian economists have concentrated on the money market because it is more directly related to monetary policy, so we now turn to explain money supply and demand.

The money supply

We have already explained the nominal supply of money M_s in Chapter 10. Here we assume a simple banking system with cash reserves held only against demand deposits, at a fixed rate rr. We also assume that the public holds currency and demand deposits as money, in the fixed ratio cu:1, just as in the case 2 example of Chapter 10 that is illustrated in Figure 10–5. The stock of outstanding currency and demand deposits is tied directly to the stock of high-powered money (the level of cash reserve assets made available to the banking system by the Bank of Canada), by a **money supply multiplier**, mm, which depends on the cash reserve ratio rr and the desired currency-to-deposit ratio cu. That is,

$$M_s = mmH, \tag{11}$$

where $mm = (1 + cu)/(cu + rr)$.

In this review chapter we will keep things simple by treating the money supply multiplier mm as fixed.

The stock of high-powered money H cannot always be assumed to be exogenous. H will rise whenever the Bank of Canada adds to its assets or reduces the government's account in the Bank of Canada. One way of reducing that

---

[6] It will help you to keep track of the symbol for money demand, if you think of it as demand for liquidity. That was Hicks' usage when he first presented Keynesian macro-economics in this format. J.R. Hicks, "Mr, Keynes and the Classics: A Suggested Interpretation," *Econometrica*, 1937, 147–59.

account is to add to official foreign exchange reserves; payment for official reserves comes from the government's account in the Bank of Canada. Under a floating exchange rate policy, changes in official reserves are not expected, so the stock of high-powered money can be assumed to be exogenous. Under a fixed exchange rate policy, changes in official reserves are expected to occur, so H will change as well unless the Bank of Canada is assumed to *sterilize* changes in official reserves by undertaking offsetting transactions of its own.[7] For now we will regard M_s as fixed in the short run but not necessarily after that.

The demand for money

The behaviour of demand for real money balances L reflects assetholders' choice between money and debt + equity. In general, that choice depends on relative yields, relative risks, and total real wealth. Here the **demand for money** is assumed to be insensitive to wealth (so that all extra wealth is put into debt + equity). Relative risks are also assumed to be constant over all periods of our analysis, so relative risks can be ignored. The yield on debt + equity is the interest rate R. Money is assumed to have zero nominal yield, but to have an implicit yield from its liquidity services — the saving of transactions costs that are possible when one has a stock of the medium of exchange on hand. The value of those liquidity services, or the amount of transactions costs to be saved, are assumed to rise with the level of each individual's volume of spending in each month. High-spenders are assumed to have more need for the 1000th dollar in their chequing accounts than are penny-pinching misers.

If we let real income Y approximate the volume of spending, a linear equation reflecting the ideas above is:

$$L = kY - hR, \tag{12}$$

where k and h are coefficients. In Equation (12), L rises with Y and falls with R.

Equilibrium and the LM curve

It is assumed that asset markets will clear, by means of changes in the interest rate R. If the demand for money is smaller than the supply of money, then Walras' law requires that the demand for debt + equity must also be bigger than the supply of debt + equity. As a result, debt + equity prices will be driven up and the interest rate R will be brought down until both markets are once more in balance. Equilibrium in the money market is shown in Figure 16–3(a), a diagram of money market equilibrium with the debt + equity yield R on the vertical axis. The real money supply M_s/P is assumed to be fixed for now, so it appears as a

---

[7] A purchase of official reserves could be offset by the Bank of Canada selling some of its bonds to the public or transferring government deposits from banks to the Bank of Canada account. As long as the Bank of Canada has assets to sell it can sterilize changes in official foreign exchange reserves.

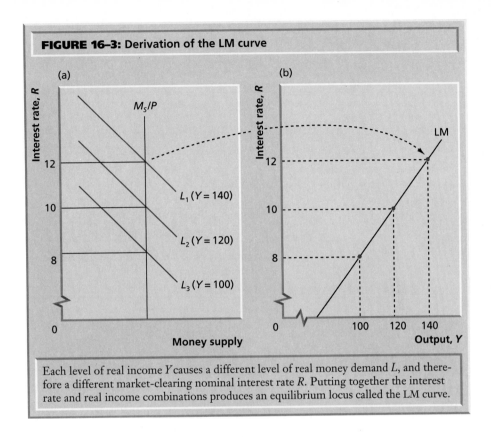

FIGURE 16–3: Derivation of the LM curve

Each level of real income Y causes a different level of real money demand L, and therefore a different market-clearing nominal interest rate R. Putting together the interest rate and real income combinations produces an equilibrium locus called the LM curve.

vertical line. Each real money demand schedule slopes downward, but higher Y levels generate higher L schedules. The equilibrium interest rate that sets each $L = M_s/P$ is found at the intersection of each L schedule with the M_s/P line.

Just as the goods market diagram generated a whole set of possible equilibrium levels of Y, so the money market diagram generates a whole set of possible equilibrium interest rate levels — one for each L schedule, and therefore one for each level of Y. Putting the combinations of Y and equilibrium R together produces the money market equilibrium locus called the **LM curve**, as shown in Figure 16–3(b). The name comes from the condition that L equal M, where M was originally used as the symbol for the real money supply M_s/P.

Algebraically, the LM curve is derived by setting $L = M_s/P$, substituting for L in Equation (12), and rearranging to get:

$$Y = (1/k)\, M_s/P + (h/k)\, R. \qquad (13)$$

The slope of the LM curve is k/h, and its horizontal intercept is $(1/k)\, M_s/P$. The LM curve will be shifted by any change in either M_s or in P.

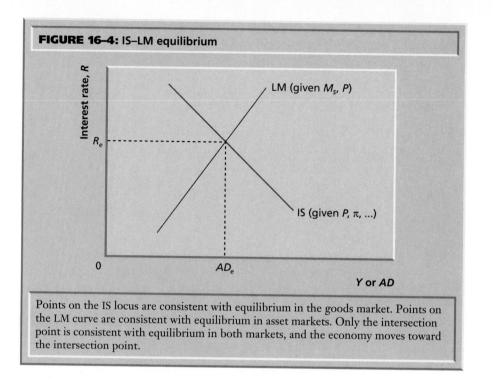

FIGURE 16–4: IS–LM equilibrium

Points on the IS locus are consistent with equilibrium in the goods market. Points on the LM curve are consistent with equilibrium in asset markets. Only the intersection point is consistent with equilibrium in both markets, and the economy moves toward the intersection point.

Joint IS and LM equilibrium

It is worthwhile pausing a moment before explaining how the exchange rate π is determined in the foreign exchange market, in order to put together the puzzle pieces we have. The IS curve shows many possible equilibrium AD levels in the goods market, one for each possible level of R. The LM curve shows many possible equilibrium levels of interest rates R in asset markets, one for each possible level of income Y. If both aggregate demand and the money market must be in equilibrium, then both IS conditions and LM conditions must be satisfied. That is, the levels of Y (or AD) and R that will be observed must lie on both the IS and the LM curves. That produces an unique joint **IS–LM equilibrium** level for both AD and for R, as shown in Figure 16–4. The joint equilibrium depends on all ingredients of both curves, so it can be changed by changes in any ingredient of either curve. Next we discuss specifically how the equilibrium will be changed by changes in the nominal exchange rate π.

SECTION 3

▨ The foreign exchange market

The **foreign exchange market** has appeared several times earlier in this book, particularly in Chapter 14, where we looked at international arbitrage with and without forward cover. The discussion in this section will be relatively crude in order to review what is commonly presented in intermediate macroeconomics. In Chapter 20 we return to this topic to consider whether a more sophisticated approach makes any difference to policy conclusions.

The foreign exchange market can be explained in the same categories as the **balance of payments** — the set of accounts that records Canadians' transactions with foreigners. All transactions in the foreign exchange market fit into one of the three accounts in the balance of payments:

1. The *current account* contains all trade flows of exports and imports.

2. The *capital account* contains all changes in asset holdings involving foreign exchange transactions. The capital account records as capital inflows all receipts of foreign exchange from foreigners to purchase Canadian assets, and as capital outflows all payments of foreign exchange by Canadians to purchase foreign assets.[8]

3. The third account is just called *net official monetary movements*. It records any changes in foreign exchange holdings of the monetary authorities (the Bank of Canada, the exchange fund account of the Department of Finance, and the Receiver General for Canada). Most official monetary movements are carried out by the Bank of Canada on behalf of the exchange fund account of the government. The exchange fund account buys and sells with funds coming from and going to the government's account in the Bank of Canada.

Current account flows

The current account provides Canada with a net supply of foreign exchange equal to net exports, which we have already discussed above in section 1:

$$X - M = X_a - mY - s\pi P. \tag{14}$$

The effect of a lower nominal exchange rate π is to improve Canada's competitive position and to increase its net export earnings. The relationship between net exports and the nominal exchange rate is as shown in Figure 16–5(a).

---

[8] The balance of payments does not reflect purchases of Canadian assets by foreigners with Canadian currency earned in Canada (for instance, in domestic subsidiaries). Such purchases affect the degree of foreign ownership and the balance of international indebtedness, but not the balance of payments and the foreign exchange market.

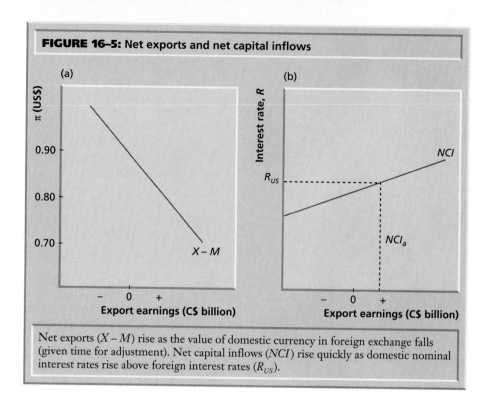

FIGURE 16–5: Net exports and net capital inflows

Net exports $(X - M)$ rise as the value of domestic currency in foreign exchange falls (given time for adjustment). Net capital inflows (NCI) rise quickly as domestic nominal interest rates rise above foreign interest rates (R_{US}).

Capital account flows

There are many different sources of capital account flows into and out of Canada, and therefore many different possible behaviours. In Chapter 14, we looked at flows of arbitrage between money market assets in different currencies; such arbitrage flows are likely to dominate other flows in the short run. Arbitrage flows respond to yield differentials between assets denominated in different currencies, including any expected currency appreciation. If arbitrage flows are large enough, they will force expected yields to be the same in each currency. Here we assume that arbitrage flows are large, but not necessarily that large. We also assume that expected currency appreciation is constant. That leaves us with a simple explanation of capital account flows: the net capital inflow NCI will rise as R rises relative to the foreign interest rate. Let the United States interest rate R_{US} stand for all foreign interest rates, since most capital flows into and out of Canada are from and to the United States. That is,

$$NCI = NCI_a + q(R - R_{US}), \tag{15}$$

where q is a constant coefficient that reflects the degree of sensitivity of capital inflows to the interest differential. Equation (15) is illustrated in Figure 16–5(b).

Net official monetary movements

Changes in official reserves (dOR) are managed by the Bank of Canada even though the reserves are mostly held in the government's exchange fund account. The Bank of Canada can choose among several policies for dOR. It could add to and sell off official reserves to support a particular target exchange rate π by mopping up excess demand and supply from current account and capital account flows. That is a **fixed exchange rate** policy, whether formally announced as such or not. Alternatively, the bank could follow a **floating exchange rate** policy, letting the exchange rate float without official intervention to find the equilibrium level that balances current and capital account flows. With a floating exchange rate official reserves will generally stay constant, so dOR will be zero.

The bank actually uses a **managed float** policy, which falls in between these two. The bank intervenes fairly frequently in foreign exchange markets to slow down rapid exchange rate movements. Such intervention is mostly automatic, coordinated in advance with other major central banks. [9] The effect of managed floating is that π takes longer to arrive at any new equilibrium after some shock to trade flows or capital flows, but the new equilibrium is still determined only by current and capital account flows. During the bank's intervention, dOR changes temporarily as in a fixed exchange rate system, but only until the new equilibrium foreign exchange rate has been reached.[10] Thereafter, dOR is zero as under a floating exchange rate system. Since we will be discussing only short- and long-run equilibrium states, we can treat a managed float as though it were simply an unmanaged float.

Equilibrium in the foreign exchange market

Equilibrium in the foreign exchange market requires that all flow demands and supplies cancel out, that is, that net exports, capital inflows, and the change in official reserves add to zero:

$$X - M + NCI + dOR = 0 .$$

Substituting our explanations for $X - M$ and for NCI,

$$(X_a - mY - s\pi P) + (NCI_a + q[R - R_{US}]) + dOR = 0 . \qquad (16)$$

Equation (16) can be rearranged as either

$$Y = (1/m)(X_a - s\pi P + NCI_a - qR_{US} + dOR) + (1/m) R,$$

---

[9] For discussion of the Bank of Canada's foreign exchange market intervention, see John Murray, Mark Zelmer, and Shane Williamson, *Measuring the Profitability and Effectiveness of Foreign Exchange Market Intervention: Some Canadian Evidence* (Ottawa: Bank of Canada Technical Report 53), March 1990.

[10] The role of official reserves in a managed float is exactly the same as the role of inventories in a firm that does not want to adjust prices immediately to balance supply and demand.

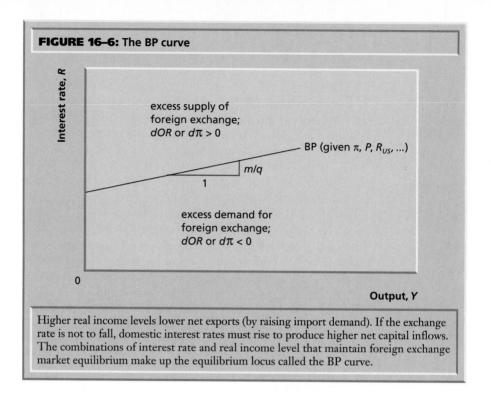

FIGURE 16–6: The BP curve

Interest rate, R

excess supply of
foreign exchange;
dOR or dπ > 0

BP (given π, P, R$_{US}$, ...)

m/q

1

excess demand for
foreign exchange;
dOR or dπ < 0

0

Output, Y

Higher real income levels lower net exports (by raising import demand). If the exchange rate is not to fall, domestic interest rates must rise to produce higher net capital inflows. The combinations of interest rate and real income level that maintain foreign exchange market equilibrium make up the equilibrium locus called the BP curve.

or

$$R = R_{US} + (1/q)(s\pi P - X_a - NCI_a - dOR) + (m/q)Y. \qquad (17)$$

Equation (17) is satisfied by changes in π under a floating exchange rate system (managed or unmanaged). It is satisfied by changes in dOR under a fixed exchange rate system.

Equation (17) can be illustrated graphically in several ways. The most common is to hold π and P constant, to set dOR to zero (so the equation implies equilibrium of private sector flows), and then to trace out what combinations of R and Y will maintain foreign exchange market equilibrium. That produces the **BP curve** derived in Figure 16–6 (named after the balance of payments). The slope of this locus is m/q, which is positive. Intuitively, the BP curve slopes upward because as higher income Y lowers net exports, a higher interest rate R is needed to raise net capital inflows by an offsetting amount. The intercept of the BP curve depends on all the variables in Equation (17) other than R and Y. In particular, the BP curve is shifted upward by increases in R_{US} (one for one), by currency appreciation, and by increases in domestic prices relative to foreign prices.

We should note what happens in the foreign exchange market if the economy is off the BP curve. When the economy is at an R, Y point above its BP curve, the interest rate R is too high, so net capital inflows are also too high;

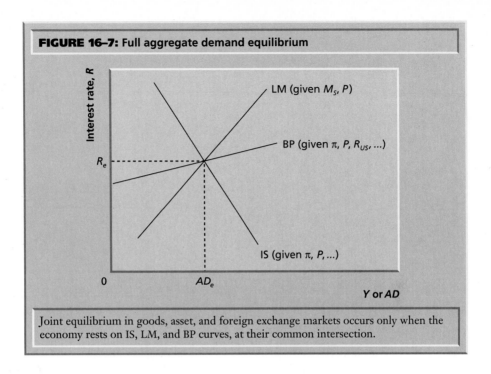

FIGURE 16–7: Full aggregate demand equilibrium

Joint equilibrium in goods, asset, and foreign exchange markets occurs only when the economy rests on IS, LM, and BP curves, at their common intersection.

there is an excess supply of foreign exchange from the private sector at the current exchange rate. One of two adjustments occurs. Under a flexible exchange rate system, π appreciates, moving the BP curve up toward the economy. Under a fixed exchange rate system, official reserves are increased (dOR becomes positive) to absorb the excess supply of foreign exchange.

SECTION 4

Equilibrium aggregate demand

We can now bring together all the ingredients of aggregate demand to generate a complete macroeconomic equilibrium. After describing this equilibrium, we explain the impact of price levels on the equilibrium and summarize the impact in an equilibrium **aggregate demand curve**.

For full macroeconomic equilibrium, the levels of aggregate demand AD and interest rates R must be such as to cause equilibria in goods, money, and foreign exchange markets. If they are not, then there will be pressures in at least one of the markets to restore equilibrium, and those pressures may cause changes in AD, Y, and R.

Joint equilibrium of all three markets will occur only at a joint intersection of all three of the IS, LM, and BP curves, as shown in Figure 16–7. At that point,

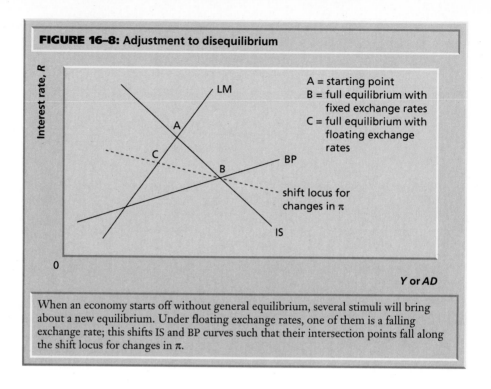

FIGURE 16-8: Adjustment to disequilibrium

A = starting point
B = full equilibrium with fixed exchange rates
C = full equilibrium with floating exchange rates

shift locus for changes in π

When an economy starts off without general equilibrium, several stimuli will bring about a new equilibrium. Under floating exchange rates, one of them is a falling exchange rate; this shifts IS and BP curves such that their intersection points fall along the shift locus for changes in π.

(1) aggregate demand is large enough to absorb all output produced, so that goods inventories do not change; (2) real money balances held by the public just absorb the real money balances that banks want outstanding; and (3) private-sector demands for and supplies of foreign exchange just balance, without any change in official reserves.

In the short run it is possible for an economy to lie at the intersection of IS and LM curves, without also being on its BP curve, as shown at point A in Figure 16-8. Such a disequilibrium in the balance of payments can continue as long as the central bank is willing to absorb excess demands and supplies of foreign exchange with changes in official reserves. However, the disequilibrium gradually causes one other adjustment in the economy as well. For instance, in Figure 16-8 the economy's IS–LM equilibrium at A is above the BP curve. In the foreign exchange market there is an excess private supply of foreign exchange each period, and this is absorbed by the central bank in positive levels of dOR. Over time, positive levels of dOR are likely to cause growth of the stock of high-powered money, which in turn will cause the LM curve to shift to the right. In the long run under such a policy, the economy would come to full equilibrium via shifts of the LM curve, at the intersection of IS and BP curves at B. That is, under fixed exchange rates, it is the money supply that adjusts to produce full equilibrium in the long run.

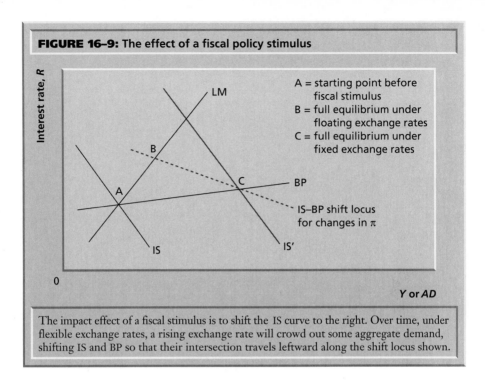

FIGURE 16–9: The effect of a fiscal policy stimulus

A = starting point before fiscal stimulus
B = full equilibrium under floating exchange rates
C = full equilibrium under fixed exchange rates

IS–BP shift locus for changes in π

The impact effect of a fiscal stimulus is to shift the IS curve to the right. Over time, under flexible exchange rates, a rising exchange rate will crowd out some aggregate demand, shifting IS and BP so that their intersection travels leftward along the shift locus shown.

If the economy starts above its BP curve under flexible exchange rates, the exchange rate π will appreciate. As it does so, it will cause both BP and IS curves to shift. The BP curve shifts upward as higher π levels worsen the competitive position of domestic producers, and reduce net exports; as increases in π reduce net exports, higher net capital inflows will be needed to maintain foreign exchange market balance, and higher domestic interest rates are needed in turn in order to raise net capital inflows. While the BP curve is shifting upward, the IS curve shifts to the left; lower net exports caused by higher π levels reduce aggregate demand and employment. The intersection points of subsequent pairs of BP and IS curves, as the exchange rate appreciates, will lie along a line called an **IS–BP shift locus**, as shown in Figure 16–8. The shift locus is flatter than the IS curve, but it still has a negative slope. The eventual full equilibrium will be reached only when both BP and IS have shifted so that their intersection also lies on the LM curve, at point C. This three-way intersection must lie below and to the left of the economy's starting point at A, since the LM curve has not shifted.

Policy impacts

It is fairly easy to extract what fixed and floating exchange rate systems imply about the impact of stabilization policies. The effects of a fiscal policy stimulus that shifts the IS curve to the right, as shown in Figure 16–9, will be greater the less the fiscal stimulus is offset by increases in either R or π. Under flexible

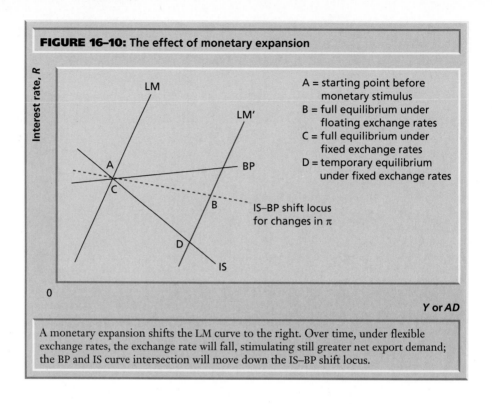

FIGURE 16–10: The effect of monetary expansion

A = starting point before
    monetary stimulus
B = full equilibrium under
    floating exchange rates
C = full equilibrium under
    fixed exchange rates
D = temporary equilibrium
    under fixed exchange rates

IS–BP shift locus
for changes in π

A monetary expansion shifts the LM curve to the right. Over time, under flexible exchange rates, the exchange rate will fall, stimulating still greater net export demand; the BP and IS curve intersection will move down the IS–BP shift locus.

exchange rates, a rightward shift of the IS curve would be accompanied by higher interest rates and currency appreciation until the economy had settled on the original LM curve with a higher BP curve, at point B. Much but not all of the fiscal stimulus would thus be offset. Under a fixed exchange rate system, on the other hand, the exchange rate cannot rise to shift the IS curve back to the left. Further, unless sterilization is complete, foreign exchange market disequilibrium would cause official reserves and also the stock of high-powered money to rise, so the LM curve would gradually move out to the right; even the interest rate would not rise much. The final equilibrium point would be further to the right along the BP curve, at point C. Fiscal policy is more powerful under fixed exchange rates.

An expansionary monetary policy would shift the LM curve to the right, as shown in Figure 16–10. Under flexible exchange rates, lower levels of R will cause depreciation of the exchange rate and will stimulate net export spending as well as investment spending. Further, leakage of domestic spending into imports will also be counteracted: any extra imports would generate further depreciation to restore foreign exchange market equilibrium, until exports had risen to match. The economy would then come to rest on the new LM′ curve at point B.

Under fixed exchange rates, a monetary policy that lowered domestic interest rates would also lower net capital inflows and cause official reserves to fall. Unless changes in official reserves are completely sterilized, the monetary base would start to fall also, shifting the LM curve back eventually to its original position. Even in the short run, aggregate demand would only expand to point D. That is, monetary policy has a larger impact under flexible exchange rates. In the extreme case under fixed exchange rates, where net capital inflows are sensitive enough to interest differentials to enforce the arbitrage equilibrium of Chapter 14, domestic monetary policy cannot hope to lower domestic interest rates below foreign interest rates at all. The capital outflow would be too big for the central bank to handle; the pressure of huge changes in official reserves would force it to abandon the policy. Such an economy could have no independent monetary policy. In Chapter 22 we consider further whether this would necessarily be a bad idea.

Price level impacts and the AD curve

We have so far explained aggregate demand behaviour on the assumption that the price level remains fixed. Over longer periods than the short run that will not be a reasonable assumption, so we must now know how changes in the price level P affect aggregate demand. This effect is summarized in the aggregate demand curve that relates AD and Y to P. We continue to assume that (1) asset markets can adjust back to equilibrium by changes in R, (2) foreign exchange markets can adjust also by changes in π or in dOR, depending on the adjustment mechanism, and (3) the output level Y adjusts to the level of AD in the goods market, without causing any price change. The last assumption is not realistic, nor is it intended to be. It is a simplifying device to allow us to analyze aggregate demand until (in Chapter 17) we are able to introduce a supply side to the model.

One impact of prices on aggregate demand is felt whether exchange rates are fixed or floating. A higher price level P lowers the real money supply M_s/P and therefore shifts the LM curve to the left. This forces interest rates upward and depresses investment spending. By itself, this is sufficient to give the aggregate demand curve a negative slope.

Under fixed exchange rates there is at least one additional effect of a change in P, and possibly two. Regardless of whether changes in official reserves are sterilized, a higher domestic price level worsens the competitive position of domestic producers and lowers net exports. If dOR is not fully sterilized, losses of official reserves will cause decreases in the stock of high-powered money, and this will reduce M_s/P still more. These impacts cause aggregate demand to be still more price-responsive.

Under flexible exchange rates, one cannot expect a direct impact of price changes on net exports. Any change in price that disturbs net exports would bring about a change in exchange rate to offset it, in order to restore foreign exchange market equilibrium. That is, other things remaining equal, π will change in response to P so as to keep the product πP constant. In this way flexible exchange rates are said to insulate domestic producers from relative price changes at home and abroad.

Other things do not remain equal, however. Lower real money supply M_s/P caused by higher prices P will force up domestic interest rates, R. As

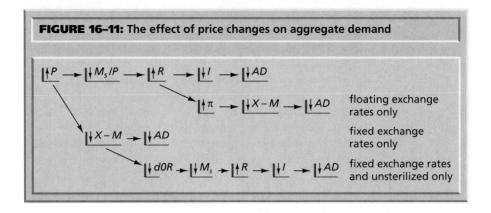

FIGURE 16–11: The effect of price changes on aggregate demand

higher R attracts higher net capital inflows, the exchange rate rises. Higher π then depresses net exports just as higher R depresses investment spending. This impact, added to the effects of higher R, makes aggregate demand quite sensitive to price levels under flexible exchange rates as well.

Figure 16–11 summarizes the channels of impact of higher prices under fixed and flexible exchange rates.

SECTION   5

◻ Summary

Aggregate demand is the sum of consumption, investment, government spending, and foreign export demand, less the import components of each. Consumption spending is explained in simple macroeconomic models as depending on current disposable income, whereas investment spending depends on the single interest rate R. Government spending is assumed to be exogenous. Net exports depend inversely on Canadian income and on our competitive position. Competitive position is measured by the ratio of Canadian to foreign prices, with Canadian prices converted to foreign currency at the current exchange rate.

Aggregate demand is consistent with goods market equilibrium only when it equals the output and income level; otherwise goods inventories will change. Equilibrium levels of aggregate demand depend on the interest rate, the exchange rate, and the price level, as well as on government spending and other exogenous components of aggregate demand.

The interest rate and the exchange rate are determined in the money market and the foreign exchange market, respectively. When both the money market and the goods market are in equilibrium, there is a single joint solution for interest rates and aggregate demand that is illustrated in the IS–LM diagram. The equilibrium still depends on the exchange rate, however.

Full equilibrium of all three markets produces an extra constraint on the IS–LM diagram, described by adding a BP curve to reflect foreign exchange market equilibrium without government intervention. The process of reaching equilibrium in the foreign exchange market either changes the exchange rate (thereby changing net exports and the IS curve); otherwise it changes official reserves and possibly the nominal money supply.

When all three markets are allowed to adjust to a new equilibrium, fiscal policy is more powerful under fixed than under floating exchange rates because a less offsetting effect on aggregate demand is induced by changes in interest rates and exchange rates. Monetary policy is more powerful under floating exchange rates because there is an extra channel of effect on aggregate demand through exchange rates and net exports. Monetary policy can have an effect under fixed exchange rates only as long as changes in official reserves can be sterilized to prevent high-powered money from returning to its original level.

Output and price are determined simultaneously by aggregate demand and aggregate supply. The aggregate demand curve derived from the aggregate demand model must have a negative slope because higher prices lower the real money supply and drive up interest rates. There are other channels of effect that cause still greater price sensitivity of aggregate demand, but they vary depending on whether exchange rates are fixed or floating.

Key Terms

aggregate demand	IS–LM equilibrium
real exchange rate	foreign exchange market
equilibrium level of	balance of payments
aggregate demand	fixed exchange rate
IS curve	floating exchange rate
Walras' law	managed float
money supply multiplier	BP curve
demand for money	aggregate demand curve
LM curve	IS–BP shift locus

Questions and Problems

1. What difference would it make to the slope of the aggregate spending line in Figure 16–1 or to the slope of the IS curve if we were to include specifically in our model a positive linkage between investment spending and income level?

2. Does the idea of an equilibrium level of demand imply that demand creates its own supply?

3. Why is the equilibrium aggregate demand multiplier for government spending on goods and services different from that for government spending on transfer payments?

4. What would be the net effect on aggregate demand and on the IS curve of a tax-financed increase in government spending on transfer payments?

5. What determines the slope of the IS curve?

6. What causes the IS curve to shift?

7. Which account of the balance of payments now dominates the foreign exchange market, and with what effect on monetary policy?

8. Would a change in the price level induce any change in your own level of demand? If so, why?

9. Why does the condition for financial market equilibrium require only that wealth be allocated and that money demand equal money supply, in the simple asset model of section 2?

10. What causes shifts of the LM curve?

11. What is the situation in financial markets when the economy is above its LM curve? What will happen in such a case?

12. Under what circumstances could the aggregate demand curve be vertical?

Suggestions for Further Reading

Dornbusch, R., S. Fischer, and G. Sparks. *Macroeconomics*, 3rd Canadian ed. Toronto: McGraw-Hill Ryerson, 1989.

Hall, Robert E., John H. Taylor, and Jeremy Rudin. *Macroeconomics*, 2nd Canadian ed. Toronto: Norton, 1990.

Parkin, Michael and Robin Bade. *Modern Macroeconomics*, 2nd ed. Scarborough, Ont.: Prentice-Hall, 1986.

Tobin, James. "A General Equilibrium Approach to Monetary Theory." *Journal of Money, Credit, and Banking* 1 (1969), 15–29.

Wilton, David A. , and David M. Prescott. *Macroeconomics: Theory and Policy in Canada*, 2nd ed. Don Mills, Ont.: Addison-Wesley, 1987.

Chapter seventeen

Aggregate Supply and Equilibrium

Keynesian and classical economists agree that an increase in the monetary base or the rate of government spending will increase nominal aggregate demand; what they disagree about is the way in which this increase will be divided between output and price level effects.

— Bennett T. McCallum[1]

This chapter offers a review of aggregate supply theory. There are three different, competing ways of explaining aggregate supply, so this chapter builds three different models. The choice among them is a major source of controversy in macroeconomics. After a review of these aggregate supply theories, we add back the aggregate demand curve and look at the kinds of equilibrium that result.

Section 1 deals with supply in the long run; for this period there is a consensus that the classical model is still the relevant one. Section 2 looks at the new Keynesian approach to supply in the short run. Section 3 looks at the new classical approach in the short run. Section 4 considers expectations explicitly, to see what difference rational expectations make to aggregate supply behaviour under each of the two short-run approaches. Section 5 extends the aggregate supply models to explain unemployment and inflation rates, directly, by rescaling axes and introducing the Phillips curve. Section 6 puts together aggregate demand and supply models to look at equilibrium behaviour in short and long runs.

---

[1] Bennett T. McCallum, "Postwar Developments in Business Cycle Theory: A Moderately Classical Perspective," *Journal of Money, Credit, and Banking*, August 1988, Part 2, 459.

You should learn in this chapter:

1. how the supply of inputs and the production function determine output in the long run, independent of the general price level;

2. how new Keynesians add assumptions of price-setting and short run disequilibrium determination of employment to explain short-run output responses to aggregate demand shifts;

3. how the new classical school keep the assumption that all wages and prices adjust to clear markets, as in an auction, and conclude that only unanticipated price changes affect output levels;

4. the distinction between backward-looking adaptive expectations and forward-looking rational expectations;

5. how to extend the aggregate supply models to relate inflation and unemployment rather than output and price levels;

6. how the different theories of aggregate supply, in combination with the model of aggregate demand of Chapter 16, produce equilibrium output and price levels in short and long runs.

SECTION 1

▣ The classical long-run model

There is substantial agreement on the model relevant for the long run, a model that dates back to David Ricardo in the first half of the nineteenth century.[2] Several key assumptions are made in the **classical model**:

1. All prices and wages adjust to clear their respective markets — not an implausible assumption in the long run.

2. All markets are sufficiently competitive or contestable that prices are forced close to marginal costs.

3. For simplicity, there is only one good (with price P) and one kind of labour (with nominal wage Wa).

It follows from the assumption of competition and contestability that producers will be forced to make full use of whatever capital equipment, natural resources, and workers they choose to employ. If inputs are fully utilized, then no extra output can be provided without extra inputs. It follows from profit maximization that producers will provide extra output only if the price for extra output exceeds the marginal costs of extra inputs. To find how high a price is needed to attract

---

[2] Professor James Ahiakpor of St. Mary's University in Halifax notes that some classical economists intended their model for the short run as well. J. Ahiakpor, "Ricardo on Money," *History of Political Economy*, 1985, 17–30.

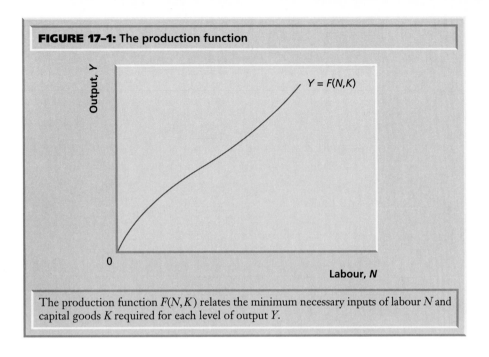

FIGURE 17–1: The production function

The production function $F(N,K)$ relates the minimum necessary inputs of labour N and capital goods K required for each level of output Y.

extra output, we need to understand marginal costs for the economy as a whole, in the long run.

Part of marginal cost behaviour is explained by the **production function**, which shows how many extra inputs are needed for each extra unit of output; part is explained by the behaviour of input prices as use of inputs changes. The production function is usually shown as a general function relating output Y to inputs of labour N and capital goods services K:

$$Y = F(N, K),$$

where F refers to an unspecified mathematical relationship. In general, higher levels of each input generate higher levels of output, as is shown for labour and output in Figure 17–1. The slope of the relationship in Figure 17–1 measures the extra output per unit of labour added, and the reciprocal of that ratio is the marginal labour requirement for each unit of extra output. Looking at a similar relationship for output and capital inputs would reveal the marginal capital inputs required for extra output.

Input prices for labour and capital are determined in the markets for labour and capital goods. Capital goods are produced as part of the output of the goods market, which has been assumed homogeneous for simplicity. The price of capital reflects the costs of producing capital goods. These costs are basically labour costs and the costs of machine tools used to produce capital goods. The costs of machine tools in turn reflect labour costs and the cost of capital inputs used to produce machine tools, and so on. When we trace all the costs back through

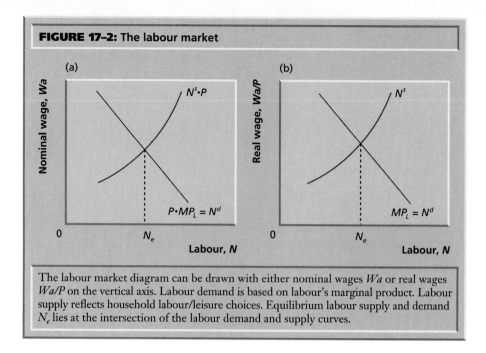

FIGURE 17–2: The labour market

The labour market diagram can be drawn with either nominal wages Wa or real wages Wa/P on the vertical axis. Labour demand is based on labour's marginal product. Labour supply reflects household labour/leisure choices. Equilibrium labour supply and demand N_e lies at the intersection of the labour demand and supply curves.

enough stages of production, we are left with just labour costs. In the long run, the nominal wage Wa will determine the costs of labour and capital inputs to generate the marginal cost of extra output. To explain Wa itself we must look at the labour market.

The labour market

The demand for labour is derived from firms' supply of output. Firms in contestable markets hire workers to the point at which the value of their marginal product ($P{\cdot}MP_L$) equals their nominal wage Wa; alternatively, workers are hired to the point where their marginal product MP_L is equal to the real wage Wa/P. On a **labour market diagram** such as Figure 17–2, the labour demand curve is the value-of-marginal-product schedule if Wa is on the vertical axis. It is the marginal-product-of-labour schedule if it is the real wage Wa/P on the vertical axis.[3]

The supply of labour by households reflects households' choices between leisure and working for consumption, both now and later. The real wage Wa/P is the opportunity cost of leisure; the higher the opportunity cost, the less leisure is consumed, and so the aggregate supply of labour increases with higher real

---

[3] In the short run the marginal product of labour is given by the slope of the (short-run) production function. In the long run some of the extra output accompanying extra labour inputs is attributable to extra capital inputs.

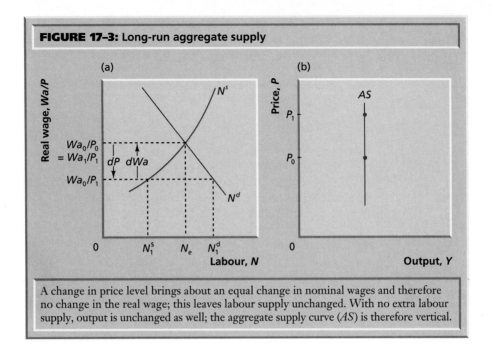

FIGURE 17–3: Long-run aggregate supply

A change in price level brings about an equal change in nominal wages and therefore no change in the real wage; this leaves labour supply unchanged. With no extra labour supply, output is unchanged as well; the aggregate supply curve (*AS*) is therefore vertical.

wages. In the long run to which the classical model applies, households have no difficulty knowing both Wa and P, nor do they get confused between nominal and real wages: it is real wages that count. Workers have no "money illusion." Because all labour is homogeneous in this simple model, there is no room for any concern by workers about relative wages.

Equilibrium aggregate supply

The intersection of the labour demand and supply curves in Figure 17–2 determines both the market-clearing real wage Wa/P and the equilibrium employment level N_e. The level of employment determines the level of output, from the production function. The **equilibrium aggregate supply curve** can now be derived by considering what happens if a change in the demand for output were to raise or lower the price level P.

Consider the effect of higher demand for goods, which drives P upward from P_0 to P_1. Firms would immediately see the higher price as exceeding marginal costs, and they would want to (hire more workers to) expand output. The labour market diagram tells the same story, but in a different way. A higher price level P initially lowers the real wage to Wa_0/P_1, making extra employment profitable for the firm. Firms want to increase their quantity of labour demanded, moving further down the labour demand curve to N_1^d, as shown in Figure 17–3.

Households also see that the real wage is lower at Wa_0/P_1, but they are not as enthusiastic. In fact, some of them decide to stay in bed or go fishing rather than go to work. They decrease their quantity of labour supplied, moving further down their aggregate labour supply curve to N_1^s in Figure 17–3. There is now excess demand for labour of $N_1^d - N_1^s$. The nominal wage will rise to Wa_1 to clear the market. Higher nominal wages will raise the real wage Wa/P until both firms and households have moved back into balance. This occurs at the original real wage, that is, $Wa_1/P_1 = Wa_0/P_0$. The original real wage generates the original level of employment N_e. With the original level of employment comes the original level of output. Aggregate supply is therefore not changed as a result of higher price levels. The aggregate supply curve is vertical.

Before we leave the long-run classical supply curve we should note a few of its other properties. It is not sensitive to price, but it is sensitive to any change in the production function. The same level of employment will mean higher output levels if either technology improves, or some other input quality is increased. Further, the level of employment itself will change if a change in technology affects the marginal product of labour. Finally, note that in the classical model there is no involuntary unemployment. All workers who want work at the going nominal wage (all those joining the labour supply curve up to the equilibrium wage) are employed. Those not employed are those who do not want to work at the current wage. Such people join the labour supply curve only above the equilibrium wage.

SECTION 2

▣ Short-run supply: the new Keynesian model

It is easy to justify the assumption that all prices and wages clear their respective goods and labour markets in the long run. In the long run there is plenty of time to adjust, regardless of the price and wage-setting mechanism. In the short run, however, the assumption of market-clearing wages and prices is not as easy to justify. The **new Keynesian model** is built on the observations that there are no auction-market mechanisms in most goods and labour markets that would change prices and wages quickly enough to keep markets cleared in the short run. Instead, one of the obvious features of the labour market is that most wage rates are fixed for periods of a year or more.[4] **Collective agreements** between firms and unions, and **implicit wage contracts** between firms and non-unionized skilled employees both provide for wages that will not be changed until the next contract or salary review date, which may be six months or a year or more in the future. In the short run, after a contract is signed, nominal wages are fixed.

---

[4] See John H. Taylor, "Staggered Wage Setting in a Macro Model," *American Economic Review*, May 1979, 108–13, or Stanley Fischer, "Long-term Contracts, Rational Expectations, and the Optimal Money Supply Rule," *Journal of Political Economy*, February 1977, 191–206 for early versions of new Keynesian models.

Many prices behave in much the same way as wages, though we do not need that assumption to present the basic new Keynesian model.[5]

The new Keynesian model adds one more feature observed in modern labour markets in the short run — that the level of employment is by and large determined by employers even when demand for labour exceeds supply. That is, if firms want to employ more labour than households want to supply at the current contract wage, managers ask workers to work longer hours, and the workers do so. If firms want to employ less labour than households want to supply, it is again the firms that determine the employment level.

Labour is not quite homogeneous in the new Keynesian model, since different groups of workers negotiate their wage contracts at different times. There are some other differences between groups of workers to make them less than perfectly substitutable in production. Nevertheless, firms will substitute some cheaper workers for more expensive ones if the wages of different groups get out of line.

It is assumed in the new Keynesian model that negotiators of wage contracts try to negotiate a nominal wage that will clear expected labour demand and supply in their particular market over the life of their contracts.[6] Thus negotiators must forecast changes in the aggregate price P, and also any changes in labour demand and supply that would influence the equilibrium real wage over the life of their contracts.

The new Keynesian assumptions create different supply situations, depending on whether the new contract revision date is far off or in the current period. We now consider each situation in turn, and then look at what happens when there are both types of contracts in force.

The extreme Keynesian case: fixed nominal wages

If the revision date of the wage contract is beyond the short run, then the nominal wage Wa is effectively fixed for the current period. This latter case was investigated by Keynes in the 1930s, and so is known as the extreme Keynesian case.

Figure 17–4 derives the short-run supply response for firms with fixed nominal wages. In this example, the fixed nominal wages were negotiated in the past with some expectation in mind of prices and of any changes in the

[5] Arthur Okun referred to these markets as price-tag markets, which gives an idea of their prevalence. A. Okun, *Prices and Quantities* (Washington, D.C.: Brookings Institution, 1981), 263ff. Maurice Levi and Albert Dexter note that in Canada many prices are set explicitly by regulatory authorities such as public utility commissions, which are even slower to respond to the level of demand than the rest of the fix-price sector. "Regulated Prices and Their Consequences," *Canadian Public Policy*, March 1983, 24–31.

[6] Parkin and Bade use this assumption, for instance, in *Modern Macroeconomics*, 2nd ed. (Scarborough, Ont.: Prentice-Hall, 1986). They derive it from J.A. Gray, "Wage Indexation: A Macroeconomic Approach," *Journal of Monetary Economics*, April 1976, 221–35.

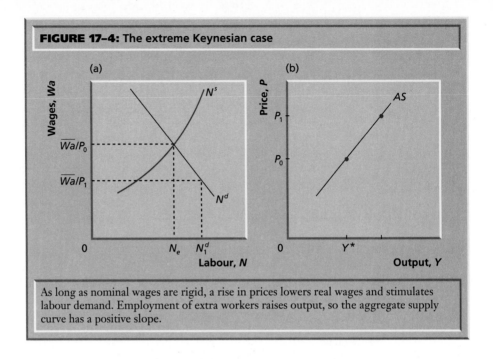

FIGURE 17–4: The extreme Keynesian case

As long as nominal wages are rigid, a rise in prices lowers real wages and stimulates labour demand. Employment of extra workers raises output, so the aggregate supply curve has a positive slope.

equilibrium real wage. Bargaining pressures would have caused such expectations to be reflected (in advance) in the negotiated wage.

Given a negotiated nominal wage, an unexpected price increase from P_0 to P_1 lowers the real wage to Wa/P_1 and raises the quantity of labour demanded to N_1^d. It also lowers the quantity of labour households would want to supply if they had the choice, but in the short run they do not; managers ask workers to work longer hours, and workers do so in the new Keynesian model. Employment therefore increases to N_1^d. From higher employment comes higher output. Since the higher price level P has caused higher output, the supply curve in Figure 17–4(b) is positively sloped rather than vertical.[7]

If a price increase occurs that was expected much earlier, when these contracts were still being negotiated, there would be little net impact on the real wage, and little impact on employment and output. For instance, in 1990 many Canadian unions negotiated into their contracts a wage increase to offset the price increase that was widely forecast to be caused by the introduction of the Goods and Services Tax in January 1991. To the extent that their negotiation was successful, their real wages are not affected by the price increase that occurred in January 1991.

---

[7] Just how flat the supply curve is depends also on how quickly input costs rise in the short run with extra output — that is, it also depends on the slopes of short-run marginal cost curves for firms, as in microeconomics.

Currently negotiated contracts

Currently negotiated contracts are negotiated to clear labour markets for the workers represented, but there is a consideration not present in the classical model: concern over relative wages. Because there are other workers whose wages are temporarily fixed, the workers currently negotiating will change their wages less than they otherwise would. In particular, their response to a rise in prices P is to demand higher nominal wages, but not enough to restore the original real wage level. To do so would cause too much substitution of other, cheaper workers for themselves. As a result, real wages are allowed to fall somewhat when prices rise, and firms increase employment. With higher employment, output rises as well. The supply curve for firms currently negotiating wage contracts therefore also has a positive slope.

Aggregate supply with overlapping contracts

In the labour markets of most industrial countries, different groups of workers negotiate their wage contracts at different dates and for different periods, so there are **overlapping wage contracts**. When wage contracts overlap, part of the labour force has fixed nominal wages because their contracts have already been signed, while the rest have flexible wages because their contracts are up for negotiation. In the short run, the aggregate supply curve will reflect an average of the responses of each group. Higher unexpected price levels will increase output levels, particularly of goods produced by workers whose nominal wages are fixed. The aggregate supply curve will be steeper than in Figure 17–4, but not vertical. Higher expected price levels will have some effect, but less than in Figure 17–4.

We should note a few features of this aggregate supply curve. First, involuntary unemployment is quite possible, as is overfull employment. Both layoffs and overtime will occur as demand fluctuates. Second, expectations make a significant difference to supply responses. It therefore matters how we explain which changes in price are expected and which are not. Section 4 addresses this issue explicitly.

SECTION 3

Short-run supply: the new classical model

The new Keynesian theory assumes that wages do not all clear labour markets in the short run. The alternative approach is to assume as a modelling strategy that they do.[8] For instance, even if nominal wages do not change, workers might

---

[8] The new classical approach has been presented by many authors. The first and most influential was Robert E. Lucas, "Some International Evidence on Output–Inflation Tradeoffs," *American Economic Review*, 1973, 326–334. For a more polemic presentation, see R.E. Lucas and T.J. Sargent, "After Keynesian Economics," in *After the Phillips Curve: Persistence of High Inflation and High Unemployment* (Boston: Federal Reserve Board of Boston, Conference Series No. 19, 1978).

Hybrid Models and Asymmetry

In practice, there are markets with rigid prices and wages, and markets with flexible prices and wages. Sir John Hicks has called them fix-price and flex-price markets.[a] In labour markets, Okun has labelled them **career and casual labour markets**.[b] In career labour markets both employers and employees go out of their way to maintain what are seen as long-term relationships, in order to avoid the substantial costs that arise from allowing a high turnover of staff (search costs, loss of productivity, loss of pension benefits, etc.). Among the steps they take is to keep nominal wages in line with other wages elsewhere. Firms also do not lower employees' real wages in the short run

FIGURE 17–5: The asymmetric supply curve

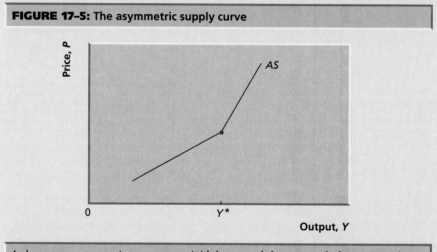

As long as wages or prices are more rigid downward than upward, the economy's response to demand shocks will be asymmetrical. Price and wage responses will be greater for positive demand shocks. Output responses will be more vigorous for negative demand shocks.

adjust the quality of their work to fit whatever real wages they are paid. Firms with fixed price lists might offer secret discounts. In the **new classical model**, all markets are assumed to be always in equilibrium. All transactions are assumed to be undertaken willingly by both parties, unlike overtime work and layoffs in the new Keynesian approach.

The new classical approach builds on a different short-run constraint: that less information is available in the short run than in the long run. In particular, it is assumed that workers receive information about their own nominal wage immediately, but they receive information about the aggregate price level only with a lag. When households need to use an aggregate price to assess what real wage is implied by any nominal wage, they must use an expectation of the current price level, P^e. They can replace P^e with P as soon as accurate information about just because unemployment is temporarily higher; the higher turnover costs to firms from disgruntled employees would more than offset short-term savings in wage costs. Only in casual labour markets for largely unskilled workers, where turnover is less expensive, do managers take advantage of any slack in labour markets in order to lower real wages.

In such a realistic but hybrid economy, the outcome usually lies somewhere between that of the new classical and new Keynesian models. The major difference between these hybrid models and what we have seen so far is that there is an **asymmetrical adjustment** to increases and decreases in demand. When demand increases, firms using casual labour raise nominal wages immediately to attract more workers. Firms using career labour must also raise wages to keep their workers from starting to look elsewhere. When demand falls off for what is expected to be only a short while, firms using casual labour will lower nominal wages, but firms using career labour will not do so for fear of losing workers they will not be able to replace later. Instead, firms using career labour will reduce output. As a result, output falls more when prices fall than output rises when prices rise. The aggregate supply curve is steeper above the long-run equilibrium output Y^* than below it. Figure 17–5 shows an example.[c]

Hybrid models such as Okun's are more realistic and produce a richer set of predictions about labour market behaviour than the new classical and new Keynesian models, but they are much more complex to use.

[a] Hicks introduced this convenient distinction in *Capital and Growth* (Oxford: Oxford University Press, 1965), 76–83.
[b] Arthur Okun, *Prices and Quantities* (Washington, D.C.: Brookings Institution, 1981), 81ff.
[c] Richard Lipsey argued that belief in this asymmetry was one of the beliefs that separated monetarists and Keynesians. "The Understanding and Control of Inflation: Is There a Crisis in Macro-economics?" *Canadian Journal of Economics*, November 1981, 545–76.

P becomes available, but that is only later, after the fact. Firms, on the other hand, use their own product price to calculate real wages, and they know their own product price immediately.

The effect of any change in price in the new classical model depends on whether the change in price is or is not accompanied by a change in the expected price P^e.

The effect of anticipated price changes

If a price increase is *anticipated*, both P and P^e rise by the same amount. As in the long-run classical model, illustrated in Figure 17–3, firms and workers both see the real wage as having fallen. Firms see the real wage as falling to

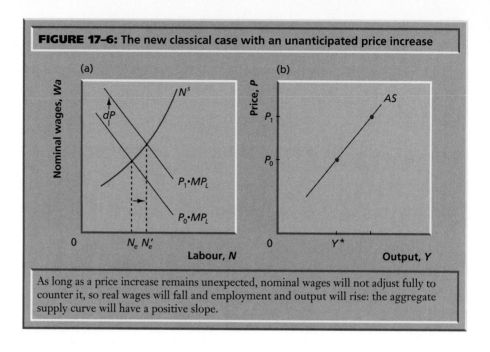

FIGURE 17–6: The new classical case with an unanticipated price increase

As long as a price increase remains unexpected, nominal wages will not adjust fully to counter it, so real wages will fall and employment and output will rise: the aggregate supply curve will have a positive slope.

$W a_0 / P_1$. Households see it as falling to $W a_0 / P_1^e$, which is the same as $W a_0 / P_1$ in Figure 17–3. Firms want to expand employment to N_1^d. Households want to cut back their labour supply to N_1^s and spend more time fishing. The excess labour demand drives nominal wages up to $W a_1$, the level at which the original real wage is re-established. At the original real wage, employment remains at the original level, so output cannot have changed. Since output does not respond to price changes, the aggregate supply curve is vertical. That is, for anticipated price changes, the new classical model produces the same outcome in the short run as the classical model produces in the long run. Figure 17–3 illustrates both cases.

The effect of unanticipated price changes

For any price increase that is *unanticipated* (and that can include just the unanticipated part of a partially anticipated price change), the change in P is not accompanied by a change in P^e. Firms notice that their real wage costs have fallen, so they want to hire more workers. Households do not notice that their real wage has fallen, so the quantity of labour they supply does not fall.

In Figure 17–6 the labour market diagram is drawn as in Figure 17–2(a), with nominal wages on the vertical axis. The labour demand curve shifts up and down proportionately with actual changes in product price P. The labour supply curve shifts up and down proportionately with changes in expected product price P^e.

An unanticipated price increase shifts firms' labour demand curve upward, but not households' labour supply curve. At the original level of employment, the value of marginal product now exceeds the nominal wage level, and firms want to hire more workers. There is now an excess demand for labour. Nominal wages rise to clear the labour market. As they do, firms' desire to employ more workers falls off somewhat, but households are willing to work longer hours; some fishing plans are shelved in favour of extra job search. Equilibrium employment rises to N_e'. Higher employment means higher output. That is, the aggregate supply curve is positively sloped rather than vertical.[9]

Note the implied definition of the short run in the new classical model: the short run is a period short enough that workers cannot find out about the aggregate price level, so they cannot realize they have made a mistake. The length of the short run reflects lags in recognizing and acting on information. In financial markets, such lags are measured in hours.

SECTION 4

Adaptive and rational expectations

Expectations play a major role in both new Keynesian and new classical models. In the new classical model, workers must form expectations of the aggregate price level in order to assess what real wage is implied by available nominal wage offers. In the new Keynesian model, workers and firms must form expectations of future prices, and future labour market conditions, in order to negotiate long-term wage contracts. So far we have not said much about how those expectations are formed. We have merely shown that if the expectations remain fixed, changes in nominal wages will indeed cause extra output. But will such expectations stay fixed? We need to know how expectations are formed.

Adaptive expectations

The simplest assumption about expectations formation is that we expect in the future what we have already seen. Thus we form our estimates of price level P in the next period by looking backwards at what P was yesterday and is today. If prices rose in the past, we expect that future prices will also be higher. But we cannot foresee changes in future prices until *after* they have occurred in the present. Such expectations are adaptive, in that they adapt, after the fact, to what we observe happening.

Adaptive expectations are not the only possible kind of expectations. One could imagine many others: using Tarot cards or poker dice, forecasts from *The*

---

[9] Just how much extra output is made available depends on the slopes of the labour supply curve (up which the labour demand curve slides) and of the production function (up which the economy slides as employment is increased).

The New Classical "Price Surprise" Supply Function

A more simplified version of the new classical model is sometimes used that dispenses with labour markets. Robert E. Lucas of the University of Chicago has constructed a streamlined model economy in which all firms are essentially farms, each producing a different crop and using all of the economy's output as inputs (seed, fertilizer, machinery, food, etc.).[a]

FIGURE 17-7: The price surprise supply function

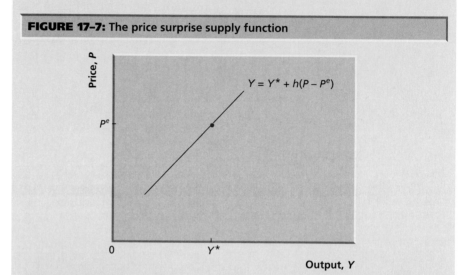

$$Y = Y^* + h(P - P^e)$$

This aggregate supply curve reflects only unanticipated price movements, and only for as long as they are unanticipated; otherwise output reverts to the natural rate Y^*.

Financial Post, wishful thinking, listening to one's brother-in-law, using leading indicator series, and so on. Some of these others would be forward-looking, in that they use today's observations of important variables, such as the nominal money supply or the unemployment level, to infer what will probably happen to the aggregate price level tomorrow.

Rational expectations

The most extreme forward-looking hypothesis assumes that households and firms behave in goods and labour markets in the same way that the efficient markets hypothesis predicts for behaviour of investors in financial markets (see Chapter 14, section 1); that is, that households and firms take into account all available information, including the conventional wisdom about how the economy works, to form their expectations of the future. Adding such expectations, known as **rational expectations**, has a dramatic effect on the predictions of the new classical model.

Let p be each firm's individual crop price, and let P be the aggregate price level that measures the average cost of firms' inputs. Each firm will increase its output if its crop price p rises relative to the average input price P, and will decrease its output if the opposite happens. Firms receive up-to-date information on their own crop price p, but they receive information on the aggregate (input) price level P only with a lag. In making their output decisions, firms must use expected input prices P^e. When P actually rises, firms will immediately observe only the rise in their own crop price p. If firms assume from observing a rise in p that P has not changed (that is, if the price increase is unanticipated), then p/P^e will have risen and firms will expand output. The aggregate supply curve will have a positive slope. If firms infer from rising p that P has also risen, then P^e will rise as p does and the ratio p/P^e does not change. Neither does output. The aggregate supply curve is vertical.

In this model the only part of a price increase that matters to output is the unanticipated part, the price surprise. The model is summarized by the **"price surprise" supply function** illustrated in Figure 17–7:

$$Y = Y^* + h(P - P^e),$$

where Y^* is the long-run equilibrium output level and h is a constant coefficient.

---

[a] R.E. Lucas, Jr., "Some International Evidence on Output–Inflation Tradeoffs," *American Economic Review*, 1973, 326–34.

If price expectations in any model are to be rational, then firms and households must use as their expected future price level P^e whatever the model itself predicts. Households in a new classical model must use the new classical model's predictions, while households and firms in the new Keynesian model must use the new Keynesian model's predictions.

In the new classical model, news about or predictions of a surge of demand next year would cause (rational) expectations of a rise in the aggregate price level. When aggregate demand does increase, raising actual prices P and nominal wages Wa, the rising nominal wages would not be interpreted by households as higher real wages, so there would be no increase in labour supply or output. The aggregate supply curve would be vertical. Any announced demand stimulus from the government would therefore have no effect on output or employment — only on the price level and inflation. Unannounced policy stimuli would still affect output as long as the stimuli could not be predicted on some other basis. Since it is difficult to argue that unannounced and unpredictable policy is ever desirable, the effect of adding rational expectations to the new classical model is to make all sensible stabilization policy incapable of affecting employment. This policy ineffectiveness proposition is a quite startling conclusion, one that has earned the new classical school a lot of attention.

In the new Keynesian model, news about or predictions of a surge of demand next year can not be used currently by workers whose wage contracts are not renegotiated until next year (call them the "delayed group"). Those currently negotiating wage contracts (the "current group") would expect prices to rise, but they would not expect nominal wages to rise by as much. They would expect real wages to fall, and employment and output to increase. Nominal wages would not be expected to rise as much as prices because (a) workers in the delayed group are locked into their contracted nominal wage until next year, and (b) workers in the current group will not insist on maintaining their real wage constant when that means getting too far out of line with real wages of the delayed group. Next year workers in the delayed group take the demand surge into account in renegotiating their contracts, and they build higher P^e into nominal wage levels. However, they also allow real wage levels to fall somewhat to stay more in line with the current group. Employment and output therefore stay somewhat higher than the original level even next year.

In the new Keynesian model, therefore, announced or predictable stabilization policies will have an effect on output and employment even under rational expectations. The difference that rational expectations makes in the new Keynesian model is mainly that announced policies will have their effects on nominal wages in advance. As soon as a demand surge comes to be expected, nominal wages currently being negotiated will reflect it even if aggregate demand is not due to change until near the end of the contract period.[10] For instance, the announcement of fiscal restraint for the next few budgets would lower nominal wage settlements immediately in civil service contracts being negotiated. A similar effect appears in models of the term structure of interest rates, discussed in Chapter 14: expectations of lower short-term interest rates in the future are reflected immediately in today's long-term interest rates.

SECTION 5

Inflation and unemployment

So far in this chapter we have explained price and output levels. However, public discussion of macroeconomic policy is almost always couched in terms of inflation and unemployment rates. To make our price–output models relevant

---

[10] In the same way we observe that the announcement of any major investment project in an area affects property prices in that area well before the investment activity takes place.

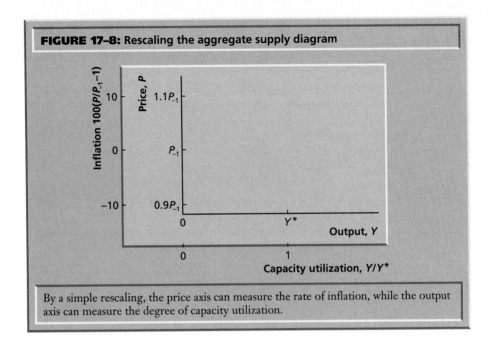

FIGURE 17-8: Rescaling the aggregate supply diagram

By a simple rescaling, the price axis can measure the rate of inflation, while the output axis can measure the degree of capacity utilization.

for policy discussions we must be able to extend them so they will explain inflation and unemployment directly. That is the task of this section.

Some of this task can be achieved simply by rescaling the aggregate supply diagram. First, let each output level on the output axis be divided by the long-run equilibrium output level Y^*. The horizontal axis of the aggregate supply diagram now measures the degree of capacity utilization rather than output. Figure 17–8 illustrates the change.

Second, we can rescale the price axis into an inflation axis in three steps. Let each price level be divided by the price level of last period, P_{-1}. Then subtract 1 from each value on the vertical axis, and multiply each remaining value by 100. What those operations produce is the inflation rate (in percentage form) that is implied by each possible current price level, given the previous period's price level. Figure 17–8 also illustrates this change.

A short-run aggregate supply curve drawn with rescaled axes now relates the inflation rate to the degree of capacity utilization. Higher capacity utilization implies higher inflation in the short run if the aggregate supply curve is positively sloped. If the aggregate supply curve is vertical, then attempts to raise capacity utilization simply generate higher inflation.

In order to focus on unemployment rather than capacity utilization, we use a relationship between the two that is known as **Okun's law** after the economist who first noticed it, Arthur Okun. Corresponding to each degree of capacity utilization is a degree of utilization of the potential labour force (and of the capital stock, for that matter).[11] Corresponding to the long-run equilibrium rate of capacity utilization (1 on the horizontal axis of Figure 17–8) is a long-run equilibrium level of unemployment U^*. This unemployment represents the long-run equilibrium proportion of the labour force between jobs. Okun's law is the hypothesis that changing the degree of capacity utilization changes the rate of unemployment in the opposite direction, at a constant rate, as in

$$Y/Y^* - 1 = 2.5(U^* - U),$$

where U and U^* are in decimal form, and the Okun's law coefficient is 2.5.

With Okun's law assumed, we can interpret any effect of higher rates of capacity utilization as being also the effect of lower rates of unemployment. For instance, the curve in Figure 17–9(a) asserts that higher capacity utilization drives up inflation rates in the short run. In Figure 17–9(b), the matching curve asserts instead that lower unemployment rates drive up inflation rates. The two assertions are merely two versions of the same story.

The curve in Figure 17–9(b) is known as a **Phillips curve**. The original Phillips curve related unemployment to wage inflation, but Richard Lipsey quickly extended Phillips' analysis to price inflation.[12] The curve shown in Figure 17–9(a) is a form of aggregate supply curve. Because its logic is the same as that of the Phillips curve, it is sometimes referred to as the **PEP curve** (for price expectations augmented Phillips curve).[13] Others refer to it as an expectations-augmented aggregate supply (EAS) curve.

For both curves in Figure 17–9, any non-vertical slope is due to workers operating as though with a fixed expectation of the price level P^e. In the new classical model, the Phillips and PEP curves will be vertical unless workers' expectation of inflation $[(P^e - P_{-1})/P_{-1}]$ does not change as actual inflation does. In the new Keynesian model the Phillips and PEP curves are not vertical because some wages were fixed in the past on the basis of past (and therefore fixed) expectations of inflation.

Both of the curves drawn in Figure 17–9 reflect the assumption of 5 percent expected inflation. If a higher expected inflation rate is assumed — for instance,

---

[11] Layoffs of capital are not as obvious as layoffs of workers when recession hits (except to firms renting out capital equipment on short-term leases), but capital layoffs are the rule rather than the exception. When firms drop to a single shift, for instance, they idle their equipment at the same time that they idle their workers. When workers are rehired, the equipment is brought back into service. The labour:capital ratio is flexible, to be sure, but mainly in the long run.

[12] A.W. Phillips, "The Relation Between Unemployment and the Rate of Change of Money Wages in the United Kingdom, 1861–1957," *Economica*, November 1958, 283–99; R.G. Lipsey, "The Relation Between Unemployment and the Rate of Change of Money Wages in the United Kingdom, 1861–1957: A Further Analysis," *Economica*, February 1960, 1–31. For a modern specification of this relationship in Canada, see W.C. Riddell and Philip Smith, "Expected Inflation and Wage Changes in Canada," *Canadian Journal of Economics*, August 1982, 377–94.

[13] For instance, this is the label used by David A. Wilton and David M. Prescott in *Macroeconomics: Theory and Policy in Canada*, 2nd ed. (Don Mills, Ont.: Addison-Wesley, 1987).

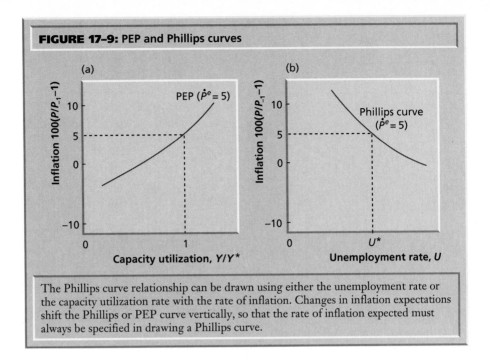

FIGURE 17-9: PEP and Phillips curves

The Phillips curve relationship can be drawn using either the unemployment rate or the capacity utilization rate with the rate of inflation. Changes in inflation expectations shift the Phillips or PEP curve vertically, so that the rate of inflation expected must always be specified in drawing a Phillips curve.

7 percent — the relevant Phillips and PEP curves will be higher than those in Figure 17–9 by the 2 percent margin of extra expected inflation. As expected inflation rates change over time, therefore, the economy's Phillips and PEP curves shift in step.

SECTION 6

Short- and long-run equilibria

We conclude this chapter by putting aggregate demand and supply together to explain short- and long-run equilibria of output and prices.

Long-run equilibrium

In the long run, aggregate supply curves are vertical at a long-run equilibrium output level determined by (a) labour market equilibrium, and (b) the production function. Only one output level is possible, and that is entirely determined by the supply curve. Aggregate demand serves only to determine the price level P, as shown in Figure 17–10.

The process of adjustment of demand and output to Y^* can be illustrated with an IS–LM–BP diagram on which a vertical long-run output constraint has been superimposed, as shown in Figure 17–11. Let the economy start with

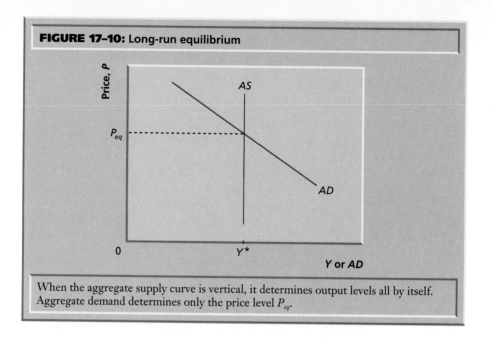

FIGURE 17–10: Long-run equilibrium

When the aggregate supply curve is vertical, it determines output levels all by itself. Aggregate demand determines only the price level P_{eq}.

output at Y^* but with aggregate demand at the intersection of IS–LM–BP, at point A. This could be caused by too high a price level. Prices of goods would be driven downward by the excess supply of goods. Nominal wages would fall with prices of goods to keep real wages constant, so neither employment nor output would change. Lower prices, however, would raise the real money supply M_s/P. The LM curve would shift to the right and interest rates would fall. Lower interest rates would increase investment spending and aggregate demand.

Greater investment spending would be reinforced by increases in net export demand, although the channel of influence would depend on the exchange rate system in force:

1. Under *fixed exchange rates*, lower domestic prices would stimulate net exports directly, and would shift both BP and IS curves to the right. Their new intersection points at lower price levels would lie along the dotted line labelled "IS–BP shift locus." If exchange market intervention were not sterilized, the domestic money supply would also be increased as extra official reserves added to the stock of high-powered money; the LM curve would be pushed further to the right. Eventually, after falling prices and interest rates had caused enough leftward shifts of the LM, IS, and BP curves, aggregate demand would reach aggregate supply at B, where the IS–BP shift locus intersects the aggregate supply line.

2. Under *floating exchange rates*, lower interest rates would cause a lower exchange rate, which in time would raise net exports. Again, both the IS and BP curves would be shifted to the right, their intersections tracing along

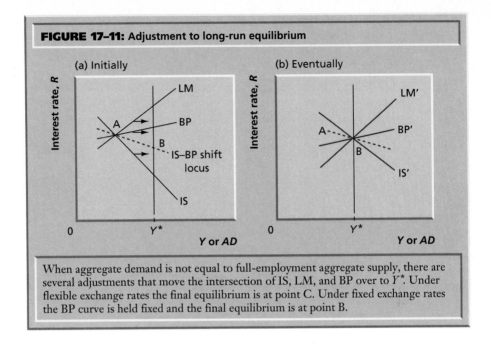

FIGURE 17–11: Adjustment to long-run equilibrium

(a) Initially

(b) Eventually

When aggregate demand is not equal to full-employment aggregate supply, there are several adjustments that move the intersection of IS, LM, and BP over to Y^*. Under flexible exchange rates the final equilibrium is at point C. Under fixed exchange rates the BP curve is held fixed and the final equilibrium is at point B.

the same IS–BP shift locus. The eventual equilibrium would be at the same point B.

The quantity theory model

Since, in the long run, output levels are fixed at Y^*, and demand serves only to fix the price level, it is worth looking for a simpler model that can be used to explain just the price level. The **quantity theory model**, which was used by macroeconomists before Keynes's *General Theory of Employment, Interest, and Money* appeared in 1936, is such a model.[14]

The quantity theory originally maintained that prices had to adjust to whatever level would balance money supply with money demand. Money demand was alleged to be a fixed fraction of nominal income. The fraction is $1/V$, where V is the velocity of money, the number of transactions per dollar of money per year. Real income is fixed at Y^*, so nominal income is PY^*. If nominal money supply M_s is fixed, then P must settle at the level needed to get

$$M_s V = PY^*,$$

or, rearranging,

$$M_s/P = (1/V)Y^*.$$

---

[14] See Irving Fisher, *The Purchasing Power of Money* (New York: Macmillan, 1911).

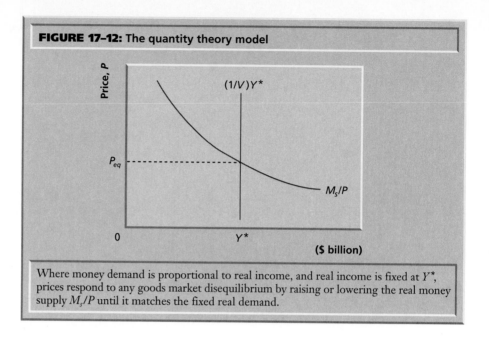

FIGURE 17–12: The quantity theory model

Where money demand is proportional to real income, and real income is fixed at Y^*, prices respond to any goods market disequilibrium by raising or lowering the real money supply M_s/P until it matches the fixed real demand.

Figure 17–12 illustrates the quantity theory model on a diagram showing the demand and supply of real money balances, with price P on the vertical axis. The demand for money is $(1/V)Y^*$, which is not sensitive to the price level. The real money supply falls as price P rises, and only the equilibrium price level P_{eq} will clear the market.

The quantity theory view will not work as in Figure 17–12, however, if the demand for money also depends on the rate of interest, as we assumed in Chapter 16. In this case there are many potential money demand curves to put in Figure 17–12, and the quantity theory no longer gives us a single prediction of the equilibrium price level.

Short-run equilibrium

In the short run, aggregate supply curves have some positive slope for all unanticipated price changes. For anticipated price changes, aggregate supply is vertical in the new classical model, but is still positively sloped in the new Keynesian model. Figure 17–13 illustrates these short-run situations. For convenience, the same positively sloping aggregate supply curve has been used to describe three separate situations: the new classical case with unanticipated demand shocks, and the two new Keynesian cases with anticipated and unanticipated demand shocks.

Both AS and AD curves determine output and price levels where the AS curve has positive slope. Where the short run supply curve is vertical, the AS curve determines the output level and the AD curve determines the price

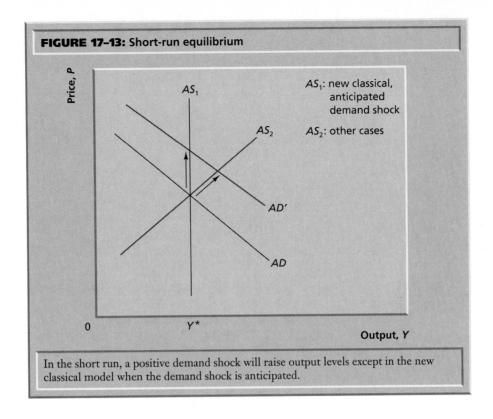

FIGURE 17–13: Short-run equilibrium

In the short run, a positive demand shock will raise output levels except in the new classical model when the demand shock is anticipated.

level, as in the long-run case described in Figure 17–10. Anticipated shifts in aggregate demand will therefore cause changes in both output and prices in the new Keynesian model, but only changes in prices in the new classical model. Unanticipated changes in demand cause changes in both output and prices in both models.

A more transparent but more complex way of seeing demand and supply interact in the short run is by putting together the IS–LM–BP diagram with the PEP curve, as shown in Figure 17–14. A fall in aggregate demand, for instance due to a 3 percent slower growth in the money supply, appears in Figure 17–14 as a leftward shift of the LM curve to LM'. Equilibrium demand would move from point A to point B under flexible exchange rates. Lower aggregate demand would lower inflation from point C to point D along the short-run PEP curve in Figure 17–14(b), if inflationary expectations were fixed in the short run.

In the new classical case, the news that money supply growth was slowing down by 3 percent would cause expected inflation also to slow down by 3 percent. The short-run, fixed-expectations PEP curve now relevant would be a PEP curve 3 percent lower. With 3 percent lower expectations, actual inflation would also drop 3 percent. The real money supply would not drop at all. Instead of the LM curve shifting to the left, the fixed-expectations PEP curve would drop

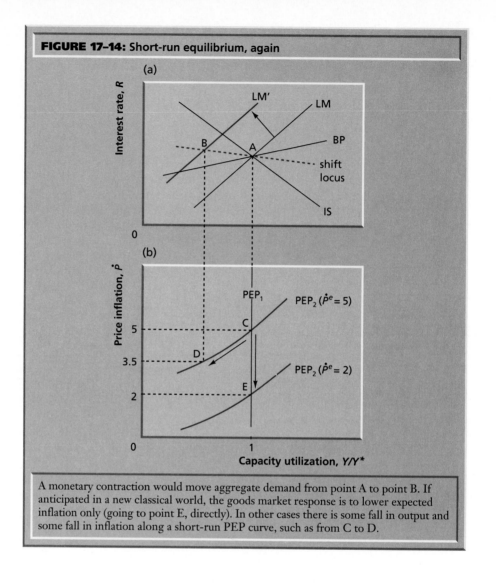

FIGURE 17–14: Short-run equilibrium, again

A monetary contraction would move aggregate demand from point A to point B. If anticipated in a new classical world, the goods market response is to lower expected inflation only (going to point E, directly). In other cases there is some fall in output and some fall in inflation along a short-run PEP curve, such as from C to D.

3 percent. The economy would move to 3 percent less inflation with no change in unemployment at all. This is of course a scenario the Bank of Canada would love to see in practice.

SECTION 7

▣ Summary

Aggregate supply reflects the supply of inputs into production, especially the supply of labour. In the long run, the supply of labour will depend on the real wage level, and changes in the price level will not have the power to influence real wages. The aggregate supply curve will be vertical.

In the short run, there are two quite different approaches to modelling behaviour of labour markets. The new Keynesian approach assumes that the labour market is characterized by overlapping, long-term wage contracts. In the short run, the nominal wages of some firms and workers will be fixed. During the life of each contract, employment is determined by firms. Demand shocks will therefore cause price changes that will be met by higher employment and output, even if the demand shock is anticipated.

The new classical approach assumes full market clearing in each period, so that the labour market is always in equilibrium. However, there are some information constraints that prevent households from being fully informed about the general price level, so they will rationally but mistakenly respond to unanticipated demand shocks by changing their labour supply in the same direction.

When the assumption of rational expectations is added to the new classical model, the class of unanticipated shocks that will produce positive supply responses dwindles to only those that can not be forecast from the past performance of the economy. This rules out all sensible stabilization policy, for instance. Adding rational expectations to the new Keynesian model has a much less startling effect.

The aggregate supply relationship can be recast into a relationship between rates of capacity utilization or unemployment, and rates of price inflation. The Phillips curve describes that relationship. The logic of short- and long-run aggregate supply responses transfers fully and easily to short- and long-run Phillips curves: changes in output and employment do not accompany changes in inflation in the long run, but they may in the short run.

Putting aggregate demand and supply together determines equilibrium output and price levels. In the long run, output is determined by supply and price level is determined by demand. In the short run both sides of the market usually determine both outcomes jointly. For anticipated demand shocks in the short run in a new classical world, however, the long-run conclusions still hold.

Key Terms

classical model	asymmetrical adjustment
production function	new classical model
the labour market	price surprise supply function
equilibrium aggregate supply	adaptive expectations
new Keynesian model	rational expectations
collective agreements	Okun's law
implicit wage contracts	the Phillips curve
overlapping wage contracts	the PEP curve
career and casual labour markets	quantity theory model

Questions and Problems

1. Classical analysis of the long run suggests that aggregate demand will not be able to influence the output level unless somehow it affects technology or labour supply. Is either of these extra effects likely?

2. What is the importance of the distinction between anticipated and unanticipated shocks (for instance, fiscal shocks)?

3. From what you know of goods markets, do you think suppliers receive their demand information mainly in the form of price news, or volume news? Why one and not the other?

4. Give three examples each of flex-price and fix-price markets.

5. Which is more important to you in picking a summer job (assuming you have a choice, that is): relative wages or real wages? Which is more important to your parent or parents in choosing their jobs?

6. Are rational expectations in goods and labour markets any less likely than in financial markets? Explain.

7. How long would the economy remain on a sloping short-run Phillips curve under the new classical, new Keynesian, and hybrid models? That is, how long is the short run in each of these models?

8. Why is the quantity theory model no longer an acceptable short-cut summary model for macroeconomic analysis?

Suggestions for Further Reading

Dornbusch, R., S. Fischer, and G. Sparks. *Macroeconomics*, 3rd Canadian ed. Toronto: McGraw-Hill Ryerson, 1989.

Lipsey, Richard G. "The Understanding and Control of Inflation: Is There a Crisis in Macro-economics?" *Canadian Journal of Economics*. November 1981, 545–76.

Lucas, Robert E. "Some International Evidence on Output–Inflation Trade-offs," *American Economic Review*, 1973, 326–334.

Okun, Arthur. *Prices and Quantities*. Washington, D.C.: Brookings Institution, 1981.

Parkin, Michael and Robin Bade. *Modern Macroeconomics*, 2nd ed. Scarborough, Ont.: Prentice-Hall, 1986.

Taylor, John H.. "Staggered Wage Setting in a Macro Model," *American Economic Review*. May 1979, 108–113.

Wilton, David A. and David M. Prescott. *Macroeconomics: Theory and Policy in Canada*, 2nd ed. Don Mills, Ont.: Addison-Wesley, 1987.

Chapter eighteen

Business Cycles

Chapters 16 and 17 have derived the aggregate demand and aggregate supply curves that make up the basic macro model of the economy. At the end of Chapter 17 we also looked at short- and long-run equilibria for the economy by putting aggregate demand and aggregate supply together. In order to discuss stabilization policy, however, we need to explain more than just the short- and long-run equilibria. We also need to understand the medium-term behaviour of the economy — the time path of moving short-run equilibria that the economy traces out on its way from the short run to the long run. This time path shows irregular fluctuations known as business cycles. The new Keynesian and new classical models offer quite different views about the factors that cause business cycles, and what can or should be done about them. We need to be aware of both views before we leave the macro review.

Section 1 provides some basic information on the business cycles that have been observed in the past. Section 2 provides the new Keynesian explanation. Section 3 provides the new classical explanation and a brief discussion of relevant evidence.

You should learn in this chapter:

1. the basic features of fluctuations in output growth, price levels, unemployment rates, and inflation that have occurred in the past;

2. the new Keynesian explanation of those fluctuations as being mainly responses to shocks to aggregate demand;

3. the new classical explanation of those fluctuations as being mainly responses to shocks to aggregate supply.

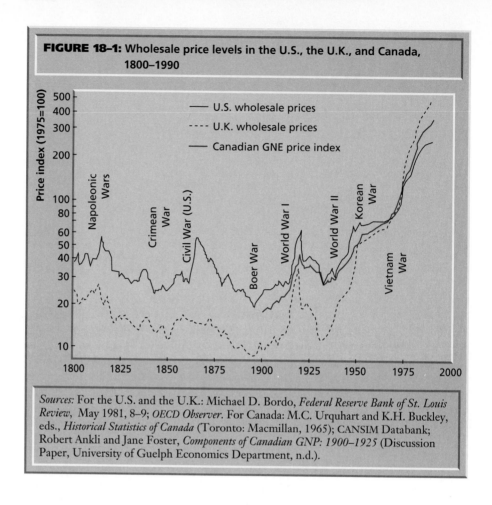

FIGURE 18–1: Wholesale price levels in the U.S., the U.K., and Canada, 1800–1990

Sources: For the U.S. and the U.K.: Michael D. Bordo, *Federal Reserve Bank of St. Louis Review,* May 1981, 8–9; *OECD Observer.* For Canada: M.C. Urquhart and K.H. Buckley, eds., *Historical Statistics of Canada* (Toronto: Macmillan, 1965); CANSIM Databank; Robert Ankli and Jane Foster, *Components of Canadian GNP: 1900–1925* (Discussion Paper, University of Guelph Economics Department, n.d.).

SECTION 1

☐ The business cycle record

Fluctuations in output growth rates over time are given the collective name of **business cycles.** Associated with cycles of output growth are cycles in price levels, unemployment rates, inflation rates, real wage rates, and many other measures of economic performance. The record of fluctuations in these variables is reviewed briefly in this section.

Price levels

To start with a very long-run perspective, Figure 18–1 shows the time path of fluctuations in wholesale price levels for the United States and the United Kingdom since 1800, and for Canada since 1900.

For the 145 years up to 1945, price levels clearly followed a pattern of rising during wars and declining thereafter. That pattern appears during the Napoleonic Wars (1803–15), the Crimean War (1853–56), the American Civil War (1861–65), and the First World War (1914–18). Price levels also rose, though less markedly, during the Second World War (1939–45) and the Vietnam War (1965–75). What is striking about the last two cases is that after 1945 the price level no longer fell; at best it only stopped rising. Coincidentally or not, it was in 1944–45 that voters recognized and Western governments acknowledged government responsibility for stabilization policy. [1]

Another feature of price changes both before and after 1945 is that they have been sluggish: rates of price change have varied considerably, but not quickly. Several years of rapid inflation have been followed by several years of slow inflation, and vice versa.

Output growth

Figure 18–2 shows the growth rates of real output in the United States and Canada since 1900. Output growth has fluctuated widely, in patterns that have been cyclical, but not regular. Several boom years have tended to be followed by a slowdown, several slow-growth years by a boom. It appears for both countries in Figure 18–2 that output growth has been much more stable after 1945 than before. [2] The length of cycles has not changed much, however. Canadian and U.S. output growth rates were very similar in most years, as one might have expected from the enormous importance to Canada of trade with the United States, and from the integration of Canadian and U.S. financial markets. Shocks to U.S. demand are quickly transmitted to Canada through trade flows, and monetary policies have generated similar interest rates on both sides of the border.

Unemployment rates and inflation

Both unemployment rates and inflation rates are implicit in Figures 18–1 and 18–2. Price inflation is the rate of change per year of the price series in Figure 18–1. Output growth implies employment growth except to the extent that extra output is the result of increased labour productivity. If the growth of labour productivity stays relatively constant, reflecting a more or less continual process of adoption of better technology in thousands of different firms each year, and if the growth of the labour force changes as sluggishly as the growth of population

---

[1] In a series of acts, such as Canada's Full Employment Act of 1944, Western governments pronounced their commitment to stabilization policy. In West Germany, the government's commitment to avoiding inflation was written into the constitution.

[2] This is the subject of some dispute. Christina Romer contends that most of the difference is a statistical illusion created by the imputation techniques that were used to assemble pre-1945 aggregate output figures. See C. Romer, "Spurious Volatility in Historical Unemployment Data," *Journal of Political Economy*, February 1986, 1–37.

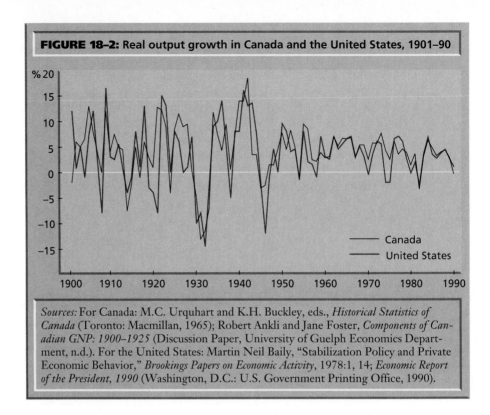

FIGURE 18–2: Real output growth in Canada and the United States, 1901–90

Sources: For Canada: M.C. Urquhart and K.H. Buckley, eds., *Historical Statistics of Canada* (Toronto: Macmillan, 1965); Robert Ankli and Jane Foster, *Components of Canadian GNP: 1900–1925* (Discussion Paper, University of Guelph Economics Department, n.d.). For the United States: Martin Neil Baily, "Stabilization Policy and Private Economic Behavior," *Brookings Papers on Economic Activity*, 1978:1, 14; *Economic Report of the President, 1990* (Washington, D.C.: U.S. Government Printing Office, 1990).

of working age, then years of rapid output growth in Figure 18–2 imply years of falling unemployment; years of slow output growth must be years of rising unemployment.

Unemployment rates and inflation rates are plotted against each other in Figure 18–3 for each year since 1954, to show their relative timing over the business cycle. The unemployment rate is of prime-age males and the inflation rate is of the consumer price index excluding food. The outcomes of successive years are connected to form a time path starting in 1954.

One of the striking features of Figure 18–3 is the generally circular, clockwise motion of the time path. A year of low unemployment is likely to be followed by another year of low unemployment, but several such years are likely to be followed by years of high unemployment. The same is true for inflation. Peaks and troughs of unemployment and inflation do not coincide completely; while inflation troughs just when unemployment peaks, inflation peaks two or three years after unemployment troughs. High unemployment does not seem to reduce inflation unless unemployment is at the same time rising.

A second feature of Figure 18–3 is that the average unemployment rate around which the time path moves appears to have risen substantially between the 1960s and the 1980s. If average unemployment rates reflect the willingness of workers to remain unemployed in order to search for better jobs, then twice

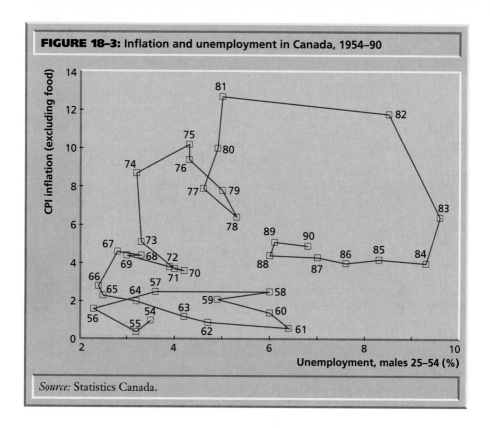

FIGURE 18–3: Inflation and unemployment in Canada, 1954–90

Source: Statistics Canada.

as large a share of prime-age males were willing to remain unemployed and to search in the 1980s as were willing to do so in the 1960s.

The third feature of Figure 18–3 is how long the cyclical fluctuations have lasted. From the few complete cycles and the fragments of others in Figure 18–3, it looks as though the economy takes about a decade to go full circle; that is much, much longer than anyone's definition of the short run.

SECTION 2

▢ The new Keynesian explanation

As explained in Chapter 17, the new Keynesian approach assumes that most wages and also some prices are fixed in the short run, and that firms are free to raise and lower output and employment in the short run both above and below the long-run equilibrium level. In this section we address the medium-run effects on prices and output, once output is moved off the long-run equilibrium level. Finally, we discuss the implications for government stabilization policy of the cyclical changes described by the new Keynesian model.

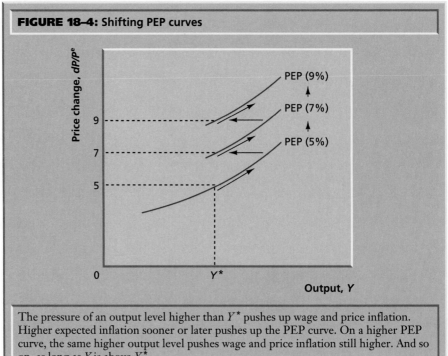

FIGURE 18–4: Shifting PEP curves

The pressure of an output level higher than Y^* pushes up wage and price inflation. Higher expected inflation sooner or later pushes up the PEP curve. On a higher PEP curve, the same higher output level pushes wage and price inflation still higher. And so on, as long as Y is above Y^*.

Shifting PEP curves

In the medium run, the economy has time to shift from one PEP curve to another. This section explains how such shifts cause inflation to accelerate or decelerate whenever output rises above or falls below the long-run equilibrium output level.

First, consider a simple new Keynesian framework with two groups of workers, A and B, who negotiate their two-year contracts in alternate years. Assume that both groups start at the long-run equilibrium level with 5 percent wage increases in their most recent contracts. When bargaining, both groups can see clearly what is happening in the current year, but they must predict the economic environment for the second year of their contract.

Now let there be a positive **aggregate demand shock** that drives up the prices of output. Firms expand along the short-run PEP curve in Figure 18–4. Workers in group A, currently negotiating, foresee higher inflation and insist on higher nominal wages in their contract. Assume they are able to secure 7 percent. Workers in group B are locked in at 5 percent; for them real wages fall, overtime hours mount up, and fishing trips must be put off. The assumption that group B is locked into 5 percent wage increases for the short run is crucial to the short-run PEP curve. That assumption is given in parentheses following the curve's label in Figure 18–4.

In the next year, group B gets to renegotiate and it is group A that is locked into a contract. However, group A is locked in at a wage increase of 7 percent rather then 5 percent. The short-run PEP curve that is relevant now is 2 percent higher than the PEP curve that was relevant in the first year. If output is still above the long-run equilibrium level Y^* (that is, if there is another unexpected demand shock), then group B will not only catch up with group A, but will also be able to take advantage of the second demand shock to get even more — say 9 percent, as in Figure 18–4. In the third year group B will be locked in at 9 percent and group A will renegotiate to catch up for the unexpected demand shock of year 2. The economy will be operating on a still higher, 9 percent PEP curve.

In short, the economy moves up the PEP curve diagram like a climber on a rope ladder, hand over hand from one rung to the next, as long as unexpected positive demand shocks continue.

The second possible reason for shifts from one PEP curve to another, following output changes, is that workers revise backward-looking **inflation expectations**. With backward-looking expectations, the change in inflation from 5 to 7 percent in Figure 18–4 is unexpected. Because workers in group A do not foresee the extra inflation, they do not insist on as large a nominal wage increase in their contract. The PEP curve is therefore flatter than with forward-looking expectations. Later, of course, they learn of their mistake. When they do, their revision of expectations causes the flatter PEP curve to shift up by the amount of extra inflationary expectations. If group A bargains every two years, this upward shift of the PEP curve will occur in the third year; that is when the group's contract next can be renegotiated.

As actual inflation exceeds what workers expect on signing contracts, workers will insist on higher nominal wage settlements to make up lost ground. Actual inflation will exceed what workers expected whenever output is above the long-run equilibrium level, almost by definition: extra output is possible only if real wages fall, which means that prices rise faster than nominal wages. This will occur only if workers can not foresee the inflation at time of contract negotiation. PEP curves therefore shift between successive short runs whenever the economy is off the long-run equilibrium output level Y^*.

Accelerationism and the NAIRU

The pattern of adjustment in Figure 18–4 makes the new Keynesian model one of a class of **accelerationist models**, in which inflation accelerates as long as output Y is maintained above the long-run equilibrium level Y^*, and decelerates as long as Y is less than Y^*. Put differently, inflation accelerates as long as unemployment U is held below the long-run equilibrium level U^*. For that reason, U^* is known as the non-accelerating inflation rate of unemployment, or **NAIRU**.[3]

[3] Y^* could be called the non-accelerating rate of output, or NAIRO, but usually it is not. For a review of the NAIRU, see David E. Rose, *The NAIRU in Canada: Concepts, Determinants, and Estimates* (Ottawa: Bank of Canada Technical Report No. 50, December 1988).

Exactly what it takes to keep output above Y^* or unemployment below NAIRU depends on what is assumed about expectations. If expectations are adaptive — that is, backward-looking — then any demand shock that is different from the past will cause unexpected current price changes, higher output, and lower unemployment. If expectations are rational, then the demand shock must have been unpredictable to generate more than just price and nominal wage changes. Unpredictable demand shocks are less frequent than demand shocks that are merely different from the past.

Putting the accelerationist result together with the aggregate demand model gives rise to cyclical fluctuations in inflation and capacity utilization of the sort recorded in Figure 18–3. Figure 18–5 illustrates this, using a closed-economy IS–LM model for simplicity instead of the full IS–LM–BP model. The economy starts at A in both (a) and (b). Expectations are adaptive. An unexpected demand shock in the first year (for instance, from an export boom or an election spending binge) shifts the IS curve to the right, generating higher aggregate demand and interest rates in part (a). The economy moves up the PEP curve in part (b) to higher capacity utilization and price inflation. The economy's new short-run equilibrium by the end of the first year is at B in both (a) and (b).

By the second year, faster price inflation has shrunk the real money supply M_s/P, so that the LM curve has been shifted to the left. Aggregate demand is crowded out somewhat by higher interest rates. In (a), the short-run equilibrium moves to C. In (b), the PEP curve is shifted up by, for example, 2 percent; workers previously locked in renegotiate their wage contracts to take into account the surprisingly high inflation observed in the first year, at point B. On the higher (7 percent) PEP curve, the aggregate demand level at point C in part (a) therefore generates 8 percent inflation at point C in part (b). Inflation still accelerates in the second year even though output growth has fallen, because output and capacities utilization levels are above Y^*.

In subsequent years the economy follows a circular, counterclockwise path shown beyond point C on the PEP curve diagram as the twin forces of changing real money supply and changing wage contracts or inflation expectations shift the LM and PEP curves from one short-run situation to the next. The circular path centres around the long-run equilibrium levels of output and inflation. The long-run equilibrium inflation rate is determined by the rate of change of the nominal money supply. If money supply growth is given at 5 percent in Figure 18–5, then the height of the long-run equilibrium centre for the circular path (point A in part (b)) is also 5 percent.

The new Keynesian story depends heavily on expectations and how quickly they adjust. With perfect foresight, aggregate demand shocks would never be allowed to move real wages out of line in the first place, so the short run would always be at Y^* and U^*. In a world of imperfect information, however, there will always be surprises. If we respond quickly to surprises, we will not stay off long-run equilibrium output levels for long, and inflation will not have long to accelerate or decelerate. If we negotiate long-term contracts, or adjust our

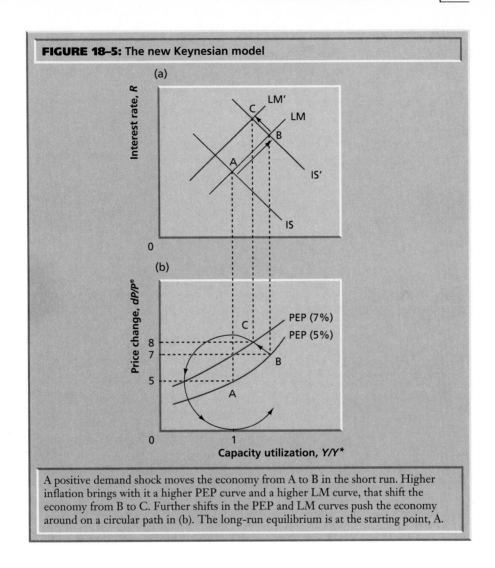

FIGURE 18–5: The new Keynesian model

(a)

(b)

A positive demand shock moves the economy from A to B in the short run. Higher inflation brings with it a higher PEP curve and a higher LM curve, that shift the economy from B to C. Further shifts in the PEP and LM curves push the economy around on a circular path in (b). The long-run equilibrium is at the starting point, A.

expectations slowly, or both, output can exceed the long-run equilibrium level for several years.[4]

---

[4]Arthur Okun believed that the benchmark of "normal" wage increases used in contract negotiations and salary reviews was adjusted only slowly and in the light of past experience. A. Okun, *Prices and Quantities* (Washington, D.C.: Brookings Institution, 1981). For a discussion of the source of wage rigidities in the Canadian economy, see W.C. Riddell, "The Responsiveness of Wage Settlements in Canada, and Economic Policy," *Canadian Public Policy*, March 1983, 9–23. For an unflattering comparison of the Canadian and foreign economies in this respect, see C.L. Barber and John C.P. McCallum, *Controlling Inflation* (Toronto: James Lorimer, for the Canadian Institute for Economic Policy, 1982), Chapters 4 and 5.

Reprinted with permission — The Toronto Star Syndicate.

Implications for stabilization policy

The new Keynesian model suggests that government **stabilization policy** is possible and can be socially useful. The starting point for this conclusion is that the cyclical response of output and inflation in the new Keynesian model is not socially desirable. High unemployment is largely involuntary, the result of layoffs rather than of workers' plans for longer fishing trips. Higher inflation is disturbing to households' financial plans, especially when it can not be foreseen. There is a *prima facie* case that anything governments can do to keep inflation down and unemployment at the NAIRU will improve social welfare. If governments have policy instruments that themselves generate demand and supply shocks, and if such tools can be used quickly enough, policymakers can hope to counter other demand and supply shocks, or at least to speed up the economy's responses to return to long-run equilibrium all the sooner. However, neither assumption can be taken for granted in practice, as we shall see in Chapters 22 and 23.

   In fact, the government is bound to affect the cyclical process to some extent because government itself is part of the aggregate demand model. Government spending, taxes, and the nominal money supply all affect aggregate demand and all must be determined in practice by some sort of rule or decision process. In Chapter 16 we assumed that government spending G and the nominal money supply M_s are held fixed, but we also assumed that tax revenue T rises with real income levels. Actual governments vary all three policy levers (spending, the nominal money supply, and taxes) in predictable but more sophisticated ways than that. The government's policy rules for G and M_s can be added to the model of aggregate demand described in Chapter 16. Such policy rules affect the short-run equilibrium and also expectations behaviour. Both impacts will affect the medium-run cyclical path of the economy. The question for stabilization policy is what policy rules generate the greatest stability of output and prices, and what side-effects there are on other aspects of the economy. We address this issue in more detail in Chapter 22.

SECTION 3

New classical explanations

The new classical model is built on the assumption of constant market-clearing in both goods and labour markets.[5] In the new classical model presented in Chapter 17, output levels deviate from the long-run equilibrium only because of misperceptions by workers of what has happened to the general price level, and the deviations last only as long as the misperceptions last. There is not much of a cyclical story to tell with this model as a result of demand shock surprises, because the disturbance to output does not last long enough unless people are very slow to realize what is going on around them in the economy.

Some new classical economists, however, have developed other explanations for cyclical changes in output levels. In this section we describe two of them: intertemporal substitution of labour supplies between periods, and technological shocks to the production function. Finally, we discuss the implications of these two explanations for government stabilization policy.

Intertemporal substitution of labour

The explanation of the business cycle in terms of **intertemporal substitution of labour** uses the logic of the life-cycle model of Chapter 7, but for the intertemporal allocation of labour and leisure rather than of consumption. Higher interest rates, it is argued, cause households not only to delay consuming goods, but also to delay some leisure and work longer hours in the current period. The extra income earned from this extra work in the current period can then buy extra future leisure, such as in earlier retirement. That is, higher interest rates are predicted to cause a greater supply of labour.

It follows that any positive demand shock, such as a surge in government spending or in investment spending, will also increase labour supply as long

---

[5] For a presentation and a critique of the real business cycle approach to cycles, see Charles I. Plosser, "Understanding Real Business Cycles," and Gregory N. Mankiw, "Real Business Cycles: A New Keynesian Perspective," both in *Journal of Economic Perspectives*, Summer 1989, 51–91.

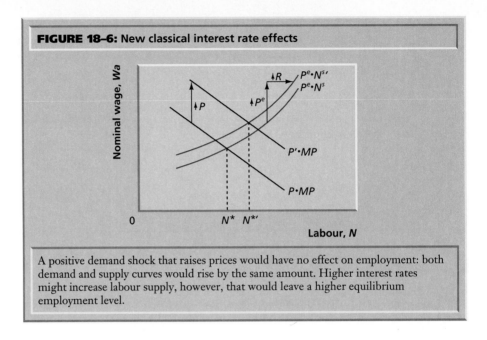

FIGURE 18–6: New classical interest rate effects

A positive demand shock that raises prices would have no effect on employment: both demand and supply curves would rise by the same amount. Higher interest rates might increase labour supply, however, that would leave a higher equilibrium employment level.

as it increases interest rates. With extra labour supply being generated by higher interest rates, employment and output can expand even if expectations are rational and price increases are correctly foreseen; the new classical model does not have to rely on misperceptions of price increases to generate extra labour supply. With significant intertemporal substitution of labour, any positive demand shock will not increase the equilibrium nominal wage as much as the price level. Real wages will therefore fall, and equilibrium employment will rise from N^* to $N^{*\prime}$, as shown in Figure 18–6.

There are two difficulties with this new classical argument. First, it implies that a stimulative monetary policy, which lowers interest rates, would also lower employment and output. That is not what we observe. Second, there is little empirical support for the idea that significant amounts of leisure or labour supply are reallocated between periods in response to changes in interest rates.[6] Choices between fishing trips now versus next year are seldom influenced by the level of interest rates.

Real business cycle theory

The third new classical approach to explaining business cycles abandons any attempt to explain them as responses to demand shocks of any kind. Instead,

---

[6] See, for example, Gregory N. Mankiw, "Real Business Cycles: A New Keynesian Perspective," *Journal of Economic Perspectives*, Summer 1989, 80–91.

real business cycle theorists have advanced **aggregate supply shocks** to explain almost all business cycle fluctuations in output and employment.

Supply shocks shift the production function. Technological progress is a kind of supply shock that shifts production functions upward. Most economists think of this process as fairly smooth and continuous when aggregated over thousands of firms in hundreds of different industries. However, there could be discontinuous jumps in technology. One such was during and after the OPEC oil price increases of 1974 and 1979–80, as whole economies scrambled to adopt less energy-intensive techniques.

The real business cycle theory argues that booms are periods of rapid technical progress, while recessions are periods of slow technical progress. Technical progress affects employment through the **marginal product of labour**. Rapid technical progress shifts the marginal product of labour upward, as shown in Figure 18–7. With a higher marginal product of labour, firms hire more workers and pay higher real wages to get them. Fishing trips are postponed. Output growth rises, even faster than employment. A drop in marginal product would lower real wages and cause the opposite reactions.[7]

Two features make the real business cycle explanation attractive. The first and most compelling to academic economists is that it uses the same microeconomic model of rational individual decision-making that is at the core of most theoretical economics, thereby adding consistency to economics.

The second attractive feature is that technology may move with the kind of fits and starts necessary to explain real output fluctuations. When economists try to identify the sources of economic growth, large and variable residuals remain after the influence of growing inputs of labour and capital have been accounted for. Those residuals are properly called just "unexplained sources of output growth," but many economists have for years thought of them as being due to technical progress. It is understandable that real business cycle theorists would adopt them as measures of technical change, in the absence of anything better. It is the case that these residuals are strongly cyclical just like output growth — big in booms and small in recessions. If this interpretation of these residuals as **technology shocks** is accepted, then real business cycle theorists have a tenable, but radically different explanation of the output fluctuations in Figure 18–2.

Policy implications

New classical equilibria always clear markets. Firms and households act with the best information they can obtain, in ways they think best for themselves. No transaction is involuntary. If markets are competitive or contestable, then the outcomes are not easy to improve upon. Governments could improve upon

---

[7] For a recession to occur and unemployment to rise in the real world, it is not necessary that technology actually worsen, shifting the production function down. It is enough that technical progress does not shift the marginal product of labour curve out to the right as fast as labour force growth is shifting the labour supply curve. In such cases the real wage will fall and so will employment relative to the labour force.

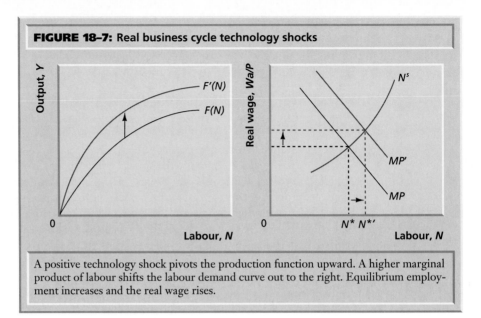

FIGURE 18-7: Real business cycle technology shocks

A positive technology shock pivots the production function upward. A higher marginal product of labour shifts the labour demand curve out to the right. Equilibrium employment increases and the real wage rises.

such outcomes if governments had special information that firms and households did not have, but there are few such situations where government's best course would not be just to pass on their special information in a press release; firms and households could then take account of the new information in the way each found most appropriate. It is hard to make a case for government stabilization policy being necessary or even effective in such economies.

The real business cycle explanation suggests that business cycles do not impose significant costs on society anyway, so there is little need for stabilization policy. In particular, it explains rising unemployment simply as the result of workers voluntarily taking extra leisure, such as longer fishing trips, in response to lower real wages; it does not explain rising unemployment as more workers being laid off against their wishes. The only role for stabilization policy is to lower and stabilize inflation, unless there is some way in which the rate of technical progress can be affected by policy. Aside from that, according to the real business cycle theory, the job of government is to provide necessary public services and keep out of the private sector's way.

Some evidence

The facts are generally kinder to the new Keynesian theory than they are to the real business cycle theory. The most important flaw in the real business cycle is that the nature of unemployment does not fit the new classical explanation. Most of the extra unemployment encountered in growth slowdowns is created by layoffs rather than by voluntary resignations implied by new classical theory. It is

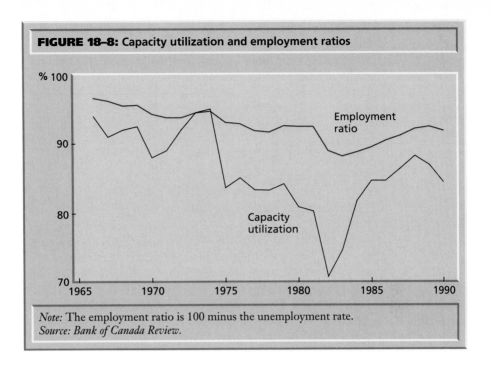

FIGURE 18–8: Capacity utilization and employment ratios

Note: The employment ratio is 100 minus the unemployment rate.
Source: Bank of Canada Review.

difficult to accept that layoffs (particularly when concentrated among employees without seniority) reflect merely the desires of plant workers to take more leisure.

It is even more difficult to accept that fluctuations of capacity utilization of plant and equipment are voluntary; fixed capital equipment cannot go fishing. Yet Figure 18–8 shows that capacity utilization fluctuates even more than the employment ratio of employment to labour force.

Finally, the economic growth residuals that real business cycle theorists interpret as "technology shocks" can be interpreted just as easily by new Keynesian theorists to reflect only labour hoarding by employers. In the hybrid model of Chapter 17 we sketched the logic for employers not wanting to lower nominal wages in recessions: staff turnover would increase, which would impose substantial costs on employers. Similarly, firms may decide not to lay off some valuable employees in a business downturn even when they cannot be fully utilized, for fear of being unable to replace them later when business picks up again.[8] Such **labour hoarding** causes employment to fall less rapidly than output in recessions. It also causes employment to rise less rapidly than output in the early stages of a recovery; firms use up their reserve of underutilized labour before hiring extra workers. Labour hoarding in recessions would cause labour productivity to fall, just as is observed. Using up hoarded labour in recoveries

---

[8]Note that this behaviour implies that firms move off the production function in the short run.

would cause labour productivity to rise, just as is observed. In other words, the data interpreted by real business cycle theorists as evidence for technology shocks are interpreted by new Keynesian theorists as simply part of a sluggish employer response to demand shocks. Those data are therefore consistent with both theories.

SECTION 4

Summary

There are important fluctuations in output, prices, unemployment, inflation, and real wages over a series of short runs, which together make up the business cycle. It is the medium-run period of the business cycle that is most relevant to stabilization policy, rather than either the short or the long runs. A look at the time path of unemployment and inflation suggests that a full business cycle could take around a decade.

There are two explanations of business cycles in modern macroeconomics. The new Keynesian explanation involves both demand and supply changes. On the supply side, short-run PEP curves shift over time because of changing assumptions as one short-run situation is replaced by another. PEP curves rise when output exceeds the long-run equilibrium level, and they fall when output falls below the long-run equilibrium level. On the demand side, inflation lowers aggregate demand cumulatively, as long as inflation exceeds money supply growth, and increases aggregate demand when the opposite is true, by lowering or raising the real money supply. The combination of changes in demand and supply produces a circular pattern of adjustment of output and inflation in a succession of short runs. The length of time taken in such adjustment patterns depends heavily on lags in expectations formation and in negotiation of wage contracts.

The real business cycle theory, one of three new classical explanations of business cycles, explains business cycles as the equilibrium responses of fully rational economic agents to cyclical supply shocks due to changes in technology. Changes in technology affect employment through changes in the marginal product of labour.

The new Keynesian theory suggests that business cycles are socially wasteful departures from long-run equilibrium that should be mitigated. The new classical theory imagines the business cycle as an equilibrium phenomenon that can not easily be improved upon by stabilization policy, even if stabilization policy could have any predictable effect.

Key Terms

business cycles
aggregate demand shocks
inflation expectations
accelerationist models
NAIRU
stabilization policy

intertemporal substitution
  of labour
real business cycle theory
aggregate supply shocks
marginal product of labour
technology shocks
labour hoarding

Questions and Problems

1. Redraw Figure 18–3 roughly, with capacity utilization on the horizontal axis instead of the unemployment rate.

2. What do you expect to happen to tuition fees next year? On what do you base your expectations?

3. Must increases in expected inflation always push up actual inflation by the same amount? Why or why not?

4. What is the definition of the NAIRU? How would you go about estimating it?

5. If you had to choose between new classical and new Keynesian short-run models to predict output and inflation one year from now, which would you pick? Three years from now? Five years from now?

6. How do the new Keynesian and real business cycle theorists derive such dramatically different policy implications from explaining the same data?

7. Explain how the cartoon model in this chapter is or is not consistent with first the new Keynesian and then the new classical story of response to a spending stimulus.

Suggestions for Further Reading

Carmichael, H. Lorne. "Efficiency Wage Models of Unemployment: A Survey." *Economic Inquiry*, 1990.

Dornbusch, R., S. Fischer, and G. Sparks. *Macroeconomics*, 3rd Canadian ed. Toronto: McGraw-Hill Ryerson, 1989.

Gordon, Robert J. "What Is New Keynesian Economics?" *Journal of Economic Literature*, September 1990, 1151–1190.

Lipsey, Richard G. "The Understanding and Control of Inflation: Is There a Crisis in Macro-economics?" *Canadian Journal of Economics*, November 1981, 545–76.

McCallum, Bennett T. "Real Business Cycle Models," in R. J. Barro, ed. *Handbook of Modern Business Cycle Theory*. New York: Wiley, 1988.

Okun, Arthur. *Prices and Quantities*. Washington, D.C.: Brookings Institution, 1981.

Parkin, Michael and Robin Bade. *Modern Macroeconomics*, 2nd ed. Scarborough, Ont.: Prentice-Hall, 1986.

Plosser, Charles I. "Understanding Real Business Cycles." *Journal of Economic Perspectives*, Summer 1989, 51–71.

Mankiw, Gregory N. "Real Business Cycles: A New Keynesian Perspective." *Journal of Economic Perspectives*, Summer 1989, 72–91.

Rose, David E. *The NAIRU in Canada: Concepts, Determinants, and Estimates*. Ottawa: Bank of Canada Technical Report No. 50, December 1988.

Wilton, David A. and David M. Prescott. *Macroeconomics: Theory and Policy in Canada*, 2nd ed. Don Mills, Ont.: Addison-Wesley, 1987.

Chapter nineteen

The Money Market in Macroeconomics

In the macroeconomic review presented in Chapters 16–18, the treatment of financial matters was very simplified. In particular, the explanation of money demand and supply in Chapter 16 was kept short and the number of variables was kept to the bare minimum. In this chapter we explain money demand and supply more thoroughly and discuss how the macroeconomic model of Chapters 16–18 is affected when the treatment of money is more sophisticated.

Section 1 looks briefly at definitions of the broad and narrow money supply, and at why one might prefer one to the other. Section 2 explains the various theories that have been advanced to explain the demand for money. Section 3 briefly reviews the evidence of many tests of the money demand relationships predicted by these theories. Section 4 discusses the supply of money. Section 5 considers the impact of a more sophisticated explanation of the money market on the behaviour of the macro model of aggregate demand from Chapter 16.

You should learn in this chapter:

1. the criteria for distinguishing and for choosing between narrow and broad definitions of money;
2. the range of pre-Keynesian and post-Keynesian theories of the demand for money;
3. how to derive the predictions of the inventory theory of the transactions demand for money, in particular;
4. the main conclusions from decades of research which has tested each theory of the demand for money;
5. the sources of interest sensitivity of the supply of money;
6. the effect of adding interest-sensitive money supply, expected inflation, and many financial markets to the macroeconomic model of Chapters 16–18.

SECTION 1

Broad versus narrow moneys

Money redefined

The definitions of money were introduced in Chapter 2, and were summarized in Figure 2–1. The **narrow money supply**, M1, includes the major assets that are commonly accepted as means of payment: currency in circulation outside banks, and Canadian-dollar demand deposits in chartered banks (excluding federal government deposits). **Broad money supply** measures (M2, M3, and M2+) add in other kinds of deposits that are not commonly used as media of exchange, but which can be easily converted into deposits that are. M2 adds in personal savings deposits and non-personal notice deposits. M2+ goes further by adding in similar deposits of near banks as well. M3 adds in non-personal term deposits and those foreign currency deposits of residents that are recorded within Canada. Until the post-World War II era broad money was not important, because the range of time deposits available was much narrower than it is today. Early explanations of money demand therefore focused on narrow money and the roles played by media of exchange. That is still true to a surprising extent.

Choosing between broad and narrow moneys

In building a macro model one must first choose between narrow and broad money measures. They cannot all be used at once. The grounds for preferring one definition of money over another depend on the roles that the money supply must fill in macroeconomic models. Some definitions of money supply perform these roles better than others.

Definitions of money supply have three possible roles in macro models. The first is to generate an LM curve, so that we can tell which of the many possible goods market equilibria on the IS curve will actually occur. A good definition of money for this role will leave us with a demand for and a supply of money that are almost fully explained by just a few variables, and in particular by monetary policy actions of the central bank. If either money demand or supply are explained by many variables or are largely unexplained, then the LM curve itself will reflect that uncertainty by shifting around a lot over time quite independently of monetary policy. If the LM curve is subject to a lot of variation, then it is not of great use in predicting equilibrium demand levels. The macro model of which it is part will be a poor predictor.

The second role for a money supply definition is to help in analyses of monetary policy. Since monetary policy operates through changes in the quantity of high-powered money H, the money supply should be closely related to H. The broad definitions of money have an advantage here, since it is broad moneys that are most clearly related to H: broad money definitions come closer to including all and only deposits subject to legal or prudential cash reserve requirements, whereas narrow money excludes the huge time deposit category. It is therefore possible that the supply of narrow money could change without any change in H (if the part of H needed for time deposits drops), and vice versa.

The third role for a money supply measure is to reveal to the central bank what is happening to output growth. In practice, information on real output becomes available only with a lag; early estimates contain large errors. The conduct of stabilization policy is made easier if some readily available figure such as a measure of the money supply can be used to infer what is currently happening to real output. If a money supply measure is to serve as an indicator of output levels, it must have two properties: first, it must be available quickly; second, the demand for money thus defined must depend on real income and only a few other variables. M2+, the broad money aggregate that includes near-bank deposits, lacks the first property because credit union deposits are available only with a three-month lag. The other money supply measures are all available weekly and with almost no error; which of them is best hinges on which is most fully explained by real income and prices and a handful of other variables.

We now review the range of variables that have been thought to explain the demand for broad and narrow money.

SECTION 2

■ The demand for money: theory

The **demand for money** is a topic with as venerable a history as any topic in economics.[1] What has powered the long and vigorous debate over the demand for money is that the market for money is the market through which central banks intervene to influence the economy. Central banks adjust the money supply up and down. Whether they can have any influence over the rest of the economy by doing so depends crucially on the nature of money demand. One (extreme case) theory of money demand implies that money does not matter at all, while an opposite extreme view implies that only money matters.

In this section the history of theories of money demand is divided into two basic parts: early views that concentrated on the transactions role of money, relating money demand to prices and real income; and later views that added a role for interest rates.

Early views on the demand for money: the quantity theory

The **quantity theory** of the demand for money goes back centuries, but it was best explained by Irving Fisher at the turn of the century.[2] Fisher started with

---

[1] For years the best source for this history has been David Laidler, *The Demand for Money: Theories, Evidence, and Problems*, 3rd ed. (New York: Harper and Row, 1985).

[2] Irving Fisher, *The Purchasing Power of Money* (New York: Macmillan, 1911).

the assumption that money is demanded for transactions purposes (that is, there is a **transactions demand** for money) and the observation that money (M) must change hands whenever there is a transaction in the economy. If money changes hands at a constant *velocity of circulation V*, then one can simply calculate what stock of money is required if a given volume of transactions T is to take place at a given average price level P. Algebraically, this produces the *quantity equation*:

$$MV = PT. \tag{1}$$

Quantity theorists believed that velocity was indeed relatively constant over short periods of time, reflecting payments technology and habits. With that extra assumption, the demand for money becomes simply proportional to prices and the volume of transactions in the economy. The volume of transactions is not an easy concept to measure, so later theorists replaced it with the level of real income and output, Y. This yielded the income version of the quantity theory:[3]

$$MV' = PY, \tag{2}$$

where V' is the income velocity of money.

The Cambridge quantity theory

Fisher's quantity theory started from aggregates: total transactions, total money stock, and the average price level. In contrast, all later theories of money demand have started from the microeconomic, individual level and have then aggregated across all individuals to explain aggregate behaviour. The first to approach money demand this way were the neoclassical economists at Cambridge University, led by Alfred Marshall and A.C. Pigou.[4] They asked how much of one's wealth a person would want to hold as money. Money demand, they thought, would be a fairly constant proportion k of nominal income PY, both for individuals and in aggregate. The proportion k reflected payments technology and habits, and also the level of interest rates on alternative assets. However, Cambridge theorists thereafter ignored or at least played down the role of interest rates. This was probably because in the United Kingdom, long-term interest rates had not changed more than 100 basis points in total over the whole period from 1832 to 1913; it is easy to ignore a variable that does not vary.[5]

---

[3] The major difference between T and Y is that T includes all intermediate transactions and all trading of existing assets, while Y measures only net value-added transactions. The volume of asset trading on secondary stock and bond markets can change dramatically from year to year, and the amounts involved are huge. Other differences are unlikely to cause major differences in fluctuations of the two series even over periods as long as a few decades.

[4] See, for instance, A.C. Pigou, "The Value of Money," *Quarterly Journal of Economics*, 1917, 38–65.

[5] For a picture of this amazing stability, see Kenneth L. Fisher, *The Wall Street Waltz: 90 Visual Perspectives* (Chicago: Contemporary Books, 1987), 111.

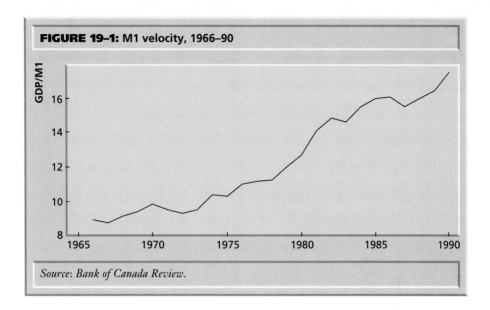

FIGURE 19–1: M1 velocity, 1966–90

Source: Bank of Canada Review.

Because payments technology and habits change only gradually, the Cambridge economists regarded k as fairly stable in the short run. The Cambridge theorists therefore used a money demand equation in which interest is ignored, and in which aggregate money demand (M) is proportional to nominal income PY. The Cambridge equation is

$$M = kPY. \qquad (3)$$

The Cambridge equation produces the same result as the income version of the quantity equation, with income velocity V' replaced by $1/k$.

Since the 1920s, however, neither interest rates nor the velocity of circulation has been at all constant. Figure 19–1, for instance, shows the velocity of circulation for Canada since 1968, as measured by the ratio of nominal gross domestic product to M1. Observing unstable velocities around them, economists were pressed to go beyond the quantity theory approximation.

Sources of interest sensitivity: Keynes's speculative demand

Keynes was the first to add interest rates as an explicit determinant of the demand for money. He did so by adding a new category of demand for money: a **liquidity preference** or **speculative demand** by speculators who shift back and forth between risky speculation in stocks and bonds and safe liquidity in money.[6] Keynes basically accepted the Cambridge logic that the transactions demand for money is proportional to nominal income, but he split it into a regular,

---

[6] J.M. Keynes, *The General Theory of Employment, Interest and Money* (London: Macmillan, 1936).

transactions part and an irregular, precautionary part. The logic of precautionary demand was not clearly spelled out, however. It was Keynes's liquidity preference or speculative demand that revolutionized the theory of money demand.

Two key assumptions underlay Keynes's speculative demand for money. The first was that a large group of investors can choose only between long-term assets (call them bonds) and money. Bond market speculators invest to reap capital gains on bonds. They hold their wealth in bonds only when bond prices are expected to rise. Speculators plan to hold money instead when bond prices are expected to fall. Bond prices move opposite to yields. Speculators will therefore hold large money balances when bond yields are expected to rise, and small money balances when bond yields are expected to fall.

What is required to complete the theory is an explanation of speculators' expectations. Keynes's second assumption is that speculators have some relatively fixed expectation of future prices and yields, determined essentially by what has been "normal" in the past. Such expectations are sometimes referred to as *inelastic expectations*. It follows that as actual yields rise further and further, more and more speculators come to see them as being above expected future levels, ripe for a fall; they act on that belief by shifting their wealth out of money into bonds, in order to profit from the expected rise in bond prices. Money demand falls.

Economists no longer believe that expectations are necessarily or even reliably inelastic. The period of stable long-term yields experienced in the United Kingdom in the nineteenth and early twentieth centuries has not been repeated since, so it is no longer plausible to assume that investors have any fixed expectation of "normal" long-term yields. Without inelastic expectations, however, Keynes's speculative demand theory does not imply any particular direction of interest sensitivity of the demand for money. An increase in interest rates could cause money demand either to rise or to fall.

Today it is also no longer realistic to assume that wholesale bond market investors would invest their funds in currency or chequing deposits to ride out expected bearish periods in bond markets. Instead they would use short-term interest-bearing assets such as treasury bills, bankers' acceptances, or short-term term deposits.[7] Households, to the extent they do speculate on fluctuations of asset yields, would use savings deposits as their safe asset rather than currency or chequing deposits. Keynes's speculative demand could therefore explain the demand for the interest-bearing parts of broad money, but not the demand for either of the two assets included in narrow money.

Tobin's liquidity preference as risk aversion

The Tobin–Markowitz or mean-variance model of portfolio choice was presented in section 4 of Chapter 9 as the basis of modern thinking about choices under risk. Tobin first presented this model as an alternative to Keynes's

---

[7] The jargon of financial market professionals reflects this fact. The term "cash" has come to refer to treasury bills rather than currency and chequing deposits.

speculative demand — that is, to explain the demand for money without requiring inelastic expectations.[8]

The logic of Tobin's explanation is fairly simple. Money is the riskless asset in the Tobin–Markowitz model described in Chapter 9, Figure 9–4. All lenders choose some combination of money and risky assets in their portfolios, the proportion of money rising with each lender's degree of risk aversion. Since portfolio combinations are assumed not to depend on portfolio size, the demand for money is a constant proportion of the portfolio and thus of wealth. When interest rates on risky assets rise or when interest rates on money fall, so that the opportunity cost of money rises, the slope of each lender's efficient set in Figure 9–4 steepens. With steeper efficient sets, lenders marginal reward for risk-taking is increased. As long as substitution effects outweigh income effects, lenders will respond by putting more of their funds in risky assets and by reducing their holdings of money. Thus the demand for money responds negatively to yields on non-money assets, just as in Keynes's theory.

Tobin's theory explains demand for money only if money is the only risk-free asset. For both firms and households, money market assets and short-term time deposits are effectively risk-free assets. Both dominate currency and chequing deposits where either is used simply as a store of value and not as a medium of exchange. Tobin's theory therefore explains the demand for short-term liquid assets, including some time deposits in broad money, rather than the demand for narrow money. Tobin's model is justly famous for introducing risk analysis to the economics profession, but is less useful now as a part of money demand theory.

Friedman's modern quantity theory

In 1956 Milton Friedman extended his permanent-income theory of consumption spending to explain money demand. In this **modern quantity theory**, Friedman asserted that money yields liquidity services of some sort (without specifying them in detail), and that households demand those services just like other services.[9] The demand for liquidity services is assumed to be proportional to total consumption, other things being equal. In Friedman's permanent-income theory, total consumption is proportional to total wealth, where total wealth is the present discounted value of total lifetime resources. Total wealth includes and is dominated by human wealth. As a proxy for total wealth, Friedman used the concept of permanent-income, the level stream of lifetime income that totally exhausts total wealth. Other things being equal, therefore, the demand for money is proportional to permanent income.

Other things are not always equal, of course. The demand for liquidity services drops when the price of those services rises, just like any other part

---

[8]J. Tobin, "Liquidity Preference as Behavior Toward Risk," *Review of Economic Studies*, February 1958, 65–86. Widely reprinted.

[9]"The Quantity Theory of Money: A Restatement," in M. Friedman, ed., *Studies in the Quantity Theory of Money* (Chicago: University of Chicago Press, 1956).

of consumption. The price of liquidity services is the net opportunity cost of holding money rather than other interest-bearing assets. The demand for liquidity services and for money therefore drops whenever relative yields on non-money assets rise. Many assets are potential substitutes for money, so many yields are relevant as opportunity costs of money. Even the expected inflation rate is relevant, as an expected nominal yield on holding stocks of consumer goods. Friedman's analysis of money demand is expressed in real terms, so nominal money demand is proportional to the price level.

To summarize, Friedman's theory predicts that the demand for money will be proportional to permanent income and will fall as the net opportunity costs of money rise. The unobservable permanent income has usually been specified empirically as a weighted average of current and past observed real income levels. A result of this specification is that economists have assumed long time lags in the response of money demand to changes in observed income. Increases in observed income raise permanent income only gradually, so they raise money demand only gradually as well. It follows that while money demand changes proportionally with observed real income in the long run, it changes much less than proportionally in the short run. Finally, the nature of liquidity services is not specified, so Friedman's analysis fits for both narrow money and broad money assets.

The Baumol–Tobin inventory theory

In 1952 and 1956, respectively, William Baumol and James Tobin applied the logic of profit-maximizing inventory holdings to the case of money holdings. The application of this **inventory theory** has provided a specific and plausible justification for the interest sensitivity of the demand for money. It has also generated a rich and detailed set of predictions about money demand behaviour, most of which have been borne out in tests. The logic of inventory theory applies most directly to holdings of currency and demand deposits, unlike Keynes's speculative demand and Tobin's liquidity preference explanations. The Baumol–Tobin model is worth developing in some detail.[10]

We start with the assumption that money balances are held as a kind of buffer stock to bridge gaps between income receipts and expenditure. By analogy, inventories of goods and raw materials are held by business firms as buffers between stages of production and sales; inventories of groceries are held by households as buffers between consumption and shopping activities. Households generally receive income less continuously than they spend, while business firms may do just the opposite. Both have income-spending gaps to be buffered.

Money balances are a part of wealth, so any funds held as money are funds not held in non-money, interest-bearing forms. The problem of how much to

---

[10] W.J. Baumol, "The Transactions Demand for Cash: An Inventory Theoretic Approach," *Quarterly Journal of Economics*, November 1952, 545–56 (widely reprinted); James Tobin, "The Interest Elasticity of the Transactions Demand for Cash," *Review of Economics and Statistics*, August 1956, 241–47.

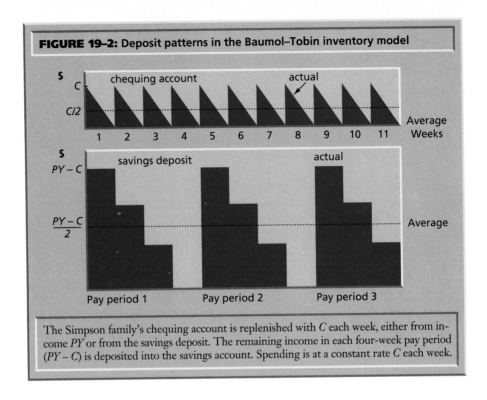

FIGURE 19–2: Deposit patterns in the Baumol–Tobin inventory model

The Simpson family's chequing account is replenished with C each week, either from income PY or from the savings deposit. The remaining income in each four-week pay period ($PY - C$) is deposited into the savings account. Spending is at a constant rate C each week.

hold as money can be analyzed as the problem of how much wealth to keep invested in non-money assets. There are benefits and costs. The benefit of holding non-money assets is the extra yield available. The cost of holding non-money assets rather than money is the cost of not having money balances on hand when needed: that cost is the lesser of (a) the utility loss from having to postpone desired spending until more income comes in, or (b) the costs of arranging to convert some other asset into money to replenish money holdings every time they run out. The optimal average money holding is the one that maximizes net benefit or profit from investing in non-money assets.

The Baumol–Tobin model is illustrated with a sawtooth diagram as shown in Figure 19–2. It shows the pattern of money (chequing deposit) and non-money asset (savings deposit) holdings for a specific household (the Simpsons). In Figure 19–2 the Simpsons are assumed to receive nominal income PY every four weeks, to spend continuously, and to top up the chequing account each week with a deposit C equal to one-quarter of income PY. Whatever income is not kept back as cash is left in a savings deposit to earn interest. The average money balance held over each week is $C/2$. The savings deposit balance starts after payday at $PY - C$, and then drops by C at regular intervals until it reaches zero just before the next payday; the average savings deposit balance is $(PY - C)/2$. If the extra interest available on non-money assets is R per pay period, the savings deposit earns $R(PY - C)/2$ in extra interest.

Baumol generalized the Simpsons' situation in Figure 19–2 and specified what the profit from investment in non-money assets would look like.[11] He assumed the following: nominal monthly income is PY; savings deposits earn R percent per month more than money; the chequing deposit is topped up by C at regular intervals (either out of income on paydays or by withdrawals from the savings account at other times); and the cost of depositing to or withdrawing from the savings deposit is a fixed nominal amount Pb, where P is the general price level and b is the real value of time taken by the Simpsons and by bank staff to handle savings account deposits and withdrawals.

The Simpsons' profit from their savings deposit investment is interest earnings less savings deposit transactions costs. Interest earnings are $R(PY - C)/2$, as above. Transactions costs are the cost per transaction Pb multiplied by the number of savings deposit transactions PY/C (for one deposit and $(PY/C) - 1$ withdrawals). The net profit F is

$$F = R(PY - C)/2 - Pb(PY/C). \qquad (4)$$

The Simpsons' problem is how frequently to make trips to the bank to top up the chequing account. The more frequently they go, the smaller the topping up amount C and the larger the average amount invested $(PY - C)/2$, but the greater the number of transactions charges. The level of C that maximizes the net profit F is the amount such that (using calculus)

$$dF/dC = 0 = -R/2 + PbPY/C^2. \qquad (5)$$

By rearranging this equation, the optimal level of C that maximizes profits (and therefore satisfies the equation above) can be written as

$$C^* = P(2bY/R)^{1/2}, \qquad (6)$$

where C^* is the amount added to money balances when they run out. The average money holding is $C^*/2$ for any individual. Money demand for all households and firms will be the sum of the average amounts for each household and firm, provided that fluctuations in individual money holdings around the average cancel each other out during the pay period. The average nominal money demand M per household is therefore

$$M = C^*/2 = P(bY/2R)^{1/2}. \qquad (7)$$

The Baumol–Tobin result in Equation (7) predicts very specifically that money demand will be proportional to the price level, but that it will rise only with the square root of real income. Money demand also falls as the (square root

---

[11] Baumol's analysis also applies without significant change to the opposite situation (opposite to that of the Simpsons) of business firms that receive income continuously and spend only at discrete intervals such as paydays or month ends.

of the) interest rate rises.[12] That is, money demand has a price elasticity of 1.0, a real income elasticity of $1/2$, and a net interest elasticity of $-1/2$. Money demand also rises with the square root of the real transactions cost b, which can be thought of as reflecting the real wage level.[13]

Extensions and applications of the inventory model

The simple, streamlined model above can be extended in many ways to reflect reality more closely.[14] The extensions make little difference to the results obtained. In almost all of the extensions, money demand varies proportionally with the price level and less than proportionally with real income and has a net interest elasticity of $-1/2$.

It is fairly easy to apply the inventory model to real world situations, for instance to predict the effect of financial innovations. As a first example, the relative interest rates paid on savings deposits in Canada changed dramatically in 1979; for households, savings deposits are the main alternative to narrow money, so their yields represent the variable R in Equation (7). Until 1979 Canadian households earned zero interest on savings deposits held only for short periods, because the interest was calculated only on the minimum monthly or quarterly balance. After 1979, savings deposits paid interest on each day's balance. This innovation raised the effective level of R abruptly. Household money demand dropped significantly.

---

[12] The interest rate R is the net opportunity cost of holding money, the difference between the expected yield on non-money assets and that on money. Both yields matter to demand for money, as in Friedman's modern quantity theory approach.

[13] The relevance of real wages was added in D.S. Dutton and W.P. Gramm, "Transactions Costs, the Wage Rate, and the Demand for Money," *American Economic Review*, September 1973, 652–65, and Thomas R. Saving, "The Value of Time and Economies of Scale in the Demand for Cash Balances: A Comment," *Journal of Money, Credit, and Banking*, February 1974, 122–24. This idea has been extended recently in Kevin Dowd, "The Value of Time and the Transactions Demand for Money," *Journal of Money, Credit, and Banking*, February 1990, 51–64.

[14] Tobin, for instance, independently considered a version of Baumol's problem with a variable transactions cost instead of just a lump-sum cost. "The Interest Elasticity of the Transactions Demand for Cash," *Review of Economics and Statistics*, August 1956, 241–47. Edgar L. Feige and Michael Parkin extend Baumol's model to allow for real capital and commodity holdings as well as bonds and money in "The Optimal Quantity of Money, Bonds, Commodity Inventories, and Capital," *American Economic Review*, June 1971, 335–49. Robert Clower and Peter Howitt used a sort of mathematics different from Baumol's to see how transactions demand would behave if the pattern of receipts and expenditures varied, in "The Transactions Theory of the Demand for Money: A Reconsideration," *Journal of Political Economy*, 1978, 449–66. Merton Miller and Dale Orr considered the case of random changes in cash flows, in "The Transactions Demand for Money by Firms," *Quarterly Journal of Economics*, 1966, 413–35. Jurg Niehans has extended Baumol's analysis to allow formal choice of receipt and expenditure pattern as part of the decision problem in *The Theory of Money* (Baltimore: Johns Hopkins Press, 1978), chapter 2.

As a second innovation, banks introduced cash management accounts for business firms, starting in 1976. These accounts provided free, automatic transfers of funds from interest-earning accounts to chequing accounts, as needed to cover cheques written. This lowered the transactions cost Pb to zero in Equation (7). Firms responded as predicted, by holding zero money balances.

As a final example, one can apply this model to countries where inflation proceeds at rates such as 1 percent *per day*. If chequing accounts pay zero interest, the opportunity cost of holding money (that is, R) is 1 percent per day. In this case, cash balances will be held to near zero. Families will therefore spend a lot of time (going to the bank each afternoon) to make sure that no funds lie idle overnight.[15]

Precautionary demand for money

A further, unique extension of inventory theory adds uncertainty about receipts and payments. In this extension, following Keynes, money balances held for just the possibility of future transactions needs are classified as **precautionary demand** rather than *transactions* demand.[16] The analysis of this case is similar to that of inventory theory in some ways, however, as are the results.

Consider a family firm (Simpco) that is uncertain about the size of future income-spending gaps that money balances might be needed to cover. Assume that there is some known or estimated probability distribution of possible income-spending gaps in the next period. The only necessary property of this distribution is that probabilities decrease for larger gaps, as shown in Figure 19–3(a).

Each *extra* dollar of money balances held by Simpco has a potential benefit and a probability of realizing the benefit. The potential benefit is saving some expensive alternative response such as cutting spending or selling off some other asset. Assume that the expense to be avoided is a fixed brokerage fee b. The probability of realizing that benefit just because of holding $1 more is the probability of the income-spending gap being exactly $1 bigger than the previous money balance M_0. If the spending gap is bigger than $M_0 + 1$, the brokerage cost will be incurred anyway because some non-money assets will have to be sold. If the spending gap is only M_0 or smaller, the extra $1 of money balances would not be needed. The probability of realizing the benefit from the $(M_0 + 1)$th dollar of money holdings is shown in Figure 19–3 as the height of the probability distribution at $M_0 + 1$.

---

[15] I am indebted to Dr. Arnon Boneh for this application, which reflects his family's response to similar Israeli inflation in the 1980s.

[16] The theory of precautionary demand has developed, after Keynes, from the approach of Don Patinkin in *Money, Interest and Prices*, 2nd ed. (New York: Harper and Row, 1965), chapter 5. Laidler provides a concise summary of the theory in *The Demand for Money: Theories, Evidence, and Problems*, 3rd ed. (New York: Harper and Row, 1985), 63ff.

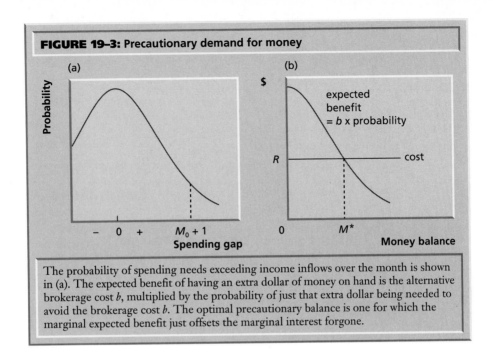

FIGURE 19–3: Precautionary demand for money

The probability of spending needs exceeding income inflows over the month is shown in (a). The expected benefit of having an extra dollar of money on hand is the alternative brokerage cost b, multiplied by the probability of just that extra dollar being needed to avoid the brokerage cost b. The optimal precautionary balance is one for which the marginal expected benefit just offsets the marginal interest forgone.

The *expected* benefit of each extra dollar of money balances is the product of the potential benefit and its probability. When plotted in Figure 19–5(b), the expected benefit is the part of the probability distribution in (a) to the right of zero, with the vertical axis multiplied by the fixed brokerage cost b.

The cost of holding extra money balances is net interest forgone for as long as it could have been earned. Assume for simplicity that spending gaps would require selling off other assets only very near the end of the period, so extra interest could have been earned at rate R percent for the whole period had each dollar of money balance been invested instead. The opportunity cost of money balances is then a straight line of height R, as shown in Figure 19–3(b).

Simpco's optimal precautionary balance lies at the intersection of marginal benefit and expected marginal cost, at M^*. The precautionary demand therefore depends on all the determinants of M^* in Figure 19–3. A higher interest rate R pushes the expected marginal cost curve upward and reduces M^*; that is, the interest elasticity of precautionary money demand is negative. A higher brokerage cost b shifts the expected marginal benefit of holding money balances upward proportionally and raises M^*; that is, the elasticity of precautionary money demand with respect to transactions costs is positive. Nothing is necessarily implied about the effect of higher real income or prices, however; both could imply more widely dispersed potential spending gaps, which would both widen and flatten the probability distribution of Figure 19–3(a). It is not clear what a wider but flatter probability distribution would do to the optimal M^* at the intersection point of marginal benefit and marginal cost. Precautionary demand theory therefore generates some of the same results as the inventory theory approach, but it does not have as large or as specific a set of predictions.

▢ The demand for money: evidence

Many economists have tested money demand relationships against historical data, for just about every economy that has produced data and for both narrow and broad money. These results have been reviewed periodically by Professor David Laidler of the University of Western Ontario. This section provides a brief summary of the main results.[17] To give the flavour of those results, Table 19–1 reports data from one recent study by two Bank of Canada economists of the demand for broad money as measured by M2 and M2+, estimated over the period 1970 to 1985.[18]

Some of the results in Table 19–1 are typical of other evidence on the demand for money.

1. Prices, real incomes, and interest rates are important. Interest rates on money substitutes have negative signs, whereas those on money assets (90-day bank deposits) have positive signs. These results are almost universal.

2. All variables take a long time to have an effect. There is nothing like the instantaneous effect that the efficient markets theory leads us to expect in, say, the stock market. The trust company deposit yield, for instance, takes almost six months to have any effect at all. Also, the lags in Table 19–1 are shorter than in many studies.

3. Income elasticities are positive but less than 1.0. A 10 percent rise in real income raises money demand only 4.7 percent for M2, and 6.9 percent for M2+. Such income elasticities are common for narrow money; broad money such as M2 usually has elasticities close to 1.0.

---

[17] See David Laidler, *The Demand for Money: Theories, Evidence and Problems*, 3rd ed. (New York: Harper and Row, 1985) for a comprehensive review of the evidence from many countries.

[18] Tim McPhail and Francesco Caramazza, *La demande de M2 et M2+ au Canada: quelques resultats recents* (Ottawa: Bank of Canada Working Paper 90–3, February 1990). An extension of this work and many further results are reported in Caramazza, Doug Hostland, and Stephen Poloz, *The Demand for Money and the Monetary Policy Process in Canada* (Ottawa: Bank of Canada Working Paper 90–5, May 1990).

TABLE 19-1: The demand for broad money, M2 and M2+

	M2	M2+
Price elasticity (after 12 months)[a]	1.00	1.00
Real income elasticity (after 12 months)	0.47	0.69
Interest rate semi-elasticities[b]		
90-day commercial paper (after 9 months)	−1.50	−1.70
90-day trust company deposits (after 16 months)	−2.65	
both together	−4.15	−1.70
90-day bank deposits (after 15 months)	4.00	−1.44
all three yields together	−0.15	−0.26

[a]The number of months shown after each variable is the maximum lag length for that variable, after which any change has had full effect on money demand.

[b] Semi-elasticity coefficients are the rate of change of money demand (in percent) per 100 basis point change in the interest rate(s). For instance, a rise in the 90-day commercial paper rate from 8 to 9 percent per year would lower demand for M2 by 1.5 percent; a similar rise in all interest rates would lower M2 demand by only 0.15 percent.

Source: Kim McPhail and Francesco Caramazza, *La demande de M2 et M2+ au Canada: quelques resultats recents* (Ottawa: Bank of Canada Working Paper 90–3, February 1990). The same results are reported by Caramazza in the *Bank of Canada Review*, December 1989, 1–19.

4. Price elasticities are assumed to be exactly 1.0 rather than estimated to have that value. All theories predict price elasticity of 1.0, and all studies support that prediction, even if not as strongly as we might wish.[19]

5. Interest semi-elasticities are fairly small individually, but the net effect of changing all three yields together (which is the common situation in practice) is very small indeed. This supports the idea that only the net interest differential matters. It also implies that broad money demand is insensitive to changes in the general level of interest rates that do not also cause changes in relative yields. In practice, most movements in interest rates are of the type where all yields move together.

Some properties of money demand behaviour are not conveyed by the results in Table 19–1. These include:

1. Measures of financial wealth are important in explaining the demand for money if real income is left out. When real income is left in, however, financial wealth tends to have a relatively insignificant impact on the demand for

---

[19] William White of the Bank of Canada concluded, from an earlier, thorough investigation, that price and income levels have moved too closely together over time to allow us to separate out the impact of price changes and income changes. *The Demand for Money in Canada and the Control of Monetary Aggregates: Evidence from the Monthly Data* (Ottawa: Bank of Canada, 1976).

money. We can infer that increases in financial wealth increase demand for other assets, but not for money.

2. Opportunity yields are always important in studies of money demand. It is not possible to identify which particular opportunity yield is the most important, but neither is it necessary. All of the yields on substitute short-term assets move together as a rule and presumably all of them have some impact. Using any one or two of the many available short-term yields therefore reflects fairly well the combined impact of all of them.

3. There have been few tests of the impact of expected inflation on the demand for money, except indirect ones. Where it is included specifically (however it is estimated, since expectations are unobservable), it has the expected negative elasticity as befits an opportunity yield. Even where expected inflation is not introduced explicitly, some part of it appears implicitly since expected inflation is partly reflected in nominal yields on money substitutes (see the discussion of the Fisher effect in section 6 of Chapter 14).

4. The real wage rate is significant as a measure of the transactions costs of depositing and withdrawing money balances. Higher real wages raise the demand for money balances in the United States, as predicted by the Baumol–Tobin inventory theory model.

5. There have been very few tests of the importance of relative risk variables for the demand for money. Most researchers have probably felt there was little evidence of changes in relative risks, or that it was impossible to measure, or both. Professors Alan Gregory and James Mackinnon have provided an exception in testing explicitly for the effect of the postal strikes of 1976 and 1979 on the demand for money in Canada.[20] Postal strikes cause sudden and sharp increases in uncertainty about future income receipts, which sharply increased the demand for money in these two periods.

Lags and stability

To those familiar with the rapid adjustments that are common in the rest of the financial system, one of the surprising features of money demand is how long it takes to adjust to changes in income, prices, and relative yields. A theory that reconciles slow response of money and rapid response of other financial markets is the idea of **buffer stocks**.[21] This idea is that stocks of inventories are held to buffer other flow processes that are expensive to adjust in the short run, such as the flows of production, income, or spending. For instance, if inventories of finished goods can be allowed to rise or fall whenever sales move below or

---

[20] A. Gregory and J. Mackinnon, "Where's My Cheque? A Note on Postal Strikes and the Demand for Money in Canada," *Canadian Journal of Economics*, November 1980, 683–88.

[21] For elaboration of this idea, see David Laidler, "The Buffer Stock Notion in Monetary Economics," *Conference Proceedings Supplement to the Economic Journal*, 1984, 17–34.

above production, respectively, then firms can avoid the expense of adjusting their production levels. If inventories of money balances can be allowed to rise or fall whenever spending needs are less than or greater than income, respectively, then households can avoid the pain of adjusting either their labour supply or their spending.

The buffer stock idea introduces explicitly the adjustment costs of changing production, income, or spending. In general it is assumed that such adjustment costs rise more than proportionally with the scale of adjustment required. For example, the costs of speeding up production by 100 units are assumed to be more than twice as large as the costs of raising production by only 50 units. If that is the case, then when firms and households must change their inventories of money, they will do so slowly through small changes in income or spending, rather than quickly through large changes in income or spending. It follows that when, for instance, a decrease in interest rates increases the level of money balances that households want, actual money balances held may rise quite slowly in response.

Economists have found it difficult to establish from past evidence how quickly money demand adjusts to changes in income, prices, and interest rates. Estimates made over the period from the 1950s to 1973 did very poorly in forecasting money demand in the next three years; estimates made over the period from the 1960s to the late 1970s did poorly in forecasting over 1980–81. In economic jargon, the demand for money function seems to be *unstable*. David Laidler has argued that the problem is truly intractable, because we cannot easily separate out how money demand is adjusting to prices from how prices are adjusting to money supply — and the latter is a process that changes significantly over time depending on expectations behaviour. Money demand behaviour itself has changed over time as banks and near banks have pioneered new payments arrangements such as automated tellers, pre-authorized bill payments, general credit cards, daily-interest savings accounts, interest-bearing demand deposits, and the like. Such innovations can make past evidence of money demand behaviour irrelevant to figuring out how money demand will behave in the present and the future. In practice, financial innovations since 1970 have affected M1 demand strongly, but not the demand for broad money.

SECTION 4

Money supply behaviour

Equilibrium in the money market requires that demand for money equal the money supply. Section 2 explained the demand for money. This section explains the supply of money, by looking more deeply into the simple bank deposit expansion multiplier that was used in Chapter 16. In particular, more attention is paid to how the choices of firms, households, and banks might be affected by changes in interest rates.

If banks issue only demand deposits and if public currency holdings are always proportional to demand deposits, then the nominal money supply M_s will be a fixed multiple of the stock of high-powered money H, as in Chapter 16:

$$M_s = (1 + cu)/(rr + cu) H, \qquad (8)$$

where cu is the currency to deposit ratio and rr is the required reserve ratio on demand deposits. If H is fixed and cu and rr are constants in Equation (8), then M_s is fixed also. But M_s can be endogenous.

Policy rules and money supply

The money supply can be endogenous in two ways. First, the supply of high-powered money H can be determined by the central bank in a way (that is, by a policy rule) that depends on other variables in the economy. So far, we have assumed that H is exogenous, but that is extremely unlikely in the real world. Central banks do not operate by setting H levels and then adjusting them every so often. Instead, they manage H in order to maintain target levels of interest rates in the short run of a few weeks, in order to maintain target levels of assorted monetary aggregates in the longer run of a few months, and in order to maintain target levels of prices and real income over periods of several quarters. In other words, H is tied to interest rates R, to rates of growth of monetary aggregates, and ultimately to inflation and real income growth. H is far from exogenous. Adding endogenous H to macro models can greatly complicate such models when monetary policy rules influence expectations formation, so we do not do that until Chapter 22.

Variable ratios of time to demand deposits

The other source of endogeneity in the money supply is the **money supply multiplier** itself. Either rr or cu may not be constant. We start with rr. In modern financial systems, banks have outstanding time deposits that are many times larger than total demand deposits. In Chapter 10 we considered this case, but we assumed that the public held time deposits in a fixed ratio to demand deposits; what emerged was simply a slightly more complicated but still constant money supply multiplier. It is now time to be more realistic, by allowing the **ratio of time to demand deposits** to vary.

Let t be the public's holdings of time deposits as a multiple of its holdings of demand deposits. The ratio t will rise as time deposit yields rise relative to demand deposit yields (that is the prediction of all the money demand theories of section 2). Time deposit yields, as mentioned above, fluctuate with the general level of yields on other financial assets. Time deposits absorb high-powered money, at a rate equal to the required cash reserve ratio rr_t on time deposits. Higher time deposit interest rates therefore imply a greater absorption of H to support time deposits, and less of H available to support demand deposits. This has opposite effects on narrow and broad money.

The narrow money supply M1 will fall as t rises. Figure 19–4 shows the effect of higher interest rates on narrow money supply; part (b) of this diagram

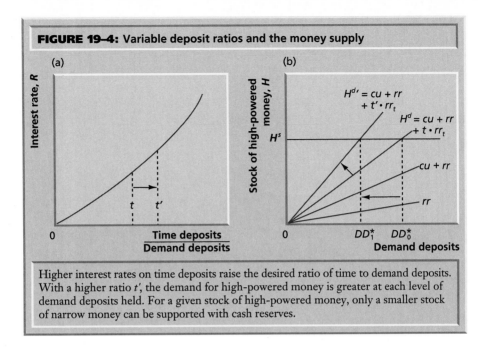

FIGURE 19–4: Variable deposit ratios and the money supply

(a)

(b)

Interest rate, R

Stock of high-powered money, H

$H^{d'} = cu + rr + t' \cdot rr_t$

$H^d = cu + rr + t \cdot rr_t$

H^s

$cu + rr$

rr

t t'

$\dfrac{\text{Time deposits}}{\text{Demand deposits}}$

DD_1^* DD_0^*

Demand deposits

Higher interest rates on time deposits raise the desired ratio of time to demand deposits. With a higher ratio t', the demand for high-powered money is greater at each level of demand deposits held. For a given stock of high-powered money, only a smaller stock of narrow money can be supported with cash reserves.

was introduced in Chapter 10. Part (a) shows that higher interest rates, including higher time deposit yields in particular, will raise the ratio t as households shift their wealth. Part (b) shows that the total demand for reserves *per dollar of demand deposits* rises as each demand deposit is accompanied by more time deposits. Total high-powered money is therefore absorbed at a lower total of demand deposits. The narrow money supply (demand deposits and currency) is therefore lower for a given stock of H. That is, higher interest rates cause the narrow money supply to shrink.

Broad money will rise as interest rates rise. This idea can be best understood if broad money as a whole is considered as having a single reserve requirement that is a weighted average of that on each kind of asset (100 percent for currency, 10 percent for demand deposits, and either 3 or 0 percent for time deposits). The demand for high-powered money in Figure 19–5 reflects the average reserve requirement for broad money as a whole:

$$M_s = (1/rr_{av}) H. \tag{9}$$

When higher interest rates raise the relative weight of time deposits in broad money, the average reserve requirement falls. For a given level of H, the broad money supply rises, as shown in Figure 19–5. The broad money supply is therefore increased by higher interest rates.

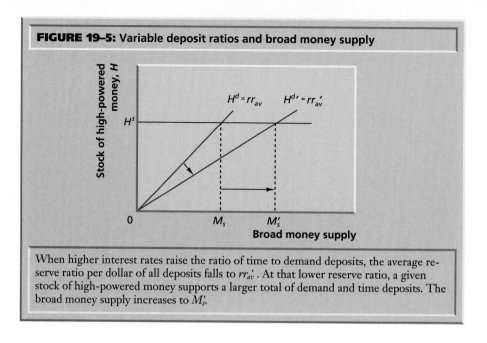

FIGURE 19–5: Variable deposit ratios and broad money supply

When higher interest rates raise the ratio of time to demand deposits, the average reserve ratio per dollar of all deposits falls to rr_{av}'. At that lower reserve ratio, a given stock of high-powered money supports a larger total of demand and time deposits. The broad money supply increases to M_s'.

Changes in the currency–deposit ratio *cu*

Prior to July 1980, chequing deposits in Canada did not have market-sensitive yields, so that the net opportunity cost of holding currency versus demand deposits did not change. The choice of **currency–deposit ratio** reflected only other features (such as relative convenience) that change only slowly. For the purposes of modelling short-run macroeconomic behaviour, it was sensible to assume that *cu* was fixed.

Since 1980 the ratio *cu* has varied significantly over short periods, as shown in Figure 19–6. Now that chequing deposits can pay interest at market-sensitive rates, changes in interest rates do change the net opportunity cost of holding money in currency rather than chequing deposits, and we can expect *cu* to fall as interest rates rise.[22] The effect on supply of either narrow or broad money is very similar to the effect on supply of broad money of raising the ratio of time to demand deposits. With lower currency holdings per dollar of both narrow and broad money, the average reserve ratio rr_{av} is lowered and a given stock of high-powered money supports a larger money supply. To the extent that households and firms are holding demand deposits with market-sensitive yields, therefore, higher interest rates cause both narrow and broad money supplies to rise.

---

[22] Note from Figure 19–6 that the rise in *cu* in 1983 followed an abrupt drop in the level of yields in 1982.

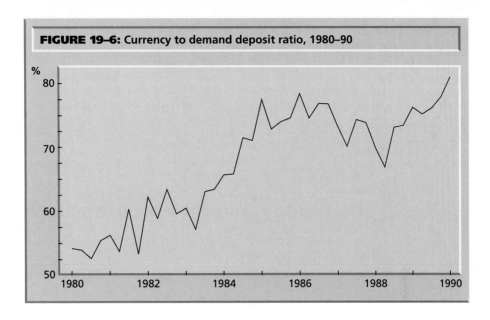

FIGURE 19–6: Currency to demand deposit ratio, 1980–90

Excess cash reserves

Banks can also change the actual reserve ratio rr by holding varying amounts of **excess cash reserves**. The amount of excess cash reserves that a bank wants to hold reflects the opportunity cost of excess cash reserves — the spread between the yield on other short-term assets and the yield on cash reserves. Since cash reserves have had a yield of zero percent, Canadian banks have consistently held zero excess cash reserves. In the new Bank Act to be introduced in 1992, the government plans to remove the cash reserve requirement from banks over a two-year period. It seems likely that even then, the banks will not hold significant excess cash reserves; as long as cash reserves earn zero percent, other short-term assets will always seem preferable.

Banks do have decisions to make that can influence the money supply, however. In most countries, banks can change the money supply by borrowing extra cash reserves from the central bank and thereby increasing total high-powered money H. Banks will tend to do so when the yield they can earn on short-term assets exceeds the yield they must pay to borrow from the central bank. In Canada, chartered banks have done very little such borrowing from the Bank of Canada, for two reasons. First, the cost of borrowing from the Bank of Canada — the **Bank rate** — is fixed automatically each week at 25 basis points above the yield on 90-day treasury bills, making it higher than at least that short-term asset. Second, the Bank of Canada has discouraged such borrowing (and the chartered banks have not insisted) even when some short-term assets have had yields above the Bank rate; this has been the most important use of the Bank of Canada's power of **moral suasion**, which we discuss further in Chapter 21.

For both reasons, the stock of high-powered money H in Canada has not been sensitive to interest rates because of the banks' behaviour.

Under the current revision of the Bank Act, the Bank of Canada has replaced this use of moral suasion by a system of penalty borrowing rates (roughly twice the Bank rate) for any use of borrowed reserves.[23] Such penalty rates will automatically discourage any bank from borrowing extra cash reserves, almost regardless of yields on short-term assets.

SECTION 5

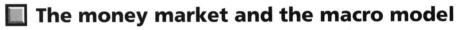

The money market and the macro model

This chapter has considered more sophisticated explanations of money demand and money supply. In this section we look at the impact of the new explanations on the asset market equilibrium condition — the LM curve — in the macro model of Chapter 16.

Money demand changes

By and large, the conclusions of our more sophisticated inspection of money demand support almost all of the assumptions made about money demand in Chapter 16. Nominal money demand does appear to be proportional to price levels, so it does make sense to talk of demand for real cash balances. The demand for real cash balances does indeed depend on real income and interest rates, and with the signs assumed in Chapter 16. Financial wealth does not affect money demand significantly. The real wage rate affects money demand, but not significantly. Many different interest rates may affect money demand, but since they largely move together, the bulk of money demand behaviour can be explained by just two or three interest rates, as shown in Table 19–1.

Broad money is more sensitive to movements of individual financial yields than is narrow money, which is to be expected; time deposits are much closer substitutes for treasury bills than are currency and chequing deposits. However, Figure 19–7 shows that interest rates on broad money deposits and on close substitutes generally do not move separately; they move together. In particular, the yield on time deposits moves so closely with yields on money market assets that the net opportunity cost of broad money hardly changes at all. This means that changes in the general level of interest rates do not cause significant changes in the net opportunity cost of broad money, and therefore do not cause significant changes in the demand for broad money. That is, broad money demand is almost insensitive to the general level of interest rates.

---

[23] This system is presented in the *Bank of Canada Review*, May 1991, and analyzed by David Longworth in *Optimal Behaviour of Direct Clearers in a World with Zero Reserve Requirements* (Ottawa: Bank of Canada, mimeo, May 1989).

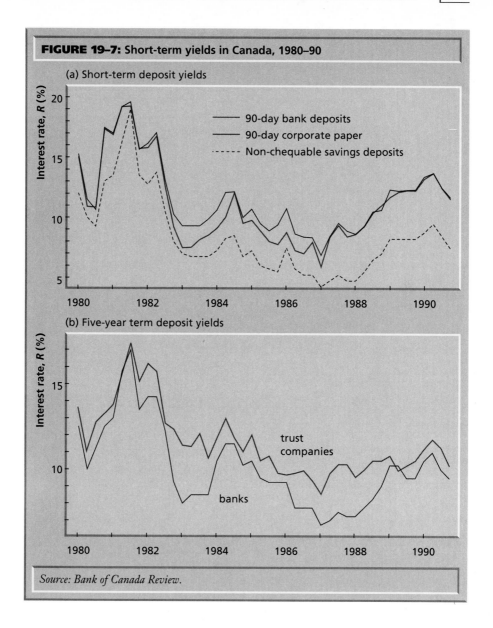

FIGURE 19–7: Short-term yields in Canada, 1980–90

(a) Short-term deposit yields

90-day bank deposits
90-day corporate paper
Non-chequable savings deposits

(b) Five-year term deposit yields

trust companies

banks

Source: Bank of Canada Review.

The interest insensitivity of broad money means that the LM curve derived for broad money should be quite steep—almost vertical for the M2 and M2+ estimates reported in Table 19–1. Even when a rise in interest rates does raise net opportunity costs, the interest sensitivity of demand for broad money is not large enough to make the LM curve less than steep.

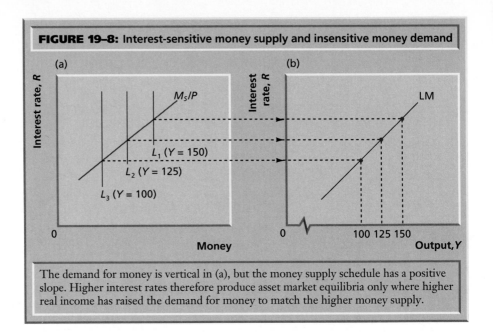

FIGURE 19–8: Interest-sensitive money supply and insensitive money demand

The demand for money is vertical in (a), but the money supply schedule has a positive slope. Higher interest rates therefore produce asset market equilibria only where higher real income has raised the demand for money to match the higher money supply.

Money supply changes

The considerations of section 4 suggest that we should think of nominal money supply as rising with interest rates. On the money market diagram, therefore, the real money supply is no longer a vertical line but rather a positively sloping one. When this conclusion is put together with the proposition that broad money demand is almost insensitive to the general level of interest rates, what emerges as an extreme case is illustrated in Figure 19–8.

In Figure 19–8(a) there are different but vertical money demand curves for different real income levels. There is one real money supply curve, which has a positive slope. In the money market diagram used in Chapter 16 to derive the LM curve, by contrast, the money supply curve was vertical and money demand curves had a negative slope. As far as the LM curve is concerned, however, it makes no difference which of the two curves slopes as long as the difference between the slopes stays the same. The outcome from Figure 19–8(b) is an LM curve of the normal, upward-sloping variety. Its slope now depends on the income sensitivity of money demand and the interest sensitivity of money supply, but otherwise its behaviour is more or less as described in Chapter 16.

Expected inflation and real versus nominal yields

In the explanation of money demand and supply, the interest rates that matter are **nominal interest rates**. The interest rate measured on the vertical axis of the LM curve diagram in Figure 19–9 is therefore a nominal interest rate. In Chapter 16, however, the interest rate that affects real investment spending by

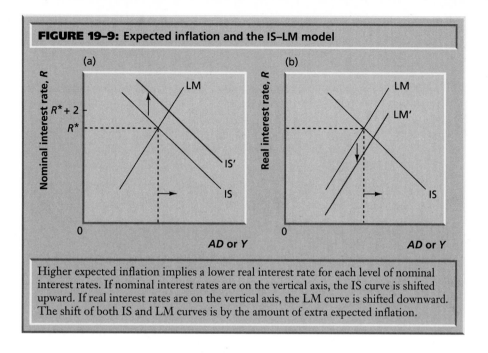

FIGURE 19–9: Expected inflation and the IS–LM model

Higher expected inflation implies a lower real interest rate for each level of nominal interest rates. If nominal interest rates are on the vertical axis, the IS curve is shifted upward. If real interest rates are on the vertical axis, the LM curve is shifted downward. The shift of both IS and LM curves is by the amount of extra expected inflation.

business firms is surely a **real interest rate** — the nominal interest rate less the rate of inflation.[24] Business firms will continue to borrow at high nominal interest rates as long as they expect future inflation almost as high.

It is inconsistent to have two different definitions of yield on the same vertical axis for the IS–LM diagram. As long as expected inflation does not change, the error is not serious: changes in nominal rates will still imply equal changes in real rates and vice versa. However, expected inflation is a subjective expectation that certainly does change. In order to remedy the problem, Figure 19–9(a) draws the IS–LM diagram using the nominal interest rate on the vertical axis for both curves. Since the real interest rate is the nominal rate less the expected inflation rate, any increase in expected inflation lowers the real interest rate that is implied by any given nominal interest rate. For a given nominal interest rate, therefore, the IS curve shifts outward to the right whenever the expected inflation rate rises. A new variable, the expected inflation rate, is added to the determinants of the IS curve and therefore of aggregate demand.

One can remedy the problem as in Figure 19–9(b) also, by drawing both IS and LM curves against the real interest rate on the vertical axis. In this case it is the LM curve that shifts (downward) when expected inflation increases.

---

[24] One can argue that much of the interest sensitivity of aggregate demand is to nominal interest rates (for instance, demand for housing that is financed by mortgages). The logic of this section requires only that some aggregate demand respond to real rather than to nominal interest rates.

For example, assume that expected inflation of 5 percent changes to 7 percent. Each nominal interest rate now implies a real interest rate 2 percentage points lower and each real interest rate implies a nominal rate 2 percentage points higher. In Figure 19–9(a), an IS–LM diagram with nominal interest rates on the vertical axis, the IS curve shifts upward by 2 percentage points; the investment demand that occurred at each previous nominal interest rate now occurs at a nominal interest rate 2 percentage points higher. In Figure 19–9(b), with real interest rates on the vertical axis, the LM curve falls 2 percentage points; the money demand that occurred at each previous real rate now occurs only if the real rate is lowered 2 percent to give the previous nominal rate. In Figure 19–9(a) and (b), the effect is to increase aggregate demand and to decrease real yields.

Adding extra financial markets

The crudest feature of macroeconomic treatment of financial markets is that it aggregates all financial markets into only two: the market for money and the market for everything else. That aggregation allows us to summarize asset market equilibrium in a single curve, the LM curve. What difference does it make if we consider a whole spectrum of financial markets, as was done for the first 15 chapters of this book?

The answer was provided by James Tobin in 1969, in his **general equilibrium approach** to monetary theory.[25] We can add in markets for bank loans, mortgages, stocks, and as many other assets as we wish. The result would be a (large) model of aggregate demand with many interest rates rather than just one. There would not be a single LM curve, but rather a number of them; each would have a different interest rate on the vertical axis, and each would require an extra assumption about how other interest rates varied or stayed put when the interest rate on the vertical axis changed.

The major benefits of a model with many financial markets are (a) it allows us to be explicit about which interest rates will affect the interest-sensitive part of the macro model, and (b) it allows those different interest rates to move independently if that is a property of the economy being modelled. Such a model makes explicit the many different steps of cause and effect between the central bank changing the supply of high-powered money, at one end of the financial system, and the response of real spending to some long-term yield or asset price at the other end.

The major drawback of models that include many financial assets is that they are much more complex. Increasingly, yields in the Canadian financial system (and abroad) move together rather than independently. The more that is true, the more sensible it is for macroeconomic modellers to move toward the other extreme of collapsing all closely related interest rates into a single, representative rate, as described in Chapter 16.

---

[25]James Tobin, "A General Equilibrium Approach to Monetary Theory," *Journal of Money, Credit, and Banking*, 1969, 15–29.

Typically, large-scale models that do break down the financial system into several different financial markets do not require each financial market to reach its own separate equilibrium. Instead, such models use the short-cut of assuming sufficient arbitrage that the different equilibrium yields are always kept in line with each other according to some "normal" yield structure, as explained in Chapter 14. A term structure equation is then estimated to relate long-term yields to short-term yields, another interest rate equation to relate mortgage loan yields to bank loan yields or treasury bill rates, and so on. If just one yield (such as the treasury bill yield) is used as a benchmark for the rest of the financial system, then this benchmark yield is the one that will be influenced directly by monetary policy, inflation, investment booms, and the other ingredients of an IS–LM model.

SECTION 6

Summary

This chapter has explored money demand and supply to see what revisions might be made to the macroeconomic model if one were to take a more sophisticated view of the market for money than was adopted in Chapters 16–18.

First, a choice needs to be made between using narrow money and broad money. Given the purposes for which a money market is needed in macroeconomics, either type of money definition can be used. Which one is the best is the one whose demand explanation is the most stable over time.

Explanations of the demand for money started off with the use of money for transactions. The quantity theory in both its versions (classical and Cambridge) focused entirely on transactions balances. Subsequent theories related the demand for money to interest rates as well. Keynes's speculative demand for money related it to the difference between observed interest rates and some subjective expectation of future rates. All subsequent theorists have related the demand for money to the net difference between interest rates on non-money assets and the yield on money (if any).

The Baumol–Tobin inventory theory of the demand for money predicts that the optimal average inventory of money balances will be proportional to prices, positively related to real income (but less than proportionally) and to real wages, and negatively related to the net opportunity cost of money. Friedman's permanent-income theory of money demand predicts much the same set of results, though less specifically. An extension of inventory theory to explain precautionary demand for money produces some of the same predictions.

Evidence of money demand behaviour supports the predictions of the Baumol–Tobin theory surprisingly well, though it is also more or less consistent with Friedman's less specific predictions. Demand for money specifications were not very stable in the 1970s and early 1980s, unfortunately. Perhaps the biggest surprise from estimates of money demand functions is the slowness with which money demand responds to incomes, prices, and relative yields.

Money supply is not fixed and exogenous, as is usually assumed in intermediate macroeconomics. Instead, it is generally responsive to interest rates. Such responsiveness occurs both because the central bank changes the supply of high-powered money, and because the money supply multiplier is interest-sensitive.

The major differences that a more sophisticated approach to modelling money markets make to the macroeconomic model are (a) to replace the interest sensitivity of money demand with interest sensitivity of money supply as the explanation of much of the upward slope of the LM curve; (b) to add expected inflation as a determinant of aggregate demand; and (c) to recognize that any model of asset market behaviour is incomplete until the behaviour of the central bank has been included.

Key Terms

narrow and broad money supply	buffer stocks
	money supply multiplier
demand for money	ratio of time to
quantity theory	demand deposits
transactions demand	currency–deposit ratio
liquidity preference	excess cash reserves
speculative demand	Bank rate
modern quantity theory	moral suasion
inventory theory	nominal and real interest rates
precautionary demand	general equilibrium approach

Questions and Problems

1. Of the three criteria for choice between definitions of money, which are the most important for purposes of macroeconomic policy, and why?

2. If you suddenly won a lottery and had your financial wealth rise abruptly, what proportion of it would you choose to hold in narrow money assets, on average, over the next year? Is this greater or less than the proportion of money in your existing financial wealth?

3. How much money do you hold, on average in a typical week, as a fraction of your weekly expenditures? Why do you not hold twice as much or half as much instead?

4. What money demand curve would Tobin's mean-variance model imply for a risk-seeking individual?

5. How could narrow money have been less stable than broad money, when broad money includes a wider range of assets?

6. Even if you never left home without your American Express card, would you also need to carry money balances?

7. What does the addition of interest sensitivity of the supply of money do to the slope of the LM curve?

8. Why is it that broad money is more sensitive to movements of relative yields, but its LM curve is steeper than that using narrow money?

9. In 1982–83, actual inflation in Canada dropped by 5 percent. Expected inflation dropped about the same amount. What impact did the latter have on the economy's IS curve between 1982 and 1983 (other things being equal)?

Suggestions for Further Reading

Caramazza, Francesco, Doug Hostland, and Stephen Poloz, *The Demand for Money and the Monetary Policy Process in Canada*. Ottawa: Bank of Canada Working Paper 90–5, May 1990.

Laidler, David. "The Buffer Stock Notion in Monetary Economics." *Conference Proceedings Supplement to the Economic Journal*, 1984, 17–34.

——. *The Demand for Money: Theories, Evidence, and Problems*, 3rd ed. New York: Harper and Row, 1985.

Tobin, James "A General Equilibrium Approach to Monetary Theory." *Journal of Money, Credit, and Banking*, 1969, 15–29.

Chapter twenty

Interest Parity and Wealth Effects in Macroeconomics

The macroeconomic model of Chapter 16 was simplified not only in its assumptions about the money market. First, the implications of arbitraging capital flows were ignored in determining the exchange rate. Second, the model ignored various feedback effects that affect aggregate demand through changes in the capital stock and in wealth. This chapter therefore reconsiders these two parts of the aggregate demand model of Chapter 16 to make it more consistent financially.

Section 1 looks more closely at the uncovered arbitrage condition assumed in Chapter 16 as the basis for the BP locus (the foreign exchange market equilibrium condition). Section 2 looks at a stock effect introduced early into Keynesian models: the capital stock adjustment explanation of investment spending. Section 3 looks at the feedback effects of wealth on aggregate demand when wealth is changed by interest rates, income, or fiscal policy. Section 4 looks at the feedback effects of wealth on aggregate demand when wealth is changed by inflation. Each section first explains the new feature being added to the model, and then analyzes its effect on aggregate demand behaviour.

You should learn in this chapter:

1. how the exchange rate affects capital flows rather than net exports in the short run;

2. how the interest parity theory adds uncertainty to the model through the expected future exchange rate;

3. how real investment spending becomes only temporary, and therefore more volatile, once it is explained as spending to adjust the capital stock;

4. how Tobin's q model makes real investment spending also sensitive to speculative swings in stock market prices;

5. how wealth is held and valued in Canada, and how changes in wealth are likely to affect aggregate demand;

6. how changes in price levels can affect aggregate demand through changes in the real value of nominal wealth.

SECTION 1

Interest parity and capital flows

In Chapter 16 we assumed that net export demand is sensitive to the exchange rate π. Net capital inflows, although admitted to be large, were assumed to be "not reliably affected" by π. As a result, it is net exports that respond to changes in π in Chapter 16, so that any change in π will have a direct impact on aggregate demand.

This story is not consistent with a conclusion of Chapter 14, however, that capital flows are sufficiently sensitive to international yield differentials to keep both covered and uncovered interest parity conditions satisfied. In this section we will see that the uncovered interest parity condition does indeed imply a reliable effect of changes in π on capital flows.

The description of the foreign exchange market in Chapter 16 also overstated the speed with which exports and imports react to π. Indeed, the dramatic decline in the value of the U.S. dollar after 1985 took so long to affect the U.S. trade deficit that economists had time to become concerned, to hold symposia, and even to publish the proceedings.[1] Trade flows do respond to exchange rate changes, but not quickly. Most trade flows require the prior establishment of supplier–customer relationships, which cannot be done quickly. In sectors where there is rivalry among firms, a rise in exchange rate that is seen as temporary will sometimes be absorbed by export suppliers through accepting lower prices, in order to protect hard-won market shares.

The reconsideration of the foreign exchange market mechanisms in this section will lead us to conclude that the model of Chapter 16 is not appropriate for a short run of less than a year, although it is still appropriate after that. Instead of π affecting aggregate demand directly in the short run through net exports, in this section π will affect only capital flows. Effects on net exports will be felt only later. The key to understanding this new exchange market adjustment is the uncovered interest parity condition.

Uncovered interest parity

The **uncovered interest parity** condition, as discussed in Chapter 14, starts with the idea that investors who are considering investments at home or abroad will prefer the investment with higher expected yield. Risk-averse investors will

---

[1] For instance, *Brookings Papers on Economic Activity*, 1987:1.

insist on some extra yield premium on the investment abroad to compensate for exposure to foreign exchange risk. If the risk premium for foreign exchange risk exposure is very small, which it will be if the risk is not systematic, then arbitrage flows of lending by such investors will cause expected yields to be almost identical.

To see what this means, consider the choice between a U.S. and a Canadian asset to be held for one year. A Canadian investing in New York would have to sell Canadian dollars at the current **spot exchange rate** π and buy them a year from now at the uncertain future spot rate π^e. His or her yield would be R_{US} (the nominal yield on U.S. assets) less any expected appreciation of the Canadian dollar over the year, $(\pi^e - \pi)$. Arbitrage will cause the yield on U.S. assets to equal the yield R on Canadian assets. The uncovered interest parity condition is

$$R = R_{US} - \text{ expected appreciation of the C\$}, \tag{1}$$

where R_{US} is the nominal yield on U.S. assets before conversion into Canadian dollars. The expected appreciation of the Canadian dollar must be expressed in annual percentage terms in Equation (1), so that it will be in the same units as the interest rate terms. Let π be exactly 100 for convenience; then $\pi^e - \pi$ measures expected appreciation in annual percentage terms. We can rearrange and restate the uncovered interest parity condition as

$$R - R_{US} = \pi - \pi^e; \tag{2}$$

that is, the simple interest differential is matched by the expected depreciation of the Canadian dollar.

Uncovered interest parity in Equation (2) ties the **expected future exchange rate** depreciation to the simple interest differential $R - R_{US}$. If exchange rates are flexible, as they have been outside the European Community since 1973, uncovered arbitrage forces changes in $\pi - \pi^e$ to match changes in $R - R_{US}$. If R rises by 2 percent, arbitrage will raise the spot exchange rate π relative to its expected future value π^e, until 2 percent more depreciation is expected. This arbitrage is in the form of large-scale, short-term capital inflows.

Figure 20–1 shows the capital flow schedule implied by large-scale uncovered arbitrage on the assumption that π^e is constant. Small differences in π from the level where $\pi - \pi^e$ just offsets the simple interest differential cause huge capital inflows; the net capital inflow (NCI) schedule is almost flat. Each level of simple interest differential has its own NCI schedule, at a height to offset $(R - R_{US})$. To complete the exchange market model, add in a net import schedule. This schedule will be vertical to reflect the fact that foreign trade flows do not respond at all quickly. Where there is no official intervention by changing official reserves, the equilibrium condition in the foreign exchange market is that net exports match net capital inflows:

$$NCI + X - M = 0 \quad \text{ or } \quad NCI = M - X, \tag{3}$$

(where X and M represent exports and imports, respectively), so that the equilibrium exchange rate lies at the intersection of the NCI schedule and the

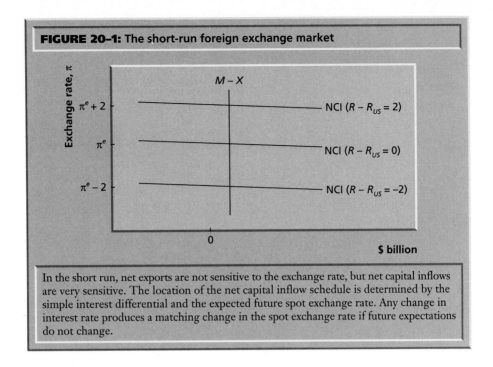

FIGURE 20-1: The short-run foreign exchange market

In the short run, net exports are not sensitive to the exchange rate, but net capital inflows are very sensitive. The location of the net capital inflow schedule is determined by the simple interest differential and the expected future spot exchange rate. Any change in interest rate produces a matching change in the spot exchange rate if future expectations do not change.

$M - X$ schedule. Here we ignore changes in official reserves because we wish to find the equilibrium exchange rate without exchange market intervention.

The result of Figure 20–1 is that in the short run to which this diagram refers, the exchange rate is determined entirely by the height of the NCI schedule, that is, by the simple interest differential and expected future exchange rate. Shifts in simple interest differentials, by themselves, have immediate and equal effects on the exchange rate. Changes in expected future exchange rate likewise drag the spot exchange rate along in order to keep the arbitrage condition satisfied.

It follows that if the expected future exchange rate π^e is fixed because the economy operates on a fixed exchange rate system, as within most of the European Community, then a rise of x percent in R must lead to an x percent rise in the spot exchange rate π. If R rises x percent and the expected future exchange rate is not fixed, as occurs in floating exchange rate systems, then the spot exchange rate must rise x percent, *plus* whatever change there is in the expected exchange rate. For instance, on 18 January 1990, the Bank of Canada lowered the Bank rate by only 29 basis points. The Canadian dollar plummeted 1.7 percent (170 basis points) within the week. At most 29 basis points of the drop in the exchange rate were to keep up with the narrowing interest differential $R - R_{US}$; the rest was to keep up with the plummeting expected exchange rate π^e. Despite a subsequent rise in the Bank rate above its pre-January 18 level, the Canadian dollar continued to slide a further 1.5 cents over the next two weeks; further drops in the expected exchange rate dragged the spot rate down as well.

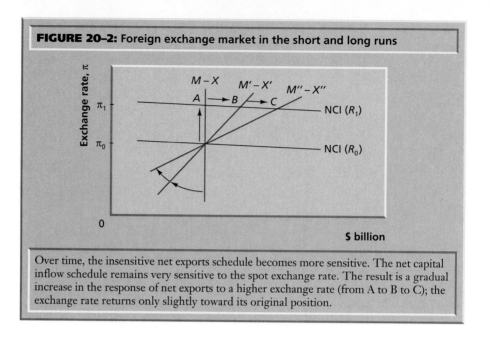

FIGURE 20-2: Foreign exchange market in the short and long runs

Over time, the insensitive net exports schedule becomes more sensitive. The net capital inflow schedule remains very sensitive to the spot exchange rate. The result is a gradual increase in the response of net exports to a higher exchange rate (from A to B to C); the exchange rate returns only slightly toward its original position.

Changes in expectations formation will clearly have a big impact on exchange rate behaviour. Unfortunately we know little about exchange rate expectations except that they adjust very quickly. The foreign exchange market is close to an efficient market, so its behaviour is very difficult to forecast.[2]

In the longer run of one or more years, net imports do respond to changes in the exchange rate. The net import schedule in Figure 20-2 becomes flatter as more time is allowed for adjustment following a change in π. In Figure 20-2 an increase in R is assumed that pushes the NCI schedule upward by the same percentage amount, as implied by uncovered interest parity. At the initial equilibrium exchange rate π_0 there would be huge excess demand from eager potential capital inflows. In a floating exchange rate system the exchange rate would rise immediately to π_1 to clear the market. In the short run there would be no change in the volume of either net capital inflows or net imports; net imports have not had time to adjust, and the rise in π has choked off the incentive for any extra capital flows. Over time, net imports gradually respond to the higher exchange rate. As they do so, the exchange rate drops to induce matching net capital inflow, but only a very small drop below π_1 is required because the net capital inflow curve is almost flat. The exchange market moves from equilibrium at A to equilibrium at B and then, later, at C. If arbitrage flows are large, the exchange rate at C will be almost the same as that at A. It is mainly the size of net imports and net capital inflows that changes.

---

[2] For a review of what we do know, see David Backus, "The Exchange Rate: Separating the Wheat from the Chaff," *Canadian Journal of Economics*, November 1984, 824–846.

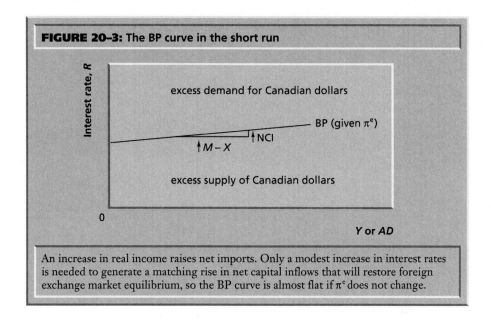

FIGURE 20–3: The BP curve in the short run

An increase in real income raises net imports. Only a modest increase in interest rates is needed to generate a matching rise in net capital inflows that will restore foreign exchange market equilibrium, so the BP curve is almost flat if π^e does not change.

What is unexplained in the model is the expected exchange rate. One of the spectres that haunts the nightmares of central bankers is the possibility that arbitrageurs will have elastic expectations; that is, that they will respond to falling exchange rates by expecting still more depreciation. If arbitrageurs do have elastic expectations, those expectations would be self-fulfilling: arbitrageurs would shift their NCI schedules down as quickly as they lowered their expected future exchange rates, thereby lowering spot exchange rates. Falling spot exchange rates would cause expectations of further decreases, and so on. Only massive intervention by central banks (if they have enough foreign exchange reserves) or dramatic increases in domestic interest rates to offset expected depreciation would stop the process. The January 1990 episode is a case in point; the Bank of Canada reversed its interest rate decrease within two weeks and added a further 89 basis point increase by mid-February to stop the fall in the Canadian dollar.

The effect of interest parity on the macro model

The slope of the BP curve depends on exchange rate expectations behaviour. If the expected exchange rate changes as much as or more than the spot exchange rate, the foreign exchange market is unstable (as in the central banker's nightmare). If expected exchange rates are not affected by changes in the spot exchange rate (the most plausible and least masochistic assumption, but still only an assumption), the BP curve becomes almost horizontal, as shown in Figure 20–3. When higher real income Y raises net imports $M - X$, it now takes only a tiny change in interest rate to raise the net capital inflow by enough to restore balance in the foreign exchange market.

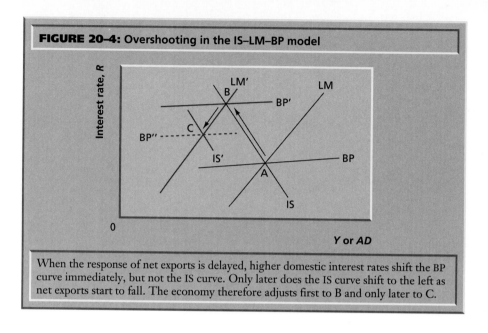

FIGURE 20–4: Overshooting in the IS–LM–BP model

When the response of net exports is delayed, higher domestic interest rates shift the BP curve immediately, but not the IS curve. Only later does the IS curve shift to the left as net exports start to fall. The economy therefore adjusts first to B and only later to C.

The new element added to the BP curve is the expected future exchange rate. If π^e falls, the old exchange rate will no longer be an equilibrium level; there would be huge capital outflows fleeing from the larger expected depreciation $\pi - \pi^e$. In order for the net capital inflow to get back into balance with an unchanged flow of net imports, the interest rate R would have to be higher by as much as π^e had fallen. The level of R that maintains foreign exchange market equilibrium at an unchanged exchange rate would now be higher. The BP curve would therefore be shifted upward by a fall in the expected future exchange rate.

The implications of being off the BP curve are the same as before: excess demand for Canadian dollars if the economy is above it, excess supply if it is below it. When capital flows are as sensitive as the uncovered interest parity theorem requires, the volume of excess demand or supply is likely to be huge. A central bank planning to maintain a disequilibrium exchange rate will therefore need enormous reserves to offset or absorb huge private capital flows. Central banks in fixed exchange rate systems will also have real trouble sterilizing changes in official reserves to prevent them from affecting the money supply when the changes are so large.

Changes in the exchange rate cause the same shifts of the IS and BP curve as in Chapter 16, except that shifts of the IS curve are delayed beyond the short run. Initially, a change in π affects only net capital inflows, which are not part of aggregate demand for goods. Initially, therefore, changes in π do not affect the IS curve. Only later, as net imports start to respond to changes in π, will the IS curve also start to shift. The result is an **overshooting** of both exchange rate and interest rate, as Figure 20–4 shows.

In Figure 20–4 the real money supply is reduced, shifting the LM curve to the left, to LM′. The path of the economy is from starting point A, to B, and finally to C. An initial interest rate increase (to B) causes an immediate rise in π of the same amount because of the huge net capital inflow pressure in the foreign exchange market. With the higher exchange rate the BP curve rises to BP′, intersecting the new LM curve and the original IS curve at B. Over time, higher π starts to raise net imports and also to shift the IS curve to the left. As the IS curve shifts to IS′, both output and interest rates fall. As interest rates fall, so does the exchange rate and the BP curve. The long-run equilibrium will be reached at some point such as C. The path of the exchange rate is to rise initially above its long-run equilibrium level, and then to drift back down again as net imports start to respond. The same is true of the interest rate.

Expectations and fixed exchange rates

The **Bretton Woods system** (1944–73) was based on fixed exchange rates.[3] Members of the system (and this included almost all Western market economies) were expected to maintain their exchange rates within 1 percent on either side of the **official parity level** they had chosen. Initially capital flows presented no problems in exchange rate management, because exchange controls severely limited capital flows from most nations. Exchange market intervention by central banks was more than sufficient to keep them in line.

By the early 1960s, however, capital flows started to cause crisis after crisis in the fixed exchange rate system, because of the behaviour of expectations. The problem was that central banks were obliged to support exchange rates in a crisis right up to the last moment; then a "fundamental disequilibrium" was declared and the exchange rate was "repegged" closer to a new equilibrium level. Exchange rate adjustments were large when they occurred, and the signs of imminent depreciations were obvious to all: persistent current account deficits accompanied by falling official foreign exchange reserves. By postponing exchange rate adjustments, the central banks set themselves up for massive speculation by private investors. Highly levered speculators stood to make huge gains if they were right, and tiny losses if they were wrong; if they were wrong, they lost no more than brokerage costs and possibly some forgone interest for a few months. The more massive the speculation, the shorter the time a central bank had before adjusting the official parity, and the less fixed the fixed exchange rate mechanism became. Over time, capital flows became ever more massive. Now, with most exchange controls eliminated, hundreds of billions of dollars' worth of exchange transactions occur every day. Such flows could quickly overwhelm the combined reserves of central banks.

Because they can no longer fight capital flows, central banks have been forced to make use of them instead. To support an exchange rate now, central

---

[3] Canada was on this system only briefly, from 1944 to 1950 and again from 1962 to 1970. We were the exception in letting our exchange rate float the rest of the time.

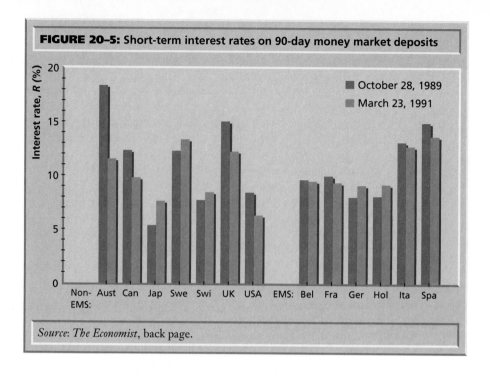

FIGURE 20–5: Short-term interest rates on 90-day money market deposits

Source: *The Economist*, back page.

banks must keep their interest rates adjusted to the uncovered interest parity level. That is, in order to maintain fixed exchange rates, central banks must give up independent interest rate policies. They must coordinate their monetary policy with those of other countries with whom their exchange rates are fixed. The evidence of such coordination can be seen in Figure 20–5. Members of the European Monetary System (the EMS) have had to coordinate their interest rates, while other countries have not, in order to keep the EMS exchange rates in line.[4] Belgium, France, Germany, and the Netherlands will allow their mutual exchange rates to fluctuate only within a 2.5 percent band. Spain, Italy, and (as of 1991) the United Kingdom will allow their exchange rates with other EMS countries to fluctuate within 6 percent. Non-EMS members are unrestricted. Figure 20–5 shows that the tighter the exchange rate commitment, the closer are the nominal interest rates. Figure 20–5 also shows that having to stay in step with one's neighbours causes more sluggish movements (that is, more stability) of individual EMS members' interest rates.

---

[4]The EMS is a system of fixed exchange rates between member countries, combined with jointly floating rates with outside countries.

SECTION 2

◼ Investment and capital stock adjustment

A second change to make the macro model more realistic has little to do with the foreign exchange rate; it is to recognize the volatility of domestic spending on new real capital assets—real investment demand. Investment demand is demand for newly produced housing, plant, equipment, and inventories to add to the stock inherited from the previous year (the previous year's capital stock less depreciation). That is, investment is **capital stock adjustment**. Whenever real investment spending is greater than that needed to to replace existing equipment that wears out, the economy's stock of capital increases. Whenever real investment falls below what is needed for replacement, the economy's stock of capital falls.

Capital stock adjustment implies a finite response of investment to the interest rate. When lower interest rates induce firms to add more capital, investment spending will stay high only as long as it takes to adjust actual capital up to the new desired level. Thereafter, investment spending will fall back to just the replacement level. In Manitoba, for instance, provincial investment spending is buoyant while Manitoba Hydro is adding to its hydro capacity by building dams on the Nelson River, but every time a hydro dam is completed, investment spending falls off abruptly until the next one is started.

Capital stock adjustment also implies that investment spending will be very sensitive to the level of capacity utilization. It is when existing capacity is being fully utilized that firms wish they had more capacity and set about adding it. Conversely, once capacity has been increased relative to demand, expansion plans will be put on the shelf for a while. Such behaviour of investment spending makes it a source of great instability in aggregate demand. It kicks in at full capacity just when stabilization policymakers would like to cool the economy down, and it kicks out as soon as the economy heads into recession.

As an example, consider North American newsprint capacity and demand, illustrated in Figure 20–6. When North American and export demand was very close to output capacity in 1979, producers started building new mills to expand capacity (by 12 percent on the East coast, by 44 percent on the West coast). Their expansion, plus the 1981–82 recession, caused a glut of capacity and low profit margins until 1987. By then, demand growth had caught up to capacity again, and producers announced plans to build new mills to expand capacity (coincidentally, the plans added up to 12 percent capacity expansion on the East coast, and 44 percent on the West coast). This expansion, plus the recession of 1990–91, seems likely to repeat the cycle for the 1990s. Where such behaviour is systematic rather than random across many sectors, it can cause aggregate demand growth to be volatile.

Housing demand is slightly different from business investment in that many young households are constrained by their current incomes. Young households starting out generally have much higher income expectations for their later years than their relatively low current starting salaries. That is, their permanent income

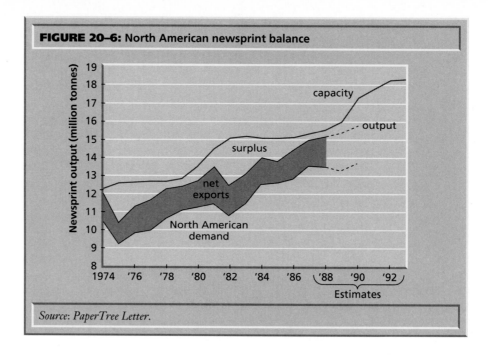

FIGURE 20–6: North American newsprint balance

Source: PaperTree Letter.

is much higher than their initial income. Yet they are often not able to find lenders to finance the kind of house appropriate to their permanent income: the interest and principal payments on the necessary mortgage loan would take up so large a portion of their (temporarily) smaller current income that lenders would think the default risk too high. The result of this borrowing constraint is that spending on housing is partly tied to current income just as consumption is tied to current income in the simple Keynesian consumption function.

Tobin's *q* theory of investment

James Tobin has added a financial market flavour to investment theory by telling the story partly from the vantage point of suppliers of capital goods.[5] **Tobin's *q* theory** explains directly the output of those capital goods not built to order but built on speculation, such as most real estate development and much resource development. Tobin's story is that capital goods producers will produce whenever the market price they expect is greater than their costs, as always in microeconomics. Dividing the expected market price of capital goods by the cost of production gives Tobin's *q* ratio. Tobin's story in terms of *q* is that producers will build capital goods for sale whenever the *q* ratio is greater than 1.0.

---

[5] James Tobin, "A General Equilibrium Approach to Monetary Theory," *Journal of Money, Credit, and Banking*, 1969, 1:15–29.

The behaviour of q can be understood by looking at its ingredients separately. The expected market price of new capital assets P_k is the equilibrium price at which the current stock of capital assets will be willingly held. Our theory of financial markets predicts that equilibrium will be the present discounted value of the expected receipts from such assets. Expected receipts from new capital assets are what we call in microeconomics the expected marginal value product of capital (that is, price of goods multiplied by marginal product of capital, $P \times MP_k$). For continually replaced capital assets, and assuming constant expected marginal products for simplicity, the relationship between the price of a capital good and its marginal value product is the same as that between the price and the yield of a bond that lasts forever (a perpetual bond):[6]

$$P_k = (P \times MP_k)/R_k, \qquad (4)$$

where R_k is the yield required on assets with this degree of risk, in fractional form. The cost of production of capital assets reflects the cost of newly produced goods and services generally in the economy, so the aggregate price level P is a good proxy for it. The q ratio is therefore:

$$q = P_k/P \qquad (5)$$

By substituting for P_k from Equation (4), we get

$$q = MP_k/R_k. \qquad (6)$$

that is, Tobin's q will fall as the interest rate rises and as the marginal product of capital falls. Tobin's story of Equation (5) can also explain much of the business investment spending that is done to order. Firms wanting to expand can choose to do it by building new capacity from scratch, or by buying up existing capacity. Buying up existing firms means taking over existing firms by buying up their shares and taking on their debts. Which of the two routes is cheapest will depend on the ratio of (a) the price of debt + equity of existing firms in capital markets, and (b) the cost of newly produced capital goods. The cost of new capacity is reflected in the aggregate price level for new output. The price of an existing firm's assets is the present discounted value of earnings on shares and of interest payments on outstanding debts. When the ratio of (a) to (b) is less than 1.0, firms will find it cheaper to expand by acquisition. When the ratio exceeds 1.0, firms find it cheaper to build from scratch. Any inflation of stock market prices relative to the aggregate price level will therefore cause greater building of new capacity and less takeover activity. Some fluctuations in stock market prices reflect general

---

[6] This equation assumes that the portion of the asset's gross revenue set aside as depreciation allowances is used to repair or replace worn-out parts of the real asset so that the investment lasts indefinitely, like a perpetual bond. The logic is not changed if the real asset does not last to infinity as a perpetual bond does, but the pricing formula is made much more complex. The marginal product of capital MP_k is defined as net of the depreciation allowance.

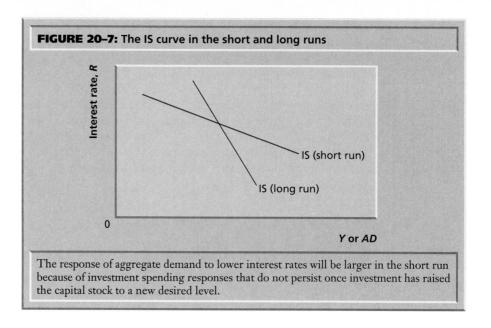

FIGURE 20–7: The IS curve in the short and long runs

The response of aggregate demand to lower interest rates will be larger in the short run because of investment spending responses that do not persist once investment has raised the capital stock to a new desired level.

changes in interest rates, that affect all assets; other fluctuations reflect changes in expected future sales, the variable that is so important in the capital stock adjustment theory.

Effects of capital stock adjustment on the macro model

Capital stock adjustment and Tobin's q theory imply three changes to the macro model of Chapter 16:

1. Investment spending is sensitive to income directly in the case of housing, and indirectly where plant and equipment spending is sensitive to the level of capacity use. This means that feedback effects from income to aggregate demand are not confined to consumption spending. There can be powerful feedback effects through investment demand as well.

2. The response of investment (for instance, to lowered interest rates) is only temporary. It is self-reversing once capacity has been adjusted to the desired level; at that point investment spending would revert to just replacement investment. The self-reversing response of investment spending gives rise to or perpetuates cycles in aggregate demand. One way of incorporating this response into the aggregate demand model is to recognize that the IS curve has long- and short-run versions, as shown in Figure 20–7. The short-run version is more sensitive to interest rates than the long-run version. The long run in this case is a period long enough that new capacity can be completely installed, so that many new investment spending programs initiated because of lower interest rates will have run their course and stopped.

3. Investment spending is volatile because it is driven so strongly by expectations. This adds uncertainty to any forecast of aggregate demand. Tobin's idea that stock market valuation also plays a role adds even more uncertainty.

SECTION 3

Wealth effects

Wealth has already been introduced as a factor in the life-cycle permanent-income theory in Chapter 7. In that theory, total wealth as a constraint on lifetime consumption is dominated by human wealth rather than by the non-human wealth recorded in the national balance sheet accounts as net private domestic wealth. Non-human wealth has also attracted a lot of attention from macroeconomists, however. In this section we first define non-human wealth, then we identify what might cause it to change, and finally we examine how aggregate demand might be affected if and when wealth does change.

Defining private domestic wealth

Private domestic wealth or net worth W can be defined (from the national balance sheet accounts in section 2 of Chapter 5) as the market value of total real assets K, less net debt to the rest of the world F, plus net debt owed by the government sector. All other financial assets are both issued and held by members of the private sector, so they cancel each other out when liabilities are subtracted from assets to calculate wealth for the entire private sector.

The government sector's net debt is the public's holdings of government bonds (B), plus the stock of high-powered money (H), less the government's holdings of real assets (K_g). H is a convenient measure of those government bonds held directly by the central bank, but held indirectly by the public (that is, after intermediation) in the form of central bank currency and cash reserves against deposits.[7]

Private domestic wealth is therefore, in nominal terms,

$$W = K - F + (B + H - K_g). \qquad (7)$$

If we now let K_p be the market value of privately held real assets (that is, $K - K_g$), and if we divide by P to get real values, real private domestic wealth, W/P, is:

$$W/P = (K_p - F + B + H)/P. \qquad (8)$$

---

[7] Cash reserves against deposits are also not held directly by the public; the public holds only the deposits issued by banks to finance their cash reserve assets. Ultimately, after "washing out" all intermediary transactions, households have assets equivalent to H.

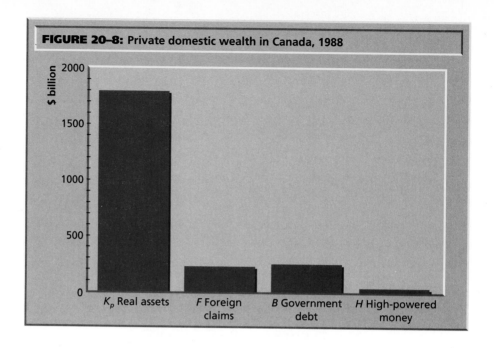

FIGURE 20–8: Private domestic wealth in Canada, 1988

Figure 20–8 shows that for the Canadian economy as of 1988, K_p is huge, F and B are relatively small, and H is tiny. H is so small that changes in it have no significant wealth effect; even a doubling of H would raise W by only 1.2 percent. A doubling of B or of F would raise W by only about 15 percent. Thus we ignore H in the rest of this chapter, and we will not give much emphasis to government bonds either.

The value of W can be explained using only a few variables: K_p, F, and B are each valued at market prices that reflect the present discounted value of a stream of expected income. If all the streams are fixed nominal payments, and perpetual, the market value of each is the annual stream divided by the appropriate discount rate. Those market values would then be sensitive to the discount rate. Much of government debt is in the form of short-term treasury bills whose market values do not fluctuate nearly as much as would be suggested by the formula for a perpetual bond.[8] However, their values do fall when interest rates rise, and vice versa. The level of high-powered money H is a fixed nominal value that is insensitive to interest rates.

If we let k, f, and b stand for the flows of income from K_p, F, and B in Equation (7), and assume them constant and perpetual for convenience, and if we let the appropriate discount rates be R_k, R_f and R, then real private domestic wealth can be written

---

[8] For a perpetual bond with coupon payment C, and yield R, its price P is determined by the equation $P = C/R$, so a fall in R from, say, 0.08 to 0.04 will double the price of the bond.

$$W/P = [(k/R_k) - (f/R_f) + (b/R) + H]/P. \tag{9}$$

It follows from Equation (9) that what will change real private domestic wealth are interest rates (R, R_k, and R_f), the flow of earnings on real capital (k) and to foreigners (f), the flow of interest on government debt (b), the level of high-powered money (H), and the price level (P). The flow of earnings k from the capital stock will be raised by net investment spending. The flow of earnings f paid abroad will be raised by net capital inflows. The flow of government bond interest b will be raised by government deficits.

Most discussions of wealth effects in macro models focus on changes in the level of wealth caused by changes in interest rates and prices. Changes in the flows k, f, and b are normally small or slow enough that little impact will be felt in any short-run period. In the rest of this section we discuss effects of interest rate changes on aggregate demand through changes in wealth, and review a controversy about whether government bonds B should even be counted as part of wealth. Discussion of effects of prices on aggregate demand through changes in real wealth are deferred to section 4.

Intermediation and the valuation of wealth

The definition of private domestic wealth, given above, can be as simple as it is only because of much cancelling out of financial intermediation. Where households own debts of banks, banks own debts of firms, and firms own real capital assets, offsetting debts and financial assets of the private sector as a whole can be cancelled out, leaving households "owning" the real capital assets actually held by firms. Firms and banks thus become irrelevant. This **washing out of financial assets and debts** is correct accounting, but it can be misleading when imported into macro models.

One problem is that the process of transmutation of assets by intermediaries is likely to alter some of the price variability of assets held at different stages of intermediation. For instance, fluctuations in the price of real assets held by firms may not be passed through fully to banks holding the firms' liabilities, and still less to households holding deposits in banks. Similarly, pension fund contributors are almost all unaware of fluctuations in the market value of bonds and mortgages held for them in pension funds. Changes in the market value of W therefore may not even be perceived by households, let alone responded to.

Another problem of the accounting definition of wealth is that it washes out firms as though they could take no actions independently of their ultimate owners, households; only the balance sheets of households are assumed to matter. However, if there is any financing constraint on firms, as is likely, the structure of their balance sheets can be important to their borrowing and spending, and we do not want them washed out.

Wealth effects on aggregate demand

The theories advanced in Chapters 7, 16, and 19 suggest that changes in wealth will affect both consumption and investment, and possibly also the demand for money. Higher household wealth levels should raise consumption, other things being equal, because households will feel that their futures are more secure and will feel less need to save for the future out of current income; that is the central message of the life-cycle permanent-income hypothesis of Chapter 7. The impact is fairly small, however. Ando and Modigliani, for example, first estimated a marginal propensity to consume out of wealth of 0.06 (roughly equal to consuming the real yield each year).[9]

Higher wealth or equity levels of firms will affect investment spending through lower debt–equity levels. If firms are subject to borrowing constraints that are based on what lenders see as maximum prudent debt–equity ratios, an increase in equity lowers debt–equity levels and eases their borrowing constraint.[10] The impact of easing borrowing constraints will be large where it occurs. For example, if the average debt–equity ratio is 0.8, then each extra dollar of extra equity value permits an extra $0.80 of extra borrowing.[11] If firms are indeed constrained, then they will want to spend more and will do so once they get the chance. All that prevents the effect of wealth on investment spending from being huge is that most firms are not constrained from borrowing. For those firms not constrained, it is not clear that a change in the value of business equity would have any effect on their spending either way.

Evidence on the behaviour of the demand for money, discussed in Chapter 19, suggests that the effects of changes in wealth on the demand for money are tiny; we therefore ignore them.

Are wealth changes visible?

In Chapter 7 we looked closely at household asset portfolios to see whether any significant part of them is subject to fluctuations in prices such as might be caused by changes in yields. We concluded that few of the assets held directly by households, in Canada at least, are valued at market prices or are sensitive to fluctuations in market value. The major exceptions are the family home and the value of pension fund entitlements. Since the values of assets actually held by households are not very sensitive to interest rate levels, interest rate feedback effects on aggregate demand through impacts on household wealth will be small.

Impacts on firms will be more noticeable. Firms' debts are all recorded at book values that are close to the final redemption prices of those debts. The book value does not change with the level of current interest rates on similar debts. Therefore any fluctuations in asset values will not be offset by matching fluctuations in debt values and will cause equal fluctuations in equity instead.

---

[9] A. Ando and F. Modigliani, "The 'Life Cycle' Hypothesis of Saving: Aggregate Implications and Tests," *American Economic Review*, March 1963.

[10] James Tobin, *Asset Accumulation and Economic Activity* (Chicago: University of Chicago Press, 1980).

[11] The average debt–equity ratio is 0.81 in the national balance sheet accounts for 1988 for non-financial private corporations.

Fluctuations in equity can interact with borrowing constraints to affect business investment spending. For instance, higher current interest rates will lower both asset values and equity; lower equity will make borrowing constraints still tighter and lower investment spending for constrained firms.

Are government bonds net wealth? Barro's Ricardian equivalence theorem

Households can be surprised if their wealth is changed by extra government deficits, since government decisions are made outside household plans to some extent. Whether households or firms even regard government debt as net wealth is a controversial issue today in macroeconomics. The controversy appears under the heading of the **Ricardian equivalence theorem**, put forward by Robert Barro.[12]

A proper definition of wealth for forward-looking households and firms would include all future obligations as liabilities, subtracting them all from total assets. Robert Barro has protested that we do not do that with the tax liabilities that accompany government bonds. Rational individuals, he argues, would recognize that governments must eventually raise taxes to pay interest on any extra bonds that are issued to finance deficits. Rational households would consider those extra taxes as a form of liability. The present discounted value of the extra future taxes would then exactly offset the value of government bonds. The government sector would contribute nothing to private domestic wealth from any amount of deficit spending. This idea of the equivalence of public debt interest and of the taxes to pay that interest is named after David Ricardo (1772–1823), an early and eminent classical economist, but its resurgence in modern macroeconomics has been entirely due to Robert Barro. Its message is that there are zero wealth effects either from deficit spending or from changes in interest rates.

The idea that deficit spending would have zero effect on wealth may change when we consider where extra government bonds are likely to be held after a round of deficit spending. Extra bonds could be held domestically if domestic saving absorbed them. Some of them would merely replace the debts of private firms if those firms were crowded out of financial markets by government borrowing. Some of the bonds would be held abroad. The flow of funds identity from Chapter 4 establishes that in equilibrium, the entire government sector deficit $(G - T)$ must be matched by the private sector surplus $(S - I)$ plus the current account deficit $(M - X)$ or net capital inflow (NCI):

$$(G - T) = (S - I) + (M - X)$$
$$= (S - I) + NCI. \qquad (10)$$

---

[12] Robert J. Barro, "Are Government Bonds Net Wealth?" *Journal of Political Economy*, 1974, 1095–117.

Under some circumstances, the entire extra issue of government bonds could end up being held outside the country, so the private domestic sector would have only the extra tax liabilities to contemplate, and none of the extra future interest receipts. In a new classical model where output levels are not budged from the natural level by demand shocks such as extra government spending, private sector saving would not be raised by income increases, as it would in a new Keynesian model. If the central bank was also reluctant to allow interest rates to rise to crowd out investment spending, as in a fixed exchange rate situation, then the private sector surplus could not rise at all to offset a greater public sector deficit. The whole impact would be on net imports, which would be matched by a net capital inflow. Foreigners would receive the extra government bond interest in the future, while domestic residents would pay the taxes. Private domestic wealth would fall on both counts, other things remaining equal.

Critics of Barro's theorem have argued that we do not recognize future tax liabilities as faithfully as we count up our Canada Savings Bonds, for example, so there would still be some net wealth effect from government bond issues. If foreigners hold all the bonds, however, the wealth effect would have to be negative. A middle-of-the-road position is that some of the newly issued bonds would be held domestically, and that future taxes to pay interest on all newly issued bonds would be imperfectly recognized. The result of such a pair of assumptions is that the net effect of government bond issues on private domestic wealth and on spending would be fairly small.

Wealth effects in the macro model

When we stand back and look at the effects of financial wealth, it is easy to see why they are typically left out of macro models. Few of the channels of effect we have looked at seem likely to be important. In many cases, changes in wealth due to changes in interest rates go unobserved by the households they are supposed to affect. The response of firms is likely to be greater. Wealth changes from the government bond issues that accompany deficit spending are partly felt abroad and are partly offset by the prospect of higher future taxes, so that the net impact on domestic aggregate demand is probably negligible.

To the extent that interest rates do induce wealth effects, this adds (marginally) to interest rate effects already included in the macro model. They make the IS curve slightly flatter.

SECTION 4

Price level effects revisited

Chapter 16 summarized aggregate demand behaviour in an aggregate demand curve relating demand to the price level. The negative slope of this curve was explained by two effects: lower real money supply raising interest rates, which depresses investment spending; and either higher exchange rates or higher prices (depending on the exchange rate mechanism) lowering net exports. In this section we discuss how higher price levels also affect aggregate demand by lowering the real value of fixed nominal wealth. The impact of higher price levels on aggregate demand turns out to depend on whether the higher price level was expected or not, so this section discusses the two situations separately.

Expected price changes

If a price increase is expected, lenders will be able to insist on some nominal interest rate increase as an **inflation premium** to compensate for the lower purchasing power they will get back for each dollar loaned. The compensation will not be complete, as we explained in Chapter 14, because lenders do not have any close substitute asset to shift to which is not affected by expected inflation; in particular, Canadian lenders have no indexed bond market to turn to when expected inflation rises. Nevertheless, as higher prices lower the purchasing power of financial assets, a higher stream of nominal interest repairs some of the damage.

The tax system makes inflation premiums even less adequate to offset inflation. All nominal interest income is taxed regardless of whether it is an inflation premium or not. Even if nominal interest rates rise by as much as expected inflation, the amount left after personal income tax does not. There will be a negative net effect on wealth and therefore on aggregate demand.

Those locked into existing fixed nominal contracts, particularly holders and issuers of term loans and bonds and longer-term mortgages, will feel a double impact from rising rates of inflation. Holders of such assets will suffer a loss in purchasing power equal to the inflation rate, but also a further capital loss in nominal market value because of the higher yields offered on newly issued assets. Issuers of these same assets gain what holders lose, except that debtors seldom think of their debts in terms of market value; almost all debts are recorded at book value, which generally lies somewhere in the narrow range between the issue price and the redemption value. These impacts of faster inflation are one-shot and temporary; nominal interest rates rise when expected inflation rises, but not again even if the inflation persists.

Higher inflation skews cash flows for firms in several ways. The net effect on firms is likely to decrease their equity and investment spending. First, fixed depreciation schedules decline in real value over time, cumulatively. That exposes more of corporate income to profits tax and leaves less for shareholders. Second, the inflation premium in nominal interest rates is deductible from gross revenue in calculating profits, exposing less of corporate income to tax (though more to bondholders). Third, higher nominal interest rates will seriously impair the cash flow position of some firms even if the real interest costs are no higher. The reason is that an increase in expected inflation can increase nominal interest costs much more quickly than it increases firms' revenues. Over time, if the expected inflation materializes, borrowers' revenues will gradually catch up with their higher but constant nominal interest payments. To start with, however, borrowers' liquidity may be so constrained that they cannot even finance assets that in the long run are good investments.

Unexpected price changes

Unanticipated price increases lower real wealth by lowering the real values of government bonds. There is no obvious impact on the value of real capital assets: higher nominal earnings per share due to inflation should more or less offset the lower purchasing power of each nominal dollar. Unexpected inflation also transfers real wealth from creditors to debtors by devaluing all the financial assets that are washed out in calculating net wealth. (In the Canadian national balance sheet for 1988, these assets amounted to $3300 billion for 1988, over one and a half times the value of private domestic wealth.) Creditors can be expected to reduce consumption and to increase saving in order to restore wealth levels. Debtors will have smaller real liabilities relative to real income or any real assets, so they will find it less risky to expand their borrowing. In general, we can think of the creditors as households and the debtors as firms.

If the net effect of redistribution of wealth is zero (that is, if impacts on creditors and debtors cancel each other out), then the effects of unexpected price changes on aggregate demand through wealth effects are small. A rough calculation explains this point. From the life-cycle permanent-income model we can expect consumption spending to be proportional to total wealth, human and non-human. Private domestic wealth is only about 15 percent of total wealth defined to include human wealth, so a 1 percent increase in private domestic wealth increases total wealth and consumption by only 0.15 percent. Now government bonds are only 14 percent of private domestic wealth; a 1 percent increase in the value of government bonds therefore raises private domestic wealth by only 0.14 percent and total wealth and consumption by only $0.14 \times 0.15 = 0.02$ percent. This is indeed a tiny effect.

If there is to be a significant effect of inflation on aggregate demand via wealth, it must come by affecting borrowing contraints on debtors, as first suggested by Tobin and more recently by Mark Gertler and others.[13] Faster inflation lowers the real value of debts, lowers debt–equity ratios, and causes the supply of bank credit to **constrained debtors** to loosen up. The result, for what Tobin calls liquidity-constrained firms, is a surge in the demand for capital assets that is much larger than will likely be offset by the lower consumption of creditors. The net real wealth effect of an unanticipated price level increase is therefore likely to be an increase rather than a decrease in aggregate demand.[14]

---

[13] See for instance, Mark Gertler, "Financial Structure and Aggregate Economic Activity: an Overview," *Journal of Money, Credit and Banking*, August 1988, Part 2, 573.

[14] Note the contrast with the case of expected inflation, in which case higher nominal interest rates are likely to cause a cash flow squeeze that would more than offset the prospect of lower real debt principal values in the short run.

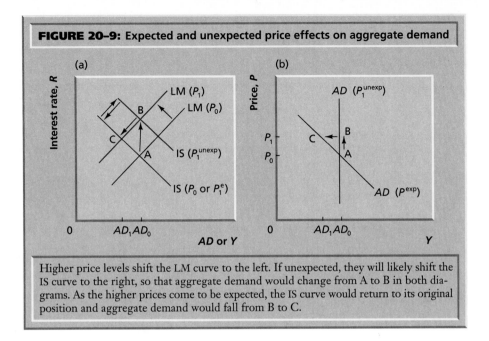

FIGURE 20-9: Expected and unexpected price effects on aggregate demand

Higher price levels shift the LM curve to the left. If unexpected, they will likely shift the IS curve to the right, so that aggregate demand would change from A to B in both diagrams. As the higher prices come to be expected, the IS curve would return to its original position and aggregate demand would fall from B to C.

The effect of inflation on the macro model

The effects of changes in price levels on aggregate demand through wealth effects depend critically on whether the price increase is expected or not. If inflation is expected, the impact is likely to be negative but not large. If inflation is unexpected, the impact is likely to be positive. Changing price levels will therefore shift the IS curve in opposite directions depending on inflation expectations. The likely time path is for inflation to be at first unexpected and then expected; the IS curve would be shifted first to the right and then to the left. The result for aggregate demand is a demand curve that is less responsive to the price level at first, and more responsive later. Figure 20–9 illustrates these effects.

SECTION 5

☐ Summary

This chapter introduces several sophisticated aspects of financial systems that were ignored in the macro model of Chapters 16 to 18. These add greater realism to the macro model, but they do not all affect aggregate demand behaviour significantly.

The foreign exchange market is recast to show how net capital inflows rather than net exports respond to the exchange rate in the short run. This is implicit in the uncovered interest arbitrage rationale for net capital inflows even in the intermediate macro model, so it should not be left out. The change leaves the BP curve intact but more sensitive to interest rates. It also delays the response of aggregate demand to changes in the exchange rate, and adds another volatile expectations variable to the model: the expected future exchange rate.

Recognizing the capital stock adjustment rationale behind investment spending makes that part of aggregate demand quite unstable. Investment responses become only temporary, and sensitive to expected future sales levels. A connection between investment and capacity utilization is sensible but presents no problem for the macro model: it is just one more positive income feedback. Adding Tobin's "q theory" rationale for investment provides a direct role for stock market valuation, an extra source of volatility in investment spending.

Adding financial wealth effects to the macro model makes surprisingly little difference. If private domestic wealth is the measure of that wealth that should be relevant, then the wealth impacts from changes in either interest rates, or extra deficits, or even changes in the price level are quite modest. The Ricardian equivalence theorem even questions whether to call government bonds an ingredient of wealth, since they should be offset in each household's notional balance sheet by extra future tax liabilities.

More significant impacts are likely to come from the effect of asset and debt revaluation on the tightness of borrowing constraints facing debtors. Changes in wealth for such firms can produce changes in spending of roughly the same size as the change in wealth. This effect will probably predominate if inflation is unexpected. If inflation is expected and is accompanied by higher nominal interest rates, the cash flow effects of high nominal interest rates on existing debt are likely to choke off any extra borrowing even if inflation is simultaneously lowering debt–equity ratios. Wealth effects can therefore cause the aggregate demand curve to be flatter if inflation is expected, and steeper if it is not.

Key Terms

uncovered interest parity	Tobin's q theory
spot exchange rate	private domestic wealth
expected future exchange rate	washing out assets and debts
overshooting	Ricardian equivalence
Bretton Woods system	theorem
official parity levels	inflation premiums
capital stock adjustment	constrained debtors

Questions and Problems

1. How does the short-run behaviour of the NCI curve in Figure 20–1 depend on the assumption we make about the process of forming expectations of future spot exchange rates? Show the effect of some other alternatives.

2. Why was it that speculators stood to make huge gains and only tiny losses when speculating against weak currencies under the Bretton Woods system?

3. Explain why it is that investment is so much more important than consumption spending in generating cycles.

4. Explain which financial intermediaries are likely to pass on to creditors the effects of fluctuations in market value of their assets.

5. What assumptions are required for the Ricardian equivalence theorem to hold? Are those assumptions realistic?

Suggestions for Further Reading

Ando, Albert and Franco Modigliani. "The 'Life Cycle' Hypothesis of Saving: Aggregate Implications and Tests." *American Economic Review*, March 1963.

Barro, Robert J. "Are Government Bonds Net Wealth?" *Journal of Political Economy*, 1974, 1095–117.

Gertler, Mark. "Financial Structure and Aggregate Economic Activity: An Overview." *Journal of Money, Credit and Banking*, August 1988, Part 2, 559–88.

Tobin, James. "A General Equilibrium Approach to Monetary Theory." *Journal of Money, Credit, and Banking* 1 (1969), 15 29.

——. *Asset Accumulation and Economic Activity*. Chicago: University of Chicago Press, 1980.

PART SIX

Stabilization Policy in Canada

Chapter twenty-one

Monetary Policy Tools and Options

Chapters 16–20 provided a number of explanations of how the macroeconomy works. In all of them, monetary policy has effects on the macro model through changes in the supply of cash reserve assets or high-powered money H. This chapter explains how monetary policymakers can set about changing H, and discusses the effects of the various other powers given to and exercised by the Bank of Canada.

You should learn in this chapter:

1. what powers and responsibilities the Bank of Canada has;
2. how the Bank of Canada manages the supply of cash reserve assets available to the banking system;
3. exactly how the cash reserve requirements of chartered banks are determined;
4. how the Bank of Canada's other powers affect its ability to conduct monetary policy.

SECTION 1

The Bank of Canada

The organization, functions, and powers of the **Bank of Canada** (hereafter referred to as the Bank) were well stated in the Bank's own submission to the Royal Commission on Financial Management and Accountability in March 1978. This section quotes extensively from that submission and its appendix.[1]

---

[1] Extracts are reprinted from the *Bank of Canada Review*, June 1978.

Organization of the Bank of Canada

The Bank of Canada was set up in 1934 by the Bank of Canada Act and has been owned entirely by the government since 1938. Each year the Governor of the Bank reports to the Minister of Finance, and each year the Bank's considerable profits (entirely from seigniorage, the printing of money) flow directly into the government's coffers.

> The responsibility for the affairs of the Bank of Canada rests with a Board of Directors composed of the Governor, the Senior Deputy Governor, and twelve directors appointed from diversified occupations for three-year terms by the Minister of Finance with the approval of the Governor-in-Council [that is, Cabinet]. The Deputy Minister of Finance is also a member of the board but does not have the right to vote. ... No director can be a director, officer, or shareholder of a chartered bank, ... or an investment dealer that acts as a primary distributor for new Government of Canada securities. The directors appoint the Governor and the Senior Deputy Governor, also with the approval of the Governor-in-Council, for seven-year terms during good behaviour. ... The Board normally meets seven times a year. Between its meetings an Executive Committee, composed of the Governor, the Senior Deputy Governor, two other directors and the Deputy Minister of Finance (without a vote), acts for the Board and has all the powers of the Board.
>
> The presence of the Deputy Minister of Finance on both the Board of Directors and the Executive Committee provides a formal channel of communication between the Bank of Canada and the Department of Finance. It is supplemented by many other close contacts of a less formal character.
>
> The Governor is Chairman of the Board and Chief Executive Officer of the Bank and handles the direction and control of the Bank's affairs on behalf of the Board.

These passages give the impression of a central bank run by a board of directors, much like other corporations.

> A number of factors tend, however, to focus responsibility on the Governor. ... Since other directors [other than the Governor and Senior Deputy Governor] are expected to devote only a small part of their time to the affairs of the Bank and are not required to be expert in the field of monetary policy, it would not be reasonable to look to them to formulate monetary policy. ... In practice, the Governor and the Senior Deputy Governor, with the assistance of their senior officers, formulate and conduct monetary policy, direct the other business of the Bank, and report to the Board and Executive Committee at the regular meetings. On the basis of these reports ... the Board has the responsibility for satisfying itself that the Bank is being well run in all major respects or for taking initiatives to improve the situation.

The preceding passages give the impression that monetary policy is the preserve of the Governor and the Senior Deputy Governor. In almost all circumstances this is accurate. However,

> … the fact that the Bank of Canada operates with a large measure of independence does not mean that the Government can be relieved of the ultimate responsibility for monetary policy. … The [Bank of Canada] Act now provides for regular consultation between the Governor and the Minister of Finance and for a formal procedure whereby, in the event of a disagreement between the Government and the Bank which cannot be resolved, the Minister with the approval of the Governor-in-Council may issue a directive to the Bank as to the monetary policy it is to follow.[2]
>
> The directive must be in writing, in specific terms, applicable for a specified period and published forthwith. This provision of the Act makes it absolutely clear that the Government must take the ultimate responsibility for monetary policy but the Bank is in no way relieved of its responsibility so long as a directive is not in effect. …
>
> Although it is not possible to foresee all of the conditions which might give rise to the issuance of a directive to the Bank, it seems most likely that one result would be the resignation of the Governor since a directive would hardly be necessary if he felt he could in good conscience carry out the policy favoured by the Government. For the independent status of the Bank to be meaningful, therefore, the Governor must be prepared at all times to insist on the policies which the Bank believes to be right and to be ready to resign in the event that he is overruled by a directive.

The net result of this special procedure for a directive to the Bank (a procedure that has never been used) has been to make the Minister of Finance very cautious about publicly expressing anything but support for the policies of the Bank. Any hint of disagreement, publicly expressed, might force the Minister into using a directive. The use of a directive would bring about the Governor's resignation and start a crisis that would do serious damage to the Minister's political career. That is a cost ministers of finance will incur only if they are completely convinced the Bank is in serious error. Under all other circumstances the Governor is free to formulate and defend his monetary policy unopposed (in public) by the Minister of Finance. Any objections the government has will be conveyed privately through the Deputy Minister's participation on the board and executive committee, or through the regular consultations of the Governor with the Minister of Finance.

---

[2] This provision was put into the Bank of Canada Act in 1967, following a misunderstanding between Governor James Coyne and the Diefenbaker government in 1960–61 over who had the final responsibility for monetary policy. The effect of the provision, paradoxically, has been to give the Governor of the Bank greater discretion than before. See J.L. Granatstein, "The Untouchables," *Saturday Night*, April 1983, for a clear and colourful account of how central bankers have interacted with governments in Canada.

Internally, the Bank has several operating departments that carry out its day-to-day securities business, and several research departments that keep abreast of changes in financial markets and of research into macroeconomic behaviour. A large, well-qualified staff in these departments (including many of the brightest graduates of money and banking courses) generate a flood of research memoranda and regular forecasts from several large-scale econometric models of the economy. Once a week all of the Bank's senior staff (the Governor, deputy governors, advisors, and department chiefs) assemble to review the state of the economy and to discuss the current policy stance in the light of it. It is in this body of well-informed experts that monetary policy initiatives are formulated.

The degree of independence of central banks from their parent governments varies widely between countries. The German Bundesbank is the most independent, the Bank of England quite dependent, and the U.S. Federal Reserve somewhere in between. The Bank of Canada is closer to the Bundesbank's situation than to that of the Bank of England. The issue at stake is seen to be the time horizon used in making monetary policy decisions: it is assumed that governments will tend to take into account mainly short-run impacts up to the next election, while independent central bankers appointed for long terms will take a longer view.

Objectives and functions

The objectives of the Bank of Canada are laid out somewhat vaguely in the preamble to the Bank of Canada Act:

> To regulate credit and currency in the best interests of the economic life of the nation, to control and protect the external value of the national monetary unit and to mitigate by its influence fluctuations in the general level of production, trade, prices, and unemployment, so far as may be possible within the scope of monetary action, and generally to promote the economic and financial welfare of the Dominion.

The Bank of Canada is also the fiscal agent for the federal government. This role is mostly irrelevant to monetary policy, except that as a by-product it gives the Bank one additional means of influencing the financial system. The job of fiscal agent includes:

1. handling all federal government receipts and payments, as holder of the government's chequing account;
2. transferring the government's deposit funds between its chequing account (in the Bank of Canada) and its non-chequing, interest-bearing deposit accounts (in the chartered banks);
3. issuing and underwriting all government bond and treasury bill offerings;
4. buying and selling foreign currency assets in the name of the **exchange fund account**, a fund held in the name of the Minister of Finance.

The Bank of Canada functions as the bank of settlement for the Canadian payments system. This means that the Bank of Canada holds deposits of all clearing members of the payments system with which net clearing balances can be settled at the end of each day.[3]

The Bank of Canada also functions as a backstop to the financial system, as lender of last resort to chartered banks, to other members of the Canadian Payments Association (CPA), to federal and provincial governments, and to money market jobbers. This function allows the Bank to keep default risk levels low, but has little relevance for stabilization policy.

The Bank of Canada is a financial intermediary, although a special one charged with a range of extra service functions as the government's fiscal agent. Table 21–1 shows the composition of the Bank of Canada's balance sheet in April 1991. Almost all of its assets are in interest-earning debts of the federal government. Over 98 percent of the Bank's debt pays no interest. The Bank of Canada's interest spread is therefore the same as its asset yield. Profit is not in any way the goal of the central bank, but central banking has always been very profitable, even after allowing for large research departments and expensive activities as fiscal agent. In 1990, for instance, the profit of the Bank of Canada was almost two-thirds as large as that of all chartered banks put together, with less than one-twentieth of the assets.

SECTION 2

▨ Cash reserve management

The Bank of Canada has an effective monopoly of **cash reserve assets**, also known as **high-powered money**. As discussed in Chapter 11, the Bank Act currently specifies that chartered banks must hold a certain legal minimum amount of cash reserve assets per dollar of each type of deposit liability. Even when this provision is removed (which will be by the end of 1994), a by-law of the Canadian Payments Association requires that all direct clearing members of the CPA hold their cash reserves for clearing purposes as deposits in the Bank of Canada, and the direct clearers will always have some minimum desired clearing balance. In addition, all deposit-taking institutions will continue to need substantial quantities of Bank of Canada notes (one of the cash reserve assets) in their branches and automated teller networks. By varying the total of cash reserve assets available relative to the total required by the banking system — an action known as **cash reserve management** — the Bank of Canada can influence the level of short-term interest rates and the amount of deposit liabilities that banks make available to the rest of the economy. In this section we will look at how the

---

[3] Smaller members of the Canadian Payments Association have their cheque-clearing losses settled through a clearing member, rather than through the Bank of Canada. The smaller members keep their clearing balances with the clearing member instead of with the Bank of Canada.

TABLE 21–1: Balance sheet of the Bank of Canada, April 3, 1991

	$ million	Percent
Assets		
Government of Canada securities:		
treasury bills	10 738	46.6
bonds	10 024	43.5
of which, held under purchase and resale agreements	242	1.1
Advances to CPA members	171	0.7
Foreign currency securities and deposits	1611	7.0
Other assets	486	2.1
Total assets	23 029	100.0
Liabilities and Equity		
Notes in circulation	20 374	88.5
of which, held by banks	3 881	16.9
held by public	16 493	71.6
Canadian-dollar deposits	2 312	10.0
of which, Government of Canada	12	0.1
chartered banks	1 703	7.4
other CPA members	124	0.5
other	473	2.1
Foreign currency liabilities	193	0.8
Other liabilities and equity	151	0.7

Source: Bank of Canada, *Weekly Financial Statistics.*

Bank of Canada manages the level of cash reserves of the banking system, and how chartered banks can react.

Sources and uses of cash reserve assets

To see how the Bank manages the total of cash reserve assets, look at a simplified version of the Bank of Canada's balance sheet in Table 21–2. Total cash reserve assets, labelled H in Chapter 16 (for the stock of high-powered money), consists of currency in circulation outside banks (CUR) and chartered bank reserves (CBR). The stock of high-powered money plus the other liabilities (OL) and the **government deposits** (GD) make up total liabilities of the Bank of Canada. Total liabilities must by definition equal total assets: government treasury bills and bonds (TB) plus advances (ADV) plus foreign currency assets (FCA) plus other assets (OA).

    In equation form:

$$Assets = CUR + CBR + GD + OL \tag{1}$$

TABLE 21–2: Simplified balance sheet of the Bank of Canada

Assets		Liabilities	
Treasury bills and bonds	TB	Currency held by public	CUR
Advances to money market and CPA members	ADV	Currency and deposits held by chartered banks	CBR
Foreign currency assets	FCA	Government deposits	GD
Other assets	OA	Other liabilities	OL

The stock of high-powered money H is the sum of CUR and CBR in Table 21–2, so Equation (1) can be rewritten:

$$Assets = H + (GD + OL).$$

So

$$
\begin{aligned}
H &= Assets - (GD + OL) \\
&= (TB + ADV + FCA + OA) - (GD + OL).
\end{aligned}
\tag{2}
$$

Managing the stock of high-powered money is therefore equivalent to managing the items on the right-hand side of Equation (2).

An alternative way of looking at cash reserve management is to focus just on chartered bank reserves, CBR. These are by definition equal to the stock of high-powered money less currency in circulation outside banks. We can derive a chartered bank reserve equation simply by subtracting CUR from each side of Equation (2):

$$CBR = TB + ADV + FCA + OA - GD - OL - CUR. \tag{3}$$

The Bank of Canada's week-to-week monetary policy consists of mainly of monitoring all the items on the left-hand side of Equation (3), and then adjusting the items under the Bank's control as needed to leave CBR at the desired level. The desired level of CBR is thought of in terms relative to the level of CBR chartered banks are required to hold under the Bank Act: a level of CBR greater than what is required causes interest rates to fall, while a level less than required causes interest rates to rise. One can describe Bank of Canada policy in fact as one of managing *excess* cash reserves of banks, rather than managing total cash reserves. The upcoming Bank Act revision will reduce the levels of CBR that banks require, but there is so far no reason to expect a change in the Bank of Canada's basic approach of conducting monetary policy by managing excess cash reserves.

To appreciate the Bank's position in managing CBR it will help to discuss the kind of variation to be expected in each item on the left-hand side of Equation (3) for CBR, and the extent to which each can be controlled by the Bank.

Advances. Advances to money market dealers through purchase and resale agreements (PRAs), or to members of the Canadian Payments Association can

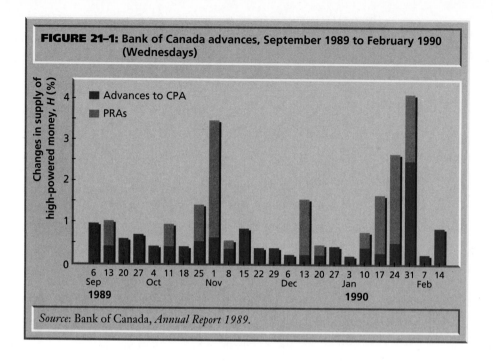

FIGURE 21–1: Bank of Canada advances, September 1989 to February 1990 (Wednesdays)

Source: Bank of Canada, *Annual Report 1989*.

cause significant changes in CBR, but only over very short periods; advances and PRAs are both very short-term arrangements that unwind themselves automatically in one or two weeks. Figure 21–1 shows a sample of the volatility of advances, from late 1989 to early 1990. On occasion, such as late January 1990 when the Bank of Canada was supporting the Canadian dollar with a sharp run-up in interest rates, advances can cause large and abrupt changes in the supply of cash reserve assets.

Foreign currency assets. The Bank of Canada does not have complete control over its foreign currency assets, because it has specific agreements with other major central banks to intervene to dampen fluctuations in the price of the Canadian dollar in each major currency. That is, much of the Bank's exchange market intervention is precommitted rather than discretionary. Most of that intervention is undertaken through the government's exchange fund account, but sometimes the Bank's own foreign currency assets are involved as well. In January–February 1990, for instance, the Bank ran its holdings of foreign currency assets down to zero in four weeks. It is fair to regard foreign currency assets as largely uncontrollable and occasionally volatile.

Government deposits. All payments from or to the federal government first go into or out of the government's deposit account in the Bank of Canada. This happens whether the payments are for current taxes and expenditures, for redemptions of maturing bonds or treasury bills, or for purchases of newly issued bonds. Purchases and sales of foreign exchange for the government's

TABLE 21–3: Monetary policy actions, January 1991

Balance sheet item	Change ($ billion)	Effect on Bank of Canada deposits of chartered banks
(a) *Uncontrollable items*		
Advances	−0.1	−0.1
Currency held by the public	−0.9	0.9
Currency held by banks	−1.6	1.6
Net foreign exchange assets	−1.3	−1.3
Other assets	0.3	0.3
Other liabilities	0	0
total effect		1.3
(b) *Controllable items*		
Treasury bills not held under PRAs	−0.4	−0.4
Government of Canada deposits	0	0
total		−0.4
(c) *Net effect on chartered banks' deposits in the Bank of Canada*		0.9

Sources: Bank of Canada, *Annual Report* 1990, p. 51; *Bank of Canada Review*, Table B1. Components may not add due to rounding.

exchange fund account also cause large flows into and out of the government's deposit account in the Bank of Canada.[4] The Bank of Canada has no trouble offsetting these fluctuations with transfers to or from the government's accounts in chartered banks, so government deposits are firmly under the Bank's control.

Currency in circulation. Currency in circulation changes both seasonally (more at Christmas and towards August) and randomly. Fortunately, random fluctuations of public currency holdings from month to month are seldom more than 1 percent of total chartered bank reserves. Seasonal fluctuations are much larger but present no problem because they are so predictable.

The Bank of Canada controls its holdings of treasury bills TB as well as the size of the government deposit GD in Equation (3). It can therefore counter changes in other items with any combination of changes in TB or GD. Table 21–3 shows, for example, the changes used in January 1991. By month-end the Bank wanted banks' deposits in the Bank of Canada to rise by $0.9 billion from its level of the previous month. As it happened, changes in uncontrollable items would have caused an increase of $1.3 billion, so the Bank of Canada

---

[4] For instance, the government's account in the Bank of Canada rose to $507 million on 14 February 1990, from $10 million the previous week; this was at the end of a large three-week slide of the Canadian dollar.

FIGURE 21–2: Shift of treasury bills from the Bank of Canada to chartered banks

Bank of Canada				Chartered banks	
Assets		**Liabilities**		**Assets**	**Liabilities**
Treasury bills	−100	Government deposits	−100 +100	Treasury bills +100 Reserves −100	
		Chartered bank deposits	−100		

arranged an offsetting reduction of $0.4 billion by reducing its holdings of treasury bills (TB). For this month, GD was left unchanged.

We now discuss the mechanisms for changing the Bank's holdings of both treasury bills and government deposits.

Changing *TB* by open-market operations

Open-market operations are Bank of Canada purchases and sales of government securities. Actual open-market operations almost all involve treasury bills rather than bonds. The Bank of Canada buys bonds only at the time of issue, as part of being the government's underwriter, and holds them to maturity.

Open-market operations are almost all purchases rather than sales. There are so many treasury bills outstanding that huge amounts come due each week (about $1 billion for the Bank of Canada alone). Holdings of treasury bills can be reduced or increased simply by buying less or more, respectively, than are maturing that week. The weekly treasury bill auction is therefore the centrepiece of monetary policy action.[5] The Bank of Canada, as underwriter of each treasury bill issue, has the reserve bid in each treasury bill auction, so it can easily arrange to end up buying exactly the quantity it wants; only the other bidders have to wait to see how many of their bids are filled.[6]

The consequences of treasury bill auctions for the stock of high-powered money can be illustrated with T-accounts for the central bank and the chartered banks for two different cases. T-accounts are simplified balance sheet

---

[5] In between auctions the Bank can buy and sell directly from dealers, or it can initiate "special PRAs" or their reverse, sale and repurchase agreements (SRAs). These are seldom used, however. In 1989, for instance, Special PRAs were outstanding on only 31 days, and SRAs on only 5. Bank of Canada, *Annual Report*, 1989, 35, 57.

[6] See Chapter 6 for a full description of the treasury bill auction.

FIGURE 21–3: Sale of treasury bills by the government to the Bank of Canada; proceeds spent immediately

Bank of Canada				Chartered banks		
Assets		Liabilities		Assets		Liabilities
Treasury bills	+100	Government deposits	+100 −100	Reserves +100		Deposits +100
		Chartered bank deposits	+100			

presentations including only the items that change as a result of the transactions being studied.

Case 1. New treasury bills are auctioned in amounts just large enough to replace maturing issues, so that total treasury bills outstanding do not change (Figure 21–2). Assume that the Bank of Canada buys $100 million less than it has maturing. Others (assume they are chartered banks) must be buying $100 million more than they have maturing.

Bank of Canada holdings of treasury bills fall $100 million, banks' holdings rise by $100 million. The government's Bank of Canada deposit rises by $100 million as the banks pay for their extra treasury bills, and falls by $100 million to pay the Bank of Canada for its net $100 million excess of maturing treasury bills. The banks pay for their extra treasury bills by drawing down their deposits in the Bank of Canada, so chartered bank reserves fall by $100 million.

Had the Bank of Canada instead bought $100 million more treasury bills than it had maturing, all the signs in Figure 21–2 would be reversed. Chartered bank reserves would have risen by $100 million.

Case 2. New treasury bills are auctioned to raise $100 million more than the value of maturing treasury bills (Figure 21–3). Assume that the money raised will be spent almost immediately, and that the treasury bills are bought by the Bank of Canada.

The Bank of Canada increases its treasury bill holdings and the government's Bank of Canada deposit by $100 million. As the government spends the money, the extra $100 million is deducted from its account and added to private sector accounts in chartered banks. After the government's cheques have been cleared, chartered bank deposits in the Bank of Canada rise by $100 million. Chartered bank reserves have increased.

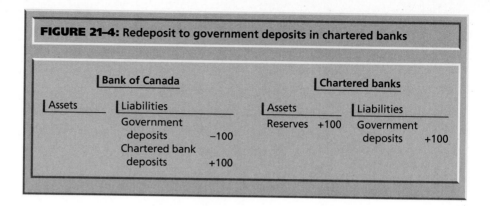

FIGURE 21–4: Redeposit to government deposits in chartered banks

Changing *GD* by federal deposit transfers (drawdowns and redeposits)

The Bank of Canada prefers federal deposit transfers to open-market operations for changing chartered bank cash reserves. Transfers between the government deposit in the Bank of Canada and government deposits in chartered banks are no different in principle from those of any individual who shifts funds from one type of deposit to another. However, because one deposit is in the Bank of Canada and the others are in chartered banks, transfers of federal deposits will change the level of chartered bank reserves. Transfers to federal deposit accounts in chartered banks (known as **redeposits**) will increase bank cash reserves; transfers to the federal deposit account in the Bank of Canada (known as **drawdowns**) will decrease bank cash reserves. In each case cash reserves will change by the amount of the transfer.

Figure 21–4 shows the T-account entries for a $100 million redeposit. Chartered banks increase the government deposit by $100 million and the Bank of Canada adds $100 million to their deposits with the Bank of Canada. On the Bank of Canada's balance sheet the deposit owing to the federal government is reduced by $100 million and deposits owing to the chartered banks rise by $100 million. Chartered bank reserves have increased.

There are two reasons for preferring federal deposit transfers over open-market operations. First, in using federal deposit transfers the Bank of Canada does not intervene directly in any financial market to buy or sell, so it does not run the risk of causing a distortion in relative yields. Such a risk is always present for large open-market operations, since the Bank of Canada cannot spread its purchases and sales over a wide range of different assets such as commercial paper or provincial bonds. Second, federal deposit transfers are easy and they affect bank cash reserves the next day.

FIGURE 21–5: Foreign exchange swap

Bank of Canada		Exchange Fund Account	
Assets	**Liabilities**	**Assets**	**Liabilities**
Foreign currency assets +100	Government deposits +100	Foreign currency assets −100	Debt to government −100

Foreign exchange swaps

There is a limit to the size of federal deposit transfers that is possible if one of the types of deposit account is very small. Redeposits of federal government balances in chartered banks cannot be large if the government's Bank of Canada account itself is not very large. Typically, that account has not been large. Yet the Bank of Canada's main need has been to increase chartered bank reserves, which calls for just such redeposits. **Foreign exchange swaps** with the federal government's exchange fund account (EFA) are one answer to this problem.

Foreign exchange swaps serve to boost the federal government's account in the Bank of Canada without the need for extra taxes or bond issues. The Bank of Canada buys up some of the foreign currency assets held as official foreign exchange reserves by the exchange fund account. Normally, one would expect the EFA's Canadian-dollar deposit in the Bank of Canada to be increased by the value of the foreign asset sale, but the EFA holds no Canadian-dollar deposits anywhere. Instead, any Canadian funds received by the EFA are automatically repaid to the government to reduce the EFA's debt to the government (the debt that "finances" the EFA's entire holding of foreign currency assets, in an accounting sense); the Canadian-dollar funds received by the EFA therefore increase the government's deposit in the Bank of Canada. Now that the government has a larger Bank of Canada deposit, larger redeposits can be made to raise CBR. Figure 21−5 illustrates the accounting steps involved.

SECTION 3

⬛ Cash reserve requirements

What the Bank aims to do with cash reserve management is to change the banks' *excess* cash reserves. Chartered banks use excess cash reserves to buy up extra treasury bills and other money market assets in the short run. These purchases drive down short-term yields and expand the money supply through the normal deposit expansion process. Those are the outcomes the Bank of

Canada wants to achieve. Thus, what matters in cash reserve management is not the absolute level of cash reserves, but only whether cash reserves are above or below the level the banks wish to hold. The level that Canadian banks wish to hold is just high enough to meet the legal **cash reserve requirement**, and no higher. In this section we look at the legal cash reserve requirements in detail. These requirements are in transition between the levels of the 1980 cash reserve requirement and the zero specified in the new Bank Act. We will discuss the 1980 Bank Act first, and then the changes to be made in the new Bank Act. The new Bank Act provisions will be phased in over 24 months following the Act's proclamation in late 1991 or 1992.

The 1980 Bank Act

Cash reserve requirements are specified in the Bank Act as various percentages of deposit liabilities outstanding. The percentages have been 10 percent of Canadian-dollar demand deposits, 3 percent of foreign currency deposits held by Canadian residents, 2 percent of reservable Canadian-dollar term and notice deposits, plus 1 percent more for amounts over $500 million, and 0 percent for all other deposits. Reservable term and notice deposits are defined to exclude all term deposits that at time of issue were not redeemable within one year of the date of issue. In April 1991 the weighted average reserve requirement on reservable deposits was 3.79 percent.

Regulations issued under authority of the Bank Act spell out exactly how cash reserve requirements are to be met. The effect of these regulations is that required reserves for the current month are based on measures of deposits and Bank of Canada notes as of roughly six weeks earlier. For instance, the **statutory deposit** totals to be used in calculating required cash reserves for January are the average of Wednesday deposit totals from the second half of November and the first half of December. The *statutory* level of vault cash (the name given to chartered banks' holdings of Bank of Canada notes) to be used in calculating January's holdings of cash reserves is measured as the average of actual vault-cash holdings on those same four Wednesdays. Only holdings of Bank of Canada deposits are calculated using levels from January. That is, the level of reserves required and the level of vault cash that will be counted in those reserves are both known and fixed in advance of the month for which the reserve requirement must be met.

It may help to see cash reserve requirements in equation form. If we ignore the detail about the first $500 million of reservable notice and term deposits having a 1 percent lower reserve ratio, the cash reserve requirement is

$$CBR = (BCD + VC^*) > (0.10\,DD^* + 0.03\,FCA^* + 0.03\,TND^*), \qquad (4)$$

where BCD is Bank of Canada deposits, VC is vault cash, DD is Canadian-dollar demand deposits, FCA is foreign currency deposits of residents, TND is reservable Canadian-dollar term and notice deposits, and the asterisk denotes statutory (that is, lagged) measurement. Subtracting VC^* (the statutory measure of vault cash) from both sides of Equation (4) gives the cash reserve constraint for the only component of cash reserves that banks can adjust during the current month:

$$BCD > (0.10\,DD^* + 0.03\,FCA^* + 0.03\,TND^*) - VC^*. \qquad (5)$$

Chartered banks must keep at least enough Bank of Canada deposits on hand to make up the difference between total required reserves and statutory vault cash.

Finally, regulations under the 1980 Bank Act further specify that the Bank of Canada deposit holdings of each bank need satisfy Equation (4) only on average over each of two two-week **reserve-averaging periods** in the month. Bank of Canada deposits can be below the requirement on some of the days, provided that for the whole averaging period the cumulative excess holding is positive. Equation (4) is therefore better described in this way: the cumulative sum of daily excess cash reserve holdings over the whole averaging period must be greater than or equal to zero.

Cash reserve strategies of chartered banks

Each chartered bank thus knows in advance of each month exactly what the cumulative sum of its daily Bank of Canada deposits must be in order to meet the cash reserve requirement, and each bank directs its liquid asset management toward ensuring that the constraint is met with only the minimum to spare. When the cumulative sum of daily Bank of Canada deposits rises or falls relative to the desired amount, the chartered bank normally adjusts its reserve holdings by purchases or sales of money market assets that take effect the next day. For the last day of the averaging period, however, next-day adjustment is not good enough; clearing losses that reduced the cumulative excess to below zero would have to be made up on the same day by expensive borrowing from the Bank of Canada. "Each bank therefore tries to accumulate over the averaging period a cushion of cumulative excess cash reserves greater than or equal to the largest random clearing loss it anticipates on the last day of the averaging period."[7]

The effect of adding dozens of foreign bank subsidiaries to the Canadian banking system has been to raise excess cash reserves to about twice their previous level. Still the level of excess cash reserves is tiny. In 1988–91 excess cash reserves averaged only 0.06 percent of reservable deposits.

Cash reserve requirements under the new Bank Act

Cash reserve requirements are to be phased out in the new Bank Act.[8] There are two major changes. First, only direct-clearing members of the CPA will have

---

[7] W.R. White, *Management by the Canadian Banks of Their Domestic Portfolios, 1956– 1971: An Econometric Study* (Ottawa: Bank of Canada, 1975), 124.

[8] "The Implementation of Monetary Policy in a System with Zero Reserve Requirements," *Bank of Canada Review*, May 1991, 23–34.

any need for settlement balances in the Bank of Canada. Other deposit-takers will need only vault cash (for their automated teller machines and for normal dealings with their public) and some settlement balance in a deposit with the institution through which their cheques are cleared. Second, only direct-clearing members will be required to maintain settlement balances that average to zero over each month, in addition to whatever vault cash they find prudent.[9] Direct clearers will have a strong incentive to aim very close to that zero average because either alternative will be very expensive. Any excess settlement balance is a sum that could have been invested; its cost is the overnight loan rate that could have been earned otherwise. Any shortfall in the average settlement balance would have to be met by both an overdraft loan at the time of the negative balance (from the Bank of Canada, at Bank rate), and by an advance from the Bank at the end of the averaging period (also at Bank rate); its net cost would be twice Bank rate less whatever was earned on the liquid assets that the direct clearer could have sold to avoid the shortfall in the first place.

If direct clearers do aim at a zero average balance, then the Bank of Canada can be confident that any extra Bank of Canada deposits it creates will be treated as excess settlement balances — that is, that they will be promptly used to make more overnight loans in order to earn interest, thereby influencing the overnight loan rate. In the words of the Bank itself,

> The structure outlined above would permit the Bank of Canada to influence short-term interest rates in a way very similar to that under the current system. That is, by using redeposits or drawdowns to vary the quantity of settlement balances above or below the levels desired by direct clearers, the Bank of Canada could induce downward or upward pressure on very short-term interest rates.[10]

SECTION 4

Other policy tools

The Bank of Canada has other policy tools available besides cash reserve management, but they are relatively unimportant even in the short run. These other policy tools include: (1) changing the *secondary* reserve requirement imposed on chartered banks; (2) setting the Bank rate; (3) advising the federal government on debt management policy (that is, on adjusting the relative supplies of various maturities of federal debt); (4) foreign exchange market intervention; and (5) using moral suasion to produce or prevent certain specific lending or borrowing practices by banks and other intermediaries.

---

[9] The averaging period will end on the second Wednesday of each month.

[10] "The Implementation of Monetary Policy in a System with Zero Reserve Requirements," *Bank of Canada Review*, May 1991, 26.

Secondary reserve requirements

The **secondary reserve requirement** (soon to be abolished) is rather like the human appendix: a useless organ carried over from a much earlier period when it maybe did have some purpose. Banks are required under the 1980 Bank Act to hold an amount of secondary reserve assets at least equal to a specified percentage of their Canadian-dollar deposit liabilities. Secondary reserve assets include excess cash reserve assets, federal treasury bills, and day loans to money market dealers. Secondary reserve requirements were introduced informally by the Bank of Canada in 1955, and have been included in the Bank Act since 1967. The Bank of Canada can raise or lower the secondary reserve ratio by 1 percent per month. There is no secondary reserve requirement at all under the new Bank Act.

Changing the secondary reserve requirement has no useful effect on the economy, and it interferes arbitrarily with competition among banks and near banks, so it has not been used since 1977. An increase in the level of the secondary reserve requirement forces a reallocation of chartered banks' asset portfolios away from other assets and into secondary reserve assets. In effect this means a move into treasury bills and out of general loans. Back when secondary reserve requirements were introduced, bank loans were the only source of short-term credit for most firms. If some of the banks' lending power could be soaked up in larger treasury bill holdings, the growth of business lending could be slowed significantly. Now that business firms can borrow abroad, or from non-banks, or through bankers' acceptances in the money market, the only effect of erecting a barrier to the growth of bank loans would be to steer a larger part of business lending to these other channels; there would be little change in total business lending. Chartered banks think a large part of their profit comes from business lending, so they are not at all keen on the central bank using a policy tool that would divert that business to rival institutions.

So the secondary reserve ratio is left at 4 percent, a level that was only half of what banks wanted to hold anyway in 1990. Its abolition is long overdue.

The Bank rate

The **Bank rate** is the minimum rate at which the Bank of Canada will make advances to members of the Canadian Payments Association. In practice, the Bank makes few such advances (see Table 21–1). Such loans are intended to be last-resort financing, to be used only when other cash reserve adjustments are exhausted. To keep advances as a last resort, they are made only after direct clearers have financed shortfalls with an overdraft, itself at close to the treasury bill rate. The Bank rate is made a penalty rate, 25 basis points higher than the average yield on the latest weekly auction of treasury bills; that guarantees a negative spread for any bank financing liquid assets with advances from the Bank of Canada.

The Bank rate has been set to float with market yields ever since March 1980. Up to that point it was posted by the Bank of Canada with occasional adjustments.

The Bank of Canada's announcements of Bank rate changes became the source of so much political heat (especially in parliament the day after each announced increase), and served to focus on the Bank of Canada so much of the anguish caused by higher rates generally, that in 1980 the Bank pegged the Bank rate to the average yield on treasury bills in the weekly auction.

Debt management

As the fiscal agent of the federal government, the Bank of Canada advises on the proper structure of the public debt and the proper composition of current borrowing. This advice on **debt management** can be used as a vehicle for interest rate management, since changes in the relative amounts of various types of debt outstanding will influence relative interest rates in financial markets. At least in principle it will. In practice, the term structure of the federal debt has so far made little difference to the term structure of interest rates on federal debt. In Chapter 14 we reviewed evidence on the behaviour of relative interest rates in short- and long-term parts of government debt markets. The evidence shows that arbitrage between short- and long-term debt markets is large enough that changes in relative supplies have tiny effects on relative yields. Figure 21–6 illustrates the arbitrage involved. Large changes in borrowers curves have tiny effects on yields because lenders curves are almost horizontal over a large range.[11] A large refunding of treasury bills with long-term bonds would shift the vertical borrowers curves as in Figure 21–6, but there would be little change in the short–long interest differential to show for it.

Nevertheless, the Bank of Canada does report that in February 1989 it bought three-month treasury bills and sold an equal amount of still shorter-term bills precisely in order to counter upward pressure on the highly visible three-month treasury bill rate.[12] This is an example of debt management, so debt management *is* practised occasionally despite the conventional wisdom that arbitrage makes it useless.

Foreign exchange market intervention

We have discussed foreign exchange market intervention in Chapter 16. The Bank of Canada does intervene on a regular basis in the foreign exchange market, because it fears that exchange rates might "snowball" without such dampening interventions. The conventional wisdom and almost all of the evidence suggests that there is little, if any, impact of such intervention by itself; there will be some effect only if intervention is also allowed to cause a change in high-powered money (that is, if it is not sterilized). The uncovered interest parity condition, for instance, implies that central bank intervention could have no effect at all on

---

[11] The lenders curves are each horizontal at the level of yield that provides the same risk-adjusted return on both short and long-term bonds.

[12] Bank of Canada, *Annual Report* 1989, 36.

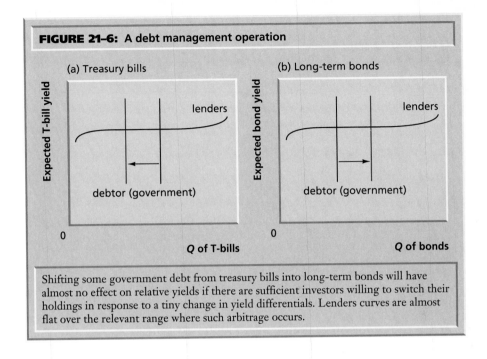

FIGURE 21-6: A debt management operation

(a) Treasury bills

(b) Long-term bonds

Shifting some government debt from treasury bills into long-term bonds will have almost no effect on relative yields if there are sufficient investors willing to switch their holdings in response to a tiny change in yield differentials. Lenders curves are almost flat over the relevant range where such arbitrage occurs.

the spot exchange rate unless it also affected the expected future exchange rate in the same direction. Otherwise, offsetting arbitrage would immediately absorb central banks' actions as soon as they began to influence the spot exchange rate.[13]

Moral suasion

As a tool of monetary policy, **moral suasion** is vaguely defined. In 1978 the Governor of the Bank described it and its use in these terms:

> Moral suasion consists in requesting the banks, and possibly other financial institutions and market participants, to allocate credit, set interest rates, or otherwise conduct their operations in conformity with particular, specified monetary policy objectives rather than solely in the light of their own assessments of current market conditions. ... So far as I am concerned, the Bank of Canada does not now, and probably will not in the future, rely to any great extent on moral suasion. ... Moral suasion is only useful for a short period of time, and in unusual circumstances in which the need for

---

[13] For arguments to this effect from within the Bank, see John Murray and Ritha Khemani, *International Interest Rate Linkages and Monetary Policy: A Canadian Perspective* (Ottawa: Bank of Canada Technical Report 52, 1989).

some special type of action is evident to the affected parties and is ultimately in their own best interest.[14]

This passage suggests that moral suasion would not be very effective if it ran counter to the profitability of banks. Most recorded uses of moral suasion have not done so. In fact, many uses of moral suasion have increased bank profits by reducing price competition among banks. After the 1967 Bank Act revision, the Bank of Canada frequently intervened in vigorous competition between chartered banks for large-scale term deposits, to ask the big banks to compete *less* vigorously. From May 1972 to January 1975 the intervention took the form of the Winnipeg Agreement: banks agreed to observe a ceiling on interest rates on large term deposits of up to one year to maturity.

Moral suasion has generally been effective on the few occasions it has been used. There have been exceptions, however. In 1970, for instance, the Minister of Finance stated explicitly that the banks should not engage in equipment leasing, either directly or through subsidiaries. In 1973 the banks started buying into leasing companies anyway, getting around the Bank Act restriction on ownership of non-bank companies by using exempt companies with a share capital of less than $5 million.[15] On other occasions when the Bank has attempted to use moral suasion on non-bank intermediaries, the attempt was ignored. It seems likely that with globalization of financial markets, the Bank of Canada will find itself increasingly unable to use moral suasion to achieve changes in Canadian financial flows: the Bank will find that the institutions to be persuaded will no longer be all Canadian.

SECTION 5

Summary

The Bank of Canada is the body charged with primary responsibility for designing and carrying out monetary policy in Canada, in pursuit of fairly general objectives set out in the Bank of Canada Act. The Governor of the Bank of Canada and his senior administrative staff bear most of the burden. At the same time, the Minister of Finance has both the power and the responsibility to overrule the Governor should the Minister ever conclude that monetary policy is in serious error.

The Bank serves as banker, securities underwriter, and fiscal agent for the federal government. The Bank is lender of last resort to chartered banks and other members of the Canadian Payments Association, as well as to governments

---

[14]Opening Statement by Gerald K. Bouey, Governor of the Bank of Canada, before the House of Commons Standing Committee on Finance, Trade, and Economic Affairs, 28 November 1978, *Bank of Canada Review*, December 1978, 3–8.

[15]See H.H. Binhammer and J. Williams, *Deposit-taking Institutions: Innovation and the Process of Change* (Ottawa: Economic Council of Canada, 1976), 80.

and to money market dealers. The Bank is the sole issuer of cash reserve assets (currency and Bank of Canada deposits) for the economy.

The main tool of monetary policy is the management of excess chartered bank reserves. The Bank of Canada does this through open-market operations and through drawdowns and redeposits of federal government deposits in the chartered banks.

The Bank of Canada's other monetary policy levers are much more limited and less important. The Bank has been able to adjust the secondary reserve requirement, change the Bank rate, change the structure of federal debt outstanding, intervene to buy and sell in the foreign exchange market, and use what moral suasion it can muster to persuade banks and others to adopt particular lending policies. The first of these levers is ineffective and will disappear, but even the others are not very powerful compared to cash reserve management.

Key Terms

Bank of Canada	foreign exchange swaps
exchange fund account	cash reserve requirements
cash reserve assets	statutory deposits
high-powered money	reserve-averaging periods
cash reserve management	secondary reserve requirement
government deposits	Bank rate
open-market operations	debt management
redeposits and drawdowns	moral suasion

Questions and Problems

1. What control, implicit or explicit, does the government have over the Bank of Canada?

2. Why is the Bank of Canada so profitable?

3. Bond holdings of the Bank of Canada are very large, and the federal deposit is very small. Does it follow that the Bank relies more on open-market operations than on federal deposit transfers to increase the monetary base?

4. List four sources of uncertainty facing the Bank in its attempts to control the money supply by controlling the stock of high-powered money.

5. What uncertainty do banks face in meeting their legal cash reserve requirement?

6. What would be the effect on Canadian high-powered money if the German central bank withdrew some of its deposits in the Bank of Canada (and was paid in Deutschemarks)?

7. What are the similarities between the effects of a change in secondary reserve requirements and the effects of debt management policy?

8. How is moral suasion different from collusion in an informal cartel?

Suggestions for Further Reading

Bank of Canada. *Annual Report*. Annual.

Binhammer, H.H. *Money, Banking and the Canadian Financial System*. Toronto: Methuen, 5th ed. 1988 or later edition.

Boreham, Gordon F. with Ronald G. Bodkin. *Money, Banking and Finance: The Canadian Context*. Toronto: Holt, Rinehart & Winston, 1988.

Department of Finance. *Quarterly Economic Review*.

Martin, Peter. *Inside the Bank of Canada's Weekly Financial Statistics: A Technical Guide*. Vancouver: Fraser Institute, 1989.

Minister of Finance. *Budget Speech*. Occasional.

Shearer, Ronald A., John Chant, and David Bond. *The Economics of the Canadian Financial System*, 2nd ed. Scarborough, Ont.: Prentice-Hall Canada, 1984.

The Financial Post, *The Globe and Mail Report on Business*, and the *Financial Times* all have commentary from time to time on stabilization policy actions of the Bank of Canada.

Chapter twenty-two

Monetary Policy Rules

T he problem of economic policy, as I have observed it for forty years ... is what to do when you don't know what to do, which is the usual situation.

— *Herbert Stein, Chairman of the Council of Economic Advisers under U.S. President Nixon*[1]

In Chapters 16–18 we discovered that the behaviour of inflation, output, and employment in a modern open economy can be described by slow cycles. Even without policy changes, a full business cycle from boom to boom might take a decade or so. Unless one believes completely in the real business cycle explanation of output fluctuations, it seems there are many variations in output and income that the economy could do without. We also discovered that management of total cash reserve assets, H, is likely to have significant effects on income and prices in the short run and on prices in the long run. The channels of effect are described in Chapters 16–20.

In this chapter we ask what kind of management of cash reserve assets or high-powered money is best for the economy. The question is dealt with in several parts. Section 1 examines what aspects of the economy's performance monetary policy should be concerned about. What are the proper goals of stabilization policy, and which of those goals are the proper focus of monetary policy? Section 2 asks the next question after some consensus has been reached on the proper goals for monetary policy: which alternative rule for determining H will maximize the achievement of those goals? Will it be a rule that allows for

---

[1] Herbert Stein, "Comments on Recent Developments in Macroeconomics," *Journal of Money, Credit, and Banking*, August 1988. Part 2, 451.

feedback from the current state of the economy to the level of H, or will it not? If there is to be feedback, which economic variables will be allowed to affect H and which will not? Section 3 discusses the extent to which the central bank should be precommitted to any chosen rule, rather than being free to change its behaviour to better fit unforeseen circumstances. Section 4 presents two rules that have been derived for a central bank that must conduct its policy in an economy rife with uncertainty.

You should learn in this chapter:

1. the source of the costs incurred by society when the economy falls short of the two main objectives of high capacity utilization and low inflation;

2. the logic that must be used in assigning different policy tools to different targets;

3. several of the possible rules that could be used to form monetary policy, and how they affect the stability of output in an uncertain economy;

4. the costs that can be incurred when policymakers are not committed in advance to explicit rules, and when the public knows this in forming its expectations of future policy;

5. the proper response of policymakers when policy actions themselves generate uncertainty.

SECTION 1

◼ Policy goals

In Chapter 15 we discussed two approaches to the analysis of policy objectives. One is the rational politics approach pioneered by James Buchanan and Ronald Coase.[2] The rational politics approach presents politicians and their subordinate government departments as pursuing their own objectives with the tools of public policy, basically minimizing the risk of losing office by using policy tools to generate benefits for influential constituent or interest groups.

The second and more traditional approach to thinking about government policy objectives is to assume that the government is trying to maximize social welfare. Subsidiary, or operational, goals are then derived from that grand premise. Policy derived from the social welfare approach can claim to be optimal policy, since governments are assumed to know that voters will turf them out of office if such optimal policies are not followed. Civil servants are not subject to that threat, but they are assumed to be disinterested servants of the public good.

Economists tend to follow the second approach in thinking about macro-economic policy goals. This chapter will do so as well.

---

[2] A good exposition is in George Stigler, *The Citizen and the State* (Chicago: University of Chicago Press, 1977).

The social loss function

Stabilization policy is designed to reduce instability of output and price levels, because instability causes losses to society in the form of a reduced standard of living or greater uncertainty. Social losses L arise, for instance, from output Y or inflation dP/P being different from target levels Y^T and zero, respectively.[3]

Risk-averse policymakers will care about (a) any *expected* deviation of output from its target level and the *expected* inflation rate and (b) the volatility of possible output levels and inflation rates. The social losses caused by these two features of output and inflation can be summarized in a **social loss function**, an equation that explains which economic behaviours generate social losses. In general algebraic form, the social loss function might be written:

$$L = L[\,(E(Y) - Y^T,\ E(dP/P),\ \sigma_Y,\ \sigma_{dP/P})\,], \qquad (1)$$

where $E(\ )$ denotes an expected value of the variable within the brackets, and σ_Y and $\sigma_{dP/P}$ are the standard deviations of output, and of inflation. All four arguments inside the square brackets of Equation (1) are "bads;" that is, each adds to more of the social loss.

Policymakers may also be concerned about volatility of interest rates (R) and exchange rates (π), since these are particularly important both to financial institutions and to the financial plans of households and firms. Policymakers are not likely to have any target level for the interest rate or the exchange rate except in the short run as a means of changing aggregate demand, but high volatility of either over time is likely to be considered undesirable.[4]

A full objective function for stabilization policymakers may therefore contain six ingredients, as in Equation (2):

$$L = L[\,E(Y) - Y^T,\ E(dP/P),\ \sigma_Y,\ \sigma_{dP/P},\ \sigma_R,\ \sigma_\pi\,], \qquad (2)$$

where σ_R and σ_π are the standard deviations of R and π, respectively.

The weights given to each element in Equation (2) will reflect roughly the relative social costs imposed by high levels of that element. It seems likely that

---

[3] The level of employment, unemployment, or capacity utilization could be substituted for the level of output in the short run, since those four measures track one another fairly closely. In a growing economy, the target income level Y^T will rise with growth of capacity.

[4] Peter Howitt of the University of Western Ontario emphasizes in his critique of monetary policy that changes in interest rates and exchange rates are the means by which monetary policy has effect; limiting the volatility of interest rates and exchange rates may amount to limiting the vigour with which monetary policy can be conducted. *Monetary Policy in Transition: A Study of Bank of Canada Policy, 1982–85* (Scarborough, Ont.: C.D. Howe Research Institute, 1986), p.18.

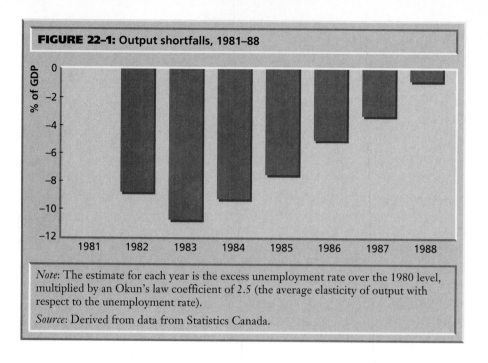

FIGURE 22–1: Output shortfalls, 1981–88

Note: The estimate for each year is the excess unemployment rate over the 1980 level, multiplied by an Okun's law coefficient of 2.5 (the average elasticity of output with respect to the unemployment rate).

Source: Derived from data from Statistics Canada.

the marginal social cost rises for each element in (2) as its level rises. That is, doubling any element will more than double the social cost incurred.[5]

The social costs of excess capacity

The **costs of excess capacity** (when $Y < Y^T$) are basically the forgone value of output that could have been produced had unemployed labour and idle capital resources been fully used instead. If capacity output is $600 billion, as in 1989, each 1 percent shortfall in output is $6 billion wasted — a waste that is repeated for every year that the shortfall continues. A recession and recovery is likely to mean anywhere from 4 to 20 percent-years worth of such waste: the latter means $120 billion at the capacity level of 1989. The total costs of a recession are clearly very large. Figure 22–1 for instance shows a rough estimate of the output forgone because of the severe 1981–82 recession.

---

[5] Professor Henri Theil has suggested a quadratic loss function as a good approximation of the government policymakers' loss function. For example,

$$L = a_1 (Y - Y^T)^2 + a_2 [dP/P - (dP/P)^T]^2,$$

where the coefficients a_1 and a_2 are both positive. *Economic Forecasts and Policy* (Amsterdam: North-Holland, 1961). Remember from Appendix 9–1 that households are often assumed to have a quadratic utility function in portfolio theory.

Output not produced is only a rough estimate of the cost of slow output growth. A more sophisticated measure will include several adjustments.[6] Social costs will be reduced by the value of nonrenewable resources that are saved for the future as a result of lower current output. The cost will be reduced by the value of nonmarket activity (going fishing, painting the house, spending more time with the children) that the unemployed may engage in during periods of unemployment. The cost will be increased by the value of job skills lost by the unemployed and by the value equivalent of the greater uncertainty that unemployment adds to the lives of all who feel their job security threatened. It is likely that extra slack in the economy also lowers the rate of capital formation; with less capital per worker, output per worker will be lower for all future periods; the present discounted value of this cost can be very large. Finally, the social cost could be reduced to allow for the fact that with extra slack there are fewer shortages in the economy—themselves a source of both inefficiency and uncertainty. The net result of all the extra adjustments is not clear, but undoubtedly the costs of a recession are very large.

The costs of slack and unemployment are of course borne mainly by the unemployed. Society does reallocate some of the burden of a shortfall in output growth by handing out unemployment insurance benefits, and occasionally by government bailouts of firms on the brink of bankruptcy. However, that assistance repairs only a fraction of the damage done to the individual victims of a recession, and it does not reduce the total burden on society.

The costs of inflation

The social **costs of inflation** are less visible than the costs of excess capacity, and therefore they are harder to measure. There is vigorous dispute about whether they are larger or smaller than the costs of the excess capacity that would be generated by a recession. The costs of inflation come from inefficient financial arrangements that absorb otherwise useful time and resources, from unnecessary production of barren inflation hedges, from undesirable wealth redistribution, and from reduced investment and lower growth rates that may be caused either by greater uncertainty about price information or by greater tax burdens on capital income.[7]

---

[6]For a good discussion of these adjustments, see Arthur Okun, *Prices and Quantities* (Washington, D.C.: Brookings Institution, 1981), 297–98, or David A. Wilton and David M. Prescott, *Macroeconomics: Theory and Policy in Canada*, 2nd ed. (Don Mills, Ont.: Addison-Wesley, 1987), or Orley Ashenfelter, "The Withering Away of a Full Employment Goal," *Canadian Public Policy*, March 1983, 112–25.

[7]For further discussion of inflation costs, see Stanley Fischer and Franco Modigliani, "Toward an Understanding of the Effects and Costs of Inflation," *Weltwirtschaftliches Archiv*, 114, 1978, 810–33, or S. Fischer, "Towards an Understanding of the Costs of Inflation II," in Karl Brunner and A. Meltzer, eds., *The Costs and Consequences of Inflation* (Carnegie-Rochester Series in Public Policy vol. 15, 1981), or Jack Selody, *The Goal of Price Stability: A Review of the Issues* (Ottawa: Bank of Canada Technical Report No. 54, May 1990).

Inefficient financial arrangements (shoe-leather costs)

Inflation makes for inefficient financial arrangements by putting a tax on money, the so-called inflation tax. Because money pays no interest, inflation reduces its real value each year as though it were taxed at the inflation rate. Rational money-holders respond by shifting their portfolios out of money and into interest-earning assets. In corporations (which hold most of the money supply in Canada) this adjustment is known as tighter cash management. Financial vice-presidents hire more assistants to collect the firm's revenues faster and to keep the funds invested in Eurodollar deposits and other exotic investments right up to the time the money is needed for purchases. Banks co-operate by setting up computer routines that invest corporations' excess demand deposit balances overnight.

In early discussions of the costs of inflation (before bank computerization), the main extra cost of such transactions was thought of as extra trips to the bank, so the costs have come to be known as **shoe-leather costs**. The extra transactions costs due to inflation could be approximated roughly as the annual salary costs of all the extra financial staff of Canadian corporations added since 1960, over and above those needed just to service a growing volume of real output. The entire finance, insurance, and real estate sector employs only 4 percent of the labour force, so this extra cost has to be small as a share of GNP. It is, however, a recurring cost rather than a once-only cost. Peter Howitt suggests that shoe-leather costs are at least 0.1 percent of GDP per percentage point of inflation per year for as long as the inflation lasts, and possibly much higher.[8]

Barren inflation hedges

Because of the inflation tax on money, some investors are persuaded to shift more of their wealth from money into real assets. If these new real assets are produced to satisfy this demand and are used at the same time in production or as consumer durables (for instance, as gold jewellery, fine art, or housing), then society has a net gain in value or output capacity. However, if the real assets are barren like gold bars — that is, if they are held just because of their anticipated capital gains and are not used in either production or consumption — then society has wasted resources in producing them. Without inflation, the demand for those real stores of value could have been met instead by money, which is costless to produce.

This effect of inflation is as though we were all persuaded by some slick salesperson that we should breathe our air through oxygen masks instead of directly from the atmosphere. The cost of barren inflation hedges can be

---

[8] Peter Howitt, "Zero Inflation as a Long-Term Target for Monetary Policy," in Richard G. Lipsey, ed. *Zero Inflation: The Goal of Price Stability* (Scarborough, Ont.: C.D. Howe Research Institute, 1990, 74–75). The estimate of 0.1 percent of GDP comes from the assumptions that (a) without any inflation nominal interest rates would be lower, (b) more money would be held at lower interest rates, and (c) the area under the money demand curve is a proper measure of the services that would have been provided by that extra money holding. The estimate was by Paul M. Boothe and Stephen S. Poloz, "Unstable Money Demand and the Monetary Model of the Exchange Rate," *Canadian Journal of Economics*, November 1988, 785–98.

approximated as the cost of mining and later protecting all the gold and silver and any other barren real assets used only as hedges against inflation. It seems likely that this cost is small relative to those that follow — particularly as the cost of production is a once-only cost.

Wealth redistribution

Inflation redistributes income by taxing net creditors with fixed-yield assets and subsidizing net debtors with fixed-yield debts. We saw in Chapter 14 that nominal yields adjust to compensate partially for expected inflation, though apparently before-tax real yields fall a little and after-tax yields fall a lot. Nominal yields do not adjust at all for unexpected inflation. Further, nominal yields cannot adjust on existing fixed-yield assets; holders and issuers can adjust their nominal yields only when the asset matures and is replaced.

It is hard to estimate the social cost of such redistribution of wealth. Total wealth is not much affected, as we saw in Chapter 20. The main cost is in the extra uncertainty that such redistribution imposes on individuals (the same uncertainty that Robin Hood imposed when he took up residence in Sherwood Forest). As an extreme but thoroughly modern case, consider Peru in 1989. Its inflation rate was 2700 percent in 1989; despite efforts to protect themselves, workers saw their wages rise only 2640 percent, so their real wages fell 60 percent. This is Robin Hood in reverse, robbing the poor instead of the rich. The extra uncertainty could have other serious consequences if it leads to lower investment spending, and therefore a permanently lower capital stock and possibly a lower growth rate of GDP; this consequence is not firmly established, however.

Extra uncertainty about price information

An even less visible effect of inflation is the uncertainty it causes about how to interpret price information. When we are not sure whether price changes are relative price changes (and therefore important market signals to reallocate resources) or part of a general price change (and therefore not a market signal to reallocate resources), we will tend to make inefficient decisions and lower the economy's productivity. This system-wide effect can generate costs that cumulate to totals many times larger than current GDP, but there are no good estimates so far.

It can be argued that the rate of inflation need not generate uncertainty about price levels if the inflation rate is steady. However, Figure 22–2 shows that average levels of inflation and the variability of inflation have gone hand in hand since 1952 in advanced industrial economies such as Canada, so that argument is not supported.

Higher real taxes

A more visible impact of inflation is to reduce the real value of fixed-nominal-value tax shelters such as depreciation allowances for real capital investment. When the real value of this shelter is reduced, the tax burden on real capital assets rises. Investment in new real capital assets drops, and with it drops real output growth. As has been mentioned, the costs of permanently lower output levels can add up to totals several times larger than annual GDP.

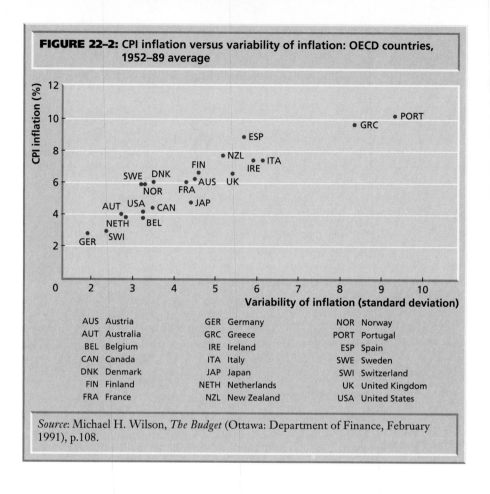

FIGURE 22–2: CPI inflation versus variability of inflation: OECD countries, 1952–89 average

AUS	Austria	GER	Germany	NOR	Norway
AUT	Australia	GRC	Greece	PORT	Portugal
BEL	Belgium	IRE	Ireland	ESP	Spain
CAN	Canada	ITA	Italy	SWE	Sweden
DNK	Denmark	JAP	Japan	SWI	Switzerland
FIN	Finland	NETH	Netherlands	UK	United Kingdom
FRA	France	NZL	New Zealand	USA	United States

Source: Michael H. Wilson, *The Budget* (Ottawa: Department of Finance, February 1991), p.108.

Howitt's estimates of the costs mentioned above are large enough to suggest that the only sensible long-run inflation target is zero. His is not the only opinion, however. Olivier J. Blanchard and Stanley Fischer comment in their advanced macroeconomics textbook:

> Despite an impressive array of models in which inflation is socially costly, there appears to be professional consensus (which we believe is less justified that it was a decade ago) that economics cannot justify the weight put on low inflation as a goal of monetary policy.[9]

---

[9] O.J. Blanchard and S. Fischer, *Lectures on Macroeconomics* (Cambridge, Mass.: MIT Press, 1989), 569.

Note: The figure digging his way to deficit reduction is then-Finance Minister Michael Wilson. The Bank of Canada should have been shown as driving the snowblower.

Source: Phil Mallette, *The Financial Post*, September 18, 1989, p. 14.

Assignment of policy tools

Identifying the proper goals for stabilization policy is not the whole story for monetary policy, however. There is still the issue of how to allocate goals to different stabilization policies. Should monetary policy be used only for some of the goals above, and if so, for which ones? The **assignment of policy tools** was originally recognized as a problem by Robert Mundell in the context of a government having as its two objectives the maintenance of internal balance (full employment) and external balance (equilibrium in the balance of payments), with **fiscal and monetary policy** as its two tools. The same problem may arise when the two goals are different, however.

In Mundell's original problem it does matter how the tools are allocated. Each policy tool must be dedicated to that objective that it has a comparative advantage in controlling; otherwise the economy may be dynamically unstable. In open economies that wish for some reason to target the exchange rate (which must be done by targeting the differential between domestic and foreign interest rates), monetary policy must be assigned to look after the interest and exchange rates, and the other goals must be looked after by fiscal policy. The opposite allocation would lead to ever wilder fluctuations in both employment and interest rates after any initial shock moves the economy off its equilibrium.

In the short run, the logic of the assignment problem does not apply if the targets to be achieved are for inflation and unemployment. It makes no sense to suggest that fiscal policy should be devoted to the unemployment rate, and monetary policy to the inflation rate. The reason is that both fiscal and monetary policy affect inflation and unemployment through the same basic channel: changing aggregate demand. It makes no difference to the impact of aggregate demand on inflation and unemployment that fiscal policy shifts aggregate demand through the IS curve, while monetary policy shifts it through the LM curve. The relative impacts of either monetary or fiscal policy on unemployment and inflation are determined by the slope of the short-run aggregate supply curve, which is presumably the same for both policies. It *is* sensible to discriminate between monetary and fiscal policy on grounds of other side-effects, such as impact on the long-run capital stock or the regional distribution of impacts, but not on the ground that either is relatively more efficient in influencing inflation or unemployment.

In the long run, however, monetary policy does have an important comparative advantage in controlling inflation. As Professor Howitt cautiously puts it:

> Over periods as short as one or two years, inflation and monetary expansion are not closely correlated. But whenever a country has experienced severe inflation over several years, it also has had a rate of monetary expansion significantly in excess of the rate of growth of real output, on average, for several years.[10]

It follows that in the long run, monetary policy must be assigned to the goal of low inflation rather than to some other goal. Otherwise the goal of low inflation cannot be achieved at all.

Even incomes policies, such as wage and price controls, do not have a comparative advantage over monetary policy in lowering inflation except in the very short run of a year or so. Incomes policies are ineffective in lowering inflation by themselves; they are complements to restrictive monetary policy rather than alternatives.[11]

SECTION 2

■ Choice of policy rules

Given a goal for monetary policy, what operating rule for high-powered money H will best achieve it? The first economist to address this problem was William Poole in 1970; his approach has been followed more or less since then in

---

[10] P. Howitt, *Monetary Policy in Transition*, 12.

[11] See, for instance, the discussion in David A. Wilton and David M. Prescott, *Macroeconomics: Theory and Policy in Canada*, 2nd ed. (Don Mills, Ont.: Addison-Wesley, 1987), 350ff.

numerous extensions.[12] Poole compared two extreme monetary rules: the first is to keep H fixed and exogenous (a fixed-H rule); the second is to change H to accommodate all changes in money demand from whatever source, so as to keep the interest rate R unchanged (a fixed-R rule).[13] Poole's original analysis raises most of the important issues involved in choice of policy rules. It can also be illustrated on a simple IS–LM curve diagram.

Poole's model

There are three steps to illustrating Poole's argument using the IS–LM model. The first is to add uncertain demand shocks of two sorts. One sort ("**IS shocks**") causes shifts of the IS curve; they are reflected by adding a random error term to the IS equation derived in Chapter 16. The other sort are "**LM shocks**"; they cause shifts of the LM curve and are reflected by adding a random error term to the LM curve equation in Chapter 16. IS shocks can be caused by changes in taxes, government spending, export demand, or the exchange rate (at a given domestic interest rate, such as would be caused by changes in foreign interest rates or in expectations of future exchange rates). LM shocks can be caused by changes in the money supply multiplier, by changes in relative yields among money substitutes, by financial innovations, by postal strikes, or by changes in financial risks. IS shocks arise in the real sector, LM shocks in the financial sector.

The second step is to recognize that different rules for determining H produce different LM curves. The LM curve for the **fixed-H monetary rule** looks familiar. Holding H constant and exogenous is the assumption we used to derive the LM curve in Chapter 16. With a **fixed-R monetary rule**, however, the LM curve becomes horizontal. Figure 22–3 shows how the LM curve is derived in the fixed-R case. The money supply is set at whatever level will match money demand at the unchanged target interest rate R^T. When real income (or prices or anything else) increases the demand for money, the money supply is increased also. Different real income levels therefore all produce money market equilibrium at the same interest rate R^T.

The third step is to recognize part of the uncertainty in which monetary policy is conducted. Policymakers cannot quickly and accurately observe the current level of real or even nominal income. For example, Statistics Canada

---

[12] William Poole, "Optimal Choice of Monetary Instruments in a Simple Stochastic Macro Model," *Quarterly Journal of Economics*, 1970, 197–216. This approach to stabilization policy has been extended to an open economy by Gordon Sparks in "The Choice of Monetary Policy Instruments in Canada," *Canadian Journal of Economics*, 1979, 615–25, and to include supply shocks in Peter S. Sephton, "The Choice of Monetary Policy Instruments in Canada: An Extension," *Canadian Journal of Economics*, February 1987, 55–60.

[13] The counterpart of the fixed-H rule in the real world is Milton Friedman's recommendation from 1959 on that the stock of high-powered money be left to grow at 4 percent per year—roughly the growth rate of output capacity each year. Fixed-R rules for the short term are implicit in any government decision not to allow rapid demand growth in any year to force interest rates upward. Fixed-R rules are seldom advanced explicitly for more than short terms, but often for several short terms in a row.

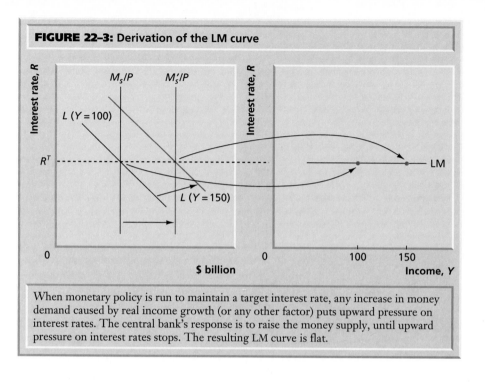

FIGURE 22–3: Derivation of the LM curve

When monetary policy is run to maintain a target interest rate, any increase in money demand caused by real income growth (or any other factor) puts upward pressure on interest rates. The central bank's response is to raise the money supply, until upward pressure on interest rates stops. The resulting LM curve is flat.

releases its first estimates of aggregate output only two months after the end of the period being measured, and revises its first estimate one or more times thereafter — sometimes substantially. The Bank of Canada can observe the interest rate currently and without error, but it cannot find out where the economy is on the horizontal axis of the IS–LM curve diagram until much later. As a result, the Bank cannot tell immediately whether a rise in interest rates is due to a rightward shift of the IS curve (which would raise real income levels) or a leftward shift of the LM curve (which would lower real income levels).

Shifts of IS and LM curves with fixed-*H* and fixed-*R* rules

Now consider and compare the response of aggregate demand to IS shocks under the two monetary rules. Figure 22–4 shows both types of LM curves (LM_H if H is fixed; LM_R if the interest rate R is fixed), intersecting at the target interest rate R^T. The target demand level AD^T will occur if the IS curve is in its expected position IS^e. However, IS shocks could produce actual IS curves and aggregate demand levels to the right or left of IS^e and AD^T respectively, as shown in Figure 22–4. With reserves fixed (along LM_H), surges in the demand for goods are partly crowded out by rising interest rates. With the interest rate fixed (along LM_R), there is no crowding out; the range of possible aggregate demand outcomes is correspondingly wider. That is, a fixed-*H* monetary rule automatically stabilizes

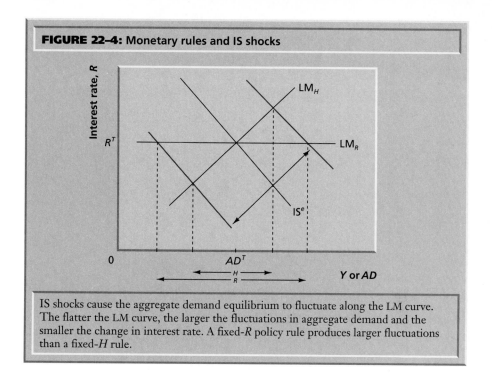

FIGURE 22–4: Monetary rules and IS shocks

IS shocks cause the aggregate demand equilibrium to fluctuate along the LM curve. The flatter the LM curve, the larger the fluctuations in aggregate demand and the smaller the change in interest rate. A fixed-R policy rule produces larger fluctuations than a fixed-H rule.

aggregate demand more than a fixed-R rule when demand shocks are of the IS-shock type.

When demand shocks are to the LM curve, the fixed-interest rule is better. Figure 22–5 shows the result of LM shocks when the IS curve is certain. With the level of H fixed, any positive shock to the demand for money shifts the LM curve to the left and drives up interest rates. Higher interest rates reduce aggregate demand. With the interest rate fixed instead, the positive money demand shock is automatically accommodated by changes in cash reserves. There is no change in interest rates and therefore no change in aggregate demand. The fixed-R rule completely offsets LM shocks, whereas the fixed-H rule transmits them from the financial sector to the real sector.

IS and LM shocks with an intermediate rule

Figures 22–4 and 22–5 show that each rule is the best under some circumstances. Which of the two rules is better overall depends on whether IS or LM shocks are the most important sources of disturbance to aggregate demand. Of course these two monetary rules are not the only rules to choose from. Poole went on to consider whether there might be some combination rule that would perform better than either extreme — one where H changes to some extent with feedback from the economy but not as much as with the fixed-interest rate rule.

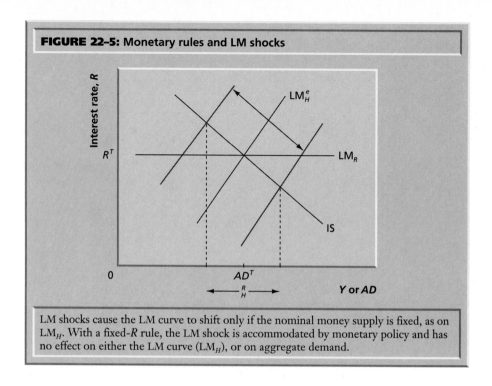

FIGURE 22–5: Monetary rules and LM shocks

LM shocks cause the LM curve to shift only if the nominal money supply is fixed, as on LM_H. With a fixed-R rule, the LM shock is accommodated by monetary policy and has no effect on either the LM curve (LM_H), or on aggregate demand.

How to choose an optimal combination of fixed-H and fixed-R rules is best explained by imagining that the Bank knows that both goods and financial markets are subject to shocks, and is able to detect these shocks at first only by their effects in financial markets; timely estimates of current aggregate demand are not available for a month or two.[14] Imagine that the Bank has set H at a level that is expected to generate an equilibrium interest rate level R^e and the targeted aggregate demand level AD^T, as shown in Figure 22–6. Then assume that the Bank actually observes upward pressure in the money market driving interest rates to R'.

For R' to be the new equilibrium interest rate, either the IS or the LM curve or both must have shifted from the expected positions in Figure 22–6 to raise their intersection to R'. For the Bank to know how to respond, it must decide which curves have shifted and by how much. If the IS curve has raised R by shifting to the right, then monetary policy should be restrictive; H should be lowered until the LM_H curve intersects the revised IS curve at AD^T again. If instead the LM curve has shifted to the left, then cash reserves should be increased

---

[14] This explanation of the logic and intuition behind Poole's argument is given by Stephen F. Leroy and David E. Lindsey, "Determining the Monetary Instrument: A Diagrammatic Exposition," *American Economic Review*, December 1978, 929–34.

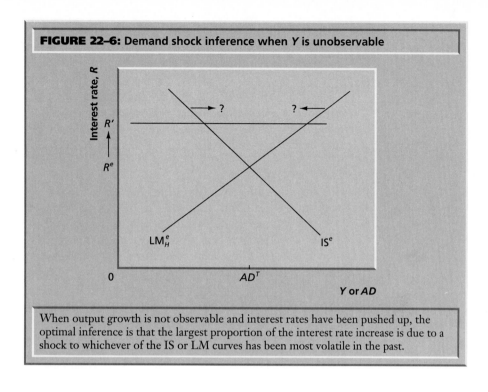

FIGURE 22–6: Demand shock inference when Y is unobservable

When output growth is not observable and interest rates have been pushed up, the optimal inference is that the largest proportion of the interest rate increase is due to a shock to whichever of the IS or LM curves has been most volatile in the past.

to return the LM curve to its original position; otherwise the Bank will find it has allowed a financial disturbance to cause a recession in the real sector.

The Bank's best guess is to assume that the change in interest rate is due to shifts in both IS and LM, in proportions determined by the relative instability of the IS and LM curves in the past. The larger the IS shocks have been in the past, the more of the unexpected rise in R is blamed on the IS curve and the more the Bank of Canada moves to offset what is seen as a disturbance to aggregate demand. The larger LM shocks have been in the past, the more of the rise in R is blamed on the LM curve and the more the Bank moves to offset what is now seen as mainly a financial market disturbance.

Poole's argument brings out two features of monetary rules. First, different monetary rules cause monetary policy to react to different shocks. Under a fixed-R rule, the amount of H created reacts to both IS and LM shocks. Under a fixed-H rule, monetary policy does not react to anything. Different monetary rules can be described and analyzed by the kind of shocks allowed to affect H, and the kind of shocks ignored. Second, the optimal policy will require some feedback from the economy to help the Bank guess what kinds of shocks are occurring.

The question in the real world is which feedback to use. Each month policymakers are deluged with new data, and never do all the data point the same way. Given enough time, the Bank will rely on the feedback of output growth and inflation figures, since those are its ultimate targets. But in the short run of two to six months, the Bank is not sure what is happening to output growth and inflation, and so it needs guidance from other kinds of feedback.

Other monetary rules

Three monetary rules have been suggested other than fixed-R and fixed-H. Each forces monetary policy to react automatically to a different set of shocks, over the short period during which output and inflation outcomes are unknown.

A fixed exchange rate rule

In the 1990s, with sufficient arbitrage to enforce uncovered interest parity, a **fixed exchange rate rule** effectively forces the central bank to set domestic real and nominal interest rates at the world interest rate level.[15] Feedback in the form of changes in U.S. interest rates causes domestic interest rate targets to change in step. Any feedback about domestic conditions does not influence the target interest rate at all; it is all accommodated (for IS shocks) or offset (for LM shocks) by changes in H. Fixed exchange rate rules tend to be long-term commitments, set up so that governments have little discretion to tinker or deviate.

A fixed exchange rate rule makes good sense if for some reason we trust foreign central bankers more than we trust our own, and if we expect foreign economies to experience much the same shocks we will. In the United Kingdom, for example, whose central bank is not very independent of the Cabinet and its short-term political pressures, the adoption of a fixed exchange rate to the Deutschemark is attractive precisely because it commits British monetary policy to follow the same course as that of the German Bundesbank; the Bundesbank has been seen as the most independent and the most anti-inflationary of central banks.

A nominal income rule

The **nominal income rule** calls for varying the growth of H opposite to the growth of nominal income. When faster nominal income growth rates are observed, decreases in H will drive interest rates and exchange rates up and slow nominal income growth down again. As long as nominal income growth is on target, H will be allowed to grow at the same rate as real capacity. That is, H will have feedback only from nominal income. Nominal income growth feedback is slow in coming, only slightly faster than separate feedback on its two ingredients of output growth and inflation. Monetary policy must therefore operate blind or use some other feedback for the two months it takes to produce nominal income figures. On the other hand, feedback on nominal income is more closely related

---

[15] *The Report of the Working Group on Exchange Market Intervention*, commissioned at the Versailles Summit of 1982, concluded that exchange market intervention had little impact unless it was unsterilized—that is, accompanied by changes in domestic high-powered money (Paris, March 1983, 69). In other words, foreign exchange management policy cannot be separated from the regular monetary policy of managing high-powered money.

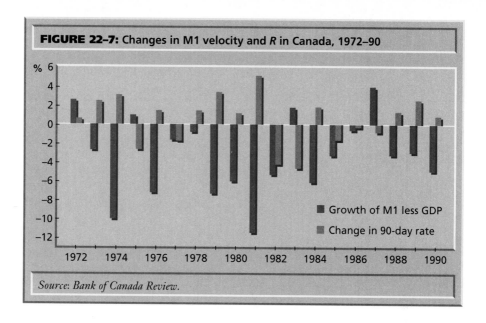

FIGURE 22–7: Changes in M1 velocity and *R* in Canada, 1972–90

■ Growth of M1 less GDP

■ Change in 90-day rate

Source: Bank of Canada Review.

to the two targets of output growth and inflation than to any other feedback, and is therefore less likely to be misleading.

Narrow and broad money rules

The third alternative, the use of **narrow or broad money rules,** is to let the growth of *H* respond to feedback from growth of a broad or narrow money aggregate such as M2, M2+, M3, or M1. All of the monetary aggregates except M2+ are available weekly, with no errors or later revisions. It is hoped that a sufficiently vigorous response of monetary policy to such feedback would move *R* and the exchange rate π in time to stabilize growth of aggregate demand. Monetary rules tend to be couched in specific terms, namely to keep the monetary aggregate itself growing at some target rate (on average, over several months at a time). This presents a problem for narrow monetary aggregates because the growth of M1 demand responds to the general level of interest rates as well as to nominal income growth. A constant growth rate of M1 therefore does not imply even nearly constant growth of nominal income when interest rates are changing. Figure 22–7, for instance, shows how changes in the 90-day commercial paper rate in Canada are associated with large gaps between M1 growth and nominal income growth over the last two decades.

In his review of Bank of Canada policy in the mid-1980s, Professor Howitt favours using feedback from M2 or M2+. Recall from Chapter 19 that the demand for broad money is almost insensitive to the general level of interest rates; demand for M2 is sensitive to interest rate differentials on time deposits and non-money assets, but such differentials do not change much, if at all, as the general level of interest rates rises and falls. The feedback of faster M2 growth is more likely

FIGURE 22–8: Monetary policy decisions

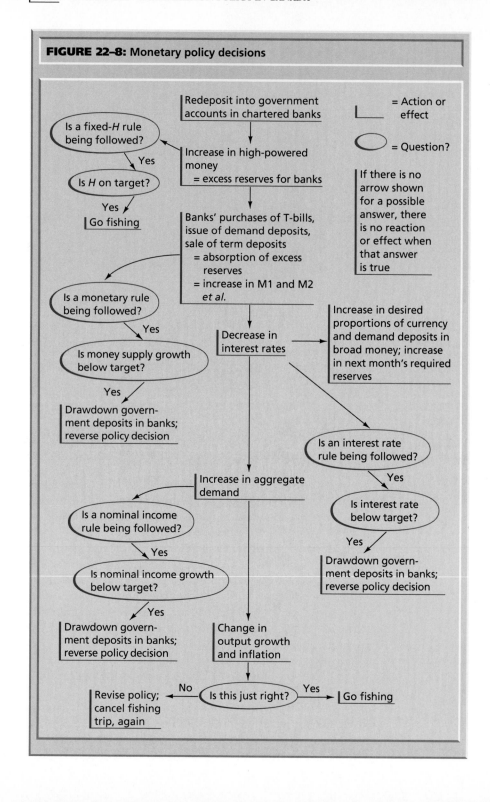

than M1 to reflect faster growth of prices or output, and is therefore a more appropriate signal for monetary policy to react to until the truth about prices and output is revealed a few months later.

A comparison of monetary rules

Each of the five monetary rules discussed in this section uses different information, and each is invoked at a different point in time. Figure 22–8 may help to put these monetary rules into perspective by tying each to a different stage of impact of monetary policy.

The five feedback rules are subject to varying amounts of "noise." Noise occurs, like static in a radio or TV signal, when the indicator used as feedback (for instance, M2 or nominal income) rises or falls independently of movements in output and inflation. Nominal income is subject to the least amount of noise since nominal income growth is made up of output growth and inflation. Unfortunately, nominal income is also the slowest source of feedback. Fixed-H and fixed-R rules are subject to the most noise but are also very quick; each can be monitored daily. Monetary rules lie in between: they are subject to more noise than a nominal income rule, but all except M2+ are available weekly (M2+ is not available until well after output and inflation figures become available).

In practice, the difference between daily and weekly monitoring is not significant. Monetary policy can fail to respond to an aggregate demand shock for up to a month without even hostile observers being able to detect the impact. Only when the failure lasts for several months does it become serious. Of the two types of monetary aggregates used for monetary rules, broad money has been the least subject to noise over the last two decades because financial innovations in payments arrangements and in paying daily interest have affected mainly narrow money totals and not broad money totals. The financial innovations of the future may not be of that type, of course.

There is one other property of different feedback rules that may matter. The feedback rule being followed may influence public expectations of inflation; we have seen in Chapter 17 that public expectations of inflation may be vital to actual inflation. If there is a feedback rule known to be in effect that automatically resists any speed-up of inflation (as do the fixed-H rule, the nominal income rule, and both monetary rules) then the public may expect less inflation in the future than would otherwise be true.

It is hard to assess the significance of this last argument. Howitt, for one, does not believe that expectations of inflation are what drive wage increases in the short run: nominal wage increases in his view are mainly to catch up with wages of workers in other groups. As he puts it,

> Most Canadians simply do not have a firm belief that monetary policy is the primary determinant of the rate of inflation. Even those who hold such a belief do not have anything approaching the sort of detailed quantitative knowledge concerning the connection between monetary policy and inflation that it would take to make accurate, short-term predictions of

inflation based on the future course of monetary policy. Certainly no one I know has such knowledge. Thus, even if firms and workers were able to predict accurately the future course of monetary policy, it is unlikely that many would pay much attention to those predictions when setting their prices and wages.[16]

The experience of 1975–81 supports Howitt's view. In that period the Bank of Canada was following an explicit monetary rule whose impact on inflationary expectations should have been to lower them; the Bank's policy promised to tighten the screws until aggregate demand collapsed. Yet there was no sign until 1981 of expectations being influenced at all by this policy threat even though it had been made some five years earlier and had been repeated constantly by Bank officials. On the other hand, financial market professionals watch the Bank of Canada quite closely when trying to forecast interest rates in the short run, and the fate of aggregate demand is often inferred from interest rate forecasts.

SECTION 3

◼ Rules versus discretion: the value of precommitment

An important debate is now under way in monetary economics about how binding the rules for stabilization policy ought to be. The debate reached a political crescendo in the early 1980s when U.S. President Reagan championed the cause of an amendment to the U.S. Constitution that would have obligated the government to follow a fiscal rule of balancing the budget. In economic theory the pivotal event was a demonstration by Robert Barro and David Gordon that full precommitment to a monetary rule can open up some desirable options for the economy that will remain closed if policymakers insist on keeping some **policy discretion**.[17] Barro and Gordon's argument is worth repeating because it shows clearly a constraint on policymaking that is not considered in the mainstream macro model of Chapters 16–20: a constraint imposed by the private sector's expectations of government policy.

To illustrate the effect of **policy expectations**, assume as in Figure 22–9 that the central bank can move the economy along a short-run aggregate supply curve whose position shifts with each change in the public's inflationary expectations. There exists a whole family of such supply curves, one for each possible expected inflation rate. Assume also that the central bank has a set of preferences shown by

---

[16] P. Howitt, *Monetary Policy in Transition*, 16.

[17] Robert Barro and David Gordon, "A Positive Theory of Monetary Policy in a Natural Rate Model," *Journal of Political Economy*, 1983, 589–610. Their article built on an argument first advanced by F. Kydland and E.C. Prescott in "Rules Rather than Discretion: The Inconsistency of Optimal Plans," *Journal of Political Economy*, 1977, 473–92.

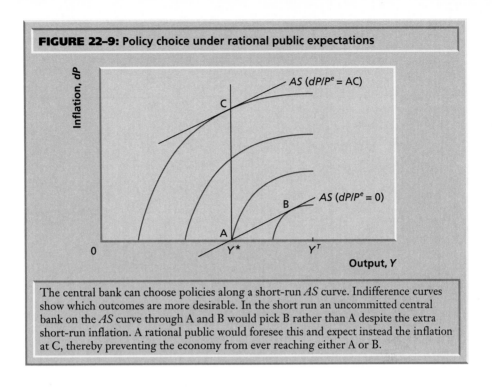

FIGURE 22-9: Policy choice under rational public expectations

The central bank can choose policies along a short-run *AS* curve. Indifference curves show which outcomes are more desirable. In the short run an uncommitted central bank on the *AS* curve through A and B would pick B rather than A despite the extra short-run inflation. A rational public would foresee this and expect instead the inflation at C, thereby preventing the economy from ever reaching either A or B.

the set of indifference curves centred around the point of maximum social welfare where $Y = Y^T$ and $dP/P = 0$. It is critical to this argument that the target level of output Y^T be greater than the natural rate of output Y^*, as shown in Figure 22–9; Y^T can be thought of as "full employment."

The public determines which short-run aggregate supply curve the central bank faces, because it is the public's expectations of inflation that matter to the aggregate supply curve. Now the public forms its expectations by imagining what sort of policy choice the central bank is likely to make.

If the central bank has locked itself into a policy of not allowing output levels to rise above the natural level Y^*, then the rational point for the central bank to choose at Y^* will be the point of zero inflation at A. If the central bank is so locked in, the public will expect that rational outcome of zero inflation; the central bank will then face the lowest aggregate supply curve shown in Figure 22–9, and the economy will be at A.

Discretion and cheating

On the other hand, if the central bank is not locked into a policy constraining Y to Y^*, then the central bank would be tempted to exploit any reputation it had for staunch resistance to inflation by cheating on it: by moving up along the economy's short-run supply curve to higher output levels, whenever the supply curve is flatter than the indifference curves. The extra inflation caused in the short

This argument for rules over discretion has many other applications in everyday life. For instance, both students and professors would be better off if there were no final examinations. Yet students seem to need the incentive of the exam to work properly. Thus, one's first thought is that the optimal policy would be a discretionary one in which the professor promises an exam and then, near the end of term, breaks that promise. This way the students would work and learn but would avoid the trauma of the exam, and the professor would avoid the marking. The problem is that students can anticipate such a broken promise (especially if there is a history of this behavior), so we opt for a "rules without feedback" approach — exams no matter what.

— William Scarth, *Macroeconomics: An Introduction to Advanced Methods* (Toronto: Harcourt Brace Jovanovich, 1988), p. 82.

run is more than compensated for by the extra output achieved. For instance, the central bank would not want to stay at A when it could achieve a better combination in the short run by sliding up to B. Now the public (first its economic analysts, then its journalists, then the rest) can see this logic as well as the central bank, so the public will not believe that zero inflation is likely. The only inflation rate the public will accept as likely is one at which extra inflation is so painful that the central bank will not be tempted to add any more by raising Y above the natural rate. That occurs only at C in Figure 22–9, where the social indifference curve is tangent to the short-run aggregate supply curve. The inflation rate at C will be the public's expected inflation rate. The aggregate supply curve through C is the one along which the central bank must choose, and C is the best point on that curve. C is not nearly as good as A for the economy, so allowing the central bank discretion has left the economy worse off.

Assessment of Barro and Gordon's argument

The logic of Barro and Gordon's argument is inescapable. The applicability of the model to the real world of monetary policy is open to question on several counts.

First, there is Howitt's question of whether the public's expectation of inflation is influenced in advance by expectations of monetary policy conduct. It is obvious that the general public is not much aware of the central bank, let alone what it is doing currently; it is only in third-year university courses that the issue is even brought up. If the public forms its expectations of inflation on the basis of advice from "experts" who are well aware of central bank policy, however, the general public's expectations can be indirectly influenced as Barro and Gordon assume.

Howitt also argues that in the case of Canada at least, the short-run sluggishness of prices (which is what makes the aggregate supply curve less than vertical) is not due to expectations behaviour, but rather to the sluggish adjustment of wages as workers catch up with other groups in Canada's decentralized, uncoordinated, staggered pattern of wage negotiations. Whether public expectations of inflation are influenced by central bank policy is irrelevant if those expectations do not influence wages in the short run. Over time, however, wage demands will speed up if the central bank does consistently choose points such as B over points such as A in Figure 22–9, because some workers will raise wage demands as actual inflation exceeds what is expected, and other workers will follow them to catch up. Howitt's argument delays the effect described by Barro and Gordon, but that is all.[18]

Second, the response by the central bank in Barro and Gordon's model seems too short-sighted. If the central bank is known to take into account not only the short-run output and inflation consequences of choosing B, but also the long-run consequence of ending up at C for many years because of public mistrust, professional central bank watchers could expect the central bank to eschew the short-run benefit of B for the greater long-run benefit of A. Such watchers would keep inflationary expectations of zero inflation. If they could influence others in the economy to expect the same, the central bank could have the best of both worlds: discretion to change its behaviour in the future, but also public faith that it would not exploit that discretion to the public's disadvantage. The economy could reach point A even without full precommitment by the central bank.

Acceptance of the second argument above leads into a third proposition, that discretion does confer some advantages not shown in Figure 22–9. Both Howitt and Lawrence Summers of Harvard University argue that the central bank must expect the unexpected, that there will be special circumstances, as yet unforeseen, where some response will be better than none.[19] The October 1987 stock market crash, higher interest rates in the economies of major trading partners, war in the Middle East, the failure of a large financial intermediary — the list of possible emergencies is long. Precommitment to any manageable rule prevents any response to such emergencies.

---

[18] Note that the sluggish adjustment of wages to faster inflation is an institutional response that is itself endogenous. We allow sluggishness because we live in an economy where, so far, sluggishness has not cost us much. If inflation were to speed up as a result of some new monetary rule, we would speed up our wage response as well. This is an example of the Lucas critique, that simulating the effect of changes in policy rules must take into account changes in economic structure that are tied in any way to existing policy rules. Robert E. Lucas, Jr., *Econometric Policy Evaluation: A Critique* (Carnegie-Rochester Series on Public Policy vol. 1, 1976), 19–46. In 1990, for instance, some unions built COLA clauses without ceilings into their wage contracts, precisely because they foresaw an acceleration of inflation when the federal Goods and Services Tax was introduced in January 1991. Such COLA clauses speed up the wage response to inflation.

[19] L. Summers, "Comments on 'Postwar Developments in Business Cycle Theory: A Moderately Classical Perspective'," *Journal of Money, Credit, and Banking*, August 1988, Part 2, 472–75.

Note that this argument is not an argument against rules. It is merely an argument for allowing monetary policy response to shocks not explicitly provided for in whatever rule is chosen for normal circumstances.

SECTION 4

Treatment of uncertainty

Governments and central banks face several kinds of uncertainty. Government policymakers are uncertain about exactly how the economy works, despite the conviction with which many economists put forth their own explanations. The government is not sure of the size of aggregate demand multipliers or the size of supply responses. Since the government cannot be sure of the levels of many of the exogenous variables in its own economic forecasting models, it must expect the unexpected. Policymakers know there are lags in the responses of output, employment, and price levels to both demand and supply shocks, but they do not know how long those lags will be. Finally, measurement of aggregate demand and output levels occurs so slowly and is subject to so much revision that policymakers are uncertain about even the current state of the economy; their measurements lag several months behind. From this perspective, running monetary policy is much like steering a long freighter in the fog.

What account should policymakers take of these uncertainties?

The certainty-equivalent rule

The proper reaction to all this uncertainty is not simply to hide under the bed. Some kinds of uncertainty do not matter to the conduct of stabilization policy. These kinds of uncertainty increase risks in the economy, but the risks are not affected by the conduct of stabilization policy. Uncertainties about the levels of all exogenous variables (future wealth, foreign interest rates, expectations of investors, and so on) are of this type. Optimal policy strategy in the face of this type of uncertainty is to make an unbiased estimate of the effects of policy changes on the target variables and then to proceed as if that estimate were known for certain; for obvious reasons, this is known as the **certainty-equivalent approach**.[20] Theil has shown that, even where changes in the policy or in exogenous variables affect output and inflation with long and possibly uncertain lags, the errors from the certainty-equivalent approach will be less serious than the errors from any other approach.

---

[20]H. Theil, *Economic Forecasts and Policy* (Amsterdam: North-Holland, 1961). See also Pierre Fortin, "Monetary Targets and Monetary Policy in Canada: A Critical Assessment," *Canadian Journal of Economics*, November 1979, 631; Fortin suggests on the basis of U.S. results that Canadian forecasters may well produce unbiased forecasts of real GNP growth up to four quarters ahead.

> My economic advisers were seldom in agreement — but they were never in doubt.
>
> — *Former U.S. President Richard M. Nixon*

Brainard's rule of caution

Optimal stabilization policy is affected if there is uncertainty about the effect of policy tools. This type of uncertainty matters because the level of uncertainty about economic performance of the economy must increase as the size of policy change increases. William Brainard of Yale University demonstrated in 1967 that optimal policy will be more cautious in the face of this type of uncertainty.[21] His demonstration of the **rule of caution** is worth repeating both because of the light it sheds on optimal policymaking and because it is a useful application of the mean-variance approach of Chapter 7 to decisions outside the area of portfolio choice.

In the simplest case, we assume there is only variable of interest, the change in income dY. Assume there is only one demand management tool, the change in high-powered money dH. Let dH affect dY with a multiplier effect a that is uncertain. Let a have an expected value E_a and standard deviation σ_a. The change in income in any period will be:

$$dY = a\,dH + u, \tag{3}$$

where u is a residual term reflecting the impact of all other variables that affect dY. Assume policymakers' objective is to minimize the quadratic social loss function

$$L' = [\,E(dY - dY^T)\,]^2,$$

which is equivalent to the mean-variance loss function

$$L = L[\,E(dY) - dY^T, \sigma_Y\,], \tag{4}$$

where σ_Y is the standard deviation of dY around its expected value.

In the simplest case, where the residual term u is certain, uncertainty about the policy multiplier is the only source of uncertainty about dY, and σ_Y is proportional to the size of policy dose:

$$\sigma_Y = dH\,\sigma_a. \tag{5}$$

This situation is described in Figure 22–10. The opportunity set available to policymakers is given by the upward-sloping line starting at u when dH is zero.

---

[21] William C. Brainard, "Uncertainty and the Effectiveness of Policy," *American Economic Review*, 1967, 411–25.

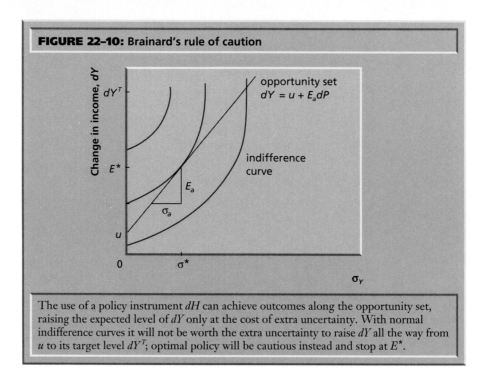

FIGURE 22–10: Brainard's rule of caution

The use of a policy instrument dH can achieve outcomes along the opportunity set, raising the expected level of dY only at the cost of extra uncertainty. With normal indifference curves it will not be worth the extra uncertainty to raise dY all the way from u to its target level dY^T; optimal policy will be cautious instead and stop at E^*.

The slope of the opportunity set is E_a/σ_a; each 1-unit increase in dH raises $E(dY)$ by E_a and raises σ_Y by σ_a.

The central bank's social indifference curves are shown as converging on the best possible outcome of all at $dY = dY^T$ and $\sigma_Y = 0$. The optimal policy dose produces the combination E^* and σ^* at the point of tangency of the opportunity set with the highest indifference curve. What is important about this optimal point is that E^* is less than dY^T. The optimal policy dose dH^* falls short of the level that would fully achieve the target. Optimal policy is cautious in the face of uncertainty about policy effects, because more aggressive policy adds to uncertainty.

If we relax the requirement that all the rest of the world be certain, so that the residual u in Equation (3) is no longer certain, the analysis becomes more complex, but the rule of caution still holds under plausible assumptions.

Brainard's analysis raises the important and largely unanswered question of which policies have the most certain impact. Certainty of impact is likely to be associated with directness of impact and with accumulated experience in the use of the policy instrument. Government spending, for instance, has a closely predictable effect on aggregate demand, whereas monetary policy does not, because monetary policy affects aggregate demand only indirectly through effects on interest rates, exchange rates, and wealth.[22] Milton Friedman and Anna Schwartz, on the other hand, sought to increase the perceived reliability of monetary policy by documenting the effects of money supply changes over more than a century of U.S. history.[23] The world has little experience with incomes policies, by contrast, so even their staunchest advocates are uncertain about how effective they would be.

It follows from the Lucas critique that any policy action affecting the structure of the economy (such as switching from an income tax to a consumption tax) may make the economy's past responses irrelevant as guides for future policy because such policy actions would change the process of forming rational expectations.[24] Until we know how (unobservable) expectations formation is affected by any policy change, we cannot be certain of the effects even of policies used before. Lucas' message is therefore that policy effects are bound to be more uncertain than our econometric estimates suggest.

SECTION 5

Summary

The objectives of stabilization policy are generally conceived to be stabilization of output, employment, and inflation, at high levels for output and employment and at low levels for inflation. Stability of the interest rate and the exchange rate may also be desirable to reduce uncertainty in private-sector decisions and to maintain investors' confidence in financial markets. Of these objectives, lowering inflation is the one objective to which monetary policy must be assigned in the long run.

There are a range of possible monetary rules to guide management of high-powered money in the short run when it is not clear just what kind of shocks the economy may be experiencing. Each rule allows a slightly different set of shocks to affect policy. The rules that allow the most appropriate set of shocks to affect policy are also the rules that are least readily implemented in the very short run — the very period for which monetary rules are most needed.

---

[22] Monetarists have sometimes argued that monetary policy has direct effects on aggregate demand, independently of interest rates. The Bank of Canada's view is that it "has never uncovered any links between the supply of base money (or any other measure of the money supply) and the price level or the rate of economic activity that are not attributable, directly or indirectly, to the movement of interest rates or the exchange rate." Gordon Thiessen, *The Canadian Experience with Monetary Targeting* (Ottawa: Bank of Canada, May 5, 1982), 2.

[23] M. Friedman and A. Schwartz, *A Monetary History of the United States, 1867–1960* (Princeton: Princeton University Press, 1963).

[24] Robert E. Lucas, Jr., "Econometric Policy Evaluation: A Critique," in Karl Brunner and Alan H. Meltzer, eds. *The Phillips Curve and the Labor Market* (Amsterdam: North-Holland, 1976), 19–46.

There is an argument for advance commitment to some monetary rule, to gain the benefits of being able to influence expectations favourably. On inspection it seems likely that those benefits can also be gained without irrevocable commitment, thereby keeping the benefits of some flexibility in a world full of unexpected shocks.

The Bank of Canada must choose its policy strategy in an environment that is subject to several different types of uncertainty. The Bank is uncertain about all of the exogenous variables that affect aggregate demand and supply, about many of the impacts of its own policies, and often about the use that will be made of other stabilization policies. If the effect of policy itself is uncertain, then policymakers will find it desirable to be cautious in their policy actions.

Key Terms

social loss function
costs of excess capacity
costs of inflation
shoe-leather costs
assignment of policy tools
fiscal and monetary policy
IS and LM shocks
fixed-H and fixed-R
   monetary rules

fixed exchange rate rule
nominal income rule
narrow and broad money rules
policy discretion
policy expectations
certainty-equivalent approach
rule of caution

Questions and Problems

1. What weights would you give to the various components of the social loss function in Equation (2) of this chapter? Would your weights as Minister of Finance be influenced by lobby groups? Which lobby groups would you expect to push for higher weights for price stability? For stability of real growth?

2. Is it plausible that the value of extra leisure activities could ever exceed the value of output forgone as a result of extra unemployment?

3. Are the costs of unemployment reduced by unemployment insurance, or merely redistributed?

4. If it is possible to remove inflation by reducing aggregate demand, how long will the costs and the benefits last from doing so?

5. Why should monetary policy respond at all to feedback from the economy other than feedback in the form of output growth and inflation?

6. What is to be gained from the Bank of Canada committing itself publicly to some particular feedback rule? What is to be lost?

7. Is uncertainty a sufficient reason for doing nothing with stabilization policy? If not, what is an appropriate response to uncertainty?

8. Professor Lucas has argued in a famous critique of policy simulations that merely announcing a new policy rule will change the structure of the economy. How does this argument undermine the logic of Poole's optimal (combination) monetary rule, if at all?

Suggestions for Further Reading

Barro, Robert and David Gordon. "A Positive Theory of Monetary Policy in a Natural Rate Model." *Journal of Political Economy*, 1983, 589–610.

Brainard, William C. "Uncertainty and the Effectiveness of Policy." *American Economic Review*. 1967, 411–25.

Courchene, Thomas J. *Money, Inflation, and the Bank of Canada*, Montreal: C.D. Howe Research Institute, 1975.

———. *The Strategy of Gradualism*. Montreal: C.D. Howe Research Institute, 1977.

———. *Money, Inflation, and the Bank of Canada*, Vol. 2. Montreal: C.D. Howe Research Institute, 1981.

Howitt, Peter. *Monetary Policy in Transition: A Study of Bank of Canada Policy, 1982–85*. Scarborough, Ont.: C.D. Howe Institute, 1986.

Leroy, Stephen F. and David E. Lindsey. "Determining the Monetary Instrument: A Diagrammatic Exposition." *American Economic Review*, December 1978, 929–34.

Lipsey, Richard G., ed. *Zero Inflation: The Goal of Price Stability*. Scarborough, Ont.: C.D. Howe Institute, 1990.

Poole, William. "Optimal Choice of Monetary Instruments in a Simple Stochastic Macro Model." *Quarterly Journal of Economics*, 1970, 197–216.

Riddell, W. Craig. *Dealing with Inflation and Unemployment in Canada*. Toronto: University of Toronto Press for the MacDonald Commission, 1986.

Sargent, John, research coordinator. *Postwar Macroeconomic Developments*. Toronto: University of Toronto Press for the MacDonald Commission, 1986.

Sparks, Gordon R. "The Theory and Practice of Monetary Policy in Canada," in John Sargent, research coordinator. *Fiscal and Monetary Policy*. Toronto: University of Toronto Press for the MacDonald Commission, 1986, 54–83.

The Record of Monetary Policy, 1971–90

T here is precious little information embedded in the current economic data to help us resolve our uncertainties over the future course of events. Like the two central characters in Samuel Beckett's play, *Waiting for Godot*, who take as faith that a rational structure for events exists, we analysts wait patiently for another data point and the possibility that meaningful connections will emerge.

— *Federal Reserve Bank of Cleveland, Economic Trends, March 1990*

This chapter moves on from discussion of possible monetary rules to look at what has actually been done with monetary policy in Canada. The transition is complex because of differences in context. Actual monetary policy is conducted in growing rather than static economies, and actual monetary policy is conducted in a world experiencing very specific shocks that do not always fit neatly into economists' categories. Other stabilization policies used with monetary policy often have lives of their own rather than being pliable allies. The aim of this chapter is to overcome these difficulties in order to demonstrate how actual policy can be analyzed using the concepts developed so far. The demonstration will also show us (with hindsight) examples of both the costs and benefits of the monetary rules used by the Bank of Canada.

Section 1 discusses the objectives given by the Bank for its monetary policy, and then adapts the LM curve diagram to fit a growing economy. From the adapted LM curve diagram we derive net M2 growth as a rough measure of monetary policy actions. Sections 2–4 use this measure to discuss the conduct of anti-inflationary monetary policy over the three periods 1971–1975,

1975–1981, and 1981–1990.[1] Section 5 discusses the use of monetary policy to counter shocks that cause instability in the financial system.

You should learn in this chapter:

1. how to adapt the IS–LM diagram to analyze a growing economy;

2. the monetary rules used by the Bank of Canada since 1970;

3. how monetary rules have accommodated or failed to accommodate different shocks to the economy since 1970.

SECTION 1

▢ Objectives and measures of monetary policy

The loudly and frequently stated goal of the Bank of Canada (hereafter referred to more simply as "the Bank") is to lower and keep down the rate of inflation (to preserve the value of money, as the Bank prefers to put it). In speeches, annual reports, and testimony before parliamentary committees, Bank officials repeat the argument that lowering inflation is a prerequisite to healthy output growth, that zero inflation is the only credible target, and that monetary policy is the tool that must be assigned to the task.[2] For instance,

> The unique contribution that monetary policy can consistently make to good economic performance is to ensure that Canadians can conduct their economic affairs with the benefit of a money they can trust. This means that monetary expansion needs to be limited so that money will retain its value. ...[3]

The only other goals that the Bank mentions from time to time are the prevention of large changes ("disorder") in financial and exchange markets. Bank officials are anxious about the possibility of rapid decreases in exchange rates, and particularly anxious when aggregate demand levels are high; they fear that such

---

[1] We start with 1971 because the situation of the Bank of Canada before 1971 was quite different from that which it faces now. From June 1962 to May 1970 Canada was on a fixed exchange rate. Before June 1962 Canada was one of the few advanced economies on a floating exchange rate, but in that period international capital flows were only a pale reflection of what central banks must deal with today; most countries had exchange controls to prevent arbitrage between currencies.

[2] For a critical discussion of the Bank's argument, see Robert F. Lucas, "The Bank of Canada and Zero Inflation: A New Cross of Gold?" *Canadian Public Policy*, March 1989, 84–95. For a response from the Bank, see Jack Selody, *The Goal of Price Stability: A Review of the Issues* (Ottawa: Bank of Canada Technical Report No. 54, May 1990).

[3] Bank of Canada, *Annual Report 1989* (Ottawa: Bank of Canada), 7.

depreciations will raise domestic prices enough to start off a wage–price spiral that will be very expensive to stop.

Strategic thinking about the use of monetary policy tends to be the same in the United States as in Canada. During 1990, four of the twelve presidents of the U.S. Federal Reserve Banks (parts of the U.S. central banking system, referred to as "the Fed") testified in favour of a proposed Congressional resolution that would remove any flexibility the Fed has to pursue any goal other than price stability, and that would set an explicit timetable for achieving that goal. In particular, the resolution would exclude as a goal the achievement of either maximum employment or moderate long-term interest rates, both of which are included as goals in the Fed's current legislation.[4]

Our discussion of Canada's monetary policy in the past is divided into two parts: its use to combat inflation in three periods (in sections 2–4) and then its use to stabilize the financial system (in section 5). First, however, we discuss how to measure monetary policy in a growing economy.

Measures of monetary policy

Macroeconomists think of monetary policy as shifting the LM curve, usually in the context of a static model. It will be useful for us to have an **indicator of monetary policy** by the Bank of Canada that could be interpreted as shifting the LM curve of the Canadian economy one way or the other. Since the Canadian economy is dynamic rather than static (that is, its output capacity grows more or less steadily over time), we also need to adapt the static LM curve into a **dynamic LM curve**.

Indicators of monetary policy are usually the growth rate of some definition of the money supply. Growth rates faster than price inflation are interpreted as shifting the economy's LM curve to the right, and growth rates below price inflation as shifting it to the left. There are several different definitions of the money supply that could be used. Here we follow Howitt and use a measure based on M2.[5] M2 has two desirable properties for our purposes. First, over the period since 1971, it appears that the demand for M2 has been more stable than the demand for narrow money (M1). Financial innovations of this period have mainly caused shifts in the composition of M2 rather than shifts into and out of M2 assets; the growth rate of M2 has not been much affected. Second, M2 demand is more or less insensitive to the general level of interest rates; while M2 demand is sensitive to both own rates (that is, yields on assets included in M2) and opportunity rates (yields on other, substitute assets), these two rates tend to move together most of the time. As a result, the demand for M2 is normally

---

[4] Federal Reserve Bank of Cleveland, *Economic Trends*, March 1990, 3.

[5] Peter Howitt, *Monetary Policy in Transition: A Study of Bank of Canada Policy, 1982–85* (Scarborough, Ont.: C.D. Howe Research Institute, 1986), 44f.

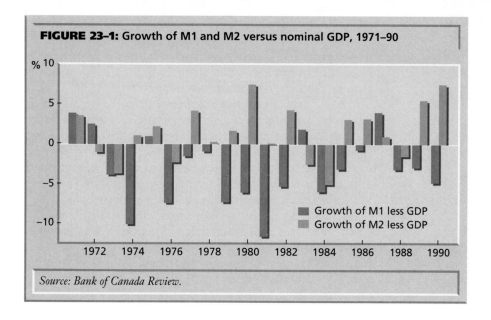

FIGURE 23–1: Growth of M1 and M2 versus nominal GDP, 1971–90

Growth of M1 less GDP
Growth of M2 less GDP

Source: *Bank of Canada Review.*

more or less proportional to the growth of nominal income.[6] The growth rate of nominal income is always the sum of inflation and real output growth. This is not true of M1, which is also sensitive to the general level of interest rates. As evidence, Figure 23–1 shows that both M1 and M2 frequently grew at rates different from nominal income, but also that the discrepancies were much greater and more variable for M1 than for M2.[7]

Monetary indicators in a dynamic economy

Using M2 growth by itself as an indicator of monetary policy is likely to be misleading in discussing a real economy whose output capacity grows over time. When we think of an expansionary or contractionary monetary policy in a growing economy, we usually think of that policy as raising or lowering the degree of capacity utilization rather than just the level of output. In an economy in which output capacity and demand grow at 3 percent, for instance, monetary policy would have to allow M2 growth to accommodate at least three percent growth of output, as well as any current inflation, just to keep nominal interest

---

[6] If income elasticity of demand for broad money is less than 1.0, as some evidence suggests, then demand for M2 grows slightly less than proportionally with nominal income. This discrepancy will be small in most years and is ignored here.

[7] In their exhaustive study of different monetary aggregates, Hostland *et al.* found that the rate of growth of M2 was the best leading indicator of inflation. Doug Hostland, Stephen Poloz, and Paul Storer, *An Analysis of the Information Content of Alternative Monetary Aggregates* (Ottawa: Bank of Canada Technical Report No. 48, 1987).

rates constant. In order to identify whether monetary policy was expansionary or contractionary in any period, therefore, we should compare the current inflation rate with the excess of M2 growth over the growth of capacity, rather than with total M2 growth.[8] In order to simplify such comparisons for the rest of this chapter, the indicator of monetary policy will be M2 growth less capacity growth.[9] It will be referred to as **net M2 growth**. Net M2 growth would be expansionary if it exceeds inflation, and contractionary if it is less than inflation.

Net M2 growth can be interpreted as shifting an LM curve to the right when expansionary, and to the left when contractionary, if we make one adjustment to the IS–LM diagram. The adjustment is to measure the degree of capacity utilization (that is, actual output/full-capacity output) rather than just output on the horizontal axis, as shown in Figure 23–2. A rightward shift of the LM curve in Figure 23–2 is expansionary: it raises demand relative to capacity. To shift such an LM curve to the right requires M2 to grow faster than inflation plus capacity growth, which means net M2 growth faster than inflation. To shift the LM curve to the left requires M2 growth less than inflation plus capacity growth, or net M2 growth less than inflation.

Before we review actual monetary policy in the past, we should first acknowledge some sources of error in using just net M2 growth and inflation to measure the stance of monetary policy. Even the demand for M2 does not depend only on prices and output levels; there are a few other factors that occasionally cause demand for M2 to grow at a different rate than the sum of inflation and output. These include postal strikes, changes in relative yields on M2 assets and important M2-substitutes such as Canada Savings Bonds, and changes in relative risk levels in the economy. Each of these will cause one-shot deviations in M2 growth from the sum of inflation and output growth.[10] For the LM curve of Figure 23–2 to stay put in years of such monetary shocks, net M2 growth must match inflation plus any extra M2 demand growth caused by the shock. When such shocks occur, it is incomplete to measure monetary policy only by comparing net M2 growth and inflation.

The seriousness of this problem depends on how stable the demand for M2 has been over the period since 1970. Over the period 1970–85, Kim McPhail and

---

[8] Implicitly, this assumes that 1 percent extra M2 is required to accommodate 1 percent extra real output. Measures of the output elasticity of M2 demand are usually somewhat less than 1, so the growth rate of M2 less the growth rate of output capacity will tend to understate the degree of stimulus provided by actual monetary policy.

[9] In calculating net M2 growth, average output growth over the period 1971–89 is used as an estimate of capacity growth. Average unemployment rates of prime-age males are similar at both ends of the period, so capacity must have grown at close to the same rate as output.

[10] 1989 provides an example of changes in relative yields, when yields on Canada Savings Bonds (CSBs) proved uncompetitive. In early 1989 an unusually large wave of CSB redemptions caused a flood of demand into personal time deposits and swelled M2 growth. The October 1987 stock market crash provides an example of risk changes, in this case also swelling demand for M2 assets.

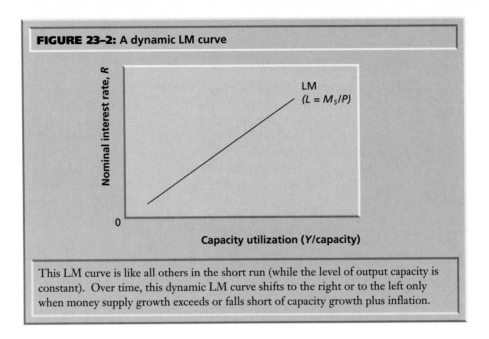

FIGURE 23–2: A dynamic LM curve

LM
$(L = M_S/P)$

Nominal interest rate, R

Capacity utilization (Y/capacity)

This LM curve is like all others in the short run (while the level of output capacity is constant). Over time, this dynamic LM curve shifts to the right or to the left only when money supply growth exceeds or falls short of capacity growth plus inflation.

Francesco Caramazza of the Bank of Canada found demand for M2 to be quite stable, but that was after they had allowed for postal strikes and two other one-time shocks.[11] Jean-Marie Dufour and Daniel Racette concluded in their survey of empirical evidence for the MacDonald Commission that demand for M2 was more stable than demand for M1.[12] Here we will be using only annual data, so one-time errors to monthly figures will be averaged out. We should conclude that our measure of monetary policy is incomplete and subject to some error, but less incomplete and subject to smaller errors than if we had used net M1 growth instead.

[11] Kim McPhail and Francesco Caramazza, *La demande de M2 et M2+ au Canada: quelques resultats recents* (Ottawa: Banque du Canada, 1990, Document de travail 90–3). These and other results are discussed further in Francesco Caramazza, Doug Hostland, and Stepen Poloz, *The Demand for Money and the Monetary Policy Process in Canada* (Ottawa: Bank of Canada, Working Paper 90–5), May 1990.

[12] Jean-Marie Dufour and Daniel Racette, "Monetary Control in Canada," in J. Sargent, research coordinator, *Fiscal and Monetary Policy* (Toronto: University of Toronto Press for the MacDonald Commission, 1986), 199–256.

SECTION 2

▣ The early 1970s

Figure 23–3 summarizes key parts of the story of Canadian monetary policy for the whole period from 1971 to 1990.[13] Part (a) shows net M2 growth and the inflation rate. Capacity growth is taken as a constant, so the time path of net M2 growth is exactly parallel to that for M2 growth itself. Part (b) shows the behaviour of two intermediate links between monetary policy and the inflation rate: changes in a typical short-term interest rate (on 90-day commercial paper, $R\,90$) and in the trade-weighted average real exchange rate of the Canadian dollar against other Group of Ten (G-10) currencies. Part (c) shows a measure of the stimuli from the fiscal policies of federal and other governments (provincial and local governments and hospitals).

The fiscal stimuli in (c) measure the *increase* in structural, primary budget deficits as a percentage of GDP.[14] Positive values represent extra deficits that are not the automatic result of either changes in capacity utilization, nor of changes in interest payments on the (growing) public debt. Such extra deficits can be taken as a crude proxy for the exogenous, active component of fiscal policy.

Monetary and fiscal policy

Figure 23–3(a) shows that in the years 1971–1974, net M2 grew much faster than inflation. The nation's LM curve of Figure 23–2 was moved quickly out to the right even as inflation accelerated. Monetary policy was very expansionary, and the inflation rate obliged by speeding up dramatically. The OPEC oil price increase is often blamed in the public mind for this inflation eruption, but monetary policy was accommodating faster inflation long before OPEC members quadrupled their prices in 1974. As new Keynesian theory predicts, following such a policy caused aggregate demand and output to grow well ahead of capacity growth — 400 basis points ahead in 1973. The long-run impact of faster inflation quickly followed (as is predicted by *all* macroeconomic theories). In 1975 net M2 growth merely accommodated inflation, but by then the inflation being accommodated had soared to 10.8 percent.

Can any of the blame be put on fiscal policy? Figure 23–3(c) shows that fiscal policies were mildly expansionary to start with, mildly contractionary by 1974,

---

[13] For a thorough discussion of this and the following period, see Tom Courchene's monographs for the C.D. Howe Research Institute, especially *Monetarism and Controls: The Inflation Fighters* (Montreal, 1976). For the official Bank of Canada view, see the Bank's *Annual Reports*.

[14] Structural deficits are actual deficits with the effect of abnormal capacity utilization taken out (that is, they are "cyclically adjusted"). Primary deficits are actual deficits calculated without counting interest on the public debt as expenditure. Primary structural deficits are actual deficits calculated with both adjustments. All estimates are provided by the federal Department of Finance.

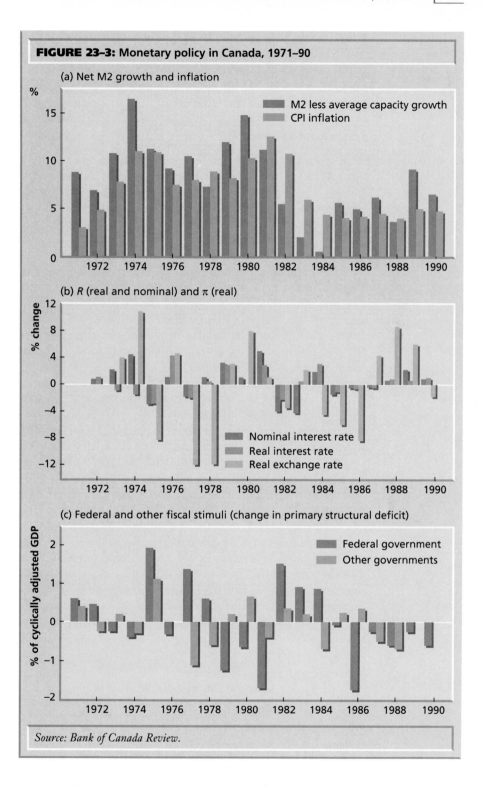

FIGURE 23–3: Monetary policy in Canada, 1971–90

(a) Net M2 growth and inflation

(b) R (real and nominal) and π (real)

(c) Federal and other fiscal stimuli (change in primary structural deficit)

Source: Bank of Canada Review.

and then very expansionary in 1975 at both federal and provincial levels. Only in 1975 can the blame be shifted to fiscal policy. In 1975 a decline in demand in the private sector was offset by fiscal stimuli, even though inflation was at double-digit levels and clearly the nation's number one economic concern.

The monetary rule

The **monetary policy rule** being followed in this episode was clearly *not* to keep an eye on net M2 growth — or on any other monetary aggregate, for that matter. The short-run (week-to-week) rule in this period, as in all periods, was to keep nominal interest rates at target levels. The more important medium-term (month-to-month) rule in this period was to raise target nominal interest rate levels whenever excess capacity became too small, and the unemployment rate was used as the main indicator of excess capacity. Unfortunately, shocks occurred to both nominal interest rates and to the unemployment rate, and the Bank of Canada's monetary rule passed both of them on to affect output and inflation. By the time the shocks were recognized as such, the damage had already been done.

The shock to nominal interest rates was the acceleration of expected inflation. When expected inflation accelerates, any given nominal interest rate implies a lower real interest rate. Much of aggregate demand is sensitive to real rather than to nominal interest rates. The effect of accelerating expected inflation is therefore to shift the IS curve to the right at each nominal interest rate. During such a shock, mere increases in nominal interest rates are not sufficient evidence that aggregate demand is being crowded out; nominal interest rates must increase at a faster rate than expected inflation. In fact, actual (*ex post*) real interest rates before tax fell from 2.3 percent in 1971 to −0.2 percent in 1973 and −2.9 percent in 1975. Anyone inferring, as the Bank did, that monetary policy was tight just from seeing rising nominal interest rates in 1973 and 1974 was way off the mark.

The shock to the unemployment rate was the massive enrichment of unemployment insurance benefits in 1972. This change greatly decreased the net opportunity cost of searching for jobs in the labour market. Predictably, more Canadians would be found unemployed and looking for work at each level of capacity use after the change, so the relationship between capacity use and the unemployment rate was shifted. In macroeconomic jargon, the **non-accelerating inflation rate of unemployment** (NAIRU) rose; later estimates have shown that it rose by about 2 percent.[15] As capacity utilization grew in 1971–73, the unemployment rate did not reflect it by falling as it normally would have done; instead the unemployment rate merely stayed put. Policymakers and their

---

[15] For a discussion of this episode, see David A. Wilton and David M. Prescott, *Macroeconomics: Theory and Policy in Canada*, 2nd ed. (Don Mills, Ont.: Addison-Wesley, 1987), 325ff; or C. Green and J.-M. Cousineau, *Unemployment in Canada: The Impact of the Unemployment Insurance Act* (Economic Council of Canada, 1976); or M.W. Keil and J.S.V. Symons, "An Analysis of Canadian Unemployment," *Canadian Public Policy*, March 1990, 1–16.

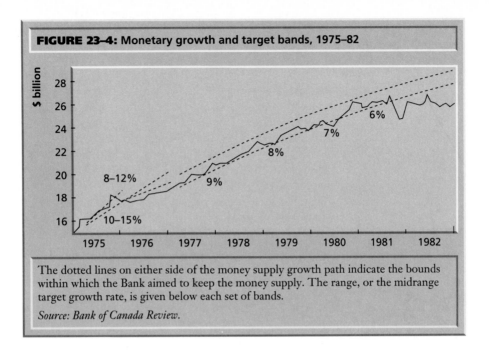

FIGURE 23–4: Monetary growth and target bands, 1975–82

The dotted lines on either side of the money supply growth path indicate the bounds within which the Bank aimed to keep the money supply. The range, or the midrange target growth rate, is given below each set of bands.

Source: Bank of Canada Review.

public overestimated the amount of slack in the economy, because unemployment was well above what had been considered "full employment" in the 1960s.

The monetary rule of looking at the unemployment rate as the main indicator of the degree of slack in the economy, and at nominal interest rates as the main indicator of the tightness of money markets, proved grossly inadequate with the particular shocks experienced in 1971–75. Something better was promised in September 1975.

SECTION 3

The strategy of gradualism, 1975–82

In September 1975, with double-digit inflation already a painful fact of life, the Governor of the Bank of Canada announced a dramatic change of tactics. Henceforth the Bank would adjust its short-term interest rate targets from week to week in order to keep the growth of narrow money supply (M1) within explicitly stated target bands (on average, and over longer periods of several months). The target bands were to be lowered to just the rate of capacity growth over a period of five years or so — that is, gradually rather than immediately. The policy was immediately described as a monetarist one, and gradualist rather than "cold-turkey." Figure 23–4 shows the target bands for M1 growth and the actual time path of M1 growth over the period.

The **strategy of gradualism** was carried out in the context of two other policy initiatives, two adverse supply shocks, and of course fiscal policy stimuli. The first policy initiative lasted from 1975 to 1978: the federal government established the Anti-Inflation Board (AIB) as an incomes policy to lower expectations and nominal wage increases; the AIB policy is credited with lowering wage increases (and therefore price inflation) by about 2 percent below what would otherwise have occurred.[16] The second policy initiative was the oil pricing agreement under the National Energy Program of 1981, which both raised domestic oil prices and removed most of the incentives for exploration and development that had caused the energy boom in western Canada. The adverse supply shocks were (a) OPEC's doubling of the market price of oil in 1979–80, and (b) unstable agricultural prices; in 1976 a collapse in the price of meat held consumer price inflation down, but in 1978–79 food price explosions pushed consumer price inflation up, just as in 1973–74. Finally, federal fiscal policy was expansionary in both 1977 and 1978, even though it was largely offset by the fiscal stance of provincial and local governments. Only in 1979 and again in 1981 was federal fiscal policy strongly contractionary.

Despite the adverse supply shocks, the Bank more than achieved its stated target for M1 growth for the period 1975–82. Figure 23–4 shows that M1 growth slowed gradually and persistently. From late 1980 on to the end of 1982 M1 hardly grew at all. The Bank was able to adjust nominal interest rates to the levels needed to keep M1 growth within or below the target bands.

Figure 23–5 repeats the series in Figure 23–3 for just the years 1975–82. Part (a) shows what was actually happening to monetary policy using the net M2 growth measure. Net M2 growth still *more* than accommodated inflation in every year except 1978 and 1981. LM curves were being shifted out to the right rather than back to the left. The nominal interest rates shown in (b) actually fell in 1977; they increased sharply only in 1979 and then further in 1981. *Ex post* real interest rates rose sharply in 1976 (becoming barely positive again), then dropped over 2 percentage points in 1977 before rising sharply in 1979 and then further in 1981. With such a monetary policy it was not surprising that the real exchange rate fell abruptly in late 1976, and kept on falling to the end of 1978; only when real interest rates were raised in 1979, and the second oil-price shock hit Canadian export prices, did the real exchange rate rise.

In short, aggregate demand was not being restrained much, if at all, by either monetary or fiscal policy during the AIB period. Inflation did not slow down until after both monetary and fiscal policy became far more contractionary in 1979 and 1981. Only by 1981 did monetary and fiscal policy manage to overcome the legacy of earlier years and shift the economy's IS and LM curves far enough to the left to reduce inflation. By then, however, there was no incomes policy in

---

[16] For a description and assessment of the Anti-Inflation Board program, see David A. Wilton and David M. Prescott, *Macroeconomics: Theory and Policy in Canada*, 2nd ed. (Don Mills, Ont.: Addison-Wesley, 1987), chapter 13.

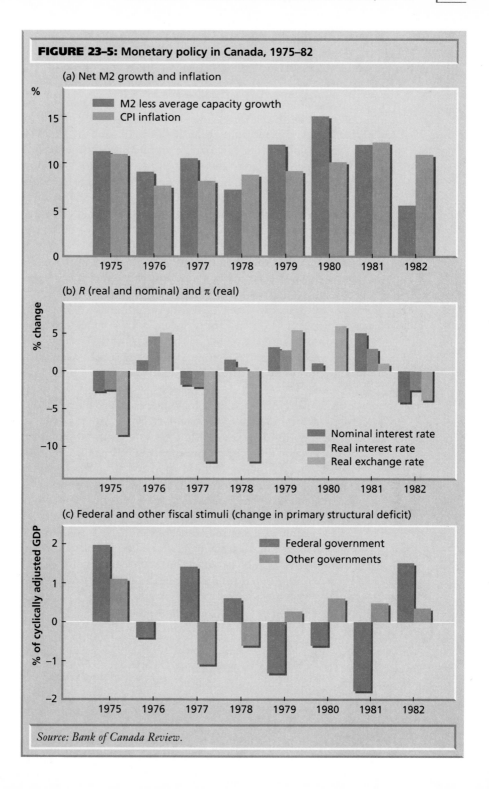

FIGURE 23–5: Monetary policy in Canada, 1975–82

(a) Net M2 growth and inflation

(b) *R* (real and nominal) and π (real)

(c) Federal and other fiscal stimuli (change in primary structural deficit)

Source: Bank of Canada Review.

place to help the economy slow down inflation without a massive or prolonged recession.[17]

The monetary rule and the LM shock

The difficulty in this period was an instance of Murphy's law: once the Bank of Canada picked its monetary rule, fate dealt out just the kind of **LM shock** to which that rule is vulnerable. The Bank naturally thought that its policy would shift the LM curve persistently to the left if inflation did not slow down as quickly as its targets were lowered. Indeed, the Bank hoped that the public would believe in government announcements of anti-inflation policy and lower their inflationary expectations quickly. In that case inflation could fall as fast as the Bank's money growth targets.

Unfortunately, after 1975 narrow money was the object of several important financial innovations that dramatically slowed growth of M1 demand. Banks started paying daily interest on non-chequable and then chequable savings deposits in 1979 and 1980; they also provided day's-end transfer of excess corporate demand deposits into overnight time deposits, first in 1976 for their biggest customers, and then in 1981 for medium-sized customers. Both innovations caused the official measure of M1 balances demanded to fall significantly. Howitt reports a cumulative estimate of at least a 28 percent drop in M1 demand over the period 1976–81 because of these innovations; a massive LM shock.[18]

Any decrease in demand for money at unchanged income and interest rate levels shifts the LM curve out to the right, in the same way that an expansionary monetary policy does. By holding to its growth targets for narrow money and not recognizing the innovations, the Bank of Canada unwittingly accommodated these rightward shifts of the LM curve at a time when it wanted just the opposite. By the time the Bank had recognized the LM shock for what it was, estimated its effect, and acted on its estimate, the incomes policy was over and inflation had surged back to the levels of 1975.

The Bank of Canada had recognized the serious problems of its narrow money indicator by 1981, and abandoned it officially by early 1982.[19] Aggregate demand was restrained by enormous increases in nominal interest rates in 1981. The economy headed into recession in mid-year. Output spiralled downward

---

[17] In June 1982 an incomes policy was imposed that limited wage increases for federal employees and in federal Crown corporations to 6 percent and then 5 percent in the next two years. This "6 and 5" program was too little and too late; by this time many businesses were already announcing wage freezes for their management personnel, if not layoffs or bankruptcy.

[18] Peter Howitt, *Monetary Policy in Transition*, 46. The estimate was made by a Bank of Canada economist in 1983.

[19] For a good discussion of the Bank's decision to abandon its M1 strategy, see Tom Courchene, *No Place To Stand?* (Montreal: C.D. Howe Research Institute, 1983).

for a year and a half, ending up some 4.5 percent below the level of mid-1981. The strategy of gradualism had been abandoned in favour of the cold-turkey alternative.

SECTION 4

◼ Recession and recovery, 1981–90

The recession of 1981–82 did to inflation what the strategy of gradualism could not. The very tight monetary policy of 1981 pricked the bubble of inflationary expectations on which much of the growth of 1979 and 1980 had depended. Firms built up large debt loads in 1979–80 whose future burden was bearable only if inflation stayed high. Once double-digit inflation was no longer expected, in 1982–83, investment spending collapsed. Corporations could no longer afford to buy new capital assets. With declining output levels, firms found themselves with a lot of excess capacity and did not want new capital assets anyway.[20] Many firms concentrated entirely on staying out of bankruptcy, using every available dollar of cash to pay down debts and improve balance sheets. Business investment spending did not pick up until 1985.

Figure 23–6 repeats the record of these years. Inflation fell during 1983 and 1984 from 11 percent to 5 percent. Inflationary expectations must have dropped as well. As inflationary expectations fell, the real interest rate implied by each nominal rate rose; that further depressed investment spending. Fiscal policy worked to push aggregate demand in the opposite direction. Figure 23–6(c) shows that the federal government generated large fiscal stimuli in 1982–84, although these were countered by provincial government fiscal restraint in 1984.

Figure 23–6(a) shows that monetary policy was tight through 1984. In each year, net M2 growth was as far below inflation in each year as it had been above inflation in 1972–74.[21] That is, the economy's LM curve was shifted further to the left each year to 1984. The net effect of monetary restrictions and the collapsing IS curve in 1982–83 was a drop in real interest rates in 1982, followed by flat real interest rates in 1983. Part (b) shows that continued monetary restraint brought sharply rising real interest rates only in 1984, by which time the IS curve had stopped collapsing. Nominal interest rates fell in 1982–83 by the drop in real rates of 1982 plus a further 6 percent in 1982–83 to reflect lower inflationary expectations. By 1984 the further decline in inflation was not enough to offset the effects of contractionary monetary policy, so nominal rates rose again.

---

[20] This is an example of the classic investment accelerator mechanism at work in a downturn.

[21] McPhail and Caramazza report evidence of an LM shock in 1982–84 that lowered M2 growth about 2 percent per year over the period. Such an LM shock would account for only half of the shortfall of net M2 growth below inflation in Figure 23–6(a). *La demande de M2 et M2+ au Canada: quelques résultats recents*.

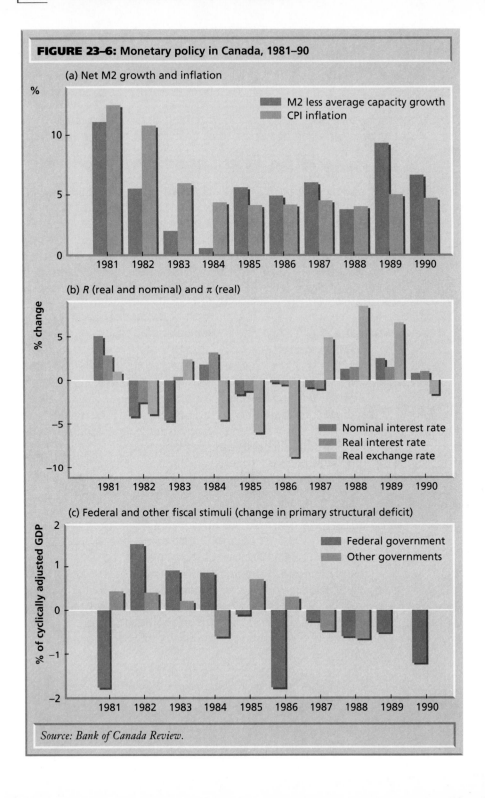

FIGURE 23–6: Monetary policy in Canada, 1981–90

(a) Net M2 growth and inflation

■ M2 less average capacity growth
■ CPI inflation

(b) *R* (real and nominal) and π (real)

■ Nominal interest rate
■ Real interest rate
■ Real exchange rate

(c) Federal and other fiscal stimuli (change in primary structural deficit)

■ Federal government
■ Other governments

Source: Bank of Canada Review.

What monetary rule?

It is not clear what monetary rule the Bank of Canada was following in this period. The M1 rule had been abandoned. Aggregate demand had been so weakened by the end of 1982 that there could be no doubt that inflation would soon decline. The continuation of monetary restraint in 1983–84 has been interpreted by Howitt as meaning that the M1 rule had been replaced by a rule of (nominal) exchange rate stability — effectively the same as being in a fixed exchange rate system, except that it was kept secret.[22] After 1984, he argues, the Bank shifted to something like a broad money rule.

The period 1985–90

From 1985 to 1990, the pattern of Canadian monetary policy was on the whole the opposite of that in 1982–84. With the passage of time after 1983, the IS curve was pushed steadily to the right: existing excess capacity shrank over time because of depreciation, obsolescence, and output growth; corporate balance sheets were steadily improved by several years' ploughing back of all profits to pay down debts; accumulation of technological change (especially microcomputer technology) piled up potential new projects for firms to invest in; the Free Trade Agreement opened up new markets to expand into and new competition to prepare against; and the development of new methods of financing such as junk bonds also eased financing for some firms. Private sector investment demand began to pick up speed after 1984.

In contrast to this private sector buoyancy, federal fiscal policy turned contractionary in 1985 and 1986. Figure 23–6(c) shows that provincial and local governments turned contractionary in 1986 to 1988. Part (a) shows that monetary policy turned mildly expansionary: net M2 growth at least accommodated inflation from 1985 through 1987.[23]

The result of recovering investment demand and permissive monetary policy was a rapid recovery of output levels and falling interest rates (both real and nominal) in 1985–87. Capacity utilization levels also recovered quickly, but only in 1988–89 did the Bank stop accommodating inflation. Nominal and real interest rates rose significantly from late 1988 through early 1990. Bank of Canada officials stated publicly that inflation had to be brought down to zero, and they realized that unemployment rates, though high, were not much if at all above the NAIRU by 1987. Only the stock market crash of October 1987, which caused widespread belief in a softening of aggregate demand growth, stayed the

---

[22] Peter Howitt, *Monetary Policy in Transition*, 99.

[23] The introduction of better yields for high-balance savings deposits in 1986 and again in 1988 constituted an LM shock that could explain some of the more rapid M2 growth in 1987 and 1989. The LM shock also explains how the modest shortfall of net M2 growth below inflation in 1988 could have caused such a significant increase in interest rates. "Monetary Aggregates in Canada: Some Recent Developments," *Bank of Canada Review*, February 1990, 3–15.

restrictive monetary policy as long as late 1988. The short-run impact in 1989–90 came in the form of slower output growth and then recession, lasting into 1991. The inflation rate continued high into 1991 and was actually boosted to 6.8 percent in January 1991 because of the introduction of the new federal Goods and Services Tax in that month. The Bank of Canada has actually predicted as this is written that the inflation rate will fall to 5 percent by the end of 1991 and then to 3 percent in 1992.

Response to the 1989 LM shock

The experience of 1989 provides an example of the perils of any monetary rule and the benefits of being flexible. During 1989, M2 growth of 13.1 percent substantially exceeded the 7.5 percent growth in nominal income; so did growth of M2+. At the same time, the amount of Canada Savings Bonds outstanding shrank by one-fifth after a wave of early redemptions in early 1989 and a relatively small-scale CSB sales campaign in the fall. There appears to have been a large, positive LM shock to M2 growth, in the form of a shift into bank term deposits from CSBs, because of a change in the relative yields of CSBs and term deposits. High-balance savings account yields, for instance, moved from being well below to being above CSB yields in late 1988.

Had the Bank been following a rigid M2 growth strategy like its M1 strategy of 1975–81, it would initially have reacted to the faster M2 growth by raising interest rates much more dramatically in early 1989 than it did. Instead, it recognized that the faster M2 growth was at least partly due to an LM shock, and therefore should not be passed on by higher interest rates that would have affected output levels. The Bank of Canada is in some sense following an M2 rule, but not as rigidly as it followed the M1 rule earlier. At the same time the Bank is also following many other monetary and credit aggregates to help it detect quickly just such LM shocks as the one described above.[24]

The Bank's flexibility in following its own M2 rule is further illustrated by the fact that it attributed only 1 percent extra M2 growth in 1989 to the drop in CSB holdings. That still left a great deal of inflationary net M2 growth unexplained by the LM shock, implying extra inflation for 1990 and beyond. Instead of reacting by imposing vigorous increases in interest rates, the Bank chose to do nothing. It explained away the excess M2 growth with the vague phrase that it "reflects accumulation of inflationary pressures resulting from the vigorous pace of total spending since 1987" (*Annual Report*, 1989, 23). Such an interpretation of money demand is not

---

[24] Two technical reports by Bank of Canada staff in 1987 and 1988 investigated no less than 46 monetary aggregates and 25 measures of credit to isolate those with the best connections to growth of output and inflation. See Doug Hostland, Stephen Poloz, and Paul Storer, *An Analysis of the Information Content of Alternative Monetary Aggregates*, and Leslie Milton, *An Analysis of the Information Content of Alternative Credit Aggregates* (Ottawa: Bank of Canada, Technical Reports 48 and 49, 1987 and 1988).

consistent with the Bank's own reported estimate of how M2 demand behaves;[25] for better or for worse, the Bank is pursuing its M2 rule with large amounts of discretion.

SECTION 5

 # Financial market stability

The Bank of Canada has some responsibility for the smooth functioning of financial markets in Canada. It also has strong self-interest in the matter: **financial market stability** is necessary if the Bank's influence over a few short-term yields is to be faithfully transmitted to the whole range of yields in Canada. The Bank of Canada pursues this objective in many ways, including the use of its lender of last resort facilities. On occasion, the objective of financial market stability also affects monetary policy. The Bank's defence of financial market stability through monetary policy is visible in several episodes between 1979–82 and 1985–90.

Reaction to U.S. fixed-reserves strategy, 1979–82

The first episode is the period from October 1979 to September 1982. During this period the U.S. Federal Reserve Board (the Fed) adopted a radical change in its conduct of monetary policy. The Fed fixed the week-to-week growth of high-powered money at target rates and allowed interest rates to adjust as needed to bring money markets into equilibrium. Previously the target from week to week had been interest rates, with reserves doing most of the adjusting rather than interest rates. Interest rates became many times more volatile from month to month after October 1979 than they had been before, as Figure 23–7 shows.

Faced with sudden **interest rate volatility** in the United States, and relatively uninhibited capital flows between Canada and the United States, the Bank of Canada faced a dilemma: if Canadian interest rates were held stable, arbitrage lending flows across the border would cause the exchange rate to fluctuate even more dramatically than before. For the exchange rate not to fluctuate dramatically, Canadian interest rates would have to move at least part of the way with U.S. interest rates.

Canadian interest rates did move with U.S. interest rates, but not as far. Figure 23–7 shows that the big changes in the U.S. interest rates were accompanied by smaller but opposite swings in the Canadian–U.S. interest differential: the Bank of Canada followed the U.S. lead only part way. This policy prevented exchange rate volatility from becoming much worse than before.

---

[25] The technical note explaining M2 demand in the *Bank of Canada Review* (December 1989) can be taken as the Bank's official view.

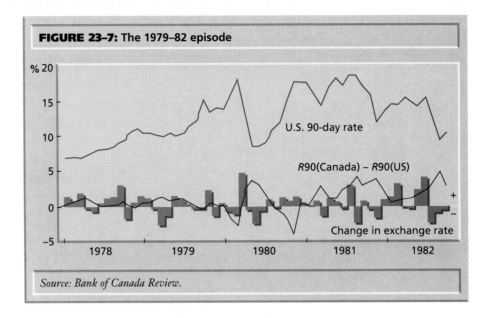

FIGURE 23–7: The 1979–82 episode

U.S. 90-day rate

R90(Canada) – R90(US)

Change in exchange rate

Source: *Bank of Canada Review.*

Exchange rate and stock market crises, 1985–1990

Figure 23–8 shows four other occasions between 1985 and 1990 when the Bank of Canada responded by changing Canadian short-term interest rates vigorously to protect financial market stability. Three were responses to dramatic changes in the exchange rate, and one to a dramatic drop in stock market prices.

In each of early 1985, early 1986, and early 1990 the exchange rate started to fall very rapidly. Fearing the financial and inflationary consequences of a volatile exchange rate, the Bank of Canada stepped in and instead raised the Canada–U.S. interest differential abruptly.[26] The sharp upward spikes in the interest rate series are clear in Figure 23–8(a). In early 1990 the Bank's action added to an already very high interest differential. Covered interest parity in each of these three instances had been disturbed by a drop in arbitrageurs' expectations of future spot exchange rates; the Bank of Canada restored covered interest parity by raising domestic interest rates instead of letting arbitrageurs restore the parity by an even larger drop in the spot exchange rate. Exchange rate changes in Figure 23–8(b) were kept within a "normal" range. In early 1987 the same problem arose in the opposite direction: the Canadian dollar strengthened too quickly against

---

[26] The financial consequences, in the Bank's view, could have been (a) a significantly higher exchange risk premium in the yields paid by borrowers of Canadian dollars in international markets, and (b) elastic expectations of future spot exchange rates over a significant range, making the exchange market unstable over that range. If the exchange market were unstable, monetary policy would probably have to be devoted almost full-time to stabilizing it; effectively, a fixed exchange rate regime. Howitt, for one, finds these fears exaggerated at best. *Monetary Policy in Transition*, chapter 6.

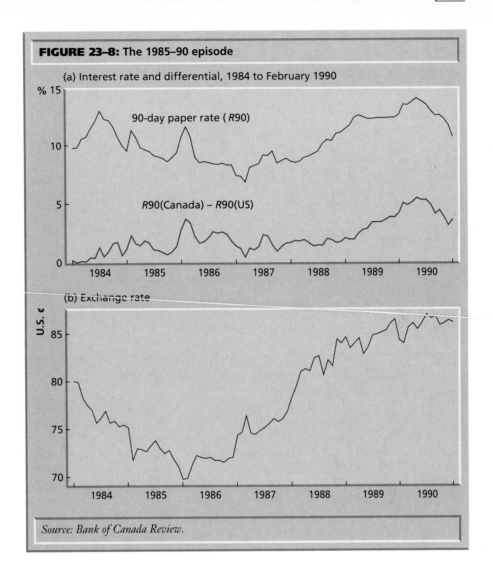

FIGURE 23–8: The 1985–90 episode

(a) Interest rate and differential, 1984 to February 1990

(b) Exchange rate

Source: Bank of Canada Review.

other currencies. The Bank's response was to reduce sharply the Canada–U.S. interest differential.

The fourth occasion when the Bank of Canada intervened to maintain financial market stability was after the stock market crash of October 1987. Stock prices around the world fell by enormous amounts on the two days of 19 and 20 October, 1987. The decline was enough to cause widespread fears that some large investment dealers might fail, taking other firms with them. Central banks around the world immediately tried to shore up the liquidity of investment dealers by stepping up monetary growth and lowering interest rates. The effect is visible in

Figure 23–8(a) as a reversal of what had been a series of steep increases in interest rates since early 1987.

These episodes are examples of the sort of event that could not have been foreseen nor provided for in any of the automatic monetary rules discussed in Chapter 22. They are examples of the sort of benefit that Summers and Howitt argue can be gained only if the central bank is left with some discretion to deviate from whatever monetary rule it may have previously announced.

SECTION 6

■ Summary

Bank of Canada monetary policy over the period 1971–90 has gone through at least three separate episodes, each characterized by different monetary rules and different shocks to the economy.

The stance of monetary policy is summarized by looking at M2 growth net of capacity growth, relative to the inflation rate. Monetary policy that generates net M2 growth faster than current inflation is labelled expansionary. M2 is used because it is more stably related to output growth and inflation than are the available alternatives, and Canadian monetary policy has been focused on inflation since 1971.

In the early 1970s the Bank of Canada was misled by a large supply shock to the unemployment rate, and by IS shocks from changing inflationary expectations. The result was growth of net M2 at rates much faster than inflation. Only in 1975 were the misleading shocks seen for what they were and reacted to properly.

From 1975 to 1981 the Bank of Canada adopted a monetary rule of slowing the growth of M1 in order to lower the inflation that had been generated in 1971–75. Unfortunately, monetary policy remained expansionary despite the Bank's good intentions. Large decreases in demand for M1 due to financial innovations converted what was to have been gradual, cumulative monetary restraint into a policy that instead lowered real and nominal interest rates. Only in 1979 and then again in 1981 did monetary policy succeed in raising real interest rates.

The period since 1981 can be divided into two parts. During the recession of 1981–82 and right up to 1985, monetary policy was restrictive. By 1984 monetary policy actually generated substantial increases in real interest rates. Inflation continued to fall until 1984.

From 1985 to 1988, monetary policy was mildly expansionary. Only after that did it turn restrictive, though it might have done so earlier had the October 1987 stock market crash not occurred to stall the change in policy. Accommodating monetary policy in 1985–88 not only did not force inflation down any further, as the Bank wished, but allowed inflation to accelerate in 1989.

From time to time the Bank's basic strategy of fighting inflation is set aside to respond to sudden shocks that would otherwise impair the stability of

Canadian financial markets. On several occasions in the 1980s the Bank has changed domestic interest rates abruptly to slow down what would otherwise be too large and sudden changes in the exchange rate. On other occasions it has changed interest rates and money supply growth rates to alleviate concerns over solvency or to smooth the effects of turbulent foreign interest rate swings.

Key Terms

indicators of monetary policy	strategy of gradualism
dynamic LM curve	LM shock
net M2 growth	financial market stability
monetary policy rules	foreign interest rate volatility
non-accelerating inflation rate of unemployment (NAIRU)	

Questions and Problems

1. How fast must the Bank of Canada allow the nominal money supply to increase in order not to have the nominal interest rate rise between one year and the next?

2. What assumptions are being made about the demand for money in your answer to the previous question?

3. What was gradual about the strategy of gradualism? What were the alternatives? Which was preferable, in retrospect?

4. Was the monetary rule being followed in the early 1970s a bad rule for any occasion, or just the wrong rule for that particular period? Explain.

5. Was non-federal fiscal policy a help or a hindrance to monetary policy on average over the period 1971 to 1989?

6. Why did the strategy of gradualism have to be abandoned in 1982?

7. What are the important differences between having the Bank of Canada follow an M1 rule, an M2 rule, and an M2+ rule?

Suggestions for Further Reading

Bothwell, Robert, Ian Drummond, and John English. *Canada Since 1945.* Toronto: University of Toronto Press, 1989.

Howitt, Peter. *Monetary Policy in Transition: A Study of Bank of Canada Policy, 1982–85.* Scarborough, Ont.: C.D. Howe Institute, 1986.

Lucas, Robert F. "The Bank of Canada and Zero Inflation: A New Cross of Gold?" *Canadian Public Policy*, March 1989, 84–95.

Riddell, W. Craig. *Dealing with Inflation and Unemployment in Canada*. Toronto: University of Toronto Press for the MacDonald Commission, 1986.

Sargent, John, research coordinator. *Postwar Macroeconomic Developments*. Toronto: University of Toronto Press for the MacDonald Commission, 1986.

Sparks, Gordon R. "The Theory and Practice of Monetary Policy in Canada," in John Sargent, research coordinator, *Fiscal and Monetary Policy*. Toronto: University of Toronto Press for the MacDonald Commission, 1986, 54–83.

PART SEVEN

The International Financial System

Chapter twenty-four

The International Financial System

Throughout this book the Canadian economy has been treated as part of the international financial system. Canadian wholesale credit markets have been tied in to world credit markets via arbitrage for decades. First lenders and now borrowers as well shift between countries for a few basis points of extra yield advantage. Securitization of loans and pooling of many different financial institutions into partnerships in venture capital and merchant banking firms have meant that even the ordinary corporate bank loan customer can now end up borrowing some of its funds indirectly from such unlikely sources as foreign pension funds. The other side of the coin is that capital flows have come to dominate foreign exchange markets and much of monetary policy.

Canada's large and growing financial integration with the rest of the world shows clearly in Figure 24–1, which measures how the **rest-of-the-world (ROW) sector** has accumulated assets and debts in Canada. Canadians borrow extensively from foreigners, and foreigners borrow extensively from us. We buy foreign currency assets both for short and long terms, and foreigners buy Canadian-dollar assets for short and long terms. In addition, there are very large flows of foreign currency payments and receipts to pay for exports and imports of goods and services; for 1988, the combined total of these flows was over $310 billion — half of Canada's gross domestic product. The exchange rate at which these foreign currency payments are made has important effects on Canadian output and inflation.

This chapter does not need to explain the impact of the rest of the world on the Canadian economy; that has been done in the appropriate places in previous chapters. What this chapter does need to do is to pull together the strands of some previous discussions and fill in some gaps, in order to provide a comprehensive view of the international financial system. Readers should be able to see it as a macro-financial system in its own right, rather than simply as a background to the Canadian financial system.

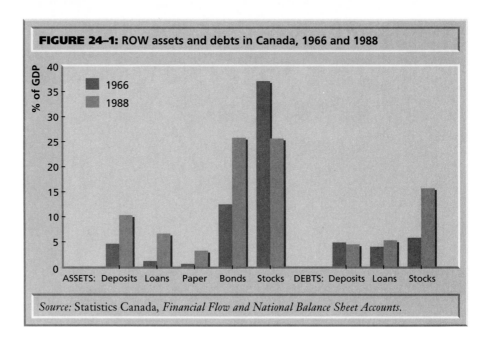

FIGURE 24-1: ROW assets and debts in Canada, 1966 and 1988

Source: Statistics Canada, *Financial Flow and National Balance Sheet Accounts.*

You should learn in this last chapter:

1. the major components of the international financial system;
2. the criteria for assessing the performance of the world financial system;
3. how the international financial system has performed on each of these criteria, especially in arranging for adequate growth of the world money supply.

SECTION 1

▢ The world financial system

Figure 24–2 illustrates the **international flow of funds** through the world financial system; this figure is basically the same as that for the Canadian financial system in Figure 4–1. Funds flow from surplus nations to deficit nations either directly or indirectly. Surplus nations are those with current account surpluses; the use of the surpluses in Figure 24–2 is recorded in the balance of payments as the nation's net capital outflow. Participants in this world financial system, as both lenders and borrowers, are individuals, corporations, central banks, and governments. Within each nation there are always some individuals and corporations lending in the world financial system, and others borrowing. The nation's net capital outflow represents just the net lending of members of that nation in the world financial system. Gross lending and borrowing flows are many times larger than the net capital flows of Figure 24–2.

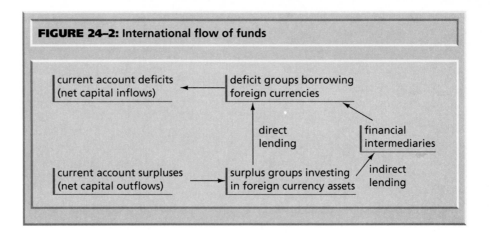

FIGURE 24–2: International flow of funds

In the middle of the international financial system are the intermediaries, making it possible for lenders to buy kinds of assets that are different from the promissory notes supplied by the borrowers. Most of the intermediaries in the international financial system are banks of some sort, dealing in assets and debts with maturities of up to five years. The only major financial institutions that make long-term international loans are official international lending agencies like the International Bank for Reconstruction and Development, better known as the **World Bank**.

Some of the assets held in this world financial system are part of the **world money supply**. Most world money is in the form of U.S.-dollar demand deposits held in U.S. banks, where it also serves as part of the U.S. money supply. The vast bulk of assets held in the world financial system are near moneys, denominated usually in U.S. dollars but sometimes in Japanese yen, German marks, French francs, or British pounds sterling. Most of the near moneys are term deposits issued by Eurobanks (banks operating in the Eurodollar market) or by banks in the U.S. Some of the near moneys are U.S. money market assets such as U.S. government treasury bills or short-term corporate paper. The remainder are bonds and promissory loan notes issued by traders, large and medium-size corporations, and governments that borrow abroad. The average term of the loans is longer than the average term of deposits, but most of the loans have floating interest rates tied to a benchmark deposit rate known as the London interbank offer rate (LIBOR), so a mismatch of asset and liability maturities does not mean that there is great volatility in interest spreads. Securitization has made the loans resaleable rather than illiquid, in contrast to domestic personal loans.

One of the confusing aspects of the world financial system is its overlap with the U.S. domestic financial system. The U.S. dollar is the key currency of international trade transactions, and U.S.-dollar demand deposits are the main medium of exchange in world trade. As a result, all U.S.-dollar money and near money can also be world money and near money. In principle, the demand for U.S. dollars for domestic transactions by U.S. residents is not part of the world financial system, and the demand for U.S. dollars for international transactions with nonresidents is part of it, but that principle can be difficult to apply in practice.

The role of the world financial system in channelling savings from surplus groups to deficit groups is clear in Figure 24–2. This role was dramatic in the years 1974–76 and 1979–82 as the OPEC nations became a huge surplus group almost overnight and as a host of less-developed countries became a huge deficit group, borrowing to finance their basic consumption needs for oil. The strains of channelling those funds occupied bankers for most of the 1980s in the form of massive debt reschedulings, postponements, defaults, and other problems with their Third World debts. The other major transfer of savings in the 1980s was from German and Japanese savers to U.S. borrowers; that took place on a huge scale but with little apparent strain.

Figure 24–2 does not show the role of the world financial system in providing an international payments mechanism to allow individuals to pay foreign bills without a great deal of fuss, and it does not show how the growth of the world money supply is arranged. We will postpone the topic of world money supply growth until section 4, but we will deal with the world payments mechanism in the next section.

SECTION 2

Foreign exchange markets and institutions

The currency of world trade is mainly U.S.-dollar demand deposits issued by U.S. banks, which are transferred by cheque or bank draft. Some deposits in other currencies are used, but the bulk are U.S.-dollar demand deposits.

Individuals and corporations in each nation have access to U.S. dollars mainly through their own domestic foreign exchange market, which is usually run by the private banks and some private foreign exchange brokers.[1] Private-sector banks in turn buy and sell foreign exchange at a wholesale level among themselves, with the central bank's traders, and with traders in other nations' foreign exchange markets.

The Canadian foreign exchange market

The Canadian foreign exchange market is different from most in that there are few private foreign exchange brokers acting as agents; the major banks run the foreign exchange market as principals through an **interbank foreign**

---

[1] In countries with foreign exchange controls, the foreign exchange market may effectively be a department of government or the central bank instead.

exchange market whose brokers are salaried employees of the Canadian Bankers' Association.[2]

Most foreign exchange is bought and sold in Canada within individual banks. Exporters and those Canadians selling assets for foreign currency sell their foreign exchange to their regular bank. Banks resell foreign currencies to importer customers and to those buying assets for foreign currency, at a price higher by 0.5 to 1 percent (the bank's expense and profit margin). If a bank's customers were to bring in for sale exactly the amount and mix of currencies that other customers wanted to buy, the bank would not need an interbank market. The bank would deposit the foreign exchange it received into its accounts with foreign banks (these are known as **correspondent accounts**), and issue draughts or money orders on those same accounts for the foreign exchange it sold.

However, it is unlikely that any one bank will have coming in from customers each day exactly the amount and mix of currencies it has sold. When there is a mismatch, the individual bank will allow its inventories of individual currencies to be run up or run down, but within narrow limits. Outside those limits the bank will go to the interbank market: it will sell off correspondent deposits in those currencies of which it has too much, and buy correspondent deposits in currencies of which it has too little.

The interbank market operates as an electronic auction on computer screens like the NASDAQ (National Association of Securities Dealers' Automatic Quotation) or CATS (Computer-Assisted Trading System) systems for stocks. Through agencies in London, Tokyo, and elsewhere, the interbank market operates round the clock. It is not only for spot (immediate) exchange transactions but also for forward exchange. The display of bid and offer rates for the various currencies includes bids and offers for spot delivery and for assorted future delivery dates up to ten years ahead.[3]

The role of the Bank of Canada

Today the Bank of Canada sits on the sidelines of Canada's foreign exchange market, basically just leaning against any sudden movements in exchange rates in order to slow them down. This is known as "leaning against the wind." Figure 24–3 shows Bank of Canada activity in the foreign exchange market; the Bank leans against increases in the value of the Canadian dollar by buying

---

[2] One private foreign exchange broker set up shop in Toronto in 1975; two more started business in 1978. They operate on commission (0.025 percent for large transactions); the interbank market has no commission, but banks operate on spreads generally larger than that.

[3] The Toronto, Winnipeg, and Chicago futures markets deal in foreign currency futures as competitors to the interbank forward-exchange market. The futures contracts are standardized and have commission charges. Forward-exchange arrangements are more customized, are paid for by spreads, and are generally not available to speculators. Forward-exchange contracts are available even in retail amounts as small and as specific as $3647.

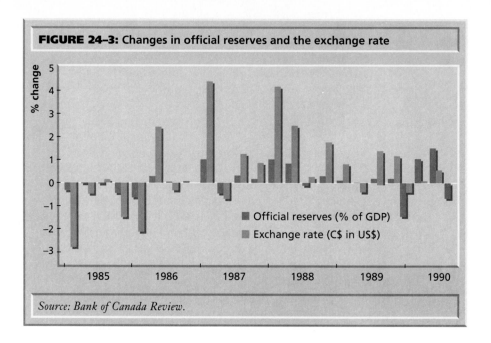

FIGURE 24–3: Changes in official reserves and the exchange rate

■ Official reserves (% of GDP)
■ Exchange rate (C$ in US$)

Source: Bank of Canada Review.

foreign exchange to add to official reserves, and against decreases by doing the opposite. Much of the Bank of Canada's exchange market activity is carried out automatically under agreements between central banks about stabilizing each others' currencies. When large changes in exchange rates are needed, central banks must change domestic interest rates instead.

Over the past 20 years the Bank of Canada's influence has shrunk because the scale of capital flows has grown much faster than has the scale of official foreign exchange reserves. In the early 1970s official reserves were 40 percent of outstanding foreign-owned, fixed-income securities. By 1989 that ratio was down to 10 percent.

For the period 1962–70 the Bank of Canada accepted a responsibility under the **Bretton Woods system** to intervene as often as necessary to keep the exchange rate within 1 percent on either side of 92.5 cents U.S. per Canadian dollar. Under the **European Monetary System (EMS)**, West European governments have agreed to maintain their exchange rates within narrow limits relative to each others' currencies, but not with the rest of the world. Under the European Monetary Union of 1992 that agreement will become much tighter and will cover all countries in the European Community. Effectively there will be a single currency. Fixed exchange rate systems therefore have a long history that is still relevant. At the centre of this history are the Bretton Woods agreement and GATT.

Bretton Woods, GATT, etc.

At the Bretton Woods conference in Bretton Woods, New Hampshire, in 1944, 40 countries agreed to an organization of international payments after World War II that would prevent the self-defeating cycle of currency devaluations and erection of import barriers that had occurred in the 1930s. The nations agreed that exchange rates should be pegged within 1 percent of a parity rate and maintained there by central banks' buying or selling foreign exchange to meet any excess demand or supply. That is, central banks were to run a two-way price support scheme for the price of their currency. Only if the nation had a "fundamental disequilibrium" at the central parity rate would the parity rate be changed. This system was maintained with increasing difficulty until early 1973, when most of the major trading nations abandoned defence of any central parity rate and let their currencies float.

The **General Agreement on Tariffs and Trade (GATT)** is an outgrowth of the Bretton Woods conference that sets out acceptable codes of conduct for trade in goods and services. It is an executive agreement of the participating governments that prohibits import controls and quotas, export subsidies, and barriers to the free international movement of capital funds. Not all members live up to the code at all times, but GATT does reduce the chances of a round of self-defeating attempts by member nations to protect domestic jobs at the expense of employment in the economies of their trading partners (that is, attempts to export domestic unemployment to their trading partners).

The two international agencies that coordinate central banking are the International Monetary Fund in Washington and the Bank for International Settlements in Basle, Switzerland. The **International Monetary Fund (IMF)** was started in 1947 as a specialized agency of the United Nations to monitor and assist in setting and maintaining central parity exchange rates. The participating nations realized that defence of parity exchange rates would require each central bank to have adequate reserves, so the IMF was set up as a central pool of foreign exchange reserves upon which all nations could draw. Each member nation contributes its quota: some in gold or other convertible foreign exchange, most in its own currency. In return, each nation can borrow foreign exchange up to and later beyond its quota. As a member's borrowing increases, its borrowing becomes subject to increasingly stringent conditions.

Many further arrangements have been made since 1947 to raise the foreign exchange reserves available to central banks for exchange rate management. The purpose of the Bretton Woods scheme was to enable central banks to defend fixed exchange rates, in order to give national governments time and elbow room for whatever domestic adjustments were needed to remove current account deficits. Now, with floating exchange rates and enormous capital flows, the purpose of the IMF borrowing privileges is more modest: merely to allow central banks to slow down or delay exchange rate movements so that foreign exchange markets do not become even more unstable.

Over time, the increase in world foreign exchange reserves has not nearly kept pace with the increase in either world trade flows or international capital flows. Many central banks and governments have also borrowed foreign exchange reserves from Eurobanks. For instance, the Canadian government arranged $5.5 billion in stand-bys in 1977 and 1978, in addition to borrowing $2.2 billion dollars and German marks from the international bond markets.

From a longer-term perspective, the most important change in provision of international reserves has been the introduction of **special drawing rights (SDRs)**. These "deposits" with the IMF were originally redeemable at a fixed price in gold, then in U.S. dollars, and now in a basket of currencies. They are still available only to central banks and a few other international institutions, but their convertibility enables central banks to economize on other forms of foreign exchange reserves. The most important aspect of SDRs is that they are issued by a stroke of the pen. They are a world paper money issued by a world central bank. SDRs are an important advance for the world financial system just as the development of central-bank fiat currency was important for Canada's domestic financial system. The use of SDRs is still relatively small, but so was the use of Dominion Notes when the Canadian government first issued them at the time of Confederation. Now at least the world has in place a mechanism that can adapt the stock of world money cheaply and reliably to meet the needs of world trade.

The **Bank for International Settlements (BIS)** in Basle, Switzerland, is an older cousin of the IMF. It was set up in 1930 by central banks of the industrialized countries, who remain its directors. It is essentially a central bankers' cooperative bank designed to do collectively what the central banks by themselves would find difficult. The BIS handles and coordinates foreign exchange swaps between member central banks, and it extends collective but limited guarantees to act as a lender of last resort for the Eurocurrency market banks. Because the latter are playing an ever larger role in the world financial system, the lender-of-last-resort function is becoming increasingly important for world financial confidence; confidence is necessary for performance in the financial world. The BIS was therefore the originator of the common regulation on bank capital adequacy, to be implemented in 1992 (see Chapter 11, section 4). The BIS has also established an international code of conduct to prevent money laundering for criminal activities, and is at work on capital adequacy standards for investment dealers.

Eurocurrency market regulation

The other ingredients of the international financial system are the **Eurocurrency markets** for short- and long-term assets. These markets have been discussed in Chapters 5 and 6 as extensions of Canadian financial markets (or vice versa). That discussion will not be repeated here.

One international issue raised by Eurocurrency markets is that of regulation for solvency: typically, such regulation has fallen between stools. Because the banks are generally transacting with foreigners and in a currency not that of the host country, the host countries have not felt much need to regulate the bank intermediaries, so the costs of doing Eurocurrency business are small. There are no reserve requirements where the deposits are held in foreign subsidiaries, no deposit insurance premiums, few reporting requirements, few taxes, and intense competition. Until the BIS arranged for common international bank capital requirements, these were loose as well. Margins between loan rates and deposit rates are therefore very small (0.5 to 1 percent), and deposit rates are often considerably higher than in domestic markets. When the reserve requirement in domestic financial markets is 3 percent, for instance, and loan assets yield 15 percent, the reserve requirement lowers average asset earnings for domestic assets (loans plus reserves) by 0.45 percent; domestic deposit yields must be 0.45 percent lower just to give the domestic bank the same spread as on Eurocurrency business. For large-scale accounts of many millions, 0.45 percent is a large difference, so it is understandable that intermediaries have flocked to the Eurocurrency markets to do their international business.

The plan to unite the European Community nations into a single market by 1992 is providing a powerful stimulus to uniform security legislation, which will tighten up the regulation of the Eurocurrency markets. European Community nations have had to agree on minimal standards for both domestic and foreign activity in order to establish a single market in financial services.

SECTION 3

⬜ Performance of the world's financial system

The international financial system poses both microeconomic and macroeconomic problems, quite apart from the problem each member nation has in deciding whether to fix or float its exchange rate. In this section we will consider these problems by looking at the goals of an international financial system and then seeing how they are or are not met.

There could be many different goals for the world financial system, but minimum goals must include the following:

1. it should provide an efficient payments mechanism for international transactions;
2. it should transfer savings efficiently from surplus groups to deficit groups, with at least no worsening of the world's distribution of incomes and wealth;
3. it should at least not reduce what equity there is in the world distribution of income and wealth;
4. it should provide for adequate growth of the world money supply in line with the needs of world trade.

Some of these goals have been met more satisfactorily than others.

The world payments mechanism

The **world payments mechanism** is efficient. The use of a single currency for almost all international trade provides all of the benefits of a single unit of account. With a single currency, traders are more easily able to keep track of relative values of goods and services from different economies, so there is a saving in information costs. The use of the currency of the major trading nation as that single, key currency enables still more savings. When the pound sterling was the major international currency, before World War I, world traders could make use of the existing British banking system to handle payments and receipts. No separate world banking structure was needed. After World War II, the U.S. dollar became the key international currency because the United States was the largest trading nation. Payments in world trade are made mostly by transfers of U.S.-dollar demand deposits in New York banks, so the existing U.S. financial system handles most of the payments mechanism. The international trade still conducted in pounds sterling or in French francs is similarly paid for through the British and French banking systems.

The system of payments by transfer of demand deposits is relatively efficient and is becoming more efficient. Most transfers are still made by cheque, bank draft, or telex, but large-scale transfers are made electronically through networks like CHIPS (Clearing House Interbank Payments System) or the SWIFT system (Society for Worldwide Interbank Financial Telecommunication; both are discussed in Chapter 2). Almost all major banks now record their deposit balances on computer, so that most international payments will soon be made electronically at almost zero marginal cost. This is a far cry from sending gold under armed guard to settle international debts, as was once done.

Gold has largely been replaced as a medium of exchange in international trade. It is still very important as a store of value internationally and will likely continue to be so for many decades, but it is now seldom used for making payments, even among central banks.[4] Given the relatively high costs of adding to world reserves of gold versus adding to stocks of paper money, this is indeed an efficient development.

The most significant innovation in the world payments mechanism has been the introduction of special drawing rights on the International Monetary Fund as an international paper money for payments among central banks. There is no world government with the power to declare SDRs as legal tender, which would ensure their acceptability as media of exchange, but the members have agreed on a set of rules for holding and transferring SDRs that do more or less the same thing.[5] The SDR is valued at the average of a basket of currencies and is therefore

---

[4] In September 1975 the members of the IMF agreed to abolish the official price of gold and to sell off or give back one-third of the IMF's total gold holdings. The proceeds of gold sales have been used to set up the IMF Trust Fund for soft loans to developing countries.

[5] Central banks can use their allocated SDR quotas to buy whatever foreign currencies they wish. Canada had used SDR 630 million of its 780 million quota in this way as of April 1982. We are not obligated to buy those SDRs back from the other central banks to which we have transferred them, but on average over a five-year period our SDR holdings must be at least 15 percent of our allocated quota. For Canada this means SDR 117 million at our current quota level. On the other hand, no country is obliged to accept SDRs in

automatically more stable than the value of the typical currency in that basket. Fifteen countries take advantage of this stability and peg their currencies to the SDR.[6] Currently the SDR balances of central banks are to world money what the Bank of Canada deposits of chartered banks are to the domestic Canadian money supply, but the SDR's role could easily be expanded should there be a need to take pressure off some of the other assets serving as international moneys (U.S. dollars in particular).

The other consideration in the international payments mechanism, besides its efficiency, is its risk level. Some foreign exchange rates are not tied together. Where the risk is worthwhile, traders can cover in forward-exchange markets for periods that now stretch up to ten years into the future. Most international trade transactions require only a few months of forward cover, between arranging the transaction and receiving payment, and for such short periods the forward-exchange markets have generally functioned smoothly and reliably.

Efficiency in transfer of savings

At first blush, the world financial system seems amazingly efficient compared with the financial systems of individual nations. The Eurocurrency market in particular is subject to intense competition from dozens of large banks from many countries. These banks operate on the slimmest of margins and make reasonable returns on equity only because of large leverage.[7]

On the other hand, it was the large international banks that made possible the huge overextension of credit to the Third World nations, in the period 1974–1980, that the latter could not service in the 1980s. The international financial system did succeed in recycling the surpluses of the oil-rich nations to eager lenders, but with so little prudence that the borrowing nations are still weighed down by their debt load. Effectively, too much of the savings of the OPEC countries was transferred to the Third World in 1974–80, and now the Third World borrowers are having to struggle to transfer some of it back.

The other major transfer of savings in the 1980s has been more successful. The United States has run large current account deficits to finance even larger budget deficits throughout the 1980s, while the German and Japanese economies have run large current account surpluses. The international financial system has been successful in channelling the savings of Germany and Japan into U.S.-

---

exchange for its own currency in an amount greater than three times its allocated quota. There is a charge for the use of SDRs, and an interest payment on SDR holdings above the quota.

[6] There are also Eurobond issues denominated in SDRs. These represent the use of the SDR merely as an international unit of account, and not as a medium of exchange or a store of value.

[7] Margins between prime loan rates and deposit rates in London were roughly 1.25 percent for developed countries and 2.5 percent for less-developed countries in 1974–76. By the period 1979–81, competition had slimmed these margins to only 0.5 percent and 0.68 percent, respectively. Adam Smith, *Paper Money* (New York: Dell, 1981), 300.

dollar assets for a decade, and in doing so without major disturbances in foreign exchange markets.

Equitable world distribution of income and wealth

In the Canadian economy there is a general presumption that income redistribution should be brought about mainly through taxes and transfer payments and that the financial system should merely be neutral, providing equal access to all and discriminating only by credit risk.

For the world financial system, however, this presumption does not hold. Income disparities between nations are huge, and there is no tax or transfer mechanism to remove those disparities. There is only world aid and the provision of soft loans on relatively generous terms. The world financial system is therefore under pressure to be very non-neutral, and to make loans to less developed countries on humanitarian grounds.

The Eurobanks have little room in their interest spreads for consideration of factors other than the credit risks of borrowers. The other international lenders are official institutions, more capable of bias toward poorer countries. The World Bank, for instance, was set up for just this purpose.

The International Monetary Fund has been the subject of pressure on this point since 1970 as SDRs have been created out of thin air and credited to member nations. The pressure on the IMF has been to have the credits go mainly to the poorer nations rather than mainly to the richer industrialized countries. The pressure has not been successful. Allocations so far have been just in proportion to IMF quotas, that favour the richer trading nations. The IMF did arrange a special oil facility to help with oil-related deficits in 1974–76, raising US$6.9 billion from OPEC nations and from some industrialized countries. The IMF also has a Trust Fund, established in 1977 with the proceeds of sales of one-sixth of the IMF's gold holdings, for special credits to developing nations. Finally, many if not most of the special credit facilities are designed to accommodate the poorer countries rather than the richer ones.

SECTION 4

◻ Growth of the world money supply

The least successful aspect of the world financial system's performance has been its inability to provide for growth of the world money supply in line with the needs of world trade. This has been a sore point for at least several hundred years, however, and the current international financial system is better than its predecessors by a large margin even if it is still unsatisfactory.

A gold-based money supply

In the nineteenth century the medium of exchange for most international trade came to be pound-sterling deposits in London banks. Trade was arranged through bills of exchange drawn on these banks and payable at maturity from deposits in these banks. The volume of deposits outstanding was tied to the banks' available cash reserves, which consisted of gold and Bank of England notes. The issue of Bank of England notes was also tied to Bank of England gold holdings (an arrangement known as the **gold standard**), so adequate growth of the world money supply depended on adequate growth of Britain's gold holdings. For much of the nineteenth century that growth was not adequate. World gold stocks grew by fits and starts with each new gold discovery, and between those discoveries world monetary growth could occur only if Britain increased its share of the total world gold stock. The result was long periods of falling price levels and slow output growth, particularly in the last quarter of the century. (The falling price level is shown in Figure 18–1.) Even now the physical stock of gold grows at less than 3 percent per year.

The U.S. dollar in shortage and glut

Since 1945 the key international currency has been the U.S. dollar. U.S. dollars are supplied to the rest of the world in exchange either for goods sold to U.S. residents or for foreign assets sold to U.S. residents. Both sources generate U.S. balance of payments deficits, on current account or capital account, or both. In short, the United States receives goods or assets from foreigners in exchange for merely increasing its monetary base and allowing banks to create new U.S.-dollar deposits.

This ability to get something for nothing is known as **seigniorage** and is enjoyed by the issuers of any money that is not full-bodied, as we discussed in Chapter 2. As a measure of the U.S. advantage, the external liabilities of the U.S. totalled US$1098 billion as of 1989. This is a rough estimate of the huge amount of foreign goods, services, and assets bought since 1945 simply by issuing new U.S. dollars.

For a while after 1945 there was a problem of insufficient international money because the U.S. ran huge trade surpluses while other, war-damaged economies were getting back on their feet. The trade surpluses sucked the U.S.-dollar deposits out of the rest of the world in the same way that the trade surpluses of France sucked specie out of the colony of New France in the seventeenth and eighteenth centuries (as described in Chapter 4). The rest of the world was left with too little world money to finance its trade. Marshall Plan aid from the U.S. to these economies helped to recirculate money with which other nations could buy U.S. goods, and in so doing it lubricated the world trade system.

In the 1950s the supply of U.S. dollars in world trade was sufficient even though world trade grew very rapidly. The U.S. balance of payments deficits grew to keep pace, mostly in the capital account via foreign borrowing in New York.

In the 1960s the United States ran into the gold constraint implied in any version of the gold standard. The U.S. was not on the gold standard domestically; residents were forbidden to hold gold in bullion or specie, and the U.S. money supply could be increased even if official U.S. gold holdings did not increase. Nonresidents could convert their U.S.-dollar assets into gold at $35 per ounce, however, and that promise initially explained a large part of foreigners' willingness to continue holding U.S.- dollar assets. Gradually, over the late 1950s and 1960s, the volume of U.S.-dollar assets held by nonresidents grew, until it was much larger than the total of U.S. gold reserves. The gold backing of the U.S. dollar began to look shaky even for nonresidents.

The volume of nonresident holdings of U.S.-dollar assets grew because the U.S. economy ran persistent deficits in its balance of payments. Its trading partners grew more competitive, and U.S. corporations stepped up their expansion abroad. The U.S. deficits could have been eliminated by a devaluation of the U.S. dollar, by restrictive domestic monetary policy, or by trade barriers, but the U.S. government was unwilling to allow any of these. Instead, the U.S. compounded the problem by stepping up its deficits: it waged an expensive war in Vietnam without any major increase in taxes. The results were even larger balance of payments deficits and even faster growth of nonresidents' holdings of U.S. dollars. The U.S. government was taking maximum advantage of its seigniorage by fighting the Vietnam War partly with resources of other countries, bought with newly printed world money.

Holders of U.S. dollars did not need to hold their wealth in that form. They could instead use the dollars to buy up U.S. land or the stock of U.S. companies, thereby returning the funds to the U.S. financial system. They could convert the dollars to gold or to their own domestic currency. In the latter case foreign central banks ended up holding the dollars, since under the Bretton Woods system those central banks had to buy up any excess supply of dollars in their foreign exchange markets. More and more of the surplus U.S. dollars came to be held by foreign central banks as private holders became more convinced that the U.S. dollar would have to be devalued.[8] By 1971, U.S. gold reserves were only one-sixth as large as official liabilities of the U.S. to foreigners.

The shift to floating exchange rates and paper money

The crunch came in August 1971 when U.S. President Nixon suspended convertibility of the dollar into gold, slapped on a temporary import surcharge, and abandoned any defence of the dollar's value in foreign exchange markets.

---

[8] This caused some protest abroad. The printing of money by the U.S., and the automatic purchase of that money by the Bank of France (as well as by other central banks) in order to defend the U.S.-dollar exchange rate, conferred on the U.S. what General de Gaulle regarded as "an exorbitant privilege." The Bank of France was essentially lending on demand to the U.S., and the loan was being used in part to finance investment abroad by the U.S. As one commentator has put it, "What was to stop the Americans from printing money and buying up France?" Smith, *Paper Money*, 147.

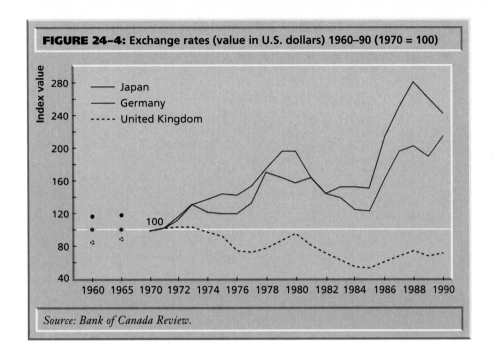

FIGURE 24–4: Exchange rates (value in U.S. dollars) 1960–90 (1970 = 100)

Source: Bank of Canada Review.

In the Smithsonian Agreement of December 1971 the dollar's value in gold was lowered, while those of several other currencies were raised. By March 1973 even these measures were not enough, and all major currencies were allowed to float. Central banks were no longer obliged to buy up unwanted amounts of world money, only to see it devalued months later.

Nixon's action of August 1971 removed the gold constraint from the supply of U.S. dollars to nonresidents. Since then there has been no explicit limit to the creation of world money. The world now has a problem that is just the opposite of that of the gold standard system of the last century. With the U.S. dollar still the main form of world money and with few close substitutes, the United States can and does create more world money simply by running up large balance of payments deficits at the expense of the rest of the world. The rest of the world cannot refuse to accept the U.S. dollars as long as dollars are the international medium of exchange. Holders can use the dollars to buy up U.S. assets, or exchange them for foreign currencies and force the dollar exchange rate down, or just hold the dollars in Eurodollar deposits (that is, interest-earning near-money deposits) at good interest rates. In the 1980s the Japanese and German investors who financed most of the huge U.S. current account deficits of that decade chose all three alternatives at one time or another. Their choices caused substantial swings in the value of the U.S. dollar, as Figure 24–4 shows.

Alternative world moneys

The unsatisfactory state of the world money supply has given rise to a search for better ways of providing it. The problem with using a key currency as the medium of exchange has been that the key-currency country must act against its own short-term self-interest in not exploiting its seigniorage. At the present time, the United States gets only a share of the benefits from proper growth of world money, but all of the benefits of exploiting seigniorage.

In national financial systems without any discipline from a gold standard, the solution to providing a proper domestic money supply has been to have an elected government responsible for providing an adequate money supply and to throw that government out of power if it fails to do so, rather than to entrust the matter to any private group such as bankers. The world's nations have started on a similar route by having the International Monetary Fund issue special drawing rights on the agreement of the world's governments. This is collective action, essentially, by all of the parties who will suffer if the volume of world money is not adequate. So far, however, SDRs are only a limited form of international money, useful only for transactions between central banks.[9]

The solution toward which the world seems to be moving is that suggested by Keynes at the Bretton Woods conference in 1944: a system of paper money created by a world central bank on the agreement of world governments. The value of the paper money would be based on the value of a basket of currencies, and its issue would be subject to no constraints other than the consensus of all governments affected. This is a reasonable international approximation of the system Canada has for controlling its domestic money supply. In Europe, the twelve member nations of the European Community are blazing the trail by negotiating towards a common central bank; it seems likely that they will also negotiate binding procedures to coordinate fiscal policy. This example may spread beyond Europe.

SECTION 4

Summary

The Canadian financial system is embedded in a broader world financial system, much as the Canadian economy is embedded in a world economy. There are some obviously international financial institutions that give concrete structure to the world financial system, such as the International Monetary Fund (IMF), the Bank for International Settlements (BIS), and the General Agreement on Tariffs and Trade (GATT).

The rest of the world financial system is more amorphous. Central banks and private commercial banks in each nation play a role internationally by

---

[9] The European currency unit (ECU) is a parallel form of international currency that is made up of European currencies in fixed weights. Its use is limited at present.

servicing the needs of their customers for foreign exchange and by trading in foreign currency assets. Even more amorphous is the Eurocurrency market run through banks usually operating out of their home jurisdictions in currencies other than that of the host country. These banks make up a very competitive set of suppliers of short- to long-term deposits and compete equally vigorously for loan customers.

The world financial system is a financial system like any other, and its performance can be assessed. The logical criteria are how well it performs its functions of (a) providing a world payments mechanism, (b) transferring surpluses from primary lenders to primary borrowers, and (c) providing neither more nor less money than is needed for world trade. The world financial system scores fairly well in transferring funds and providing a payments mechanism.

The major difficulty of the world financial system has been in providing for the right growth of international money. As long as the U.S. dollar is the main key currency, the United States is free to increase the world's money supply too rapidly without suffering all of the consequences, particularly if other nations attempt to hold their exchange rates fixed. It is possible that the IMF's special drawing rights will gradually grow to fill much of the U.S. dollar's place in world trade, in which case at least the issue of SDRs will be a collective decision rather than the prerogative of one nation.

Key Terms

rest-of-the-world sector	International Monetary Fund
international flow of funds	(IMF)
World Bank	special drawing rights (SDRs)
world money supply	Bank for International
interbank foreign exchange	Settlements (BIS)
market	Eurocurrency markets
correspondent accounts	world payments mechanism
Bretton Woods system	gold standard
European monetary system	seigniorage
General Agreement on Tariffs	
and Trade (GATT)	

Questions and Problems

1. How is the international financial system different from a national financial system, in (a) its roles and (b) its institutions?

2. What is the world money supply, and why is it held?

3. Why is the recycling problem for the world financial system more difficult than the domestic recycling problem for a national financial system?

4. In what ways are SDRs money?

5. Who have been the recipients of the benefits of world seigniorage, and how have they come to receive those benefits?

6. Does the United States still receive seigniorage benefits now that the world is operating on a floating exchange rate system? Explain.

7. The "Lucas critique" states that changing government policy rules causes changes in other parts of the economy's structure, and that such structural changes must be recognized to forecast properly the effects of changing policy rules. In light of this, discuss whether the change from fixed to floating exchange rates in 1973 has anything to do with liberalization of capital flow restrictions (which have made global financial markets possible).

Suggestions for Further Reading

Binhammer, H.H. *Money, Banking and the Canadian Financial System*, 5th ed. Toronto: Methuen, 1988.

Boreham, Gordon F. with Ronald G. Bodkin. *Money, Banking, and Finance: The Canadian Context*. Toronto: Holt, Rinehart and Winston, 1988.

McMillan, Alexander. *An Introduction to Canadian Financial Markets: An Analytical Approach*. Scarborough, Ont.: Prentice-Hall Canada, 1989.

Meier, Gerald M. *Problems of a World Monetary Order*, 2nd ed. New York: Oxford University Press, 1982.

Neave, Edwin H. *Canada's Financial System*. Toronto: Wiley, 1981 (or later edition).

Sampson, Anthony. *The Money Lenders*. New York: Hodder and Stoughton, 1982.

Shearer, Ronald A., John Chant, and David Bond. *The Economics of the Canadian Financial System*, 2nd ed. Scarborough, Ont.: Prentice-Hall Canada, 1984 (or later edition).

Smith, Adam. *Paper Money*. New York: Dell, 1981.

GLOSSARY

A

Accelerationist model: Model of aggregate demand and supply behaviour in which inflation accelerates or decelerates whenever the unemployment rate is below or above the NAIRU.

Accelerator mechanism: Dynamic mechanism in which changing investment spending adds to other fluctuations in aggregate demand growth.

Acceptance business: Taking over the management and collection of clients' accounts receivable, either for a fee or by buying the accounts receivable at a discount from face value.

Actuarial reserve: Present value of an insurance company's liabilities to policyholders.

Adaptive expectations: Expectations formed by looking backward at what has happened in the recent past.

Adverse selection: Selection of a group of insured such that the group has a higher probability of the event insured against than does the general population.

Aggregate demand (AD): Real demand for goods and services during a year; real gross national expenditure, excluding unplanned inventory accumulation.

Aggregate demand multiplier: Rate of change in equilibrium aggregate demand per dollar of change in an exogenous determinant of aggregate demand.

Aggregate supply (AS): Level of output of real goods and services in a year; real gross domestic product.

Alberta treasury branches (ATBs): System of provincially owned and operated financial institutions in Alberta, performing all the functions of a bank.

Amortized value: Form of book value of an asset that spreads any capital gain between the purchase price and redemption value over the entire lifetime of the asset.

Annuity: Asset providing a steady, fixed stream of payments, either for life (life annuity) or for a definite period.

Annuity value: Amount per annum, in perpetuity, that is equivalent to a fixed lump sum.

Arbitrage: Flow of funds from one financial market to another in response to differences in relative expected yields.

Arbitrage models: Models of relative yield structures that rely on arbitrage to hold the structures in place.

Army bills: Form of paper currency issued by the colonial government to finance the War of 1812.

Asset-backed securities: Assets that are generalized claims on a portfolio of other financial assets such as a pool of mortgages.

Asset-market equilibrium locus, or LM curve: A line joining combinations of real income and nominal interest rate at which asset markets are in equilibrium.

Asset portfolio: Collection of assets held.

Assignment rule: Assignment of stabilization policy tools to stabilization policy targets according to each policy tool's comparative advantage in achieving targets.

Automated clearing and settlement system (ACSS): Personnel, equipment, and procedures to process each day's cheques from receiving to paying banks, and to transfer net amounts owed between clearing banks.

Automatic transfer service, cash management account, or zero-balance banking: Arrangements under which banks transfer funds from customers' chequing deposits to earn more interest until needed to cover cheques written.

B

Balance of payments: Record of all of a nation's receipts and payments involving foreign currency during a year.

Bank Act: Federal act that regulates banks.

Bank for International Settlements (BIS): Central bankers' bank in Basle, Switzerland, responsible for coordinating agreements among central banks and other financial regulators in advanced industrial economies. *See* Basle Agreement.

Bank of Canada: Central bank for Canada that issues all cash reserve assets for the banking system.

Bank of settlement: A (central) bank holding those deposit balances of other banks that are used to make settlements between those other banks.

Bank rate: Minimum rate at which the Bank of Canada will lend to members of the Canadian Payments Association; fixed at 0.25 percent above the average yield on the most recent weekly treasury bill auction.

Bankers' acceptances: Large, short-term trade credits whose payment has been guaranteed by a bank (for an acceptance fee).

Bankruptcy: The declared state of being unable to pay one's debts.

Barter: Exchange of goods and services directly for other goods and services, without the use of any medium of exchange.

Barter exchange: A network in which barter can take place without simultaneous exchange.

Basis point: One-hundredth of a percentage point.

Basket clause: Clause in some financial institutions' legislation specifying what percentage of total assets (how large a basket) can be invested in specific assets generally prohibited elsewhere in the regulations.

Basle Agreement: Agreement among financial regulators of most advanced industrial countries on minimum standards of capital adequacy for banks; agreed upon in 1988, in force by 1992.

Bear market: A market dominated by those expecting falling prices, called bears.

Bearer instrument: An asset whose ownership is not registered, but transferred simply by passage from hand to hand.

Best-efforts underwriting: Underwriting without a fixed guarantee of price to the issuer. *See* Bought-deal underwriting.

Beta: Measure of volatility of an asset's yield relative to that of the market index.

Blended payments: Level payments over the life of a loan that combine interest and repayment of principal.

Book value: The value of an asset or liability actually recorded on the balance sheet of the holder or issuer; usually market value or amortized value or historical cost.

Borrower–lender diagram: Diagram that shows the borrowers curve and the lenders curve for a particular asset.

Borrowers curve: Curve relating (a) the amount of a particular debt that borrowers want to leave outstanding to (b) the yield expected or promised on that debt. *See also* Lenders curve.

Bought-deal underwriting: Underwriting with a fixed guarantee of price to the issuer. *See* Best-efforts underwriting.

BP curve: Equilibrium locus for the foreign exchange market, on an IS–LM diagram.

Bretton Woods system: Fixed exchange rate system agreed on at the Bretton Woods conference in 1944; abandoned in 1973.

Broad money: Narrow money plus close substitutes for narrow-money assets.

Broad money rule: Monetary rule in which short-term interest rates are changed to keep the growth rate of broad money near a target path.

Buffer stock: Stock of assets that can be run up or down to avoid more frequent adjustment of output or spending or other assets instead; inventories and money are the two assets most frequently used.

Bull market: A market dominated by those expecting rising prices, called bulls.

Buyback: Purchase and resale agreement between a money market dealer and lenders other than the Bank of Canada.

C

Caisses populaires: Quebec or francophone credit unions.

Call option: A contract entitling but not obligating the holder to buy the underlying asset at the option's strike price on or before the option's expiry date.

Callable: Redeemable before maturity (at one or more call dates) at the discretion of the issuer.

Cambridge equation: $M = kPY$, where k is a constant in the short run.

Canada Deposit Insurance Corporation (CDIC): Federal Crown corporation that insures retail deposits in banks and most near-banks.

Canada Mortgage and Housing Corporation (CMHC): Federal Crown corporation that insures many residential mortgages and lends directly in a few specific parts of the housing market.

Canada Pension Plan (CPP): Mandatory pension plan to which all full-time workers and employers outside Quebec contribute, that lends all contributions directly to provinces.

Canadian Payments Association (CPA): Association of all financial institutions that issue transferable deposits in Canada; operator of the automated clearing and settlement system.

Capacity use or utilization: Ratio of actual output to full-capacity output.

Capital account: Record of all foreign currency receipts and payments for transactions not involving currently produced goods and services.

Capital adequacy: Adequacy of the ratio of equity to assets. *See also* Leverage ratio.

Capital asset pricing model (CAPM): Model in which each asset's equilibrium expected yield depends only on its beta and the yield on the risk-free asset.

Capital consumption or depreciation : Decrease in the value of an asset due to wear and tear.

Capital consumption or depreciation allowance: An estimate of the decrease in value of a real asset due to wear and tear; used to shelter some of gross income from income tax.

Capital gains income: Income or extra wealth received in the form of an increase in the market value of assets held.

Capital market line: Relationship relating equilibrium expected yields and betas of different assets.

Capital markets: Markets for long-term financial assets.

Capital ratio: Ratio of equity to assets.

Capital stock adjustment: Investment spending to adjust actual capital stock to desired levels; source of the accelerator mechanism.

Career labour market: Labour market for those skilled workers and managers for whom turnover costs are high, both to employers and to employees.

Cash management account, or zero-balance banking: *See* Automatic transfer service.

Cash reserve assets: Assets eligible to satisfy cash reserve requirements; under the 1980 Bank Act Canadian coin and Bank of Canada notes, plus chartered bank deposits in the Bank of Canada. Same as Monetary base and High-powered money.

Cash reserve management: Changing the supply of cash reserve assets to leave banks with more or less excess cash reserves than they want.

Cash reserve requirement: Requirement in the Bank Act of 1980 that banks have at least a specified minimum level of cash reserves on hand for every dollar of deposits used to finance assets; to be abolished in the 1991 Bank Act.

Cash surrender value: Amount to be paid out to each policyholder upon surrender of an insurance policy; approximately equal to the value of the policy reserve for each policy.

Casual labour market: Labour market for workers for whom turnover costs are low, both to employers and to employees. *See also* Career labour market.

Central parity rate: Exchange rate at the centre of the band that the government is committed to maintain, under fixed exchange rate systems such as the Bretton Woods system and the European Monetary System.

Centrals: The central credit unions or caisses populaires that act as central banker to the locals. *See also* Locals.

Certainty-equivalent approach: Treating uncertain forecasts of future exogenous variables as though they were certain, in choosing stabilization policy settings.

Characteristic equation: Equation relating an asset's actual yield to the market portfolio yield; source of the asset's beta.

Chartered banks: Firms chartered under the federal Bank Act.

Chattel mortgage: Loan secured with a claim or mortgage on movable goods such as a car or boat.

Clearing: Processing cheques and other payment orders after they are deposited or cashed.

Clearing House Interbank Payments System (CHIPS): International clearing and settlement system operated through the Federal Reserve Bank of New York.

Clearing members: Larger members of the Canadian Payments Association that hold settlement balances in the Bank of Canada for clearing purposes.

Closed-end mutual funds: Mutual funds whose shares are not redeemable.

Closed mortgage: Mortgage loan that is not repayable before maturity.

Collateral: Asset pledged as security for a loan, to be seized by the creditor in event of default.

Commercial banking: The business of making unsecured, short-term, self-liquidating loans to finance inventories, with funds borrowed by issue of short-term deposits or banknotes.

Commercial paper: Short-term, nonredeemable loan notes issued by large, well-known corporations with little default risk.

Commodity exchange standard: A monetary system with token money convertible into a commodity that is not itself used as money.

Commodity standard: Monetary system in which the medium of exchange is a commodity with non-monetary uses.

Common stock or shares: Shares held by ultimate owners of a firm, who share in the residual profits of the firm without limit.

Conflict of interest: Situation in which a decision maker represents two or more different groups whose interests call for different, mutually exclusive actions.

Constrained debtors: Debtors who would borrow more and spend more if only lenders would agree to lend them more.

Consumer price index: Average level of prices of goods and services bought by consumers, set to equal 100 at some benchmark date.

Contagion effects: Liquidity difficulties passed on from a firm in trouble to other firms, just because the other firms are seen by the lending public as somehow similar.

Contingent payments: Payments that are required only if a specific situation or contingency occurs.

Contractual savings firms: Firms that take in funds from households under contracts for regular investment of savings amounts.

Convertible: Exchangeable for some other asset such as common shares, at the holder's discretion, at a set conversion rate.

Core capital: Under the Basle Agreement, shareholders' equity excluding preferred shares and all loss reserves.

Correlation coefficient: Coefficient measuring the degree and direction of a linear association between two variables over time.

Correspondent accounts or deposits: Deposits held by domestic banks in other banks abroad, that are used by domestic banks to make foreign currency payments for customers.

Cost of forward cover: The cost of hedging foreign exchange contracts; determined by forward exchange premiums or discounts, and expressed usually in percent per annum.

Cost of living adjustment (COLA) clause: Clause in collective agreements providing for automatic increase in wage levels in line with changes in the consumer price index.

Coupon rate: Bond yield defined as the interest coupon divided by the face value.

Covariance: A measure of joint variation of two yields around their respective expected yields.

Covered interest differential: Simple interest differential less the cost of forward cover.

Covered interest parity: Cost of forward cover exactly offsetting the simple interest differential; covered interest differential of zero.

Credit rating: Default risk classification of an asset by a rating agency such as Moody or Standard & Poor.

Credit rationing: Allocation of credit among similar loan customers on grounds other than willingness to pay the interest rate charged.

Credit risk: Risk of the borrower not paying in full and on time.

Crowding out: Suppression of other components of aggregate demand by an expansion of one component—usually government spending.

Currency drain: Leakage of extra high-powered money into extra currency holdings of the public.

Currency swap: Exchange of interest obligations in one currency for interest obligations in a different currency.

Current account: Part of the balance of payments including trade in currently produced goods and services plus transfer payments involving foreign currencies.

Current yield: Interest or dividends expressed as a percentage of current market price.

D

Day loan (day-to-day loan): Loan note issued by money market dealers to a bank, extendible one day at a time.

Debentures: Bonds that do not have any specific real property pledged as collateral; also the name given to term deposits of some mortgage loan companies.

Debit card: A general-purpose payments card, the use of which authorizes immediate payment from the user's chequing account.

Debit float: Value of cheques deposited and credited to receivers' accounts but not yet debited from the payors' accounts.

Debt management: Managing the composition of government debt.

Default risk: Risk of the borrower not paying on time and in full.

Defined-benefit pension plan: A pension plan promising specific pensions at retirement not contingent on the asset value of the pension fund.

Demand deposits: Deposits withdrawable on demand.

Demand loan: Loan repayable on demand at the discretion of the lender, with no fixed repayment schedule.

Demand management policy: Use of demand management tools to achieve desired growth of aggregate demand.

Demand management tool: Any stabilization policy variable under the government's control that influences aggregate demand.

Demand shock: Any disturbance to aggregate demand not caused through a change in the price level.

Deposit administration plan: One type of pension plan managed by an insurance company.

Deposit expansion model: Model that explains banks' issue of deposits as tied mechanically to the level of cash reserve assets available, and to nothing else.

Deposit expansion multiplier: Ratio of change in total deposits outstanding to change in high-powered money.

Deposit insurance: Insurance of depositors against default by the deposit-issuing institution.

Deposit-takers: Financial intermediaries that finance most of their assets by issuing deposits of some sort.

Depreciation: *See* Capital consumption.

Direct borrowing and lending: Borrowing by a primary borrower directly from a primary lender.

Direct clearers: *See* Clearing members.

Disclosure rules: Regulations that force intermediaries and others to disclose publicly all relevant details of loans being solicited.

Discounted present value: *See* Present discounted value.

Discounting: Selling a claim on future payments, at the present discounted value of those future payments.

Disintermediation: A shift of lending away from debts of intermediaries and toward debts of primary borrowers.

Diversification: Combining several assets with different payment streams.

Dividend yield: *See* Current yield.

Dominion Notes: Currency issued by the federal government between Confederation and the startup of the Bank of Canada in 1935.

Double coincidence of wants: Requirement for any barter transaction to take place; coincidence must be simultaneous for pure barter, but not for a barter exchange.

Drawdowns: Transfers of the federal government's deposit balances from its accounts in the chartered banks to its account in the Bank of Canada.

Dynamic efficiency: Allocation of savings to the most productive forms of investment.

Dynamic LM curve: An LM curve drawn with capacity use replacing income.

E

Economies of scale: Reductions in operating costs or risks per dollar of assets, due to a larger scale of operations.

Economies of scope: Reductions in operating costs or risks per dollar of assets, due to a wider variety of operations.

Effective annual interest rate: Annual interest rate including compounding.

Efficient frontier or set: The upper left edge of the feasible set of combinations of portfolio risk and expected yield.

Efficient markets hypothesis: Hypothesis that market participants use all available information in arriving at expectations about future asset prices.

Efficient risky portfolio: The single collection of risky assets that, in various combinations with the risk-free asset, produces the efficient frontier.

Elastic expectations: Expectations of a future situation that adjust more than fully with changes in the current situation.

Elasticity: ratio of the percentage change in a response variable (e.g., the demand for money) to the percentage change in a stimulus variable (e.g., the level of real income).

Endogenous: Determined within the model, not given from outside.

Endowment point: The point on a diagram of intertemporal consumption choice whose coordinates are the current and future incomes with which the individual is endowed.

Equilibrium locus: Set of points at which an equilibrium could occur.

Equity: Equal treatment of equals; also, a synonym for wealth or net worth.

Equity premium: Extra yield required to persuade investors to hold the risky portfolio rather than the risk-free asset.

Estate, trust, and agency (ETA) business: Business of trust companies as instructed agent for others (executor, trustee, agent).

Eurobanks: Banks operating in the Eurocurrency market.

Eurocurrency market: Wholesale market for foreign currency assets (bonds, deposits, and loans), in a currency other than that of the host country; no longer confined to Europe.

European monetary system (EMS): Fixed exchange rate system supported by some members of the European Community since 1979.

Excess cash reserves: Cash reserve assets held over and above those required.

Exchange fund account (EFA): Fund of the Minister of Finance holding most of Canada's official foreign exchange reserves; managed by the Bank of Canada.

Exogenous: Determined outside the model; given or predetermined.

Expectations-augmented Phillips curve: Phillips curve that shifts with changes in expected future inflation.

Expected utility: Probability-weighted average of possible utility levels.

Expected yield: A weighted average of possible yields, with relative probabilities serving as weights; the midpoint of a probability distribution of possible yields.

Extendible: With a maturity date that can be extended.

F

Face value: Promised repayment value of an asset.

Factoring and acceptance business: *See* Acceptance business.

Feasible set: Set of all possible outcomes (for instance, of expected yield and portfolio variance).

Federal deposit transfers: *See* Drawdowns.

Fedwire: System for handling large-scale payments and securities transfers, both in the United States and internationally; operated through the U.S. Federal Reserve System.

Fiat money: An item that serves as money because the government orders it so.

Fiduciary money: Token money that the holders trust will be convertible into some form of commodity money such as specie.

Finance company: Intermediary that finances short-term loans of various sorts, generally

by issuing short-term paper in the money market.

Finance paper: Short-term, nonredeemable loan notes issued by finance companies, secured by blocks of consumer loans.

Financial flow accounts: Record of savings, investment, lending, and borrowing by sectors of the economy.

Financial futures: Futures contracts in financial assets.

Financial institution or intermediary: Firm that borrows in order to relend.

Financial intermediation: Borrowing in order to relend.

Financial lease: Long-term lease of a real asset, for a period covering almost all of the asset's working life.

Fiscal impulse: Change in primary, structural government surplus.

Fiscal stimulus: Change in primary, structural government deficit.

Fisher effect: Increase in nominal interest rates caused by greater expected inflation.

Fixed-H rule: Monetary rule that keeps the stock of high-powered money constant.

Fixed-installment debt: Debt with a fixed, regular payment blending together interest and principal repayments.

Fixed-R rule: Monetary rule that keeps the nominal interest rate constant.

Fix-price markets: Markets in which prices are set, usually by the seller; such prices are generally not responsive to demand changes in the short run.

Flex-price markets: Markets in which prices fluctuate to balance supply and demand on a daily basis, as in an auction.

Float: *See* Debit float.

Floating exchange rate: Exchange rate not maintained by a central bank near an official parity rate.

Floating-rate notes: Short- to medium-term notes issued in the Eurocurrency markets by large borrowers, at yields tied to LIBOR.

Floating rates: Yields on existing assets that change immediately with some benchmark yield such as LIBOR or the prime rate.

Flow: Rate of activity, measured over a period of time.

Flow equilibrium: Balance of flows, such as borrowing and lending, or of saving and investing.

Flow of funds identity: That savings of all sorts must equal investment spending (including unplanned investment).

Forced saving: Saving that borrowers must do to build up the equity for minimum down payments on assets they would otherwise finance entirely by borrowing.

Foreign exchange risk: A specific form of income risk, the uncertainty being due to quotation of payments in a foreign currency.

Foreign exchange swaps: Swap of foreign currency assets in the exchange fund account for government deposits in the Bank of Canada; a technique used by the Bank of Canada to allow greater redeposits.

Foreign saving: Net capital inflow.

Forward contract: Contract obligating the holder to buy or sell at the contract price on or before the forward date; usually involving foreign exchange.

Forward markets: The markets for forward contracts, generally between customers and banks.

Forward rate agreement: Contract to borrow or lend a stated amount at the forward contract interest rate on or before the forward contract date.

Four-pillar system: System of four separate activities (banking, insurance, underwriting, and corporate trustee activity) undertaken by four separate groups.

Fundamental analysis: Forecasting future asset returns by looking at what determines the incomes and expenses of the companies issuing the assets; contrasted with technical analysis.

Funded pension plan: A pension plan whose assets at least match the expected present discounted value of liabilities to future pension recipients.

Futures contract: Contract obligating the holder to buy or sell at the contract price at a specified future delivery date.

Futures markets: Organized exchanges on which futures contracts are traded for commodities and financial assets.

G

General Agreement on Tariffs and Trade (GATT): International code of conduct for trade and capital transactions.

General equilibrium: The state of simultaneous equilibrium in all markets.

General insurance: Property and casualty insurance; other than life insurance.

Generalized claim: A claim on part of the total return of a pool of assets, without specific claim on any one asset.

Government deposits: Deposits held by the federal government both in the Bank of Canada and in the chartered banks; the assets used for drawdowns and redeposits.

Gresham's law: Bad money drives out good.

Gross real investment: Net real investment plus capital consumption allowances.

Gross saving: Net saving plus capital consumption allowances.

Group annuity: A pension plan managed by an insurance company.

Guaranteed investment certificate (GIC): Name given to some term deposits of trust companies.

H

Hedging: Arranging one's portfolio such that the fluctuations in one asset's yield offset exactly the fluctuations in other assets' yields.

Hedging markets: Markets for options, swaps, insurance, and futures contracts, that can be used to offset (hedge) specific risks in portfolios of other assets.

High-powered money: The total stock of cash reserve assets; the same as the monetary base.

Holding-period yield: Yield calculated over the asset holder's planned holding period, not necessarily to maturity of the asset.

Human wealth: Capitalized present value of current and expected future real labour income.

I

IMF quota: Amount of foreign exchange that each IMF member country can draw on from the International Monetary Fund.

Income debentures: Bonds whose interest payments are conditional on satisfactory profits for the issuing company.

Income effect: Effect of a change in real income on quantity demanded, holding relative prices constant.

Income risk: Uncertainty over the stream of future nominal payments to be made by the borrower, other than that due to default risk.

Income velocity of circulation: The number of times the money supply changes hands during a year in a *final* sale of goods and services.

Incomes policy: Policy to affect wage- and price-setting behaviour directly.

Indenture agreement: Agreement between a bond issuer and the bondholders about terms and conditions of a bond issue.

Index options: Options written with as underlying asset a notional portfolio made up just like a stock market index (e.g., the TSE 300).

Indexed bond: A bond whose principal value and interest coupons are adjusted proportionally to the general price level.

Indicator of monetary policy: A measure that changes reliably as monetary policy becomes more or less restrictive (e.g., the difference between net M2 growth and the inflation rate).

Indifference curve: A curve joining together all points on a diagram with the same level of satisfaction or utility.

Indirect borrowing: Borrowing by a primary borrower from a financial intermediary.

Indirect lending: Lending by a primary lender to a financial intermediary.

Indirect taxes: Taxes levied on goods or assets, rather than on individuals.

Inelastic expectations: Expectations of a future situation that adjust less than fully with changes in the current situation.

Inflation: Rate of change in the price level per year.

Inflation hedge: An asset whose nominal yield adjusts fully with inflation, whose real yield is unaffected by changes in the inflation rate.

Inflation premium: The extra nominal interest rate added to fixed-nominal-value assets to compensate lenders for expected future inflation.

Inflation risk: Uncertainty of future purchasing power because of uncertainty of future price levels.

Inflation tax: Reduction in the real value of money holdings each year due to inflation.

Information costs: The costs of acquiring information about a particular kind of financial asset.

Insider trading: Buying or selling by any individual in possession of company-specific material information not publicly released.

Insolvency: *See* Bankruptcy.

Installment debts: Consumer debts that provide for repayment in a series of level, blended payments of interest and principal.

Institutional markets: Wholesale financial markets in which financial institutions are the main participants.

Insurance company: A company that issues insurance policies as its liabilities.

Insured plan: A pension plan managed by an insurance company.

Interbank foreign exchange market: The centre of the wholesale foreign exchange market, where the banks trade with each other and large customers.

Interest coupon: The dollar amount payable on a bond each period, sometimes specified on a series of coupons attached to the bond certificate itself.

Interest rate swaps: Swaps of one kind of interest obligation for a different type, e.g., of floating-rate interest for fixed-rate interest.

Intermediation: *See* Financial intermediation.

International Monetary Fund (IMF): Official international lending agency, creator of special drawing rights.

Intertemporal choice: Choice between consuming in one period and consuming in some different period.

Intertemporal labour substitution: Substitution of work today for work in the future; the source of some supply responses in the new classical theory.

Inventory theory: An explanation of demand for transactions balances in which agents treat money as an inventory of spending power between income receipts.

Investment bank: A financial institution arranging and providing longer-term financing for new and existing firms.

Investment companies: Financial institutions that invest in longer-term securities of non-financial firms; they include venture capital firms and holding companies.

Investment dealers: Firms that specialize in trading financial assets either as brokers or from their own inventories, in money and capital and hedging markets.

Investment demand: Demand for currently produced real assets — housing, plant, equipment, and inventories.

IS curve: Line joining all combinations of output Y and interest rate R at which the goods market is in equilibrium.

IS shock: Any disturbance to the IS curve.

IS–BP shift locus: Locus of intersections of the IS and BP curves as the real exchange rate changes.

J

Jobbers: Firms accepting bids and making offers as principals, in order to make a market operate smoothly; a subgroup of investment dealers.

Junk bonds: Bonds with credit ratings below investment grade (B and below).

L

Legal tender: Assets that must by law be accepted in payment of debts.

Lenders curve: Curve relating (a) the amount of a particular asset that lenders want to hold to (b) the yield expected or promised on that debt.

Letters patent: A company charter granted (in the case of banks) by the Minister of Finance rather than by the legislature itself.

Leverage constraints: Constraints on borrowing that are imposed by lenders' concerns about borrowers' leverage ratios.

Leverage ratio: Ratio of assets to equity.

Leveraged buyout: Purchase of shares of a firm with borrowed funds.

Life annuity: Stream of fixed annual payments that continues for life.

Life-cycle theory: Forward-looking theory of savings behaviour that generally assumes a "humped" pattern of earnings over the household's expected future lifetime.

Line of credit: Commitment by a bank to lend up to the line of credit ceiling, whenever the customer wishes.

Liquidity: The property of being convertible to cash at short notice and without significant cost.

Liquidity-constrained firms: Firms that want to spend more on new capital than their lenders are willing to provide.

Liquidity-preference theory: Theory that expected holding-period yields will be identical except for an increasing liquidity premium added to longer-term yields.

Liquidity premium: Extra expected yield provided on less liquid assets, relative to more liquid assets.

Liquidity risk: Borrowers' uncertainty about availability of credit in the future.

LM curve, or asset market equilibrium locus: Line joining combinations of real income and nominal interest rate at which asset markets are in equilibrium.

LM shock: Any disturbance to the LM curve.

Loan guarantee schemes: Schemes in which the government offers to guarantee specific types of loans against default risk, in order to encourage others to do the actual lending.

Locals: Local credit unions or caisses populaires.

London interbank offer rate (LIBOR): The rate charged on loans between banks in the Eurocurrency market in London; the benchmark deposit yield in the Eurodollar market.

Long term: Longer than short term, which is up to one year in most contexts; also refers to over five years.

Loss reserves: Special portion of equity set aside to reflect the probable shortfall of loan repayments below the book value of loans.

Lucas critique: That any change in stabilization policy rules in particular will change expectations formation, and therefore how the economy responds to policy stimuli.

M

M1: Canadian currency and coin outside banks plus Canadian-dollar demand deposits in chartered banks.

M1A: M1 plus chequable Canadian-dollar notice deposits in banks.

M2: M1A plus Canadian-dollar notice and personal fixed-term deposits in banks.

M2+: M2 plus deposits of near banks.

M3: M2 plus Canadian-dollar nonpersonal fixed-term deposits in banks, plus residents' foreign currency deposits held in Canada.

Making a market: What jobbers do.

Managed float: Floating exchange rate arrangement in which the central bank intervenes to slow down rapid exchange rate movements.

Margin deposit: Deposit given to the broker as security for completion of a futures contract.

Margin loans: Loans extended to investment dealers' customers to finance part of their purchases of stocks and bonds.

Marginal efficiency of investment: The rate of return on new investment projects.

Marginal rate of substitution: Slope of an indifference curve.

Marginal rate of time preference: Proportional extra marginal utility from consumption now rather than in the next period.

Marginal social cost: The social opportunity cost of a particular use of resources.

Marginal social utility: Change in social welfare from a particular use of resources.

Market portfolio: Portfolio consisting of assets held in the same proportions as exist in total for the whole financial system.

Market risk: Uncertainty about the future price that financial markets will put on an asset.

Matching: Arranging for asset yields and debt costs to fluctuate together.

Mean-variance model: *See* Tobin–Markowitz theory.

Medium of exchange: An item regularly accepted in exchange for other goods and services.

Merchant bank: Financial institution that arranges for all kinds of financing for customer firms, including underwriting securities issues.

MM proposition: *See* Modigliani–Miller proposition.

Modern quantity theory: Demand for money theory advanced by Milton Friedman, using the permanent-income concept.

Modigliani–Miller proposition: That the total value of the firm's debts (including its shares) will not be affected by the debt:equity mix, unless tax exposure varies with the debt-equity mix.

Monetary authorities: Bank of Canada, Minister of Finance, and Receiver-General of Canada.

Monetary base: Total stock of cash reserve assets; same as high-powered money.

Monetary rule: A statement or equation explaining how monetary policy will be conducted in the event of various possible future shocks.

Money: Whatever assets are used as money; *See* Broad money and Narrow money.

Money illusion: That nominal values are the same as real values.

Money market: Wholesale market for short-term, liquid assets.

Money market dealers: Investment dealers who trade money market assets.

Money purchase pension plan: A pension plan promising only as large an annuity as the assets of the pension plan will purchase at retirement.

Money supply multiplier: Ratio of money supply to the stock of high-powered money.

Moral hazard: Chance that the odds of an event insured against will be raised by conscious efforts of the insured parties.

Moral suasion: Use of the central bank's influence to persuade bankers and others into particular courses of action.

Mortgage-backed securities: Assets that are generalized claims on the payment stream from a pool of (insured) mortgage loans, and secured by those mortgage loans.

Mortgage loan: Loan, usually long-term, secured in event of default by a prior claim on some real estate asset.

Mortgage loan company: Deposit-taking intermediary that holds mainly mortgages.

Mutual fund: Fund invested in a pool of assets, financed by the issue of undifferentiated shares or units. *See also* Open-end or Closed-end mutual funds.

Mutual insurance companies: Insurance companies owned by their participating policyholders, who elect the board of directors.

N

NAIRU (non-accelerating-inflation rate of unemployment): *See* Natural rates.

Narrow money: All regularly reported assets that are widely used as media of exchange.

Narrow money rule: Monetary rule in which short-term interest rates are changed in order to keep narrow money growth on or near some target growth path.

NASDAQ system: The National Association of Securities Dealers Automatic Quotation system, an electronic network for trading unlisted stocks in the United States.

National balance sheet accounts: Consolidated balance sheets for all sectors of the economy.

Natural rates of unemployment (NAIRU), output, and capacity use: The levels of output, unemployment, and capacity use at which inflation will tend neither to accelerate nor decelerate.

Near bank: Financial institution operating in the same markets as banks, but without a bank charter; mainly credit unions and trust companies.

Net asset value (of a mutual fund): The sum of current market values of all assets held, less any debts outstanding, all divided by the number of shares outstanding.

Net business saving: Business profits less taxes and dividend payments; the same as retained earnings in any year.

Net capital inflow: Difference between foreign purchases of domestic assets and domestic purchases of foreign assets (financial and nonfinancial).

Net M2 growth: M2 growth less the rate of growth of capacity (4 percent in Chapter 23).

Net official monetary movements: Record of all changes in foreign exchange holdings of the Bank of Canada, the exchange fund account, and the Receiver-General of Canada.

Net real investment: Net increase in holdings of real assets.

Net saving, or saving: Change in wealth over any period not caused by (a) changes in market values of assets or debts, or (b) (for corporations only) new issues of shares.

Net worth, wealth, or equity: Total assets less total debts. In the national balance sheet, shares are considered a debt of corporations to their owners.

Networking: Selling the financial services or debts of one firm through the branches of another.

New classical model: Macroeconomic model in which all markets clear in each period, generally with rational expectations as well.

New Keynesian model: Macroeconomic model in which wages and prices do not adjust quickly enough to clear all markets in each period.

Nominal income rule: A monetary rule that promises to respond to short-run shocks according to whether they raise or lower growth of nominal income.

Nominal yields: The yields reported in the financial press, without any adjustment to offset the effects of price inflation. *See also* Real yields.

Non-accelerating inflation rate of unemployment (NAIRU): *See* Natural rates.

Nonsystematic risk: *See* Unsystematic risk.

Normal distribution: A particular, bell-shaped probability distribution with the largest probabilities in the centre of the distribution.

Notice deposits: Deposits for which the issuer can legally require notice of withdrawal.

Numeraire, or unit of account: The good whose value serves as the standard of measurement for values of all other goods and services.

O

Official parity level: *See* Central parity rate.

Official reserves: Holdings of foreign exchange assets by the monetary authorities.

Okun's law: That each 1 percentage point of extra unemployment rate means (currently) 2.5 percentage points less output.

Open-end mutual funds: Mutual funds for which new shares are issued to any new lender, and old shares are redeemable at the current net asset value.

Open-market operations: Purchases and sales of treasury bills by the Bank of Canada.

Open mortgage: A mortgage loan whose principal can be repaid early, in whole or in part, without any extra compensation to the lender.

Opportunity yields: Yields on other assets that could have been held instead of the asset being analyzed.

Optimal policy rule: The announced strategy for use of a policy that minimizes variance of the target variable.

Option: A right but not an obligation to do something on or before an expiry date.

Option theory approach: An approach that seeks to break down complex financial assets into combinations of more elementary assets such as risk-free loans and options of various sorts.

Originating lender: The lender who first arranged a loan, which may then be discounted to other lenders.

Overlapping wage contracts: Wage contracts that are not all negotiated at the same time, so that some contracts are always in force while others are being negotiated.

Overshooting exchange rates: Pattern of equilibrium adjustment in which spot exchange rates initially adjust beyond their eventual equilibrium level and then gradually return.

Over-the-counter (OTC) market: The market for stocks not listed on one of the stock exchanges, traded from brokers' offices rather than on the floor of a stock exchange. *See* NASDAQ.

Own yield: Yield on the asset being analyzed. Contrast with the opportunity yield.

P

Paper standard: A monetary system in which token moneys are not convertible into anything of intrinsic value.

Par value: *See* Face value.

Participating policies: Insurance policies eligible to receive a partial rebate of premiums if the company's performance is better than was assumed when the premiums were originally set.

Pay-as-you-go: Pension plan whose current benefit payments are financed by current pension contributions.

Pension fund: An arrangement for accumulating and investing pension contributions until retirement; sometimes also for paying retirement benefits.

PEP curve (Price expectations Phillips curve): *See* Expectations-augmented Phillips curve.

Permanent income: The annuity value of total lifetime resources, which is human wealth plus financial wealth.

Permanent-income theory: That consumption depends on permanent income; extended also to the demand for money.

Permanent insurance: Insurance protection to be continued for life.

Phillips curve: Curve relating rate of nominal wage or price change to the rate of unemployment or capacity utilization. *See also* Expectations-augmented Phillips curve.

Playing-card money: Special signed and stamped playing cards issued as paper money in New France.

Policy dividend: Partial rebate of premium on a participating insurance policy.

Policy ineffectiveness proposition: New classical claim that only random policy actions can hope to affect output levels even in the short run.

Policy reserve: The accumulated value of the surplus premiums contributed by holders of permanent life insurance policies, plus all earnings on that surplus.

Policy rule: *See* Monetary rule.

Portfolio choice diagram: Diagram showing the choices between risk and expected yield from different asset portfolios.

Portfolio yield: The yield on an entire portfolio of assets, as distinct from the yield on individual assets.

Posted rates: Interest rates quoted openly by financial institutions for all customers, and left at that level for a significant period.

PRA: *See* Purchase and resale agreement.

Precautionary demand: Demand for money to protect against income shortfalls or unexpected spending needs.

Preferred-habitat theory: Theory that expected holding-period yields will differ by risk premiums that reflect investors' preferences for particular (not necessarily short-term) maturities.

Preferred shares: Shares that have first call on profits for a specified dividend yield, but no more.

Premiums: Payments made by holders of insurance policies for insurance protection; excess of forward over spot price of a currency.

Present discounted value: The equivalent in the present of values receivable only in the future; the values are discounted to allow for interest that cannot be earned between the present and the future date of expected receipt.

Price surprise supply function: A new classical supply function that explains increases in output as due to producers misperceiving general price increases as relative price increases.

Primary markets: Markets for newly issued debts.

Prime loan rate: Loan rate charged by banks to important customers.

Private domestic wealth: National wealth less government wealth and net debt to the rest of the world.

Probability distribution: A graph or schedule showing the distribution of total probability of 1.0 over all possible outcomes.

Production function: The mathematical relationship between output and the minimum necessary inputs (generally of labour and capital).

Prohibitive regulation: Regulation of intermediaries that prohibits certain activities as too risky.

Province of Ontario savings offices (POSO): An Ontario government-owned, deposit-taking intermediary that lends only to its owner.

Purchase and resale agreement (PRA): Sale of a security by a money market dealer to the Bank of Canada, together with a promise to repurchase it shortly thereafter. *See also* Sale and repurchase agreement.

Pure expectations theory: That arbitrage will force expected holding-period yields to be identical on all maturities of bond.

Put–call parity: Arbitrage condition relating put and call option prices to the price of the underlying asset.

Put option: A contract entitling the holder to sell an asset at the contract's strike price on or before the contract's expiry date.

Q

q ratio: Ratio of the market price of an existing real capital asset to its replacement cost.

Quantity equation: $MV = PT$.

Quantity theory: Theory that the quantity equation holds, and that V and T are constant, so that changes in M cause only changes in P.

Quebec Pension Plan (QPP): Quebec version of the Canada Pension Plan, differing mainly in the investment of contributions.

R

Random-walk hypothesis: Same as efficient markets hypothesis.

Rational expectations: Forward-looking expectations that take into account all information available.

Rational politics approach: Theory in which government actions are chosen to maximize the probability of re-election of the party in power.

Real assets: Physical, non-financial assets such as houses or plant and equipment.

Real business cycle theory: Theory that business cycles reflect supply shocks from new technologies rather than aggregate demand fluctuations.

Real exchange rate: Nominal exchange rate multiplied by the terms of trade.

Real investment: Net increase in holdings of real assets.

Real yields or interest rates: Nominal interest rates less the expected inflation rate.

Redeemable: Repayable before maturity at the discretion of the lender.

Redeposits: Opposite of drawdowns.

Refinancing: Repaying one debt with the proceeds from issuing another.

Registered Retirement Savings Plan (RRSP): Tax-sheltered arrangement for investing individuals' savings for retirement.

Regulatory competition: Competition by regulators in different jurisdictions to attract financial business into their jurisdiction, by more permissive or more efficient regulation.

Regulatory lag: The lag between the occurrence of a problem and the time the regulators act.

Reservable deposits: Deposits of chartered banks for which the 1980 Bank Act require minimum cash reserves.

Reserve averaging period: Period over which the average of bank cash reserve assets must at least equal some minimum level.

Rest-of-the-world sector: All participants in the domestic economy or financial system that are not residents.

Retail markets: Small-scale, non-standardized markets.

Retractable: Same as redeemable.

Ricardian equivalence theorem: That households offset the value of government debt exactly with the value of future tax payments to service its interest burden.

Risk averter: One who takes on extra risk only if compensated by the prospect of greater expected yield.

Risk pooling: Combining together different risks so they can offset each other. *See also* Diversification.

Risk premium or differential: Margin of extra expected yield to compensate for extra risk.

Risk seeker: One who will give up the prospect of greater expected yield in order to take on greater risk.

Risky set: The part of the feasible set consisting of only risky asset combinations.

Rule of caution: The rule that policymakers should be cautious in their use of policies whose effects are uncertain.

S

Sale and repurchase agreement (SRA): Same as a PRA, but in the opposite direction. *See* Purchase and resale agreement.

Sales finance companies: Firms that lend to finance sales of durable goods, with chattel mortgages.

Saving, or net saving: Change in wealth or equity over any period not caused by changes in (a) market values of assets or debts, or (b) (for corporations only) new issues of shares.

Savings deposits: Household notice and term deposits.

Schedule I or Schedule A banks: Chartered banks with wide and domestic ownership.

Schedule II or Schedule B banks: Chartered banks with foreign or concentrated ownership.

Secondary markets: Markets for buying and selling previously issued financial assets.

Secondary reserve assets: Assets that chartered banks can use to meet the secondary reserve requirement: excess cash reserves, treasury bills, and day loans to money market dealers.

Secondary reserve requirement: Requirement in the Bank Act that banks' holdings of treasury bills, day loans, and excess cash reserves be at least a minimum ratio to their deposits; abolished in the new Bank Act.

Securitization: Conversion of a loan into a resalable, transferable asset for sale in secondary markets.

Segmented-markets hypothesis: Theory that there is not enough arbitrage to force holding-period yields near equality for bonds of different maturities.

Segregated funds: Mutual fund business conducted by life insurance companies, with some insurance features added.

Seigniorage: The profit from minting coins; in modern times, the profit from creating money.

Self-dealing: Lending or borrowing by owners of a financial institution to or from firms also owned by them; generally, any transaction not at arm's length.

Self-liquidating loan: Loan whose use will automatically generate the funds for repayment at maturity.

Shoe-leather costs: Costs of alternative transactions arrangements when we make do with smaller money balances because of the inflation tax on money.

Short term: Under one year.

Sinking fund: A fund built up by the bond issuer to redeem part of a bond issue before final maturity.

Smart card: A debit or credit card with a memory chip that remembers the current balance remaining to be used.

Social loss function: Equation explaining the social costs to be minimized by public policy.

Social security funds: *See* Canada Pension Plan and Quebec Pension Plan.

Social welfare approach: Theory of government behaviour in which government actions are chosen to maximize social welfare. *See also* Rational politics approach.

Special call loans: Call loans, from banks to investment dealers, that are really callable.

Special drawing rights (SDRs): International reserve currency created by the IMF and held by central banks only, that is redeemable in all other currencies.

Specie: Gold or silver coinage.

Speculative motive: Holding money in order to profit from expected price decreases in other assets.

Speculator: One who buys assets (or sells them short) in order to profit from a change in their price.

Spot market: Market for immediate delivery of an asset or commodity.

Spread: Difference between asset yields and borrowing costs for a financial institution.

Stabilization policy: Policy to stabilize aggregate demand or inflation, or both.

Standard deviation: Square root of variance.

Standard of deferred payment: Good or item used to measure values to be paid in the future.

Static efficiency: Efficient allocation of resources and distribution of outputs among consumers.

Statutory deposits: Definition of deposit totals used in the cash reserve requirement under the 1980 Bank Act.

Statutory vault cash: Definition of vault cash totals used in the cash reserve requirement under the 1980 Bank Act.

Sterilization: Offsetting of official foreign exchange transactions to prevent changes in high-powered money.

Stock: (a) Share of corporate equity; (b) level of an asset in existence at a point of time, the cumulative sum of past flows of asset creation.

Stock equilibrium: An equilibrium in which the whole outstanding stock of any asset is willingly held in asset holders' portfolios. Contrast with flow equilibrium.

Strategy of gradualism: Name given to the Bank of Canada's strategy of slowing nominal income growth gradually after 1975, using M1 growth as a guide. Abandoned as a failure by 1981.

Strike price: The buying or selling price agreed on in an option contract.

Strip bond: A bond with no interest coupons.

Substitution effect: Effect of a change in price on quantity demanded, holding real income constant.

Supplementary capital: Under the Basle Agreement, shareholders' equity plus preferred shares, debentures, and general reserves against losses.

Supply of an asset: Amount of an asset in existence; for financial assets, the amount debtors will leave outstanding at any point of time.

Supply shocks: Any disturbance to the price at which a given output level is available, other than disturbances due to changes in expectations of inflation.

Surrender value: *See* Cash surrender value.

Swap: Exchange of one asset or obligation for another asset or obligation. *See* Interest rate swaps and Foreign exchange swaps.

Syndication: Pooling by several lenders to provide a single loan.

Systematic risk: Risk caused by factors common to all or most assets in the financial system.

T

Takeover bids: Attempts to buy enough shares for at least a controlling interest in a firm.

Tax-anticipation note: Short-term loan note issued by a provincial or local government to finance spending in anticipation of tax revenue.

Tax structure of yields: The relationships between yields that are subject to different tax rates.

Technical analysis: Forecasting the future price of an asset simply from information on the past path of the asset's price.

Term insurance: Insurance to be continued only for a specified term (though often renewable thereafter).

Term loan: Loan for a specified term; not a demand loan.

Term structure of interest rates: The structure of yields to maturity on assets of different terms to maturity but otherwise identical characteristics.

Terms of trade: Ratio of export prices to import prices or of domestic to foreign prices.

Time deposits: All deposits that are not repayable on demand.

Tobin–Markowitz theory: The theory that investors act as though only the expected yield and the variance of portfolio yield were important in choosing asset portfolios.

Tobin's q: *See* q ratio.

Token money: An asset with no intrinsic value that is used as a medium of exchange.

Total lifetime resources: Human wealth plus financial wealth; the present discounted value of all expected future labour income, plus any accumulated wealth to date.

Trade credit: Credit extended by suppliers to customers for delayed payment of bills in wholesale trade.

Transactions costs: The costs of converting non-money assets to money.

Transactions demand: Demand for money that will be used to make payment in ordinary transactions.

Transitory income: Income not expected to continue into the future.

Transmutation of assets: Conversion of assets into more desirable forms by financial intermediaries, often by risk pooling.

Treasury bills (T-bills): Short-term bills without interest coupons, issued by governments, sold at a discount.

Trust company: A deposit-taking intermediary that can offer its services as a corporate trustee.

Trust funds: Funds managed by a trust company but owned by the beneficiary.

Trust units: Resalable ownership units in an investment program, used where the investment program is to be in the name of the investors rather than that of a separate corporation.

Trusteed plan: A pension plan managed by trustees representing pension plan contributors.

U

Uncovered interest parity: Equality of expected yields on similar assets in different currencies, including any expected currency appreciation.

Underlying asset: The asset that futures and option contracts propose to buy or sell if and when exercised in the future.

Underwriting: Arranging for issue and distribution of a client firm's securities, on either a best efforts or a bought deal basis.

Unit of account: *See* Numeraire.

Unlisted stock: Stock not listed for trading on the floor of a stock exchange.

Unsystematic risk: Risk that is unique to a particular asset, not due to system-wide or common factors.

V

Variance: A measure of the width of a probability distribution; a probability-weighted average of all possible squared deviations of possible outcomes from the expected outcome.

Vault cash: Canadian coin and Bank of Canada notes held by chartered banks.

Velocity of circulation: The number of times each unit of money changes hands in transactions during a year.

Venture capital company: Firm that provides long-term capital, and often management assistance, for new and expanding companies.

W

Walras' law: That equilibrium in one asset market implies equilibrium in the rest of the financial system as well.

Wealth: *See* Net worth.

Wholesale markets: Large-scale markets that usually trade in relatively standardized amounts.

Withholding tax: Tax levied directly on income at point of payment; usually levied only for income paid abroad.

World Bank: International Bank for Reconstruction and Development; an official international bank for lending to less-developed countries.

World money: Assets used for international payments.

Writing options: Issuing of new option contracts by the seller.

Y

Yield: Returns on an asset expressed as a single average annual percentage return per dollar invested.

Yield curve: Curve showing yields to maturity on government debts of different maturities, all at a particular date.

Yield to maturity: Yield calculated on the assumption the asset is held to maturity. *See* Holding-period yield.

Z

Zero-balance banking or cash management account: *See* Automatic transfer service.

INDEX